The Works of John Adams

Volume 3

JOHN ADAMS

The Works of John Adams Volume 3
Jazzybee Verlag Jürgen Beck
86450 Altenmünster, Loschberg 9
Deutschland

Printed by Createspace, North Charleston,
South Carolina, USA

ISBN: 9783849693848

www.jazzybee-verlag.de
www.facebook.com/jazzybeeverlag
admin@jazzybee-verlag.de

Editor's Note: The Page Referrals inside this book are part of the edition that was used to build this book. Due to layout changes and fonts used then and now these referrals might not be valid for this edition. We appreciate your understanding.

CONTENTS:

AUTOBIOGRAPHY. CONTINUED.

I have omitted some things in 1775, which must be inserted· Endnote 002 On the eighteenth of September, it was resolved in Congress,—

"That a secret committee be appointed to contract for the importation and delivery of a quantity of gunpowder, not exceeding five hundred tons.

"That in case such a quantity of gunpowder cannot be procured, to contract for the importation of so much saltpetre, with a proportionable quantity of sulphur, as with the powder procured will make five hundred tons.

"That the committee be empowered to contract for the importation of forty brass field pieces, six pounders, for ten thousand stand of arms, and twenty thousand good plain double-bridled musket looks.

"That the said committee be empowered to draw on the treasurer to answer the said contracts, and

"That the said committee consist of nine members, any five of whom to be a quorum.

"The members chosen, Mr. Willing, Mr. Franklin. Mr. Livingston, Mr. Alsop, Mr. Deane, Mr. Dickinson, Mr. Langdon, Mr. McKean, and Mr. Ward."

On the eighth of November, on motion,

"Resolved, That the secret committee appointed to contract for the importation of arms, ammunition, &c., be empowered to export to the foreign West Indies, on account and risk of the Continent, as much provision or any other produce, (except horned cattle, sheep, hogs, and poultry) as they may deem necessary for the importation of arms, ammunition, sulphur, and saltpetre" Endnote 003

On Wednesday, November 29th, it was Endnote 004

"Resolved, That a committee of five be appointed for the sole purpose of corresponding with our friends in Great Britain, Ireland, and other parts of the world, and that they lay their correspondence before Congress when directed.

"Resolved, That Congress will make provision to defray all such expenses as may arise by carrying on such a correspondence, and for the payment of such agents as they may send on this service. The members chosen, Mr. Harrison, Dr. Franklin, Mr. Johnson, Mr. Dickinson, and Mr. Jay."

This last provision for an agent, was contrived, I presume, for Mr. Deane, who had been left out of the delegation by the State, but instead of returning home to Connecticut, remained in Philadelphia soliciting an appointment under the two foregoing committees, as an agent of theirs, first in the West Indies, and then in France. Unfortunately Mr. Deane was not well established at home. The good people of Connecticut thought him a man of talent and enterprise, but of more ambition than principle. He possessed not their esteem or confidence. He procured his first appointment in 1774 to Congress by an intrigue. Under the pretext of avoiding to commit the legislature of the State in any act of rebellion, he got a committee appointed with some discretionary powers, under which they undertook to appoint the members to Congress. Mr. Deane being one, was obliged to vote for himself to obtain a majority of the committee. On the third of November, 1774, the representatives indeed chose Mr. Deane among others, to attend Congress the next May; but on the second Thursday of October, 1775, the General Assembly of Governor and Company left him out. On the 16th of January, 1776, the new delegates appeared in Congress· Endnote 005 To the two secret committees, that of commerce and that of correspondence, Mr. Deane applied, and obtained of them appointments as their agent. Dr. Franklin also gave him private letters, one to Dr. Dubourg of Paris, a physician who had translated his works into French, and one to

Mr. Dumas at the Hague, who had seen him in England. With these credentials Mr. Deane went, first to the West Indies, and then to France. He was a person of a plausible readiness and volubility with his tongue and his pen, much addicted to ostentation and expense in dress and living, but without any deliberate forecast or reflection, solidity of judgment or real information. The manner in which he made use of his powers we shall see hereafter. I had hitherto, however, thought well of his intentions, and had acted with him on terms of entire civility.

Within a day or two after the appointment in Congress of the committee of correspondence, Mr. Jay came to my chamber to spend an evening with me. I was alone, and Mr. Jay opened himself to me with great frankness. His object seemed to be an apology for my being omitted in the choice of the two great secret committees, of commerce and correspondence. He said in express terms, "that my character stood very high with the members, and he knew there was but one thing which prevented me from being universally acknowledged to be the first man in Congress, and that was this; there was a great division in the house, and two men had effected it, Samuel Adams and Richard Henry Lee, and as I was known to be very intimate with those two gentlemen, many others were jealous of me." My answer to all this was, that I had thought it very strange, and had imputed it to some secret intrigue out of doors, that no member from Massachusetts had been elected on either of those committees; that I had no pretensions to the distinction of the first man in Congress, and that if I had a clear title to it, I should be very far from assuming it or wishing for it. It was a station of too much responsibility and danger in the times and circumstances in which we lived and were destined to live. That I was a friend very much attached to Mr. Lee and Mr. Adams, because I knew them to be able men and inflexible in the cause of their country. I could not therefore become cool in my friendship for them, for the sake of any distinctions that Congress could bestow. That I believed too many commercial projects and private speculations were in contemplation by the composition of those committees, but even these had not contributed so much to it, as the great division in the house on the subject of independence and the mode of carrying on the war. Mr. Jay and I, however, parted good friends and have continued such without interruption to this day. [Endnote 006]

There is a secret in this business that ought to be explained. Mr. Arthur Lee, in London, had heard some insinuations against Mr. Jay, as a suspicious character, and had written to his brother, Richard Henry Lee, or to Mr. Samuel Adams, or both, and although they were groundless and injurious, as I have no doubt, my friends had communicated them too indiscreetly, and had spoken of Mr. Jay too lightly. Mr. Lee had expressed doubts whether Mr. Jay had composed the address to the people of Great Britain, and ascribed it to his father-in-law, Mr. Livingston, afterwards Governor of New Jersey. These things had occasioned some words and animosities, which, uniting with the great questions in Congress, had some disagreeable effects. [Endnote 007] Mr. Jay's great superiority to Mr. Livingston in the art of composition would now be sufficient to decide the question, if the latter had not expressly denied having any share in that address.

On Wednesday, June 12th, 1776, Congress "Resolved that a committee of Congress be appointed, by the name of a board of war and ordnance, to consist of five members, with a secretary, clerk," &c., and their extensive powers are stated. [Endnote 008] On the 13th, Congress having proceeded to the election of a committee to form the board of war and ordnance, the following members were chosen. Mr. John Adams, Mr. Sherman, Mr. Harrison, Mr. Wilson, and Mr. E. Rutledge; and Richard Peters, Esq. was elected secretary. The duties of this board kept me in continual employment, not to say drudgery, from the 12th of June, 1776, till the 11th of November, 1777, when I left Congress forever. Not only my mornings and evenings were filled up with the crowd of business before the board, but a great part of my time in

Congress was engaged in making, explaining, and justifying our reports and proceedings. It is said there are lawyers in the United States who receive five thousand guineas a year, and many are named who are said to receive to the amount of ten thousand dollars. However this may be, I don't believe there is one of them who goes through as much business for all his emoluments, as I did for a year and a half nearly, that I was loaded with that office. Other gentlemen attended as they pleased, but as I was chairman, or as they were pleased to call it, president, I must never be absent.

On Thursday, October 5th, 1775, sundry letters from London were laid before Congress and read, [Endnote 009] and a motion was made, that it be

"Resolved, That a committee of three be appointed to prepare a plan for intercepting two vessels which are on their way to Canada, laden with arms and powder, and that the committee proceed on this business immediately."

The secretary has omitted to insert the names of this committee on the journals, but as my memory has recorded them, they were Mr. Deane, Mr. Langdon, and myself, three members who had expressed much zeal in favor of the motion. As a considerable part of my time, in the course of my profession, had been spent upon the sea-coast of Massachusetts, in attending the courts and lawsuits at Plymouth, Barnstable, Martha's Vineyard, to the southward, and in the counties of Essex, York, and Cumberland to the eastward, I had conversed much with the gentlemen who conducted our cod and whale fisheries, as well as the other navigation of the country, and had heard much of the activity, enterprise, patience, perseverance, and daring intrepidity of our seamen. I had formed a confident opinion that, if they were once let loose upon the ocean, they would contribute greatly to the relief of our wants, as well as to the distress of the enemy. I became therefore at once an ardent advocate for this motion, which we carried, not without great difficulty. The opposition to it was very loud and vehement. Some of my own colleagues appeared greatly alarmed at it, and Mr. Edward Rutledge never displayed so much eloquence as against it. He never appeared to me to discover so much information and sagacity, which convinced me that he had been instructed out-of-doors by some of the most knowing merchants and statesmen in Philadelphia. It would require too much time and space to give this debate at large, if any memory could attempt it. Mine cannot. It was, however, represented as the most wild, visionary, mad project that ever had been imagined. It was an infant, taking a mad bull by his horns; and what was more profound and remote, it was said it would ruin the character, and corrupt the morals of all our seamen. It would make them selfish, piratical, mercenary, bent wholly upon plunder, &c. &c. [Endnote 010] These formidable arguments and this terrible rhetoric were answered by us by the best reasons we could allege, and the great advantages of distressing the enemy, supplying ourselves, and beginning a system of maritime and naval operations, were represented in colors as glowing and animating. The vote was carried, the committee went out, returned very soon, and brought in the report in these words:

"The committee appointed to prepare a plan for intercepting the two vessels bound to Canada, brought in a report, which was taken into consideration; whereupon,

Resolved, That a letter be sent to General Washington, to inform him that Congress having received certain intelligence of the sailing of two north-country built brigs, of no force, from England, on the 11th of August last, loaded with arms, powder, and other stores, for Quebee, without convoy, which, it being of importance to intercept, desire that he apply to the Council of Massachusetts Bay for the two armed vessels in their service, and despatch the same, with a sufficient number of people, stores, &c. particularly a number of oars, in order, if possible, to intercept the said two brigs and their cargoes, and secure the same for the use of the continent, also any other transports, laden with ammunition, clothing, or other stores, for the use of the ministerial army or navy in America, and secure them, in the most convenient places, for the purpose above mentioned; that he give the commander or commanders such instructions as are necessary, as also proper encouragement to the marines and seamen that shall be sent on this enterprise, which instructions are to be delivered to the commander or commanders, sealed up, with orders not to open the same until out of sight of land, on account of secrecy.

"That a letter be written to the said Honorable Council, to put the said vessels under the General's command and direction, and to furnish him instantly with every necessary in their power, at the expense of the Continent.

"That the General be directed to employ the said vessels, and others, if he judge necessary, to effect the purposes aforesaid; and that he be informed that the Rhode Island and Connecticut vessels of force, will be sent directly to their assistance.

"That a letter be written to Governor Cooke, informing him of the above, desiring him to despatch one or both the armed vessels of the Colony of Rhode Island on the same service, and that he use the precautions above mentioned.

"That a letter be written to Governor Trumbull, requesting of him the largest vessel in the service of the Colony of Connecticut, to be sent on the enterprise aforesaid, acquainting him with the above particulars, and recommending the same precautions.

"That the said ships and vessels of war be on the continental risk and pay, during their being so employed."

"Friday, October 6. The committee appointed to prepare a plan, &c. brought in a further report, which was read.

"Ordered, to lie on the table for the perusal of the members."

"Friday, October 13. The Congress, taking into consideration the report of the committee appointed to propose a plan, &c. after some debate,

"Resolved, That a swift sailing vessel, to carry ten carriage guns and a proportionable number of swivels, with eighty men, be fitted with all possible despatch for a cruise of three months, and that the commander be instructed to cruise eastward, for intercepting such transports as may be laden with warlike stores and other supplies for our enemies, and for such other purposes as the Congress shall direct. That a committee of three be appointed to prepare an estimate of the expense, and lay the same before the Congress, and to contract with proper persons to fit out the vessel.

"Resolved, That another vessel be fitted out for the same purposes, and that the said committee report their opinion of a proper vessel, and also an estimate of the expense.

"The following members were chosen to compose the committee. Mr. Deane, Mr. Langdon, and Mr. Gadsden.

"Resolved, That the further consideration of the report, be referred to Monday next.

"Monday, October 30. The committee appointed to prepare an estimate, and to fit out the vessels, brought in their report, which, being taken into consideration,

"Resolved, That the second vessel, ordered to be fitted out on the 13th instant, be of such a size as to carry fourteen guns and a proportionate number of swivels and men.

"Resolved, That two more vessels be fitted out with all expedition, the one to carry not exceeding twenty guns, and the other not exceeding thirty-six guns, with a proportionable number of swivels and men, to be employed in such manner, for the protection and defence of the United Colonies, as the Congress shall direct.

"Resolved, That four members be chosen and added to the former committee of three, and that these seven be a committee to carry into execution, with all possible expedition, as well the resolutions of Congress, passed the 13th instant, as those passed this day, for fitting out armed vessels.

"The members chosen, Mr. Hopkins, Mr. Hewes, Mr. Richard Henry Lee, and Mr. John Adams.

This committee immediately procured a room in a public house in the city, and agreed to meet every evening at six o'clock, in order to despatch this business with all possible celerity.

On Thursday, November 2d, Congress

"Resolved, That the committee appointed to carry into execution the resolves of Congress, for fitting out four armed vessels, be authorized to draw on the continental treasurers from time to time for as much cash as shall be necessary for the above purpose, not exceeding the sum of one hundred thousand dollars, and that the said committee have power to agree with such officers and seamen as are proper to man and command said vessels; and that the encouragement to such officers and seamen be one half of all ships of war made prize of by them, and one third of all transport vessels, exclusive of wages.

On the 8th of November, Congress

"Resolved, That the bills of sale, for the vessels ordered to be purchased, be made to the continental treasurers or those who shall succeed them in that office, in trust nevertheless for the use of the Continent or their representatives in Congress met.

On the 10th of November, Congress

"Resolved, That two battalions of marines be raised, consisting of one colonel, two lieutenant-colonels, two majors, and other officers, as usual in other regiments; that they consist of an equal number of privates with other battalions; that particular care be taken that no persons be appointed to offices, or enlisted into said battalions, but such as are good seamen, or so acquainted with maritime affairs as to be able to serve to advantage by sea when required; that they be enlisted and commissioned to serve for and during the present war between Great Britain and the Colonies, unless dismissed by order of Congress; that they be distinguished by the names of the first and second battalions of American marines, and that they be considered as part of the number which the continental army before Boston is ordered to consist of.

"Ordered that a copy of the above be transmitted to the General.

On the 17th of November,

"A letter from General Washington, enclosing a letter and journal of Colonel Arnold, and sundry papers being received, the same were read, whereupon,—

"Resolved, That a committee of seven be appointed to take into consideration so much of the General's letter as relates to the disposal of such vessels and cargoes belonging to the enemy, as shall fall into the hands of, or be taken by, the inhabitants of the United Colonies.

"The members chosen, Mr. Wythe, Mr. E. Rutledge, Mr. J. Adams, Mr. W. Livingston, Dr. Franklin, Mr. Wilson, and Mr. Johnson.

"Thursday, November 23. The committee, for fitting out armed vessels, laid before Congress a draught of rules for the government of the American navy, and articles to be signed by the officers and men employed in that service, which were read, and ordered to lie on the table for the perusal of the members.

"Saturday, November 25. Congress resumed the consideration of the report of the committee on General Washington's letter, and the same being debated by paragraphs, was agreed to as follows.

"Whereas, it appears from undoubted information that many vessels which had cleared at the respective custom-houses in these Colonies, agreeable to the regulations established by Acts of the British Parliament, have in a lawless manner, without even the semblance of just authority, been seized by His Majesty's ships of war and carried into the harbor of Boston and other ports, where they have been rifled of their cargoes, by orders of His Majesty's naval and military officers there commanding, without the said vessels having been proceeded against by any form of trial, and without the charge of having offended against any law.

"And whereas orders have been issued in His Majesty's name, to the commanders of his ships of war, 'to proceed as in the case of actual rebellion against such of the seaport towns and places, being accessible to the King's ships, in which any troops shall be raised, or military works erected,' under color of which said orders, the commanders of His Majesty's said ships of war have already burned and destroyed the flourishing and populous town of Falmouth, and have fired upon and much injured several other towns within the United Colonies, and dispersed at a late season of the year hundreds of helpless women and children, with a savage hope that those may perish under the approaching rigors of the season, who may chance to escape destruction from fire and sword; a mode of warfare long exploded among civilized nations.

"And whereas the good people of these Colonies, sensibly affected by the destruction of their property, and other unprovoked injuries, have at last determined to prevent as much as possible a repetition thereof, and to procure some reparation for the same, by fitting out armed vessels and ships of force; in the execution of which commendable designs it is possible that those who have not been instrumental in the unwarrantable violences above mentioned may suffer, unless some laws be made to regulate, and tribunals erected competent to determine the propriety of captures. Therefore, Resolved,—

"1. That all such ships of war, frigates, sloops, cutters, and armed vessels, as are or shall be employed in the present cruel and unjust war against the United Colonies, and shall fall into the hands of, or be taken by, the inhabitants thereof, be seized and forfeited to and for the purposes hereinafter mentioned.

"2. That all transport vessels in the same service, having on board any troops, arms, ammunition, clothing, provisions, or military or naval stores, of what kind soever, and all vessels to whomsoever belonging, that shall be employed in carrying provisions or other necessaries to the British army or armies or navy, that now are, or shall hereafter be, within any of the United Colonies, or any goods, wares, or merchandises, for the use of such fleet or army, shall be liable to seizure, and with their cargoes shall be confiscated." Endnote 011

I have been particular in transcribing the proceedings of this day, November 25th, 1775, because they contain the true origin and foundation of the American navy, and as I had at least as great a share in producing them as any man living or dead, they will show that my zeal and exertions afterwards in 1798, and 1799, and 1800, at every hazard, and in opposition to a more powerful party than that against me in 1775, was but a perseverance in the same principles, systems, and views of the public interest.

On Tuesday, November 28th, the Congress resumed the consideration of the rules and orders for the navy of the United Colonies, and the same being debated by paragraphs were agreed to as follows. Endnote 012 They were drawn up in the marine committee, and by my hand, but examined, discussed, and corrected by the committee. In this place I will take the opportunity to observe, that the pleasantest part of my labors for the four years I spent in Congress from 1774 to 1778, was in this naval committee. Mr. Lee, Mr. Gadsden, were sensible men, and very cheerful, but Governor Hopkins of Rhode Island, above seventy years of age, kept us all alive. Upon business, his experience and judgment were very useful. But when the business of the evening was over, he kept us in conversation till eleven, and sometimes twelve o'clock. His custom was to drink nothing all day, nor till eight o'clock in the evening, and then his beverage was Jamaica spirit and water. It gave him wit, humor, anecdotes, science, and learning. He had read Greek, Roman, and British history, and was familiar with English poetry, particularly Pope, Thomson, and Milton, and the flow of his soul made all his reading our own, and seemed to bring to recollection in all of us, all we had ever read. I could neither eat nor drink in these days. The other gentlemen were very temperate. Hopkins never drank to excess, but all he drank was immediately not only converted into wit, sense, knowledge, and good humor, but inspired us with similar qualities.

This committee soon purchased and fitted five vessels; the first we named Alfred, in honor of the founder of the greatest navy that ever existed. The second, Columbus, after the discoverer of this quarter of the globe. The third, Cabot, for the discoverer of this northern part of the continent. The fourth, Andrew Doria, in memory of the great Genoese Admiral, and the fifth, Providence, for the town where she was purchased, the residence of Governor Hopkins, and his brother Ezek, whom we appointed first captain. We appointed all the officers of all the ships. At the solicitation of Mr. Deane, we appointed his brother-in-law, Captain Saltonstall.

Sometime in December, worn down with long and uninterrupted labor, I asked and obtained leave to visit my State and family. Mr. Langdon did the same. Mr. Deane was left out of the delegation by his State, and some others of the naval committee were dispersed, when Congress appointed a committee of twelve, one from each State, for naval affairs, so that I had no longer any particular charge relative to them; but as long as I continued a member of Congress, I never failed to support all reasonable measures reported by the new committee.

It is necessary that I should be a little more particular, in relating the rise and progress of the new government of the States.

On Friday, June 2d, 1775, *Endnote 013*

"The President laid before Congress a letter from the Provincial Convention of Massachusetts Bay, dated May 16th, which was read, setting forth the difficulties they labor under for want of a regular form of government, and as they and the other Colonies are now compelled to raise an army to defend themselves from the butcheries and devastations of their implacable enemies, which renders it still more necessary to have a regular established government, requesting the Congress to favor them with explicit advice respecting the taking up and exercising the powers of civil government, and declaring their readiness to submit to such a general plan as the Congress may direct for the Colonies, or make it their great study to establish such a form of government there as shall not only promote their advantage, but the union and interest of all America.

This subject had engaged much of my attention before I left Massachusetts, and had been frequently the subject of conversation between me and many of my friends,—Dr. Winthrop, Dr. Cooper, Colonel Otis, the two Warrens, Major Hawley, and others, besides my colleagues in Congress,—and lay with great weight upon my mind, as the most difficult and dangerous business that we had to do; (for from the beginning, I always expected we should have more difficulty and danger, in our attempts to govern ourselves, and in our negotiations and connections with foreign powers, than from all the fleets and armies of Great Britain.) It lay, therefore, with great weight upon my mind, and when this letter was read, I embraced the opportunity to open myself in Congress, and most earnestly to entreat the serious attention of all the members, and of all the continent, to the measures which the times demanded. For my part, I thought there was great wisdom in the adage, "when the sword is drawn, throw away the scabbard." Whether we threw it away voluntarily or not, it was useless now, and would be useless forever. *Endnote 014* The pride of Britain, flushed with late triumphs and conquests, their infinite contempt of all the power of America, with an insolent, arbitrary Scotch faction, with a Bute and Mansfield at their head for a ministry, we might depend upon it, would force us to call forth every energy and resource of the country, to seek the friendship of England's enemies, and we had no rational hope, but from the Ratio ultima regum et rerum-publicarum. These efforts could not be made without government, and as I supposed no man would think of consolidating this vast continent under one national government, we should probably, after the example of the Greeks, the Dutch, and the Swiss, form a confederacy of States, each of which must have a separate government. That the case of Massachusetts was the most urgent, but that it could not be long before every other Colony must follow her example. That with a view to this subject, I had looked into the ancient and modern confederacies for examples, but they all appeared to me to have been huddled up in a hurry, by a few chiefs. But we had a people of more intelligence, curiosity, and enterprise, who must be all consulted, and we must realize the theories of the wisest writers, and invite the people to erect the whole building with their own hands, upon the broadest foundation. That this could be done only by conventions of representatives chosen by the people in the several colonies, in the most exact proportions. That it was my opinion that Congress ought now to recommend to the people of every Colony to call such conventions immediately, and set up governments of their own, under their own authority; for the people were the source of all authority and original of all power. These were new, strange, and terrible doctrines to the greatest part of the members, but not a very small number heard them with apparent pleasure, and none more than Mr. John Rutledge, of South Carolina, and Mr. John Sullivan, of New Hampshire.

Congress, however, ordered the letter to lie on the table for further consideration.

On Saturday, June 3d, the letter from the convention of the Massachusetts Bay, dated the 16th of May, being again read, the subject was again discussed, and then,

"Resolved, That a committee of five persons be chosen, to consider the same, and report what in their opinion is the proper advice to be given to that Convention."

The following persons were chosen by ballot, to compose that committee, namely, Mr. J. Rutledge, Mr. Johnson, Mr. Jay, Mr. Wilson, and Mr. Lee. These gentlemen had several conferences with the delegates from our State, in the course of which, I suppose, the hint was suggested, that they adopted in their report.

On Wednesday, June 7th,

"On motion, Resolved, That Thursday, the 20th of July next, be observed throughout the twelve United Colonies as a day of humiliation, fasting, and prayer; and that Mr. Hooper, Mr. J. Adams, and Mr. Paine, be a committee to bring in a resolve for that purpose.

"The committee appointed to prepare advice, in answer to the letter from the Convention of Massachusetts Bay, brought in their report, which was read and ordered to lie on the table for consideration.

"On Friday, June 9th. the report of the committee on the letter from the Convention of Massachusetts Bay being again read, the Congress came into the following resolution.

"Resolved, That no obedience being due to the Act of Parliament for altering the charter of the Colony of Massachusetts Bay, nor to a Governor or Lieutenant-Governor who will not observe the directions of, but endeavor to subvert, that charter, the Governor and Lieutenant-Governor of that Colony are to be considered as absent, and their offices vacant; and as there is no Council there, and the inconveniences arising from the suspension of the powers of government are intolerable, especially at a time when General Gage hath actually levied war, and is carrying on hostilities against his Majesty's peaceable and loyal subjects of that Colony; that, in order to conform as near as may be to the spirit and substance of the charter, it be recommended to the Provincial Convention to write letters to the inhabitants of the several places, which are entitled to representation in Assembly, requesting them to choose such representatives, and that the Assembly when chosen do elect Counsellors; and that such assembly or Council exercise the powers of government, until a Governor of His Majesty's appointment will consent to govern the Colony according to its charter.

"Ordered, That the President transmit a copy of the above to the Convention of Massachusetts Bay."

Although this advice was in a great degree conformable to the New York and Pennsylvania system, or in other words, to the system of Mr. Dickinson and Mr. Duane, I thought it an acquisition, for it was a precedent of advice to the separate States to institute governments, and I doubted not we should soon have more occasions to follow this example. Mr. John Rutledge and Mr. Sullivan had frequent conversations with me upon this subject. Mr. Rutledge asked me my opinion of a proper form of government for a State. I answered him that any form that our people would consent to institute, would be better than none, even if they placed all power in a house of representatives, and they should appoint governors and judges; but I hoped they would be wiser, and preserve the English Constitution in its spirit and substance, as far as the circumstances of this country required or would admit. That no hereditary powers ever had existed in America, nor would they, or ought they to be introduced or proposed; but that I hoped the three branches of a legislature would be preserved, an executive, independent of the senate or council, and the house, and above all things, the independence of the judges. Mr. Sullivan was fully agreed with me in the necessity of instituting governments, and he seconded me very handsomely in supporting the argument in Congress. Mr. Samuel Adams was with us in the opinion of the necessity, and was industrious in conversation with the members out of doors, but he very rarely spoke much in Congress, and he was perfectly unsettled in any plan to be recommended to a State, always inclining to the most democratical forms, and even to a single sovereign assembly, until his constituents afterwards in Boston compelled him to vote for three branches. Mr. Cushing was also for one sovereign assembly, and Mr. Paine was silent and reserved upon the subject, at least to me.

Not long after this, Mr. John Rutledge returned to South Carolina, and Mr. Sullivan went with General Washington to Cambridge, so that I lost two of my able coadjutors. But we soon found the benefit of their cooperation at a distance.

On Wednesday, October 18th, the delegates from New Hampshire laid before the Congress a part of the instructions delivered to them by their Colony, in these words:—

"We would have you immediately use your utmost endeavors to obtain the advice and direction of the Congress, with respect to a method for our administering justice, and regulating our civil police. We press you not to delay this matter, as its being done speedily will probably prevent the greatest confusion among us."

This instruction might have been obtained by Mr. Langdon, or Mr. Whipple, but I always supposed it was General Sullivan who suggested the measure, because he left Congress with a stronger impression upon his mind of the importance of it, than I ever observed in either of the others. Be this, however, as it may have been, I embraced with joy the opportunity of haranguing on the subject at large, and of urging Congress to resolve on a general recommendation to all the States to call conventions and institute regular governments. I reasoned from various topics, many of which, perhaps, I could not now recollect. Some I remember; as,

1. The danger to the morals of the people from the present loose state of things, and general relaxation of laws and government through the Union.

2. The danger of insurrections in some of the most disaffected parts of the Colonies, in favor of the enemy, or as they called them, the mother country, an expression that I thought it high time to erase out of our language.

3. Communications and intercourse with the enemy, from various parts of the continent could not be wholly prevented, while any of the powers of government remained in the hands of the King's servants.

4. It could not well be considered as a crime to communicate intelligence, or to act as spies or guides to the enemy, without assuming all the powers of government.

5. The people of America would never consider our Union as complete, but our friends would always suspect divisions among us, and our enemies who were scattered in larger or smaller numbers, not only in every State and city, but in every village through the whole Union, would forever represent Congress as divided and ready to break to pieces, and in this way would intimidate and discourage multitudes of our people who wished us well.

6. The absurdity of carrying on war against a king, when so many persons were daily taking oaths and affirmations of allegiance to him.

7. We could not expect that our friends in Great Britain would believe us united and in earnest, or exert themselves very strenuously in our favor, while we acted such a wavering, hesitating part.

8. Foreign nations, particularly France and Spain, would not think us worthy of their attention while we appeared to be deceived by such fallacious hopes of redress of grievances, of pardon for our offences, and of reconciliation with our enemies.

9. We could not command the natural resources of our own country. We could not establish manufactories of arms, cannon, saltpetre, powder, ships, &c., without the powers of government; and all these and many other preparations ought to be going on in every State or Colony, if you will, in the country.

Although the opposition was still inveterate, many members of Congress began to hear me with more patience, and some began to ask me civil questions. "How can the people institute governments?" My answer was, "By conventions of representatives, freely, fairly, and proportionably chosen." "When the convention has fabricated a government, or a constitution rather, how do we know the people will submit to it?" "If there is any doubt of that, the convention may send out their project of a constitution, to the people in their several towns, counties, or districts, and the people may make the acceptance of it their own act." "But the people know nothing about constitutions." "I believe you are much mistaken in that supposition; if you are not, they will not oppose a plan prepared by their own chosen friends; but I believe that in every considerable portion of the people, there will be found some men, who will understand the subject as well as their representatives, and these will assist in enlightening the rest." "But what plan of a government would you advise?" "A plan as nearly resembling the government under which we were born, and have lived, as the circumstances of the country will admit. Kings we never had among us. Nobles we never had. Nothing hereditary ever existed in the country; nor will the country require or admit of any such thing. But governors and councils we have always had, as well as representatives. A legislature in three branches ought to be preserved, and independent judges." "Where and how will you get your governors and councils?" "By elections." "How,—who shall elect?" "The representatives of the people in a convention will be the best qualified to contrive a mode."

After all these discussions and interrogatories, Congress was not prepared nor disposed to do any thing as yet. They must consider farther.

"Resolved, That the consideration of this matter be referred to Monday next.

Monday arrived, and Tuesday and Wednesday passed over, and Congress not yet willing to do any thing.

On Thursday, October 26th, the subject was again brought on the carpet, and the same discussions repeated; for very little new was produced. After a long discussion, in which Mr. John Rutledge, Mr. Ward, Mr. Lee, Mr. Gadsden, Mr. Sherman, Mr. Dyer, and some others had spoken on the same side with me, Congress resolved, that a committee of five members be appointed to take into consideration the instructions given to the delegates of New

Hampshire, and report their opinion thereon. The members chosen,—Mr. John Rutledge, Mr. J. Adams, Mr. Ward, Mr. Lee, and Mr. Sherman.

Although this committee was entirely composed of members as well disposed to encourage the enterprise as could have been found in Congress, yet they could not be brought to agree upon a report and to bring it forward in Congress, till Friday, November 3d, when Congress, taking into consideration the report of the committee on the New Hampshire instructions, after another long deliberation and debate,—

"Resolved, That it be recommended to the Provincial Convention of New Hampshire, to call a full and free representation of the people, and that the representatives, if they think it necessary, establish such a form of government, as in their judgment will best produce the happiness of the people, and most effectually secure peace and good order in the Province, during the continuance of the present dispute between Great Britain and the Colonies.

By this time I mortally hated the words, "Province," "Colonies," and "Mother Country," and strove to get them out of the report. The last was indeed left out, but the other two were retained even by this committee, who were all as high Americans as any in the house, unless Mr. Gadsden should be excepted. Nevertheless, I thought this resolution a triumph, and a most important point gained.

Mr. John Rutledge was now completely with us in our desire of revolutionizing all the governments, and he brought forward immediately some representations from his own State, when

"Congress, then taking into consideration the State of South Carolina, and sundry papers relative thereto being read and considered.

"Resolved, That a committee of five be appointed to take the same into consideration, and report what in their opinion is necessary to be done. The members chosen, Mr. Harrison, Mr. Bullock, Mr. Hooper, Mr. Chase, and Mr. S. Adams.

On November 4th,

"The committee appointed to take into consideration the State of South Carolina, brought in their report, which being read," a number of resolutions passed, the last of which will be found in page 235 of the Journals, at the bottom.

"Resolved, That if the Convention of South Carolina shall find it necessary to establish a form of government in that Colony, it be recommended to that Convention to call a full and free representation of the people, and that the said representatives, if they think it necessary, shall establish such a form of government as in their judgment will produce the happiness of the people, and most effectually secure peace and good order in the Colony, during the continuance of the present dispute between Great Britain and the Colonies.

Although Mr. John Rutledge united with me and others, in persuading the committee to report this resolution, and the distance of Carolina made it convenient to furnish them with this discretionary recommendation, I doubt whether Mr. Harrison or Mr. Hooper were, as yet, sufficiently advanced to agree to it. Mr. Bullock, Mr. Chase, and Mr. Samuel Adams, were very ready for it. When it was under consideration, I labored afresh to expunge the words "Colony," and "Colonies," and insert the words "State," and "States," and the word "dispute," to make way for that of "war," and the word "Colonies," for the word "America," or "States," but the child was not yet weaned. I labored, also, to get the resolution enlarged, and extended into a recommendation to the people of all the States, to institute governments, and this occasioned more interrogatories from one part and another of the House. "What plan of government would you recommend?" &c. Here it would have been the most natural to have made a motion that Congress should appoint a committee to prepare a plan of government, to be reported to Congress and there discussed, paragraph by paragraph, and that which should be adopted should be recommended to all the States. But I dared not make such a motion, because I knew that if such a plan was adopted it would be, if not permanent, yet of long duration, and it would be extremely difficult to get rid of it. And I knew that every one of my friends, and all those who were the most zealous for assuming governments, had at that time no idea of any other government but a contemptible legislature in one assembly, with committees for executive magistrates and judges. These questions, therefore, I answered by sporting off hand a variety of short sketches of plans, which might be adopted by the conventions; and as this subject was brought into view in some way or other almost every day, and these interrogatories were frequently repeated, I had in my head and at my tongue's end as many projects of government as Mr. Burke says the Abbé Sieyes had in his pigeon-holes, not however, constructed at such length, nor labored with his-metaphysical refinements. I took care, however, always to bear my testimony against every plan of an unbalanced government.

I had read Harrington, Sidney, Hobbes, Nedham, and Locke, but with very little application to any particular views, till these debates in Congress, and the interrogatories in public and private, turned my thoughts to these researches, which produced the "Thoughts on Government," the Constitution of Massachusetts, and at length the "Defence of the Constitutions of the United States," and the "Discourses on Davila," writings which have never done any good to me, though some of them undoubtedly contributed to produce the Constitution of New York, the Constitution of the United States, and the last Constitutions of Pennsylvania and Georgia. They undoubtedly, also, contributed to the writings of Publius, called the Federalist, which were all written after the publication of my work in Philadelphia, New York, and Boston. Whether the people will permit any of these Constitutions to stand upon their pedestals, or whether they will throw them all down, I know not. Appearances at present are unfavorable and threatening. I have done all in my power according to what I thought my duty. I can do no more.

About the sixth of December, 1775, I obtained leave of Congress to visit my family, and returned home. The General Court sat at Watertown, our army was at Cambridge, and the British in Boston. Having a seat in Council, I had opportunity to converse with the members of both houses, to know their sentiments, and to communicate mine. The Council had unanimously appointed me in my absence, [Endnote 016] without any solicitation or desire on my part, Chief Justice of the State. I had accepted the office because it was a post of danger, but much against my inclination. I expected to go no more to Congress, but to take my seat on the bench. But the General Court would not excuse me from again attending Congress, and again chose me a member, with all my former colleagues, except Mr. Cushing, who I believe declined, and in his room Mr. Gerry was chosen, who went with me to Philadelphia, and we took our seats in Congress on Friday, February 9th, 1776. In this gentleman I found a faithful friend, and an ardent, persevering lover of his country, who never hesitated to promote, with all his abilities and industry, the boldest measures reconcilable with prudence. Mr. Samuel Adams, Mr. Gerry, and myself, now composed a majority of the Massachusetts delegation, and we were no longer vexed or enfeebled by divisions among ourselves, or by indecision, or indolence. On the 29th of February, 1776, William Whipple, Esq. appeared as one of the delegates from New Hampshire, another excellent member in principle and disposition, as well as understanding.

I returned to my daily routine of service in the board of war, and a punctual attendance in Congress, every day, in all their hours. I returned, also, to my almost daily exhortations to the institution of Governments in the States, and a declaration of independence. I soon found there was a whispering among the partisans in opposition to independence, that I was interested; that I held an office under the new government of Massachusetts; that I was afraid of losing it, if we did not declare independence; and that I consequently ought not to be attended to. This they circulated so successfully, that they got it insinuated among the members of the legislature in Maryland, where their friends were powerful enough to give an instruction to their delegates in Congress, warning them against listening to the advice of interested persons, and manifestly pointing me out to the understanding of every one. This instruction was read in Congress. [Endnote 017] It produced no other effect upon me than a laughing letter to my friend, Mr. Chase, [Endnote 018] who regarded it no more than I did. These chuckles I was informed of, and witnessed for many weeks, and at length they broke out in a very extraordinary manner. When I had been speaking one day on the subject of independence, or the institution of governments, which I always considered as the same thing, a gentleman of great fortune and high rank arose and said, he should move, that no person who held any office under a new government should be admitted to vote on any such question, as they were interested persons. I wondered at the simplicity of this motion, but knew very well what to do with it. I rose from my seat with great coolness and deliberation; so far from expressing or feeling any resentment, I really felt gay, though as it happened, I preserved an unusual gravity in my countenance and air, and said, "Mr. President, I will second the gentleman's motion, and I recommend it to the honorable gentleman to second another which I should make, namely, that no gentleman who holds any office under the old or present government should be admitted to vote on any such question, as they were interested persons." The moment when this was pronounced, it flew like an electric stroke through every countenance in the room, for the gentleman who made the motion held as high an office under the old government as I did under the new, and many other members present held offices under the royal government. My friends accordingly were delighted with my retaliation, and the friends of my antagonist were mortified at his indiscretion in exposing himself to such a retort. Finding the house in a good disposition to hear me, I added, I would go further, and cheerfully consent to a self-denying ordinance, that every member of Congress, before we proceeded to any question respecting independence, should take a solemn oath never to accept or hold any office of any kind in America after the revolution. Mr. Wythe, of Virginia, rose here, and said Congress had no right to exclude any of their members from voting on these questions; their constituents only had a right to restrain them; and that no member had a right to take, nor Congress to prescribe any engagement not to hold offices after the revolution or before. Again I replied, that whether the gentleman's opinion was well or ill founded, I had only said that I was willing to consent to such an arrangement. That I knew very well what these things meant. They were personal attacks upon me, and I was glad that at length they had been made publicly where I could defend myself. That I knew very well that they had been made secretly and circulated in whispers, not only in the city of Philadelphia and State of Pennsylvania, but in the neighboring States, particularly Maryland, and very probably in private letters throughout the Union. I now took the opportunity to declare in public, that it was very true, the unmerited and unsolicited, though unanimous good will of the Council of Massachusetts, had appointed me to an important office, that of Chief Justice; that as this office was a very conspicuous station, and consequently a dangerous one, I had not dared to refuse it, because it was a post of danger, though by the acceptance of it, I was obliged to relinquish another office,—meaning my barrister's office—which was more than four times as profitable. That it was a sense of duty, and a full conviction of an honest cause, and not any motives of ambition, or hopes of honor, or profit, which had drawn me into my present course. That I had seen enough already in the course of my own experience to know that the American cause was not the most promising road to profits, honors, power, or pleasure. That on the contrary, a man must renounce all these, and devote himself to labor, danger and death, and very possibly to disgrace and infamy, before he was fit in my judgment, in the present state and future prospects of the country, for a seat in that Congress. This whole scene was a comedy to Charles Thomson, whose countenance was in raptures all the time. When all was over, he told me he had been highly delighted with it, because he had been witness to many of their conversations, in which they had endeavored to excite and propagate prejudices against me, on account of my office of Chief Justice. But he said I had cleared and explained the thing in such a manner that he would be bound I should never hear any more reflections on that head. No more, indeed, were made in my presence, but the party did not cease to abuse me in their secret circles on this account, as I was well informed. Not long afterwards, hearing that the Supreme Court in Massachusetts was organized and proceeding very well on the business of their circuits, I wrote my resignation of the office of Chief Justice, to the Council, very happy to get fairly rid of an office that I knew to be burdensome, and whose emoluments, with my small fortune, would not support my family.

On the 9th of February, the day on which Mr. Gerry and I took our seats for this year, sundry letters from General Washington, General Schuyler, Governor Trumbull, with papers inclosed, were read, and referred to Mr. Chase, Mr. J. Adams, Mr. Penn, Mr. Wythe, and Mr. Rutledge.

On the 14th of February, sundry letters from General Schuyler, General Wooster, and General Arnold, were read, and referred, with the papers enclosed, to Mr. Wythe, Mr. J. Adams, and Mr. Chase. On the same day,

"Congress resolved itself into a committee of the whole House, to take into consideration the report of the committee on the regulations and restrictions under which the ports should be opened after the first day of March next, and, after some time spent thereon, the President resumed the chair, and Mr. Ward reported, that the committee had taken into consideration the matter referred to them, but not having come to a conclusion desired leave to sit again, which was granted for to-morrow."

On the 15th of February,

"Sundry other letters, from General Lee, General Schuyler, and General Wooster, were referred to the committee to whom the letters received yesterday were referred.

"On the same day, Congress took into consideration the report from the committee of the whole House, and, after debate, resolved that it be recommitted.

"Resolved, That Congress will to-morrow morning resolve itself into a committee of the whole, to take into consideration the propriety of opening the ports, and the restrictions and regulations of trade of these Colonies, after the first of March next."

Friday, February 16,

"Agreeably to the order of the day, the Congress resolved itself into a committee of the whole, to take into consideration the propriety of opening the ports, &c.

"After some time spent, Mr. Ward reported, that, not having come to a conclusion, the committee asked leave to sit again; granted."

Saturday, February 17,

"The committee to whom the letters from Generals Arnold, Wooster, Schuyler, and Lee, were referred, brought in their report, which was agreed to in the several resolutions detailed in the Journal of this day. Endnote 019

"Same day, Resolved, That Mr. J. Adams, Mr. Wythe, and Mr. Sherman, be a a committee to prepare instructions for the committee appointed to go to Canada.

"Resolved, That Congress will, on Tuesday next, resolve itself into a committee of the whole, to take into consideration the propriety of opening the ports," &c.

This measure, of opening the ports, &c. labored exceedingly, because it was considered as a bold step to independence. Indeed, I urged it expressly with that view, and as connected with the institution of government in all the States, and a declaration of national independence. The party against me had art and influence as yet, to evade, retard, and delay every motion that we made. Many motions were made, and argued at great length, and with great spirit on both sides, which are not to be found in the Journals. When motions were made and debates ensued in a committee of the whole House, no record of them was made by the secretary, unless the motion prevailed and was reported to Congress, and there adopted. This arrangement was convenient for the party in opposition to us, who by this means evaded the appearance, on the Journals, of any subject they disliked. *Endnote 020*

On Monday, February 19th, Congress attended an oration in honor of General Montgomery, and the officers and soldiers who fell with him.

On Tuesday, February 20th, and on Wednesday, February 21st, means were contrived to elude the committee of the whole House.

Thursday, February 22,

"Two letters from General Washington were referred to a committee of the whole House. Accordingly Congress resolved itself into a committee of the whole, and after some time Mr. Ward reported, that the committee had come to no conclusion; and Congress resolved, that to-morrow they would again resolve themselves into a committee of the whole, to take into their further consideration the letters from General Washington.

"Friday, February 23. Resolved, That Congress will on Monday next resolve itself into a committee of the whole, to take into consideration the letters from General Washington.

Monday, February 26th, arrived, and

"A letter from General Lee was referred to Mr. McKean, Mr. John Adams, and Mr. Lewis Morris, but no resolution of Congress into a committee of the whole.

"On Tuesday, February 27. The order of the day was renewed, but nothing done.

"Wednesday, February 28. The committee to whom the letters from General Lee, &c. were referred, brought in their report. Resolved, That the consideration of it be postponed till to-morrow."

Thursday, February 29.

"A letter of the 14th, from General Washington, inclosing a letter from Lord Drummond to General Robinson, and sundry other papers, were read. Agreeable to the order of the day, the Congress resolved itself into a committee of the whole, to take into consideration the letter from General Washington of the 9th instant, and the trade of the Colonies after the first of March; and after some time, Mr. Ward reported that the committee, not having come to a conclusion, desired leave to sit again; granted.

"Resolved, That this Congress will, to-morrow, resolve itself into a committee of the whole, to take into further consideration the letter from General Washington, and the trade of the Colonies."

The very short sketch, which is here traced, is enough to show that postponement was the object of our antagonists; and the Journals for those days will show the frivolous importance of the business transacted in them, in comparison of the great concerns which were before the committees of the whole House. There was, however, still a majority of members who were either determined against all measures preparatory to independence, or yet too timorous and wavering to venture on any decisive steps. We therefore could do nothing but keep our eyes fixed on the great objects of free trade, new governments, and independence of the United States, and seize every opening opportunity of advancing step by step in our progress. Our opponents were not less vigilant in seizing on every excuse for delay; the letter from Lord Drummond, which seemed to derive importance, from the transmission of it by General Washington, was a fine engine to play cold water on the fire of independence. They set it in operation with great zeal and activity. It was, indeed, a very airy phantom, and ought not to have been sent us by the General, who should only have referred

Lord Drummond to Congress. But there were about head-quarters some who were as weak and wavering as our members; and the General himself had chosen, for his private confidential correspondent, a member from Virginia, Harrison, who was still counted among the cold party. This was an indolent, luxurious, heavy gentleman, of no use in Congress or committee, but a great embarrassment to both. He was represented to be a kind of nexus utriusque mundi, a corner stone in which the two walls of party met in Virginia. He was descended from one of the most ancient, wealthy, and respectable families in the ancient dominion, and seemed to be set up in opposition to Mr. Richard Henry Lee. Jealousies and divisions appeared among the delegates of no State more remarkably than among those of Virginia. Mr. Wythe told me that Thomas Lee, the elder brother of Richard Henry, was the delight of the eyes of Virginia, and by far the most popular man they had; but Richard Henry was not. I asked the reason; for Mr. Lee appeared a scholar, a gentleman, a man of uncommon eloquence, and an agreeable man. Mr. Wythe said this was all true, but Mr. Lee had, when he was very young, and when he first came into the House of Burgesses, moved and urged on an inquiry into the state of the treasury, which was found deficient in large sums, which had been lent by the treasurer to many of the most influential families of the country, who found themselves exposed, and had never forgiven Mr. Lee. [Endnote 021] This, he said, had made him so many enemies, that he never had recovered his reputation, but was still heartily hated by great numbers. These feelings among the Virginia delegates were a great injury to us. Mr. Samuel Adams and myself were very intimate with Mr. Lee, and he agreed perfectly with us in the great system of our policy, and by his means we kept a majority of the delegates of Virginia with us; but Harrison, Pendleton, and some others, showed their jealousy of this intimacy plainly enough at times. Harrison consequently courted Mr. Hancock and some other of our colleagues; but we had now a majority, and gave ourselves no trouble about their little intrigues. This is all necessary to show the operation of Lord Drummond's communication. I have forgotten the particulars, but he pretended to have had conversation with Lord North; talked warmly of Lord North's good will and desire of reconciliation, but had no authority to show, and no distinct proposition to make. [Endnote 022] In short, it was so flimsy a veil, that the purblind might see through it. But yet it was made instrumental of much delay and amusement to numbers.

Friday, March 1,

"Resolved, That this Congress will to-morrow resolve itself into a committee of the whole, to take into consideration the letter of General Washington, of the 14th, with the papers inclosed.

"Resolved, That the memorial from the merchants of Montreal, be referred to a committee of five. Mr. Wilson, Mr. J. Adams, Mr. W. Livingston, Mr. L. Morris, and Mr. Tilghman."

Tuesday, March 5,

"Congress resolved itself into a committee of the whole, to take into consideration the letter from General Washington, of the 14th of February, and the papers inclosed, and after some time the President resumed the chair, and Mr. Harrison reported, that the committee have had under consideration the letters and papers to them referred, but have come to no resolution thereon.

"Resolved, That the letter from General Washington, so far as it has not been considered by the committee of the whole, be referred to the committee to whom his other letters of the 24th and 30th of January were referred.

"Wednesday, March 6. A letter from General Washington, of the 26th of February, was read. Resolved, That it be referred to the committee to whom his other letters are referred. The order of the day renewed.

"Thursday, March 7. The order of the day was renewed.

"Friday, March 8. No order of the day. The committee to whom the letters from Generals Schuyler, Wooster, and Arnold, were referred, brought in their report.

"Saturday, March 9. The committee appointed to prepare instructions for the commissioners going to Canada, brought in a draught, which was read.

"Monday, March 11. Congress took into consideration the instructions to the commissioners going to Canada. Postponed.

"Tuesday, March 12. Postponed again."

Wednesday, March 13. Although the system had been so long pursued to postpone all the great political questions, and take up any other business of however trifling consequence, yet we were daily urging on the order of the day, and on this day we succeeded.

"Congress resolved itself into a committee of the whole, to take into consideration the memorial of the merchants, &c. of Philadelphia, &c. the letters from General Washington, the state of the trade of the Colonies, &c. Mr. Ward reported no resolution. Leave to sit again."

Thursday, March 14. The state of the country so obviously called for independent governments, and a total extinction of the royal authority, and we were so earnestly urging this measure from day to day, and the opposition to it was growing so unpopular, that a kind of evasion was contrived in the following resolution, which I considered as an important step, and therefore would not oppose it, though I urged, with several others, that we ought to make the resolution more general, and advise the people to assume all the powers of government. The proposition that passed was,—

"Resolved, That it be recommended to the several Assemblies, Conventions, and Committees or Councils of Safety, of the United Colonies, immediately to cause all persons to be disarmed, within their respective Colonies, who are notoriously disaffected to the cause of America, or who have not associated and shall refuse to associate to defend by arms these United Colonies against the hostile attempts of the British fleets and armies, and to apply the arms taken from such persons in each respective Colony, in the first place, to the arming the continental troops raised in said Colony; in the next, to the arming such troops as are raised by the Colony for its own defence; and the residue to be applied to the arming the associators; that the arms when taken be appraised by indifferent persons, and such as are applied to the arming the continental troops be paid for by the Congress, and the residue by the respective Assemblies, Conventions, or Councils or Committees of Safety.

"Ordered, That a copy of the foregoing resolution be transmitted, by the delegates of each Colony, to their respective Assemblies, Conventions, or Councils or Committees of Safety."

This resolution and order was indeed assuming the powers of government in a manner as offensive as the measures we proposed could have been; but it left all the powers of government in the hands of Assemblies, Conventions, and Committees, which composed a scene of much confusion and injustice, the continuance of which was much dreaded by me, as tending to injure the morals of the people, and destroy their habits of order and attachment to regular government. However, I could do nothing but represent and remonstrate; the vote as yet was against me.

Friday, March 15,

"Congress resolved itself into a committee of the whole, to take into consideration the State of New York, and, after some time, the President resumed the chair, and Mr. Harrison reported that the committee have come to certain resolutions."

These may be seen in the Journal, and relate wholly to the defence of New York.

This is the first appearance of Mr. Harrison as chairman of the committee of the whole. The President, Mr. Hancock, had hitherto nominated Governor Ward, of Rhode Island, to that conspicuous distinction. Mr. Harrison had courted Mr. Hancock, and Mr. Hancock had courted Mr. Duane, Mr. Dickinson, and their party, and leaned so partially in their favor, that Mr. Samuel Adams had become very bitter against Mr. Hancock, and spoke of him with great asperity in private circles; and this alienation between them continued from this time till the year 1789, thirteen years, when they were again reconciled. Governor Ward was become extremely obnoxious to Mr. Hancock's party, by his zealous attachment to Mr. Samuel Adams and Mr. Richard Henry Lee. Such, I supposed, were the motives which excited Mr. Hancock to bring forward Mr. Harrison.

Although Harrison was another Sir John Falstaff, excepting in his larcenies and robberies, his conversation disgusting to every man of delicacy or decorum, yet, as I saw he was to be often nominated with us in business, I took no notice of his vices or follies, but treated him, and Mr. Hancock too, with uniform politeness. I was, however, too intimate with Mr. Lee, Mr. Adams, Mr. Ward, &c. to escape the jealousy and malignity of their adversaries. Hence, I suppose, the calumnies that were written or otherwise insinuated into the minds of the army, that I was an enemy to Washington, in favor of an annual election of a General, against enlisting troops during the war, &c. &c.; all utterly false and groundless.

Saturday, March 16,

"Mr. W. Livingston brought in a proclamation for a fast on the 17th of May.

"Congress resolved itself into a committee of the whole, according to the standing order of the day. Mr. Harrison reported no resolution."

Tuesday, March 19,

"The order of the day again. Mr. Harrison reported that the committee have come to sundry resolutions, which they directed him to lay before Congress. The report of the committee being read,

"Resolved, That a committee of three be appointed to draw a declaration pursuant to said report, and lay the same before Congress. The members chosen, Mr. Wythe, Mr. Jay, and Mr. Wilson."

Mr. Wythe was one of our best men; but Mr. Jay and Mr. Wilson, though excellent members when present, had been hitherto generally in favor of the dilatory system.

"Resolved, That it be an instruction to the said committee to receive and insert a clause or clauses, that all seamen and mariners on board of merchantships and vessels taken and condemned as prizes shall be entitled to their pay, according to the terms of their contracts, until the time of condemnation."

Wednesday, March 20. Congress resumed the consideration of the instructions and commission to the deputies or commissioners going to Canada, and agreed to them as they appear in the Journals. In these we obtained one step more towards our great object—a general recommendation to the States to institute governments. Congress recommended to the people of Canada to set up such a form of government as will be most likely, in their judgment, to produce their happiness; and pressed them to have a complete representation of the people assembled in Convention, with all possible expedition, to deliberate concerning the establishment of a form of government, and a union with the United Colonies. It will readily be supposed that a great part of these instructions were opposed by our antagonists with great zeal; but they were supported on our side with equal ardor, and the acceptance of them afforded a strong proof of the real determination of a majority of Congress to go with us to the final consummation of our wishes.

Thursday, March 21. There are three resolutions which I claim. *Endnote 023*

These resolutions I introduced and supported, not only for their intrinsic utility, which I thought would be very considerable, but because they held up to the view of the nation the air of independence.

Friday, March 22,

"Congress took into consideration the declaration brought in by the committee, and, after debate, the further consideration of it, at the request of a Colony, was postponed till to-morrow."

Saturday, March 23. The Congress resumed the consideration of the declaration, which was agreed to as follows.

"Whereas the petitions of the United Colonies to the King, for the redress of great and manifold grievances, have not only been rejected, but treated with scorn and contempt, and the opposition to designs evidently formed to reduce them to a state of servile subjection, and their necessary defence against hostile forces actually employed to subdue them, declared rebellion; and whereas an unjust war hath been commenced against them, which the commanders of the British fleets and armies have prosecuted, and still continue to prosecute, with their utmost vigor, and in a cruel manner, wasting, spoiling, and destroying the country, burning houses and defenceless towns, and exposing the helpless inhabitants to every misery, from the inclemency of the winter, and not only urging savages to invade the country, but instigating negroes to murder their masters; and whereas the Parliament of Great Britain hath lately passed an act, affirming these Colonics to be in open rebellion, forbidding all trade and commerce with the inhabitants thereof, until they shall accept pardons, and submit to despotic rule, declaring their property, wherever found upon the water, liable to seizure and confiscation, and enacting that what had been done there, by virtue of the royal authority, were just and lawful acts, and shall be so deemed; from all which it is manifest, that the iniquitous scheme, concerted to deprive them of the liberty they have a right to by the laws of nature and the English constitution, will be pertinaciously pursued. It being, therefore, necessary to provide for their defence and security, and justifiable to make reprisals upon their enemies, and otherwise to annoy them, according to the laws and usages of nations, the Congress, trusting that such of their friends in Great Britain, (of whom it is confessed there are many entitled to applause and gratitude for their patriotism and benevolence, and in whose favor a discrimination of property cannot be made,) as shall suffer by captures, will impute it to the authors of our common calamities, do declare and resolve as followeth, to wit:—

"Resolved, That the inhabitants of these Colonies be permitted to fit out armed vessels, to cruise on the enemies of these United Colonies.

"Resolved, That all ships and other vessels, their tackle, apparel, and furniture, and all goods, wares, and merchandises, belonging to any inhabitant or inhabitants of Great Britain, taken on the high seas, or between high and low water mark, by any armed vessel fitted out by any private person or persons, and to whom commissions shall be granted, and being libelled and prosecuted in any court erected for the trial of maritime affairs, in any of these Colonies, shall be deemed and adjudged to be lawful prize; and after deducting and paying the wages which the seamen and mariners, on board of such captures as are merchant ships and vessels, shall be entitled to, according to the terms of their contracts, until the time of the adjudication, shall be condemned to and for the use of the owner or owners, and the officers, marines, and mariners of such armed vessel, according to such rules and proportions as they shall agree on; provided always, that this resolution shall not extend to any vessel bringing settlers, arms, ammunition, and warlike stores to and for the use of these Colonies or any of the inhabitants thereof, who are friends to the American cause, or to such warlike stores, or to the effects of such settlers. *Endnote 024*

Resolved, That a committee of five be appointed to consider of the fortifying one or more ports on the American coast in the strongest manner, for the protection of our cruisers, and the reception of their prizes; that they take the opinion of the best engineers on the manner and expense; and report thereon to Congress.

The members chosen, Mr. Harrison, Mr. J. Adams, Mr. Hewes, Mr. R. Morris and Mr. Whipple.

Resolved, That this Congress will, on Monday next, resolve itself into a committee of the whole, to take into consideration the trade of the United Colonies; and that sundry motions offered by the members from Massachusetts Bay, Maryland, and Virginia, be referred to said committee.

Here is an instance, in addition to many others, of an extraordinary liberty taken by the secretary, I suppose at the instigation of the party against independence, to suppress, by omitting on the Journals, the many motions that were made disagreeable to that set. These motions ought to have been inserted verbatim on the Journals, with the names of those who made them.

On Monday, March 25th, I made a motion, and laid it in writing on the table, in these words,—

Resolved, That the thanks of this Congress, in their own name, and in the name of the thirteen United Colonies, whom they represent, be presented to His Excellency General Washington, and the officers and soldiers under his command, for their wise and spirited conduct in the siege and acquisition of Boston; and that a medal of gold be struck in commemoration of this great event and presented to His Excellency; and that a committee of three be appointed to prepare a letter of thanks, and a proper device for the medal.

The members chosen, Mr. J. Adams, Mr. Jay, and Mr. Hopkins.

Tuesday, March 26. Congress were informed of the death of Governor Ward, and on

Wednesday, March 27th, they attended his funeral, in mourning for a month. In this gentleman, who died of the small-pox, we lost an honorable, a conscientious, a benevolent, and inflexible patriot.

Thursday, March 28. A multitude of details, but no committee of the whole house.

Friday, March 29. More trifles, but no committee of the whole.

Saturday, March 30. Ditto.

Monday, April 1. A measure of great importance was adopted; a treasury office with an auditor, and a sufficient number of clerks. On the 17th of February, Congress had resolved that a standing committee of five be appointed for superintending the Treasury; their duties were pointed out; and Mr. Duane, Mr. Nelson, Mr. Gerry, Mr. Smith, and Mr. Willing, were chosen on the committee. On this day, April 1st, the treasury was much improved in its system. No order of the day.

April 2.

"The committee appointed to prepare a letter of thanks to General Washington, and the officers and soldiers under his command, brought in a draught, which was read and agreed to.

"Ordered, That it be transcribed, signed by the President, and forwarded."

But the letter, a great part of the compliment of which would have lain in the insertion of it in the Journals, was carefully secluded. Perhaps the secretary, or the president, or both, chose rather to conceal the compliment to the General, than make one to the member who made the motion and the committee who prepared it. I never troubled myself about the Journals, and should never have known the letter was not there, if I had not been called to peruse them now, after twenty-nine years have rolled away. *Endnote 025*

April 3. Great things were done. The naval system made great progress.

April 4. We did great things again.

"Agreeable to the order of the day, the Congress resolved itself into a committee of the whole, to take into consideration the trade of the United Colonies, and after some time spent thereon, the President resumed the chair, and Mr. Harrison reported that the committee had taken into consideration the matters referred to them, and had come to sundry resolutions, which he was ordered to deliver in.

"The resolutions agreed to by the committee of the whole Congress being read,

"Ordered, To lie on the table."

April 5. Good Friday.

April 6.

"The Congress resumed the consideration of the report from the committee of the whole, and the same being twice read, and debated by paragraphs, was agreed to."

These resolutions are on the Journals, and amount to something. They opened the ports, and set our commerce at liberty, but they were far short of what had been moved by members from Massachusetts, Maryland, and Virginia. There is one resolution I will not omit.

"Resolved, That no slaves be imported into any of the thirteen Colonies."

I will not omit to remark here the manifest artifice in concealing in the Journals the motions which were made, and the names of the members who made them, in these daily committees of the whole. The spirit of a party, which has been before exposed, can alone account for this unfairness.

"A letter from General Washington of the 27th of March, and a letter from Brigadier General Heath, being received and read,

"Resolved, That the letter from General Washington, with the papers inclosed, be referred to a committee of the whole Congress."

Tuesday, April 9. No committee of the whole.

Wednesday, April 10.

"Resolved, That the letters from General Washington, be referred to a committee of the whole Congress."

April 11.

"Resolved, That a committee of three be appointed to inquire into the truth of the report respecting Governor Tryon's exacting an oath from persons going by the packet, and to ascertain the fact by affidavits taken before a chief justice, or other chief magistrate.

"The members chosen, Mr. Jay, Mr. Wythe, and Mr. Wilson."

This helped forward our designs a little.

"Resolved, That it be recommended to the several Assemblies, Conventions, and Committees or Councils of Safety of the United Colonies, to use their best endeavors in communicating to foreign nations the resolutions of Congress relative to trade."

This, also, was a considerable advance; but it would now be scarcely credited if I were to relate the struggle it cost us to obtain every one of these resolutions.

April 12. No committee of the whole.

April 13. No committee of the whole.

April 15. No committee of the whole.

Tuesday, April 16.

"Whereas, information has been this day laid before Congress, from which there is great reason to believe that Robert Eden, Esq., Governor of Maryland, has lately carried on a correspondence with the British Ministry, highly dangerous to the liberties of America;

"Resolved, therefore, that the Council of Safety of Maryland be earnestly requested immediately to cause the person and papers of Governor Eden to be seized and secured, and such of the papers as relate to the American dispute, without delay, conveyed safely to Congress, and that copies of the intercepted letters from the Secretary of State be inclosed to the said Council of Safety."

A similar resolution relative to Alexander Ross and his papers.

No committee of the whole.

Wednesday, April 17. Thursday, April 18. No committee of the whole.

Friday, April 19.

"Resolved, That a committee of seven be appointed to examine and ascertain the value of the several species of gold and silver coins current in these Colonies, and the proportions they ought to bear to Spanish milled dollars. Members chosen, Mr. Duane, Mr. Wythe, Mr. John Adams, Mr. Sherman, Mr. Hewes, Mr. Johnson, and Mr. Whipple.

"The committee to whom General Washington's letter of the 15th instant, as well as other letters, were referred, brought in their report, which being taken into consideration was agreed to, whereupon, Resolved." Endnote 026

One resolution was, that the resignation of James Warren, as paymaster-general of the army, be accepted. This gentleman had been appointed at my solicitation, Mr. Samuel Adams and Mr. Gerry concurring; our other colleagues notwithstanding.

"The committee to whom were referred the letter from General Washington of the 4th, and the letter from General Schuyler of the second, of this month, brought in their report.

"Adjourned to Monday."

Monday, April 22. A letter from the Canada Commissioners, one from General Washington of the 19th, one from General Schuyler, inclosing sundry letters and papers from Canada, and one from the committee of inspection of West Augusta, with sundry papers inclosed, were referred to Mr. R. H. Lee, Mr. J. Adams, Mr. Jay, Mr. Braxton, and Mr. Johnson.

Tuesday, April 23.

"The committee to whom the letters from General Washington, General Schuyler, and the letters from Canada, &c., were referred, brought in their report."

Wednesday, April 24. Thomas Heyward, Junior, Esq., a new member from Carolina, and an excellent one, appeared in Congress. On him we could always depend for sound measures, though he seldom spoke in public. Thomas Lynch, Junior, Esq., also appeared. Congress resolved itself into a committee of the whole, but came to no resolutions.

Thursday, April 25. Two letters from General Washington of the 22d, and 23d, were referred to Mr. R. H. Lee, Mr. J. Adams, and Mr. Hewes.

"Congress resolved itself into a committee of the whole, to take into their farther consideration, the letter from General Washington of the 27th of March last, and the papers therein inclosed, and Mr. Harrison reported that the committee had come to a resolution on the matters referred to them, which he read and delivered in."

Report read again, and postponed.

Friday, April 26. Postponed. Saturday, April 27. Ditto.

Monday, April 29. Congress resumed the consideration of the report of the committee on General Washington's letter of the 20th, and came to sundry resolutions which may be seen on the Journal.

Tuesday, April 30.

"Congress took into consideration the report of the Committee on General Washington's letter of the 24th of March, whereupon, Resolved,"

As in the Journal. Of some importance, but nothing to the great objects still kept out of sight.

"The delegates from New Jersey having laid before Congress a number of bills, counterfeited to imitate the continental bills of credit,

"Resolved, That a committee of six be appointed to consider of this matter, and report thereon to Congress. The members chosen, Mr. W. Livingston, Mr. McKean, Mr. Sherman, Mr. J. Adams, Mr. Braxton, and Mr. Duane. Adjourned to Thursday."

Thursday, May 2.

"Congress resumed the consideration of the report of the Committee on General Washington's letter of the 24th of March last, and after debate,

"Resolved, That it be recommitted, and, as the members of the former committee are absent, that a new committee be appointed; the members chosen, Mr. Dickinson, Mr. W. Livingston, and Mr. Rutledge."

The recommitment, and the names of the new committee, show the design.

Friday, May 3.

"A petition from Peter Simon was presented to Congress, and read; ordered, that it be referred to a committee of three. The members chosen, Mr. McKean, Mr. Wythe, and Mr. J. Adams.

"The committee to whom the report on General Washington's letter of the 24th of March last was recommitted, brought in their report, which was read;

"Ordered, To lie on the table."

Monday, May 6.

"Congress resumed the consideration of the report on General Washington's letter of the 24th of March, and thereupon came to the following resolution;

"Whereas, General Washington has requested directions concerning the conduct that should be observed towards commissioners said to be coming from Great Britain to America,

"Resolved, That General Washington be informed, that Congress suppose, if commissioners are intended to be sent from Great Britain to treat of peace, that the practice usual in such cases will be observed, by making previous application for the necessary passports or safe conduct, and on such application being made, Congress will then direct the proper measures for the reception of such commissioners."

It will be observed how long this trifling business had been depending, but it cannot be known from the Journal how much debate it had occasioned. It was one of those delusive contrivances, by which the party in opposition to us endeavored, by lulling the people with idle hopes of reconciliation into security, to turn their heads and thoughts from independence. They endeavored to insert in the resolution ideas of reconciliation; we carried our point for inserting peace. They wanted powers to be given to the General to receive the commissioners in ceremony; we ordered nothing to be done till we were solicited for passports. Upon the whole, we avoided the snare, and brought the controversy to a close, with some dignity. But it will never be known how much labor it cost us to accomplish it.

Then a committee of the whole, on the state of the colonies. Mr. Harrison reported sundry resolutions, which, as they stand on the Journal, will show the art and skill with which the General's letters, Indian affairs, revenue matters, naval arrangements, and twenty other things, many of them very trivial, were mixed, in those committees of the whole, with the great subjects of government, independence, and commerce. Little things were designedly thrown in the way of great ones, and the time consumed upon trifles which ought to have been consecrated to higher interests. We could only harangue against the misapplication of time, and harangues consumed more time, so that we could only now and then snatch a transient glance at the promised land. Endnote 027

Wednesday, May 8.

"The instructions given by the naval committee to Commodore Hopkins being laid before Congress and read;

"Ordered, That they be referred to a committee of seven, and that it be an instruction to the said committee to inquire how far Commodore Hopkins has complied with the said instructions, and if, upon inquiring, they shall find that he has departed therefrom, to examine into the occasion thereof; also to inquire into the situation of the governor and lieutenant-governor of Providence and the other officer brought from thence, and report what, in their opinion, is proper to be done with them.

"That the said Committee have power to send for witnesses and papers.

"The members chosen, Mr. Harrison, Mr. J. Adams, Mr. McKean, Mr. Duane, Mr. Lynch, Mr. Sherman, and Mr. W. Livingston."

There were three persons at this time who were standing subjects of altercation in Congress; General Wooster, Commodore Hopkins, and a Mr. Wrixon. I never could discover any reason for the bitterness against Wooster, but his being a New Englandman; Endnote 028 nor for that against Hopkins, but that he had done too much; nor for that against Wrixon, but his being patronized by Mr. Samuel Adams and Mr. R. H. Lee. Be it as it may, these three consumed an immense quantity of time, and kept up the passions of the parties to a great height. One design was to divert us from our main object.

A committee of the whole. Mr. Harrison reported no resolution. Leave to sit again.

Thursday, May 9. A committee of the whole. Mr. Harrison reported a resolution, which he read and delivered in. The resolution of the committee of the whole was again read, and the determination thereof, at the request of a Colony, was postponed till to-morrow.

Friday, May 10.

"Congress resumed the consideration of the resolution reported from the committee of the whole, and the same was agreed to as follows;

"Resolved, That it be recommended to the respective assemblies and conventions of the United Colonies, where no government sufficient to the exigencies of their affairs hath been hitherto established, to adopt such government as shall, in the opinion of the representatives of the people, best conduce to the happiness and safety of their constituents in particular, and America in general.

"Resolved, That a committee of three be appointed to prepare a preamble to the foregoing resolution. The members chosen, Mr. J. Adams, Mr. Rutledge, and Mr. Richard Henry Lee."

Marshall, in his Life of Washington, says, Endnote 029 "this resolution was moved by R. H. Lee, and seconded by J. Adams." It was brought before the Committee of the whole house, in concert between Mr. R. H. Lee and me, and I suppose General Washington was informed of it by Mr. Harrison, the chairman, or some other of his correspondents. But nothing of this appears upon the Journal. It is carefully concealed, like many other things relative to the greatest affairs of the nation, which were before Congress in that year.

This resolution I considered as an epocha, a decisive event. Endnote 030 It was a measure which I had invariably pursued for a whole year, and contended for, through a scene and a series of anxiety, labor, study, argument, and obloquy, which was then little known, and is now forgotten by all but Dr. Rush and a very few, who, like him, survive. Millions of curses were poured out upon me for these exertions and for these triumphs over them, by many, who, whatever their pretences may have been, have never forgotten, nor cordially forgiven me. By these I mean, not the Tories, for from them I received always more candor, but a class of people who thought proper and convenient to themselves to go along with the public opinion, in appearance, though in their hearts they detested it. Although they might think the public opinion was right, in general, in its difference with Great Britain, yet they secretly regretted the separation, and above all things the connection with France. Such a party has always existed, and was the final ruin of the federal administration, as will hereafter very plainly appear.

A committee of the whole again. Mr. Harrison reported no resolution. I mention these committees to show how all these great questions labored. Day after day consumed in debates without any conclusion.

Saturday, May 11.

"A petition from John Jacobs, in behalf of himself and others, was presented to Congress and read.

"Ordered, that it be referred to a committee of three. The members chosen, Mr. John Adams, Mr. Lee, and Mr. Rutledge.

"A committee of the whole. Mr. Harrison reported no resolution."

This day's Journal of this Committee shows with what art other matters were referred to these committees of the whole, in order to retard and embarrass the great questions.

Tuesday, May 14.

"A letter of the 11th, from General Washington, inclosing sundry papers, a letter of the 3d, from General Schuyler, and a letter of the 9th, from Daniel Robertson, were laid before Congress and read.

"Resolved, That they be referred to a committee of three. The members chosen, Mr. W. Livingston, Mr. Jefferson, and Mr. J. Adams."

William Ellery, Esq., appeared as a delegate from Rhode Island, in the place of Governor Ward, and being an excellent member, fully supplied his place. The Committee appointed to prepare a preamble, thought it not necessary to be very elaborate, and Mr. Lee and Mr. Rutledge desired me, as chairman, to draw something very short, which I did, and, with their approbation, on Wednesday, May 15th, reported the following, which was agreed to.

"Whereas, His Britannic Majesty in conjunction with the Lords and Commons of Great Britain has, by a late act of Parliament, excluded the inhabitants of these United Colonies from the protection of his crown; and whereas, no answer whatever to the humble petitions of the Colonies for redress of grievances and reconciliation with Great Britain has been, or is likely to be given, but the whole force of that kingdom, aided by foreign mercenaries, is to be exerted for the destruction of the good people of these Colonies; and whereas, it appears absolutely irreconcilable to reason and good conscience for the people of these Colonies now to take the oaths and affirmations necessary for the support of any government under the Crown of Great Britain, and it is necessary that the exercise of every kind of authority under the said Crown should be totally suppressed, and all the powers of government exerted under the authority of the people of the Colonies, for the preservation of internal peace, virtue, and good order, as well as for the defence of their lives, liberties, and properties, against the hostile invasions and cruel depredations of their enemies. Therefore,

"Resolved, That it be recommended to the respective Assemblies and Conventions of the United Colonies, where no government sufficient to the exigencies of their affairs hath been hitherto established, to adopt such government as shall, in the opinion of the representatives of the people, best conduce to the happiness and safety of their constituents in particular, and America in general.

"Ordered, that the said preamble, with the resolution passed the 10th instant, be published."

Mr. Duane called it to me, a machine for the fabrication of independence. Endnote 031 I said, smiling, I thought it was independence itself, but we must have it with more formality yet.

May 16. Thursday.

"The following letters were laid before Congress and read; one of the 1st, from the Commissioners of Congress in Canada; one of the tenth, from General Schuyler; and one without date from General Washington, inclosing a letter to him from Dr. Stringer.

"Resolved, That the letter from Dr. Stringer to General Washington, be referred to the committee appointed to prepare medicine chests; that the other letters be referred to Mr. W. Livingston, Mr. Jefferson, and Mr. J. Adams.

"Resolved, That the President write to General Washington, requesting him to repair to Philadelphia, as soon as he can conveniently, in order to consult with Congress upon such measures as may be necessary for the carrying on the ensuing campaign.

"Horatio Gates, Esq., was elected a Major General, and Thomas Mifflin, Esq., Brigadier General.

I take notice of this appointment of Gates, because it had great influence on my future fortunes. It soon occasioned a competition between him and Schuyler, in which I always contended for Gates; and the rivalry occasioned great animosities among the friends of the two Generals, the consequences of which are not yet spent. Indeed, they have affected the essential interests of the United States, and will influence their ultimate destiny. They effected an enmity between Gates and Mr. Jay, who always supported Schuyler, and a dislike in Gates of Hamilton, who married Schuyler's daughter, with which Mr. Burr wrought so skilfully, as, in 1800, to turn the elections in New York, not only against Hamilton but against the federalists. Gates's resentment against Jay, Schuyler, and Hamilton, made him turn, in 1799, against me, who had been the best friend and the most efficacious supporter he ever had in America. I had never in my life any personal prejudice or dislike against General Schuyler; on the contrary, I knew him to be industrious, studious, and intelligent. But the New England officers, soldiers, and inhabitants, knew Gates in the camp at Cambridge. Schuyler was not known to many, and the few who had heard of him, were prejudiced against him from the former French war. The New England soldiers would not enlist to serve under him, and the militia would not turn out. I was, therefore, under a necessity of supporting Gates. Mr. Duane, Mr. Jay, Colonel Harrison, &c., supported Schuyler.

On this same May 16th, it was

"Resolved, That it be recommended to the General Assemblies of Massachusetts Bay and Connecticut, to endeavor to have the battalions enlisted for two years, unless sooner discharged by Congress, in which case the men to be allowed one month's pay on their discharge; but if the men cannot be prevailed on to enlist for two years, that they be enlisted for one; and that they be ordered, as soon as raised and armed, to march immediately to Boston."

Here it is proper for me to obviate some aspersions against me, which were not the less malicious for being silly. I will not here charge the authors with wilful falsehood, because I can readily believe, that among the correspondents with the army, and the connections of my opponents, they may have heard insinuations and misrepresentations that they too easily credited. The truth is, I never opposed the raising of men during the war. I was always willing the General might obtain as many men as he possibly could, to enlist during the war, or during the longest period they could be persuaded to enlist for, and I always declared myself so. But I contended that I knew the number to be obtained in this manner would be very small in New England, from whence almost the whole army was derived. A regiment might possibly be obtained, of the meanest, idlest, most intemperate and worthless, but no more. A regiment was no army to defend this country. We must have tradesmen's sons, and farmers' sons, or we should be without defence; and such men certainly would not enlist during the war, or for long periods, as yet. The service was too new; they had not yet become attached to it by habit. Was it credible that men who could get at home better living, more comfortable lodgings, more than double the wages, in safety, not exposed to the sicknesses of the camp, would bind themselves during the war? I knew it to be impossible. In the Middle States, where they imported, from Ireland and Germany, so many transported convicts and redemptioners, it was possible they might obtain some. Let them try. I had no objection. But I warned them against depending on so improbable a resource for the defence of the country. Congress confessed the unanswerable force of this reasoning. Mr. McKean, I remember, said in Congress, "Mr. John Adams has convinced me that you will get no army upon such terms. Even in Pennsylvania, the most desperate of imported laborers cannot be obtained in any numbers upon such terms. Farmers and tradesmen give much more encouragement to laborers and journeymen." Mr. McKean's opinion was well founded, and proved to be true in experience, for Pennsylvania never was able to obtain half the complement of New England in proportion. *Endnote 032*

Monday, May 20. Lyman Hall and Button Gwinnet appear as delegates from Georgia, both intelligent and spirited men, who made a powerful addition to our phalanx.

"Certain resolutions of the Convention of South Carolina, respecting the battalions raised in that Colony; also, certain resolutions passed by the General Assembly of the said Colony, respecting the manner in which commissioners, coming from England, are to be received and treated in that Colony, were laid before Congress and read.

"Resolved, That the resolutions respecting the battalions be referred to a committee of five.

"The members chosen, Mr. John Adams, Mr. Sherman, Mr. Floyd, Mr. W. Livingston, and Mr. Morton.

"A committee of the whole. Mr. Harrison reported no resolution.

Tuesday, May 21.

"Three letters from General Washington, inclosing letters and papers of intelligence from England, and a copy of the treaties made by His Britannic Majesty with the Duke of Brunswick, for 4084 of his troops, with the Landgrave of Hesse Cassel, for 12,000 of his troops; and with the Count of Hanau, for 668 of his troops.

"A letter from William Palfrey, with a copy of his weekly account. A letter from John Langdon to General Washington. A petition from Samuel Austin, John Rowe, S. Partridge, Samuel Dashwood, and John Scollay, of Boston.

"Resolved, That the said letters, and papers, and petition, be referred to a committee of five; that the said committee be directed to extract and publish the treaties, and such parts of the intelligence as they think proper. Also, to consider of an adequate reward for the person who brought the intelligence, and that they prepare an address to the foreign mercenaries who are coming to invade America.

"The members chosen, Mr. John Adams, Mr. William Livingston, Mr. Jefferson, Mr. R. H. Lee, and Mr. Sherman.

"The committee, to whom the letter of the 10th from General Lee was referred, brought in their report, which was read, and after some debate,

"Resolved, That the farther consideration thereof be postponed till the arrival of General Washington.

"The committee to whom the letters from General Washington, Major-General Schuyler, and the commissioners in Canada were referred, brought in their report, which was read.

"Resolved, That the consideration thereof be postponed till to-morrow.

Thursday, May 23.

"Resolved, That a committee of five be appointed to confer with General Washington, Major-General Gates, and Brigadier-General Mifflin, upon the most speedy and effectual means of supporting the American cause in Canada. The members chosen, Mr. Harrison, Mr. R. H. Lee, Mr. J. Adams, Mr. Wilson, and Mr. Rutledge.

Friday, May 24.

"The committee appointed to confer with His Excellency General Washington, Major-General Gates, and Brigadier-General Mifflin, brought in their report. *Endnote 033*

"Agreeable to order, General Washington attended in Congress, and after some conference with him.

"Resolved, That he be directed to attend again to-morrow.

Saturday, May 25.

"Resolved, That a committee be appointed to confer with His Excellency General Washington, Major General Gates, and Brigadier-General Mifflin, and to concert a plan of military operations for the ensuing campaign. The members appointed, Mr. Harrison. Mr. R. H. Lee, Mr. J. Adams, Mr. Wilson, Mr. R. R. Livingston, Mr. Whipple, Mr. Sherman, Mr. Hopkins, Mr. W. Livingston, Mr. Read, Mr. Tilghman, Mr. Hewes, Mr. Middleton, and Mr. Hall.

"Congress took into consideration the report of the committee on the letter from General Washington of the 11th of May, the letter from General Schuyler of the 3d, &c., which was in part agreed to, as may be seen on the Journal.

"Resolved, That the consideration of the first paragraph in said report be postponed, and that the third and fifth paragraphs be referred to the committee appointed to confer with the Generals.

"Resolved, That the several reports on General Washington's letters, not yet considered, and the General's letters referred to a committee of the whole Congress, be committed to the committee appointed to confer with the Generals.

Thus, as postponement and embarrassment had been for many months the object, we now had all our business to go over again.

"A number of deputies from four of the Six Nations of Indians having arrived in town, and notified Congress that they are desirous of an audience,

"Resolved, That they be admitted to an audience on Monday next at eleven o'clock."

Monday, May 27.

"Agreeable to order, the Indians were admitted to an audience.

Wednesday, May 29.

"The committee appointed to confer with the Generals, brought in a report which was read and considered. Resolved, That the farther consideration of the report be postponed till to-morrow.

Thursday, May 30.

"Congress took into consideration the report of the committee appointed to confer with the Generals. Resolved, That it be referred to a committee of the whole Congress. Mr. Harrison reported one resolution relative to the defence of New York. Leave to sit again."

Friday, May 31.

"The committee of conference brought in a farther report, which was read.

"Resolved, That it be referred to the committee of the whole Congress.

"Mr. Harrison reported a request to sit again. Granted."

Saturday, June 1.

"Colonel Joseph Reed resigned his office of secretary to General Washington.

"Committee of the whole again. Mr. Harrison reported some resolutions. Leave to sit again."

Monday, June 3.

"Committee of the whole. Mr. Harrison reported sundry resolutions. Leave to sit again."

Tuesday, June 4.

"Committee of the whole. Mr. Harrison reported more resolutions. Leave to sit again. Resolutions reported postponed."

Wednesday, June 5.

"Congress took into consideration the report of the committee of the whole, whereupon, Resolved, That a committee of five be appointed to consider what is proper to be done with persons giving intelligence to the enemy, or supplying them with provisions. The members chosen, Mr. J. Adams, Mr. Jefferson, Mr. Rutledge, Mr. Wilson, and Mr. R. Livingston.

"Resolved, That Robert Hanson Harrison, Esq., have the rank of Lieutenant-Colonel in the Continental army. The General's secretary, as I suppose.

"Joseph Reed, Esq., was elected Adjutant-General."

Friday, June 7.

"Certain resolutions, respecting independency, being moved and seconded,

"Resolved, That the consideration of them be referred till to-morrow morning, and that the members be enjoined to attend punctually at ten o'clock, in order to take the same into their consideration."

It will naturally be inquired why these resolutions, and the names of the gentlemen who moved and seconded them, were not inserted on the Journals. To this question, I can give no other answer than this. Mr. Hancock was President, Mr. Harrison, chairman of the committee of the whole house, Mr. Thomson, the secretary, was cousin to Mr. Dickinson, and Mr. R. H. Lee and Mr. John Adams were no favorites of either.

Saturday, June 8.

"Resolved, That the resolutions respecting independency be referred to a committee of the whole Congress. Mr. Harrison reported no resolution. Leave to sit again.

Monday, June 10.

"Committee of the whole. Mr. Harrison reported a resolution. The resolution, agreed to in the committee of the whole Congress, being read,

"Resolved, That the consideration of the first resolution be postponed to the first day of July next, and in the meanwhile, that no time be lost, in case the Congress agree thereto, that a committee be appointed to prepare a declaration to the effect of the first resolution, which is in these words. 'That these United Colonies are, and of right ought to be, free and independent States; that they are absolved from all allegiance to the British Crown; and that all political connection between them and the State of Great Britain, is and ought to be totally dissolved.' "

Tuesday, June 11.

"Resolved, That a committee of three be appointed to consider of a compensation to the secretary for his services. The members chosen, Mr. J. Adams, Mr. Rutledge, and Mr. Hewes.

"Resolved, That the committee for preparing the declaration consist of five. The members chosen, Mr. Jefferson, Mr. John Adams, Mr. Franklin, Mr. Sherman, and Mr. R. R. Livingston. Jefferson was chairman, because he had most votes; and he had most votes, because we united in him to the exclusion of R. H. Lee, and to keep out Harrison.

"Resolved, That a committee be appointed to prepare and digest the form of a confederation to be entered into between these Colonies.

"That a committee be appointed to prepare a plan of treaties to be proposed to foreign powers.

Wednesday, June 12.

"Resolved, That the committee to prepare and digest the form of a confederation, to be entered into between these Colonies, consist of a member from each Colony. The members appointed, Mr. Bartlett, Mr. S. Adams, Mr. Hopkins, Mr. Sherman, Mr. R. R. Livingston, Mr. Dickinson, Mr. McKean, Mr. Stone, Mr. Nelson, Mr. Hewes, Mr. E. Rutledge, and Mr. Gwinnet.

"Resolved, That the committee to prepare a plan of treaties to be proposed to foreign powers, consist of five. The members chosen, Mr. Dickinson, Mr. Franklin, Mr. J. Adams, Mr. Harrison, and Mr. R. Morris.

"Congress took into consideration the report of the committee on the war-office, whereupon,

"Resolved, That a committee of Congress be appointed, by the name of a board of war and ordnance, to consist of five members." *Endnote 034*

In order to show the insupportable burden of business that was thrown upon me by this Congress, it is necessary to transcribe from the Journals an account of the constitution, powers, and duties of this board.

It was resolved,

"That a secretary and one or more clerks be appointed by Congress, with competent salaries, to assist the said board in executing the business of their department.

"That it shall be the duty of the said board to obtain and keep an alphabetical and accurate register of the names of all officers of the land forces, in the service of the United Colonies, with their rank and the dates of their respective commissions; and also regular accounts of the state and disposition of the troops in the respective Colonies, for which purpose the Generals and officers commanding the different departments and posts are to cause regular returns to be made into the said war office.

"That they shall obtain and keep exact accounts of all the artillery, arms, ammunition, and warlike stores, belonging to the United Colonies, and of the manner in which, and the places where, the same shall from time to time be lodged and employed; and that they shall have the immediate care of all such artillery, arms, ammunition, and warlike stores, as shall not be employed in actual service; for preserving whereof, they shall have power to hire proper magazines at the public expense.

"That they shall have the care of forwarding all despatches from Congress to the Colonies and armies, and all moneys to be transmitted for the public service by order of Congress, and of providing suitable escorts and guards for the safe conveyance of such despatches and moneys, when it shall appear to them to be necessary.

"That they shall superintend the raising, fitting out, and despatching, all such land forces as may be ordered for the service of the United Colonies.

"That they shall have the care and direction of all prisoners of war, agreeable to the orders and regulations of Congress.

"That they shall keep and preserve in the said office, in regular order, all original letters and papers which shall come into said office by order of Congress or otherwise, and shall also cause all draughts of letters and despatches to be made or transcribed in books to be set apart for that purpose, and shall cause fair entries in like manner to be made, and registers preserved, of all other business which shall be transacted in said office." *Endnote 035*

From this time, we find in almost every day's Journal references of various business to the board of war, or their reports upon such things as were referred to them.

Friday, June 28. A new delegation appeared from New Jersey. Mr. William Livingston and all others, who had hitherto resisted independence, were left out. Richard Stockton, Francis Hopkinson, and Dr. John Witherspoon, were new members.

Monday, July 1.

"A resolution of the Convention of Maryland, passed the 28th of June, was laid before Congress, and read, as follows: 'That the instructions given to their deputies in December last, be recalled, and the restrictions therein contained removed; and that their deputies be authorized and empowered to concur with the other United Colonies, or a majority of them, in declaring the United Colonies free and independent States; in forming a compact between them, and in making foreign alliances, &c. *Endnote 036*

"Resolved, That this Congress will resolve itself into a committee of the whole, to take into consideration the resolution respecting independency.

"That the declaration be referred to said committee.

"The Congress resolved itself into a committee of the whole. After some time, the President resumed the chair, and Mr. Harrison reported, that the committee had come to a resolution, which they desired him to report, and to move for leave to sit again.

"The resolution, agreed to by the committee of the whole, being read, the determination thereof was, at the request of a Colony, postponed till to-morrow."

I am not able to recollect whether it was on this or some preceding day, that the greatest and most solemn debate was had on the question of independence. The subject had been in contemplation for more than a year, and frequent discussions had been had concerning it. At one time and another all the arguments for it and against it had been exhausted, and were become familiar. I expected no more would be said in public, but that the question would be put and decided. Mr. Dickinson, however, was determined to bear his testimony against it with more formality. He had prepared himself apparently with great labor and ardent zeal, and in a speech of great length, and with all his eloquence, he combined together all that had before been written in pamphlets and newspapers, and all that had from time to time been said in Congress by himself and others. He conducted the debate not only with great ingenuity and eloquence, but with equal politeness and candor, and was answered in the same spirit.

No member rose to answer him, and after waiting some time, in hopes that some one less obnoxious than myself, who had been all along for a year before, and still was, represented and believed to be the author of all the mischief, would move, I determined to speak.

It has been said, by some of our historians, that I began by an invocation to the god of eloquence. This is a misrepresentation. Nothing so puerile as this fell from me. I began, by saying that this was the first time of my life that I had ever wished for the talents and eloquence of the ancient orators of Greece and Rome, for I was very sure that none of them ever had before him a question of more importance to his country and to the world. They would probably, upon less occasions than this, have begun by solemn invocations to their divinities for assistance; but the question before me appeared so simple, that I had confidence enough in the plain understanding and common sense that had been given me, to believe that I could answer, to the satisfaction of the House, all the arguments which had been produced, notwithstanding the abilities which had been displayed, and the eloquence with which they had been enforced. Mr. Dickinson, some years afterwards, published his speech. *Endnote 037* I had made no preparation beforehand, and never committed any minutes of mine to writing. But if I had a copy of Mr. Dickinson's before me, I would now, after nine and twenty years have elapsed, endeavor to recollect mine.

Before the final question was put, the new delegates from New Jersey came in, and Mr. Stockton, Dr. Witherspoon, and Mr. Hopkinson, very respectable characters, expressed a great desire to hear the arguments. Endnote 038 All was silence; no one would speak; all eyes were turned upon me. Mr. Edward Rutledge came to me and said, laughing, "Nobody will speak but you [56a] upon this subject. You have all the topics so ready, that you must satisfy the gentlemen from New Jersey." I answered him, laughing, that it had so much the air of exhibiting like an actor or gladiator, for the entertainment of the audience, that I was ashamed to repeat what I had said twenty times before, and I thought nothing new could be advanced by me. The New Jersey gentlemen, however, still insisting on hearing at least a recapitulation of the arguments, and no other gentleman being willing to speak, I summed up the reasons, objections, and answers, in as concise a manner as I could, till at length the Jersey gentlemen said they were fully satisfied and ready for the question, which was then put, and determined in the affirmative.

Mr. Jay, Mr. Duane, and Mr. William Livingston of New Jersey, were not present. But they all acquiesced in the declaration, and steadily supported it ever afterwards.

July 4.

"Resolved, That Dr. Franklin, Mr. J. Adams, and Mr. Jefferson, be a committee to prepare a device for a seal for the United States of America."

Monday, July 15.

"A letter from Mr. Jay, and two letters from the Convention of New York, of the 11th, with sundry papers inclosed, among which were the following resolutions.

"In convention of the representatives of the State of New York,

White Plains, July 9, 1776.

"Resolved, unanimously, that the reasons assigned by the Continental Congress for declaring the United Colonies free and independent States are cogent and conclusive, and that while we lament the cruel necessity which has rendered that measure unavoidable, we approve the same, and will, at the risk of our lives and fortunes, join with the other Colonies in supporting it.

"Resolved, unanimously, that the delegates of this State in the Continental Congress be, and they hereby are, authorized to concert and adopt all such measures as they may deem conducive to the happiness and welfare of America."

"Extract from the Minutes.

Robert Benson, Secretary."

This was the Convention which formed the constitution of New York, and Mr. Jay and Mr. Duane had attended it, as I suppose, for the purpose of getting a plan adopted, conformable to my ideas in the letter to Mr. Wythe, which had been published in the Spring before. I presume this was the fact, because Mr. Duane, after his return to Congress, asked me if I had seen the constitution of New York? I answered him, that I had. He then asked me if it was not agreeable to my ideas, as I had published them in my letter to Mr. Wythe. I said I thought it by far the best constitution that had yet been adopted.

The daily references to the Board of War, rendered it necessary for me to spend almost my whole time in it, on mornings, till Congress met, and on evenings, till late at night. The Journals will show some of the results of the tedious details. There is one report, which may be mentioned here.

Wednesday, July 17.

"The board of war, to whom the letter of General Washington, of the 14th, was referred, brought in their report, which was taken into consideration; whereupon,

"Resolved, That General Washington, in refusing to receive a letter said to be sent from Lord Howe, addressed to 'George Washington, Esq.,' acted with a dignity becoming his station; and therefore, this Congress do highly approve the same; and do direct that no letter or message be received, on any occasion whatsoever, from the enemy, by the commander-in-chief, or others, the commanders of the American army, but such as shall be directed to them in the characters they respectively sustain.

"Resolved, That Mr. J. Adams, Mr. Harrison, and Mr. Morris, be a committee to bring in a resolution for subjecting to confiscation the property of the subjects of the crown of Great Britain, and particularly, of the inhabitants of the British West Indies, taken on the high seas, or between high and low water mark."

Thursday, July 18.

"Resolved, That a member be added to the board of war. The member chosen, Mr. Carroll."

An excellent member, whose education, manners, and application to business and to study, did honor to his fortune, the first in America.

"The committee appointed to prepare a plan of treaties to be entered into with foreign states and kingdoms, brought in a report, which was read;

"Ordered, To lie on the table."

Friday, July 19.

"The board of war brought in a report, which was taken into consideration; whereupon, Resolved, *Endnote 039* . . .

"The committee appointed to prepare a resolution for subjecting to confiscation the property of the subjects of Great Britain, &c., brought in the same, which was read;

"Ordered, To lie on the table, and that the same be taken into consideration on Monday next.

"The committee to whom the letters from Lord Howe to Mr. Franklin, &c., were referred, brought in a report, which was taken into consideration; whereupon,

"Resolved, That a copy of the circular letters, and the declaration inclosed from Lord Howe to Mr. William Franklin, Mr. Penn, Mr. Eden, Lord Dunmore, Mr. Martin, and Sir James Wright, which were sent to Amboy by a flag, and forwarded to Congress by General Washington, be published in the several Gazettes, that the good people of these United States may be informed of what nature are the commissioners, and what the terms, with expectation of which the insidious court of Britain has endeavored to amuse and disarm them, and that the few, who still remain suspended by a hope founded either in the justice or moderation of their late king, may now at length be convinced that the valor alone of their country is to save its liberties."

Saturday, July 20.

"Resolved, That the letter from General Lee, with the papers inclosed, which were received and read yesterday, be referred to the board of war.

"A petition and memorial of Mr. Pelissier was presented to Congress, and read;

"Resolved, That it be referred to the board of war.

"Resolved, That the plan of treaties be printed for the use of the members, under the restrictions and regulations prescribed for printing the plan of confederation; and that, in the printed copy, the names of persons, places, and States, be omitted.

"The board of war brought in a report, which was taken into consideration; whereupon, Resolved, as in the Journal.

"The delegates of Pennsylvania produced credentials of a new appointment, made on the 20th of July. *Endnote 040*

"Resolved, That Dr. Franklin may, if he thinks proper, return an answer to the letter he received from Lord Howe."

Monday, July 22.

"The Congress resolved itself into a committee of the whole, to take into consideration the articles of confederation, and, after some time, the president resumed the chair, and Mr. Harrison reported that the committee have made some progress in the matter to them referred, but not having come to a conclusion, desire leave to sit again.

"Resolved, That this Congress will to-morrow again resolve itself into a committee of the whole, to take into their farther consideration the articles of confederation."

Tuesday, July 23d, was employed in making references to the board of war, and in receiving, considering, and adopting their reports, as may be seen in the Journal.

Also in a committee of the whole on the articles of confederation.

Wednesday, July 24.

"A letter from Lieutenant Colonel William Allen was laid before Congress, and read, requesting leave to resign his commission. Resolved, That leave be granted."

About this time it was that the gentlemen in the Pennsylvania proprietary interest generally left us.

"A petition from George Kills was presented to Congress and read:

"Resolved, That it be referred to the board of war.

"The Congress took into consideration the report of the committee appointed to prepare a resolution for confiscating the property of the subjects of Great Britain; whereupon,

"Resolved, That all the resolutions of this Congress passed on the twenty-third day of March last, and on the third day of April last, relating to ships and other vessels, their tackle, apparel, and furniture, and all goods, wares, and merchandises, belonging to any inhabitant or inhabitants of Great Britain, taken on the high seas, or between high and low water mark, be extended to all ships and other vessels, their tackle, apparel, and furniture, and to all goods, wares, and merchandises, belonging to any subject or subjects of the King of Great Britain, except the inhabitants of the Bermudas and Providence or Bahama Islands.

"The board of war brought in their report, which was taken into consideration; whereupon, Resolved, as in the Journal."

Among the number, I select with great pleasure the two following, namely,

"Resolved, That Colonel Knox's plan for raising another battalion of artillery, be approved, and carried into execution as soon as possible.

"Resolved, That General Washington be empowered to agree to the exchange of Governor Skene for Mr. James Lovell."

A committee of the whole on the articles of confederation, but no progress.

Then a list of letters from General Washington and others referred to the board of war.

Thursday, July 25. A memorial from sundry officers who served in Canada, referred to the board of war.

Committee of the whole on the articles of confederation.

Letter from General Washington, inclosing letters from Governor Trumbull, and a Committee of Safety of New Hampshire, referred to the board of war.

Friday, July 26. A committee of the whole on the articles of the confederation. Mr. Morton in the chair.

Monday, July 29. A long list of references to the board of war, of letters from Washington, Schuyler, Reed, Trumbull, Convention of New Jersey, Council of Massachusetts, &c.

The board of war brought in a report, which was taken into consideration, whereupon, Resolved, as in the Journal.

Committee of the whole on the articles of confederation. Mr. Morton in the chair.

Tuesday, July 30. Two reports from the board of war, with resolutions in consequence of them, as in the Journal.

Committee of the whole on the articles of confederation. Mr. Morton in the chair.

Wednesday, July 31. The board of war brought in a report, which was taken into consideration, whereupon, Resolved, as in the Journal.

A committee of the whole on the articles of confederation. Mr. Morton in the chair.

Thursday, August 1. Letters from General Mercer and General Roberdeau, referred to the board of war.

Committee of the whole on the articles of confederation. Mr. Morton in the chair.

Letters from General Washington, General Schuyler, and Colonel Dubois, referred to the board of war.

The board of war brought in two reports which were accepted, as in the Journal.

Friday, August 2. The board of war brought in a report which was accepted, as in the Journal.

The marine committee brought in a report on the conduct of Commodore Hopkins.

Committee of the whole on the articles of confederation. Mr. Morton in the chair.

Saturday, August 3.

"A letter from Neil McLean, referred to the board of war."

Monday, August 5.

"Two letters from General Washington, one from the Council of Virginia, with copies of sundry letters from North Carolina and South Carolina, inclosed; one from E. Anderson, and sundry resolutions passed by the Convention of Pennsylvania, were laid before Congress and read; referred to the board of war.

"The board of war brought in a report, which was taken into consideration; whereupon,

"Resolved, That the commanders of all ships of war and armed vessels in the service of these States, or any of them, and all letters of marque and privateers, be permitted to enlist into service, on board the said ships and vessels, any seamen who may be taken on board any of the ships or vessels of our enemies, and that no such seamen be entitled to receive the wages due to them out of the said prizes, but such as will so enlist, and that all other seamen so taken be held as prisoners of war, and exchanged for others taken by the enemy, whether on board vessels of war or merchantmen, as there may be opportunity.

"That Lieutenant-Colonel Rufus Putnam be appointed an engineer, with the rank of Colonel, and pay of sixty dollars a month."

A petition from Commodore Hopkins, for a hearing, &c.

Ordered, That the board of war furnish the committee of treasury with the names of the British officers, and other prisoners, who are entitled to the allowance made by Congress of two dollars a week, with the times of their captivity and the places where they are quartered.

"Resolved, That the pay of an assistant clerk to the board of war, be two hundred and sixty-six dollars and two thirds, a year.

"A petition from Louis de Linkensdorf, referred to the board of war.

Tuesday, August 6.

"A letter of the 5th from General Washington, inclosing copies of letters between him and General Howe, respecting the exchange of prisoners, and sundry other letters and papers; also, one from Brigadier-General Mercer of the 4th, were laid before Congress and read;

"Resolved, That they be referred to the board of war.

"A committee of the whole on the articles of confederation. Mr. Morton in the chair."

Wednesday, August 7.

"A memorial from George Measam referred to the board of war.

"A report from the board of war, as in the Journal.

"A committee of the whole on the articles of confederation. Mr. Morton in the chair."

Thursday, August 8.

"The board of war directed to see certain resolutions carried into effect.

"Resolved, That the board of war be directed to take into immediate consideration the state of the army in the Northern department, and our naval force on the lakes; and that Mr. Chase be directed to attend the said board, and give them all the information in his power; and that Mr. Williams be desired to furnish the said board with an extract of the letter he has received from Governor Trumbull, relative to the said army and naval force, and that the said board report thereon as soon as possible.

"Resolved, That to-morrow be assigned for electing four Major Generals and six Brigadier Generals.

"A committee of the whole on the articles of confederation. Mr. Morton in the chair."

Friday, August 9.

"The board of war brought in a report, which was read;

"Ordered, To lie on the table.

"Resolved, That the secret committee be directed to deliver to the order of the board of war, such articles in their possession, belonging to the continent, as in the opinion of the said board of war are necessary for the Delaware battalion.

"William Heath, Joseph Spencer, John Sullivan, Nathaniel Greene, Esqs., chosen Major Generals.

"James Reed, John Nixon, Arthur St. Clair, Alexander McDougall, Samuel Holden Parsons, and James Clinton, Esqs., Brigadiers.

"Resolved, That the hearing of Commodore Hopkins be postponed to Monday next, at eleven o'clock, and that Captain Jones be directed to attend at the same time.

Saturday, August 10.

"The board of war brought in a report which was taken into consideration; whereupon,

"Resolved, That commissions be made out, and sent to General Washington, to be delivered to the several officers recommended in the list exhibited by the said board, to fill the vacancies mentioned in the said list, excepting those persons recommended to fill the vacancies occasioned by officers being in captivity, which ought not to be filled, but to be left open until those officers shall be redeemed, and excepting the case of Lieutenant-Colonel Tyler, who is to have a commission for Colonel of the regiment lately commanded by Colonel Parsons, promoted; and that Lieutenant-Colonel Durkee have a commission of Colonel of the 20th regiment, and that Major Prentice be made Lieutenant-Colonel of the regiment in which he is now Major, and Major Knowlton, Lieutenant-Colonel of the 20th regiment.

"Resolved, That William Tudor, Judge Advocate General, have the rank of Lieutenant-Colonel in the army of the United States; and that he be ordered immediately to repair to the discharge of his duty at New York."

Monday, August 12.

"A letter from General Washington of the 8th, with sundry papers inclosed, and one from General Mercer, with one inclosed to him from Colonel Dickinson, were read.

"Resolved, That the letter from General Washington, with the papers inclosed, be referred to the board of war."

Commodore Hopkins had his hearing, as in the Journal. On this occasion I had a very laborious task against all the prejudices of the gentlemen from the Southern and Middle States, and of many from New England. I thought, however, that Hopkins had done great service, and made an important beginning of naval operations.

The record in the Journal stands as follows:

"Agreeable to the order of the day, Commodore Hopkins attended, and was admitted: when the examination taken before the marine committee, and the report of the said committee in consequence thereof, were read to him; and the Commodore being heard in his own defence, and having delivered in some further answers to the questions asked him by the marine committee, and two witnesses being at his request introduced and examined, he withdrew.

"Congress then took into consideration the instructions given to Commodore Hopkins, his examination and answers to the marine committee, and the report of the marine committee thereupon; also, the farther defence by him made, and the testimony of the witnesses; and after some debate, the farther consideration thereof was postponed."

It appeared to me that the Commodore was pursued and persecuted by that anti-New-England spirit which haunted Congress in many other of their proceedings, as well as in this case and that of General Wooster. I saw nothing in the conduct of Hopkins, which indicated corruption or want of integrity. Experience and skill might have been deficient in several particulars; but where could we find greater experience or skill? I knew of none to be found. The other captains had not so much, and it was afterwards found they had not more success. I therefore entered into a full and candid investigation of the whole subject; considered all the charges and all the evidence, as well as his answers and proofs; and exerted all the talents and eloquence I had, in justifying him where he was justifiable, and excusing him where he was excusable. When the trial was over, Mr. Ellery of Newport, came to me and said, "You have made the old man your friend for life: he will hear of your defence of him, and he never forgets a kindness." More than twenty years afterwards, the old gentleman hobbled on his crutches to the inn in Providence, at fourscore years of age, one half of him dead in consequence of a paralytic stroke, with his eyes overflowing with tears, to express his gratitude to me. He said he knew not for what end he was continued in life, unless it were to punish his friends, or to teach his children and grandchildren to respect me. The president of Rhode Island College, who had married his daughter, and all his family, showed me the same affectionate attachment.

Tuesday, August 13.

"The board of war brought in a report, which was taken into consideration, whereupon, Resolved, as in the Journal.

"A letter of the 12th, from Brigadier General Mercer, was read.

"Resolved, That it be referred to the board of war.

"Congress took into consideration the articles of war, and after some time spent thereon, the farther consideration thereof was postponed till to-morrow.

Wednesday, August 14.

"A letter of the 12th, from General Washington, with a return of the army at New York, and sundry other papers inclosed, being received, was read; also, sundry letters from England were read;

"Resolved, That the letter from General Washington, with the papers inclosed, be referred to the board of war.

"The board of war brought in a report, which was taken into consideration, whereupon, Resolved, as in the Journal."

Thursday, August 15.

"The board of war brought in a report which was taken into consideration, whereupon, Resolved, as in the Journal."

"A petition from Return Jonathan Meigs, in behalf of himself and others, was presented to Congress, and read;

"Resolved, That it be referred to the board of war.

"Congress resumed the consideration of the instructions given to Commodore Hopkins, &c.

"Resolved, That the said Commodore Hopkins, during his cruise to the southward, did not pay due regard to the tenor of his instructions, whereby he was expressly directed to annoy the enemy's ships upon the coasts of the Southern States, and that his reasons for not going from Providence immediately to the Carolinas are by no means satisfactory.

"At the request of the delegates of Pennsylvania, the farther consideration of the report was postponed till to-morrow.

Friday, August 16.

"Resolved, That a member be added to the committee to whom were referred the letters and papers respecting the murder of Mr. Parsons.

"The member chosen, Mr. J. Adams.

"Resolved, That the letters received yesterday from General Washington, General Schuyler, and General Gates, be referred to the board of war.

"Congress resumed the consideration of the instructions given to Commodore Hopkins, &c., and thereupon came to the following resolution.

"Resolved, That the said conduct of Commodore Hopkins deserves the censure of this House, and this House does accordingly censure him.

"Ordered, That a copy of the resolutions passed against Commodore Hopkins be transmitted to him."

Although this resolution of censure was not in my opinion demanded by justice, and consequently was inconsistent with good policy, as it tended to discourage an officer, and diminish his authority, by tarnishing his reputation, yet, as it went not so far as to cashier him, which had been the object intended by the spirit that dictated the prosecution, I had the satisfaction to think that I had not labored wholly in vain in his defence. *Endnote 041*

Saturday, August 17.

"Congress resumed the consideration of the report of the Committee to whom was referred Brigadier General Wooster's letter, requesting an inquiry into his conduct, while he had the honor of commanding the continental forces in Canada, which was read as follows:—

"That Brigadier General Wooster produced copies of a number of letters which passed between him and General Schuyler, and of his letters to Congress, from which it appears that he from time to time, gave seasonable and due notice of the state of the army under his command, and what supplies were in his opinion necessary to render the enterprise successful; that a number of officers and other gentlemen from Canada who were acquainted with his conduct there, and who happened to be occasionally in this city, were examined before the committee, to which letters, and the minutes of the examination of the witnesses herewith exhibited, the committee beg leave to refer Congress for further information, and report as the opinion of the committee upon the whole of the evidence that was before them, that nothing censurable or blameworthy appears against Brigadier General Wooster.

"The report being again read, was agreed to."

But not, however, without a great struggle. In this instance, again, as in many others, where the same anti-New-England spirit which pursued Commodore Hopkins, persecuted General Wooster, I had to contend with the whole host of their enemies, and with the utmost anxiety, and most arduous efforts, was scarcely able to preserve them from disgrace and ruin, which Wooster had merited even less than Hopkins. In Wooster's case, there was a manifest endeavor to lay upon him the blame of their own misconduct, in Congress, in embarrassing and starving the war in Canada. Wooster was calumniated for incapacity, want of application, and even for cowardice, without a color of proof of either. The charge of cowardice he soon confuted, by a glorious and voluntary sacrifice of his life, which compelled his enemies to confess he was a hero.

The board of war brought in a report, which was taken into consideration, whereupon, Resolved, as in all the rest of the Journal.

Monday, August 19.

"Letters from General Washington, referred to the board of war. A letter of the 14th, from Commodore Hopkins, was read, whereupon.

"Resolved, That Commodore Hopkins be directed to repair to Rhode Island, and take the command of the fleet formerly put under his care.

"Congress resumed the consideration of the articles of war, as revised by the committee for that purpose appointed, and after some time spent thereon, the further consideration thereof was postponed."

This report was made by me and Mr. Jefferson, in consequence of a letter from General Washington, sent by Colonel Tudor, Judge Advocate-General, representing the insufficiency of the articles of war, and requesting a revision of them. Mr. John Adams and Mr. Jefferson were appointed a committee to hear Tudor, and revise the articles. It was a very difficult and unpopular subject, and I observed to Jefferson, that whatever alteration we should report with the least energy in it, or the least tendency to a necessary discipline of the army, would be opposed with as much vehemence, as if it were the most perfect; we might as well, therefore, report a complete system at once, and let it meet its fate. Something perhaps might be gained. There was extant one system of articles of war which had carried two empires to the head of mankind, the Roman and the British; for the British articles of war were only a literal translation of the Roman. It would be in vain for us to seek in our own inventions, or the records of warlike nations, for a more complete system of military discipline. It was an observation founded in undoubted facts, that the prosperity of nations had been in proportion to the discipline of their forces by sea and land; I was, therefore, for reporting the British articles of war, totidem verbis. Jefferson, in those days, never failed to agree with me, in every thing of a political nature, and he very cordially concurred in this. The British articles of war were, accordingly, reported, and defended in Congress by me assisted by some others, and finally carried. They laid the foundation of a discipline which, in time, brought our troops to a capacity of contending with British veterans, and a rivalry with the best troops of France.

Tuesday, August 20.

"A letter of the 18th, from General Washington, with sundry papers inclosed, was laid before Congress and read.

"Resolved, That the same be referred to a committee of five. The members chosen. Mr. Jefferson, Mr. Franklin, Mr. Rutledge, Mr. J. Adams, and Mr. Hooper.

"A committee of the whole on the articles of confederation. Mr. Morton reported that the committee had gone through the same, and agreed to sundry articles, which he was ordered to submit to Congress.

"Ordered, That eighty copies of the articles of confederation, as reported from the committee of the whole, be printed under the same injunctions as the former articles, and delivered to the members under the like instructions as formerly."

Thus we see the whole record of this momentous transaction. No motions recorded, *Endnote 042* no yeas and nays taken down, no alterations proposed, no debates preserved, no names mentioned; all in profound secrecy. Nothing suffered to transpire, no opportunity to consult constituents; no room for advice or criticisms in pamphlets, papers, or private conversation. I was very uneasy under all this, but could not avoid it. In the course of this confederation a few others were as anxious as myself. Mr. Wilson, of Pennsylvania, upon one occasion, moved that the debates should be public, the doors opened, galleries erected, or an adjournment made to some public building, where the people might be accommodated. Mr. John Adams seconded the motion, and supported it with zeal. But no! neither party was willing; some were afraid of divisions among the people; but more were afraid to let the people see the insignificant figures they made in that assembly. Nothing, indeed, was less understood abroad, among the people, than the real constitution of Congress, and the characters of those who conducted the business of it. The truth is, the motions, plans, debates, amendments, which were every day brought forward, in those committees of the whole house, if committed to writing, would be very voluminous; but they are lost forever. The preservation of them, indeed, might, for any thing I recollect, be of more curiosity than use. Endnote 043

Wednesday, August 21.

"A petition from Prudhomme La Jeunesse was read, and referred to the board of war.

"The committee to whom part of the report from the committee on spies was recommitted, having brought in a report, the same was taken into consideration, whereupon,

"Resolved, That all persons not members of, nor owing allegiance to any of the United States of America, as described in a resolution of Congress, of the 24th of June last, who shall be found lurking as spies, in or about the fortifications or encampments of the armies of the United States, or of any of them, shall suffer death, according to the law and usage of nations, by sentence of a court martial, or such other punishment as such court martial shall direct.

"Ordered, That the above resolution be printed at the end of the rules and articles of war.

"The board of war brought in a report, which was taken into consideration, whereupon, Resolved, as in the Journal.

"Resolved, That the letter from General Washington read yesterday, and that of the 12th, with the papers inclosed, be referred to the board of war.

"Resolved, That a committee of three be appointed to revise the resolutions of Congress, respecting the place where prizes are to be carried into, and to bring in such further resolutions as to them shall seem proper.

"The members chosen, Mr. Jefferson, Mr. Morris, and Mr. J. Adams.

Thursday, August 22.

"Letters from General Washington and Schuyler, with papers inclosed, referred to the board of war.

"The board of war brought in a report, which was read.

"Ordered, To lie on the table.

"The committee to whom the letter, from General Washington, of the 18th was referred, brought in a report, which was read. Ordered, To lie on the table.

"A committee of the whole on the form of a treaty; Mr. Nelson in the chair.

"A letter from Brigadier-General Lewis; also, a letter from the Committee of Carlisle, in Pennsylvania, inclosing a memorial from the officers and prisoners there, were read and referred to the board of war.

Friday, August 23.

"A letter of the 21st, from General Washington, inclosing a copy of a letter from him to Lord Howe, together with his lordship's answer, was read.

"Resolved, That the same be referred to the board of war, with orders to publish the General's letter to Lord Howe, and His Lordship's answer.

Monday, August 26.

"Three letters of the 22d and 23d, from General Washington, with sundry papers inclosed, a letter from William Finnie, deputy quartermaster-general of the Southern department, were read and referred to the board of war.

"A letter of the 22d, from Colonel James Wilson, was read, and referred to Mr. Jefferson, Mr. Franklin, and Mr. John Adams.

Tuesday, August 27.

"A letter of the 23d, from General Mercer, was read and referred to the board of war.

"The board of war brought in a report, which was taken into consideration, whereupon, Resolved—See the several resolutions in the Journal.

"The committee to whom the letter from Colonel Wilson was referred, brought in a report, which was taken into consideration, whereupon, Congress came to the following resolutions. *Endnote 044*

"A committee of the whole on the plan of foreign treaties. Mr. Nelson reported that the committee had gone through the same, and made sundry amendments.

"Resolved, That the plan of treaties, with the amendments, be referred to the committee who brought in the original plan, in order to draw up instructions pursuant to the amendments made by the committee of the whole; that two members be added to the said committee. The members chosen, Mr. Richard Henry Lee and Mr. Wilson.

"A petition from the deputy commissary-general was read, and referred to the board of war.

Wednesday, August 28.

"Delegates from Virginia produced new credentials. George Wythe, Thomas Nelson, Richard Henry Lee, Thomas Jefferson, and Francis Lightfoot Lee, Esqs.

Thursday, August 29.

"A letter of the 27th, from R. H. Harrison, the General's secretary, and one of the 28th, from General Mercer, both giving an account of an action on Long Island, on the 27th, were read and referred to the board of war.

"The board of war brought in a report, which was taken into consideration, whereupon, Resolved—See the several resolutions in the Journal.

"Resolved, That the committee to whom the plan of treaties with the amendments was recommitted, be empowered to prepare such further instructions, as to them shall seem proper, and make report thereof to Congress.

Friday, August 30.

"A memorial from Mr. Kosciusko was read, and referred to the board of war.

Monday, September 2.

"A letter of the 31st of August from General Washington, inclosing the determination of a council of war, and the reasons for quitting Long Island, and a copy of a letter from Lord Stirling; also, one of the 23d from General Gates, with sundry papers inclosed; one from sundry field officers in the army at Ticonderoga, dated the 19th of August, with the proceedings between a court martial and Brigadier-General Arnold; also, a letter of the 23d, from Captain John Nelson, and one from Benjamin Harrison, Jr., deputy paymaster-general, with his weekly account, were read and referred to the board of war.

"Congress being informed that General Sullivan was come to Philadelphia with a design to communicate a message from Lord Howe;

"Ordered, That he be admitted and heard before Congress.

"A petition from Michael Fitzgerald, one from John Weitzell, and one from James Paul Govert, were read and referred to the board of war.

"General Sullivan being admitted, delivered a verbal message he had in charge from Lord Howe, which he was desired to reduce to writing, and then he withdrew.

"Resolved, That the board of war be directed to prepare and bring in a plan of military operations for the next campaign."

Tuesday, September 3.

"General Sullivan, having reduced to writing the verbal message from Lord Howe, the same was read as follows:—

"The following is the purport of the message of Lord Howe to Congress, by General Sullivan.

"That, though he could not at present treat with Congress as such, yet he was very desirous of having a conference with some of the members whom he would consider, for the present, only as private gentlemen, and meet them himself as such, at such place as they should appoint.

"That he, in conjunction with General Howe, had full powers to compromise the dispute between Great Britain and America, upon terms advantageous to both: the obtaining of which delayed him near two months in England, and prevented his arrival at this place, before the declaration of independency took place. That he wished a compact might be settled at this time, when no decisive blow was struck, and neither party could say that they were compelled to enter into such agreement.

"That in case Congress were disposed to treat, many things which they had not as yet asked, might and ought to be granted them, and that if, upon the conference, they found any probable ground of accommodation, the authority of Congress must be afterwards acknowledged, otherwise the compact would not be complete."

In this written statement of the message it ought to be observed, that General Sullivan has not inserted, what he had reported verbally, that Lord Howe had told him "he would set the act of Parliament wholly aside, and that Parliament had no right to tax America, or meddle with her internal polity."

"The board of war brought in a report which was read, and a number of resolutions adopted upon it, which see in the Journal."

Wednesday, September 4.

"Resolved, That the board of war be directed to call in the several recruiting parties of the German battalion, and to have them formed and armed with all possible expedition, and forwarded to New York, taking measures, and giving proper directions to have the battalion recruited to the full complement, as soon as the same can conveniently be done.

"Resolved, That the proposal made by General Howe, as delivered by General Sullivan, of exchanging General Sullivan for General Prescott, and Lord Stirling for Brigadier-General McDonald, be complied with.

"Congress took into consideration the report of the board of war, and after some time spent thereon,

"Resolved, That the farther consideration thereof be postponed till to-morrow.

Thursday, September 5.

"A petition referred to the board of war.

"Resolved. That General Prescott, and Brigadier-General McDonald be sent by the board of war, under an escort, to General Washington, to be exchanged for General Sullivan and Lord Stirling.

"Congress resumed the consideration of the report of the board of war, whereupon,

"Resolved, That General Sullivan be requested to inform Lord Howe, that this Congress being the representatives of the free and independent States of America, cannot with propriety send any of its members to confer with His Lordship in their private characters, but that, ever desirous of establishing peace on reasonable terms, they will send a committee of their body, to know whether he has any authority to treat with persons, authorized by

Congress for that purpose, in behalf of America, and what that authority is, and to hear such propositions as he shall think fit to make respecting the same.

"That the President be desired to write to General Washington, and acquaint him, that it is the opinion of Congress no proposals for making peace between Great Britain and the United States of America, ought to be received and attended to, unless the same be made in writing, and addressed to the representatives of the said States in Congress, or persons authorized by them, and if application be made to him by any of the commanders of the British forces on that subject, that he inform them that these United States, who entered into the war only for the defence of their lives and liberties, will cheerfully agree to peace on reasonable terms, whenever such shall be proposed to them, in manner aforesaid.

"Resolved, That a copy of the first of the two foregoing resolutions be delivered to General Sullivan, and that he be directed to repair immediately to Lord Howe.

"Resolved, That to-morrow be assigned for electing the committee."

Friday, September 6.

"Resolved, That General Sullivan be requested to deliver to Lord Howe, the copy of the resolution given to him.

"Resolved, That the committee 'to be sent to know whether Lord Howe has any authority to treat with persons authorized by Congress for that purpose in behalf of America, and what that authority is, and to hear such propositions as he shall think fit to make respecting the same,' consist of three.

"Congress then proceeded to the election, and the ballots being taken, Mr. Franklin, Mr. J. Adams, and Mr. Rutledge, were elected.

"Letters from General Washington, Schuyler, Gates, and Mercer, referred to the board of war.

"The board of war brought in a report. Resolutions upon it."

Saturday, September 7.

"A letter of the 5th from Charles Preston, Major of the 26th regiment, a prisoner, was read and referred to the board of war.

"Resolved, That a copy of the resolutions passed by Congress on the message brought by General Sullivan, and the names of the committee appointed, be sent to General Washington.

"Congress resumed the consideration of the report of the board of war, whereupon,

"Resolved, That all letters to and from the board of war and ordnance, or the secretary of the same, be free of all expense in the post-office of the United States, &c."

Monday, September 9.

"Resolved, That in all continental commissions and other instruments, where heretofore the words "United Colonies" have been used, the style be altered for the future to the "United States."

"The board of war brought in a report, which was read.

"Ordered, To lie on the table."

On this day Mr. Franklin, Mr. Edward Rutledge, and Mr. John Adams, proceeded on their journey to Lord Howe, on Staten Island, the two former in chairs, and the latter on horseback. The first night we lodged at an inn in New Brunswick. On the road, and at all the public houses, we saw such numbers of officers and soldiers, straggling and loitering, as gave me, at least, but a poor opinion of the discipline of our forces, and excited as much indignation as anxiety. Such thoughtless dissipation, at a time so critical, was not calculated to inspire very sanguine hopes, or give great courage to ambassadors. I was, nevertheless, determined that it should not dishearten me. I saw that we must, and had no doubt but we should, be chastised into order in time.

The taverns were so full we could with difficulty obtain entertainment. At Brunswick, but one bed could be procured for Dr. Franklin and me, in a chamber little larger than the bed, without a chimney, and with only one small window. The window was open, and I, who was an invalid and afraid of the air in the night, shut it close. "Oh!" says Franklin, "don't shut the window, we shall be suffocated." I answered, I was afraid of the evening air. Dr. Franklin replied, "The air within this chamber will soon be, and indeed is now, worse than that without doors. Come, open the window and come to bed, and I will convince you. I believe you are not acquainted with my theory of colds." Opening the window, and leaping into bed, I said I had read his letters to Dr. Cooper, in which he had advanced, that nobody ever got cold by going into a cold church or any other cold air, but the theory was so little consistent with my experience, that I thought it a paradox. However, I had so much curiosity to hear his reasons that I would run the risk of a cold. The Doctor then began a harangue upon air and cold, and respiration and perspiration, with which I was so much amused that I soon fell asleep, and left him and his philosophy together, but I believe they were equally sound and insensible within a few minutes after me, for the last words I heard were pronounced as if he was more than half asleep. I remember little of the lecture, except that the human body, by respiration and perspiration, destroys a gallon of air in a minute; that two such persons as were now in that chamber, would consume all the air in it in an hour or two; that by breathing over again the matter thrown off by the lungs and the skin, we should imbibe the real cause of colds, not from abroad, but from within. I am not inclined to introduce here a dissertation on this subject. There is much truth, I believe, in some things he advanced, but they warrant not the assertion that a cold is never taken from cold air. I have often conversed with him since on the same subject, and I believe with him, that colds are often taken in foul air in close rooms, but they are often taken from cold air abroad, too. I have often asked him whether a person heated with exercise going suddenly into cold air, or standing still in a current of it, might not have his pores suddenly contracted, his perspiration stopped, and that matter thrown into the circulations, or cast upon the lungs, which he acknowledged was the cause of colds. To this he never could give me a satisfactory answer, and I have heard that in the opinion of his own able physician, Dr. Jones, he fell a sacrifice at last, not to the stone, but to his own theory, having caught the violent cold which finally choked him, by sitting for some hours at a window, with the cool air blowing upon him.

The next morning we proceeded on our journey, and the remainder of this negotiation will be related from the Journals of Congress, and from a few familiar letters, which I wrote to my most intimate friends before and after my journey. The abrupt, uncouth freedom of these and all others of my letters in those days, requires an apology. Nothing was farther from my thoughts, than that they would ever appear before the public. Oppressed with a load of business, without an amanuensis, or any assistance, I was obliged to do every thing myself. For seven years before this, I had never been without three clerks in my office as a barrister; but now I had no secretary, or servant, whom I could trust to write, and every thing must be copied by myself, or be hazarded without any copy. The few that I wrote, upon this occasion, I copied, merely to assist my memory, as occasion might demand.

There were a few circumstances which appear neither in the Journals of Congress, nor in my letters, which may be thought by some worth preserving. Lord Howe had sent over an officer as a hostage for our security. I said to Dr. Franklin, it would be childish in us to depend upon such a pledge, and insisted on taking him over with us, and keeping our surety on the same side of the water with us. My colleagues exulted in the proposition, and agreed to it instantly. We told the officer, if he held himself under our direction, he must go back with us. He bowed assent, and we all embarked in his lordship's barge. As we approached the shore, his lordship, observing us, came down to the water's edge to receive us, and, looking at the officer, he said, "Gentlemen, you make me a very high compliment, and you may depend upon it, I will consider it as the most sacred of things." We walked up to the house between lines of guards of grenadiers, looking fierce as ten Furies, and making all the grimaces, and gestures, and motions of their muskets, with bayonets fixed, which, I suppose, military etiquette requires, but which we neither understood nor regarded.

The house had been the habitation of military guards, and was as dirty as a stable; but his lordship had prepared a large handsome room, by spreading a carpet of moss and green sprigs, from bushes and shrubs in the neighborhood, till he had made it not only wholesome, but romantically elegant; and he entertained us with good claret, good bread, cold ham, tongues, and mutton.

I will now proceed to relate the sequel of this conference: 1st, from the Journal of Congress; 2d, from the letters written to some of my friends at the time; 3d, a circumstance or two, which are not preserved in the Journals or letters.

Friday, September 13.

"The committee appointed to confer with Lord Howe, having returned, made a verbal report.

"Ordered, That they make a report, in writing, as soon as conveniently they can."

Tuesday, September 17.

"The committee appointed to confer with Lord Howe, agreeable to the order of Congress, brought in a report in writing, which was read, as follows:

"In obedience to the orders of Congress, we have had a meeting with Lord Howe. It was on Wednesday last, upon Staten Island, opposite to Amboy, where his lordship received and entertained us with the utmost politeness.

"His lordship opened the conversation by acquainting us, that, though he could not treat with us as a Committee of Congress, yet, as his powers enabled him to confer and consult with any private gentlemen of influence in the Colonies, on the means of restoring peace between the two countries, he was glad of this opportunity of conferring with us on that subject, if we thought ourselves at liberty to enter into a conference with him in that character. We observed to his lordship, that, as our business was to hear, he might consider us in what light he pleased, and communicate to us any propositions he might be authorized to make for the purpose mentioned, but that we could consider ourselves in no other character than that in which we were placed by order of Congress.

"His Lordship then entered into a discourse of considerable length, which contained no explicit proposition of peace, except one, namely. That the Colonies should return to their allegiance and obedience to the Government of Great Britain. The rest consisted, principally, of assurances, that there was an exceeding good disposition in the King and his ministers to make that government easy to us, with intimations, that, in case of our submission, they would cause the offensive acts of Parliament to be revised, and the instructions to governors to be reconsidered; that so, if any just causes of complaint were found in the acts, or any errors in government were perceived to have crept into the instructions, they might be amended or withdrawn.

"We gave it as our opinion to his lordship, that a return to the domination of Great Britain was not now to be expected. We mentioned the repeated humble petitions of the Colonies to the King and Parliament, which had been treated with contempt, and answered only by additional injuries; the unexampled patience we had shown under their tyrannical government, and that it was not till the late act of Parliament, which denounced war against us, and put us out of the King's protection, that we declared our independence; that this declaration had been called for by the people of the Colonies in general; that every Colony had approved of it, when made, and all now considered themselves as independent States, and were settling, or had settled their governments accordingly, so that it was not in the power of Congress to agree, for them, that they should return to their former dependent state; that there was no doubt of their inclination to peace, and their willingness to enter into a treaty with Britain, that might be advantageous to both countries; that, though his lordship had, at present, no power to treat with them as independent States, he might, if there was the same good disposition in Britain, much sooner obtain fresh powers from thence, for that purpose, than powers could be obtained by Congress, from the several Colonies, to consent to a submission.

"His lordship then, saying that he was sorry to find that no accommodation was like to take place, put an end to the conference.

"Upon the whole, it did not appear to your committee that his lordship's commission contained any other authority than that expressed in the act of Parliament, namely, that of granting pardons, with such exceptions as the commissioners shall think proper to make, and of declaring America, or any part of it, to be in the King's peace, upon submission; for, as to the power of inquiring into the state of America, which his lordship mentioned to us, and of conferring and consulting with any persons the commissioners might think proper, and representing the result of such conversation to the ministry, who, provided the Colonies would subject themselves, might, after all, or might not, at their pleasure, make any alterations in the former instructions to governors, or propose in Parliament any amendment of the acts complained of, we apprehended any expectation from the effects of such a power, would have been too uncertain and precarious to be relied on by America, had she still continued in her state of dependence.

"Ordered, That the foregoing report, and also the message from Lord Howe, as delivered by General Sullivan, and the resolution of Congress, in consequence thereof, be published by the committee who brought in the foregoing report.

"Ordered, That the said committee publish Lord Drummond's letters to General Washington, and the General's answers.

Two or three circumstances, which are omitted in this report, and, indeed, not thought worth notice in any of my private letters, I afterwards found circulated in Europe, and oftener repeated than any other part of this whole transaction. Lord Howe was profuse in his expressions of gratitude to the state of Massachusetts, for erecting a marble monument, in Westminster Abbey, to his elder brother, Lord Howe, who was killed in America, in the last French war, saying, "he esteemed that honor to his family above all things in this world. That such was his gratitude and affection to this country, on that account, that he felt for America as for a brother, and, if America should fall, he should feel and lament it like the loss of a brother." Dr. Franklin, with an easy air, and a collected countenance, a bow, a smile, and all that naiveté, which sometimes appeared in his conversation, and is often observed in his writings, replied, "My Lord, we will do our utmost endeavors to save your lordship that mortification." His lordship appeared to feel this with more sensibility than I could expect; but he only returned, "I suppose you will endeavor to give us employment in Europe." To this observation, not a word, nor a look, from which he could draw any inference, escaped any of the committee.

Another circumstance, of no more importance than the former, was so much celebrated in Europe, that it has often reminded me of the question of Phocion to his fellow-citizens, when something he had said in public was received by the people of Athens with clamorous applause: "Have I said any foolish thing?" When his lordship observed to us, that he could not confer with us as members of Congress, or public characters, but only as private persons and British subjects, Mr. John Adams answered somewhat quickly, "Your lordship may consider me in what light you please, and, indeed, I should be willing to consider myself, for a few moments, in any character which would be agreeable to your lordship, except that of a British subject." His lordship, at these words, turned to Dr. Franklin and Mr. Rutledge, and said, "Mr. Adams is a decided character," with so much gravity and solemnity, that I now believe it meant more than either of my colleagues, or myself, understood, at the time. In our report to Congress, we supposed that the commissioners, Lord and General Howe, had, by their commission, power to except from pardon all that they should think proper; but I was informed, in England, afterwards, that a number were expressly excepted, by name, from pardon, by the Privy Council, and that John Adams was one of them, and that this list of exceptions was given, as an instruction, to the two Howes, with their commission. When I was afterwards a minister plenipotentiary at the Court of St. James, the king and the ministry were often insulted, ridiculed, and reproached, in the newspapers, for having conducted themselves with so much folly, as to be reduced to the humiliating necessity of receiving, as an ambassador, a man who stood recorded, by the Privy Council, as a rebel expressly excepted from pardon. Endnote 045 If this is true, it will account for his lordship's gloomy denunciation of me as "a decided character." Some years afterwards, when I resided in England, as a public minister, his lordship recollected, and alluded to this conversation, with great politeness and much good humor. At the ball, on the queen's birthnight, I was at a loss for the seats assigned to the foreign ambassadors and their ladies. Fortunately meeting Lord Howe at the door, I asked his lordship where were the ambassadors' seats. His lordship, with his usual politeness, and an unusual smile of good humor, pointed to the seats, and, manifestly alluding to the conversation on Staten Island, said, "Ay! now we must turn you away, among the foreigners."

The conduct of General Sullivan, in consenting to come to Philadelphia, upon so confused an errand from Lord Howe, though his situation, as a prisoner, was a temptation, and may be considered as some apology for it, appeared to me to betray such want of penetration and fortitude, and there was so little precision in the information he communicated, that I felt much resentment, and more contempt, upon the occasion, than was perhaps just. The time was extremely critical. The attention of Congress, the army, the States, and the people, ought to have been wholly directed to the defence of the country. To have it diverted and relaxed, by such a poor artifice and confused tale, appeared very reprehensible. To a few of my most confidential friends, I expressed my feelings, in a very few words, which I found time to write, and all the letters of which I find copies in my letter book, are here subjoined, relative to this transaction, from its beginning to its end. Endnote 046

I return to the Journal of Congress.

Friday, September 13.

"Two letters, of the 7th and 11th, from General Washington, one of the 8th from General Green, and a resolution of the Committee of Safety of Pennsylvania, of the 13th, were read, and referred to the board of war.

"Two letters, of the 8th, from General Schuyler, with sundry papers inclosed, one of the 7th, from Walter Livingston, and one of the 12th of August, from Brigadier-General Armstrong, were read. Referred to the board of war.

"A committee of the whole to take into consideration a report of the board of war. Mr. Nelson reported no resolutions."

Saturday, September 14.

"A letter from R. H. Harrison, secretary to General Washington, was read. Four French officers, who arrived in the Reprisal, Captain Weeks, being recommended to Congress,

"Resolved, That they be referred to the board of war.

"The board of war brought in a report, which was taken into consideration, whereupon nine resolutions were adopted. Endnote 047

"A letter of the 9th, from General Lee to the board of war, was laid before Congress, and read."

Monday, September 16.

"A letter of the 14th from General Washington, one of the 9th from General Schuyler, inclosing a copy of one from General Gates, dated the 6th, and one of the 2d from General Gates, with sundry papers inclosed, were read, and referred to the board of war.

"A committee of the whole on a report of the board of war. Mr. Nelson reported sundry amendments, and Congress adopted the resolutions with the amendments. Endnote 048

"Resolved, That to-morrow be assigned for taking into consideration the articles of war."

Tuesday, September 17.

"Sundry resolutions being moved and seconded, in addition to those passed yesterday, relative to the new army. After debate.

"Resolved, That they be referred to the board of war.

"A letter of the 10th from Brigadier-General Lewis was read; also a letter from James Forrest was read, and referred to the board of war.

"Congress took into consideration the plan of treaties to be proposed to foreign nations, with the amendments agreed to by the committee of the whole, and the same was agreed to."

This is all that I can find in the Public Journal relative to this, one of the most important transactions that ever came before Congress. A Secret Journal was prepared, in which all the proceedings on this business were entered, which has never been published. If that Journal was honestly and faithfully kept, the progress of the plan of treaties, and the persons chiefly concerned in it, will there appear. Endnote 049

Wednesday, September 18.

"The board of war brought in a report, which was taken into consideration, and six resolutions adopted from it, which appear on the Journal. The remainder of the report postponed.

"Resolved, That the board of war be directed to prepare a resolution for enforcing and perfecting discipline in the army.

"Congress took into consideration the instructions to the commissioners, &c."

These, I suppose, were the ministers to France and other courts in Europe.

Thursday, September 19.

"The board of war brought in a report, which was taken into consideration, and five resolutions adopted from it, which see in the Journal. The last of these is in these words.

"That the commander-in-chief of the forces of these States, in the several departments, be directed to give positive orders to the brigadier-generals and colonels, and all other officers in their several armies, that the troops under their command may every day be called together and trained in arms, in order that officers and men may be perfected in the manual exercise and manœuvres, and inured to the most exemplary discipline, and that all officers be assured that the Congress will consider activity and success, in introducing discipline into the army, among the best recommendations for promotion."

This resolution was the effect of my late journey through the Jerseys to Staten Island. I had observed such dissipation and idleness, such confusion and distraction among officers and soldiers, in various parts of the country, as astonished, grieved, and alarmed me. Discipline, discipline, had become my constant topic of discourse and even declamation in and out of Congress, and especially in the board of war. I saw very clearly that the ruin of our cause and country must be the consequence, if a thorough reformation and strict discipline could not be introduced. My zeal on this occasion was no doubt represented by my faithful enemies, in great secrecy, however, to their friends in the army; and although it might recommend me to the esteem of a very few, yet it will be easily believed that it contributed nothing to my popularity among the many.

"A memorial from the Chevalier Dorre was read. Ordered, that it be referred to the board of war.

"Congress resumed the consideation of the articles of war, and after some time the farther consideration thereof was postponed."

This was another measure that I constantly urged on with all the zeal and industry possible, convinced that nothing short of the Roman and British discipline could possibly save us.

Friday, September 20.

"Congress resumed the consideration of the articles of war, which, being debated in paragraphs, were agreed to as follows:—

"Resolved, That from and after the publication of the following articles, in the respective armies of the United States, the rules and articles by which the said armies have heretofore been governed shall be, and they are, hereby, repealed."

The articles are inserted in the Journal of this day, and need not be transcribed; they are the system which I persuaded Jefferson to agree with me in reporting to Congress. They fill about sixteen pages of the Journal. In Congress, Jefferson never spoke, and all the labor of the debate on those articles, paragraph by paragraph, was thrown upon me, and such was the opposition, and so undigested were the notions of liberty prevalent among the majority of the members most zealously attached to the public cause, that to this day I scarcely know how it was possible that these articles could have been carried. They were adopted, however, and have governed our armies with little variation to this day. *Endnote 050*

"Ordered, That the foregoing articles of war be immediately published.

"Ordered, That the resolutions for raising the new army be published, and copies thereof sent to the commanding officers in the several departments, and to the Assemblies and Conventions of the respective States."

These were for raising eighty-eight battalions, with a bounty for enlisting the men during the war, granting lands, &c. *Endnote 051* The articles of war, and the institution of the army, during the war, were all my work, and yet I have been represented as an enemy to a regular army!

Monday, September 23.

"A letter, of the 20th and 21st, from General Washington; two of the 19th, from J. Trumbull; one of the 21st, from the Convention of Delaware; one of the 14th, from R. Varick; one of the 19th from Governor Livingston; also, one of the 14th, from General Schuyler, and one of the 19th, from Colonel Van Schaick, and one from Dr. William Shippen, were read.

"Ordered, That the letter from Dr. Shippen be referred to the medical committee, and the rest to the board of war.

"Two petitions, one from Colonel J. Stark, and the other from Monsieur Devourouy, were read, and referred to the board of war."

Tuesday, September 24.

"The board of war brought in a report, which was read. Ordered, To lie on the table.

"The board of war brought in a further report. Ordered, To lie on the table.

"Congress resumed the consideration of the instructions to the commissioners, and the same being debated by paragraphs, and amended, were agreed to."

These instructions were recorded only on the Secret Journal, and are not, therefore, in my power. They may be found, no doubt, at the seat of government, in the office of the Secretary of State. *Endnote 052*

Wednesday, September 25.

"Two letters from General Lee; one of the 24th of August to the President; the other, of the 27th of the same month, to the board of war, both dated at Savannah, being received, were read.

"Congress took into consideration the report of the board of war, whereupon, Resolved, &c." Endnote 053

Friday, September 27.

"Two letters, of the 24th and 25th, from General Washington, with sundry papers inclosed; one of the 20th from the Convention of New York; one of the 22d from Joseph Trumbull, one of the 25th, from Colonel John Shee, inclosing his commission; one of the 25th, from Jon. B. Smith, requesting leave to resign his office of deputy mustermaster-general, were laid before Congress, and read.

"Ordered, That the letters from General Washington be referred to a committee of five.

"The members chosen, Mr. Wythe, Mr. Hopkinson, Mr. Rutledge, Mr. J. Adams, and Mr. Stone.

"Ordered, That the secret committee deliver to the board of war the care and custody of all arms, ammunition, and other warlike stores, now under their care, or that may hereafter be imported or purchased by them for account of the United States of America."

Saturday, September 28.

"The board of war, to whom the petition of William McCue was referred, brought in a report, whereupon, Resolved, as in the Journal."

Monday, September 30.

"Resolved, That the board of war be empowered and directed, on requisition of the General or commanding officers in the several departments, to send such articles of military stores and other necessaries, which they may have in their possession, or can procure.

"Resolved, That the board of war be directed to order the three Virginia battalions, now on their march to New York, to be lodged in the barracks at Wilmington; there to remain till further orders.

"The committee to whom were referred the letters from General Washington, of the 24th and 25th instant, and the papers inclosed therein, brought in their report, which was taken into consideration; whereupon, many resolutions were passed, which appear in the Journal, and the remainder of the report postponed."

Tuesday, October 1.

"Resolved, That a committee of four be appointed to confer with Brigadier-General Mifflin.

"The members chosen, Mr. R. H. Lee, Mr. Sherman, Mr. J. Adams, and Mr. Gerry.

"Resolved, That a committee of five be appointed to prepare and bring in a plan of a military academy at the army.

"The members chosen, Mr. Hooper, Mr. Lynch, Mr. Wythe, Mr. Williams, and Mr. J. Adams."

On this same day I wrote to Colonel Knox in these words:

"This day I had the honor of making a motion for the appointment of a committee to consider of a plan for the establishment of a military academy in the army. The committee was appointed and your servant was one. Write me your sentiments upon the subject."

As this was, in my opinion, the most critical and dangerous period of the whole revolutionary war; as all that I had seen and heard and read of the state of our army, made a great impression on my mind, and aroused the most alarming apprehensions, I will conceal nothing from posterity. My own private letters to confidential friends will show my opinion at the time of the state of facts, and the measures that were necessary to retrieve our disgraces. Like Mr. Gifford, I look back with a sort of skepticism, on the application of those days, and cannot account for the possibility of finding time, amidst all my employments in Congress and the board of war, to write and copy the letters I find in my books.

If these papers should hereafter be read by disinterested persons, they will perhaps think that I took too much upon me, in assuming the office of preceptor to the army. To this objection, I can only reply by asserting that it was high time that the army had some instructor or other. It was a scene of indiscipline, insubordination, and confusion. Colonel Tudor had been my pupil as a clerk in my office as a barrister at law. Colonel Knox had been a youth, who had attracted my notice by his pleasing manners and inquisitive turn of mind, when I was a man in business in Boston. General Parsons had been my junior for three years at college, and upon terms of familiarity. I had therefore no reason to suppose that either of them would take offence at any thing I should write. Again, I had formed an opinion that courage and reading were all that were necessary to the formation of an officer. Of the courage of these gentlemen, and the officers in general, I had no doubt; but I was too well informed that most of the officers were deficient in reading, and I wished to turn the minds of such as were capable of it, to that great source of information. I had met with an observation among regular officers, that mankind were naturally divided into three sorts; one third of them are animated at the first appearance of danger, and will press forward to meet and examine it; another third are alarmed at it, but will neither advance nor retreat, till they know the nature of it, but stand to meet it. The remaining third will run or fly upon the first thought of it. If this remark is just, as I believed it was, it appeared to me that the only way to form an army to be confided in, was a systematic discipline, by which means all men may be made heroes. In this manner, in time, our American army was made equal to the veterans of France and England, and in this way the armies of France have been made invincible hitherto, and in the same way they will be ultimately conquered, or at least, successfully resisted by their enemies.

All the powers of government, legislative, executive, and judiciary were at that time collected in one centre, and that centre was the Congress. As a member of that body, I had contributed my share towards the creation of the army, and the appointment of all the officers, and, as president of the board of war, it was my peculiar province to superintend every thing relating to the army. I will add without vanity, I had read as much on the military art, and much more of the history of war, than any American officer of that army, General Lee excepted. If all these considerations are not a sufficient apology for my interference, I submit to censure. Certain it is, that these letters, and many more that I wrote, without preserving copies, were not calculated to procure me popularity in the army, but on the contrary, contributed to produce those misrepresentations which were diffused from that source against me, as well as my friend Samuel Adams and others. The General's secretaries and aids, all from the southward, Reed, Harrison, &c., &c., were young gentlemen of letters, and thought full as highly of themselves as they ought to think, and much more disrespectfully of New England, and even of Congress than they ought to have thought; they dictated letters, which were not well calculated to preserve that subordination of the military power to the civil authority, which the spirit of liberty will always require and enforce. *Endnote 054*

Some time in the month of October, 1776,—I cannot from the Journals, ascertain the day, *Endnote 055*—worn down with continual application, through all the heats of a summer in Philadelphia, anxious for the state of my family, and desirous of conferring with my constituents on the critical and dangerous state of affairs at home, I asked leave of Congress to be absent, which they readily granted.

The fragment of Autobiography left by Mr. Adams terminates here. An interval of a year takes place and then follows a paper which appears to have been commenced on the first of December, 1806, under the title of "Travels and Negotiations." The greater part of this is only an amplification of his Diary of the same period. As a selection of one or the other of these papers seemed necessary, the Diary, as the contemporaneous record, has been preferred for publication, whilst such portions of the other paper have been added as furnish interesting details. These are distinguished by being placed within brackets.

Among the papers left by Mr. Adams, is the logbook of Captain Samuel Tucker, during the voyage to France of the Frigate Boston. With this record the Diary has been compared, and such extracts from it as tend to illustrate the text have been placed in the Notes.

1777. November. When I asked leave of Congress to make a visit to my constituents and my family in November, 1777, it was my intention to decline the next election, and return to my practice at the bar. I had been four years in Congress, had left my accounts in a very loose condition, my debtors were failing, the paper money was depreciating: I was daily losing the fruits of seventeen years' industry; my family was living on my past acquisitions, which were very moderate, for no man ever did so much business for so little profit; my children were growing up without my care in their education, and all my emoluments as a member of Congress, for four years, had not been sufficient to pay a laboring man upon my farm. Some of my friends, who had more compassion for me and my family than others, suggested to me what I knew very well before, that I was losing a fortune every year by my absence. Young gentlemen who had been clerks in my office, and others whom I had left in that character in other offices, were growing rich; for the prize causes, and other controversies had made the profession of a barrister more lucrative than it ever had been before. I thought, therefore, that four years' drudgery, and sacrifice of every thing, were sufficient for my share of absence from home, and that another might take my place. Upon my arrival at my home in Braintree, I soon found that my old clients had not forgotten me, and that new ones had heard enough of me to be ambitious of engaging me in suits which were depending. I had applications from all quarters in the most important disputes. Among others, Col. Elisha Doane applied to me to go to Portsmouth, in New Hampshire, upon the case of a large ship and cargo, which had been seized, and was to be tried in the court of admiralty, before Judge Brackett.

At the trial of the cause at Portsmouth, and while I was speaking in it, Mr. Langdon came in from Philadelphia, and leaning over the bar, whispered to me, that Mr. Deane was recalled, and I was appointed to go to France. As I could scarcely believe the news to be true, and suspected Langdon to be sporting with me, it did not disconcert me. As I had never solicited such an appointment, nor intimated to any one the smallest inclination for it, the news was altogether unexpected. The only hint I ever had of such a design in Congress was this. After I had mounted my horse for my journey home, Mr. Gerry, at Yorktown, came out of the house of Mr. Roberdeau, where we lodged together, and said to me, between him and me, that I must go to France; that Mr. Deane's conduct had been so intolerably bad as to disgrace himself and his country, and that Congress had no other way of retrieving the dishonor but by recalling him. I answered that, as to recalling Mr. Deane, Congress would do as they thought fit, but I entreated him that neither Mr. Gerry nor any one else would think of me for a successor, for I was altogether unqualified for it. Supposing it only a sudden thought of Mr. Gerry, and that when he should consider it a moment he would relinquish it, I know not that I recollected it again, till Mr. Langdon brought it to remembrance. At Portsmouth, Captain Landais was introduced to me as then lately arrived from France, who gave me an account of his voyage with Bougainville round the world, and other particulars of his life. Upon my return to Braintree, I found to my infinite anxiety, that

Mr. Langdon's intelligence was too well founded. Large packets from Congress, containing a new commission to Franklin, Lee, and me, as plenipotentiaries to the King of France, with our instructions and other papers had been left at my house, and waited my arrival. A letter from the President of Congress informed me of my appointment, and that the navy board in Boston was ordered to fit out the frigate Boston as soon as possible, to carry me to France. It should have been observed before, that in announcing to me the intelligence of my appointment, Langdon neither expressed congratulation nor regret, but I soon afterwards had evidence enough that he lamented Mr. Deane's recall, for he had already formed lucrative connections in France, by Mr. Deane's recommendation, particularly with Mr. Le Ray de Chaumont, who had shipped merchandises to him to sell upon commission, an account of which, rendered to Chaumont by Langdon, was shown to me by the former, at Passy, in 1779, in which almost the whole capital was sunk by the depreciation of paper money.

When the despatches from Congress were read, the first question was, whether I should accept the commission, or return it to Congress. The dangers of the seas, and the sufferings of a winter passage, although I had no experience of either, had little weight with me. The British men-of-war were a more serious consideration. The news of my appointment, I had no doubt, were known in Rhode Island, where a part of the British navy and army then lay, as soon as they were to me, and transmitted to England as soon as possible. I had every reason to expect that ships would be ordered from Rhode Island and from Halifax to intercept the Boston, and that intelligence would be secretly sent them, as accurately as possible, of the time when she was to sail. For there always have been and still are spies in America, as well as in France, England, and other countries. The consequence of a capture would be a lodging in Newgate. For the spirit of contempt, as well as indignation and vindictive rage, with which the British government had to that time conducted both the controversy and the war, forbade me to hope for the honor of an apartment in the Tower as a state prisoner. As their Act of Parliament would authorize them to try me in England for treason, and proceed to execution too, I had no doubt they would go to the extent of their power, and practise upon me all the cruelties of their punishment of treason. My family, consisting of a dearly beloved wife and four young children, excited sentiments of tenderness, which a father and a lover only can conceive, and which no language can express; and my want of qualifications for the office was by no means forgotten.

On the other hand, my country was in deep distress and in great danger. Her dearest interests would be involved in the relations she might form with foreign nations. My own plan of these relations had been deliberately formed and fully communicated to Congress nearly two years before. The confidence of my country was committed to me without my solicitation. My wife, who had always encouraged and animated me in all antecedent dangers and perplexities, did not fail me on this occasion. But she discovered an inclination to bear me company, with all our children. This proposal, however, she was soon convinced, was too hazardous and imprudent.

It was an opinion, generally prevailing in Boston, that the fisheries were lost forever. Mr. Isaac Smith, who had been more largely concerned in the cod-fishery than any man, excepting Mr. Hooper and Mr. Lee of Marblehead, had spoken to me on the subject, and said that whatever should be the termination of the war, he knew we should never be allowed to fish again upon the Banks. My practice as a barrister, in the counties of Essex, Plymouth, and Barnstable, had introduced me to more knowledge, both of the cod and whale fisheries, and of their importance, both to the commerce and naval power of this country, than any other man possessed who would be sent abroad if I refused; and this consideration had no small weight in producing my determination.

After much agitation of mind, and a thousand reveries unnecessary to be detailed, I resolved to devote my family and my life to the cause, accepted the appointment, and made preparation for the voyage. A longer time than I expected was required to fit and man the frigate. The news of my appointment was whispered about, and General Knox came up to dine with me at Braintree. The design of his visit was, as I soon perceived, to sound me in relation to General Washington. He asked me what my opinion of him was. I answered, with the utmost frankness, that I thought him a perfectly honest man, with an amiable and excellent heart, and the most important character at that time among us; for he was the centre of our Union. He asked the question, he said, because, as I was going to Europe, it was of importance that the General's character should be supported in other countries. I replied, that he might be perfectly at his ease on the subject, for he might depend upon it, that, both from principle and affection, public and private, I should do my utmost to support his character, at all times and in all places, unless something should happen very greatly to alter my opinion of him; and this I have done from that time to this. I mention this incident, because that insolent blasphemer of things sacred, and transcendent libeller of all that is good, Tom Paine, has more than once asserted in print that I was one of a faction, in the fall of the year 1777, against General Washington. *Endnote 056*

I was almost out of patience waiting for the frigate till the thirteenth day of February, 1778.

DIARY.

1778. February 13. Friday. Captain Samuel Tucker, commander of the frigate Boston, met me at Mr. Norton Quincy's, where we dined, and after dinner I sent my baggage, and walked myself with Captain Tucker, *Endnote 057* Mr. Griffin, a midshipman, and my eldest son, John Quincy Adams, between ten and eleven years of age, down to the Moon Head, where lay the Boston's barge. The wind was very high, and the sea very rough; but, by means of a quantity of hay in the bottom of the boat, and good watch-coats, with which we were covered, we arrived on board the Boston, about five o'clock, tolerably warm and dry. On board I found Mr. Vernon, a son of Mr. Vernon of the navy board, a little son of Mr. Deane of Wethersfield, between eleven and twelve years of age, and Mr. Nicholas Noel, a French gentleman, surgeon of the ship, who seems to be a well-bred man. Dr. Noel showed me a book which was new to me. The title translated is, "The Elements of the English Tongue, developed in a new, easy, and concise Manner, in which the Pronunciation is taught by an Asemblage of Letters, which form similar Sounds in French. By V. J. Peyton.

"Linguarum diversitas alienat hominem ab homine, et propter solam linguarum diversitatem, nihil potest ad consociandos homines tanta similitudo naturæ."

St. August. De Civit. Dei.

14. Saturday. A very fine morning; the wind at north-west. At daybreak, orders were given for the ship to unmoor. My lodging was a cot, with a double mattress, a good bolster, my own sheets, and blankets enough; my little son with me. We lay very comfortably, and slept well. A violent gale of wind in the night.

15. Sunday. This morning, weighed the last anchor, and came under sail, before breakfast. A fine wind and a pleasant sun, but a sharp, cold air. Thus I bid farewell to my native shore. Arrived and anchored in the harbor of Marblehead about noon. Major Reed, Captain Gatchell, father-in-law of Captain Tucker, came on board, and a Captain Stephens, who came to make me a present of a single pistol. [He made many apologies for giving me but one. He had no more. He had lately presented to Mr. Hancock a beautiful pair, and this was all he had left. I understood they had been taken from the English, in one of the prize ships.]

16. Monday. Another storm for our mortification; the wind at north-east, and the snow so thick that the captain thinks he cannot go to sea. Our excursion to this place was unfortunate, because it is almost impossible to keep the men on board; mothers, wives, sisters, come on board, and beg for leave for their sons, husbands, and brothers, to go on shore for one hour, &c.; so that it is hard for the commander to resist their importunity. I am anxious at these delays; we shall never have another wind so good as we have lost. Congress and the navy-board will be surprised at these delays, and yet there is no fault that I know of. The commander of the ship is active and vigilant, and does all in his power, but he wants men· *Endnote 058* He has very few seamen indeed. All is as yet chaos on board. His men are not disciplined; the marines are not. The men are not exercised to the guns; they hardly know the ropes.

My son is treated very complaisantly by Dr. Noel, and by a captain and lieutenant of artillery, who are on board, all French gentlemen. They are very assiduous in teaching him French. The Doctor, Monsieur Noel, is a genteel, well-bred man, and has received somewhere a good education. He has wounds on his forehead and on his hands, which he says he received, last war, in the light-horse service. The name of the captain of artillery is Parison, and that of the lieutenant is Bégard.

Since my embarkation, Master Jesse Deane delivered me a letter from his uncle Barnabas Deane, dated 10th February, recommending to my particular care and attention the bearer, the only child of his brother, Silas Deane, Esq., now in France, making no doubt, as the letter adds, "that I shall take the same care of a child in his situation, which I would wish to have done to a child of my own, in the like circumstances. It is needless to mention his youth and helplessness, also how much he will be exposed to bad company, and to contract bad habits, without some friendly monitor to caution and keep him from associating with the common hands on board."

About the same time, another letter was delivered to me from William Vernon, Esq., of the Continental Navy Board, dated February 9, in these words: "I presume it is unnecessary to say one word, in order to impress your mind with the anxiety a parent is under in the education of a son, more especially when not under his immediate inspection, and at three thousand miles distance. Your parental affection fixes this principle. Therefore I have only to beg the favor of you, sir, to place my son in such a situation, and with such a gentleman as you would choose for one of yours, whom you would wish to accomplish for a merchant. If such a house could be found, either at Bordeaux or Nantes, of Protestant principles, of general and extensive business, I rather think one of those cities the best. Yet, if it should be your opinion that some other place might be more advantageous to place him at, or that he can be employed by any of the States' agents, with a good prospect of improving himself in such manner that he may hereafter be useful to society, and in particular to these American States, my views are fully answered. I have only one observation more to make, namely, in respect to the economy of this matter, which I am persuaded will engage your attention, as the small fortune that remains with me I would wish to appropriate for the education of my son, which I know must be husbanded; yet I can't think of being rigidly parsimonious, nor must I be very lavish, lest my money should not hold out.

"I imagine a gratuity of one hundred pounds sterling may be given to a merchant of eminence to take him for two or three years, and, perhaps, his yearly board paid for. I shall be entirely satisfied, in whatsoever may seem best for you to do, and ever shall have a grateful remembrance of your unmerited favors. And sincerely hope, in future, to have it in my power to make compensation. I wish you health, and the utmost happiness, and am, with the greatest regards, &c."

Thus I find myself invested with the unexpected trust of a kind of guardianship of two promising young gentlemen, besides my own son. This benevolent office is peculiarly agreeable to my temper. Few things have ever given me greater pleasure than the tuition of youth to the bar, and the advancement of merit.

[I was soon relieved from the principal care of it, however, for Mr. Vernon chose to remain at Bordeaux; and Mr. Deane, by the advice of Dr. Franklin, was put to Le Cœur's pension, at Passy, with my son, J. Q. A., and his grandson, Benjamin Franklin Bache, since that time, famous enough as the editor and proprietor of the Aurora.]

17. Tuesday. I set a lesson to my son, in Chambaud's French Grammar, and asked the favor of Dr. Noel to show him the precise, critical pronunciation of all the French words, syllables, and letters, which the Doctor very politely did, and Mr. John is getting his lessons accordingly, very much pleased.

The weather is fair, and the wind right, and we are again weighing anchor in order to put to sea.

Captain Diamond and Captain Inlaker came on board and breakfasted; two prisoners taken with Manly in the Hancock, and lately escaped from Halifax. Our captain is an able seaman, and a brave, active, vigilant officer, but I believe he has no great erudition. His library consists of Dyche's English Dictionary, Charlevoix's Paraguay, The Rights of the Christian Church Asserted vs. The Romish and other Priests who claim an Independent Power over it, the second volume of Chubb's Posthumous Works, one volume of the

History of Charles Horton, Esq., and one volume of the Delicate Embarrassments, a novel. I shall, at some other time, take more notice of some of these books.

18. Wednesday. Last night, about sunset, we sailed out of Marblehead harbor, and have had a fine wind from that time to this, twenty-four hours. The constant rolling and rocking of the ship, last night, made us all sick. Half the sailors were so. My young gentlemen, Jesse and Johnny, were taken about twelve o'clock last night, and have been very sea-sick ever since. I was seized with it myself this forenoon. My servant, Joseph Stevens, and the captain's Will, have both been very bad.

19. Thursday. Arose at four o'clock. The wind and weather still fair. The ship rolls less than yesterday, and I have neither felt nor heard any thing of sea sickness last night, nor this morning. Monsieur Parison, one of General Du Coudray's captains, dined with us yesterday, and made me a present of a bottle of a nice French dram, a civility which I must repay. He seems a civil and sensible man.

The mal de mer seems to be merely the effect of agitation. The smoke, and smell of sea-coal, the smell of stagnant, putrid water, the smell of the ship where the sailors lie, or any other offensive smell, will increase the qualminess, but do not occasion it.

Captain Parison says, that the roads from Nantes to Paris are very good, no mountains, no hills, no rocks, all as smooth as the ship's deck, and a very fine country; but the roads from Bordeaux to Paris are bad and mountainous.

In the morning we discovered three sail of vessels ahead; we went near enough to discover them to be frigates, and then put away. We soon lost sight of two of them; but the third chased us the whole day; sometimes we gained upon her, and sometimes she upon us. *Endnote 059*

20. Friday. In the morning nothing to be seen, but soon after, another sail discovered ahead, which is supposed to be the same. *Endnote 060*

[When the night approached, the wind died away, and we were left rolling and pitching in a calm, with our guns all out, our courses all drawn up, and every way prepared for battle; the officers and men appeared in good spirits, and Captain Tucker said his orders were to carry me to France, and to take any prizes that might fall in his way; he thought it his duty, therefore, to avoid fighting, especially with an unequal force, if he could, but if he could not avoid an engagement, he would give them something that should make them remember him. I said, and did all in my power, to encourage the officers and men to fight them to the last extremity. My motives were more urgent than theirs; for it will easily be believed that it would have been more eligible for me to be killed on board the Boston, or sunk to the bottom in her, than to be taken prisoner. I sat in the cabin, at the windows in the stern, and saw the enemy gaining upon us very fast, she appearing to have a breeze of wind, while we had none. Our powder, cartridges, and balls, were placed by the guns, and every thing ready to begin the action. Although it was calm on the surface of the sea, where we lay, the heavens had been gradually overspread with black clouds, and the wind began to spring up. Our ship began to move. The night came on, and it was soon dark. We lost sight of our enemy, who did not appear to me very ardent to overtake us. But the wind increased to a hurricane.]

21. Saturday; 22. Sunday; and 23. Monday; exhibited such scenes as were new to me. We lost sight of our enemy, it is true, but we found ourselves in the Gulf stream, in the midst of an épouvantable orage; the wind north-east, then north, and then north-west.

It would be fruitless to attempt a description of what I saw, heard, and felt, during these three days and nights. To describe the ocean, the waves, the winds; the ship, her motions, rollings, wringings, and agonies; the sailors, their countenances, language, and behavior, is impossible. No man could keep upon his legs, and nothing could be kept in its place; an universal wreck of every thing in all parts of the ship, chests, casks, bottles, &c. No place or person was dry. On one of these nights, a thunderbolt struck three men upon deck, and wounded one of them a little, by a scorch upon his shoulder; it also struck our maintop-mast· Endnote 061

Wednesday, 25. Tuesday, 24. Tuesday we spied a sail and gave her chase. We overhauled her, and, upon firing a gun to leeward and hoisting American colors, she fired a friendly gun, and hoisted the French colors of the Province of Normandy; she lay to for us, and we were coming about to speak to her, when the wind sprung up afresh of a sudden, and carried away our maintop-mast. We have been employed ever since in getting in a new one, repairing the sails and rigging, much damaged in the late storm, and in cleaning the ship and putting her in order. From the 36th to the 39th degrees of latitude, are called the squally latitudes, and we have found them to answer their character. I should have been pleased to have kept a minute journal of all that passed, in the late chases and turbulent weather; but I was so wet, and every thing and place was so wet, every table and chair was so wrecked, that it was impossible to touch a pen, or paper.

It is a great satisfaction to me, however, to recollect that I was myself perfectly calm, during the whole. I found, by the opinion of the people aboard, and of the captain himself, that we were in danger, and of this I was certain also, from my own observation; but I thought myself in the way of my duty, and I did not repent of my voyage. I confess I often regretted that I had brought my son. I was not so clear that it was my duty to expose him as myself, but I had been led to it by the child's inclination, and by the advice of all my friends. Mr. Johnson's behavior gave me a satisfaction that I cannot express: fully sensible of our danger, he was constantly endeavoring to bear it with a manly patience, very attentive to me, and his thoughts constantly running in a serious strain.

26. Thursday. I have made many observations, in the late bad weather, some of which I do not think it prudent to put in writing. A few I will set down. 1st. I have seen the inexpressible inconvenience of having so small a space between decks, as there is in the Boston. As the main deck was almost constantly under water, the sea rolling in and out of the ports and scuppers, we were obliged to keep the hatchways down, whereby the air became so hot and so dry in the 'tween-decks, that, for my own part, I could not breathe or live there; yet the water would pour down, whenever a hatchway was opened, so that all was afloat. 2d. The Boston is over-metalled; her number of guns, and the weight of their metal, is too great for her tonnage; she has five twelve-pounders, and nineteen nines. We were obliged to sail, day and night during a chase, with the guns out, in order to be ready, and this exposed us to certain inconvenience, and great danger; they made the ship labor and roll, so as to oblige us to keep the chain pumps, as well as the hand pumps, almost constantly going; besides, they wring and twist the ship in such a manner as to endanger the starting of a butt, but still more to endanger the masts and rigging. 3d. The ship is furnished with no pistols, which she ought to be, with at least as many as there are officers, because there is nothing but the dread of a pistol will keep many of the men to their quarters in time of action. 4th. This ship is not furnished with good glasses, which appear to me of very great consequence. Our ships ought to be furnished with the best glasses that art affords; their expense would be saved a thousand ways. 5th. There is the same general inattention, I find, to economy, in the navy, that there is in the army. 6th. There is the same general relaxation of order and discipline. 7th. There is the same inattention to the cleanliness of the ship, and the persons and health of the sailors, as there is at land to the cleanliness of the camp, and the health, and cleanliness of the soldiers 8th. The practice of profane cursing and swearing, so silly as well as detestable, prevails in a most abominable degree. It is indulged and connived at by

officers, and practised, too, in much a manner, that there is no kind of check against it. And I take upon me to say, that order of every kind will be lax as long as this is so much the case.

This morning, Captain Tucker made me a present of Charlevoix's History of Paraguay. Yesterday, Doctor Noel put into my hand a pocket volume, entitled "Le Géographe manuel, contenant la Description de tous les Pays du Monde, leurs Qualités, leur Climat, le Caractère de leurs Habitans, leur Villes Capitales, avec leur Distances de Paris, et des Routes qui y menent tant par Terre que par Mer; &c. &c. Par M. l'Abbé Expilly, de la Société royale des Sciences et Belles-Lettres de Nancy."

These manuals come out annually, and are to be had in any of the great towns in France.

27. Friday. A calm. As soft and warm as summer. A species of black fish, which our officers call bonitos, appeared about the ship.

One source of the disorders in this ship, is the irregularity of meals. There ought to be a well digested system for eating, drinking, and sleeping. At six, all hands should be called up; at eight, all hands should breakfast; at one, all hands should dine; at eight again, all hands should sup. It ought to be penal for the cook to fail of having his victuals ready punctually. This would be for the health, comfort, and spirits of the men, and would greatly promote the business of the ship.

I am constantly giving hints to the captain concerning order, economy, and regularity, and he seems to be sensible of the necessity of them, and exerts himself to introduce them. He has cleared out the 'tween decks, ordered up the hammocks to be aired, and ordered up the sick, such as could bear it, upon deck for sweet air. This ship would have bred the plague or the jail fever, if there had not been great exertions, since the storm, to wash, sweep, air, and purify clothes, cots, cabins, hammocks, and all other things, places, and persons. The captain, yesterday, went down into the cockpit and ordered up everybody from that sink of devastation and putrefaction; ordered up the hammocks, &c. This was in pursuance of the advice I gave him in the morning: "If you intend to have any reputation for economy, discipline, or any thing that is good, look to your cockpit."

Yesterday, the captain brought in a curiosity which he had drawn up over the side in a bucket of water, which the sailors call a Portuguese man-of-war, and to-day I have seen many of them sailing by the ship. They have some appearances of life and sensibility. They spread a curious sail, and are wafted along very briskly. They have something like guts hanging down, which are said to be in a degree poisonous to human flesh. The hulk is like blue glass. I pierced it with the sharp point of my penknife, and found it empty. The air came out, and the thing shrunk up almost to nothing.

28. Saturday. Last night and this day we have enjoyed a fine easy breeze; the ship has had no motion but directly forward. I slept as quietly and as soundly as in my own bed at home. Doctor Noel gave me a phial of Balsamum Fioravanti, for an inflammation in my eyes, which seems to be very good for them. It is very much compounded; it is very subtle and penetrating. Pour a few drops into the palms of your hands, rub it over the palm and the fingers, and then hold the insides of your hands before your eyes, and the steam which evaporates enters the eyes, and works them clear. This balsam derives its name from its author.

The ship is now in very good order, cleaned out between decks, on the main deck, in the cabin and quarter decks. The masts, yards, sails, and rigging are well repaired. The captain has just now sent written orders to the steward of the ship, to make weekly returns to him of the state of provisions, and to be very frugal of provisions and candles, which appeared to be very necessary, as near one half of the ship's stores of candles are expended.

This is Saturday night; a fortnight yesterday since I took leave of my family. What scenes have I beheld since! What anxiety have my friends on shore suffered on my account, during the north-east storm which they must have had at land!

What is this gulf stream? What is the course of it? from what point, and to what point does it flow? how broad is it? how far distant is it from the continent of America? What is the longitude and latitude of it?

March 1. Sunday. Discovered that our mainmast was sprung in two places; one beneath the main deck, where if the mast had wholly failed in the late storm, it must have torn up the main deck, and the ship must have foundered. This is one among many instances, in which it has already appeared that our safety has not depended on ourselves.

A fine wind all day and night. Somewhat sea-sick. The ship was very quiet and still, no disturbance, little noise. I hope for the future we shall carry less sail, especially of nights, and at all times when we are not in chase.

2. Monday. A fair wind still, and a pleasant morning. The color of the water, which is green, not blue, as it has been for many days past, the appearance of large flocks of gulls and various other birds, convinced the knowing ones to-day, that we were not far from the Grand Bank of Newfoundland. The captain, however, thinks it thirty-five leagues to the northwest of us.

Our mast was yesterday repaired with two large fishes, as they call them; that is, large oaken planks, cut for the purpose, and put on. It seems now as firm as ever. The sailors are very superstitious. They say the ship has been so unfortunate that they really believe there is some woman on board. Women are the unluckiest creatures in the world at sea, &c.

This evening the wind is very fresh, and the ship sails at a great rate. We are out of the reach, I hope, of the gulf stream and British cruisers, two evils which I have great aversion to.

3. Tuesday. Our wind continued brisk and fresh all the last night and this morning.

Our course is about north-east. Showers in the night and this morning. The flocks of gulls still pursuing us. This morning, Mr. Parison breakfasted with us. Our captain in gay spirits, chattering in French, Spanish, Portuguese, German, Dutch, Greek, and boasting that he could speak some words in every language. He told us he had ordered two more fishes upon the mainmast, to cover the flaws above deck. The captain, lieutenants, master, mates, and midshipmen, are now making their calculations to discover their longitude, but I conjecture they will be very wild.

The life I lead is a dull scene to me; no business, no pleasure, no study. Our little world is all wet and damp. There is nothing I can eat or drink without nauseating. We have no spirits for conversation, nor any thing to converse about. We see nothing but sky, clouds, and sea, and then sea, clouds, and sky.

I have often heard of learning a language, as French or English, on the passage, but I believe very little of any thing was ever learned on a passage. There must be more health and better accommodations.

My young friend, Mr. Vernon, has never had the least qualm of the sea-sickness since we came aboard. I have advised him to begin the study of the French tongue methodically by reading the grammar through. He has begun it accordingly, and we shall see his patience and perseverance.

4. Wednesday. Fair weather, but an adverse wind from the north-east, which obliges us to go to the southward of the southeast, which is out of our course.

[Our general intention was to make for Nantes, one of the most commercial cities of France, which I was very anxious to see, not only on account of its wealth and antiquity, and the connection of its merchants with those of Bilbao, but also as the scene of the edict of

Nantes proclaimed by Henry IV. in 1590, so much to the honor and interest of humanity, and revoked by Louis XIV. in 1685, so much to its disgrace and injury.]

5. Thursday. This morning we have the pleasantest prospect we have yet seen; a fine easy breeze from the southward, which gives us an opportunity of keeping our true course, a soft, clear, warm air, a fair sun, no sea. We have a great number of sails spread, and we go at the rate of nine knots, yet the ship has no perceptible motion, and makes no noise.

My little son is very proud of his knowledge of all the sails, and last night the captain put him to learn the mariner's compass. Oh, that we might make prize to-day of an English vessel, lately from London, with all the newspapers and Magazines on board, that we might obtain the latest intelligence, and discover the plan of operations for the ensuing campaign!

Whenever I arrive at any port in Europe, whether in Spain or France, my first inquiry should be concerning the designs of the enemy. What force they mean to send to America? where they are to obtain men? what is the state of the British nation? what the state of parties? what the state of finances and of stocks? Then the state of Europe, particularly France and Spain. What the real designs of those courts? What the condition of their finances? what the state of their armies, but especially, of their fleets? what number of ships they have fitted for the sea? what their names, number of men and guns, weight of metal, &c., where they lie, &c. The probability or improbability of a war, and the causes and reasons for and against each supposition. The supplies of clothing, arms, &c., gone to America during the past winter. The state of American credit in France. What remittances have been made from America in tobacco, rice, indigo, or any other articles?

We are now supposed to be nearly in the latitude of Cape Finistere, so that we have only to sail an easterly course.

"Finistère, Finis Terræ; c'est le cap le plus occidental, non seulement de la Galice et de l'Espagne, mais même de l'Europe; ce qui fait que les Anciens qui ne connoissoient rien au dela, lui ont donné son nom, qui signifie l'Extrêmité de la Terre, ou le bout du monde. Il y a une Ville de même nom."

This day, we have enjoyed the clearest horizon, the softest weather, the best wind, and the smoothest sea, that we have seen since we came on board. All sails are spread, and we have gone ten knots, upon an average, the whole day.

6. Friday. The wind continued in the same point, about south, all night; and the ship has gone nine knots upon an average. This is great favor.

I am now reading the Amphitryon of Molière, which is his sixth volume. Rêvai-je? do I dream? have I dreamed? I have been in a dream? J' ai rêvé? I have been in a dream. It is in the Preterit.

We shall pass to the northward of the Western Islands, and are now supposed to be as near them as we shall be. They all belong to Portugal.

7. Saturday. The same prosperous wind, and the same beautiful weather continue. We proceed in our course, at the rate of about two hundred miles in twenty-four hours. We have passed all the dangers of the American coast. Those of the Bay of Biscay remain. God grant us a happy passage through them all.

Yesterday, the ship was all in an uproar with laughter. The boatswain's mate asked one of his superior officers, if they might have a frolic. The answer was, yes. Jerry accordingly, with the old sailors, proposed to build a galley, and all the raw hands, to the number of twenty or thirty, were taken in, and suffered themselves to be tied together by their legs. When, all of a sudden, Jerry and his knowing ones were found handing buckets of water over the sides and pouring them upon the poor dupes, until they were wet to the skin. The behavior of the gulled, their passions, and speeches, and actions, were diverting enough. So much for Jerry's fun. This frolic, I suppose, according to the sailors' reasoning, is to conjure up a prize.

This morning the captain ordered all hands upon deck, and took an account of the number of souls on board, which amounted to one hundred and seventy-two; then he ordered the articles of war to be read to them. After which he ordered all hands upon the forecastle, and then all hands upon the quarter deck, in order to try experiments, for determining whether any difference was made in the ship's sailing, by the weight of the men being forward or abaft.

Then all hands were ordered to their quarters, to exercise them at the guns. Mr. Barron gave the word of command; and they spent an hour, perhaps, in the exercise, at which they seemed tolerably expert. Then the captain ordered a dance upon the main deck, and all hands, negroes, boys, and men, were obliged to dance. After this, the old sailors set on foot another frolic, called the miller, or the mill. I will not spend time to describe this odd scene. But it ended in a very high frolic, in which almost all the men were powdered over with flour, and wet again to the skin. Whether these whimsical diversions are indulged in order to make the men wash themselves, and shift their clothes, and to wash away vermin, I don't know. But there is not in them the least ray of elegance, very little wit, and a humor of the coarsest kind. It is not superior to negro and Indian dances.

8. Sunday. The same wind and weather continues, and we go at seven and half and eight knots. We are supposed to be past the Western Islands.

Mr. Barron, our first lieutenant, appears to me to be an excellent officer. Very diligent and attentive to his duty. Very thoughtful and considerate about the safety of the ship, and about order, economy, and regularity among the officers and men. He has great experience at sea; has used the trade to London, Lisbon, Africa, West Indies, Southern States, &c.

This morning, the captain ordered all hands upon quarterdeck to prayers. The captain's clerk, Mr. William Cooper, had prepared a composition of his own, which was a very decent and comprehensive prayer, which he delivered in a grave and proper manner. The officers and men all attended in clean clothes, and behaved very soberly.

The weather has been cloudy all day. Towards night it became rainy and windy, and now the ship rolls a little in the old fashion. We are about two thousand miles from Boston.

The late storm showed the beauty of Boileau's description d'une Tempéte. [As it was the first morsel of French verse, except Molière, which I ever attempted to understand, it may be inserted here.]

Comme l'on voit les flots, soulevés par l'orage,
Fondre sur un vaisseau qui s'oppose a leur rage.
Le vent avec fureur dans les voiles frémit,
La mer blanchit d'écume, et l'air au loin gémit.
Le matelot troublé, que son art abandonne,
Croit voir dans chaque flot la mort qui l'environne.
Trad. de Longin.

9. Monday. Last night the wind shifted to the north-west, and blew fresh. It is now still fairer for us than before. The weather is fine, and we go on our voyage at a great rate. Some officers think we shall reach our port by Thursday night; others, by Saturday night. But these make no account of chases and cruises, and make no allowance for the variability of the winds.

14. Saturday. I have omitted inserting the occurrences of this week, on account of the hurry and confusion we have been in. Tuesday we spied a sail, *Endnote 062* and gave her chase, we soon came up with her: but as we had borne directly down upon her, she had not seen our broadside, and knew not our force. She was a letter of marque, with fourteen guns, eight

nines, and six sixes. She fired upon us, and one of her shot went through our mizzen yard. I happened to be upon the quarter deck, and in the direction from the ship to the yard, so that the ball went directly over my head. We, upon this, turned our broadside, which the instant she saw, she struck. Captain Tucker very prudently ordered his officers not to fire. *Endnote 063*

The prize is the ship Martha, Captain McIntosh, from London to New York, loaded with a cargo of great value. The captain told me that seventy thousand pounds sterling was insured upon her at Lloyd's, and that she was worth eighty thousand. The captain is very much of a gentleman. There are two gentlemen with him, passengers, the one Mr. R. Gault, the other, Mr. Wallace of New York. Two young Jews were on board. That, and the next day, was spent in despatching the prize, under the command of the third lieutenant, Mr. Welch, to Boston. *Endnote 064* After that, we fell in chase of another vessel, and overtaking her, found her to be a French snow, from Bordeaux to Miquelon. We then saw another vessel, chased, and came up with her, which proved to be a French brig, from Marseilles to Nantes. This last cost us very dear. Mr. Barron, our first lieutenant, attempting to fire a gun as a signal to the brig, the gun burst, and tore the right leg of this excellent officer in pieces, so that the doctor was obliged to amputate it, just below the knee. I was present at this affecting scene, and held Mr. Barron in my arms, while the doctor put on the tourniquet and cut off the limb. Mr. Barron bore it with great fortitude and magnanimity; thought he should die, and frequently entreated me to take care of his family. He had an helpless family, he said, and begged that I would take care of his children. I cannot but think the fall of this officer a great loss to the United States. His prudence, his moderation, his attention, his zeal, were qualities much wanted in our navy. He is by birth a Virginian.

[He said he had a mother, a wife and children who were dependent on him, and in indigent circumstances. I promised him that as soon as I could write to America, I would recommend his family to the care of the public, as well as of individuals. I recollect to have done something of this, but the scenes of distraction in which I was soon involved, I fear prevented me from doing so much as I ought to have done; and I feel it to this hour to be one of the omissions which I ought to regret.] *Endnote 065*

19. Thursday. I have scarcely been able to stand or sit, without holding fast with both my hands upon some lashed table, some lashed gun, the side or beams of the ship, or some other fixed object, such has been the perpetual motion of the ship, arising from violent gales, and a heavy sea. In the course of the last five days, we have seen a great number of vessels, two of which, at least, if not four, were supposed to be cruisers. But here we are, at liberty as yet. The wind has been directly against us, but this morning has veered, and we now steer, at least our head lies by the compass, south-east. Who knows but Providence has favored us by the last gale, as it seemed to do by the first? By the last gale we have already escaped cruisers, as we did by the first, and possibly this violent gale from the south-east may have driven all the cruisers from the coast of Spain, and the southerly part of the Bay of Biscay, and by this means have opened a clear passage for us to Bordeaux. This is possible, and so is the contrary; God knows.

20. Friday. Yester afternoon, the weather cleared up, and the wind came about very fair. We had a great run last night. This morning, spied a sail under our leeward bow, chased, and soon came up with her, a snow from Amsterdam to Demerara and Essequibo.

I made inquiry to-day of our prisoner, Captain McIntosh, concerning the Trinity House. He says it is the richest corporation in the kingdom; that Lord Sandwich is an elder brother of it; that any master of a vessel may be made a younger brother of it, if he will; that there are many thousands of younger brothers; that this house gives permission to every vessel to take out or to take in ballast, and that a few pence, 6d. perhaps, per ton, are paid them for such license; that they have the care of all light-houses, &c.

My principal motive for omitting to keep a regular and particular journal, has been the danger of falling into the hands of my enemies, and an apprehension that I should not have an opportunity of destroying these papers in such a case. We have now so fine a wind, that a very few days will determine whether we shall meet any capital disaster, or arrive safe at port.

21. Saturday. Five weeks yesterday since my embarkation. This morning, a heavy wind and high sea. We go east, southeast.

27. Friday. On Wednesday evening Mr. Barron died, and yesterday was committed to the deep, from the quarter-deck. He was put into a chest, and ten or twelve twelve pounds shot put in with him, and then nailed up. The fragment of the gun which destroyed him was lashed on the chest, and the whole launched overboard through one of the ports, in presence of all the ship's crew, after the burial service had been read by Mr. Cooper.

In the course of the last week we have had some of the worst winds that we have felt yet.

Monday last we made the land upon the coast of Spain.

Tuesday, we run into the Bay of Saint Antonio. Four or five boats, with fifteen or sixteen men in each, came to us, out of which we took a pilot.

Upon sight of the Spanish shore, which I viewed as minutely as possible through the glasses, I had a great curiosity to go on shore; there was a fine verdure near the sea, although the mountains were covered with snow. I saw one convent; but we did not come in sight of the town. The moment we were about turning the point of the Rock to go into the harbor, a sail appeared; we put out to see who she was; found her a Spanish brig, and after this, upon repeated efforts, found it impracticable to get into the harbor. In the night the wind caught us suddenly at north-west, and we were obliged to make all the sail we could and put to sea; we steered our course for Bordeaux. Yesterday was a calm, the little wind there was directly against us. This morning the wind is a little better. We are supposed to be within thirty leagues of Bordeaux River.

28. Saturday. Last night, and this morning, we were in the thoroughfare of all the ships from Bordeaux; we had always a great number in sight. By observations, to-day, our latitude is forty-six degrees three minutes, north, about seven minutes south of the middle of the Isle of Ré; we are, therefore, about twenty leagues from the Tower of Cordouan. We have no wind; and nothing can be more tedious and disagreeable to me than this idle life.

Last evening we had two little incidents which were disagreeable: one was, the French barber, attempting to go below contrary to orders, the sentinel cut off his great toe with his cutlass, which raised at first a little ill blood in the French people who are on board, but, on inquiry, finding the fellow deserved it, they acquiesced. The other unpleasant incident was, that one of our prisoners of war, a little more elevated than usual, grew out of temper, and was very passionate with Mr. Vernon, and afterwards with Captain Palmes; but it has all subsided.

[Our English prisoners, though in general they behaved very well, were sometimes out of humor, and had made some invidious remarks upon our officers and men and their awkward conduct of the ship; and, especially on the evening of St. Patrick's day, when many of them, who had declared they would get drunk, and, I suppose, had been as good as their word, were overheard to wish to meet a British man-of-war, and hinted that we could not stand an engagement of half an hour with a British vessel of half our force, &c.]

Mr. McIntosh is of North Britain, and appears to be very decided against America in this contest; and his passions are so engaged that they easily enkindle.

Mr. Gault is an Irish gentleman, and as decided against America, in her claim of independence at least, as the other; Mr. Wallace is more reserved, cautious, silent, and secret.

Jealousies arise among our men, that the prisoners are plotting with some of our profligate people. But I believe this jealousy is groundless.

All day yesterday, and all the forenoon of this day, we have been looking out for land; about four o'clock we found it. The Isles of Ré and Oléron, between which two is the entrance into the harbor of Rochelle, which is about half way between Bordeaux and Nantes. The land is extremely flat and low. We see the Tower. The water is shoal, twenty or thirty fathoms, the bottom, sand; the reverse of the Spanish coast on the other side of the Bay of Biscay.

This afternoon a clock calm, and Mr. Goss played upon his fiddle the whole afternoon, and the sailors danced, which seemed to have a very happy effect upon their spirits and good humor. Numbers of small birds, from the shore, came along today; some of them, fatigued, alighted on our rigging, yards, &c., and one of them we caught, a little lark he was called. These birds lose the shore, and get lost, and then they fly until they are so fatigued that the instant they alight upon a ship they drop to sleep.

29. Sunday. Becalmed all last night. This morning a vast number of sails in sight; St. Martin's and Oléron in sight; many towers and windmills; land very low and level. A pilot boat, with two sails and four men, came on board, and the pilot instantly undertook to pilot us to Bordeaux. He says this ship may go up quite to the city, if she drew twenty feet of water, at high water. We are now sailing very agreeably towards our port.

The pilot says war is declared, last Wednesday, and that the pavilions *Endnote 066* were hoisted yesterday at every port and lighthouse. Quare.

There is a civil Frenchman on board whose name I never asked until to-day. His name is Quillau, Fourrier des Logis de M. Le Comte D'Artois. He was not of M. Du Coudray's corps.

The French gentlemen on board can scarcely understand our new pilot. He speaks Gascon, the dialect of Bordeaux, they say, which is not good French.

This day six weeks, we sailed from Nantasket road. How many dangers, distresses, and hair-breadth escapes have we seen!

[There was one, however, which has been omitted. One evening when we were approaching the French coast, I was sitting in the cabin, when Captain McIntosh, our prisoner, came down to me, and addressed me with great solemnity. "Mr. Adams, this ship will be captured by my countrymen in less than half an hour. Two large British men-of-war are bearing directly down upon us, and are just by. You will hear from them, I warrant you, in six minutes. Let me take the liberty to say to you that I feel for you more than for any one else. I have always liked you since I came on board, and have always ascribed to you, chiefly, the good treatment I have received, as well as my people; and you may depend upon it, all the good service I can render you with my countrymen, shall be done with pleasure."

I saw by his countenance, gestures, air, language, and every thing, that he believed what he said; that he most heartily rejoiced in his own prospect of deliverance, and that he heartily pitied me. I smiled, however, at his offers of kind offices to me, knowing full well, that his prayers and tears would be as unavailing as my own, if he should be generous and I weak enough to employ them with British officers, ministers, judges, or king, in the then circumstances of things and temper of the Britons. I made him a bow, expressive of my sense of his politeness, but said nothing. Determined to see my danger, before I would be intimidated at it, I took my hat, and marched up to the quarter-deck. I had before heard an uncommon trampling upon deck, and perceived signs of some alarm and confusion, but when upon deck I saw the two ships indeed. They both appeared larger than our frigate, and were already within musket-shot of us. The air was clear, and the moon very bright. We could see every thing, even the men on board. We all expected every moment to be hailed, and, possibly, saluted with a broadside. But the two ships passed by us, without speaking a word, and I stood upon deck till they had got so far off as to remove all apprehensions of danger from them. Whether they were two American frigates, which had been about that time in France, we never knew. We had no inclination to inquire about their business or destination, and were very happy that they discovered so little curiosity about ours.] Endnote 067

A Story.—Garrick had a relation convicted of a capital offence. He waited on His Majesty, to beg a pardon. The King asked what was the crime? He has only taken a cup too much, says Garrick, may it please your Majesty. Is that all? said the King, let him be pardoned. Gault.

A Story.—A Frenchman, in London, advertised an infallible remedy against fleas. The ladies all flocked to purchase the powder; but, after they had bought it, one of them asked for directions to use it. "Madam," says the Frenchman, "you must catch the flea, and squeeze him between your fingers until he gape, then you must put a little of this powder in his mouth, and I will be responsible he will never bite you again." "But," says the lady, "when I have him between my fingers, why may I not rub him to death?" "O, Madam, dat will do just as well den." Tucker.

We have been becalmed all day in sight of Oléron. The village of St. Denis was in sight, and multitudes of windmills and sand hills all along the shore. Multitudes of vessels in sight, French, Spanish, Dutch vessels, and English smugglers. I feel a curiosity to visit this Island of Oléron, so famous in antiquity for her sea laws; at least, I take this to be the place.

30. Monday. This morning, at 5, the officer came down and told the captain that a lofty ship was close by us, and had fired two heavy guns; all hands called; she proved to be a heavy loaded snow. The weather cloudy, but no wind. Still, except a small swell. The Tower of Cordouan, or in other words Bordeaux light-house, in sight, over our larboard bow. The captain is now cleaning ship, and removing his warlike appearances.

This day has been hitherto fortunate and happy. Our pilot has brought us safely into the river, and we have run up with wind and tide as far as Pauillac, where we have anchored for the night, and have taken in another pilot. This forenoon a fisherman came alongside, with hakes, skates, and gurnards; we bought a few and had a high regale.

This river is very beautiful on both sides; the plantations are very pleasant, on the south side especially; we saw, all along, horses, oxen, cows, and great flocks of sheep grazing, the husbandmen ploughing, &c., and the women, half a dozen in a drove, with their hoes. The churches, convents, gentlemen's seats, and the villages appear very magnificent.

This river seldom swells with freshes; for the rural improvements, and even the fishermen's houses, are brought quite down to the water's edge. The water in the river is very foul to all appearance, looking all the way like a mud puddle. The tide sets in five knots. We outrun every thing in sailing up the river. The buildings, public and private, are of stone; and a great number of beautiful groves appear between the grand seats and best plantations; a great number of vessels lay in the river.

The pleasure resulting from the sight of land, cattle, houses, &c., after so long, so tedious and dangerous a voyage, is very great. It gives me a pleasing melancholy to see this country; an honor which a few months ago I never expected to arrive at. Europe, the great theatre of arts, sciences, commerce, war! am I at last permitted to visit thy territories? May the design of my voyage be answered!

31. Tuesday. Lying in the River of Bordeaux, near Pauillac—a twenty-four gun ship close by us, under French colors, bound to St. Domingue.

A dark misty morning. My first inquiry should be, who is Agent for the United States of America at Bordeaux, at Blaye, &c.; who are the principal merchants on this river concerned in the American trade? What vessels, French or American, have sailed, or are about sailing for America? What their cargoes, and for what ports? Whether on account of the United States, of any particular State, or of private merchants, French or American?

This morning the captain and a passenger came on board the Boston, from the Julie, a large ship bound to St. Domingue, to make us a visit. They invited us on board to dine. Captain Palmes, Master Jesse and Johnny, and myself, went. We found half a dozen genteel persons on board, and found a pretty ship, an elegant cabin, and every accommodation. The white stone plates were laid, and a clean napkin placed in each, and a cut of fine bread. The cloth, plates, servants, every thing was as clean as in any gentleman's house. The first dish was a fine French soup, which I confess I liked very much. Then a dish of boiled meat. Then the lights of a calf, dressed one way and the liver another. Then roasted mutton, then fricasseed mutton, a fine salad, and something very like asparagus, but not it. The bread was very fine, and it was baked on board. We had prunes, almonds, and the most delicate raisins I ever saw. Dutch cheese, then a dish of coffee, then a French cordial; and wine and water, excellent claret with our dinner. None of us understood French, none of them English; so that Doctor Noel stood interpreter. While at dinner we saw a pinnace go on board the Boston with several, half a dozen, genteel people on board. On the quarter deck I was struck with the hens, capons and cocks, in their coops, the largest I ever saw. After a genteel entertainment, Mr. Griffin, one of our petty officers, came with the pinnace and Captain Tucker's compliments, desiring to see me. We took leave and returned, where we found very genteel company, consisting of the captain of another ship bound to Martinique, and several King's officers bound out. One was the Commandant. Capt. Palmes was sent forward to Blaye in the pinnace, to the officer at the Castle, in order to produce our commission and procure an entry and pass to Bordeaux. Palmes came back full of the compliments of the broker *Endnote 068* to the captain and to me. I shall not repeat the compliments sent to me, but he earnestly requested that Capt. Tucker would salute the fort with thirteen guns, &c., which the captain did. *Endnote 069* All the gentlemen we have seen to-day agree that Doctor Franklin has been received by the King in great pomp, and that a treaty is concluded, and they all expect war every moment.

This is a most beautiful river. The villages and country seats appear upon each side all the way. We have got up this afternoon within three leagues of the town.

April 1. Wednesday. This morning Mr. J. C. Champagne, négociant et courtier de marine, at Blaye, came on board to make a visit and pay his compliments. He says, that of the first growths of wines in the Province of Guienne there are four sorts, Chateau-Margaux, Haut-brion, Lafitte, and Latour.

This morning I took leave of the ship and went up to town with my son and servant, Mr. Vernon, Mr. Jesse, and Doctor Noel, in the pinnace. *Endnote 070* When we came up to the town we had the luck to see Mr. McCreery and Major Frazer on the shore. Mr. McCreery came on board our boat, and conducted us up to his lodgings. Mr. Pringle was there. We dined there in the fashion of the country; we had fish and beans, and salad, and claret, champagne, and mountain wine. After dinner, Mr. Bondfield, who is agent here, invited me to take a walk, which we did, to his lodgings, where we drank tea; then we walked about the town, and to see the new comédie; after this we went to the opera, where the scenery, the dancing, the music, afforded to me a very cheerful, sprightly amusement, having never seen any thing of the kind before. [Our American theatres had not then existed even in contemplation.] After this we returned to Mr. McCreery's lodgings, where we supped.

2. Thursday. Walked round the town, to see the Chamber and Council of Commerce, the Parliament which was sitting, where we heard the council. Then we went round to the shipyards, &c. Made many visits. Dined at the Hotel d'Angleterre. Visited the custom-house, the post-office; visited the commandant of the chateau Trompette, a work of Vauban's. Visited the Premier President of the Parliament of Bordeaux.

[Here I met a reception that was not only polite and respectful, but really tender and seemingly affectionate. He asked permission to embrace me a la françoise. He said he had long felt for me an affection resembling that of a brother. He had pitied me, and trembled for me, and was cordially rejoiced to see me. He could not avoid sympathizing with every sincere friend of liberty in the world. He knew that I had gone through many dangers and sufferings in the cause of liberty, and he had felt for me in them all. "He had reason," he said, "to feel for the sufferers in the cause of Liberty, because he had suffered many years in that cause himself. He had been banished for coöperating with Mr. Malesherbes, and the other courts and parliaments of the kingdom, in the time of Louis XV. in their remonstrances against the arbitrary conduct and pernicious edicts of the court, &c. &c." Mr. Bondfield had to interpret all this effusion of compliments; and I thought it never would come to an end. But it did; and I concluded, upon the whole, there was a form of sincerity in it, decorated and almost suffocated with French compliments.]

Went to the coffee-house; went to the comédie, saw Les deux Avares. Supped at Messrs. Reuilles De Basmarein and Raimbaux.

3. Friday. Waited on the Intendant. Dined at Mr. Bondfield's, and supped at Mr. Le Texier's. Our company on Thursday evening at Mr. Basmarein's were, the Count of Virelade, the son of the Premier President; Le Moine, first Commissary of the Navy; Le Moine, the son, Commissary of the Navy; Cornie, Captain of a Frigate, Knight of St. Louis; Jean Baptiste Nairac, former Deputy of Commerce from La Rochelle; Paul Nairac, a merchant; Elisée Nairac, a merchant; Latour Féger, Esq., a merchant;—Menoire, Esq., a merchant;—Couturier, Esq., a merchant; Mr. Bondfield and Major Frazer. The toasts were announced by thirteen shots, in honor of the thirteen States. The King of France, twenty-one shots. The Congress, thirteen. George Washington, three. M. De Sartine, three; General Gates, three; Marshal Broglie, three; the Count of Broglie, his brother, three; the Marquis De Lafayette, three. The glory and prosperity of the thirteen United States, thirteen. The prosperity of France, three. Eternal concord between the two nations, now friends and allies, three. The State of Massachusetts Bay, and Mr. Adams, its representative. M. D'Estaing, vice admiral. The city of Bordeaux. Mrs. Adams, three. The French and American ladies, twenty-one. The departure of Mr. Adams, when he mounted his coach, was saluted by thirteen shots. The garden was beautifully illuminated with an inscription, God save the Congress, Liberty and Adams. Endnote 071

[The conversation at and after supper was very gay, animated, cheerful and good-humored, as it appeared to my eyes and ears, and feelings; but my understanding had no share in it. The language was altogether incomprehensible. The company was more attentive to me than I desired; for they often addressed observations and questions to me, which I could only understand by the interpretation of Mr. Bondfield, and the returns of civility on my part could only be communicated to me through the same channel, a kind of conviviality so tedious and irksome, that I had much rather have remained in silent observation and reflection.]

4. Saturday. About 10 o'clock we commenced our journey to Paris, and went about fifty miles.

[During my delay at Bordeaux, Mr. McCreery informed me, in confidence, that he had lately come from Paris, where he had been sorry to perceive a dryness between the American Ministers, Franklin, Deane, and Lee. Mr. McCreery was very cautious and prudent, but he gave me fully to understand that the animosity was very rancorous, and had divided all the Americans, and all the French people connected with Americans or American affairs, into parties very bitter against each other. This information gave me much disquietude, as it opened a prospect of perplexities to me that I supposed must be very disagreeable. Mr. Lee,

Mr. Izard, Dr. Bancroft, and others whom Mr. McCreery named, were entire strangers to me but by reputation. With Dr. Franklin I had served one year and more in Congress. Mr. Williams I had known in Boston. The French gentlemen were altogether unknown to me. I determined to be cautious and impartial, knowing, however, very well, the difficulty and the danger of acting an honest and upright part in all such situations.]

5. Sunday. Proceeded on our journey more than one hundred miles.

6. Monday. Arrived at Poitiers, the city so famous for the battle which was fought here. It is a beautiful situation, and the cultivation of the plains about it is exquisite. The houses are old and poor, and the streets very narrow. Afternoon, passed through Chatellerault, another city nearly as large as Poitiers, and as old, and the streets as narrow. When we stopped at the post to change our horses, about twenty young women came about the chaise with their elegant knives, scissors, tooth-picks, &c., to sell. The scene was new to me, and highly diverting. Their eagerness to sell a knite was as great as that of some persons I have seen in other countries to get offices. We arrived in the evening at Les Ormes, the magnificent seat of the Marquis D'Argenson. It is needless to make particular remarks upon this country. Every part of it is cultivated. The fields of grain, the vineyards, the castles, the cities, the parks, the gardens, every thing is beautiful, yet every place swarms with beggars.

7. Tuesday. Travelled from Les Ormes to Mer. We went through Tours and Amboise, and several other smaller villages. Tours is the most elegant place we have yet seen. It stands upon the River Loire, which empties itself at Nantes. We rode upon a causeway made in the River Loire, for a great number of miles. The meadows and river banks were extremely beautiful.

8. Wednesday. Rode through Orleans, &c., and arrived at Paris about 9 o'clock. For thirty miles or more the road is paved, and the scenes extremely beautiful.

At Paris we went to several hotels, which were full, particularly the Hotel d'Artois, and the Hotel Bayonne. Then we were advised to the Hotel de Valois, where we found entertainment; but we could not have it without taking all the chambers upon the floor, which were four in number, very elegant and richly furnished, at the small price of two crowns and a half a day, without any thing to eat or drink; we send for victuals to the cooks. I took the apartments only for two or three days.

At our arrival last night at a certain barrier, we were stopped and searched, and paid the duties for about twenty-five bottles of wine, which we had left of the generous present of Mr. Delap, at Bordeaux.

My little son has sustained this long journey of near five hundred miles, at the rate of a hundred miles a day, with the utmost firmness, as he did our fatiguing and dangerous voyage.

Immediately on our arrival we were called upon for our names, as we were at Mrs. Rives's, at Bordeaux.

We passed the bridge last night over the Seine, and passed through the Louvre. The streets were crowded with carriages with livery servants.

9. Thursday. This morning the bells and carriages and various cries in the street make noise enough; yet the city was very still last night, towards the morning. L'hôtel de Valois, Rue de Richelieu, is the name of the house and street where I now am. Went to Passy, in a coach, with Dr. Noel and my son. Dr. Franklin presented to me the compliments of M. Turgot, lately comptroller of the finances, and his invitation to dine with him. Went with Dr. Franklin and Mr. Lee, and dined in company with the Duchess d'Enville, the mother of the Duke de la Rochefoucauld, and twenty of the great people of France.

[I thought it odd that the first lady I should dine with in France should happen to be the widow of our great enemy, who commanded a kind of armada against us, within my memory; but I was not the less pleased with her conversation for that. She appeared to be venerable for her years, and several of her observations at table, full, as I thought, of bold, masculine, and original sense, were translated to me.]

It is in vain to attempt a description of the magnificence of the house, gardens, library, furniture, or the entertainment of the table. Mr. Turgot has the appearance of a grave, sensible, and amiable man.

[I was very particularly examined by the company through my colleagues and interpreters, Franklin and Lee, concerning American affairs. I should have been much better pleased to be permitted to remain less conspicuous; but I gave to all their inquiries the most concise and clear answer I could, and came off for the first time, I thought, well enough.]

Came home and supped with Dr. Franklin on cheese and beer.

10. Friday. Dined at Monsieur Brillon's, with many ladies and gentlemen. Madame Brillon is a beauty and a great mistress of music, as are her two little daughters. The dinner was luxury, as usual;—a cake was brought in with three flags flying; on one, Pride subdued; on another, Hæc Dies in quâ fit Congressus, exultemus et potemus in eâ. Supped in the evening at Mr. Chaumont's.

[Dr. Franklin had shown me the apartments and furniture left by Mr. Deane, which were every way more elegant than I desired, and comfortable and convenient as I could wish. Although Mr. Deane, in addition to these, had a house, furniture, and equipage, in Paris, I determined to put my country to no further expense on my account, but to take my lodgings under the same roof with Dr. Franklin, and to use no other equipage than his, if I could avoid it. This house was called the Basse cour de Monsieur Le Ray de Chaumont, which was, to be sure, not a title of great dignity for the mansion of ambassadors, though they were no more than American ambassadors. Nevertheless, it had been nothing less than the famous Hotel de Valentinois, with a motto on the door, "Se sta bene, non si muove," which I thought a good rule for my conduct.

The first moment Dr. Franklin and I happened to be alone, he began to complain to me of the coolness, as he very coolly called it, between the American ministers. He said there had been disputes between Mr. Deane and Mr. Lee; that Mr. Lee was a man of an anxious, uneasy temper, which made it disagreeable to do business with him; that he seemed to be one of those men, of whom he had known many in his day, who went on through life quarrelling with one person or another till they commonly ended with the loss of their reason. He said, Mr. Izard was there too, and joined in close friendship with Mr. Lee; that Mr. Izard was a man of violent and ungoverned passions; that each of these had a number of Americans about him, who were always exciting disputes, and propagating stories that made the service very disagreeable; that Mr. Izard, who, as I knew, had been appointed a minister to the Grand Duke of Tuscany, instead of going to Italy, remained with his lady and children at Paris; and instead of minding his own business, and having nothing else to do, he spent his time in consultations with Mr. Lee, and in interfering with the business of the commission to this court; that they had made strong objections to the treaty, and opposed several articles of it; that neither Mr. Lee nor Mr. Izard was liked by the French; that Mr. William Lee, his brother, who had been appointed to the court of Vienna, had been lingering in Germany; that he called upon the ministers at Paris for considerable sums of money, and by his connection with Lee and Izard and their party, increased the uneasiness, &c. &c. &c.

I heard all this with inward grief and external patience and composure. I only answered that I was personally much a stranger to Mr. Izard and both the Lees; that I was extremely sorry to hear of any misunderstanding among the Americans, and especially among the public ministers; that it would not become me to take any part in them; that I ought to think of nothing in such a case but truth and justice, and the means of harmonizing and composing all parties.

When Mr. Lee arrived at my lodgings one morning, it was proposed that a letter should be written to Mr. Dumas, at the Hague, to inform him of my arrival; and my colleagues proposed that I should write it. I thought it an awkward thing for me to write an account of myself, and asked Dr. Franklin to write it, after we should have considered and agreed upon what should be written; which I thought the more proper, as he was the only one of us who had been acquainted with Mr. Dumas. Accordingly, on the 10th of April, the letter was produced, in these words, which I insert at full length, because it was the only public letter, I believe, which he wrote while I was with him in that commission. *Endnote 072*]

In the evening, two gentlemen came in and advised me to go to Versailles to-morrow. One of them was the secretary to the late ambassador in London, the Count de Noailles.

[This gentleman informed me that the Count de Vergennes had expressed to him his surprise that I had not been to Court. They had been informed by the police of my arrival in Paris, and had accidentally heard of my dining in company at one place and another; but when any question was asked them concerning me, they could give no answer. He supposed I was waiting to get me a French coat, but he should be glad to see me in my American coat.]

11. Saturday. Went to Versailles, with Dr. Franklin and Mr. Lee. Waited on the Count de Vergennes, the secretary of foreign affairs; was politely received. He hoped I should stay long enough to learn French perfectly; assured me that every thing should be done to make France agreeable to me; hoped the treaty would be agreeable, and the alliance lasting. I told him I thought the treaty liberal and generous, and doubted not of its speedy ratification. I communicated to him the resolutions of Congress respecting the suspension of Burgoyne's embarkation, which he read through and pronounced fort bonnes. I was then conducted to the Count Maurepas, the prime minister; was introduced by Dr. Franklin as his new colleague, and politely received.

[This gentleman, often called the King's Mentor, was near fourscore years of age, with a fresh, rosy countenance, and apparently in better health and greater vigor than Dr. Franklin himself. He had been dismissed from office and exiled to his lands by Louis XV. in 1749, and in his retirement, if not before, had obtained the reputation of a patriot, for which reason he had been recalled to court by Louis XVI. and placed at the head of affairs.]

The Palace of Versailles was then shown to me, and I happened to be present when the king passed through, to council. His Majesty, seeing my colleagues, graciously smiled and passed on. The galleries and royal apartments, and the king's bedchamber, were shown to me. The magnificence of these scenes is immense; the statues, the paintings, the every thing, is sublime.

We then returned; went into the city, and dined with the Count, where was the Count De Noailles, his secretary, and twenty or thirty others, of the grandees of France.

After dinner we went in the coach to see the royal Hospital of Invalids, the chapel of which is immensely grand, in marble and paintings and statuary. After this, we went to the École Militaire, went into the chapel and into the hall of council, &c. Here we saw the statues of the great Condé, Turenne, Luxembourg, and Saxe. Returned and drank tea at Madame Brillon's, who lent me the Voyage Pittoresque de Paris, and entertained us again with her music and her agreeable conversation.

12. Sunday. The attention to me which has been shown, from my first landing in France, at Bordeaux, by the people in authority, of all ranks, and by the principal merchants, and since my arrival in Paris, by the ministers of state and others of the first consideration, has

been very remarkable, and bodes well to our country. It shows in what estimation the new alliance with America is held.

On Friday last I had the honor of a visit from a number of American gentlemen. Mr. James Jay, of New York, brother of the Chief Justice, Mr. Johnson, brother of the Governor of Maryland, Mr.—, Mr. Amiel, Mr. Livingston, from Jamaica, Mr. Austin, from Boston, Dr. Bancroft, Mr. R. Izard. I must return the visits of these gentlemen.

This day I had the honor to dine with the Prince de Tingry, Duc de Beaumont, of the illustrious house of Montmorency. The Duke and Duchess of . . . . .

[By this time I began to catch the sense, now and then, of the conversation in society, but very imperfectly. A conversation between the Prince de Tingry and my colleagues I understood so well as to perceive that he was haranguing upon toleration and liberty of conscience. With an air of great condescension and self-complacency for his great liberality, he vouchsafed to acknowledge, that although he should ardently desire the conversion of all Protestants to the Catholic religion, yet he would not persecute them, &c.]

Edisti satis, lusisti satis, atque bibisti;
Tempus est abire tibi;

written under the picture of Sir Robert Walpole. Some one made an amendment of bribisti instead of bibisti.

13. Monday. This morning, the Duchess d'Ayen and Mad. la Marquise de Lafayette came to visit me and inquire after the Marquis.

Went to Versailles; was introduced to the levee of M. de Sartine, the minister;—a vast number of gentlemen were attending in one room after another, and we found the minister at last entrenched as deep as we had formerly seen the Count Maurepas. The minister politely received us, and showed us into his cabinet, where were all the books and papers of his office. After he had finished the business of his levee, he came into the cabinet to us, and asked whether I spoke French, and whether I understood French? The answer was, un peu, and, si on parle lentement ou doucement. He then made an apology to each of us separately, in the name of his lady, for her absence, being gone into Paris to see a sick relation. After this, we were conducted down to dinner, which was as splendid as usual; all elegance and magnificence. A large company; four ladies only. During dinner time many gentlemen came in, and walked the room, and leaned over the chairs of the ladies and gentlemen, and conversed with them while at table. After dinner, the company all arose as usual, went into another room, where a great additional number of gentlemen came in. After some time, we came off, and went to make a visit to Madame Maurepas, the lady of the prime minister, but she was out, and we left a card.

[Count de Lauraguais, who had conducted us to her apartments, wrote our card for us in the porter's book. "Messrs. Franklin, Lee, et Adams, pour avoir l'honneur de voir Madame de Maurepas." This, I believe, was the only time that I saw De Lauraguais. He spoke our language so well, and seemed to have so much information, that I wished for more acquaintance with him; but finding that he was not a favorite at court, and especially with those ministers who had the principal management of our American affairs, and hearing from Dr. Franklin and Dr. Bancroft that Mr. Lee and Mr. Izard had given offence by too much familiarity with him, I declined any farther inquiry concerning him; and I never heard that those gentlemen had any intercourse with him after that time.] *Endnote 073*

We then went to the office of the secretary of M. de Vergennes, and delivered him a copy of my commission; then went and made a visit to Madame Vergennes, who had her levee, and returned to Passy.

[This morning, Dr. Franklin, Mr. Lee, and myself, met in my chamber, and signed and sent the following letters which I had written and had copied for signature, in answer to letters received.

Benjamin Franklin
Arthur Lee
John Adams

TO JOHN ROSS.

Passy, 13 April, 1778

Sir,—
The papers you mention are in the disposition of Mr. William Lee, who is gone to Germany. It is, therefore, not in our power to comply with what you desire. Neither are we able to make you any further advances. We wish you would send us, with all convenient expedition, copies of the invoices and bills of lading for those goods which were paid for with the money we formerly furnished you. We do not think it within our province to make an entire settlement with you. The money in Mr. Schweighauser's hands, which you say is under the direction and order of Mr. R. Morris, ought to be disposed of according to those orders. The trade being now free, from this country, it seems improper to us to give the passports you ask. We are, sir, your most obedient servants,
B. Franklin,
Arthur Lee,
John Adams.

Benjamin Franklin
Arthur Lee
John Adams

TO J. WILLIAMS.

Passy, 13 April, 1778

Sir,—
We are sorry to inform you that the state of our funds admits of no further expenditure, without danger of bringing us into great difficulties. It is, therefore, our desire, that you abstain from any further purchases, and close your accounts, for the present, with as little expense as possible. We also desire to be informed when the repair of the arms is likely to be completed. You judge right in not paying the twenty-eight louis, where there is the least appearance of trick, for that would encourage a thousand more. Inclosed you have a copy of Mercier's agreement. We have not yet been able to discover that Mr. Deane has left among the papers any agreement with Mr. Monthieu, by which we can settle the difference you mention. Perhaps Mr. Monthieu may have it. We wish to avoid disputes, confusion, and expense. We may now expect many American vessels will come into the French ports; we hope you may get them to take the remainder of the goods already bought on public account, upon freight, as is done at Bilbao.

We are, sir, your most obedient humble servants,
Benjamin Franklin,
Arthur Lee,
John Adams.

Benjamin Franklin
Arthur Lee
John Adams

TO JOHN BONDFIELD.
Passy, 13 April, 1778

Sir,—
We thank you for the civility of your favor of the 30th ultimo, and shall be obliged to you for the earliest communication of any interesting news that may reach your port. We have the honor to be,
Sir, your most obedient, humble servants,
Benjamin Franklin,
Arthur Lee,
John Adams.

Benjamin Franklin
John Adams

TO JOHN P. MERCKLÉ.

Passy, 13 April, 1778

Sir,—
We have done by our friends at Amsterdam, who have followed our orders, every thing that we thought incumbent on us to do, relative to your affairs, and we do not incline to have any further concern with them. We are, sir, your most obedient servants,
B. Franklin,
John Adams.

I have inserted these letters, apparently of little importance, not only because they were some of our first essays in business, but because these transactions began to let me into the secret of the disputes and animosities among the Americans in general in France, and, especially, between my colleagues. Mr. Lee had, as yet, said nothing to me concerning these controversies. I was informed, afterwards, by others, that he had said he would be silent on this subject, and leave me to learn by experience the state and course of the public business, and judge for myself whether it had been or was likely to be done right or wrong.

Mr. William Lee, who had been a merchant in London, and I believe an alderman, had been appointed by Congress their commercial agent and a general superintendent of all their commercial affairs. Congress was our sovereign lawgiver, prince, and judge, and, therefore, whatever was done by their express authority, we, as I believed, ought to respect and obey. Mr. William Lee had appointed Mr. Schweighauser commercial agent for the United States, under him, and Mr. Schweighauser was a very solid merchant, highly esteemed by every body, and highly approved by the Court. Mr. Jonathan Williams, a relation of Dr. Franklin, whom I had known in Boston, as well as his father, uncle, and cousin, who was a clerk in my office, I had the best disposition to favor, as far as the public service and my own sense of propriety would permit. Dr. Franklin and Mr. Deane had employed him in transactions which appeared to me to be commercial, and, in this, had differed with Mr. Arthur Lee, and interfered with the province of Mr. William Lee. I, therefore, united with Mr. Lee in this and many subsequent proceedings, requiring the settlement of Mr. Williams's accounts. Dr. Franklin, finding that two of us were agreed in opinion, subscribed the letter with us.

Mr. Ross was neither appointed by Congress, by the public ministers in France, nor by Mr. William Lee, but, I suppose, was connected in trade with Mr. Robert Morris, and might have orders from him to purchase arms, or clothing, or other articles for public use, as Mr. Morris was then chairman of the commercial committee of Congress, and, some time after, appointed financier. Mr. Ross expected us to advance him money to pay for his purchases, and yet did not think himself responsible to us, or obliged to send us his accounts, vouchers, or even his powers or orders. Whatever Mr. Deane or Dr. Franklin had done before my arrival, I thought this procedure more irregular, more inconsistent with the arrangement of Congress, and every way more unjustifiable, than even the case of Mr. Williams. Mr. Arthur Lee's opinion and mine were perfectly in unison upon this point, which, Dr. Franklin perceiving, united with us in subscribing the letter. But these were grievous disappointments to Mr. Williams and Mr. Ross, and all their friends, and, consequently, occasioned grumblings against Mr. Lee and Mr. Adams.

Mercklé was a Dutchman, and another adventurer, who applied to us for assistance, without any fair claim to it. Whether he had been employed by Mr. Morris, or Congress, to purchase any thing, I know not. But we were not informed of any authority he had to require money of us, and he was, accordingly, soon answered.

Mr. Monthieu had been very confidentially connected with Mr. Deane. The famous contract for old arms, so injurious to the United States, and so dishonorable to all who had any part in it, had been made with Monthieu, who was an humble friend of M. De Sartinc. The settlement of his affairs became very troublesome to us. I made a strict inquiry of Dr. Franklin, Mr. Lee, and others, for the books of accounts, the letter books, the letters received, the copies of letters sent; but nobody knew of any. Mr. Lee said there had been no regular accounts, nor any letter book. All agreed that Mr. Deane had done the business; that he consulted Dr. Franklin only when he pleased, and Mr. Lee rarely, if ever; and that all accounts, if any had been kept, and all letters, if any had been written, were carried off, or concealed by him.

Mr. Beaumarchais was another of Mr. Deane's confidential friends. This man's character, as a writer of dramas and memoirs, is public enough. His intrigues, as developed by himself in some of his writings, are curious enough. There is one fact which came to my knowledge, which may be thought of more importance. The confidential friend of Mr. Beaumarchais at court, was the queen's treasurer. I was afterwards very formally introduced to him as a personage of great power and respectability, and, with great solemnity, informed that he was the treasurer to the queen, and the intimate friend of Mr. Beaumarchais.

Mr. Holker was the father of the Mr. Holker who came to America with Mr. Deane at the same time with Mr. Gerard, and who passed in America for a person of great consequence, and as Consul-General of France. The Holkers, father and son, were very intimate friends of Mr. Deane, but neither had any appointment from King or minister. M. le Ray de Chaumont was their patron, and their occupation wholly as merchants, or rather as manufacturers, chiefly of cotton, either in partnership with Mr. Chaumont, or wholly under his direction.

Holker's conduct to me was always civil, respectful, social, frank, and agreeable; and, as he spoke English so well, and French so tolerably, I was always glad to see and converse with him. But he was always making apologies for Mr. Deane; and it was easy to see that he regretted very much the loss of his friend, by whom he had expected to make his fortune; and, although he had no other objection to me, he found that I was not the man for his purpose.]

14. Mardi. Yesterday morning, sent for the master of the academy in this place, who came and showed me his conditions; he agreed to take my son, who accordingly packed up his things, and went to school, much pleased with the prospect, because he understood that rewards were given to the best scholars, which, he said, was an encouragement. Dancing, fencing, music, and drawing, are taught at this school, as well as French and Latin.

15. Mercredi. Went yesterday to return the visits made me by American gentlemen.

[This, I found, was an indispensable punctilio with my countrymen in France. Great offence had been taken by some of them, because Dr. Franklin had not very exactly performed this important etiquette, especially by those of them who had come over to Paris from England.]

Dined this day with Madame Helvétius. One gentleman, one lady, Dr. F., his grandson, and myself, made the company; an elegant dinner. Madame is a widow; her husband was a man of learning, and wrote several books. She has erected a monument to her husband, a model of which she has. It is herself weeping over his tomb, with this inscription.

"Toi dont l'Ame sublime et tendre,
A fait ma Gloire, et mon Bonheur,
Je t' ai perdu: près de ta Cendre,
Je viens jouir de ma Douleur."

Here I saw a little book of Fenelon's, which I never saw before, Directions pour la Conscience d'un Roi, composées pour l'instruction de Louis de France, Duc de Bourgogne.

At Madam Helvétius's we had grapes preserved entire. I asked her how? She said "Sans air." Apples, pears, &c. are preserved here in great perfection.

16. Jeudi. Doctor Franklin is reported to speak French very well, but I find, upon attending to him, that he does not speak it grammatically, and, indeed, upon inquiring, he confesses that he is wholly inattentive to the grammar. His pronunciation, too, upon which the French gentlemen and ladies compliment him, and which he seems to think is pretty well, I am sure is very far from being exact.

Indeed, Dr. Franklin's knowledge of French, at least his faculty of speaking it, may be said to have begun with his embassy to this court. He told me that when he was in France before, Sir John Pringle was with him, and did all his conversation for him, as interpreter, and that he understood and spoke French with great difficulty, until he came here last, although he read it.

Dined at M. La Ferté's. The magnificence of the house, garden, and furniture, is astonishing. Saw here a History of the Revolution in Russia, in the year 1762. This family are fond of paintings. They have a variety of exquisite pieces, particularly, a Storm and a Calm.

17. Vendredi. Dined at home with company. Mr. Platt and his lady; Mr. Amiel and his lady; Mr. Austin, Mr. Alexander, &c. After dinner went to the Long-champ, where all the carriages in Paris were paraded, which, it seems, is a custom on Good Friday.

[On this week all the theatres of Paris are shut up, and the performers forbidden to play. By this decree, whether of the Church or State, or both, all the fashionable people of Paris and its environs are deprived of their daily amusements, and lose their ordinary topics of conversation; the consequence of which is that they are si ennuyés that they cannot live. To avoid this direful calamity, they have invented this new spectacle, and have made it fashionable for every person who owns a carriage of any kind that rolls upon wheels, and all those who can hire one, to go out of town and march their horses slowly along one side of the great road to the end of it; then they come about, and return on the other side, and in this manner the carriages are rolling all day. It was asserted on that day that there was not a pair of wheels left in the city.

For some years, certain persons of equivocal reputation were observed to appear in unusual splendor in these processions, and the scandal increased from year to year, till one of the most notorious females in Paris appeared in the most costly and splendid equipage in the whole row;—six of the finest horses in the kingdom; the most costly coach that could be built; more numerous servants and richer liveries than any of the nobility or princes; her own dress in proportion. It was generally agreed to be the finest show that had ever been exhibited. This was so audacious an insult to all modest women, and indeed to the national morality and religion, that the Queen, to her honor, sent an order that if she should ever appear again, anywhere, in that equipage, she should find herself in Bicêtre the next morning. *Endnote 074* Yet even this was a modest fancy in comparison with the palace of Bellevue. This was another symptom of the pure, virtuous manners, which I was simple enough to think would not accord with our American republican institutions. To be sure, it had never yet entered into my thoughts that any rational being would ever think of demolishing the monarchy and erecting a republic in France.]

18. Samedi. This morning, the father of General Conway came to visit me and inquire after his son, as well as American affairs. He seems a venerable personage. Dined at M. Bouffet's, who speaks a little English. M. Bouffet's brother, M. le Veillard, M. Lefévre, l'Abbé de Prades, Mr. Borry, &c. were there. Called and drank tea at Madame Brillon's; then made a visit to M. Boulainvilliers and his lady, who is a kind of lord of the manor of Passy, and is just now come out to his country seat.

[A descendant of the celebrated Boulainvilliers *Endnote 075* who wrote many books, particularly on the States-General, and a Life of Mahomet. His daughter bore the title of Mademoiselle de Passy, and was certainly one of the most beautiful young ladies I ever saw in France. She afterwards married the Marquis de Tonnerre, a gentleman of great quality and fortune, since so famous for his tragical catastrophe in the beginning of the Revolution. This nobleman's character was as amiable as that of his father-in-law was otherwise. Boulainvilliers held a superb hereditary office under the Crown, which gave him very high rank and great emolument. But, although he was very rich, he was represented as oppressive, tyrannical, and cruel, as well as avaricious, to a great degree.

Mr. Franklin, who at the age of seventy odd had neither lost his love of beauty nor his taste for it, called Mademoiselle de Passy his favorite, and his flame, and his love, which flattered the family, and did not displease the young lady. After the Marquis had demanded Mademoiselle for a wife, and obtained her, Madame de Chaumont, who was a wit, the first time she saw Franklin, cried out, "Hélas! tous les conducteurs de Monsieur Franklin n'ont pas empêché le tonnerre de tomber sur Mademoiselle de Passy."

A year or two after this, in conversation with M. de Marbois, Boulainvilliers happened to be mentioned, and Marbois said he had a most detestable character. "But," said I, "he has married a daughter to a man of great character?" "Ay," says Marbois, "I suppose you will say, what signifies character in France, when the worst cannot hinder a man from marrying his daughter to a Marquis de Tonnerre?"]

19. Dimanche. [From my first arrival in France, I had employed every moment of my time, when business and company would permit, in the study of the French language. I had

not engaged any master, and determined to engage none. I thought he would break in upon my hours, in the necessary division of my time between business and study and visits, and might often embarrass me. I had other reasons, too, but none were sufficient to justify me. It was an egregious error, and I have seen cause enough to regret it. Instead of a master, I determined to obtain the best advice of those who were masters of the language, and purchase the books in which it was taught upon principle. Two 78bbes, De Chalut and Arnoux, the former a brother of the farmer-general of that name, and himself a knight of Malta, as well as of the order of St. Louis, and both of them learned men, came early to visit me. They had a house in the city, and another in the country at Passy, in our neighborhood, where they resided in summer. Whether they were spies of the court, or not, I know not, but I should have no objection to such spies, for they were always my friends, always instructive and agreeable in conversation. They were upon so good terms, however, with the courtiers, that if they had seen any thing in my conduct, or heard any thing in my conversation, that was dangerous or very exceptionable, I doubt not they would have thought it their duty to give information of it. They were totally destitute of the English language; but by one means and another they found a way of making me understand them, and sometimes by calling an interpreter, and sometimes by gibbering something like French, I made them understand me.]

Dined at home with Mr. Grand, our banker, his lady, daughter, and sons, Mr. Austin, M. Chaumont, and a great deal of other company.

Mr. David Hartley, a member of the British House of Commons, came to visit Dr. Franklin, a Mr. Hammond with him. Went with M. Chaumont in his carriage to the Concert Spirituel. A vast crowd of company of both sexes; a great number of instruments; a gentleman sung, and then a young lady.

[Mr. Ferdinand Grand was a Protestant, from Switzerland, who had a house in Paris, and a small country house near us in Passy. Himself, his lady, niece, and sons, composed as decent, modest, and regular a family, as I ever knew in France. It was, however, by M. Chaumont's influence with the Count de Vergennes and M. de Sartine, that he obtained the reputation and emolument of being the banker to the American ministers. Sir George Grand, his brother, might contribute something towards this favor, because he had kept an inn at Stockholm, when the Count de Vergennes was ambassador of France in Sweden, and accomplished the revolution in that kingdom to an absolute monarchy. This was a mere measure of economy in the French Court, because, before, it had cost them in bribes to the States more money than they could well afford. The meeting of De Vergennes with the heads of the conspiracy, had been held at Mr. Grand's inn, and he was rewarded with a cross of St. Louis, which gave him the title of Sir, as I suppose, having never heard that he had any English knighthood, although he had lived in England, where he married his daughter to the Major or Colonel who was afterwards General Provost. This lady, as I presume, is the same who afterwards married Colonel Burr, of New York, and was the mother of Mrs. Allston, of South Carolina. Sir George was connected in partnership with the house of Horneca, Fizeaux & Co., in Amsterdam, a mercantile and banking company, and who had, or were supposed to have, the favor and confidence of the French ministers of state.

This day, Mr. David Hartley, a member of the British House of Commons, with Mr. George Hammond, the father of Mr. George Hammond who was afterwards Hartley's secretary at the negotiation of the definitive treaty of peace, and after that Minister Plenipotentiary to the United States, came to visit us, under pretence of visiting Dr. Franklin. This mysterious visit, I did not at all admire. I soon saw that Hartley was a person of as consummate vanity as Hammond was a plain, honest man; but I considered both as spies, and endeavored to be as reserved and as much on my guard as my nature would admit.

Although I endeavored to behave to both with entire civility, I suppose as I did not flatter Mr. Hartley with professions of confidence which I did not feel, and of so much admiration of his great genius and talents as he felt himself, he conceived a disgust at me, and told Sir John Temple and others, after his return to London, "Your Mr. Adams, that you represent as a man of such good sense—he may have that, but he is the most ungracious man I ever saw." I had not expressed so much astonishment at his invention of fire plates and Archimedes' mirrors as he thought they deserved. I knew him to be intimate with Lord North, by his own confession, as well as by the information of Dr. Franklin and others, and although he was numbered among the opposition in Parliament, and professed to be an advocate for the American cause, yet I knew very well that opposition to the ministry was the only solid ground on which all the friendship for America that was professed in England rested. I did not, therefore, think it safe to commit myself to a man who came to us without any pretence of authority from his sovereign or his ministers. I say without any pretence of authority, because he made none. But I then supposed, and still believe, that he came with the privity, if not at the express request, of Lord North, to sound the American ministers, and see if there were no hopes of seducing us from our connection with France, and making a separate accommodation with us, *Endnote 076* the very idea of which, as the treaty was already made, appeared to me to be an insult to our honor and good faith.]

20. Lundi. My son has been with me since Saturday. The Concert Spirituel is in the Royal Garden, where was an infinite number of gentlemen and ladies walking. Dined with the Duchess d'Enville, at her house, with her daughter and granddaughter, dukes, abbots, &c. &c. &c. [Among whom was M. Condorcet, a philosopher, with a face as pale, or rather as white, as a sheet of paper, I suppose from hard study. The Duchess d'Enville and her son, the great friends of Monsieur Turgot, were said to have great influence with the Royal Academy of Sciences, to make members at pleasure, and the secrétaire perpétuel, M. d'Alembert, was said to have been of their creation, as was M. Condorcet afterwards. His gratitude, a few years after this, will be recorded in history. This family was beloved in France, and had a reputation for patriotism, that is, of such a kind of patriotism as was allowed to exist and be esteemed in that kingdom, where no man, as Montesquieu says, must esteem himself or his country too much.]

Visited Mr. Lloyd and his lady, where we saw Mr. Digges.

21. Mardi. Dined, this day, at M. Chaumont's, with the largest collection of great company that I have yet seen. The Marquis d'Argenson, the Count de Noailles, the Marshal de Maillebois, the brother of the Count de Vergennes, and a great many others; M. Foucault and Madame, M. Chaumont's son-in-law and daughter, who has a fortune of four or five thousand pounds sterling in Saint Domingo, M. Chaumont's own son, Miss Chaumont, and M. de Vilevault, the first officer under M. de Sartine.

It is with much grief and concern that I have learned, from my first landing in France, the disputes between the Americans in this kingdom; the animosities between Mr. Deane and Mr. Lee; between Dr. Franklin and Mr. Lee; between Mr. Izard and Dr. Franklin; between Dr. Bancroft and Mr. Lee; between Mr. Carmichael and all. It is a rope of sand. I am at present wholly untainted with these prejudices, and will endeavor to keep myself so. Parties and divisions among the Americans here must have disagreeable, if not pernicious, effects. Mr. Deane seems to have made himself agreeable here to persons of importance and influence, and is gone home in such splendor, that I fear there will be altercations in America about him. Dr. Franklin, Mr. Deane, and Dr. Bancroft, are friends. The Lees and Mr. Izard are friends. Sir James Jay insinuated that Mr. Deane had been at least as attentive to his own interest, in dabbling in the English funds and in trade, and in fitting out privateers, as to the public; and said he would give Mr. Deane fifty thousand pounds for his fortune, and said that Dr. Bancroft too had made a fortune. Mr. McCreery insinuated to me that the Lees were selfish, and that this was a family misfortune. What shall I say? What shall I think? It is said that Mr. Lee has not the confidence of the ministry, nor of the persons of influence here; that he is suspected of too much affection for England, and of too much intimacy with Lord Shelburne; that he has given offence by an unhappy disposition, and by indiscreet speeches before servants and others, concerning the French nation and government—despising and cursing them. I am sorry for these things, but it is no part of my business to quarrel with anybody without cause; it is no part of my duty to differ with one party or another, or to give offence to anybody; but I must do my duty to the public, let it give offence to whom it will.

The public business has never been methodically conducted. There never was, before I came, a minute book, a letter book, or an account book; and it is not possible to obtain a clear idea of our affairs.

Mr. Deane lived expensively, and seems not to have had much order in his business, public or private; but he was active, diligent, subtle, and successful, having accomplished the great purpose of his mission to advantage. Mr. Gérard is his friend; and I find that Dr. Bancroft has the confidence of persons about the ministry, particularly of the late secretary to the ambassador to Great Britain.

[In this place, it is necessary to introduce a few portraits of characters, that the subsequent narrative may be better understood.

Dr. Franklin, one of my colleagues, is so generally known that I shall not attempt a sketch of his character at present. That he was a great genius, a great wit, a great humorist, a great satirist, and a great politician, is certain. That he was a great philosopher, a great moralist, and a great statesman, is more questionable.

Mr. Arthur Lee, my other colleague, was a native of Virginia. His father had been long a counsellor under the Crown, and some time commander-in-chief of the Colony and ancient dominion of Virginia. He left several sons, Thomas, Richard Henry, William, Francis Lightfoot, and Arthur, with all of whom, except Thomas, I have been intimately acquainted. Their father had given them all excellent classical educations, and they were all virtuous men. Arthur had studied and practised physic, but not finding it agreeable to his genius, he took chambers in the temple in England, and was there admitted to practise as a barrister, and being protected by several gentlemen of rank among the opposition, was coming fast into importance. Animated with great zeal in the cause of his native country, he took a decided part in her favor, and became a writer of some celebrity by his Junius Americanus and other publications. Becoming known in America as a zealous advocate of our cause, the two Houses of the Legislature of Massachusetts Bay appointed him provisionally their agent to the court of Great Britain, in case of the death, absence, or disability of Dr. Franklin, in which capacity he corresponded with some of the members of that assembly, particularly with Mr. Samuel Adams, and with the assembly itself, transmitting from time to time information of utility and importance. After a Congress was called in 1774-5 and 6, he continued to transmit to us some of the best and most authentic intelligence which we received from England. In 1776, when the election of ministers to the court of France was brought forward, and after I had declined the nomination, and Mr. Jefferson had refused the election and appointment sent him by Congress, Mr. Arthur Lee was elected in his place. He came immediately over to Paris, and joined his colleagues in commission. His manners were polite, his reading extensive, his attention to business was punctual, and his integrity without reproach.

Mr. Ralph Izard was a native of South Carolina. His grandfather or great-grandfather was one of Mr. Locke's land-graves, and had transmitted to his posterity an ample landed estate. Mr. Izard had his education, I believe, at Westminster or Eton School, certainly at the

University of Cambridge, in England. When he came to the possession of his fortune, he married Miss De Lancey, a daughter of Chief Justice De Lancey, who was so long at the head of the party in New York, in opposition to the Livingstons, a lady of great beauty and fine accomplishments, as well as perfect purity of conduct and character through life. This accomplished pair had a curiosity to travel. They went to Europe, and passed through Italy, Germany, Holland, and I know not how many other countries. When the American war commenced, they were in England, and Mr. Izard, embracing the cause of his country with all the warmth of his character, passed with his family over to France, on his way to America. Congress had been advised, by persons who knew no better, to send a minister to the Emperor, and to the Grand Duke of Tuscany, because they were brothers to the Queen of France. In this measure there was less attention to the political interests and views of princes, than to the ties of blood and family connections. Congress, however, adopted the measure, and Mr. Izard was nominated by Mr. Arthur Middleton, in the name of South Carolina, and highly recommended for his integrity, good sense, and information. The members from New York, and other States, supported the nomination and concurred in all the particulars of his character. Mr. Izard was accordingly appointed, and when he arrived in Paris, he found his commission to the Grand Duke. With a high sense of honor and great benevolence of heart as well as integrity of principle, Mr. Izard had a warmth of temper and sometimes a violence of passions, that were very inconvenient to him and his friends, and not a little dangerous to his enemies.

Dr. Edward Bancroft was a native of Massachusetts Bay, in the town of Suffield. He had been a school-boy under Mr. Silas Deane, when he was a schoolmaster, whether in any town of the Massachusetts or Connecticut, I do not recollect. After some education, he had been bound an apprentice to a trade; but being discontented, ran away and went to sea, carrying with him some property of his master. After some years of adventures, the history of which I have not heard, he had acquired property enough to return to his native town, make his apologies to his master, pay him honorably all his demands, and then he went to sea again.

The next information I have of him is, that he was in England, and had published his Essay towards a Natural History of Guiana, which I have in a handsome volume, presented me with his own hand; and it is a work, considering the advantages of the author, of great merit. He wrote also in England the History of Sir Charles Wentworth, a novel, which no doubt was recommended to many readers, and procured a considerably better sale, by the plentiful abuse and vilification of Christianity, which he had taken care to insert into it. He had also been in the intimacy and confidence of Dr. Franklin, who had recommended him to the editors and proprietors of the Monthly Review, in which his standing share was to review all publications relative to America. This information I had from Dr. Franklin himself. I understood this very well, as I thought—to wit, that Bancroft was the ostensible reviewer, but that Franklin was always consulted before the publication. Bancroft was a meddler in the stocks as well as reviews, and frequently went into the alley, and into the deepest and darkest retirements and recesses of the brokers and jobbers, Jews as well as Christians, and found amusement as well, perhaps, as profit, by listening to all the news and anecdotes, true or false, that were there whispered or more boldly pronounced. This information I had from his own mouth. When Mr. Deane arrived in France, whether he wrote to Bancroft, or Bancroft to him, I know not, but they somehow or other sympathized with each other so well, that Bancroft went over to Paris, and became a confidential associate with his old friends, Franklin and Deane. Bancroft had a clear head and a good pen. He wrote some things relative to the connection between France and America, with the assistance of Franklin and Deane, as I presume, which were translated into French, by M. Turgot, or the Duke de la Rochefoucauld, I forget which, and printed in a publication called,

Affaires de l'Angleterre et de l'Amérique, and which were very well done. After the peace he obtained a patent in France for the exclusive importation of the bark of the yellow oak for the dyers, and then he went to England and procured a similar patent there, by both of which together he is said to have realized an income of eight hundred a year.

Another character ought to be introduced here; although he had gone to America before my arrival at Passy, and I never had an opportunity of seeing him. A letter or two may have passed between him and me, when he was Chargé des Affaires at Madrid; but no misunderstanding ever occurred between us, and I never received, to my knowledge, any injury or offence from him. He was a native of Maryland, of Scotch extraction; wherever he may have had his education, he was in England or Scotland when the Revolution commenced, and in this year, 1778, came over to Paris, and, as I was informed, commenced an opposition to all the commissioners, Franklin, Deane, and Lee, and indeed to all who had any authority in American affairs, and was very clamorous. Mr. Deane and Dr. Franklin and Dr. Bancroft, however, a little before or after his departure, found means to appease him in some degree; and, after his arrival in America, he was chosen one of the delegates, from Maryland, in Congress, where in a year or two he got an appointment as Secretary of Legation and Chargé des Affaires to Mr. Jay, when, in 1779, he was appointed minister to the court of Spain. Here he remained many years, and finally died. *Endnote 077* He had talents and education, but was considered, by the soundest men who knew him, as too much of an adventurer. What was his moral character, and what his conduct in Spain, I shall leave to Mr. Jay; but he was represented to me as having contributed much to the animosities and exasperations among the Americans at Paris and Passy. There were great divisions in Spain among the Americans, and Mr. Jay had as much trouble with his own family, Mr. Carmichael, Mr. Brockholst Livingston, and Mr. Littlepage, as I had at Paris. I shall leave this scene to be opened by the memorials of the actors in it, if any such should ever see the light.

I have now given a faint sketch of the French and American personages who had been concerned in our affairs, at and before the time of my arrival.

I may have said before, that public business had never been methodically conducted. There never was, before I came, a minute-book, a letter-book, or an account-book; or, if there had been, Mr. Deane and Dr. Franklin had concealed them from Mr. Lee, and they were now nowhere to be found. It was utterly impossible to acquire any clear idea of our affairs. I was now determined to procure some blank books, and to apply myself with diligence to business, in which Mr. Lee cordially joined me. To this end it was necessary to alter the course of my life. Invitations were sent to Dr. Franklin and me, every day in the week, to dine in some great or small company. I determined, on my part, to decline as many as I could of these, and attend to my studies of French, and the examination and execution of that public business which suffered for want of our attention every day. An invitation came from the Duke of Brancas to dine with him at his seat. I determined to send an apology; and on—]

22. Wednesday. Dined at home, and spent the day on business with Mr. Lee.

24. Friday. Dined at M. Buffaut's, with much company.

25. Saturday. Dined at M. Chaumont's with company.

26. Sunday. Dined at home.

27. Monday. Dined with M. Boulainvilliers, at his house in Passy, with generals and bishops, and ladies, &c. In the evening went to the French comedy, and happened to be placed in the first box, very near to the celebrated Voltaire, who attended the performance of his own Alzire. Between the acts, the audience called out Voltaire, and clapped and applauded him the whole time. The old poet arose, and bowed respectfully to the audience. He has yet much fire in his eyes, and vigor in his countenance, although very old. *Endnote 078*

After the tragedy, they acted Le Tuteur, a comedy, or a farce of one act. This theatre does not exceed that at Bordeaux.

[I had not been a month as yet in France, nor three weeks in Passy, but I had seized every moment that I could save from business, company, or sleep, to acquire the language. I took with me the book to the theatre, and compared it, line for line, and word for word, with the pronunciation of the actors and actresses, and in this way I found I could understand them very well. Thinking this to be the best course I could take, to become familiar with the language, and its correct pronunciation, I determined to frequent the theatres as often as possible. Accordingly, I went as often as I could, and found a great advantage in it, as well as an agreeable entertainment. But as Dr. Franklin had almost daily occasion for the carriage, and I was determined the public should not be put to the expense of another for me, I could not go so often as I wished. Another project occurred to me, to familiarize the language, which was to keep a journal in French. This was accordingly attempted, and continued for a few days, but I found it took up too much time, and what was more decisive, I was afraid to keep any journal at all, for I had reason to believe that the house was full of spies, some of whom were among my own servants; and if my Journal should fall into the hands of the police full of free remarks, as it must be to be of any value, it might do more injury to my country, than mischief to me.]

Avril vingt-huit. Mardi· *Endnote 079*

Breakfasted at home with M. Chaumont, M. Dubourg, M. Chaumont, the son, Mr. Franklin, and his grandson.

[M. Dubourg was a physician, a bachelor, a man of letters, and of good character, but of little consequence in the French world. Franklin had been introduced to him in his first visit to Paris, and Dubourg had translated his works into French. He must have been in years, for he told me he had been acquainted with Lord Bolingbroke, when he was in France. He told us a story of Cardinal Mazarin. An officer petitioned him to make him a captain of his life-guard. The cardinal answered that he had no occasion for any other guard than his tutelary angel. "Ah, sir," said the officer, "your enemies will put him to flight with a few drops of holy water." The cardinal only replied that he was not afraid of that holy water. It was a wonder that something worse had not happened to the officer, for his insinuation was nothing less than that the devil was the cardinal's only tutelary angel. Dubourg was a jolly companion, and very fond of anecdotes. He told a great number, whenever I was in his company, which were said to be excellent, but his speech was so rapid, that I could not fully understand them. One, I remember;—he told us an instance of the great presence of mind, self-command, and good nature of Marshal Turenne. He had chosen for his valet the stoutest grenadier in his army, who frequently played at hot cockles with another of his domestics, who was named Stephen. The marshal one day stooped down to look out of a window, with one of his hands upon his back. The grenadier coming suddenly into the chamber, raised his gigantic arm, and with his brawny palm, gave his master a furious blow upon his hand upon his back. The marshal drew himself in, and looked at the grenadier, who, the moment he saw it was his master, fell upon his knees in despair, begging for mercy, "for he thought it was Stephen." "Well," said the marshal, rubbing his hand, which was tingling with the smart, "if it had been Stephen, you ought not to have struck so hard," and said no more upon the subject. This story I understood, because I had read something like it in Rousseau.

Dined at home this day with Mr. Lee, who spent the day with me, upon the public business. In the evening we went to the Italian comedy, where I saw a harlequin for the first time.

29. Wednesday. Dined with the Marshal de Maillebois, with a great deal of company. Here also we were shown the marshal's amie, seated at the table with all his great company. Mr. Lee and I had a good deal of conversation with her. Mr. Lee spoke French with tolerable ease. I could say but little, but I understood her as well as any one I had heard in French. It appeared to me that the marshal had chosen her rather for her wit and sense, than personal charms. I was soon informed that this Marshal Maillebois and Marshal Broglie, had the reputation of the two most intriguing men in France, and I was the more disposed to believe it of the former, because I knew of his intrigue with Mr. Deane to be placed over the head of General Washington in the command in chief of our American army. It is proper in this place to insert an anecdote. Mr. Lee and I waited on the Comte de Vergennes one day, to ask a favor for our country. I forget what it was. The Comte said it was in the department of war. It was on one of the feasts of the cordon bleu, when the Comte had been kneeling on marble pavements in church for some hours, and his knees ached to such a degree, that he said he would take a walk with us to the minister of war, and ask the favor for us. As we walked across the court of the Castle of Versailles, we met the Marshal Maillebois. Mutual bows were exchanged, as we passed, and Mr. Lee said to the Comte de Vergennes, "That is a great general, sir." "Ah!" said the Comte de Vergennes, "I wish he had the command with you!" This escape was, in my mind, a confirmation strong of the design at court, of getting the whole command of America into their own hands, and a luminous commentary on Mr. Deane's letters, which I had seen and heard read in Congress, [Endnote 080] and on his mad contract with M. du Coudray and his hundred officers. My feelings, on this occasion, were kept to myself, but my reflection was, "I will be buried in the ocean, or in any other manner sacrificed, before I will voluntarily put on the chains of France, when I am struggling to throw off those of Great Britain." If my life should be spared to continue these memorials, more of this Marshal de Maillebois will be recorded.

After dinner we went to the Academy of Sciences, and heard M. d'Alembert, as perpetual secretary, pronounce eulogies on several of their members, lately deceased. Voltaire and Franklin were both present, and there presently arose a general cry that M. Voltaire and M. Franklin should be introduced to each other. This was done, and they bowed and spoke to each other. This was no satisfaction; there must be something more. Neither of our philosophers seemed to divine what was wished or expected; they, however, took each other by the hand. But this was not enough; the clamor continued, until the explanation came out. "Il faut s'embrasser, à la Françoise." The two aged actors upon this great theatre of philosophy and frivolity then embraced each other, by hugging one another in their arms, and kissing each other's cheeks, and then the tumult subsided. And the cry immediately spread through the whole kingdom, and, I suppose, over all Europe. "Qu'il etait charmant de voir embrasser Solon et Sophocle!" [Endnote 081]

After the Secretary's eulogies were finished, one of which, if I remember well, was upon M. Jurieu, and another upon M. Duhamel, a number of memoirs were publicly read by their authors, upon various subjects. One was upon the Art of Making good Wine. As soon as he had read the title, the audience compelled him to stop, which he did, I presume, with pleasure, for it was to hear loud applause for the choice of his subject, before they knew how he had treated it. It seemed to be a chemical analysis of all the ingredients which enter into the composition of wine, and a process by which it might be made in its greatest perfection. It was much applauded, as were the eulogies, and most of the other memoirs. I remarked, in all these compositions, a kind of affectation that surprised me. The authors seemed to search for opportunities to introduce hints and sarcastical allusions to the frivolities, vanity, affectation, follies, and prejudices of their own nation. This, I should have expected, would have been hissed, at least, if no more. But, on the contrary, nothing was more loudly applauded, and nothing seemed to produce more gayety and good humor. Is this an honorable trait, or is it not? More liberties of this kind were taken in France, I believe, than in any other country. In America, at that time, they would not have been endured. In England, some freedoms may be used with John Bull, but you must be very careful to respect his essential characteristics of integrity, good sense, sound judgment, great courage, and humanity. If you touch these, you touch an Englishman to the quick. I have somewhere read, that it is a proof of the last degree of depravity, when a nation will laugh at their own vices, and then go away and repeat them; but I have some doubt of this.]

30. Jeudi. Dined with the Marshal de Mouchy, with the Duke and Duchess d'Ayen, their daughter, the Marquise de Lafayette, the Viscountess de Maillebois, her sister, another sister unmarried, the Prussian ambassador, an Italian ambassador, and a great deal of other great company. The nobleman with whom we dined, is Philippe de Noailles, Maréchal Duc de Mouchy, Grand d'Espagne de la première Classe, Chevalier des Ordres du Roi et de la Toison d'Or, Grand-Croix de l' Ordre de Malte, nommé Lieutenant-Général de Guienne en 1768, et Commandant-en-chef dans le Gouvernement de la dite Province en 1775.

His being commander-in-chief in the Province of Guienne, was the cause of a great compliment to me. He asked me how I liked Bordeaux. I told him I found it a rich, elegant town, flourishing in arts and commerce. He asked whether I was content with my reception there. I said they had done me too much honor. He replied, he wished he had been there to have joined them in doing me honor. He lives in all the splendor and magnificence of a viceroy, which is little inferior to that of a king.

May 1. Vendredi. Aujourd'hui j'ai été diner chez Monsieur le Duc d'Ayen, le pére de Madame la Marquise de la Fayette. La maison, le jardin, les promenades, les tableaux, les garnitures, sont très magnifiques. Les tableaux de la Famille de Noailles sont anciens et nombreux.

Madame la Duchesse d'Ayen a cinq ou six enfans, contre la coutume de ce pays çi.

We were shown into the library, and all the rooms, and first suite of chambers, in the house. The library is very large, and the rooms very elegant, and the furniture very rich.

[When I began to attempt a little conversation in French, I was very inquisitive concerning this great family of Noailles, and I was told by some of the most intelligent men in France, ecclesiastics, as well as others, that there were no less than six marshals of France of this family; that they held so many offices, under the King, that they received eighteen millions of livres annually from the crown; that the family had been remarkable, for ages, for their harmony with one another, and for doing nothing, of any consequence, without a previous council and concert; that, when the American Revolution commenced, a family council had been called to deliberate upon that great event, and determine what part they should take in it, or what conduct they should hold towards it. After they had sufficiently considered, they all agreed, in opinion, that it was a crisis of the highest importance in the affairs of Europe, and of the world; that it must affect France in so essential a manner, that the King could not, and ought not, to avoid taking a capital interest and part in it; that it would, therefore, be the best policy of the family to give their countenance to it as early as possible; and that it was expedient to send one of their sons over to America to serve in her army, under General Washington. The Prince de Poix, as the heir apparent of the Duke of Mouchy, they thought of too much importance to their views and expectations, to be risked in so hazardous a voyage, and so extraordinary a service, and, therefore, it was concluded to offer the enterprise to the Viscount de Noailles, and if he should decline it, to the Marquis de la Fayette. The Viscount, after due consideration, thought it most prudent to remain at home for the present. The Marquis, who was represented as a youth of the finest accomplishments, and most amiable disposition, panting for glory, and ardent to distinguish himself in military service, most joyfully consented to embark in the enterprise. All France pronounced it to be the first page in the history of a great man.

This family was in short become more powerful than the house of Bourbon. At least, they had more influence in the army, and when they afterwards united with the Duke of Orleans, the Rochefoucaulds, the Lamoignons, and a few others, the world knows too much of the consequences. If they advised the calling of the Assembly of Notables, the wisdom of their family councils had certainly departed.] *Endnote 082*

2. Saturday. Dined at Mr. Izard's, with Mr. Lloyd and his lady, M. François, and much other company; after dinner went to the Comédic Françoise, and saw the Brutus of Voltaire, and after it the Cocher Supposé.

[As I was coming out of the box, after the representation, a gentleman seized me by the hand. I looked at him. "Governor Wentworth, sir," said the gentleman. At first, I was somewhat embarrassed, and knew not how to behave towards him. As my classmate, and friend at college, and ever since, I could have pressed him to my bosom with most cordial affection. But we now belonged to two different nations at war with each other, and, consequently, we were enemies. Both the governor and the minister were probably watched by the spies of the police, and our interview would be known the next morning at Versailles. The governor, however, relieved me from my reverie, by asking me questions concerning his father and friends in America, which I answered according to my knowledge. He then inquired after the health of Dr. Franklin, and said he must come out to Passy, and pay his compliments to him. He should not dare to see the Marquis of Rockingham, after his return, without making a visit to Dr. Franklin. Accordingly, in a day or two, he came and made us a morning visit. Dr. Franklin and I received him together; but there was no conversation but upon trifles. The governor's motives for this trip to Paris, and visit to Passy, I never knew. If they bore any resemblance to those of Mr. Hartley, his deportment and language were very different. Not an indelicate expression to us, or our country, or our ally, escaped him. His whole behavior was that of an accomplished gentleman. Mr. Hartley, on the contrary, was, at least to me, very offensive. In his conversation, he seemed to consider our treaty with France as a nullity, that we might disregard, at our pleasure, and treat with England separately, or come again under her government, at our pleasure. This appeared to me offensive to our honor, and an insult to our good faith, and, although I always endeavored to treat him with civility, I doubt not I sometimes received it somewhat "ungraciously."]

3. Sunday. Mr. Izard and lady, Mr. Lloyd and lady, Dr. Bancroft, and much other company, dined with Dr. Franklin and me, at Passy. Mrs. Izard, at my particular desire, brought her little son and two little daughters. We had all our young gentlemen, from the academy, which made a pretty show of young Americans.

[The business of the commission had been delayed and neglected in a manner that gave me much uneasiness. Franklin and Lee had been reluctant to engage in it, as I suppose, knowing that they should differ in every thing, and both of them as yet uncertain which side I should take. I had now procured my blank books, and I took the letters which we had received into my own hands; and, after making all the inquiries into the subject which I could, I wrote in my blank book the following answers. The book is fortunately in my possession, and now before me, with the letters in my hand-writing. I shall insert these letters, because they will serve, among many others, to show the number of persons who had their eyes fixed upon our little treasury, and under what a variety of pretences and pretended authorities they set up their claims upon us for money. Dr. Franklin, after he found that Mr. Lee and I agreed in opinion, and were determined to sign and send them, did not choose to let them go without his name.

Benjamin Franklin
Arthur Lee
John Adams

To M. Bersolle.

Passy, 3 May, 1778

Sir,—

Your bill upon our banker was not paid, because it was drawn without our leave, and before you had sent us the accounts to show we were your debtors; and he could not regularly pay a bill on our account, which he had not our orders to pay.

We are sir, your most obedient servants,
Benjamin Franklin,
Arthur Lee,
John Adams.

John Adams

To Mr. Moylan.

Passy, 3 May, 1778

Sir,—

We received your several letters of the 23d and 30th of March, and the 15th and 17th of April. We are obliged to you for the care you have taken respecting the sick men. We shall apply, as you advise, for the discharge of Miggins, and hope to obtain it.

We have examined M. Bersolle's accounts, and find them approved by Captain Jones and his officers, and as you have paid his draft, we shall repay you. But we wish that hereafter you would not engage us in any considerable expense, without having received our orders, after acquainting us with the occasion.

We are, sir, your most obedient, humble servants.
Benjamin Franklin
Arthur Lee
John Adams

To Mr. Ross, at Nantes.

Passy, 3 May, 1778

Sir,—

In a former letter, you wrote us that you would send us the invoices, &c., of the goods shipped on the public account, if we thought it necessary. We wrote for those which would answer for the money we had advanced to you. The reason given in yours of the 18th, for refusing them, does not appear to us at all sufficient. If it be unavoidable to separate the part from the whole, we desire the whole may be sent, agreeable to your first proposal, which will also be of use to us, by showing the nature and extent of the supplies which have been sent. We therefore expect you will comply, without any further delay, with what we desire, and which is indispensable.

You will be so good as to send us a copy of the order of the commissioners, under which you say the ship Queen of France was purchased, as we find none such here.

When you first applied to us for our assistance, and represented that you had made contracts for goods, in pursuance of orders from the committee of Congress, which contracts, if not fulfilled, would destroy your credit, and, in consequence, hurt that of the committee, it was agreed to furnish you with the sum which you desired, and which you said would be sufficient to prevent those great inconveniences, on your promise to replace it. It is now near a year since, and you have not performed that promise. The disappointment has been very inconvenient to us. Probably it was occasioned by your not receiving the remittances you expected. However, we think you should have forborne entering into any fresh contracts and embarrassments; especially, as it was not required or expected of you, by the committee, as appears by their letter to you of December 30, of which you have sent us an extract; nor have they ever desired it of us; nor did you inform us, when you made your engagements, that you had any expectation of our assistance to discharge them. A little consideration will convince you, that it is impossible for us, to regulate our own purchases and engagements, and discharge our debts with punctuality, if other people, without our participation, allow themselves to run in debt unnecessarily, as much as they please, and call upon us for payment. By our complying with such unforeseen demands, we may soon, to prevent your discredit, become bankrupts ourselves, which, we think, would be to the full as disreputable to Congress. We, therefore, now acquaint you, that we cannot give the permission you desire, of drawing on our banker for the immense sums you mention, and we desire you would not have the least dependence on aids that we have it not in our power to grant. We are, sir,

Your most obedient, humble servants,
B. Franklin,
Arthur Lee,
John Adams.]

4. Monday. Dined at M. Chaumont's, with his family, and some other company.

5. Tuesday. Am to dine at home; a great rarity and a great blessing!

At dinner alone, my servant brought me a letter.

"À Messieurs, Messieurs Franklin, Lee, et Adams, Députés des États Unis de l'Amérique, a Passy.

"De Vergennes."

I opened, and found it in these words:

Comte de Vergennes
Versailles, le 4 Mai, 1778

J'ai pris les ordres du Roi, Messieurs, au sujet de la présentation de M. Adams, votre nouveau collégue, et Sa Majesté le verra, Vendredi prochain, 8 de ce mois. J'espère que vous voudrez bien me faire l'honneur de diner ce-jour-là chez moi; je serai ravi d'avoir cette occasion de passer quelques heures avec vous, et de vous renouveler l'assurance de la très parfaite considération avec laquelle, j'ai l'honneur d'être,

Messieurs, votre très humble et très obéissant serviteur,
De Vergennes.
Messrs. Franklin, Lee, et Adams.

[I passed the whole of this day at home. Mr. Lee came in the afternoon to my apartment, and we sat down together to a serious examination of the public papers, that is, of all that we could find, and a close attention to the public business. In the evening, M. Chaumont came in, and informed me of the destination of a frigate of thirty-two guns, from Marseilles to Boston, and that I might write by her if I pleased.]

6. Wednesday. [Franklin told us one of his characteristic stories.] "A Spanish writer of certain visions of Hell, relates that a certain devil, who was civil and well-bred, showed him all the apartments in the place, among others, that of deceased kings. The Spaniard was much pleased at so illustrious a sight, and after viewing them for some time, said he should be glad to see the rest of them. "The rest?" said the demon. "Here are all the kings that ever reigned upon earth, from the creation of it to this day. What the devil would the man have?" This was not so charitable as Dr. Watts, who, in his View of Heaven, says, "Here and there I see a king." This seems to imply that kings are as good as other men, since it is but here and there that we see a king upon earth.

[The truth is, that neither then, nor at any former time, since I had attained any maturity in age, reading, and reflection, had I imbibed any general prejudice against, or in favor of kings. It appeared to me then, as it has done ever since, that there is a state of society in which a republican government is the best, and, in America, the only one which ought to be adopted or thought of, because the morals of the people, and circumstances of the country, not only can bear it, but require it. But, in several of the great nations of Europe, kings appeared to me to be as necessary as any government at all. Nor had I ever seen any reason to believe that kings were, in general, worse than other men.]

After dinner, went to the review, where the King reviewed his guards, French and Swiss, about eight thousand of them. The show was splendid, as all other shows are in this country; the carriages of the royal family were magnificent, beyond my talent at description. Returned, and drank coffee with Mr. Lee. Walked home, and drank tea with M. Chaumont's family, and spent the rest of the evening in reading Cardinal Richelieu.

8. Friday. This morning, Dr. Franklin, Mr. Lee, and Mr. Adams, went to Versailles, in order that Mr. Adams might be presented to the King. Waited on the Count de Vergennes, at his office, and, at the hour of eleven, the Count conducted us into the King's bed chamber, where he was dressing, one officer putting on his sword, another his coat, &c.

The Count went up to the King, and his Majesty turned about, towards me, and smiled; Est-ce Monsieur Adams? said the King, and then asked a question very quick, or rather made an observation to me, which I did not fully understand. The purport of it was, that I had not been long arrived. The Count Vergennes then conducted me to the door of another room, and desired me to stand there, which I did, until the King passed. The Count told the King that I did not yet take upon me to speak French. The King asked, whether I did not speak at all as yet, and passed by me into the other room.

This monarch is in the twenty-fourth year of his age, having been born the 23d of August, 1754. He has the appearances of a strong constitution, capable of enduring to a great age. His reign has already been distinguished by an event that will reflect a glory upon it in future ages, I mean the treaty with America.

[The ceremonies at this Court were very simple. A certain day of every week was called "Ambassador's day," when all the public ministers, whether ambassadors, ministers plenipotentiary, envoys, or residents, who all passed under the general title first named, went to Versailles, were presented to the King, Queen, to Monsieur, the King's eldest brother, to the Count d'Artois, the King's youngest brother, to Madame Elizabeth, his sister, and to his two aunts, who had apartments in the castle, though they lived at Bellevue. Neither the King, nor any of the royal family, commonly spoke to any of the corps diplomatique, except the first order, the ambassadors. To them they said but a few words. The Count de Mercy, ambassador from the Emperor, said he had made his court weekly in that character to Monsieur for thirty years, and had always been asked the same question, "Have you come from Paris this morning?" Seven or eight years afterwards, in England, I found the custom very different. The King and Queen must speak to everybody. This has made him the greatest talker in Christendom; but it is a slavery to which no human being should be subjected. It is but justice to say, that it was agreeable and instructive to hear him; for, let the insolent Peter Pindar say what he will, his Majesty said as many things which deserved to be remembered, as any sage I ever heard.]

We afterwards made a visit to Count Maurepas, to M. de Sartine, to the Chancellor, to M. Bertin, &c.

The Chancellor has the countenance of a man worn with severe studies. When I was introduced to him, he turned to Dr. Franklin, and said,—M. Adams est une personne célèbre en Amérique et en Europe.

We went afterwards to dinner with the Count de Vergennes. There was a full table; no ladies but the Countess. The Count's brother, the ambassador who lately signed the treaty with Switzerland, Mr. Garnier, the late Secretary to the Embassy in England, and many others,—dukes, and bishops, and counts, &c.

Mr. Garnier and Mr.—asked me, with some appearance of concern, whether there was any foundation for the reports which the Ministry had spread in England, of a dispute between Congress and General Washington. A letter, they say, has been printed, from an officer in Philadelphia, to that purport. Mr. Garnier is the first French gentleman who has begun a serious political conversation with me of any length. He is a sensible man.

9. Saturday. This morning Mr. Joy, Mr. Johonnot, and Mr. Green, came to visit me. Joy, who lived at Weymouth; Green, son of Mr. Rufus Green.

Dined with Madame Bertin.

[This lady is married to a nephew of M. Bertin, the minister, and he holds some lucrative office under the crown. She has a fine person, and an excellent understanding. She is universally reputed to be a woman of sincere piety and spotless virtue, and has inflexibly rejected the many advances which have been made to her by gentlemen who had every advantage of power, person, and fortune, to recommend them, preferring the consciousness of innocence, and the esteem of the very few, to all other considerations. Her attentions to Mr. Izard's family, and to me, were very particular, and the reason she assigned for it to other persons, was, that she understood we were domestic people. I have heard nothing about her for more than twenty years, and whether death, by the guillotine, or otherwise, has removed her, I know not.]

10. Sunday. Messieurs Brattle, Waldo, Joy, Johonnot, Green, and Austin, dined with us, at Passy. After dinner, we walked in the Bois de Boulogne, as far as the new seat of the Count d'Artois, where we saw M. Turgot, M. and Madame La Ferté, and much other company. Sunday, in this country, is devoted to amusements and diversions. There are more games, plays, and sports, of every kind, on this day, than on any other in the week.

11. Monday. Dined at Mr. Sorin's, at Passy.

12. Tuesday. Dined at Mr. Dupré's, at the Montagne. The gardens and the prospect are very fine. It lies adjoining to the seat of the President of the Parliament of Paris. We met his lady, who desired the gentlemen to show us the place, but not the whole, for she wished to enjoy our company there, at her own invitation, and she chose to reserve a part of the curiosities of the place, as an inducement to us to accept it. From this hill we have a fine view of the country, and of the King's Castle at Vincennes. My little son, and the other young Americans, at the Pension, dined with us.

13. Wednesday. Dined at M. Chaumont's, with a great deal of company. After dinner, took a walk to Chaillot, to see Mr. Lee, who had a large company of Americans to dine with him; among the rest, Mr. Fendall, of Maryland, and Dr. Smith, brother of Mr. Smith of New York, the historian.

15. Friday. Dined at Mr. Grand's, with all the Americans in Paris.

17. Sunday. Dined at home. Dr. Dubourg, and Mr. Parker, and another gentleman, dined with me.

18. Monday. Dined at M. La Ferté's country seat, at the foot of Mount Calvaire. The house, gardens, and walks, are very spacious; it lies upon the Seine, nearly opposite to that castle, whimsically called Madrid, built by Francis I. The company yesterday, were all single persons, except M. and Madame La Ferté and myself.

19. Tuesday. Dined with M. Chalut, one of the farmers-general. We were shown into the most superb gallery that I have yet seen. The paintings, statues, and curiosities, were innumerable. The old Marshal Richelieu dined there, and a vast number of other great company. After dinner, M. Chalut invited Dr. Franklin and me to go to the opera, and take a seat in his logis. We did. The music and dancing were very fine.

20. Wednesday. The French opera is an entertainment which is very pleasing for a few times. There is every thing which can please the eye or the ear. But the words are unintelligible, and, if they were not, they are said to be very insignificant. I always wish, in such an amusement, to learn something. The imagination, the passions, and the understanding, have too little employment in the opera.

Dined at Dr. Dubourg's, with a small company, very handsomely; but not amidst those signs of wealth and grandeur which I see everywhere else. I saw, however, more of sentiment, and therefore more of true taste, than I have seen in other places, where there was ten times the magnificence. Among his pictures were these:—

Les Adieux d'Hector et d'Andromaque; in which the passions were strongly marked.

La Continence de Scipion.

Le Médecin Erasistrate découvre l'amour d'Antiochus.

Développement de la Décoration intérieure et des Peintures des Plafonds de la Galerie de Versailles.

We went and drank tea with Madame Foucault, and took a view of M. Foucault's house. A very grand hotel it is, and the furniture is vastly rich; the beds, the curtains, the every thing, is as rich as silk and gold can make it. I am wearied to death with gazing, wherever I go, at a profusion of unmeaning wealth and magnificence. The Adieu of Hector and Andromache gave me more pleasure than the sight of all the gold of Ophir would. Gold, marble, silk, velvet, silver, ivory, and alabaster, make up the show everywhere.

"A certain tailor once stole a horse, and was found out, and committed to prison, where he met another person who had long followed the trade of horse-stealing. The tailor told the other his story. The other inquired, 'Why he had not taken such a road, and assumed such a disguise, and why he had not disguised the horse? 'I did not think of it.' 'Who are you, and what has been your employment?' 'A tailor.' 'You never stole a horse before, I suppose, in your life.' 'Never.' '——you! what business had you with horse-stealing? Why did not you content yourself with your cabbage?' " Franklin.

21. Thursday. Dined at home.

[The disputes between the parties had, by this time, become so well known to me, and their violence had arisen to such rancor, that whatever was done or said by Dr. Franklin, or by me when I agreed with him in opinion, was censured and often misrepresented by one party; and whatever was done or said by Mr. Lee or Mr. Izard, and by me, when I thought they were in the right, was at least equally censured and misrepresented by the other. I was so thoroughly disgusted with the service, and so fully convinced that our whole system was wrong, and that ruin to our affairs abroad, and great danger and confusion in those at home, must be the consequence of it, that I thought it my indispensable duty to represent my ideas in America. To Congress I had no justification to write, but in conjunction with my colleagues. It was impossible that we could agree in any thing. I therefore determined to write to a confidential friend in Congress, who I knew would communicate it to others who might make such use of it as the public good might require. I accordingly wrote to Mr. Samuel Adams, as follows:— Endnote 083

"Our affairs in this kingdom I find in a state of confusion and darkness, that surprises me. Prodigious sums of money have been expended, and large sums are yet due; but there are no books of account, nor any documents from whence I have been able to learn what the United States have received as an equivalent.

"There is one subject which lies heavily on my mind, and that is the expense of the commissioners. You have three commissioners at this Court, each of whom lives at an expense of at least three thousand pounds sterling a year, I fear at a greater expense. Few men in this world are capable of living at a less expense than I am; but I find the other gentlemen have expended from three to four thousand a year each, and one of them from five to six. And by all the inquiries I have been able to make, I cannot find any article of expense which can be retrenched.

"The truth is, in my humble opinion, our system is wrong in many particulars.

"1. In having three commissioners at this Court. One in the character of envoy is enough. At present, each of the three is considered in the character of a public minister plenipotentiary, which lays him under an absolute necessity of living up to this character, whereas one alone would be obliged to incur no greater expense, and would be quite sufficient for all the business of a public minister.

"2. In leaving the salaries of these ministers at an uncertainty. You will never be able to obtain a satisfactory account of the public moneys while this system continues; it is a temptation to live at too great an expense, and gentlemen will feel an aversion to demanding a rigorous account.

"3. In blending the business of a public minister with that of a commercial agent. The business of various departments is by this means so blended, and the public and private expenses so confounded with each other, that I am sure no satisfaction can ever be given to the public of the disposition of their interests, and I am very confident that jealousies and suspicions will hereafter arise against the characters of gentlemen who may, perhaps, have acted with perfect integrity, and the fairest intentions for the public good.

"My idea is this;—separate the offices of public ministers from those of commercial agents; recall, or send to some other Court, all the public ministers but one at this Court; determine with precision the sum that shall be allowed to the remaining one for his expenses, for his salary, and for his time, risk, trouble, &c.; and when this is done, see that he receives no more than his allowance. The inconveniences arising from the multiplicity of ministers and the complication of business are infinite."

This letter was received by Mr. Adams in due season, and by him communicated to Mr. Richard Henry Lee and others. Mr. Lee wrote me immediately that he had seen it, and was entirely of my opinion. It was communicated to so many members of Congress, that it produced the revolution which followed; my friends, and the friends of Mr. Arthur Lee, uniting with those of Dr. Franklin, Mr. Deane, and Mr. Izard, in introducing the new plan.

The representation in my letter of the expenses of the commissioners, related only to the state of things before my arrival. My expenses were very trifling. I had no house rent to pay separate from Dr. Franklin. I kept no carriage, and used none but that of Dr. Franklin, and that only when he had no use for it. I had very little company more than Dr. Franklin would have had if I had not been there. But, before my arrival, Mr. Deane had his house and furniture and establishment of servants, as well as his carriage, in Paris, and another establishment for his apartments in the country at Passy, and another carriage and set of horses and servants. Mr. Lee had a house, furniture, carriage, and organization of servants, at Chaillot. Dr. Franklin had his in the Basse-cour de Monsieur Le Ray de Chaumont, at what rent, I never could discover; but, from the magnificence of the place, it was universally suspected to be enormously high. Making the best estimate I could, from the representations that were made to me, I wrote as I then believed. But, after a longer residence, more experience, and further inquiry, I was convinced that I had admitted much exaggeration into the account. Nevertheless, the expenses of Mr. Deane never have been known, and never, I presume, can be known. Endnote 084

I had taken pains to persuade my colleagues to take a house in Paris, and have but one establishment for us all. Mr. Lee, whose opinion was that we ought to live in Paris, readily consented, but Dr. Franklin refused. I proposed that Mr. Lee should take apartments with us at Passy, and there was room enough for us all; and I offered to resign my apartments to him, and take others which were not so convenient; but he refused to live together, unless it were in Paris, where the Americans in general, and the French too, seemed to think we ought to live. All my proposals were therefore abortive.

Before I wrote the letter to Mr. Adams, I had many things to consider. What would be the consequence if my plan should be adopted? Dr. Franklin's reputation was so high in America, in the court and nation of France, and all over Europe, that he would undoubtedly, as he ought, be left alone at the Court of Versailles. Mr. Lee held two commissions, one to the Court of France, and one to the Court of Spain. If that to the Court of Versailles should be annulled, the other, to the Court of Madrid, would remain in force. It would, therefore, make little odds to him. I had but one, and that to the Court of Versailles. If this were annulled, what would become of me? There was but one country to which I thought it possible Congress would send a minister at that time, and that was Holland. But there was no hope that Holland would then receive a minister, and I thought Congress ought not to send one there as yet. I thought, therefore, that there was no alternative for me, but to return to America; and I very deliberately determined, that I had rather run the gauntlet again through all the British men-of-war in the Bay of Biscay, the British Channel, and the Gulf Stream, with all their storms and calms, than remain where I was, under a system and in circumstances so ruinous to the American cause. I expected, however, that Congress would make some provision for my return, by giving me orders to receive money enough for my expenses, and give me a passage in a frigate, if any one should be in France. In this last expectation alone I was disappointed.]

22. Friday. Dined at home with a great deal of company. Went after dinner to see the Misantrope of Molière, with Mr. Amiel; it was followed by the Heureusement. Called at the Microcosme; called at Mr. Amiel's, at the pension.

23. Saturday. Dined at home with company.

24. Sunday. Dined at home.

25. Monday. Dined at home.

[Business, as well as disputes, increased and multiplied upon us, and there was nobody to do any business but me, so that I found it necessary to decline invitations abroad, and dine at home as much as possible, to answer the public letters; but, after I had written them, I had trouble and delay enough in getting them signed by my colleagues. This day the following were written.

Benjamin Franklin

Arthur Lee
John Adams

TO JOHN PAUL JONES.

Passy, 25 May, 1778

Sir:—

Your favors of May 9 and 16, from Brest, we duly received. We congratulate you on your success and safe arrival at Brest, as well as on the honor you have acquired by your conduct and bravery in taking one of the king's ships.

As we have some expectation of obtaining an exchange of prisoners from England, we would advise you to keep those you have made, securely confined, though in the manner most consistent with humanity, till we have an answer from thence. For if we can get an equal number of our own seamen to man the Drake, she will be an additional strength to you in a future expedition; whereas, sending her with the prisoners to America, will not only weaken you, by the hands you must spare to navigate her and to keep the prisoners in subjection, but will also hazard their being retaken.

We should have been happy to have been early informed of the particulars of your cruise, and of the prizes you have made, of which we have no authentic advice to this hour.

Your bill of exchange in favor of M. Bersolle, for twenty-four thousand livres, which you inform us you mean to distribute among the brave officers and men to whom you owe your late success, has been presented to us by M. Chaumont.

We are sorry to inform you that we have been under the disagreeable necessity of refusing payment, and that for several reasons. 1st. Because your application should have been made to Mr. Schweighauser, who is the person regularly authorized to act as Continental agent at Brest; and we are determined that all American concerns, within our department, shall go through his hands, so long as he shall continue in the character of American agent, or at least till we shall find it necessary to order otherwise. 2dly. Because the bill is drawn for an expense, which we have no right or authority to defray. We have no authority to make presents of the public money to officers or men, however gallant or deserving, for the purpose of providing their families with clothing, or for any other purpose; nor to advance them money upon the credit of their shares of prizes; nor have we authority to advance them any part of their pay or bounties. All these things belong to Congress alone, and must be done by the proper boards in America. Our authority extends no father than to order the necessary repairs to be made to your ship, to order her to be furnished with necessary victuals, which we are ready to order Mr. Schweighauser to do, as soon as we shall be informed by you what repairs and victuals are wanted, with an estimate of the amount of the expense.

There is one thing further, which we should venture to do for the benefit of your men. Upon a representation from you of the quantity of slops necessary for them, we should order Mr. Schweighauser to furnish your ship with them; not more, however, than one suit of clothes for each man, that you may take them on board of your ship and deliver them out to the men as they shall be wanted, charging each man upon the ship's books with what he shall receive, that it may be deducted out of his pay.

Lieutenant Simpson has stated to us your having put him under arrest for disobeying orders. As a court martial must, by order of Congress, consist of three captains, three lieutenants, and three captains of marines, and these cannot be had here, it is our desire that he may have a passage procured for him, by the first opportunity, to America, allowing him whatever may be necessary for his defence. As the consequences of an arrest in foreign countries are thus extremely troublesome, they should be well considered before they are made.

If you are in possession of any resolution of Congress giving the whole of ships of war, when made prizes, to the captors, we should be obliged to you for a copy of it.

We should also be obliged to you for a particular account, in whose hands the prizes made by you are, and in what forwardness the sale of them.

We have the honor to be, sir, your most obedient, humble servants,

B. Franklin,

Arthur Lee,

John Adams.

Benjamin Franklin

Arthur Lee

John Adams

TO JONATHAN WILLIAMS.

Passy, 25 May, 1778

Sir:—

Your favors of May 11 and 18 are now before us. We shall this day acquaint Captain Jones, how far it is in our power to comply with his desires, and in what manner.

Your letter of the 18th informs us of a dispute between Mr. Schweighauser and you, concerning the disposal of the Ranger's prizes; and you are still of opinion that you have authority to interfere in the disposal of prizes, and that you should be chargeable with neglect of duty if you did not, until your former orders are recalled.

The necessities of our country demand the utmost frugality, which can never be obtained without the utmost simplicity in the management of her affairs. And as Congress have authorized Mr. William Lee to superintend the commercial affairs in general, and he has appointed Mr. Schweighauser, and as your authority is under the commissioners at Paris only, we think it prudent and necessary, for the public service, to revoke, and we do hereby revoke, all the powers and authorities heretofore granted to you by the commissioners plenipotentiary of the United States of America, at Paris, or any of them, to the end that hereafter the management of the affairs, maritime and commercial, of America, may be under one sole direction, that of Mr. Schweighauser, within his district. As to the merchandises and stores of every kind, which you have on hand at present, we leave it to your choice, either to ship them to America yourself, or to deliver them over to Mr. Schweighauser, to be shipped by him.

It is not from any prejudice to you, Mr. Williams, for whom we have a great respect and esteem, but merely from a desire to save the public money, to prevent the clashing of claims and interests, and to avoid confusion and delays, that we have taken this step.

We have further to repeat our request, that you would lay your accounts before us as soon as possible; because, until we have them, we can never know either the state of our finances, or how far the orders of Congress for stores and merchandises to be shipped to America have been fulfilled.

We are, sir, with great respect, your most obedient, humble servants,
B. Franklin,
Arthur Lee,
John Adams.

Benjamin Franklin
Arthur Lee
John Adams

TO MR. SCHWEIGHAUSER.

Passy, 25 May, 1778

Sir:—

We inclose you extracts, from our letters of this day's date, to Mr. Williams and Captain Jones, which we recommend to your attention; and we hope this arrangement will produce the order and economy so necessary to the proper conduct of public business. Our wish is, that you will give us previous notice of any extraordinary proposed expense, that we may determine, before it is incurred, how far it is consistent with our finances, it being our determination to avoid running in debt or pledging ourselves for what we cannot perform. You will be so good as to send us an account every month, and we will direct your bills upon us for the balance to be paid by our banker.

We are, with great respect, sir, your most obedient servants,
B. Franklin,
Arthur Lee,
John Adams.

In the foregoing letter was inclosed an extract of the letter to Mr. Williams, beginning with the words, "Your letter of the 18th informs us," and ending with these: "we have taken this step." Also an extract of the letter to Captain Jones, beginning with the words, "Your application should have been made," and ending with these,—"deducted out of their pay."

Benjamin Franklin
Arthur Lee
John Adams

TO JOHN BONDFIELD.

Passy, 25 May, 1778

Sir:—

Your favors of the 12th and 17th of May are before us. They contain information of an interesting nature, which we shall attend to as soon as circumstances will admit.

We thank you for the punctuality with which you from time to time furnish us with intelligence as it arises in your city, and wish for a continuance of your favors in that way.

You desire we should write you that your bills on us will be duly honored. We request that you would transmit us an account of your disbursements, and after we shall have received and examined your accounts, your bills for the balance shall be duly honored.

We must request you, as we do every other American agent, for the future to transmit to us your accounts monthly, that we may know the state of our affairs, and not run deeper in debt than we shall be able to pay, which there is no small danger of.

We have the honor to be, with great respect, sir, &c.

B. Franklin,

Arthur Lee,

John Adams.

By these letters the die was cast, and one great scene of controversy closed for the present. I had written all of them myself, and produced them to my colleagues as soon as I could get them together. I was doubtful whether Mr. Franklin would sign them, but when he saw that Mr. Lee and I would sign them without him if he refused, with his habitual wisdom he very composedly put his signature to them all; whether from a conviction in his conscience that the decision was right, or from an apprehension that upon a representation of it to Congress it would be there approved, or from both these motives together, is none of my concern. The bruit was however spread from this time, at Nantes and Brest and Bordeaux and elsewhere, that Mr. Adams had joined with Mr. Lee against Dr. Franklin. Hence some of the subsequent letters to America, that "Monsieur Adams n'a pas réussi ici, que de raison, parcequ'il s'est joint à Monsieur Lee contre Monsieur Franklin." I made as great a sacrifice of my personal feelings upon this occasion, as Mr. Franklin. Mr. Williams, his father, uncle and cousins, I considered my friends. Mr. Schweighauser was to me an entire stranger; but by the acknowledgment of everybody, French, Americans, and Dr. Franklin himself, his house was established in reputation for integrity, for capital, for mercantile knowledge, and for an entire affection to the American cause, being a Protestant and a Swiss, though long established and universally respected in France. Mr. Williams was a young gentleman without capital, and inexperienced in the commerce of France, and liable to be imposed upon by French merchants and speculators who might be envious of Mr. Schweighauser's superiority of wealth and credit, and who I well knew, were looking with longing eyes to our little deposit of money in Mr. Grand's bank. But, abstracted from all these considerations, Congress and Mr. William Lee had lawfully and regularly settled the question, and I could not reconcile it to public or private integrity to disturb it.]

26. Tuesday. Dined at M. Bertin's, the Secretary of State, at his seat in the country. Dr. Franklin, his grandson, and I, rode with Madame Bertin, the niece of the minister, in her voiture with four horses. This was one of the pleasantest rides yet. We rode near the back of Mont Calvaire, which is perhaps the finest height near Paris. Montmartre is another very fine elevation. The gardens, walks, and water-works of M. Bertin are very magnificent. He is a bachelor; his house and gardens are situated upon the river Seine; he has, at the end of his garden, a collection of rocks drawn together at a vast expense, some thousands of guineas. I told him I would sell him a thousand times as many for half a guinea. His waterworks are very curious;—four pumps going by means of two horses. The mechanism is simple and ingenious; the horses go round as in a mill; the four pumps empty themselves into a square pond which contains an acre; from this pond the water flows through pipes down to every part of the garden.

I inquired of a certain abbé, who sat next me at dinner, who were the purest writers of French? He gave me, in writing, Discours sur l'Histoire Universelle de Bossuet, La Fontaine, Molière, Racinè, Rousseau, Le Petit Carême de Massillon, Les Sermons de Bourdaloue.

29. Friday. Dined again at Monsieur La Ferté's, at the foot of Calvaire. Madame La Ferté's four sisters dined with us. Monsieur Rulhière, who has always dined with me at that house, dined there to-day; the same gentleman who wrote the History of the Revolution in

Russia. He has also written the Revolutions of Poland. I asked him who was the best historian of France? He said, Mézeray. He added, that the observations upon the history of France, by the Abbé de Mably, were excellent; he told me I might read his History of the Revolution in Russia, when I would. The inclination and the apparatus in this country for amusement is worthy of observation. There is scarcely a genteel house but is furnished with accommodations for every sort of play; every fashionable house, at least, has a billiard table, a backgammon board, a chess board, a chequer board, cards, &c.

30. Saturday. Dined at home with only Dr. Franklin's new French clerk; he has a smattering of Italian, German, and English. He says that the best Italian Dictionary and Grammar are those of Veneroni; the best German Grammar and Dictionary are those of Gottsched; the best French Prosody is the Poétique Françoise de Marmontel.

June 2. Tuesday. Went to Versailles, and found it deserted, the Court being gone to Marly. We went to Marly; met the Comte de Vergennes, and did some business; then went to Mr. De Sartine's and dined with him. His lady was at home, and dined with the company. The Prince de Montbarey dined there. Went with Madame de Sartine to the Count d'Aranda's, the Spanish Ambassador's Coffee, as they call it, where he gives ice cream and cakes to all the world. Marly is the most curious and beautiful place I have yet seen. The water-works here, which convey such a great body of water from the Seine to Versailles, and through the gardens at Marly, are very magnificent. The Royal Palace is handsome; the gardens before it are grand. There are six pavilions on each side of the garden, that is, six houses, for the use of the king's ministers, while the royal family is at Marly, which is only for three weeks. There is nothing prettier than the play of the fountains in the garden. I saw a rainbow in all its glory in one of them. The shades, the walks, the trees, are the most charming that I have seen.

[We had not time to visit Luciennes, the elegant retreat for devotion, penitence, and mortification, of Madame du Barry; and, indeed, I had been in such a reverie in the morning, in passing Bellevue, that I was not averse to postpone the sight of another object of the same kind to a future opportunity.

On the road from Paris, and from Passy to Versailles, beyond the river Seine, and not far from St. Cloud, but on the opposite side of the way, stood a palace of uncommon beauty in its architecture, situated on one of the finest elevations in the neighborhood of the river, commanding a prospect as rich and variegated, as it was vast and sublime. In a few of the first times that I went to Versailles, I had other things to occupy my attention; but, after I had passed through my ceremonies, and began to feel myself more at ease, I asked some questions about this place, and was informed that it was called Bellevue, and was the residence of the King's aunts, Adelaide and Victoire, two of the surviving daughters of Louis XV. This palace had been built, and this establishment made, by that monarch, for Madame de Pompadour, whom he visited here for twenty years, leaving a worthy woman, his virtuous queen, alone at Versailles, from whom he had sworn an eternal separation. I cannot describe the feelings, nor relate half the reflections, which this object and history excited. Here were made judges and counsellors, magistrates of all sorts, nobles and knights of every order, generals and admirals, ambassadors and other foreign ministers, bishops, archbishops, cardinals, and popes. Hither were directed all eyes that wished and sought for employment, promotion, and every species of court favor. Here Voltaire and Richelieu, and a thousand others of their stamp, obtained royal favor and commissions. Travellers, of all ranks and characters, from all parts of Europe, were continually passing from Paris to Versailles, and spreading the fame of this house, its inhabitants and visitors, and their commerce, infamous in every point of view, civil, political, moral, and religious, all over the world. The attention of all France had been turned to Bellevue more than to Paris or Versailles. Here lettres de cachet, the highest trust and most dangerous instrument of arbitrary power in France, were publicly sold to any persons who would pay for them, for any, the vilest purposes of private malice, envy, jealousy, revenge, or cruelty. Here licenses were sold to private smugglers, to contravence the king's own laws, and defraud the public revenue. Here were sold dukedoms and peerages, and even the cordon bleu of the knights of the Holy Ghost. Here still lived the daughters of the last king, and the aunts of the present. Instead of wondering that the licentiousness of women was so common and so public in France, I was astonished that there should be any modesty or purity remaining in the kingdom, as there certainly was, though it was rare. Could there be any morality left among such a people, where such examples were set up to the view of the whole nation? Yes. There was a sort of morality. There was a great deal of humanity, and what appeared to me real benevolence. Even their politeness was benevolence. There was a great deal of charity and tenderness for the poor. There were many other qualities that I could not distinguish from virtues. This very monarch had in him the milk of human kindness, and, with all his open, undisguised vices, was very superstitious. Whenever he met the host, he would descend from his coach, and down upon his knees in the dust, or even in the mud, and compel all his courtiers to follow his example. Such are the inconsistencies in the human character!

From all that I had read of history and government, of human life and manners, I had drawn this conclusion, that the manners of women were the most infallible barometer to ascertain the degree of morality and virtue in a nation. All that I have since read, and all the observations I have made in different nations, have confirmed me in this opinion. The manners of women are the surest criterion by which to determine whether a republican government is practicable in a nation or not. The Jews, the Greeks, the Romans, the Dutch, all lost their public spirit, their republican principles and habits, and their republican forms of government, when they lost the modesty and domestic virtues of their women.

What havoc, said I to myself, would these manners make in America! Our governors, our judges, our senators or representatives, and even our ministers, would be appointed by harlots, for money; and their judgments, decrees, and decisions, be sold to repay themselves, or, perhaps, to procure the smiles of profligate females.

The foundations of national morality must be laid in private families. In vain are schools, academies, and universities, instituted, if loose principles and licentious habits are impressed upon children in their earliest years. The mothers are the earliest and most important instructors of youth. The vices and examples of the parents cannot be concealed from the children. How is it possible that children can have any just sense of the sacred obligations of morality or religion, if, from their earliest infancy, they learn that their mothers live in habitual infidelity to their fathers, and their fathers in as constant infidelity to their mothers? Besides, the catholic doctrine is, that the contract of marriage is not only a civil and moral engagement, but a sacrament; one of the most solemn vows and oaths of religious devotion. Can they then believe religion, and morality too, any thing more than a veil, a cloak, a hypocritical pretext, for political purposes of decency and conveniency?]

7. Sunday. Went to Versailles, in company with Mr. Lee, Mr. Izard and his lady, Mr. Lloyd and his lady, and Mr. François. Saw the grand procession of the Knights du Saint-Esprit, or du cordon bleu. At nine o'clock at night, went to the grand couvert, and saw the king, queen, and royal family, at supper; had a fine seat and situation close by the royal family, and had a distinct, and full view, of the royal pair.

[Our objects were to see the ceremonies of the knights, and, in the evening, the public supper of the royal family. The kneelings, the bows, and the courtesies of the knights, the dresses and decorations, the king seated on his throne, his investiture of a new created knight with the badges and ornaments of the order, and his majesty's profound and reverential bow before the altar as he retired, were novelties and curiosities to me, but surprised me much less than the patience and perseverance with which they all kneeled, for two hours together, upon the hard marble of which the floor of the chapel was made. The distinction of the blue ribbon was very dearly purchased at the price of enduring this painful operation four times in a year. The Count de Vergennes confessed to me that he was almost dead with the pain of it. And the only insinuation I ever heard, that the King was in any degree touched by the philosophy of the age, was, that he never discovered so much impatience, under any of the occurrences of his life, as in going through those tedious ceremonies of religion, to which so many hours of his life were condemned by the catholic church.

The queen was attended by her ladies to the gallery opposite to the altar, placed in the centre of the seat, and there left alone by the other ladies, who all retired. She was an object too sublime and beautiful for my dull pen to describe. I leave this enterprise to Mr. Burke. But, in his description, there is more of the orator than of the philosopher. Her dress was every thing that art and wealth could make it. One of the maids of honor told me she had diamonds upon her person to the value of eighteen millions of livres; and I always thought her majesty much beholden to her dress. Mr. Burke saw her probably but once. I have seen her fifty times perhaps, and in all the varieties of her dresses. She had a fine complexion, indicating perfect health, and was a handsome woman in her face and figure. But I have seen beauties much superior, both in countenance and form, in France, England, and America.

After the ceremonies of this institution are over, there is a collection for the poor; and that this closing scene may be as elegant as any of the former, a young lady of some of the first families in France is appointed to present the box to the knights. Her dress must be as rich and elegant, in proportion, as the queen's, and her air, motions, and curtsies, must have as much dignity and grace as those of the knights. It was a curious entertainment to observe the easy air, the graceful bow, and the conscious dignity of the knight, in presenting his contribution; and the corresponding ease, grace, and dignity of the lady, in receiving it, were not less charming. Every muscle, nerve, and fibre, of both, seemed perfectly disciplined to perform its functions. The elevation of the arm, the bend of the elbow, and every finger in the hand of the knight, in putting his louis d'ors into the box, appeared to be perfectly studied, because it was perfectly natural. How much devotion there was in all this I know not, but it was a consummate school to teach the rising generation the perfection of the French air, and external politeness and good breeding. I have seen nothing to be compared to it in any other country. The House of Lords in England I thought the most likely to rival this. But seven years afterwards, when I had seen that assembly on two extraordinary occasions, the first, the introduction of the Prince of Wales to his seat in Parliament, and the second, the trial of Warren Hastings, I concluded the peers of Great Britain were too intent on the great interests of the nation, to be very solicitous about the charms of the exterior exhibition of a spectacle. The procession of the peers, and the reverences they made to the throne, in conformity to the usage of their ancestors, as they passed to their seats in Westminster Hall, were decent and graceful enough.

At nine o'clock we went and saw the king, queen, and royal family, at the grand couvert. Whether M. François, a gentleman who undertook upon this occasion to conduct us, had contrived a plot to gratify the curiosity of the spectators, or whether the royal family had a fancy to see the raw American at their leisure, or whether they were willing to gratify him with a convenient seat, in which he might see all the royal family, and all the splendors of the place, I know not; but the scheme could not have been carried into execution, certainly, without the orders of the king. I was selected, and summoned indeed, from all my company, and ordered to a seat close beside the royal family. The seats on both sides of the hall, arranged like the seats in a theatre, were all full of ladies of the first rank and fashion in the kingdom, and there was no room or place for me but in the midst of them. It was not easy to make room for one more person. However, room was made, and I was situated between two ladies, with rows and ranks of ladies above and below me, and on the right hand and on the left, and ladies only. My dress was a decent French dress, becoming the station I held, but not to be compared with the gold, and diamonds, and embroidery, about me. I could neither speak, nor understand the language in a manner to support a conversation, but I had soon the satisfaction to find it was a silent meeting, and that nobody spoke a word, but the royal family, to each other, and they said very little. The eyes of all the assembly were turned upon me, and I felt sufficiently humble and mortified, for I was not a proper object for the criticisms of such a company. I found myself gazed at, as we in America used to gaze at the sachems who came to make speeches to us in Congress, but I thought it very hard if I could not command as much power of face as one of the chiefs of the Six Nations, and, therefore, determined that I would assume a cheerful countenance, enjoy the scene around me, and observe it as coolly as an astronomer contemplates the stars. Inscriptions of Fructus Belli were seen on the ceiling and all about the walls of the room, among paintings of the trophies of war, probably done by the order of Louis XIV. who confessed, in his dying hour, as his successor and exemplar Napoleon will probably do, that he had been too fond of war. The king was the royal carver for himself and all his family. His majesty ate like a king, and made a royal supper of solid beef, and other things in proportion. The queen took a large spoonful of soup, and displayed her fine person and graceful manners, in alternately looking at the company in various parts of the hall, and ordering several kinds of seasoning to be brought to her, by which she fitted her supper to her taste. When this was accomplished, her majesty exhibited to the admiring spectators, the magnificent spectacle of a great queen swallowing her royal supper in a single spoonful all at once. This was all performed like perfect clock work; not a feature of her face, nor a motion of any part of her person, especially her arm and her hand, could be criticized as out of order. A little, and but a little, conversation seemed to pass among the royal personages of both sexes, but in so low a voice, that nothing could be understood by any of the audience.

The officers about the king's person brought him many letters and papers, from time to time, while he was at table. He looked at these. Some of them he read, or seemed to read, and returned them to the same officers who brought them, or some others.

These ceremonies and shows may be condemned by philosophy, and ridiculed by comedy, with great reason. Yet the common sense of mankind has never adopted the rigid decrees of the former, nor ever sincerely laughed with the latter. Nor has the religion of nations, in any age, approved of the dogmas or the satires. On the contrary, it has always overborne them all, and carried its inventions of such exhibitions to a degree of sublimity and pathos, which has frequently transported the greatest infidels out of themselves. Something of the kind every government and every religion has, and must have; and the business and duty of lawgivers and philosophers is to endeavor to prevent them from being carried too far.]

8. Monday. Dined with Mr. Alexander, and went to the concert.

July 4. Saturday. The Anniversary of the Declaration of American Independence. We had the honor of the company of all the American gentlemen and ladies, in and about Paris, to dine with Dr. Franklin and me, at Passy, together with a few of the French gentlemen in the neighborhood; M. Chaumont, M. Brillon, M. Veillard, M. Grand, M. Baudouin, M. Gérard, The Abbés Chalut and Arnoux, &c.

[Mr. Izard and Dr. Franklin were upon such terms, that Franklin would not have invited him, and I know not that Izard would have accepted the invitation if he had. But I said to

Mr. Franklin that I would invite him, and I believe Dr. Smith and all the rest that he omitted, and bring them all together, and compel them, if possible, to forget their animosities. Franklin consented; and I sent cards to them in my name only. The others were invited in the names of both of us. The day was passed joyously enough, and no ill humor appeared from any quarter. Afterwards, Mr. Izard said to me that he thought we should have had some of the gentlemen of that country; he would not allow those we had to be the gentlemen of the country. They were not ministers of state, nor ambassadors, nor princes, nor dukes, nor peers, nor marquises, nor cardinals, nor archbishops, nor bishops. But neither our furniture nor our finances would have borne us out in such an ostentation. We should have made a most ridiculous figure in the eyes of such company. Besides, the ministers of state never dine from home, unless it be with one another at the Castle; and we were not yet acknowledged, as public ministers, by any sovereign in Europe, but the king of France; therefore, no ambassador, or other public minister, could have accepted our invitation. I know very well that the company we had, and the society with which Dr. Franklin generally associated, were disliked and disapproved by a great body of the first and soundest people in the kingdom. Some of them had been "flétris" by a grand court martial, or court of inquiry, which had been appointed on the beginning of this reign, or the latter end of the last, consisting of the marshals of France, whose report I have read. These great people I now speak of, were, I know, very much disgusted at our living at Passy, and in the house of M. Chaumont. But this step had been taken before my arrival; and what could we do? The circle in question revolved around M. de Sartine and the Comte de Vergennes, and were countenanced probably by Comte Maurepas, whose departure from the first intention of the present king, had disgusted, and driven from court, first, M. Malesherbes, and next, M. Turgot. I have not at present the books and papers which I have seen and read; and if I had, it would be endless, as well as useless, to develop the state of parties in France, at the close of the reign of Louis XV. and at the commencement of that of Louis XVI. *Endnote 085* By these revolutions of parties, we were thrown into the hands of a set of people, whose intrigues and mercenary views involved the first years, and indeed days, of the alliance with suspicion and want of confidence. The persons and parties are all dead, I believe, and no man will probably ever look into the memorials of those times with sufficient care to distinguish the springs of actions. But I know what I say, and I know it was regretted and lamented by many of the greatest and best men in the kingdom.]

I have omitted to keep any journal for a long time, in which I have seen a great many curious things.

6. Monday. Dined with the Abbés Chalut and Arnoux. The Farmer-General, Mr. and Mrs. Izard, Mr. Lee, Mrs. Gibbs, and Mrs. Stevens, and Mr. and Mrs. Lloyd were there. After dinner, the Abbé invited us to the French Comedy, where we saw the Malheureux Imaginaire and the Parti de Chasse d'Henri quatre.

7. Mardi. Dined at St.-Leu with the Farmer-General, Chalut, the Marshal Richelieu, and many abbés, counts, marquises, &c.

John Adams

Extract of a Letter to Elbridge Gerry.

Passy, 9 July, 1778

My Dear Friend,—

It is with real astonishment that I observe the conduct of Great Britain. After all experience, and although her true interest, and her only safe plan of policy, is as obvious as the sun, yet she cannot see it. All attention to the welfare of the nation seems to be lost, both by the members of administration and opposition, and among the people at large. Tearing one another to pieces for the loaves and fishes, and a universal rage for gambling in the stocks, seem to take up all their thoughts.

An idea of a fair and honorable treaty with Congress never enters into their minds. In short, chicanery seems to have taken possession of their hearts so entirely, that they are incapable of thinking of any thing fair.

We had an example here last week. A long letter, containing a project for an agreement with America, was thrown into one of our grates. There are reasons to believe that it came with the privity of the King. You may possibly see it some time. Full of flattery, and proposing that America should be governed by a Congress of American peers, to be created and appointed by the King; and of bribery, proposing that a number, not exceeding two hundred American peers, should be made, and that such as had stood foremost, and suffered most, and made most enemies in this contest, as Franklin, Washington, Adams, and Hancock, by name, should be of the number. Ask our friend if he should like to be a peer?

Dr. Franklin, to whom the letter was sent, as the writer is supposed to be a friend of his, sent an answer, in which they have received a dose that will make them sick.

John Adams.

[This letter requires a commentary. The reasons for believing that it came with the privity of the King, were derived wholly from Dr. Franklin, who affirmed to me, that there were in the letter infallible marks, by which he knew that it came from the King, and that it could not have come from any other, without the King's knowledge. What these marks were he never explained to me. I was not impertinently inquisitive, and he affected to have reasons for avoiding any more particular development of the mystery. Many other hints have been dropped by Franklin to me of some mysterious intercourse or correspondence between the King and him, personally. He often, and indeed always, appeared to me to have a personal animosity and very severe resentment against the King. In all his conversations, and in all his writings, when he could naturally, and sometimes when he could not, he mentioned the King with great asperity. He wrote certain annotations on Judge Foster's Discourse on the Legality of the Impressment of Seamen, in the margin of the book, and there introduced his habitual acrimony against his majesty. A thousand other occasions discovered the same disposition. Among the ancient disputes between Franklin and the proprietary governors of Pennsylvania, I have read that Franklin, upon hearing of a report in circulation against his election as agent for the province at the Court of St. James, that he had no influence with the ministry, and no acquaintance with Lord Bute, broke out into a passion, and swore, contrary to his usual reserve, "that he had an influence with the ministry, and was intimate with Lord Bute." It is not generally known that the Earl of Bute was a philosopher, a chemist, and a natural historian; that he printed seven or eight volumes of natural history of his own composition, only, however, for the use of his particular, confidential friends. This kind of ambition in the Earl might induce him to cultivate the acquaintance with Franklin, as it did afterwards Rochefoucauld, Turgot, and Condorcet, in France; and, at the Earl of Bute's, some mysterious conferences between the King and Franklin might have been concerted, and, in these interviews, Franklin might have conceived himself deceived or insulted. I mention this merely as conjecture, suggestion, or surmise. Franklin's Memorials, if they ever appear, may confirm or confute the surmise, which, however, after all, will be of very little consequence.

Franklin consulted with me, and we agreed, First, to do nothing without previously informing the French Court; Secondly, as the letter was supposed to come from a friend of Franklin, at the desire, or by the orders of the King, that Franklin should write the answer.

He produced his draught to me, and it was very explicit, decided, and severe, and in direct terms asserted that, by certain circumstances in the letter, Franklin knew that it came from the King. We sent a copy of the answer to the Comte de Vergennes, as well as the original letter and project, and asked his excellency's advice, whether we should send it or not.

In the letter, the writer proposed that we should meet him at twelve o'clock precisely, in a certain part of the Church of Notre Dame, on a certain day, in order to have a personal conference upon the subject. I know not that the papers were ever returned from Versailles. We received no advice to send the answer. The day after the one appointed to meet the messenger at Notre Dame, the Comte de Vergennes sent us the report of the Police of Paris, stating that at the day, hour, and place appointed, a gentleman appeared, and, finding nobody, wandered about the church, gazing at the statues and pictures, and other curiosities of that magnificent cathedral, never losing sight, however, of the spot appointed, and often returning to it, looking earnestly about, at times, as if he expected somebody. His person, stature, figure, air, complexion, dress, and every thing about him, were accurately and minutely described. He remained two hours in the church, and then went out, was followed through every street, and all his motions watched to the hotel where he lodged. We were told the day he arrived there, the name he assumed, which was Colonel Fitz-something—an Irish name that I have forgotten—the place he came from, and the time he set off to return.

In my letter to Mr. Gerry, it is inaccurately said that Dr. Franklin sent an answer. It was written, and I supposed it would be sent, but it was not. *Endnote 086* Whether the design was to seduce us Commissioners, or whether it was thought that we should send the project to Congress, and that they might be tempted by it, or that disputes might be excited among the people, I know not. In either case, it was very weak and absurd, and betrayed a gross ignorance of the genius of American people.

An aristocracy of American peers! hereditary peers, I suppose were meant; but, whether hereditary or for life, nothing could be more abhorrent to the general sense of America at that time, which was for making every magistrate and every legislator eligible, and that annually at least.

An aristocracy of American peers! but this could not be simple. The King must have been intended to have a negative upon the laws, no doubt; but was this authority to have been executed by a viceroy to reside in Philadelphia? And were this viceroy and these two hundred peers to have made all the laws, without a representation of the people by annual or other elections? Even if there were to have been three branches to the General Government, what was to become of the State governments? All abolished, or all continued under some kind of subordination to the General Government? Any of these projects would have appeared to the people of America, at that time, as extravagant, and as tyrannical as any thing the English had done. The English were strangely infatuated with an idea that Adams and Hancock, Washington and Franklin, with a few others, in the several States, as they had influence enough to throw off the authority of Great Britain, would have influence enough to put it on again, as a man who has strength enough to throw off his cloak, may be supposed able to throw it again over his shoulders. Nothing could be more erroneous; for none of these leaders had any influence but that which was given them by the folly and temerity of Great Britain; and if any of them had adopted and advocated any such projects as these, he would not only have lost all influence in America, but been obliged to fly to England for protection among the royalists and refugees. These speculations were, however, all rendered unnecessary. Independence had been declared two years; and all America in a manner had renounced every modification of government under Great Britain for ever, fully convinced that no cordial confidence or affection could ever be restored on either side. Besides, a treaty with France had been solemnly made. America was then a virgin, and her faith sacred; and it would have been ridiculous to suppose that France would now consent that we should make a separate treaty, and become subject again to England, that the reunited kingdoms might immediately fall upon France in a new war.

We thought the whole subject so futile, that I think we never transmitted any account of it to Congress.]

14. Tuesday. Dined at Chatou, with M. Bertin, Ministre d'État. Went to see the Park, where we rambled until we were weary.

25. Saturday. It is an amusement among some people here, who understand a little English, to give samples of English sentences, hard to be pronounced. "What think the chosen judges?" "Thrust this thistle through this thumb." "An apple in each hand, and a third in my mouth," &c.

August 16. Sunday. Went to church to the Chapel of the Dutch Ambassador in Paris, where we had prayer-books, psalm-books in French, and a sermon. The preacher spoke good French, I being judge, and with much grace. I shall go again.

17. Monday. Dined at Chatou, with M. Bertin. After dinner, went to view the machine of Marly, which forces up from the river Seine all the water at Versailles and Marly. We walked up the mountain to the pavilion and dwelling-house of Madame du Barry. The situation is one of the most extensive and beautiful about Paris. The pavilion is the most elegantly furnished of any place I have seen. The house, garden, and walks, are very magnificent. Madame du Barry was walking in the garden; she sent us word she should be glad to see us, but we answered it was too late, we had so far to go. M. Le Roy of the Academy of Sciences was with us; as we returned, we had an agreeable conversation upon philosophical subjects.

18. Went to Paris with the Abbés Chalut and Arnoux. Went to see the Church of St. Roch, the splendor and magnificence of which is very striking to me. There I saw the monument of the famous Mesnager. The pomp of these churches, I think, exceeds the magnificence of the royal palaces.

M. Chalut says that the rent of this church is eighty thousand livres a year; barely the rent of the pews and chairs, and perhaps the cellars; out of this they maintain the officers of the church, and the servants and laborers that attend it, and the organist, &c.; but what becomes of the remainder he did not say.

30. Sunday. This evening had the English Gazette extraordinary, containing extracts from letters from Lord Howe and General Clinton; the first, containing an account of the arrival of the Toulon fleet, and anchoring without Sandy Hook; the other, a relation of the action of the 28th of June, in the Jerseys.

There are letters in London, as Mr. J. Wharton says, as late as the first of July.

October 7. Wednesday. Captain Richard Grinnell, of Newport, Rhode Island, says that the English have this year seventeen vessels in the Brazil whale fishery off the river Plata, in South America, in the latitude 35° south, and from thence to 40°, just on the edge of soundings off and on, about the longitude of 63° from London; that they sail in the months of September and October. Almost all the officers and men belonging to these seventeen vessels, are Americans, from Nantucket and Cape Cod, two or three from Rhode Island and Long Island. Some of these vessels, four or five, go to Greenland. The fleet sails to Greenland the last of February, or the beginning of March.

There is another whale fishery discovered lately in the Mediterranean, on the coast of Barbary, where they catch many fish. There was last year, and this year, a publication made by the ministry,—a letter from the Lords of the Admiralty to Mr. Dennis Deberdt, in Coleman Street, informing Mr. Deberdt that there should be a convoy appointed to convoy the Brazil fleet. But this is a sham, a deception; there was no convoy last year nor this. If a convoy was to be appointed, she could be of no service, as the vessels are continually changing their course in chase of whales. That she would not go further than the line, as they would then judge themselves clear of American privateers. One privateer, from twelve to twenty guns and one hundred men, would be sufficient to take and destroy this whole fleet. The beginning of December would be the best time to proceed from hence; the same time from Boston.

8. Thursday. Captain Richard Grinnell was taken and carried into Guernsey by the Speedwell cutter, Captain Abraham Bushell, of twelve guns, pierced for fourteen.

"The town of Guernsey, the capital of the island, is fortified with one fort upon an island called Castle Island, within a quarter of a mile of the town, right before it. There are between eighty and a hundred pieces of cannon in the fort, but both guns and fort in bad condition and repair, not more than fifty soldiers at a time in the fort. There are only five hundred soldiers, Highlanders, on the whole island. They have wrote to Scotland for another regiment, which they say is coming. The militia keep watch round the island; they are well armed, but are not exercised.

"They have lately built new batteries of four and six guns, in places where boats can land, and block-houses all round the island, where boats can land.

"The island is not more than ten leagues from Cape La Hogue—the French coast. About five thousand souls on the island; very bitter against the French, but treat American prisoners very well,—more like brothers than prisoners.

"There is a forty-gun ship, and two frigates of twenty-eight or thirty guns, in the harbor, before the town of Guernsey, and several cruising round the island, as they say. Two king's cutters of twelve and fourteen guns are here also. They say there are forty-six privateers, from eight to twenty guns, belonging to this island. About twenty more belonging to Jersey, Alderney, and Sark.

"The proper place to station a frigate to intercept the prizes, of sight; here, a frigate that could sail fast enough, might retake many prizes."

Captain Peter Collass, of Boston, taken on board of Barnes, by the Speedwell, of Guernsey.

"Guernsey is about twenty miles in circumference, seven or eight long, and about three or four wide. There are breast-works all round the island, and wherever there is a cove or bay where it is possible for boats or ships to come in, there is a battery of two or four guns. They reckon they can muster between four and five thousand militia. They have five hundred Highlanders, all green, just off the mountains. They have a number of invalids besides, perhaps three or four hundred. The fort in the harbor is on a rock, a musket-shot from the town; eighty-six guns in the fort, forty-two, thirty-two, down to twelves. Every parish has a field-piece or two; of late, they have received a number of field-pieces of a new construction, three-pounders, to be drawn by men over gutters, ditches, &c.

"Guernsey, Jersey, and Alderney, have between fifty and sixty privateers, small and great.

"There is a forty-gun ship, a frigate of twenty-eight or thirty guns, and two cutters of ten or twelve. A thirty-six gun frigate to cruise about ten or twelve leagues to the westward of the Island of Guernsey, might intercept their prizes going in, providing she was a fast sailer. She should keep out of sight of the island. The Guernsey men boasted that all the islands had taken prizes this war, to an amount between three and four millions."

12. Monday. Samuel Harding of Wellfleet, Cape Cod, says, "that Mr. Robert Bartholomew or Bartlemé, and Incleby, of London, are largely concerned in the whale fishery. Richard Coffin and Shubael Gardiner, of Nantucket, are concerned with them. Dennis Deberdt carries on the business for Mr. Bartholomew. One ship of forty guns, or twenty guns, would take all the fishery. There are about three boats' crews on each ship, which are twenty-four men."

22. Thursday. William Whitmarsh, Jr. born in Braintree, married and living in Marblehead, was taken prisoner on board the Yankee privateer, Captain Johnson.

"After having taken two ships, the prisoners rose upon and carried them to England; carried to Chatham and put on board the Ardent, sixty-four gun ship, Captain Middleton; next put on board the Mars, seventy-four; from thence on board the Vulture sloop for Spithead; at Spithead put on board the Belfleur, ninety. 11 October, 1776, put on board the Rippon, of sixty guns, Commodore Vernon, bound to the East Indies; sailed 24 November from Spithead, and arrived at Madras 8 June, 1777. 11th August I left the ship and went upon the Malabar coast; from thence to a Danish island; thence to Bengal; thence to a Danish factory; discharged from the Danish snow. In November, 17th, I shipped on board an East Indiaman, homeward bound. Sailed in December to Madras, arrived in January, 1778; sailed 6th February, arrived at Spithead 6th of August;—seventeen impressed; all the men on board the fleet were pressed, midshipmen, quarter-masters, and all; twenty-seven had a ticket of liberty for fourteen days. 11 September left London for Flushing, arrived 27th. 7 October at Dunkirk; never entered, and never would."

30. Friday. Last Saturday I dined with Mr. Grand, in company with M. Gébelin, author of the Monde Primitif.

November 9. Sunday. Mr. Lee read me a paragraph of a letter from London: "That Mr. D. Hartley would probably be here in the course of this month." At dinner I repeated this paragraph to Dr. Franklin, and said that I thought "Mr. Hartley's journey ought to be forbidden." The Doctor said, "he did not see how his coming could be forbidden." I replied, "we could refuse to see him," and that I thought we ought to see nobody from England, unless they came with full powers; that little emissaries were sent by the king only to amuse a certain set of people while he was preparing for his designs; that there had been enough of this. The Doctor said, "We could decline having any private conversation with him."

26. Jeudi. Went to see the palace of Bourbon, belonging to the Prince of Condé; it is a city. The apartments of the prince are very rich and elegant; the gallery has many fine paintings. But I have no taste for ringing the changes of mirrors, gold, silver, marble, glass, and alabaster; for myself, I had rather live in this room, at Passy, than in that palace, and in my cottage, at Braintree, than in this hotel at Passy.

An unlucky accident befell my servant, Stevens, in falling from the coach and being dragged by the foot upon the pavement. He was in great danger, but happily was not essentially hurt.

Dined with the Abbés Chalut and Arnoux. Returned at night and found M. Turgot, Abbé Condillac, Madame Helvetius, and the Abbé, &c.

30. Monday. Orthodoxy is my doxy, and heterodoxy is your doxy. Definitions. Franklin.

December 2. Wednesday. Captain Bernard says, there are two hundred and thirty sail of merchant ships lying at the Mother Bank, near Spithead, ready to sail to the West Indies, loaded with all kinds of provisions and dry goods, and warlike stores; they are to be joined by about thirty sail that now lay in the Downs; they are to sail the first wind after the two fleets join; the wind must be easterly; they all go to Barbadoes, where the fleet, for the windward islands, separates from that to the leeward islands; they are to be convoyed out of the Channel by twelve ships of the line, six of them to go through the voyage to the West India Islands. As they commonly exaggerate, it is probable that not so many men-of-war will go. There may be eight or nine men-of-war go out of the Channel, and perhaps two or three go through the voyage. They cannot probably spare six vessels of the line, without leaving the French masters of the seas.

1779.

February 2. Tuesday. Last Tuesday I dined in company with the Abbé Raynal and M. Gébelin, and asked them to dine with me on the then next Sunday. Accordingly the day before yesterday they both came.

Monsieur Raynal is the most eloquent man I ever heard speak in French; his voice is sharp and clear, but pleasant; he talks a great deal, and is very entertaining. M. Gébelin is much less addicted to talking. He is silent, soft, and still; his mind always upon the stretch.

4. Thursday. Breakfasted with the Abbé Raynal at his house, at his particular invitation, with a large company of gentlemen and ladies. The Abbé is more than sixty, seems worn with studies, but he has spirit, wit, eloquence, and fire enough.

5. Friday. The Duke de la Rochefoucauld, M. Turgot, Abbés Rochon, and De la Roche, dined here.

8. Monday. In conversation with Dr. Franklin, in the morning, I gave him my opinion of Mr. Deane's Address to the people of America with great freedom and perhaps with too much warmth. I told him that it was one of the most wicked and abominable productions that ever sprang from a human heart; that there was no safety in integrity against such a man; that I should wait upon the Count de Vergennes and the other ministers, and see in what light they considered this conduct of Mr. Deane; that if they and their representatives in America were determined to countenance and support by their influence such men and measures in America, it was no matter how soon the alliance was broke; that no evil could be greater, nor any government worse, than the toleration of such conduct. No one was present but the Doctor and his grandson.

In the evening I told Dr. Bancroft, to the same effect, that the address appeared to me in a very atrocious light; that however difficult Mr. Lee's temper might be, in my opinion he was an honest man, and had the utmost fidelity towards the United States; that such a contempt of Congress, committed in the city where they sit, and the publication of such accusations in the face of the universe, so false and groundless as the most heinous of them appeared to me, these accusations attempted to be colored by such frivolous tittle-tattle, such accusations made too by a man who had been in high trust, against two others, who were still so,—appeared to me evidence of such a complication of vile passions, of vanity, arrogance, and presumption, of malice, envy, and revenge, and at the same time of such wickedness, indiscretion, and folly, as ought to unite every honest and wise man against him; that there appeared to me no alternative left but the ruin of Mr. Deane or the ruin of his country; that he appeared to me in the light of a wild boar, that ought to be hunted down for the benefit of mankind; that I would start fair with him, Dr. Bancroft, and give him notice that I had hitherto been loth to give up Mr. Deane, but that this measure of his appeared to me to be so decisive against him, that I had given him up to Satan to be buffeted.

In all this it is easy to see there is too much declamation; but the substantial meaning of it is such as appears to me exactly true, and such as I will abide by, unless future evidence, which I don't expect, should convince me of any error in it.

9. Tuesday. Abbé C.

"Terruit Hispanos, Ruiter, qui terruit Anglos
Ter ruit in Gallos, territus ipse ruit."
"Cum fueris Romæ, Romano vivito more;
Si fueris alibi, vivito sicut ibi."

Any thing to divert melancholy and to soothe an aching heart. The uncandor, the prejudices, the rage, among several persons here, make me sick as death.

Virtue is not always amiable. Integrity is sometimes ruined by prejudices and by passions. There are two men in the world who are men of honor and integrity, I believe, but whose prejudices and violent tempers would raise quarrels in the Elysian fields, if not in Heaven. On the other hand, there is another, whose love of ease and dissipation will prevent any thorough reformation of any thing, and his silence and reserve render it very difficult to do any thing with him. One of the others, whom I have allowed to be honest, has such a bitter, such a sour, in him, and so few of the nice feelings, that God knows what will be the consequence to himself and to others. Besides, he has as much cunning and as much secrecy.

Called at M. Garnier's; he not at home. At Mr. Grand's; he and his son began about the Address, *Endnote 087*—bien faché, &c. I said, coolly, that I was astonished at the publication of it, without sending it to Congress; that I believed Mr. Lee a man of integrity, and that all suggestions of improper correspondences in England were groundless; that my brother Lee was not of the sweetest disposition, perhaps, but he was honest; that virtue was not always amiable. M. Grand replied, Il est soupçonneux, il n'a du confiance en personne, il croit que tout le monde est—I can't remember the precise word. I believe this is a just observation. He has confidence in nobody; he believes all men selfish, and no man honest or sincere. This I fear is his creed, from what I have heard him say. I have often, in conversation, disputed with him on this point; however, I never was so nearly in his situation before. There is no man here that I dare trust at present. They are all too much heated with passions and prejudices and party disputes. Some are too violent, others too jealous, others too cool and too reserved at all times, and at the same time, every day, betraying symptoms of a rancor quite as deep. The wisdom of Solomon, the meekness of Moses, and the patience of Job, all united in one character, would not be sufficient to qualify a man to act in the situation in which I am at present; and I have scarcely a spice of either of these virtues.

On Dr. Franklin the eyes of all Europe are fixed, as the most important character in American affairs, in Europe: neither Lee nor myself are looked upon of much consequence. The attention of the Court seems most to Franklin, and no wonder: his long and great reputation, to which Lee's and mine are in their infancy, are enough to account for this; his age and real character render it impossible for him to search every thing to the bottom; and Lee, with his privy council, is evermore contriving: the results of their contrivances render many measures more difficult.

11. Thursday. When I arrived in France, the French nation had a great many questions to settle. The first was, Whether I was the famous Adams? Le fameux Adams? Ah, le fameux Adams. In order to speculate a little upon this subject, the pamphlet entitled "Common Sense," had been printed in the "Affaires de l'Angleterre et de l'Amérique," and expressly ascribed to Mr. Adams, the celebrated member of Congress—le célèbre membre du Congrès. It must be further known, that although the pamphlet, Common Sense, was received in France and in all Europe with rapture, yet there were certain parts of it that they did not choose to publish in France. The reasons of this any man may guess. Common Sense undertakes to prove that monarchy is unlawful by the Old Testament. They therefore gave the substance of it, as they said; and, paying many compliments to Mr. Adams, his sense and rich imagination, they were obliged to ascribe some parts to republican zeal. When I arrived at Bordeaux, all that I could say or do would not convince anybody but that I was the fameux Adams. "C'est un homme célèbre. Votre nom est bien connu ici." My answer was, It is another gentleman, whose name of Adams you have heard; it is Mr. Samuel Adams, who was excepted from pardon by General Gage's proclamation. "Oh non, Monsieur, c'est votre modestie."

But when I arrived at Paris, I found a very different style. I found great pains taken, much more than the question was worth, to settle the point that I was not the famous

Adams. There was a dread of a sensation; sensations at Paris are important things. I soon found, too, that it was effectually settled in the English newspapers that I was not the famous Adams. Nobody went so far in France or England as to say that I was the infamous Adams. I make no scruple to say that I believe both parties, for parties there were, joined in declaring that I was not the famous Adams. I certainly joined both sides in this, in declaring that I was not the famous Adams, because this was the truth.

It being settled that he was not the famous Adams, the consequence was plain; he was some man that nobody had ever heard of before, and therefore a man of no consequence—a cipher. And I am inclined to think that all parties, both in France and England,—Whigs and Tories in England, the friends of Franklin, Deane, and Lee, in France,—differing in many other things, agreed in this, that I was not the famous Adams.

Seeing all this, and saying nothing,—for what could a man say?—seeing also that there were two parties formed among the Americans, as fixed in their aversion to each other as both were to Great Britain, if I had affected the character of a fool, in order to find out the truth and to do good by-and-by, I should have had the example of a Brutus for my justification; but I did not affect this character. I behaved with as much prudence and civility and industry as I could; but still it was a settled point at Paris and in the English newspapers that I was not the famous Adams; and therefore the consequence was settled, absolutely and unalterably, that I was a man of whom nobody had ever heard before,—a perfect cipher; a man who did not understand a word of French; awkward in his figure, awkward in his dress; no abilities; a perfect bigot and fanatic.

It is my indispensable duty to tell the Count de Vergennes that I think one great cause of this horrid address of Mr. Deane, is Mr. Franklin's certificate in his favor that he is an able and faithful negotiator, and that Mr. Franklin was deceived in this; that Mr. Franklin's knowledge actually in America, for a great many years, has not been long; that he was upright in this, but deceived; that there are such certain and infallible proofs of vanity, presumption, ambition, avarice, and folly, in Mr. Deane, as render him very unworthy of confidence, and therefore that Dr. Franklin has been deceived.

12. Friday. My mind has been in such a state, since the appearance of Mr. Deane's Address to the People, as it never was before. I confess it appeared to me like a dissolution of the constitution. It should be remembered that it first appeared from London in the English papers; then in the Courier de l'Europe; and we had not received the proceedings of Congress upon it. A few days after, Dr. Franklin received from Nantes some Philadelphia papers, in which were the pieces signed Senex and Common Sense, and the account of the election of the new President, Mr. Jay. When it was known that Congress had not censured Mr. Deane for appealing to the people, it was looked upon as the most dangerous proof that had ever appeared of the weakness of government, and it was thought by some that the confederation was wholly lost. I confess it appeared terrible to me indeed; it appeared to me that it would wholly lose us the confidence of the French Court. I did not see how they could ever trust any of us again; that it would have the worst effects upon Spain, Holland, and in England, besides endangering a civil war in America. In the agony of my heart I expressed myself to one gentleman, Dr. Bancroft, with perhaps too much warmth. But this day Dr. Winship arrived here from Brest, and soon afterwards the aide-de-camp du Marquis de Lafayette, with despatches from Congress, by which it appears that Dr. Franklin is sole plenipotentiary, and of consequence that I am displaced: The greatest relief to my mind that I have ever found since the appearance of the address. Now business may be done by Dr. Franklin alone; before, it seemed as if nothing could be done.

13. Saturday. There is no such thing as human wisdom; all is the providence of God. Perhaps few men have guessed more exactly than I have been allowed to do upon several

occasions; but at this time, which is the first, I declare, of my whole life, I am utterly at a loss to foresee consequences.

March 3. Wednesday. Went to Versailles, in order to take leave of the ministry. Had a long conversation with the Count de Vergennes in French, which I found I could talk as fast as I pleased.

I asked him what effect the peace of Germany would have upon our war. He said, he believed none, because neither the Emperor nor the King of Prussia were maritime powers.

I asked him, whether he thought that England would be able to procure any ally among the northern powers; that Congress would be anxious to know this. He said, I might depend upon it, and assure Congress, that, in his opinion, England would not be able to procure any; that on the contrary the northern powers were arming, not indeed to war against England, but to protect their commerce.

Quant a l'Espagne, Monsieur? Ah! Je ne puis pas dire.

Called on M. de Sartine, who was not at home. Called on M. Genet. M. Genet's son went with me and my son to see the Menagerie.

4. Thursday. Walked with Mr. Jennings to Calvaire with my son.

12. Friday. About one o'clock arrived at Nantes, at l' Hôtel de la Comédie, after a journey of near five days, having set off from Passy, Monday, the 8th. This journey, which was by Versailles, is through the most barren and least cultivated part of France. After dinner, I had the honor to be visited by the following American gentlemen: Mr. Williams, Mr. Williams my pupil, Mr. Lloyd, Mr. Ridley, Mr. Wharton, Mr. Lee, Mr. Dobrée, Mr. Mease, Captain Jones, Lieutenant Brown, Mr. Ingraham, Mr. Cummings, Mr. Bradford. Mr. John Lloyd is a sensible man; he says that the French officers of Marine consider convoys as a disgraceful service. They hate to be ordered to convoy merchant vessels; that when a convoy is ordered, the officer is negligent, and the merchant does not complain. The marine officers, and police officers, and custom-house officers, are connected together; and if a merchant complains, he is marked out as an obnoxious person, and advantages are taken of him, so that he holds his tongue.

April 14. Wednesday. At Nantes—Hôtel de la Comédie, Rue Bignon. Walked this morning with my son over all the bridges. There are several islands in the river, and they have built bridges from one to another, and houses upon the islands. There are fine meadows on each side; and the mixed appearance of houses, meadows, water, and bridges, is very uncommon and amusing. The first island is built on with very fine houses, all stone; the stone of this place is very durable, which that of Paris is not.

I dined on Monday with Mr. Schweighauser; Tuesday with Mr. Johnson; *Endnote 088* last evening at the Comédie, where we had the Barbier de Séville and L'Épreuce nouvelle. The stage here is not like that of Paris; a poor building, the company on the stage, great part of it, and not very clean nor sweet. The actors indifferent.

Last evening I supped for the first time with the company in the house. Had a good deal of conversation with a gentleman on the subject of the alliance and the war. He said, "It is not for us merchants to judge of the interests of the State. The Court must conduct all political affairs; but it would have been better for us, the trade, if this alliance had not been, provided that would have avoided a war. We have had so many vessels taken, that many houses and individuals are ruined."

I told him that much of this trade had grown out of the connection with America; that the commerce of France was on a more respectable footing than it would have been, if harmony had continued between Great Britain and America, even after all their losses; that the loss to trade was not so great, because if half their cargoes arrived, they sold them for near as much as the whole would have produced, if it had all arrived; besides, that a great deal was insured in England. That there would have been a war between England and France, if harmony had continued between England and America; for the two nations were seldom at peace more than ten or twelve years together. That if a war had happened, in that case the maritime power, as well as commerce of France, would have been in danger of entire destruction; that it was essential to the interest of France that there should be a separation between England and America. He asked what subject there was or would have been for war between England and France. I told him a subject could never be wanting. The passions of the two nations were so strong against each other, that they were easily enkindled; and the English would have been so haughty, that France could not have borne it. He seemed pleased with the conversation, and convinced by the argument. But I find there is more coolness, both in the marine and the trade, than there was a year ago. Americans were more caressed and courted then than now. Yet they all think they must go on, and they think justly.

I have neglected my Journal. Drank tea, and spent the evening at Mr. Johnson's, with him and the two Messrs. Williams. Had some conversation with Mr. Johnson on the subject of a free port. The question was between Nantes and Lorient. Johnson is in favor of Nantes. The advantages of the river, and of the foreign merchants settled there, are his chief argument. You have the productions and the manufactures of Paris, and the whole country, at Nantes by water, by means of the Loire.

15. Thursday. Dined at home.

16. Friday. Dined with Mr. Williams; Mr. Johnson there. Walked after dinner along the river and about the town.

17. Saturday. Yesterday and to-day, in the forenoon, assisted my son in translating Cicero's first Philippic against Catiline.

Nantes is pleasantly situated on the river, and there are several agreeable prospects. The view from the front windows in the row of houses along the river is very beautiful. Mr. Schweighauser crawled up three pair of stairs to visit me this morning.

18. Sunday. Dined at Mr. Schweighauser's. About six o'clock in the evening, Captain Landais came into my chamber. The Alliance is safe arrived at St.-Nazaire with her prisoners.

22. Thursday. Yesterday morning embarked at Nantes with Mr. Hill, the first lieutenant, and Mr. Park, who is captain of marines, and my son. We stopped and dined at Port-Launay. After dinner crossed over to Pélerine, where we went to the house of a Mr. Carmichael, a Scotchman, who lives by salting beef and making bacon for the navigation of this river. This man, I suppose, was a Jacobite, who fled in 1745. We reached no farther than Paimbeuf, where we went ashore, and slept at a tavern.

This day we arrived safe on board the Alliance, and sent off to the cartel ship all the British prisoners. Thus, by my excursion to Lorient and Brest, I have accomplished successfully the expedition of the frigate, and the exchange of the prisoners; and have happily joined the ship, and got my son and baggage on board. The frigate lies at St.-Nazaire, where are several French vessels of war, but none so large as the Alliance.

My idea of the beauty, the wealth, and convenience of Nantes and Paimbeuf, and indeed of the country on both sides of the river, is much heightened, since my return from Brest, having taken a more leisurely view of it. I thought it my duty to come down, although the weather was disagreeable, and the wind contrary and very strong, because I found the British prisoners had not been discharged from the frigate, and could not be, until an order went down, and because I feared that other business would be neglected, and my not being ready alleged as an excuse for it. But I was obliged to leave Joseph Stevens sick of the measles at the tavern. This was a painful circumstance to me, although I took all the precautions in my power, by speaking to Mr. Schweighauser, Mr. Dobrée, Captain Landais, and Dr. Winship, to look to him, and engaged a careful woman to nurse him. I hope he will be well in a few days. He must have taken the infection at Brest, where he imprudently exposed himself, I fear, on shore. The distemper, it seems, is prevalent in this kingdom, at present; the Queen of France is said to be ill of it.

I have now had an opportunity of seeing Bordeaux, Nantes, Lorient, and Brest, and the intermediate countries. I could wish to have seen Rochefort and Rochelle. At Brest, I visited the commandant, whose name I have forgot, the Count d'Orvilliers, who is the marine General, and Monsieur de la Porte, who is the Intendant of the Marine. At Lorient, I did not visit the intendant nor commandant; nor at Nantes.

The zeal, the ardor, the enthusiasm, the rage, for the new American connection, I find, is much damped among the merchants, since the loss of so many of their East and West India ships. The adventurers to America have lost so many ships, and have received so small returns for those which went safe, that they are discouraged; and I cannot learn that any expeditions are formed or forming for our country. But all their chagrin cannot prevent the Court from continuing the war. The existence of French commerce and marine both, are at stake; they are wholly undone without American independence.

The pleasure of returning home is very great. But I confess it is a mortification to leave France. I have just acquired enough of the language to understand a conversation, as it runs at a table, at dinner or at supper, and to conduct all my affairs myself, in making journeys through the country, with the postmasters, postilions, tavern-keepers, &c. &c. I can go to a shop and examine the goods, and understand all the prattle of the shop-keeper, or I can sit down with a gentleman who will have a little patience to speak a little more distinctly than common, and to wait a little longer for my sentences than common, and maintain a conversation pretty well. In travelling, the best way is to dine and sup at the taverns with the company, avec les autres, as they express it. You meet here a vast variety of company, which is decent, and after a few coups de vin, their tongues run very fast, and you learn more of the language, the manners, the customs, laws, politics, arts, &c. in this way, perhaps, than in any other. You should preserve your dignity, talk little, listen much, not be very familiar with any in particular, for there are sharpers, gamblers, quack-doctors, strolling comedians, in short, people of all characters, assembled at these dinners and suppers, and, without caution, you may be taken into parties of pleasure and diversion which will cost you very dear.

Were I to come to France again, I would wait on the intendant, commandant, mayor, &c. of every place. I would dine and sup at the taverns with the company. I would go to the palais, and hear the causes; and to the Comédie, and hear the plays; and that as constantly as possible. I would go to church whenever I could hear a sermon. These are the ways to learn the language; and if to these are added a diligent study of their grammars, and a constant use of their best dictionaries, and reading of their best authors, a man, in one year, may become a great master of it. After all, if a man's character would admit of it, there is much of the language to be learned at the shops. The female shop-keepers are the most chatty in the world. They are very complaisant, talk a great deal, speak pretty good French, and are very entertaining. I took a walk this morning to the back part of the little town of Paimbeuf, and found behind it a pleasant country prospect, with one beautiful country seat of a gentleman in sight.

25. Sunday. Fair weather again. My time has been employed since I have been on board, in writing answers to my letters from Paris, Bordeaux, Passy, &c. and in assisting my son to translate into English, which he does in writing, Cicero's first Philippic against Catiline, which we have gone more than half through. He is also translating into English the French Preface of the Abbé d'Olivet, to his translation of the Philippics of Demosthenes and the Catilinaries of Cicero. Are these classical amusements becoming my situation? Are not

courts, camps, politics, and war, more proper for me? No; certainly, classical amusements are the best I can obtain on board ship, and here I cannot do any thing or contrive any thing for the public.

A boat came on board to-day with a custom-house officer, to examine and give an acquit—a caution for a chest of tea which is on board, belonging to somebody, I know not whom. I have been here so long, that I find the cabin to be rather a trite séjour. It is dull to be here alone. Tully's Offices and Orations are an agreeable amusement; but toujours Tully is as bad as toujours Perdreaux, and infinitely worse than toujours "sa femme," alluding to the anecdote of Henry IV. which I was told by the Abbé Raynal.

26. Monday. Spent the morning in translating with my son the Carmen Seculare and the notes.

There is a feebleness and a languor in my nature. My mind and body both partake of this weakness. By my physical constitution I am but an ordinary man. The times alone have destined me to fame; and even these have not been able to give me much. When I look in the glass, my eye, my forehead, my brow, my cheeks, my lips, all betray this relaxation. Yet some great events, some cutting expressions, some mean hypocrisies, have, at times, thrown this assemblage of sloth, sleep, and littleness into rage a little like a lion. Yet it is not like the lion; there is extravagance and distraction in it that still betray the same weakness.

28. Wednesday. Went up to Nantes from Mendon or St.-Nazaire, before wind and tide, in four hours. This morning, by Captain Landais, who came on board, I received a letter from Dr. Franklin inclosing one from M. de Sartine, both expressing a desire that the Alliance might not sail for some time, and that I would take my passage home with M. le Chevalier de la Luzerne, the new Ambassador, in one of the king's frigates.

This is a cruel disappointment,—to exchange May for July, and the Alliance for another frigate, is too much. Lodged at the Hôtel de St. Julien, where I find the accommodations better than at l'Hôtel de la Comédie. Dined at the hotel with a number of Navy officers, several with the Cross of St. Louis. Drank tea at Mr. Johnson's; had much conversation with him about consuls and agents. He thinks one consul enough for the kingdom, with power of deputation; that a duty of so much per ton be levied on all ships entering a French port, for the relief of unfortunate Americans, prisoners, shipwrecked persons, &c.; that no man should be discharged from a ship, but by the consul; that six, ten, or twelve merchants, should be appointed to inspect the consul's accounts once in three months.

May 7. Friday. Mr. O. of Paimbeuf, Colonel Weibert and Mr. Ford, dined in the cabin. O. speaks English perfectly, appears to have read much, is an adorer of Rousseau and Buffon. Weibert is silent, has something little in his face and air, and makes no great discovery of skill or science. Ford talks as much as ever.

I undertook to sound our engineer this evening, and find he has knowledge; he says one should begin with the architecture of Vignola, and draw the five orders, the Doric, Ionic, Tuscan, Corinthian, and Composite; begin with a pedestal, then the column, then the capital, then the ornaments; from civil you may go to military architecture, and naval if you will. He made many observations to my son about the ink, the instruments, the pens, the manner of holding the hand, sitting to the light of day, or candle, &c. which show that he knows something of these sciences. He is a désignateur. He never had a master, he says. This evening arrived Captain Jones from Baltimore. He sailed 28th March; brings nor newspapers nor news; no despatches from Congress; no letters, but to Mr. Johnson, and a packet for Bordeaux.

9. Sunday. The pilot came on board this morning from St.-Nazaire, and pronounced it unsafe to go out with this wind. F. this morning fell to talking. "Above half the gentlemen of

Paris are atheists, and the other half deists. Nobody goes to church but the common people." "I wish I could find one honest man among their merchants and tradesmen," &c.

"Mr. F." says I, "let me be so free as to request of you, when you arrive in America, not to talk in this style. It will do a great deal of harm. These sentiments are not just; they are contracted prejudices; and Mr. Lee and Mr. Izard have hurt themselves and the public too by indulging in a similar language." F. "O! I am no hypocrite." Thus this prater goes on. Yesterday he wanted me to get him a passage on board the French frigate that I am to go in. I told him I did not think it would be practicable; and I hope it will not, for I don't wish such a man to go in the ship.

At dinner, much conversation about the electrical eel, which gives a shock to a ring of persons, like the touch of a bottle or conductor. What is the name of this fish? The magnet is nothing but iron ore, somebody said at table, and that the tendency towards the pole is in all iron. This afternoon, a Mr. Watkin, a disciple of the great Whitefield, as he calls himself, performed divine service upon the quarter-deck. He is not learned; but his prayer was very good, for the United States and their allies, their army and general, their navy, and this ship and her commander. His sermon also was passable.

Our captain talks much about Batavia,—is an admirer of the Dutch settlement in the East Indies. This gentleman has been disappointed in love, and in his ambition; disappointed in the promotion to which he aspired, and in a marriage of which he thought himself sure. He has not so much activity, despatch, and decision, as I could wish. He seems not to know how to gain or preserve the affections of his officers, nor yet how to keep them in awe. Complaisance, firmness, and steadiness, are necessary to the command of a ship. Whether it is his imperfect knowledge of the language, or his absence of mind, when poring upon his disappointments, or any defect in his temper or judgment, I know not; but this happy mixture seems to be wanting. His lieutenants are smart men, quick and active, not lettered, it is true, but good seamen and brave.

10. Monday. This morning the wind at south-east. The pilot came on board. The Alliance unmoored and set sail for Lorient. A gentle breeze, fair weather, and moderately warm. The First Lieutenant. "I have made by this war one hundred and twenty pounds of prize money, for which I got six months' imprisonment, and spent the little that I had. This is all I have got by the war. The sand-droguers and chimney-sweepers in Boston have all turned merchants and made fortunes."

Ingraham. "Otis says, when the pot boils, the scum rises to the top." Ego. "The new cider, when it ferments, sends all the pomace, worms, bruised seeds, and all sorts of nastiness, to the top. People of fortune have spent their fortunes, and those who had none, have grown rich."

When I arrive, I must inquire concerning Congress, enemy's army, Rhode Island, New York, Georgia, our army, our currency, Massachusetts Bay, Boston, &c.

11. Tuesday. Sailing by Belle-Ile, which the English took last war, after a defence of six weeks, with about nine hundred men.

Dr. W. told me of Tucker's rough, tarry speech about me, at the navy board: "I did not say much to him at first, but—and—my eyes, I found him after a while as sociable as any Marblehead man." Another of Hinman,—that he had been treated with great politeness by me, and his first attention must be to see Mrs. Adams, and deliver her letters.

12. Wednesday. Landais *Endnote 089* is jealous of every thing, jealous of everybody, of all his officers, all his passengers; he knows not how to treat his officers, nor his passengers, nor anybody else. Silence, reserve, and a forbidding air, will never gain the hearts, neither by affection, nor by veneration, of our Americans. There is in this man an inactivity, and an indecision, that will ruin him; he is bewildered,—an absent, bewildered man, an embarrassed

mind. This morning he began, "You are a great man, but you are deceived. The officers deceive you; they never do their duty but when you are on deck; they never obey me but when you are on deck. The officers were in a plot against me at Boston, and the navy board promised to remove them all from the ship, and yet afterwards let them all come on board."

M. Chaumont and his son are here, and have been fifteen days; but no Chevalier de la Luzerne, nor any French frigate. *Endnote 090*

As I sit in my quarter-gallery, we are sailing directly into Port-Louis, at Lorient, before a fine, pleasant breeze. There is a strong fortification at the entrance of this harbor, at which we were hailed, and asked whence, where, name of vessel, captain, &c. What an advantage to Nantes would such a port and harbor as this be? Went ashore. Captain Landais, myself, and son, went on board the Poor Richard. *Endnote 091* Saw Captain Jones and his officers, Mr. Moylan, Captain Cazneau, Captain Young, &c. Went to visit M. Grondell, Commandant des Troupes de terre; found there M. Thevenard, Commandant du Port, M. Desaudiée, India merchant. Went then to visit M. le Ray de Chaumont, who has been here fifteen days with his son. Went then to visit M. Grandville, Commissaire-General du Port; then to the Commissaire des Classes. Was very politely received by all those gentlemen, and Captain Landais treated with particular respect. I spoke very freely to M. Chaumont about my situation; told him I was ill-treated; that I had many jealousies and suspicions; that I suspected it was an intrigue.

13. Thursday. Went on shore, and dined with Captain Jones at the Epée Royale; M. Amiel, Mr. Dick, Dr. Brooks, officers of the Poor Richard, Captain Cazneau, Captain Young, Mr. Ingraham, Mr. Blodgett, Mr. Glover, Mr. Conant, Messrs. Moylans, Mr. Mease, Mr. Nesbit, Mr. Cummings, and Mr. Taylor, made the company, with Captain Landais, myself, and my son. An elegant dinner we had, and all very agreeable. No very instructive conversation; but we practised the old American custom of drinking to each other, which I confess is always agreeable to me. Some hints about language, and glances about women, produced this observation;—that there were two ways of learning French commonly recommended,—take a mistress, and go to the comedy. Dr. Brooks, (in high good humor): "Pray, sir, which in your opinion is the best?" Answer, in as good humor: "Perhaps both would teach it soonest; to be sure, sooner than either. But," continued I, assuming my gravity, "the language is nowhere better spoken than at the comédie. The pulpit, the bar, the Academy of Sciences, and the faculty of medicine,—none of them speak so accurately as the French Comédie."

After dinner, walked out with Captains Jones and Landais, to see Jones's marines, dressed in the English uniform, red and white; a number of very active and clever sergeants and corporals are employed to teach them the exercise, and manœuvres and marches, &c.; after which, Jones came on board our ship. This is the most ambitious and intriguing officer in the American navy. Jones has art and secrecy, and aspires very high. You see the character of the man in his uniform, and that of his officers and marines, variant from the uniforms established by Congress,—golden button-holes for himself, two epaulettes,—marines in red and white, instead of green. Eccentricities and irregularities are to be expected from him. They are in his character, they are visible in his eyes. His voice is soft and still and small; his eye has keenness and wildness and softness in it. *Endnote 092*

14. Friday. On board all day, ill of a cold. Many gentlemen came on board to visit me. A Dr. Brooks, surgeon to the Poor Richard, drank tea with me. He seems to be well acquainted with philosophical experiments. I led him to talk upon this subject. He had much to say about phlogiston, fixed air, gas, &c.; about absolute and sensible heat, experiments with the thermometer, to show the absolute and sensible heat in water, air, blood, &c.

Finding he had ideas of these things, I led him to talk of the ascent of vapors in the atmosphere, and I found he had considered this subject. He mentioned a natural history of North and South Carolina, by Catesby, in four volumes, folio, with stamps of all the plants and animals; price twenty-five guineas. He mentioned a Dr. Erving, and a Dr. Black of Glasgow, as great philosophers, whose hints Priestley had taken. This Dr. Brooks is a gentleman of family, whose father has a great fortune and good character in Virginia. *Endnote 093* Mr. Dick, captain of marines on board of Jones, is also of good family and handsome fortune in Virginia. Mr. Gimat came on board to visit me, aide-de-camp of the Marquis de la Fayette.

15. Saturday. Went on shore, and dined with Captain Jones at the mess at L'Epée Royale, Mr. Hill, Captain Cazneau, Captain Young, Mr. Dick, Dr. Brooks, and Mr. Gourlade, &c. and another aide-de-camp of the Marquis. Gourlade married a Scotch lady. Captain Jones this morning showed me a letter from Lieutenant Browne, desiring, or rather apologizing for leaving the ship, because of the word, first, in Mr. Amiel's commission. I said I thought Mr. Browne could not serve under Mr. Amiel; it would be, in a manner, giving up the claims of many lieutenants, whose commissions were dated between his and Mr. Amiel's, as well as his own, and would expose him to censure; that the word, first, was agreed to be inserted by the commissioners, because we expected that either we or Captain Jones would fill up the commissions to the other lieutenants of that ship, and it was intended to give him an assurance that he should be the first on board that ship. It was not so well considered as it ought to have been, to be sure, but could not now be helped. That, however, the word, first, was void; it could not supersede the date of any former commission. M. Amiel was so urgent to have it in, that it was agreed to, perhaps too inconsiderately.

After dinner, took a walk out of town; returned, and went to view the two churches, the least of which has some fine paintings,—St. Joseph, St. Joachim, the Virgin feeling the babe leap in her womb at the sight of Elizabeth, and many others; some handsome marble pillars, and two fine statues in plaster of Paris. In the evening, Captain Landais chagrined,—suspecting plots among his officers against him,—had written to Dr. Franklin, relating things to him, &c. &c. Mr. Blodgett came in, and said he had one chest in the ward-room, which the officers had ordered him to take away; but as he had but one, and they so many, he ventured to wait for the captain's orders; that the officers were now about to treat him better, conscious that they could not treat him worse. To-day they invited him to dine in the ward-room; but he begged Mr. Degge not to invite him; they had d—d him, and he could not dine there, yet did not love to refuse,—he begged off. Such is the danger of favoritism in the government of a ship, as well as of a state! I have had the pleasure to restore this ship to peace and harmony, and am persuaded it would have continued; but when I leave here, I see plainly all will become unhappy again. There is such a mixture of ductility and obstinacy in the government of her, as will not keep her together. A tender heart and an obstinate will sometimes go together. The captain has told Mr. Blodgett of my advice, that he should not live in the cabin; this will raise his resentment against me, and B. will be his idol still; *Endnote 094* yet he will continue to be excluded the cabin, which will make it worse for what I know. The captain is not of an accommodating humor nor temper. His resolutions, when taken, are without conditions or exceptions, and unalterable as one would think, yet sometimes too easily and too entirely altered. My presence has had some degree of awe upon the captain and all the other officers; it has made them endeavor to respect one another; but the fire is not extinguished; it will break out again.

Landais said, honor and delicacy are his second God,—he shall die poor and despised, not by those who know him. This is an honest man; but chagrin and disappointment are visible in every thing about him; he is incapable of all art; has no address or dexterity at all in managing men.

P. F. this morning was upon his fights and battles; at such a time he fought in N. C.; such a time in, &c.; once he fought half an hour in his shirt tail; then he got his rheumatism,—O! his groin, his swelling, his pains in his legs, knees, joints, shoulders, his fever and ague,—if we should have a battle, and he should be sick and killed in his bed!—he had rather be killed ten times upon the quarter-deck, &c.

Colonel Weibert tells a story, that at Angers a bishop has been found unconsumed and uncorrupted, after being buried many years; they buried him up again, and he is to be dug up again after a certain time, and if found entire, is to be made a saint; his preservation is to be a miracle; whereas the truth is, there is salt where he lies; this the Colonel calls sottise.

16. Sunday. Went on shore, and dined with Mr. Moylan; Jones, Landais, Chaumont, père et fils, Moylan frère, Mease, made the company. Mease made a sensible observation, namely, that he ever found five out of six of the people of England supporting the measures of government; that the people of America had been deceived by their friends in England, by writing that the people were against these measures.

Letters from England, received to-day, say, that the last propositions of Spain, for an accommodation, have been rejected by government, with a kind of humor that we have been long used to. Went after dinner, with M. Chaumont, to the house of M. Bouvet, an old officer of Marine, a Croix de St. Louis, to see the model of a seventy-four gun ship, that he was twenty years in making with his own hand. Every spar, block, rope, iron, and timber, in the true proportions; it is fine, comme une tabatière. In his shop he has all his tools, his chisels, his files, &c. and his turning wheel, glasses, mathematical instruments, &c.

Colonel Weibert told us this evening of some very ancient and curious pictures at La Flêche. 1. In one situation you see Henry IV.; in another, at a small distance, you see one of his mistresses; in another, a second mistress. In one picture, viewed from one point, you see a man; from another point, a beast. C. L. told us of a curious grate at Nantes, which is ancient, and nobody knows how it was made; he also entertained us with an account of the Indians at Otaheite, the most dexterous thieves in the world, but the best-natured people. M. Bougainville's people sold them iron, nails, &c. for very great prices,—a hog for a deck nail, and a fowl for a board nail. He related several instances of their ingenuity in picking pockets, and stealing nails and bits of iron—one of their priests picked his pockets of all the nails in it, which was all his money—and a droll relation of a single combat between the priest and the Indian that carried him over the river on his shoulders for a nail, which consisted in clenching their hands together, and pushing, until the priest fell back, when the other gave him a fillip upon his forehead or nose, which was the triumph, and decided the question about the property of the nail. My son could not comprehend why they should be so fond of iron. He was told that iron made the principal difference between savage and civilized nations; that all arts and manufactures depended upon iron, &c.

17. Monday. Landais gave us an account of St. George at Paris,—a mulatto man, son of a former governor of Guadaloupe, by a negro woman. He has a sister married to a farmer-general. He is the most accomplished man in Europe, in riding, running, shooting, fencing, dancing, music. He will hit the button,—any button on the coat or waistcoat of the greatest masters. He will hit a crown-piece in the air with a pistol-ball.

M. Gimat came on board to go to Port-Louis with Captain Landais. The affectation in the eyes, features, laugh, air, gait, posture, and every thing of this gentleman, is so striking, that I cannot but think I see—or—whenever I see him. Affectation proceeds from vanity. Ease is the opposite. Nature is easy and simple. This man thinks himself handsome. His eyes, his complexion, his teeth, his figure, his step and air, have irresistible charms, no doubt, in his mind.

Landais will never accomplish any great thing. He has honor, delicacy, integrity, and, I doubt not, courage and skill and experience; but he has not art; and I firmly believe there never was, or will be, a great character, without a great deal of art. I am more and more convinced, every day, of the innocence, the virtue, and absolute necessity of art and design. I have arrived almost at forty-four, without any. I have less than Landais, and, therefore, shall do less things than even he. This evening, Landais said that mathematicians were never good company. That mathematics made a man unhappy; that they never were good writers. I said no, nor the lawyers; it had been often observed that lawyers could not write. Landais said that observation is not just; there are many other instances of that besides you. This looks like art, but was too obvious.

I said the Roman lawyers were good writers. Justinian's Institutes were pure as classics; several French lawyers had been fine writers, as Cochin, &c.; and some English lawyers, as Bacon, Clarendon, Cowper, Blackstone; but it was a common observation in England, and I found it as common in Paris, that lawyers were generally bad writers.

18. Tuesday. On board all day, reading Don Quixote.

19. Wednesday. Pleasant. My state is tedious enough, waiting for the Chevalier, and losing time and wind. Expectation is a painful posture of the mind; and suspense, which is a little different, is worse.

This of Lorient is a fine port and harbor. Men-of-war can come up to the wharf, and they commonly lie not far from it; but there are no such pleasant prospects of the country as in Boston harbor.

20. Thursday. Went ashore. Met a servant of M. Chaumont on the wharf, who presented me his master's compliments and an invitation to dine, which I accepted. He lodges at Monsieur —, who, with his lady and daughter of six years, an officer of the navy, Mr. C., myself, and son, made the company. A rich dinner for so small a company. The little daughter of six years showed the effects of early culture. She sung at table, at my desire, several songs, with great ease and judgment; she behaved as easily as her mother; her wit flowed, and her tongue run. Her countenance was disciplined; her eyes and lips were at her command; she was very respectful to the company, and very attentive to decency. M. Chaumont went afterwards with me to see a magazine of medicines belonging to the King, a very large store, in order to get some Jesuit's bark, the best kind of which I found was seventeen livres a pound. Found a Courier de L'Europe of the 7th May. Palliser acquitted, though reprehended—not unanimously nor honorably. Moultrie's letter of the 4th February to Lincoln, and Putnam's to Washington of 2d March. It is said in this paper that one hundred and twenty-one privateers and letters of marque, from six to thirty-six guns, have been fitted out at New York; one thousand nine hundred and seventy-six guns, nine thousand six hundred and eighty men; and that they have taken one hundred and sixty-five prizes. This must be exaggerated.

The 1st of May, the fleet at Portsmouth, of more than four hundred sail, for New York, Quebec, Newfoundland, and Ireland, put to sea, convoyed by six ships of the line, besides frigates and armed transports.

21. Friday. Mr. Ingraham and Mr. Merrick dined with me in the cabin.

22. Saturday. Colonel Weibert drank tea with me alone this evening. I had a long, free, and familiar conversation with him in French; and he made me the compliment several times to say that I spoke French very well,—that I understood French perfectly; that I had happily succeeded, très heureusement réussi, in learning French; that I spoke it fluently, &c. This flattery was uttered with as much simplicity as the Duchess d'Enville's. I understood him

perfectly, every word he said, although he commonly speaks very indistinctly. He says that he was several times with the Solicitor-General Wedderburne in London; that Wedderburne speaks and writes French very correctly; that he told him he had spent a dozen years at Paris, and made many journeys there besides; that he treated him with great politeness, beaucoup d'honnêteté; that he had a list of all the American prisoners, with notes against their names; that he brought letters for Wedderburne to some of the family of M. de Noailles, the late ambassador; that we have many friends in London; that he liked London better than Paris, because the walking was better, the streets were cleaner, and there were accommodations on each side for people on foot; that he has been two hundred leagues to see his father and family, who live in Champagne, near the frontiers of the Queen of Hungary's dominions. He ran over the streets in Paris that were commonly the most embarrassed with carriages. C'est un Cahos, &c. He has promised to look for me after Vignola's Architecture, &c. We fell upon the subject of religion and devotion on board the men-of-war. Every French man-of-war has a chaplain, who says prayers morning and evening regularly. I wished that ours were as regular. We fell upon the subject of swearing. I asked him if the French sailors swore. He said, chaque instant, every moment; that Henry IV. swore a great deal,—ventre Saint-Gris; literally, holy grey belly. I asked him if this originally alluded to the Vierge. He believed not. I told him that most of the oaths had originally relation to religion, and explained to him, zounds, G—d's zounds,—his wounds, God's wounds; s'blood and wounds, his blood and wounds, relating to Christ. He said this made him shudder. Ma foi,—faith,—par dieu, &c. It is amazing how men get the habit of using these words without thinking. I see no difference between French and English on this account. This afternoon, Captain Landais brought seven or eight French gentlemen on board to see the ship, who all admired her. They were genteel, well-bred men. This man has a littleness in his mien and air; his face is small and sharp, so that you form a mean opinion of him from the first sight; yet his eye is good. He maintained a good character among the American prisoners; and you find by close conversation with him, that he has a good deal in him of knowledge.

23. Sunday. Waited in the morning on M. Chaumont. Agreed to go to-morrow morning on board the Sensible, to make my visit to the commander. Went to the lodging of Mr. Ingraham and Blodgett, where about eight or ten Americans breakfast every morning and drink punch every evening. Took a walk with Mr. Ingraham about the town, and then went and dined with Mr. Puchelberg. This is a modest and a decent German. He says there is no Protestant church here,—all is levity, légèreté. He says this town is perdu; amour, jeu, et vin ruin all the women; the women drink brandy like water. He says that France is capable of nourishing forty-eight or fifty millions of people; but it is not half cultivated; the people are light and lazy. At Bordeaux there are forty thousand Protestants, but have no church. The workmen, artisans, &c. are Protestants. This man has a laugh and a grin and a bow that are very particular; his grin is good-natured, his laugh is complaisant, his bow is awkward, to the last degree. The peasants in this country are lazy, and no wonder; for those who work the whole year in planting vines, and in making wine, are obliged to drink water. There are many Protestants here who ne croient rien; ils sont athées.

24. Monday. Went with M. Chaumont to make my visit to the Captain of the Sensible, the frigate in which I am to embark, and was civilly received. Went next on board the Pallas, where we breakfasted with the officers, and then viewed the ship. Went next on board the Poor Richard, and took another look at her. Went ashore and dined with Captain Jones. The Captain of the Pallas dined there, and an officer of his marines; Mr. Mease, Mr. Dick, Mr. Hill, Captain Park, &c. The Sensible has twenty-eight twelve-pounders upon one deck.

June 1. Tuesday. Dined on shore at the coffee-house, with Jones, Landais, the two aide-de-camps of the Marquis de la Fayette, Captain Cotineau.

2. Wednesday. Dined on board the Sensible, at the invitation of the Captain, M. Chavagnes, with M. Thevenard, M. Grandville, M. Chaumont, &c. &c.

On fait et défait, mande et contremande. "A strong fleet is necessary to defend the port of Brest." This observation, which I had never heard before, struck me. The dry-docks might be destroyed, the stores burnt or demolished, the magazines destroyed, &c. unless the place could be defended by the castle and other fortifications, with the land forces.

8. Tuesday. Yesterday I sent one boat with some of my things, and this morning another with the remainder, on board the Sensible. Landais has torn open the old sore, and, in my opinion, has now ruined the peace of this ship. He has an unhappy mind; he must ever have something to complain of, something to peeve and fret about. He is jealous.

12. Saturday. Last night, the Chevalier de la Luzerne arrived, and took lodgings at the Epée Royale, in a chamber opposite to mine, up two pair of stairs. He did me the honor, together with Monsieur Marbois, his secretary, or rather the secretary of the commission, to come into my chamber this morning, and invited me to dine with him in his chamber, with my son. The Ambassador, the Secretary, M. Chaumont, my son, and myself, made the company. The Chevalier informs me that he dined with me once at Count Sarsfield's. I went in the morning to the lodging of Monsieur Marbois. He was out; but I found his two clerks; one of them speaks English very well. They observed to me that I had been waiting a long time. I said, yes, long enough to have made a sentimental journey through the kingdom. This pleased the English secretary very much. He said Yorick's "Sentimental Journey" was a very fine thing,—a charming piece. I said, yes; and that Sterne was the sweetest, kindest, tenderest, creature in the world; and that there was a rich stream of benevolence, flowing like milk and honey, through all his works. M. Marbois showed me a paper from Philadelphia of the 16th February, in which is a long piece with the name of Mr. Paine. In it is the letter, which I remember very well, from M. D. proposing Prince Ferdinand or M. B. to command in chief; the name was mentioned of a Marshal, who I have often heard say was one of the greatest generals in Europe. *Endnote 095* This is curious,—bien extraordinaire—one of the gentlemen said. After dinner, I took a walk in the wood. Beggars, servants, garçons, filles, décrotteurs, blanchisseuses; barges, bateaux, bargemen, coffee-houses, taverns, servants at the gates of woods and walks; fruit, cakes, ice-creams, spectacles, tailors for setting a stitch in clothes, waiters for running with errands, cards, &c.; cabin boys, coach hire, walking-canes, pamphlets, ordonnances, carts.

17. Thursday. At six o'clock this morning, Monsieur Chavagnes, Captain of the Sensible, sent his canot on shore for me and mine, and here I am in full possession of my apartment. Sailed about three o'clock in company with the Bonhomme Richard, Captain Jones, the Alliance, Captain Landais, the —, Captain Young, the —, Captain Cazneau, the Courier de L'Europe, Captain —.

The Three Friends, Captain Coleman, belonging to Mr. Williams, of Nantes, which is loaded with a large quantity of the Chevalier's baggage, was missing. The Chevalier discovered a good deal of sensibility at this. The whole fleet is obliged to wait for this Captain Coleman, and lose this fair wind. The Chevalier has an apartment about eight feet long and six wide, upon the starboard-side of the quarterdeck. I have another of the same dimensions, directly opposite to him, on the larboard; next behind the Chevalier, is the cabin of the Captain, Monsieur Chavagnes; next behind me, is the cabin of the second in command of the frigate; and behind us all, at the stern, is a larger room, the passage-way to which lies between the Chevalier's and the Captain's cabin on one side, and mine and the second's on the other. In this larger room, which extends the whole width of the quarter-deck, all the company loll and converse by day. Monsieur Marbois and my little son hang their cots there, and sleep at night. All the officers, and all the company, dine below, in what is called the grand cabin. The Chevalier is a large and a strong man; has a singular look with his eyes,—shuts his eyelids, &c. M. Marbois, the secretary, is a tall, genteel man, and has a countenance extremely pleasant; he has the appearance of delicacy in his constitution. M. Marbois has two persons with him, one a French secretary, the other a secrétaire interprète, who speaks and writes English. The Maître d'Hótel has his wife with him. She seems a well-bred woman. We are to speak English. This is the agreement; but there are so few who can speak a word of English, that nine-tenths of the conversation, in spite of our intentions and engagements, runs into French. We have on board a Dictionary of the Marine, so that we shall soon understand the names of things and actions on board. Brown, of the manufactory, is on board, as pilot for the American coast. He has received fifty guineas for it; such is the reward for making a stand manfully, ten or eleven years ago. I told the story to the Chevalier, who was much pleased with the narration. Mr. Hill, also, first hieutenant of the Alliance, is on board; but I know not by whose influence. Captain Jones or M. Chaumont probably.

18. Friday. This morning, The Monsieur, a French privateer, which sailed out from Lorient as we went into it in the Alliance, came in with four English prizes, having made six this cruise. She and her prizes saluted the Sensible, and their salutes were returned. Received a card from Mr. Williams third, apologizing for the Three Friends,—that the pilot refused to take charge of her until the morning. I asked a gentleman how he slept. "Very badly, dans la Sainte Barbe." "Il faut chercher ce mot là," said I, "dans le Dictionnaire de la Marine." He ran and brought it, and found la Sainte Barbe to be the gun-room. "Connoissez vous l'étymologic, Monsieur?" said he. "Que non?" said I. Sainte Barbe is the tutelary saint of the canonniers,—gunners. Each trade has its patron. The shoemakers have Saint Crispin, &c.; and the gunners Sainte Barbe. The Sainte Barbe, therefore, is the gun-room, or the salle d'armes,—place of arms. There are nine persons who sleep in the Sainte Barbe. The serruriers have chosen Saint Cloud for their patron. M. Marbois discovered an inclination to-day to slide into conversation with me. I fell down the stream with him as easily as possible. He thought the alliance beneficial to both countries, and hoped it would last for ever. I agreed that the alliance was useful to both, and hoped it would last. I could not foresee any thing that should interrupt the friendship. Yes, recollecting myself. I could foresee several things that might interrupt it. "Ay! what were they?" I said it was possible a king of France might arise, who, being a wicked man, might make attempts to corrupt the Americans. A king of France hereafter might have a mistress that might mislead him, or a bad minister. I said I could foresee another thing that might endanger our confederation. "What was that?" The Court of France, I said, might, or their ambassadors or consuls might, attach themselves to individuals or parties in America, so as to endanger our Union. He caught at this with great avidity, and said it was a great principle not to join with any party. It was the King's determination and the Chevalier's, not to throw the weight of the French Court into the scale of any individual or party. He said he believed, or was afraid, it had been done; but it was disapproved by the King, and would not be done again. He said that the Chevalier and himself would have the favor of the greatest part,—the generality of the honest people in France,—although there would be individuals against them. He said he hoped the United States would not think of becoming conquerors. I said it was impossible they should for many ages; it would be madness in them to think of conquering foreign countries, while they had an immense territory near them uncultivated; that if any one State should have a fancy for going abroad, it would be the interest of all the rest, and their duty, to hinder her. He seemed to be pleased with this. He said we would explain ourselves wholly on the passage. I said, with all my heart; for I had no secrets. All this conversation was in French; but he understood me very well, and I him. He said M. Gérard was a man of wit, and had an advantage of them in understanding the language very well, and speaking it easily. I said, I

believed not much. I had heard it affirmed by some that M. Gérard spoke English perfectly; but by others very indifferently; that it was often affirmed that Mr. Franklin spoke French as fluently and elegantly as a courtier at Versailles; but every man that knew, and spoke sincerely, agreed that he spoke it very ill. Persons spoke of these things according to their affections. He said it was flattery,—that he would not flatter,—it was very true that both Mr. F. and I spoke French badly. A cutter and a lugger hove in sight about noon, and dogged about all the afternoon. M. Marbois began with me again this afternoon,—inquired who was Dr. Bancroft? who Dr. Berkenhout? &c. &c.

18. Friday. The orders are to breakfast at ten, dine at five, and sup at ten.

19. Saturday. The two privateers which were in sight yesterday, are so still, with two others. Our Captain at length laid to, hoisted his colors, and fired a gun as a challenge. One of them hoisted English colors, and fired a gun, which I suppose was accepting the challenge. Our Captain gave her two broadsides, for the sake of exercising his men; and some of his balls went beyond her, some before, and some behind her; I cannot say that any one hit; but there were two which went so well, that it is possible they might. It is certain they were frightened; for, upon our wearing to give her chase, all four of them were about in an instant, and ran. But, at evening, there were several others in sight.

20. Sunday. Two privateers have been in sight all this day; one advanced, and fired several guns, in order to make us hoist our colors; but Captain Chavagnes would not do them that honor; they are afraid to come near; but this it is, every day we have a number in sight, so that there is no chance for a vessel to pass without convoy. Our Captain, M. Chavagnes, has a cross of St. Louis, and one of his midshipmen has a cross of St. Louis; his second has none. He is a youth of eighteen or nineteen, an enseigne du vaisseau, and very able for his years. He has a fine countenance.

The Chevalier de la Luzerne and M. Marbois are in raptures with my son. They get him to teach them the language. I found this morning the Ambassador seated on the cushion in our state-room, M. Marbois in his cot, at his left hand, and my son stretched out in his, at his right. The Ambassador reading out loud, in Blackstone's Discourse at his entrance on his Professorship of the Common Law at the University, and my son correcting the pronunciation of every word and syllable and letter. The Ambassador said he was astonished at my son's knowledge; that he was a master of his own language, like a professor. M. Marbois said, your son teaches us more than you; he has point de grâce, point d'éloges. He shows us no mercy, and makes us no compliments. We must have Mr. John.

This evening had a little conversation with the Chevalier upon our American affairs and characters,—Mr. Samuel Adams, Mr. Dickinson, Mr. Jay,—and upon American eloquence in Congress and assemblies, as well as in writing. He admired our eloquence. I said that our eloquence was not corrected. It was the time of Ennius with us. That Mr. Dickinson and Mr. Jay had eloquence; but it was not so chaste, nor pure, nor nervous, as that of Mr. Samuel Adams. That this last had written some things that would be admired more than any thing that has been written in America in the dispute. He inquired after Mr. Dickinson, and the reason why he disappeared. I explained, as well as I could in French, the inconsistency of the Farmer's Letters, and his perseverance in that inconsistency in Congress, Mr. Dickinson's opposition to the Declaration of Independency. I ventured, as modestly as I could, to let him know that I had the honor to be the principal disputant in Congress against Mr. Dickinson upon that great question; that Mr. Dickinson had the eloquence, the learning, and the ingenuity, on his side of the question; but that I had the hearts of the Americans on mine; and, therefore, my side of the question prevailed. That Mr. Dickinson had a good heart, and an amiable character; but that his opposition to independency had lost him the confidence of the people, who suspected him of timidity and avarice, and that his opposition sprung from those passions; but that he had since turned out with the militia against the British troops, and, I doubted not, might in time regain the confidence of the people. I said that Mr. Jay was a man of wit, well-informed, a good speaker, and an elegant writer. The Chevalier said, perhaps he will not be President when we arrive; he accepted only for a short time. I said I should not be sorry to hear of his resignation, because I did not much esteem the means by which he was advanced to the chair; it appearing to me that he came in by the efforts of a faction, at that moment dominant by means of an influence which I was afraid to mention; that I did not care to say what I thought of it.

We fell into a great deal of other conversation this evening, upon literature and eloquence, ancient and modern,—Demosthenes, Cicero, the poets, historians, philosophers, the English, Bacon, Newton, Milton, &c. He said Milton was very ancient. I said, No; in the reign of Charles and the protectorship of Cromwell, and the reign of Charles II. He thought it was much more ancient. I said there were three epochs in the English history, celebrated for great men,—the reign of Elizabeth, the reign of Charles I. and the interregnum, and the reign of Queen Anne. The Chevalier said Lord Bolingbroke was a great man. I said, Yes; and the greatest orator that England ever produced. M. Marbois, upon this, said it would be easy in France to produce an orator equal to Bolingbroke. I asked, Who? Jean Jacques? No, Malesherbes. Malesherbes's orations might be placed on a footing with Demosthenes and Cicero.

21. Monday. This morning I found M. Marbois recovered of his sea-sickness. I fell into conversation with him about his illness; advised a dish of tea, which he readily accepted; told him he must learn to drink tea in America, in order to please the ladies, who all drank tea; that the American ladies shone at the tea-table. He said he had heard they were very amiable, and of agreeable conversation. I said, Yes; but they could not dance, nor sing, nor play music, nor dress so well as the European ladies; but they had wit and sense and virtue. After a great deal of chat like this, I asked him,—Sir, you mentioned last night Malesherbes's orations. Who, and what was Malesherbes? He said, Malesherbes was president of the court of aids, during the disputes between the late King and the Parliament of Paris; that he made his orations in the course of those disputes; that most of them were not printed,—only a few of the latter ones were printed in the newspapers; that he was banished by the late King, with the Parliament, and after the accession of the present King was recalled and made one of his ministers, in which place he continued eighteen months; but, finding things were likely to take a turn not perfectly agreeable to his mind, and that he could not continue in place with honor, he resigned, and lives a private life in Paris, and is happy. He is the son of a late Chancellor de Lamoignon who was a famous man. He goes by the name of Lamoignon. He died about five years ago, and it was thought his son would take the same name of Lamoignon; but he chooses to go by that of Malesherbes. He is a great man, an intimate friend of M. de Turgot. M. Malesherbes is uncle to the Chevalier de la Luzerne. I have dined twice within a few weeks past with Mr. Franklin, at the house of M. Malesherbes, and once with him at Mr. Franklin's. The acquaintance was formed upon occasion of the appointment of the Chevalier de la Luzerne to go to America. I lamented that I had not seen M. Malesherbes; said that I had the pleasure to dine often with M. Turgot at his house and at ours; that Mr. Franklin was very intimate with M. Turgot, who I thought was a very good man. "Yes," says M. Marbois, "but a little too systematical, and a little too enthusiastical." I said enthusiasm was sometimes a very good quality, at least, very useful. "Not for a minister," says M. Marbois. "Yes, for a minister, in some cases and circumstances." "Ay," says he, "at some times, when he can communicate his enthusiasm to all about him. But at others, when his enthusiasm will be opposed by millions of people of great weight, it will not do." I am very happy to hear of these connections. I shall discover more of them yet. This

M. Marbois is one of the best informed and most reflecting men I have known in France. I warrant I shall have much pleasure in his conversation.

About three o'clock, the Chevalier and I walking upon deck, he took me under the arm, and told me he had something to communicate to me, which he had bound himself in honor not to communicate while he was in France.

"Les Espagnols viennent de se déclarer." "Comment?" said I. "Aux Anglois," said the Chevalier. They have declared, that the Court of London having rejected all the propositions for peace which they had made, they were now determined to declare themselves on the side of France, and to assist them with all their force, by land and sea, in every part of the world; and accordingly they have ordered seventeen ships of the line, or nineteen, to join the Comte D'Orvilliers, making up fifty sail in the whole. They have a minister in America, at Congress. And they are to concert with Congress all their military operations, without saying any thing about the independence of America. "Je ne comprend pas la politique d'Espagne," said I. [This instantly struck me disagreeably. I am jealous of some scheme. The subtlety, the invention, the profound secrecy, the absolute silence of these European courts, will be too much for our hot, rash, fiery ministers, and for our indolent, inattentive ones, though as silent as they.] This within crotchets was not said, but is a reflection of my own. The Chevalier added,—the basis of every proposition for peace that Spain has made, was an acknowledgment of the independence of America.

He added further,—we, that is, the French, have within this month offered, that if the English would withdraw their troops from New York, Rhode Island, and Long Island, all things should remain as they were.

Note. This I don't understand. What becomes of Georgia? What was to become of the sea war? &c.

The Chevalier added,—this was rejected by the Court of London. By this it appears the Court of Spain have given Mr. Lee the go-by; they may have made a treaty with Congress by their ambassador there. I said the English would make great depredations upon the Spanish trade. "How?" says the Chevalier. "By their little cutters and luggers," said I. "O! the Spaniards," said he, "don't make an active commerce like the French. Their commerce is made in large vessels, and always well escorted." This news operates upon my mind like the affair of Saratoga. It is not good enough, and, therefore, the disappointment makes me melancholy. The Chevalier said one other thing worth remembrance. He said that the Americans did not know what their commerce with France would be. The great and able merchants had not yet traded to America. "Who is it," said he, "that has traded to America, but a parcel of little rascals, petits coquins, and adventurers, who have sold the worst merchandises for great prices?" This conversation was all in French, and may not be perfectly translated, but I believe it is.

I have much satisfaction in reflecting, that in all the conversations I have yet had with the Chevalier, no unguarded word has escaped me. I have conversed with that frankness that makes a part of my character, but have said nothing that I did not mean to say. I find a gentleman in the suite of the Chevalier, in the character of interpreter and English master, who has written a large volume upon English pronunciation and accent. His name is Carré.

20. Tuesday. We have had a fine wind ever since we came out of Lorient; but it blows fresher to-day than ever; yet we go but about five knots, because, being obliged to wait for the Three Friends and the Foudroyant, which sail slow, we cannot carry sail. With all our sails we might now go eleven knots. This is mercantile politics, in getting the Chevalier's baggage on board those ships.

M. Marbois, with whom I fell into conversation this afternoon very easily upon deck, said a great many things that deserve notice. He said that Mr. Franklin had a great many friends among the gens de lettres in France, who make a great impression in France; that he had beaucoup d'agrément, beaucoup de charlataneríe; that he has wit, but that he is not a statesman. That he might be recalled at this moment, and, in that case, that his opinion was, he would not return to America, but would stay in Paris. That he heard many of the honest people in France lament that I left France, particularly the Count—and the Marquis de—; that I might possibly return to France, or to some other part of Europe; that the Court of France would have confidence in any gentleman that Congress should have confidence in; that there ought to be a chargé des affaires, or a secretary, and a successor pointed out, in case of the death of Dr. Franklin.

M. Marbois said some were of opinion, that as I was not recalled, I ought to have staid until I was. I told him that if Congress had directed me to return, I would have returned; if they had directed me to stay until further orders, I should have staid. But, as they reduced me to a private citizen, I had no other duties but those of a private citizen to fulfil, which were to go home as soon as possible, and take care of my family. Mr. Franklin advised me to take a journey to Geneva; my own inclinations would have led me to Holland; but I thought my honor concerned to return directly home. He said I was right.

In the evening I fell into chat with the Chevalier. He asked me about Gouverneur Morris. I said it was his Christian name; that he was not governor. The Chevalier said he had heard of him as an able man. I said he was a young man, chosen into Congress since I left it; that I had sat some years with his elder brother in Congress; that Gouverneur was a man of wit, and made pretty verses; but of a character très léger. That the cause of America had not been sustained by such characters as that of Gouverneur Morris, or his colleague, Mr. Jay, who also was a young man about thirty, and not quite so solid as his predecessor, Mr. Laurens, upon whose resignation in the sudden heat Mr. Jay was chosen. *Endnote 096* That Mr. Laurens had a great landed fortune, free from debt; that he had long experience in public life, and an amiable character for honor and probity; that he is between fifty and sixty years of age.

23. Wednesday. This forenoon, fell strangely, yet very easily, into conversation with M. Marbois. I went up to him. "M. Marbois," said I, "how many persons have you in your train, and that of the Chevalier, who speak the German language?" "Only my servant," said he, "besides the Chevalier and myself." "It will be a great advantage to you," said I, "in America, especially in Pennsylvania, to be able to speak German. There is a great body of Germans in Pennsylvania and Maryland. There is a vast proportion of the city of Philadelphia of this nation, who have three churches in it, two of which, one Lutheran, the other Calvinist, are the largest and most elegant churches in the city, frequented by the most numerous congregations, where the worship is all in the German language." "Is there not one Catholic?" said M. Marbois. "Not a German church;" said I. "There is a Roman Catholic church in Philadelphia, a very decent building, frequented by a respectable congregation, consisting partly of Germans, partly of French, and partly of Irish." "All religions are tolerated in America," said M. Marbois; "and the ambassadors have in all courts a right to a chapel in their own way; but Mr. Franklin never had any." "No," said I, laughing, "because Mr. Franklin had no"—I was going to say what I did not say, and will not say here. I stopped short, and laughed. "No," said M. Marbois; "Mr. Franklin adores only great Nature, which has interested a great many people of both sexes in his favor." "Yes," said I, laughing, "all the atheists, deists, and libertines, as well as the philosophers and ladies, are in his train,—another Voltaire, and thence—" "Yes," said M. Marbois, "he is celebrated as the great philosopher and the great legislator of America." "He is," said I, "a great philosopher, but as a legislator of America he has done very little. It is universally believed in France, England, and all Europe, that his electric wand has accomplished all this revolution. But nothing is more groundless. He has done very little. It is believed that he made all the American

constitutions and their confederation; but he made neither. He did not even make the constitution of Pennsylvania, bad as it is. The bill of rights is taken almost verbatim from that of Virginia, which was made and published two or three months before that of Philadelphia was begun; it was made by Mr. Mason, as that of Pennsylvania was by Timothy Matlack, James Cannon, and Thomas Young, and Thomas Paine. Mr. Sherman, of Connecticut, and Dr. Franklin made an essay towards a confederation about the same time. Mr. Sherman's was best liked, but very little was finally adopted from either, and the real confederation was not made until a year after Mr. Franklin left America, and but a few days before I left Congress." "Who," said the Chevalier, "made the Declaration of Independence?" "Mr. Jefferson, of Virginia," said I, "was the draughtsman. The committee consisted of Mr. Jefferson, Mr. Franklin, Mr. Harrison, *Endnote 097* Mr. R. and myself; and we appointed Jefferson a sub-committee to draw it up"

I said that Mr. Franklin had great merit as a philosopher. His discoveries in electricity were very grand, and he certainly was a great genius, and had great merit in our American affairs. But he had no title to the 'legislator of America.' M. Marbois said he had wit and irony; but these were not the faculties of statesmen. His Essay upon the true means of bringing a great Empire to be a small one, was very pretty. I said he had wrote many things which had great merit, and infinite wit and ingenuity. His Bonhomme Richard was a very ingenious thing, which had been so much celebrated in France, gone through so many editions, and been recommended by curates and bishops to so many parishes and dioceses.

M. Marbois asked, are natural children admitted in America to all privileges like children born in wedlock? I answered, They are not admitted to the rights of inheritance; but their fathers may give them estates by testament, and they are not excluded from other advantages. "In France," said M. Marbois, "they are not admitted into the army nor any office in government." I said, they were not excluded from commissions in the army, navy, or state, but they were always attended with a mark of disgrace. M. Marbois said this, no doubt, in allusion to Mr. F.'s natural son, and natural son of a natural son. I let myself thus freely into this conversation, being led on naturally by the Chevalier and M. Marbois on purpose, because I am sure it cannot be my duty, nor the interest of my country, that I should conceal any of my sentiments of this man, at the same time that I do justice to his merits. It would be worse than folly to conceal my opinion of his great faults.

24. Thursday. M. Marbois told a story of an ecclesiastic, who pronounced a funeral oration on Marshal Saxe. He compared him to Alcides, who balanced long whether he should follow the path of virtue or of sloth, and at last chose the former. But Saxe, after balancing long, did better by determining to follow both, that is, pleasure and virtue.

This evening I went into our state-room, where I found M. Marbois alone. "M. Marbois," said I, "what books are the best to give a stranger an idea of the laws and government of France?" "I shall surprise you, sir," said M. Marbois, "and I shall make you laugh; but there is no other but the Almanach Royal." "You say this," said I, laughing, "on purpose to make me laugh." "No," says he, "there is no droit public in France. There are different customs and prerogatives in different provinces. But if you wish I should talk with you more seriously, there are several books in which there are some good notions upon this subject. There are four volumes, by Boulainvilliers, of observations sur l'Ancien Gouvernement de France, and four volumes more, by the Abbé de Fleury, on the same subject." He ran over a great deal more concerning the salique law, and the capitula regum Francorum, &c. which I will be more particular with him about another time. I mentioned Domat. He said it was excellent on the civil law, but had little on the droit public. "How happened it," said I, "M. Marbois, that I never saw you at Paris?" "You have," said he. "Ay, where?" said I; "I don't remember it." "I dined with you," said he, "at the Count Sarsfield's." I said there was a great deal of company, but that I had never seen any one of them before; they were all strangers; but I remember the Count told me they were all men of letters. "There were four ladies," said M. Marbois, "the handsomest of whom was the Countess de la Luzerne, the wife of the Count de la Luzerne. The Count himself was there, who is the eldest brother of the Chevalier de la Luzerne. There was another lady there, who is not handsome, and was never married. She is a sister." "She was the lady who sat at my left hand at table," said I, "and was very sociable. I was charmed with her understanding, although I thought she was not handsome. There was a gentleman there, who asked me if the Mahometan religion was tolerated in America. I understood he had been in Constantinople, as ambassador, or secretary to some embassy. And there was a bishop there, who came in after dinner." "Yes," said he, "he is the bishop of Langres; another brother of the Chevalier de la Luzerne." "I fell," said I, "unaccountably, into a dispute with that bishop. He sat down by me, and fell into conversation about the English, and their conduct in America. In the course of the conversation, I said it was the misfortune of the English, that there was no consistent character among those in opposition to the Court; no man who would adhere to his principles. The two Howes were in opposition to the ministry and the American measures, but when the honor and emoluments of command were offered them, they accepted to serve under that Ministry, and in support of those measures; even Keppell, who refused to serve against America, was induced to serve against France, who were only supporting the Americans. The Bishop said it was the will of the King that must control public officers. I said, an officer should beg to be excused or resign, rather than serve against his conscience. He said the king's will must govern. I said it was a doctrine I could not understand. There was a gentleman present who attended to our conversation in silence till this, when he said, laughing, 'C'est une doctrine ecclésiastique, Monseigneur L'Evéque,' " "This bishop," said M. Marbois, "is no slave; he is a man of free sentiments; he is duc et pair. There are three bishops who are dukes and peers, and three others who are counts and peers, who are always present at the consecration of our kings. The Bishop of Langres is one. The Dukes of Normandy and of Burgundy used to be present, but as there are not any at present, Monsieur and the Count d'Artois represented them at the consecration of the present King, about four years ago. The origin of the custom is not known." "The Chevalier de la Luzerne," said I, "is of a high family." "Yes," said M. Marbois, "he is of an ancient family, who have formerly had in it cardinals and maréchals of France, but not lately. They are now likely to regain their splendor, for the three brothers are all very well at Court."

28. Monday. We have been favored in our voyage, hitherto, beyond my utmost expectations. We have enjoyed a succession of favorable winds and weather from the time of our leaving Lorient to this moment.

The discipline on board this ship is a constant subject of speculation to me. I have seen no punishments inflicted, no blows struck, nor heard scarcely an angry word spoken from the captain to any of his officers, or from any of the officers to the men. They live together in greater intimacy and familiarity than any family I ever saw. The gaillard, or quarter-deck, seems to be as open to the foremast men as the captain. Captain, all other officers, the ambassador, his train, common sailors, and domestic servants, are all walking upon deck, and sitting round upon seats on it, upon a footing of perfect equality, that is not seen in one of our country town meetings in America. I never saw so much equality and levelling in any society whatever. Strange contrast to a British, or even an American frigate. Landais is a Great Mogul in comparison of Chavagnes. One of the officers has favored me with the following:

État Major de la Frégate du Roi, la Sensible.

Messieurs, Bidé de Chavagnes, Capitaine de Vaisseau, Commandant la Frégate.

Le Chevalier de Goësbriand, Enseigne de Vaisseau, Lieutenant de Frégate pour la campagne.

Le Chevalier d'Arriardant, idem.

Le Chevalier de Pincaire, idem.

Le Chevalier du Bréville, idem.

Gardes de la Marine.

Messieurs, Le Chevalier de Guerivière. La Roche de St. André.

Bergerac, Chirurgien-Major.

Le Père Usem, Capucin et Aumonier.

The diversions on board the ship are very curious. The officers and men sing and dance in a ring round the capstan on the quarter-deck, in fine weather. The men are in parties at cards in all parts of the ship.

30. Wednesday. M. Marbois, this morning, upon my inquiry, told me that the Chevalier de la Luzerne is the grandson of the famous Chancelier de Lamoignon, by his mother's side; that the Maréchal Broglie is a cousin to the Chevalier. He also told me, that he himself, M. Marbois, was born in Metz; that his relatives live in Metz, where the Comte de Broglie is commandant; that going lately to Metz, to be admitted a counsellor in Parliament, he journeyed in company with the Comte.

July 2. Friday. Walking this afternoon with M. Marbois upon the quarter-deck, I said frankly to him, that I had expected M. Garnier would have been sent to America; that I had observed some things in the conduct of B. and C. which made me conjecture and believe that they were planning to have M. Garnier succeed M. Gérard; that there was a great intimacy between B. and M. Garnier. "Between ourselves," said M. Marbois, "I believe that was a reason why he did not go. M. Garnier is a man of spirit, and has a great deal of merit; in England he did us good service, and he speaks English very well, and understands affairs very well; but in this affair of his going out upon this embassy, I cannot reconcile his conduct with a man of spirit." I said I had had the pleasure of some acquaintance with M. Garnier; that he did me the honor to visit me several times, and I had several long conversations with him alone; that I was much pleased with his knowledge of our affairs from the beginning, and with his manners; but I thought him too much connected and attached to a particular circle, particularly to B., to whom he seemed to me to have a blind attachment. "There is reason to believe," said M. Marbois, "that Dr. Franklin is not too much pleased with the appointment of the Chevalier. What is the reason of the attachment of Dr. Franklin to B.?" *Endnote 098* "Because B. is devoted to Mr. D. and because he is the only American at Paris who loves him; all the Americans but him are, at present, very bitter against Franklin; he would probably be very glad to get his grandson secretary, but as I fancy he must think him too young to obtain the appointment, he will join with Mr. D. in endeavoring to get B. D. I know, from authentic information, is endeavoring to get B. appointed; that B. was so irregular and eccentric a character, and his conduct in American affairs had been such, that I confessed I had an entire distrust of him; that, at present, he and M. C. *Endnote 099* had in a manner the direction of American affairs; that Congress might as well appoint M. C. their ambassador, but that he had not the brains for the management of such affairs." M. Marbois said, "In fact, he had the management, but it was altogether improper; that the King would never suffer any of his subjects to represent foreign courts at his," &c. The Chevalier came up and said, as our Court would take it amiss if an American minister should meddle in the cabals or intrigues at Versailles, so the United States should resent a

French minister's taking a part in any disputes among them; that there was no need of policy between France and the United States; they need only understand one another—rien que s'entendre. I said, that in my youth I had often heard of the address and intrigues of the French Court, but I could sincerely say, I had found more intrigue and finesse among my own countrymen at Paris, than among the French. "It is true," said the Chevalier; "our Court at some periods of our history have mis beaucoup de ruse dans leur politique, but this had never any better effect than to make us distrusted by all mankind."

4. Sunday. This morning, having stepped out of my cabin for a few minutes, I found upon my return that the compliments of the following gentlemen were left chez moi, on the anniversary of American independence,—Le Chevalier de la Luzerne, M. de Marbois, M. Bidé de Chavagnes, Capitaine des Vaisseaux du Roi de France, commandant la Sensible, Le Chevalier de Goésbriand, the second in command, M. de la Forest, M. Otto, M. Restif, M. Carré.

I returned compliments to the Chevalier and the gentlemen, and thanks for their kind congratulations on my country's independence, and sincerely wished, as this was the foundation of the happy alliance between France and America, that the latest posterity of both countries might have reason to rejoice in it.

16. Friday. Since I have been in this ship I have read Robertson's History of America, in four volumes, in French, and four volumes of the Espion Anglois, in a series of Letters from my Lord All-Eye to my Lord All-Ear. I am now reading Les Négotiations de Monsieur le President Jeannin. He was ambassador from Henry IV. at the Hague, at the beginning of the seventeenth century, and is reputed one of the ablest and faithfulest ambassadors that France ever had. D'Ossat, Jeannin, and D'Estrades, are the three first. I am pleased with this work, as well because of the similitude between the circumstances of the United Provinces at this time and those of the United States at present, as on account of the wisdom, the prudence, and discretion and integrity of the minister.

The Espion Anglois is extremely entertaining, but it is ruined by an intermixture of debauchery and licentious pleasure. It is vastly instructive to a stranger, in many curious particulars of the political state of France; gives light upon many characters, but probably has much obloquy.

17. Saturday. Three days past we have sounded for the Grand Bank, but have not found it. By the reckonings of all the officers we ought to be now ten leagues upon the Bank.

It is surprising to me that we have not seen more fish; a few whales, a few porpoises, and two sharks are all we have seen. The two sharks we caught with a shark-hook and a bit of pork for a bait; we cut up the first, and threw overboard his head and entrails, all of which the other, who was playing after the ship, snatched at with infinite greediness, and swallowed down in an instant; after we had taken him, we opened him, and found the head and entrails of his companion in him.

M. Marbois is indefatigable; as soon as he is up, he reads the Correspondence of M. Gérard for some hours. The Minister it seems has furnished them with a copy of all M. Gérard's Letters, which appear to be voluminous. After this, he reads aloud to M. Carré, M. Otto, M. Restif, or M. Forest, one of Congreve's or Garrick's plays; then he writes some hours.

He is unwilling to let me see Gérard's letters, or what he writes.

20. Tuesday. I was struck with these words in a letter from President Jeannin to M. Bellegarde, of 28 January, 1609:

"Si le roi est content de ma conduite, et de la diligence et fidélité dont j'use pour exécuter ponctuellement ce qu'il m'a commandé, c'est déja une espèce de récompense qui donne grande satisfaction à un homme de bien; et quand il ne m'en aviendra rien de mieux, j'en accuserai plûtot mon malheur que le défaut de sa bonne volonté. Aussi suis je si accoutumé à travailler beaucoup, et profiter peu, que j'en ai acquis une habitude qui me rend plus capable de souffrir patiemment la rudesse de cette mauvaise fortune, sans m'en plaindre ni murmurer."

It is said that Henry IV. although he honored Jeannin with his confidence and trusts, yet recompensed him very ill, notwithstanding the magnificent rewards he gave to Sully, whose modesty and delicacy did not hinder him from asking for them.

30. Friday. We are not yet arrived to the Bank of St. George. Calms, contrary winds, &c. detain us. Saw a whale spouting and blowing and leaping to-day in our wake,—a grampus, they say.

31. Saturday. Found bottom this morning on St. George's Bank. The weather, the wind, the discovery of our longitude, give us all fine spirits this morning. The wind is good as we could wish it. We are now about to pass the day and night of greatest danger; by the present appearances we are highly favored, but appearances are often deceitful. At the moment I am writing, a thick fog comes up on all sides, as if directed specially to conceal us from our enemies. I am not so presumptuous as to flatter myself that these happy circumstances are all ordered for the preservation of this frigate, but not to remark them would be stupidity, not to rejoice in them would be ingratitude. If we should be prospered so much as to arrive well, what news shall we find public or private? We may find disappointment on shore; but our minds should be prepared for all.

The Sensible arrived at Boston on the 2d of August. Mr. Adams repaired immediately to his residence at Braintree, where an election was about to take place of a representative to the Convention called to frame a constitution for Massachusetts. The following entry is taken from the records of the town:

"1779. August 9. Voted, To send only one delegate to represent them in the Convention appointed to be convened at Cambridge on the first day of September next, for the purpose of forming a new constitution.

"Then the Hon. John Adams, Esq. was chosen for that purpose."

Of the labors of Mr. Adams in the Convention, no trace is to be found in the Diary, which does not appear to have been resumed until the moment, when, under a new commission from Congress, he once more embarked in the vessel which had brought him out.

November 13. Saturday. Took leave of my family, and rode to Boston with my son Charles, nine years of age last May. At four o'clock went on board the French frigate, the Sensible; Mr. Thaxter, my son John, twelve years old last July, and my servant Joseph Stevens, having come on board in the morning. I find the frigate crowded with passengers and sailors, full three hundred and fifty men. They have recruited a great number here.

16. Tuesday. Found a grammar entitled Élémens de la Langue Angloise, ou Méthode pratique, pour apprendre facilement cette Langue, par M. Siret. A Paris chez Ruault, Libraire, Rue de la Harpe, près de la Rue Serpente, 1773. Avec Approbation et Permission.

24. Wednesday. On the Grand Bank of Newfoundland. A few days ago we spoke an American privateer, the General Lincoln, Captain Barnes. Wrote letters by him to my family. Mr. Dana *Endnote 100* wrote, Mr. Thaxter, Mr. John, and several others. Heard since I came on board several hints concerning—the son of—; that he has made a great fortune by privateering, by trade, by buying sailors' shares, and by gambling; that he has won of—a great sum of money,—whom nobody pities; that—has lost reputation by the appointment of—, which is probable; that the son has made money by knowing what was wanted for the navy, and purchasing it in great quantities, and then selling it to the Board; that the agent,—, has made a great fortune; that his wife is a great Tory. Anecdotes of her conversation; that—

would certainly be hanged, if it was not that she was a Tory; "nasty poison, paper money, &c. &c.; not to put that nasty paper with our other money." Jer. A. is a very different man from his brother J.—none of the wit, humor, or fun, none of that volatile genius appears; there is a softness and a melancholy in his face, which indicates a goodness—not intemperate or vicious, to appearance.

25. Thursday. Arose at four. A fair wind and good weather. We have passed the Grand Bank. Sounded yesterday afternoon, and found bottom in thirty fathoms of water, on the easternmost edge of the Bank.

26. Friday. "Leur Gouvernement, (des Bataviennes,) fut un mélange de monarchie, d'aristocratie, et démocratie. On y voyoit un chef, qui n'étoit proprement que le premier des citoyens, et qui donnoit moins des ordres que des conseils. Les grands, qui jugeoient les procès de leur district et commandoient les troupes, étoient choisis comme les rois dans les assemblées-générales. Cent personnes, prises dans la multitude, servoient de surveillans à chaque comte, et de chefs aux differens hameaux. La nation entière étoit, en quelque sorte, une armée toujours sur pied; chaque famille y composoit un corps de milice qui servoit sous le capitaine qu'elle se donnoit."

December 5. Sunday. We are now supposed to be within one hundred leagues of Ferrol, or Corunna, to one of which places we are bound. The leak in the frigate, which keeps two pumps constantly going, has determined the Captain to put into Spain. This resolution is an embarrassment to me. Whether to travel by land to Paris, or wait for the frigate? whether I can get carriages, horses, mules, &c.? what accommodations I can get upon the road? how I can convey my children? what the expense will be? are all questions that I cannot answer. How much greater would have been my perplexity, if the rest of my family had been with me! The passage of the Pyrenees is represented as very difficult; it is said there is no regular post; that we must purchase carriages and horses, &c. I must inquire.

7. Tuesday. About eleven o'clock discovered land,—two large mountains; one sharp and steep, another large and broad. We passed three capes,—Finistère, Torinana, and Villano.

Yesterday, the Chevalier de la Mollion gave me some nuts, which he called noix d'acajou; they are the same which I have often seen, and which were called cooshoo nuts; the true name is, acajou nuts; they are shaped like our large white beans; the outside shell has an oil in it that is corrosive, caustic, or burning. In handling one of these shells enough to pick out the meat, I got a little of this oil on my fingers, and afterwards inadvertently rubbing my eyes, especially my left, I soon found the lids swelled and inflamed up to my eyebrows.

8. Wednesday. Got into Ferrol, where we found the French ships of the line. Went on board of that commanded by the General, Count de Sade. Went ashore; visited the Spanish General Don Joseph St. Vincent; took a walk about town; saw a great number of Spanish and French officers. Returned on board the frigate.

9. Thursday. Came on shore with all my family. Took lodgings. Dined with the Spanish Lieutenant-General of the Marine, with twenty-four French and Spanish officers. Don Joseph is an old officer, but has a great deal of vivacity and bonhomie.

The difference between the faces and air of the French and Spanish officers is more obvious and striking than that of their uniforms. Gravity and silence distinguish the one; gayety and vivacity and loquacity the other. The Spanish are laced with a broad and even gold lace; the French with scalloped. The French wigs and hair have rows of locks over the ears; the Spanish one. The French bags are small; the Spanish large. The Spaniards have, many of them, very long hair cued, reaching down to their hams almost; they have all a new cockade, which is made up of two,—a red one and a white, in token of the union of the two nations. Went to the Comedy, or Italian Opera; many officers, few ladies; music and dancing tolerable; the language, Italian—not understood. A dull entertainment to me. This evening the French Consul arrived from Corunna, and was introduced to me at my chamber by the French Vice-Consul at this place; both made me the politest offers of assistance of every sort.

10. Friday. Supped and slept at my lodgings. Breakfasted on Spanish chocolate, which answers the fame it has acquired in the world. Everybody congratulates us on our safe arrival at this place. The leak in the Sensible increases since she has been at anchor; and everybody thinks we have been in great danger.

13. Monday. Yesterday I walked about the town; but there is nothing to be seen excepting two churches, and the arsenals, dry docks, fortifications, and ships of war.

The inconvenience of this harbor is, the entrance is so narrow that there is no possibility of going out but when the wind is one way, that is, southeast, or thereabouts.

The three French ships of the line here are,—the Triomphant, the Souverain, and the Jason; the first of eighty guns, the second seventy-four, the third sixty-four.

M. le Comte de Sade is the Chef d'Escadre or General; M. le Chevalier de Gras Préville is the Capitaine de Pavillon; M. le Chevalier de Glandevès is Captain of the Souverain; M. de la Marthonie commands the Jason.

14. Tuesday. Walked to the barracks and dry docks, to show them to Charles. The stone of which these works are made is about as good as Braintree south-common stone. Went into the Church of St. Julien, which is magnificent; numbers of dévots upon their knees. This afternoon we cross the water to go to Corunna.

We have lodged en la Calle de la Madalena, junto coca, en casa de Pepala Botoneca. The chief magistrate of this town is the Corregidor. Last evening, and the evening before, I spent in conversation with the Consul, on the law of nations and the writers on that law, particularly on the titles in those authors concerning ambassadors and consuls. He mentioned several on the rights and duties of ambassadors and consuls, and some on the etiquette and formalities and ceremonies. I asked him many questions. He told me that the office of consul was regulated by an ordinance of the King: but that some nations had entered into particular stipulations with the King; that the consuls of different nations were differently treated by the same nation; that as Consul of France he had always claimed the privileges of the most favored nation; that he inquired what privileges were enjoyed by the consuls of England, Italy, Germany, &c. &c.; that there is for the province of Galice a sovereign court of justice, which has both civil and criminal jurisdiction; that it is without appeal in all criminal cases, but in some civil cases an appeal lies to the Council; that there is not time for an application for pardon, for they execute forthwith; that hanging is the capital punishment; they burn sometimes, but it is after death; that there was lately a sentence for parricide; the law required that the criminal should be headed up in a hogshead with an adder, a toad, a dog, a cat, &c. and cast into the sea; that he looked at it, and found that they had printed those animals on the hogshead, and that the dead body was put into the cask; that the ancient law of the Visigoths is still in use, with the institutes, codes, novelles, &c. of Justinian, the current law and ordonnances of the King; that he will procure for me a passport from the General or Governor of the Province, who resides at Corunna, which will secure me all sorts of facilities as I ride the country; but whether through the kingdom, or only through the province of Galice, I don't know.

I have not seen a chariot, coach, phaëton, chaise, or sulky, since I have been in the place. Very few horses, and those small, poor, and shabby. Mules and asses are numerous, but small. There is no hay in this country; the horses, &c. eat straw,—wheat straw. The bread, the cabbages, the cauliflowers, apples, pears, &c. are good; the beef, pork, poultry, &c. are good; the fish are good,—excellent eels, sardines, and other fish, and tolerable oysters, but not like ours.

There has been no frost yet. The verdure in the gardens and fields is fresh. The weather is so warm that the inhabitants have no fires nor fireplaces but in their kitchens; they tell us we shall have no colder weather before May, which is the coldest month in the year. Men and women and children are seen in the streets with bare feet and legs, standing on the cold stones in the mud, by the hour together. The inhabitants of both sexes have black hair and dark complexions, with fine black eyes; men and women have long hair ramillied down to their waists, and even sometimes to their knees. There is little appearance of commerce or industry, except about the King's docks and yards and works. Yet the town has some symptoms of growth and prosperity; many new houses are building of stone, which comes from the rocky mountains round about, of which there are many. There are few goods in the shops, little show in their market or in their exchange. There is a pleasant walk a little out of town, between the Exchange and the barracks. There are but two taverns in this town. Captain Chavagnes and his officers are lodged in one, at six livres each per day; the other is kept by a native of America, who speaks English and French, as well as Spanish, and is an obliging man. Here we could have lodged at a dollar a day each; but we were obliged to give one hundred and twenty-nine dollars for six days, besides the barber, and a multitude of other little expenses, and besides being kept constantly unhappy by an uneasy landlady.

Finding that I must reside some weeks in Spain, either waiting for a frigate, or travelling through the kingdom, I determined to acquire the language, to which purpose I went to a bookseller, and purchased Sobrino's Dictionary, in three volumes in quarto, and the Grammatica Castellana, which is an excellent Spanish grammar in their own tongue, and also a Latin grammar in Spanish, after which, Monsieur de Gras made me a present of a very handsome grammar of the Spanish tongue in French, by Sobrino. By the help of these books, the children and gentlemen are learning the language very fast. To a man who understands Latin it is very easy. I flatter myself that in a month I should be able to read it very well, and to make myself understood, as well as understand the Spaniards. The Consul, and Mr. Linde, an Irish gentleman, a master of a mathematical academy here, say that the Spanish nation in general have been of opinion that the revolution in America was of bad example to the Spanish Colonies, and dangerous to the interests of Spain, as the United States, if they should become ambitious, and be seized with the spirit of conquest, might aim at Mexico and Peru. The Consul mentioned Raynal's opinion, that it was not for the interest of the powers of Europe, that America should be independent. I told the Irish gentleman that Americans hated war; that agriculture and commerce were their objects, and it would be their interest, as much as that of the Dutch, to keep peace with all the world, until their country should be filled with population, which could not be in many centuries; that war, and the spirit of conquest, was the most diametrically opposite to their interests, as they would divert their attention, wealth, industry, activity, &c. from a certain source of prosperity, and even grandeur and glory, to an uncertain one, nay, to one that it is certain they could never make any advantage of; that the government of Spain over their colonies had been such, that she never could attempt to introduce such fundamental innovations as those by which England had provoked and compelled hers to revolt, and the Spanish constitution was such as could extinguish the first sparks of discontent, and quell the first risings of the people; that it was amazing to me, that a writer so well informed as Raynal, could ever give an opinion that it was not for the interest of the powers of Europe that America should be independent, when it was so easy to demonstrate that it was for the interest of every one except England. They could lose nothing by it, but certainly would every one gain something, many a great deal. It would be a pretty work to show how France, Spain, Holland, Germany, Russia, Sweden, Denmark, would gain; it would be easy to show it.

15. Wednesday. This morning we arose at five or six o'clock. Went over in a boat, and mounted our mules, thirteen of them in number, and two muleteers; one of whom went before for a guide, and the other followed after to pick up stragglers. We rode over very bad roads and very high mountains, where we had an extensive country, appearing to be a rich soil, and well cultivated, but with few plantations of trees,—some orange trees and some lemon trees, many nut trees, a few oaks, &c. We dined at Hog Bridge, about half way, upon provision made by the French Consul, whose attention and politeness have been very conspicuous; so has that of the Vice-Consul at Ferrol. We arrived at Corunna about seven o'clock, and put up at a tavern kept by persons who speak French. An officer who speaks English, kept open the gate for us to enter, attended us to our lodgings, and then insisted on our visiting the General, who is Governor of the province, and a Colonel, who commands under him, and is Military Governor of the town. These are both Irish gentlemen. They made many professions of friendship to our cause and country. The Governor of the province told me he had orders from Court to treat all Americans as their best friends. They are all very inquisitive about Mr. Jay's mission,—to know who he is? where he was born? whether ever member of Congress? whether ever president? when he embarked? in what frigate? where he was destined? whether to France or Spain, and to what port of France,—Brest, Lorient, or Nantes?

The General politely invited me to dine; said that Spaniards made no compliments, but were very sincere. He asked me when this war would finish? I said pas encore; but when the Kings of France and Spain would take the resolution to send twenty or thirty more line of battle ships to reinforce the Comte d'Estaing, and enable him to take all the British forces and possessions in America.

16. Thursday. This morning, the Governor of the province of Galice, and the Governor of the town of Corunna, came to my lodgings at the Hôtel du Grand Amiral, to return the visit I made them last evening. His Excellency invited me to dine with him to-morrow with all my family. He insisted upon seeing my sons; said I run a great risk in taking with me my children; he had passed not far from my country, in an expedition against the Portuguese; that he and every thing in his power was at my service, &c.; that he did not speak English, &c. I told him I was studying Spanish, and hoped that the next time I should have the honor to see his Excellency, I should be able to speak to him in Spanish. He smiled and bowed. He made some inquiries about American affairs, and took leave. Mr. Dana and I walked about the town, saw the fortifications, the shipping, the market, barracks, &c. and returned.

After dinner, Mr. Trask and his mate, of a schooner belonging to the Tracys, of Newburyport, who have been obliged by bad weather and contrary winds to put in here from Bilbao, came to visit me. I gave them letters to Congress and to my family. The French Consul came in, and Mr. Dana and I walked with him to the Tour de Fer. This is a very ancient monument. It is of stone, an hundred feet high; it was intended for a lighthouse, perhaps, as it commands a very wide prospect of the sea; it sees all the vessels coming from the east and from the west. There was formerly a magnificent staircase, escalier, winding round it in a spiral from the ground to the top; and it is said that some general once rode to the top of it in a coach, or on horseback; but the stairs are all taken away, and the stones employed to pave the streets of Corunna. The mortar, with which the stones are cemented, is as hard as the stones themselves, and appears to have a large mixture of powdered stone in it. There are in this town three convents of monks and two of nuns. One of the nunneries is of capuchins, very austere; the girls eat no meat, wear no linen, sleep on the floor, never on a bed; their faces are always covered up with a veil, and they never speak to anybody.

17. Friday. The Consul conducted me to the sovereign court of justice. There are three halls,—one of civil jurisdiction, another of criminal, and a third of both. The three youngest

judges are the criminal judges. The Consul introduced me to the President and the other judges, and to the Attorney-General, in their robes. The robes, wigs, and bands, both of the judges and lawyers, are nearly like ours at Boston. The President and other judges and the Procureur du Roi treated me with great ceremony; conducted me into the place in the prison, where the prisoners are brought out who have any thing to say to the judges; waited on me into each of the three halls; showed me the three folio volumes of the laws of the country, which are the laws of the Goths, Visigoths, Ripuarians, &c. incorporated on the Corpus Juris. There are no seats for anybody in the halls but for the judges; everybody stands. The President told me, that on Monday next, there would be an interesting cause; invited me to come; said he would receive me in character, and place me by the side of himself on the bench, or, if I chose to avoid this parade, he would order an officer to show me a convenient place to see and hear. Soon after, a part of an Irish battalion of troops was drawn up before the court house, and made a fine appearance. Dined with the Governor of the province of Galicia,—Mr. Dana, Mr. Thaxter, Mr. Allen, and myself. By the help of two Irish officers, I had much conversation with the Governor, who speaks only Spanish. We sent for our book of maps, and showed him the position of New York and Rhode Island and the possessions of the English there, &c. Went with the Consul into a Convent of Franciscans; walked into the church, and all about the yards and cells. Here are the cells of jealousy, hatred, revenge, envy, malice, intrigue, &c. said the Consul. There is more intrigue in a chapter of monks for the choice of a prior, than was employed to bring about the entire revolution in America. A monk has no connections nor affections to soften him, but is delivered up to his ambition, &c. The inscriptions over the cells, in Latin verse, were ingenious, and good morals. Drank tea with the Consul; the Attorney-General was there, and Mr. Lagoanere and the Captain of the French frigate.

18. Saturday. Walked all round the town, round the wharves, slips, &c. on the water, and round the walls against the country. Afternoon,—walked to see the artillery; twelve stands of arms, cannon, bombs, balls, mortars, &c. have been all packed up for some time; by the last post, orders arrived to put up five thousand more in the same manner, ready to embark, nobody knows where. Saw the magazines, arsenals, shops, &c.; carpenters, wheelwrights, blacksmiths, &c.; shown us by the Commandant of Artillery, the Consul's brother-in-law. The Consul's address is Déstournelles, Consul de France à la Corogne. The Governor of the town is Patricio O'Hara. The Governor of the province is Don Pedro Martin Sermenio.

Went into the church of a convent; found them all upon their knees, chanting the prayers to the Virgin, it being the eve of the Sainte Vierge. The wax candles lighted, by their glimmerings upon the paint and gildings, made a pretty appearance, and the music was good.

19. Sunday. Dined with Monsieur Déstournelles, the French Consul, in company with all my family, the Regent or President of the Sovereign Court of the province of Galicia, the Attorney-General, the Administrator of the King's Revenue of Tobacco, and the Commandant of Artillery, Mr. Lagoanere, &c. We had every luxury. But the wines were Bordeaux, Champagne, Burgundy, Sherry, Alicant, Navarre, and Vin de Cap, the most delicious in the world. The Chief Justice and Attorney-General expressed a great curiosity to know our forms of government; and I sent to my lodgings, and presented each of them with a copy of the Report of the Committee of the Convention of Massachusetts Bay. They said they would have them translated into Spanish, and they should be highly entertained with them. I have found the pork of this country to-day and often before, the most excellent and delicious, as also the bacon, which occasioned my inquiry into the manner of raising it. The Chief Justice informed me, that much of it was fatted upon chestnuts, and much more upon Indian corn, which was much better; but that in some provinces of Spain they had a peculiar kind of acorns, growing upon old pasture oaks, which were very sweet, and produced better

pork than either chestnuts or Indian corn; that there were parts of Spain where they fatted hogs upon vipers; they cut off their heads, and gave the bodies to their swine, and they produced better pork than chestnuts, Indian corn, or acorns.

These gentlemen told us that all kinds of grain would come to a good market in this country, even Indian corn, for they never raised more than their bread, and very seldom enough; pitch, tar, turpentine, timber, masts, &c. would do; salt-fish, spermaceti candles, &c. rice, &c. Indigo and tobacco come from their own colonies. The Administrator of the King's Tobacco told me that ten million weight was annually consumed in Spain in smoking. We inquired concerning the manner of raising the King's revenue. We were told that there were now no farmers-general in Spain; that they had been tried and found prejudicial, and abolished; that all was now collected for the King; that he appointed collectors for particular towns or other districts; that duties were laid upon exports and imports, and taxes upon lands. We inquired the manner of raising the army; found that some were enlisted for a number of years; that others were drafted by lot for a number of years; and that a number of years' service entitled to several valuable privileges and exemptions; but the pay was small. The Consul gave me two volumes, Droit Public de France, Ouvrage Posthume de M. l'Abbé Fleury, composé pour l'Education des Princes, et publié avec des Notes, par J. B. Daragon, Prof. en l'Université de Paris.

20. Monday. Went to the Audiencia, where we saw the four judges sitting in their robes; the advocates in theirs, a little below; and the attorneys lower down still. We heard a cause argued. The advocates argued sitting; used a great deal of action with their hands and arms, and spoke with eagerness; but the tone of oratory seemed to be wanting.

Inscribed over the Cell of a Monk at Corunna.

"Si tibi pulchra domus, si splendida mensa, quid inde?
Si species auri, atque argenti massa, quid inde?
Si tibi sponsa decens, si sit generosa, quid inde?
Si tibi sint nati, si prædia magna, quid inde?
Si fueris pulcher, fortis, divesve, quid inde?
Longus servorum si serviat ordo, quid inde?
Si doceas alios in quâlibet arte, quid inde?
Si rideat mundus, si prospera cuncta, quid inde?
Si prior aut abbas, si rex, si papa, quid inde?
Si rota fortunæ te tollat ad astra, quid inde?
Annis si felix regnes mille, quid inde?
Tam cito prætereunt hæc omnia, quæ nihil inde?
Sola manet virtus, quâ glorificabimur inde.
Ergo deo servi; quia sat tibi provenit inde;
Quod fecisse volens in tempore quo morieris
Hoc facias juvenis, dum corpore sanus haberis.
Quod nobis concedas, deus noster. Amen."

22. Wednesday. Drank tea at Signor Lagoanere's. Saw the ladies drink chocolate in the Spanish fashion. A servant brought in a salver, with a number of tumblers of clean, clear glass, full of cold water, and a plate of cakes, which were light pieces of sugar. Each lady took a tumbler of water and a piece of sugar, dipped her sugar in her tumbler of water, eat the one, and drank the other. The servant then brought in another salver, of cups of hot chocolate. Each lady took a cup and drank it, and then cakes and bread and butter were

served; then each lady took another cup of cold water, and here ended the repast. The ladies were Señora Lagoanere, and the lady of the Commandant of Artillery, the Consul's sister, and another. The Administrator of the King's Tobacco, the French Consul, and another gentleman, with Mr. Dana, Mr. Thaxter, and myself, made the company.

Three Spanish ships of the line and two French frigates came into this harbor this afternoon. A packet arrived here yesterday from Havana. The Administrator gave me a map of Gibraltar, and the Spanish ships about it by sea, and lines by land.

Orders of Ecclesiastics.—Dominicans, Franciscans, Augustines, only, at Corunna. Nuns of Ste. Barbe, Capuchins.

24. Friday. Dined on board the Belle Poule with the officers of the Galatea and the Belle Poule.

25. Saturday. Christmas. Went to the Palace at eleven o'clock to take my leave of his Excellency. Mr. O'Hara, the Governor of the town, went with me. The General repeated a thousand obliging things which he had said to me when I first saw him and dined with him.

26. Sunday. At half after two we mounted our carriages and mules, and rode four leagues to Betanzos, the ancient capital of the kingdom of Galicia, and the place where the archives are still kept. We saw the building, a long, square, stone building, without any roof, opposite the church. There are in this place two churches and two convents. The last league of the road was very bad, mountainous, and rocky to such a degree as to be very dangerous. Mr. Lagoancre did us the honor to bear us company to this place. It would appear romantic to describe the house, the beds, and the people.

27. Monday. Travelled from Betanzos to Castillano. The roads still mountainous and rocky. We broke one of our axletrees, early in the day, which prevented us from going more than four leagues in the whole.

The house where we lodge is of stone, two stories high. We entered into the kitchen,—no floor but the ground, and no carpet but straw, trodden into mire by men, hogs, horses, mules, &c. In the middle of the kitchen was a mound, a little raised with earth and stone, upon which was a fire, with pots, kettles, skillets, &c. of the fashion of the country, about it. There was no chimney. The smoke ascended, and found no other passage than through two holes drilled through the tiles of the roof, not perpendicularly over the fire, but at angles of about forty-five degrees. On one side was a flue oven, very large, black, smoky, and sooty; on the opposite side of the fire was a cabin filled with straw, where I suppose the patron della casa, that is, the master of the house, his wife, and four children, all pigged in together. On the same floor with the kitchen was the stable; there was a door which parted the kitchen and stable, but this was always open, and the floor of the stable was covered with miry straw like the kitchen. I went into the stable, and saw it filled on both sides with mules belonging to us and several other travellers, who were obliged to put up by the rain.

The smoke filled every part of the kitchen, stable, and other parts of the house as thick as possible, so that it was very difficult to see or breathe. There was a flight of steps of stone, from the kitchen floor up into a chamber, covered with mud and straw; on the left hand, as you ascended the stairs, was a stage built up about half way from the kitchen floor to the chamber floor; on this stage was a bed of straw on which lay a fatting hog. Around the kitchen fire were arranged the man, woman, four children, all the travellers, servants, muleteers, &c. The chamber had a large quantity of Indian corn in ears, hanging over head upon sticks and pieces of slit work—perhaps an hundred bushels; in one corner was a large bin full of rape seed or colza; on the other side, another bin full of oats. In another part of the chamber lay a bushel or two of chestnuts, two frames for beds, straw beds upon them, a table in the middle. The floor had never been washed nor swept for an hundred years; smoke, soot, dirt everywhere; two windows in the chamber, that is, port-holes, without any glass; wooden doors to open and shut before the windows. Yet, amidst all these horrors, I slept better than I have done before since my arrival in Spain.

28. Tuesday. Went from Castillan to Baamonde. The first part of the road very bad; the latter part tolerable. The whole country we have passed is very mountainous and rocky. There is here and there a valley, and here and there a farm that looks beautifully cultivated; but in general the mountains are covered with furze, and are not well cultivated. I am astonished to see so few trees; scarce an elm, oak, or any other tree to be seen; a very few walnut trees, and a very few fruit trees.

At Baamonde we stop until to-morrow, to get a new axletree to one of our calashes. The house where we now are is better than our last night's lodgings. We have a chamber for seven of us to lodge in. We shall lay our beds upon tables, seats, and chairs, or the floor, as last night. We have no smoke, and less dirt; but the floor was never washed, I believe. The kitchen and stable are below as usual, but in better order. The fire in the middle of the kitchen; but the air holes pierced through the tiles of the roof draw up the smoke, so that one may sit at the fire without inconvenience. The mules, hogs, fowls, and human inhabitants live, however, all together below, and cleanliness seems never to be thought of. Our calashes and mules are worth describing. We have three calashes in company; in one of them I ride with my two children, John and Charles; in another, go Mr. Dana and Mr. Thaxter; in a third, Mr. Allen and Sam Cooper Johonnot. Our three servants ride on mules. Sometimes the gentlemen mount the servants' mules; sometimes the children; sometimes all walk. The calashes are like those in use in Boston fifty years ago; there is finery about them in brass nails and paint; but the leather is very old, and never felt oil since it was made; the tackling is broken, and tied with twine and cords, &c.; but these merit a more particular description. The furniture of the mules is equally curious. This country is a hundred years behind the Massachusetts Bay in the repair of roads, and in all conveniences for travelling. The natural description of a mule may be spared. Their ears are shorn close to the skin; so are their necks, backs, rumps, and tails, at least half way to the end; they are lean, but very strong and sure-footed, and seem to be well shod. The saddles have large ears, and large rims or ridges round behind; they have a breastplate before, and a breech-band behind; they have large wooden stirrups made like boxes in a semicircular form, close at one end, open at the other, in which you insert your foot, which is well defended by them against rain and sloughs; the wooden boxes are bound round with iron. We have magnificent curb bridles to two or three; the rest are guided by halters; and there is a halter as well as a curb-bridle to each of the others. There are wallets or saddle-bags on each, made with canvas, in which we carry bread and cheese, meat, knives and forks, spoons, apples, and nuts. Mr. Lagoanere told us, that the original of the affair of St. Jago was this: A shepherd saw a bright light there in the night. Afterwards it was revealed to an archbishop that St. James was buried there. This laid the foundation of a church; and they have built an altar on the spot where the shepherd saw the light. Some time since, the people made a vow, that if the Moors should be driven from the country, they would give so much of the income of their lands to St. James. The Moors were driven away, and it was reported that St. James was in the battle on horseback, with a drawn sword, and the people fulfilled their vows by paying the tribute; but lately a Duke of Alva, a descendant of the famous Duke, has refused to pay for his estate, which has occasioned a law suit, which is carried by appeal to Rome. The Duke attempted to prove that St. James was never in Spain. The Pope has suspended it. This looks like a ray of light. Upon the supposition that this is the place of sepulture of St. James, there are great numbers of pilgrims who visit it every year, from France, Spain, Italy, and other parts of Europe, many of them on foot. St. Jago is called the capital of Galicia, because it is the seat of the archbishop, and because St. James is its patron; but Corunna is in fact the capital, as it is the residence of the governor, the audiencia, &c. &c.

30. Thursday. At Lugo, where we arrived yesterday. We passed yesterday the river Minho, which originates in the Mountains of Asturias, and flows through Portugal. We went to see the Cathedral at Lugo, which is very rich. A youth came to me in the street, and said he was a Bostonian, a son of Mr. Thomas Hickling; went a privateering in an English vessel, and was taken by the Spaniards; unfortunately taken, he said. Unfortunately enlisted, I said. He wanted to make his fortune, he said. Out of your country, and by fighting against your country? said I. Two Irish gentlemen came to pay their respects to me,—Michael Meagher O'Reilly and Lewis O'Brien. O'Brien afterwards sent me a meat-pie and a minced-pie and two bottles of Frontenac wine, which gave us a fine supper.

Arrived at Gallego in very good season, having made six leagues and a half from Lugo. Mountainous, but not dangerous as heretofore. About a league back we passed over a large bridge, over a river called Caracedo, which empties itself into the Minho, not far from Lugo.

I see nothing but signs of poverty and misery among the people. A fertile country, not half cultivated, people ragged and dirty, and the houses universally nothing but mire, smoke, fleas, and lice. Nothing appears rich but the churches; nobody fat but the clergy. The roads, the worst without exception that ever were passed, in a country where it would be easy to make them very good. No symptoms of commerce, or even of internal traffic; no appearance of manufactures or industry.

We are obliged in this journey to carry our own beds, blankets, sheets, pillows, &c.; our own provisions of chocolate, tea, sugar, meat, wine, spirits, and every thing that we want. We get nothing at the taverns but fire, water, and salt. We carry our own butter, cheese, and, indeed, salt and pepper, too.

31. Friday. Rode from Gallego to Sebrero, seven leagues. The journey, yesterday and to-day, has been very agreeable; the weather remarkably fair and dry; and the roads not so bad as we expected. There is the grandest profusion of wild, irregular mountains, that I ever saw; yet labored and cultivated, every one to its summit. The fields of grain are all green. We passed a range of mountains that were white with snow; and there were here and there banks of snow on the mountains we passed over, but no frost at all in the ground. We are now on the highest ground of all, and within gun-shot of the line between Galice and Leon. The houses all along are small, and of stone; some covered with brick tile, some with tile of stone, but chiefly with thatch. They interweave a shrub, of which they make brooms, among the straw, and bind both together with withes. These thatched roofs are very numerous, but universally dirty and smoky. The people wear broad-brimmed hats or caps made of woollen cloth, like their coats, jackets, and breeches, which are all of a color, made of black sheep's wool, without dyeing. The Mauregatos are dressed particularly in a greasy leathern jacket, &c.; but these people will be hereafter more exactly described. Endnote 101 The mules, the asses, the cattle, sheep, hogs, &c. of this country, ought to be more particularly remarked.

1780.

January 1. Saturday. Arrived at Villafranca, seven leagues. The road at first was very bad,—steep, sharp pitches, ragged rocks, &c. We then came into the road of Leon, which is made seemingly out of a rock; it was an excellent road for a league and a half. We then came to a river, and travelled along the banks of it for some leagues. This way was as bad as the other was good,—miry, rocky, up and down, until we came into a new road, about two leagues from Villafranca. Here we found a road again, made entirely by art, at an immense expense; but it seems to be made for ever. They are going on with the work. This work is an honor to the nation. It shows that improvements are coming in, and that attention is paid to the ease, convenience, utility, commerce, &c. of the people. The country we have travelled over to-day is the greatest curiosity I ever beheld,—an uninterrupted succession of mountains of a vast height. The river Valcarce flows between two rows of mountains, rising on each hand to a vast height—the most grand, sublime, awful objects; yet they are cultivated up to their highest summits. There are flourishing fields of grain on such steep declivities, near the summits of mountains, as I cannot conceive it possible for horses or cattle to stand upon them to plough. It must be done with mules; and I know not even how these, or men either, could stand. The houses are uniformly the same through the whole country, hitherto,—common habitations for men and beasts; the same smoky, filthy holes; not one decent house have I seen from Corunna. We passed this day the ruins of an ancient castle of the Moors, on the summit of one of the steepest and one of the highest and one of the most rugged mountains. There are in Villafranca three parish churches, one convent of men, and one of women. There is an old brick castle, built in feudal times, when lord was at war with lord—a defence against lances, bows and arrows, and no more; possibly against musket balls.

This evening I bought a mule, saddle, bridle, &c. for sixty-two dollars and a half.

A Description of my Postilion.

A little hat covered with oil cloth, flapped before; a black silk cap of curious work, with a braided tail hanging down his back in the Spanish fashion; a cotton handkerchief, spotted red and white, around his neck; a double-breasted short jacket and breeches.

2. Sunday. Rode from Villafranca del Vierzo, Rio Pte. We dined at Ponferrada. We passed through several villages, and over bridges and rivers. We passed Campo de Narraya, Cacabelos, Rio P. and Ponferrada, where we dined. The country grows smoother.

3. Monday. Rode to Astorga. We passed through the town and country of the Mauregatos. The town is small, stands on a brook in a great plain. We met coaches and genteel people as we went into Astorga.

4. Tuesday. Found clean beds and no fleas for the first time in Spain. Walked twice round the walls of the city, which are very ancient. Saw the road to Leon and Bayonne, and the road to Madrid. There is a pleasant prospect of the country from the walls. Saw the market of vegetables, onions, and turnips—the largest I ever saw—cabbages, carrots, &c.; saw the market of fuel, wood, coal, turf, and brush. Saw numbers of the Mauregato women, as fine as squaws, and a great deal more nasty; crucifixes, beads and chains, ear-rings and finger-rings, in silver, brass, glass, &c. about their necks, &c. Saw the cathedral, which is the most magnificent I have yet seen in Spain. Saw the parliament-house or Casa del Ciudad, where the Corregidor and city magistrates assemble to deliberate, and to execute the orders of the king.

This day was brought me the Gazette de Madrid of the 24th of December, in which is this article:

"Coruña, 15 de Diciembre. Hoy mismo han llegado á esta Plaza el Caballero Juan Adams, miembro del Congreso Americano y su Ministro Plenipotenciario á la Corte de Paris, y Mr. Deane, Secretario de Embaxada, quienes salieron de Boston, el 15 de Noviembre ultimo, á bordo de la Fregata Francesa de Guerra la Sensible, que entró en el Ferrol el dia 8 del corriente. Trahe la noticia de que habiendo los Ingleses evacuado a Rhode Island y retirado todas sus tropas a Nueva Yorck, los Americanos tomaron posesion de todos los puestos evacuados."

The Names of the Owner of the Post-Chaises, the Postilions, and the two Lads on Foot, who are with me and my Suite.

Senior Raymon San, the owner of all the post-chaises and the mules that draw them, and the man with whom Mr. Lagoanere made the contract.

Senior Eusebio Seberino, the postilion that drives my chaise.

Diego Antonio, the postilion that drives Mr. Allen and S. C. Johonnot.

Josef Diaz, the postilion that drives Mr. Dana and Mr. Thaxter.

The writer educated at St. Jago.

Juan Blanco. Bernardo Bria.

This afternoon a genteel Spaniard came to my lodgings to offer me all sorts of services and good offices, and to inquire if I wanted any kind of assistance, or if I wanted cash. Said he had received a letter from Mr. Lagoanere, at Corunna, desiring him to afford me every aid in his power, and to furnish me with money if I wanted. I thanked him, and desired him to thank Mr. Lagoanere, but to assure him that I wanted nothing, and that I had got so far very well.

5. Wednesday. Rode from Astorga to Leon, eight leagues. This is one great plain; the road very fine; great flocks of sheep and cattle. The sheep of a handsome size, the fleeces of wool thick, long, and extremely fine; the soil rather thin and barren. We passed several small villages. The vast range of Asturias Mountains covered with snow on our left; the weather as pleasant as could be, though cold; some frost and ice on the roads. We passed the river and bridge, or bigo, which in the spring, when swelled with the freshets of melted snow from the mountains of Asturias, is a very great river. Leon, which we entered in the night, has the appearance of a large city.

6. Thursday. Went to view the Cathedral, which is magnificent, but not equal to that at Astorga, if to that at Lugo. It was the day of the Feast of the King, and we happened to be at the celebration of high mass. We saw the procession of the bishop and of all the canons, in rich habits of silk, velvet, silver, and gold. The bishop, as he turned the corners of the church, spread out his hand to the people, who all prostrated themselves on their knees as he passed. Our guide told us we must do the same; but I contented myself with a bow. Went to see the Council Chamber of the Bishop and Chapter, hung with crimson damask; the seats all round, crimson velvet. This room and a smaller, where the bishop sometimes took aside some of the canons, were very elegant.

Saw the Casa del Ciudad, and the old castle of King Alphonsus, which is said to be one thousand nine hundred and thirty-six years old; it is of stone, and the work very neat. But there is no appearance of commerce, manufactures, or industry. The houses are low, built of brick and mud and pebble-stones from the fields. No market worth notice. Nothing looks either rich or cheerful but the churches and churchmen. There is a statue of Charles V. in this church, but very badly done. There is a school of St. Mark, as it is called,—an institution for the education of noble youths, here in mathematics and philosophy.

Dined in Leon. Got into our carriages and upon our mules about one o'clock to proceed on our journey. Passed the new bridge of Leon, which is a beautiful new piece of work; it is all of stone. The river which comes down from the mountains of Asturias is not now very large; but in the spring, when the snows melt upon the mountains, it is swelled by the freshes to a very great size. This river runs also down into the kingdom of Portugal. Not long after, we passed another bridge and river, which the peasants told me to call Rio y Puente de Villarente. This river also comes down from the Asturias, and flows down into Portugal. We passed through several very little villages, in every one of which we saw the young people, men and women, dancing a dance that they call fandango. One of the young women beats a machine, somewhat like a section of a drum; it is covered with parchment. She sings and beats on her drum, and the company dance, with each a pair of clackers in his and her hand. The clackers are two pieces of wood cut handsomely enough, which they have the art to rattle in their hands to the time of the drum. They had all, males and females, wooden shoes in the Spanish fashion, which is, mounted on stilts. We stopped once to look, and a man came out with a bottle of wine and a glass to treat us. We drank his wine in complaisance to his urbanity, though it was very sour; and I ordered our guide to give him something. We stop to-night at a village called Mansilla, through which runs another large river from the Asturias, stretching down to Portugal. A great stone bridge over it appears to have been half carried away by the water in some freshet. This was once a walled city. The towers are yet standing all round the town, and the ruins and fragments of the wall, and the appearance of a fosse round it. The towers were all made of small, round stones, not bigger than two fists, which is the only kind of stone to be had here. The cement is the ancient, which is as hard and as durable as the stones themselves. I went upon the top of one of the towers with Mr. D., Mr. A., and Mr. Charles. The town appears to be gone to decay, yet there are four or five churches here still.

There are in Leon two convents of Franciscans, one of Dominicans, one of St. Claudio Benito. One convent of nuns of St. Benito, one of the Conception, one of Descalzas, one of Recoletas.

Canonigos.

Casa de San Isidoro, one; one casa de San Marcos; nine parish churches, including the cathedral.

The grandee, who is the proprietor of the land in and about Leon, is the Comte de Luna, a descendant from the ancient kings of Leon. He resides in Madrid, and receives about sixty thousand ducats, or about thirty thousand dollars a year of rent from the tenants, partly in cash, and partly in grain. He has a secretary and some other agents, who reside at Leon, to collect his rents. The grandees of Spain all reside at Madrid. Former kings, in order to break up the barons' wars, called all the nobles to Court, and gave them employments.

I have not seen a chimney in Spain, except one of the French Consul at Corunna; one or two half imitations of chimneys in the kitchen are all that I have seen. The weather is very cold; the frosts hard, and no fire when we stop, but a few coals or a flash of brush in the kitchen, full of smoke and dirt, and covered with a dozen pots and kettles, and surrounded by twenty people looking like chimney-sweepers.

8. Saturday. Rode from San Juan de Sahagun to Paredes de Nava. We have passed through a village every league. The villages are all built of mud and straw; they have no timber, nor wood, nor stone. The villages all appear going to decay. Every village has churches and convents enough in it to ruin it and the whole country round about it, even if they had nothing to pay to the king or the landlord; but all three together, church, state, and nobility, exhaust the people to such a degree, I have no idea of the possibility of deeper wretchedness. There are in this little village four parish churches and two convents; one of monks, and one of nuns of the order of St. Francis. The parish churches and their curates are supported here by the tithes paid by the people. They pay every tenth pound of wool, every tenth part of wine, grain, honey; in short, of every thing. The good curates sometimes alleviate the severity of this by compositions or modus. The archbishop has power to do every thing for the good of the people, that is, to make new parishes, or alter old ones, at his pleasure. There are but four archbishops in Spain. The Archbishop of St. Jago has one hundred and eighty thousand ducats of rent a year. This war is popular in Spain; the clergy,

the religious houses, and other communities have offered to grant large sums to the King for the support of it. The English had become terrible to them. From Astorga to this place, the face of the country is altered; it is a plain. But there is little appearance of improvement, industry, or cultivation. No trees of any kind scarcely; no forest, or timber, or fruit trees. Scarcely any fences, except a few mud walls for sheepfolds.

11. Tuesday. Arrived at Burgos. We came from Sallada el Camino, four leagues. We had fog and rain and snow all the way; very chilly and raw. When we arrived at the tavern, (which is the best in the city, as I am informed, and my servant went to examine the others,) we found no chimney. A pan of coals in a chamber, without a chimney, was all the heat we could get. We went to view the cathedral, which is ancient and very large. The whole building is supported upon four great pillars, the largest I ever saw. Round the great altar are represented our Saviour, from the scene of his agony on the mount, when an angel presents him the cup, to his crucifixion between two thieves, his descent from the cross, and his ascension into heaven. The chapels round the great altar are the largest I have seen. Round the altar the several stages are represented: 1. The Agony in the Garden; 2. Carrying the Cross; 3. Crucifixion between Two Thieves; 4. Descent; 5. Ascension. There is no archbishopric at Burgos. There was one, which made five, but the king abolished it; and now there are but four in the whole kingdom. There is a chapel of St. Jago. Went into three booksellers' shops to search for a chart or map of Spain, but could find none, except a very small and erroneous one in a Compendio of History of Spain. It is five and twenty years that I have been almost constantly journeying and voyaging, and I have often undergone severe trials, great hardships, cold, wet, heat, fatigue, bad rest, want of sleep, bad nourishment, &c. &c. but I never experienced any thing like this journey. Every individual person in company has a great cold. We go along sneezing and coughing, as if we were fitter for an hospital than for travellers on the road. My servant and all the other servants in company behave worse than ever I knew servants behave; they are dull, inactive, unskilful. The children are sick, and in short my patience was never so near being exhausted as at present. Mr. Thaxter is as shiftless as a child; he understands no language, neither French nor Spanish; and he don't seem to think himself obliged to do any thing but get along and write his journal. In short, I am in a deplorable situation indeed. I know not what to do. I know not where to go. From this place we go to Monasterio, which is four leagues; from thence to Birviesca, which is four more; from thence to Santa Maria del Corbo, which is two more; from thence to Corbo, which is one; thence to Pancorbo, which is two, where the road parts to Vittoria and to Bilbao.

Thirteen leagues to the parting of the roads.

I have taken a walk about the town a little. A river runs directly through the town, and there are several bridges over it. There is a great number of monasteries in it. There is an old ruined castle on a hill. But I have not had time to see much. There is a little appearance of business here; some trades. We passed through several villages this day, and rode along a river, and arrived at Birviesca. The country a little more hilly than for some time past; but it has a naked and poor appearance.

12. Wednesday. Arrived at Birviesca, where there are two convents; one of men, the other of women, both Franciscans, and two parish churches.

The tavern we are in is a large house, and there are twelve good beds in it for lodgers; yet no chimneys, and the same indelicacy as in all the others,—smoke and dirt; yet they give us clean sheets. A Spanish kitchen is one of the greatest curiosities in the world, and they are all very much alike.

13. Thursday. Rode from Birviesca to Pancorbo, where we dined. We passed through Corbo, which is a little village with half a dozen other small villages in sight. In every one of

them is a church. Pancorbo is at the beginning of the rocks. There is the appearance of an ancient carriage-way up the steepest part of the rocks. We passed between the rows of mountains, consisting wholly of rocks, the most lofty and craggy precipices that I ever saw. These rocky mountains made the boundary between the ancient Castile and Biscay. Pancorbo is the last village in old Castile. At Puente de la Rada we were stopped by a number of officers, and asked if we had a passport. I produced my passport of the Governor of Galicia; they read it with much respect, and let us pass. We came four good leagues this afternoon, and are now at Ezpexo.

We are now at the best public house that I have seen. Yet the kitchen is a Spanish kitchen, like all the others, and there is no chimney in the house. There is not a tavern we have been in, but is filled with religious prints and images. The chamber where I now write has two beds; at the head of each is a delft vessel for holy water, aqua santa or aqua benita; at the head of each also is a neat cross, about nine inches long, with an image of Jesus Christ in some metal,—tin, bell-metal, pewter,—upon it. Upon the wall is a picture of la Vierge de Montcarmel or Virgo Maria de Monte Carmelo; a great number of others, that I have not patience to transcribe. From Ezpexo, where we are now, we go to Orduña, which is four leagues, and to Bilbao, which is six.

14. Friday. Rode from Ezpexo to Orduña, four leagues. The road is made all the way at a great expense; but the descent of the mountains of Orduña is a great curiosity. These mountains are chiefly rocks of a vast height. But a road has been blown out of the rocks from the height of the mountains, quite down into the valley. After winding round and round a great way, and observing the marks of the drills remaining in the rocks, the road at last came to a steep, where the only method of making a road for a carriage up and down is by serpentining it. There is a fertile valley, and well-cultivated, at the feet of these mountains, in the centre of which is the village of Orduña.

In this narrow space they have crowded two convents; one of Frailes, the other of Monjas. I saw the lazy drones of Franciscans at the windows of their cells, as we passed. At the bottom of the mountains we had a small toll to pay for the support of the road. The Administrator sent to search our trunks; but we sent him our passports, which produced a polite message by his clerk, that he had seen my name in the Gazette; that he was very glad I was arrived; wished me success and prosperity, and desired to know if I wanted any thing, or if he could be any way useful to me. I returned the message, that I was obliged, &c., but wanted nothing. In the afternoon we followed the road which pursues the course of a little river, which originates in the mountains of Orduña, and rode down between two rows of mountains to Lugiano, where we put up for the night, four leagues from Bilbao. It is as dirty and uncomfortable a house as almost any we have seen. We have met, to-day and yesterday, great numbers of mules loaded with merchandises from Bilbao. The mules and their drivers look very well in comparison of those we have seen before. Their burdens are salted-fish, sardines, cod, and a sort of fish that we see here very plenty, called besugo. They carry also horseshoes, ready made, in Bilbao, to sell in various parts of the kingdom. The mountains of Biscay, of Bilbao, of Orduña and Pancorbo, for by these names they are called, are the most remarkable that I have seen. Philip V. made the first carriage-road through those of Pancorbo; the present King has done most to those of Orduña. It was a vexatious thing to see the beautiful valley of Orduña devoured by so many hives of drones. It is a beautiful, a fertile, and a well-cultivated spot, almost the only one we have yet seen in Biscay capable of cultivation.

15. Saturday. Followed the road by the side of the river, between two rows of mountains, until we opened upon Bilbao. We saw the Sugar Loaf some time before. This is a mountain

in the shape of a pyramid, which is called the Sugar-Loaf. The town is surrounded with mountains.

The tavern where we are is tolerable, situated between a church and a monastery. We have been entertained with the music of the convent since our arrival.

Soon after our arrival, Captain Babson and Captain Lovat made us a visit. Lovat is bound for America the first wind, and Babson very soon, both in letters of marque.

Took a walk down the river, which is pleasant enough. While we were absent upon our walk, Mr. Gardoqui and son came to visit me.

16. Sunday. Reposed and wrote.

17. Monday. Dined with the two Messrs. Gardoquis and a nephew of theirs. After dinner, the gentlemen accompanied us to the parish church over the way; then to the old parish church of St. Jago, which was certainly standing in the year 1300. The high altar appears very ancient, wrought in wooden figures, the work very neat. The choir and the sacristy, &c. as in all others. We then went to the Chambers of the Board of Trade. This is a curious institution; on a certain day, annually, in the beginning of January, all the merchants of Bilbao meet, write their names on a ball or ballot, which is put into a box, from whence four are drawn by lot. These four name a certain number of counsellors or senators. But this must be further inquired into. This board of trade first endeavors to make all disputing merchants agree; if they cannot succeed, application must be made to the board, by petition in writing. It is then heard and determined, subject to an appeal somewhere. There is no consul here from France, England, or Holland, nor any other nation. The Board of Trade oppose it. The chamber is hung round with pictures of the present King and Queen, the late King and Queen, &c.; with pictures of the Royal Exchange, London, the Exchange of Amsterdam, of Antwerp, &c. Captains Babson, Lovat, and Wickes, dined with us. I spoke to Mr. Gardoqui in behalf of fifteen American prisoners escaped from Portugal, and he consented to furnish them clothes to the amount of six dollars a man. I told him I had no authority, and that I could not assure him repayment, but I believed Congress would do all in their power to repay him.

There is an academy at Bergara for the youth of Biscay, Guipuscoa, and Alava. Yesterday, a Mr. Maroni, an Irish gentleman, came to visit me.

The lands in Biscay are chiefly in the hands of the people,—few lordships. The Duke of Berwick and the Duke de Medina Cœli have some estates here, but not considerable. In the spring freshes, the water is deep enough upon 'change and in the streets for vessels of one hundred tons to float.

18. Tuesday. Spent the day in walking about the town. Walked round the wharf upon the river, through the market. Saw a plentiful market of fruit and vegetables, cabbages, turnips, carrots, beets, onions, &c.; apples, pears, &c.; raisins, figs, nuts, &c. Went as far as the gate where we entered the town; then turned up the mountain, by the stone stairs, and saw fine gardens, verdure, and vegetation. Returned, and viewed a bookseller's stall; then walked in succession through every street in the town. Afterwards met Messrs. Gardoquis, who went with us to show us a number of shops,—glass-shops, china-shops, trinket-shops, toy-shops, and cutlery-shops. I did not find any thing very great. There are several stores and shops, however, pretty large and pretty full.

19. Wednesday. Went down the river, on a visit to the Rambler, a letter of marque of eighteen guns, belonging to Mr. Andrew Cabot, of Beverly, Captain Lovat, Commander; and the Phœnix, a brig of fourteen guns, belonging to Messrs. Tracys at Newburyport, Captain Babson, Commander. We were honored with two salutes of thirteen guns each, by Babson, and with one by Lovat. We dined at the tavern on shore, and had an agreeable day. Went to

see a new packet of the King's on the stocks, and his new ropewalks, which are two hundred and ten fathoms long.

20. Thursday. [Although we endeavored in Bilbao to take as much exercise as possible, and to amuse ourselves as well as we could, and although the attention and hospitality of the house of Gardoqui had done every thing in their power to oblige us, our residence in this place was, nevertheless, very far from being comfortable. We were all sick with violent colds and coughs; some of the servants and children were so ill, that we lived under gloomy apprehensions of being detained a long time, and perhaps losing some of our company. The houses here, as well as everywhere else, were without chimneys, fires, or windows; and we could find none of those comforts and conveniences to which we had been all accustomed from the cradle, nor any of that sweet and quiet repose in sleep, upon which health and happiness so much depend. On the twentieth, however, we summoned resolution enough to take our departure from Bilbao, and passing over a mountainous country and very bad roads, arrived at the river, or rather the brook, that divides Spain from France. The houses in Biscay and Guipuscoa appeared to be larger and more convenient than those in Galicia, Castile, or Leon, but the public houses were much the same. In the last house in Spain we found one chimney, which was the only one we saw since we left that in the house of M. Déstournelles, the French Consul in Corunna. In our course we saw a few villages, and particularly Fontarabia, at a distance. We reached St. John de Luz, the first village in France, and there we dined; and never was a captive escaped from prison more delighted than I was; for every thing here was clean, sweet, and comfortable, in comparison of any thing we had found in any part of Spain.

23. Sunday. We arrived at Bayonne. Here we paid off our Spanish guide, with all his train of horses, calashes, wagon, mules, and servants. To do them justice, they had always shown a disposition to assist and be friendly to the utmost of their power; and we had no cause to complain of any improper behavior in any of them. I was obliged to sell my mule, for which I was very sorry, as he was an excellent animal, and has served me very well. I sold him for what he cost me. We purchased a post-chaise, and hired some others for our journey. I made my visit to the Governor, and received his in return.

25. Tuesday. We commenced our journey to Bordeaux. There is so much heath and uncultivated land, and so many desolate places between Bayonne and Bordeaux, that the journey could not be very pleasant. It is a region where one might expect to meet robbers; but the police of France was so vigilant and decisive, that nothing of that kind was heard of at that time in any part of France. The road in general was better, because it was smoother than in any of the great paved roads of the kingdom. We found the entertainment at all the inns comfortable; the horses and carriages as alert and convenient as they are commonly in France; and I was too happy to be very anxious to make observations on minor things.

29. Saturday. We arrived at Bordeaux. We had met couriers, and received letters on the road, inviting us to alight at all the principal inns in Bordeaux. The reputation of entertaining the American Ambassador must have been the motive to all this zeal; for our number was so small, that the profit to be made of us could not be great. As all the public houses were alike unknown to me, I ordered our postilion to drive us to the best house in the city, and left it to his judgment to determine.

30. Sunday. We dined at the Hôtel d'Angleterre, at the invitation of Mr. Bondfield, in company with Sir Robert Finlay, M. Le Texier, and others. In the evening we went to the Comedy, where we saw Amphitryon and Cartouche.]

31. Monday. Mr. A. L. at Paris, Mr. I. at Amsterdam, Mr. W. L. at Brussels.

February 1. Tuesday. Dined yesterday at the Hôtel d'Angleterre, with Mr. MacCreery, Mr. Delap, Mr. Vernon, Mr. Bondfield and my company, at the invitation of Sir Robert Finlay.

Towards evening, Mr. Cabarrus came in with the news of the blow struck by Rodney upon the Spaniards off Gibraltar.

5. Saturday. On Wednesday, the second of February, we took post for Paris, and on Friday, the 4th, arrived at Coué, where we lodged; but in the night it rained and froze at the same time, until the roads were a glare of ice, so that the postilions informed us it was impossible for their horses, which in this country are never frosted, to go. We passed by Angoulême yesterday morning, and encircled almost the whole town. It stands upon a high hill, and is walled all round; a fine, airy, healthy situation, with several streams of water below it, and fine interval lands. The river Charente runs by it. The lands are chiefly cultivated with vines, from Bordeaux to this place, which offered but a poor prospect in the winter in some places. Wheat is sown, and vines planted, alternately, in ridges. Great numbers of the vineyards are in a soil that has the greatest appearance of poverty. It is a red loam, intermixed with so many pebbles, or small stones, of a reddish color, that it looks like a heap of stones or a dry gravel. One would think there was not earth enough for the vines to take root. Other vineyards are in a black sand intermixed with a few small stones; others in fine, black, fat, mellow mould. The numerous groves, parks, and forests, in this country, form a striking contrast with Spain, where the whole country looks like a man's face that is newly shaved; every tree, bush, and shrub, being pared away.

[The first insinuation of the propriety, expediency, and necessity, of appointing a minister plenipotentiary, to reside in Europe, ready to negotiate a peace whenever he might be invited to it, was made to Congress a year before this time, by M. Gérard, the French Minister at Philadelphia, by the authority of the Count de Vergennes. But Congress had neglected it, whether from a general opinion that the time had not yet arrived when there was a necessity for it, or whether from the difficulty of agreeing on a minister, I know not. The suggestion was renewed by the Chevalier de la Luzerne, upon his arrival in Philadelphia. In both cases, it was the expectation of the French Ministry, that Dr. Franklin would be elected. In this respect, Congress disappointed them. In another point too, that is, in the commission to make a treaty of commerce with Great Britain, Congress had gone further than the French Ministry intended. Alone as I was in both commissions, and feeling the whole weight of the trust reposed in me, I determined to proceed with the utmost caution, deliberation, and prudence; to do nothing which should excite the smallest jealousy in the French Court, or give our enemies, the English, the least advantage of the United States or their allies. But something appeared to be incumbent on me to do.

Accordingly, I began by writing to the Count de Vergennes the following letter:

John Adams

TO THE COUNT DE VERGENNES.

Paris, 12 February, 1780

Sir:—

Having obtained permission from your Excellency yesterday, when I did myself the honor to wait on you at Versailles, to write on the subject of my mission, I have now the honor to acquaint you, that on the 29th day of September last, the Congress of the United States of America did me the honor to elect me their plenipotentiary to negotiate a peace with Great Britain, and also to negotiate a treaty of commerce with that kingdom; and Mr. Francis Dana, member of Congress, and of the Council of Massachusetts Bay, secretary to both commissions.

As I was not at Congress when this transaction took place, I am not able to inform your Excellency very particularly of the rise and progress of it. But from conversation with gentlemen at Boston, who were members of Congress, and from private letters, I learned in general, that it was not the result of any sudden deliberation, or the fruit of any particular event of the war, prosperous or adverse, but a measure that has been more than a year under consideration, and finally agreed to on this principle, that as it was uncertain at what time the belligerent powers might be disposed to treat of peace, which could not be concluded without a minister from the United States, it would save a great deal of time for this power to have a minister in Europe fully authorized to treat, and in concert with ministers from the other powers at war, conclude a peace with Great Britain, and a treaty of commerce consistent with that already made with His Most Christian Majesty, and such others as might be made with other powers. I am persuaded it is the intention of my constituents, and of all America, and I am sure it is my own determination, to take no steps of consequence in pursuance of my commissions, without consulting his Majesty's ministers. And as various conjectures have been, and may be made, concerning the nature of my appointment and powers, and as it may be expected by some, that I should take some measures for announcing these to the public, or at least to the Court of London, I beg the favor of your Excellency's opinion and advice upon these questions:

1. Whether, in the present state of things, it is prudent in me to acquaint the British Ministry that I am arrived here, and that I shall be ready to treat, whenever the belligerent powers shall be inclined to treat?

2. Whether it is prudent in me to publish in any manner, more than the journals of Congress may have already done, the nature of my mission?

3. Or whether to remain on the reserve, as I have hitherto done since my arrival in Europe?

If any propositions should be made to me directly or indirectly from the British Ministry, I shall not fail to communicate them, without loss of time, to your Excellency, and I beg the favor of your Excellency, as I am the only person in Europe who has authority to treat of peace, that if any propositions on the part of Great Britain, should be made to his Majesty's ministers, that they may be communicated to me, at least as far as they may relate to the interest of the United States.

Although I am not confined by commissions, nor instructions, nor by any intimations from Congress to reside in any one place in Europe more than another, yet my own inclinations, as well as those of the public, would be most gratified, and the public service most promoted, by my residing here. I must, therefore, request his Majesty's protection and permission to reside in this kingdom for some time, with or without assuming any public character, as your Excellency may think most advisable.

I have the honor to be, &c.

John Adams.

I shall here insert the answer of the Count de Vergennes, although it is not exactly in the order of dates. It was in French, and the following is a literal translation:

Count De Vergennes

COUNT DE VERGENNES TO JOHN ADAMS.

Versailles, 15 February, 1780

Sir:—

I have received the letter, which you did me the honor to write me on the 12th of this month. I think, before I reply to the different points on which you consult me, that it is proper to wait for the arrival of M. Gérard, because he is probably the bearer of your instructions, and will certainly be able to make me better acquainted with the nature and extent of your commission. But in the mean time, I am of opinion, that it will be prudent to conceal your eventual character, and above all, to take the necessary precautions, that the object of your commission may remain unknown to the Court of London. For the rest, Sir, you may be assured, that his Majesty sees you with pleasure in his dominions, that you will constantly enjoy his protection, and the prerogatives of the law of nations, and that I in particular shall be eager to give you proofs of my confidence, as well as of the sentiments with which I have the honor to be, &c.

De Vergennes.

I request the reader to read attentively the foregoing letter from the Count de Vergennes, and make his own observations upon it, before he reads mine, and then say whether I had reasons for the following reflections which presented themselves irresistibly to my mind at that time, and which I have ever since thought, and still think, well founded.

1. The instructions of a sovereign to his ambassador are a secret and a confidential communication between them; a sacred deposit, committed by the master to the servant, which the latter is under the strongest ties of honor, fidelity, and conscience, to preserve inviolate, until he has an express permission or injunction to reveal it.

2. The Count de Vergennes had been employed in several embassies, and he had sent, and, in the name of his master, instructed many ambassadors. In short, his life had been spent in diplomatic courses. He could not, therefore, be ignorant of the sacred nature of instructions, or the obligations of ambassadors to keep them to themselves.

3. The Count had been so long in the habit of intrigues to obtain the instructions from foreign courts to their ambassadors, and probably paying for them very dear, that he had forgotten that the practice was not lawful.

4. The Count had probably instructed M. Gérard, by some means or other, to penetrate into the secrets of Congress, and obtain from some of the members, or some of the secretaries or clerks, copies of the most confidential communications between Congress and their ministers.

5. The Count expected that M. Gérard had succeeded, and would soon arrive with the trophies of his success. Of this success, however, I have doubts. Mr. Jay, with whom M. Gérard went to Europe in the same ship, can tell the world, if he will, as he has told me, the arts and importunities, even to rudeness and ill-manners, which he employed with him to obtain his instructions. If he had been successful in Pennsylvania in obtaining instructions, he would not have been so zealous to procure a duplicate copy from Mr. Jay.

6. The Count might imagine that I was so little read in the law of nations and the negotiations of ambassadors, and had so little experience in the world, or, to use one of his own expressions on another occasion, so much bonhomie, that, upon the intimation in his letter, I would, in all simplicity and naiveté, send him a copy of my instructions.

7. Some alarming ideas were excited by the consideration that my sovereign was an assembly of more than fifty members; and fifty incorruptible men, all capable of containing a secret, was not always to be expected. For the honor of that Congress, however, it is but justice to say, that I believe their secrets were as well kept as secrets ever were by any government in the world.

8. The nature of my instructions I was not at all satisfied with, and was consequently more determined to keep them from the French, as well as English and other courts. The

articles relative to the boundaries of the United States and to the fisheries were by no means agreeable to me; and I had already reasons enough to suspect, and, indeed, to believe, that the French Court, at least the Count de Vergennes, would wish me to go to the utmost extent of them in relinquishing the fisheries, and in contracting the boundaries of the United States; whereas, on the contrary, it was my unalterable determination to insist on the fisheries, and on an ample extension of our boundaries, as long as my instructions would justify me. I foresaw that if these instructions were communicated to the French, they would have it in their power, in case of a negotiation, to impart them to the British ambassador, and encourage him to insist on his part, on terms that would greatly embarrass me, and ultimately injure my country in very essential points.

Whether it was consistent with the character of a great or an honorable statesman to give me so early and so just cause of jealousy of his intentions, or not, those of the Count de Vergennes were too manifest to be mistaken in his letter. His aim plainly was to obtain from me copies, not only of my commissions, but of my most secret and confidential instructions. I was determined, however, to express no surprise, but to comply with his wishes so far as I could, with honor and safety, and no farther. I wrote him the following letter:

John Adams

TO THE COUNT DE VERGENNES.

Paris, 19 February, 1780

Sir:—

I have received the letter, which your Excellency did me the honor to write me on the 15th of this month, and lest I should not have explained sufficiently in my letter of the 12th, the nature and extent of my commissions, I have now the honor to enclose attested copies of both, as well as of that to Mr. Dana.

With regard to my instructions, I presume your Excellency will not judge it proper, that I should communicate them any further than to assure you, as I do in the fullest manner, that they contain nothing inconsistent with the letter or spirit of the treaty between his Majesty and the United States, or the most perfect friendship between France and America, but, on the contrary, the clearest orders to cultivate both. I have hitherto conducted according to your advice, having never communicated to any person since my arrival in Europe, the nature of my mission, excepting to your Excellency and Dr. Franklin, to whom it was indeed communicated by a resolution of Congress, and to him in confidence. I shall continue to conceal, as far as may depend upon me, my actual character, but I ought to observe to your Excellency, that my appointment was as notorious in America as that of Mr. Jay, or Dr. Franklin, before my departure. So it is probably already known to the Court of London, although they have not regular evidence of it. I mention this, lest some persons might charge me with publishing what I certainly did not publish.

I thank your Excellency for the assurances of his Majesty's protection, and of your confidence, which it shall be my study and endeavor at all times to deserve.

I have the honor to be, &c.

John Adams.

To this letter I received an answer, of which the following is a literal translation:

Count De Vergennes

COUNT DE VERGENNES TO JOHN ADAMS.

Versailles, 24 February, 1780

Sir:—

I have received the letter, which you have done me the honor to write me the 19th of this month. Your full powers, of which you have been pleased to send me a copy, are perfectly conformable to what M. Gérard has written to me about them, and they leave us nothing to wish for, as to the form or matter. I think there will be no inconveniency in informing the public of the principal object of your mission, I mean the future pacification. It will be announced in the Gazette of France, when that shall make mention of your presentation to the King and royal family, and it will depend on you to give your eventual character a greater publicity, by having it published in the Dutch papers. I could only wish, that you would be so kind as to communicate the article to me before you transmit it. With regard to the full powers, which authorize you to negotiate a treaty of commerce with the Court of London, I think it will be prudent not to communicate them to any body whatever, and to take all possible precautions, that the British Ministry may not have a premature knowledge of them. You will surely, of yourself, feel the motives, which induce me to advise you to this precaution, and it would be needless to explain them.

With regard to your instructions, Sir, I am satisfied that they have for their certain and invariable basis, the treaties subsisting between the King and the United States. M. Gérard has assured the King of it, in the most positive manner, and his Majesty does too much justice to the uprightness of Congress, and to the stability of the sentiments which they have hitherto manifested, to have ever entertained, or to entertain, the least doubt on this subject. This way of thinking will convince you, Sir, that we have no need of seeing your instructions, to appreciate properly the principles and dispositions of Congress towards Great Britain.

I have the honor to be, &c.

De Vergennes.

I again request the particular attention of the reader to this letter. The Count evades ingeniously enough his improper attempt to draw out my instructions from their concealment. But his anxiety to have my commission to negotiate a treaty of commerce with Great Britain concealed, excited some surprise and some perplexity. I was not clear that I suspected his true motives. The United States were clearly at as full liberty to negotiate concerning commerce as concerning peace. In both they must be governed by their treaties with France, but not in one more than the other. However, time brought to light what I but imperfectly suspected. The Count meditated at that time, no doubt, what he soon carried into execution with too much success,—his intrigues with Congress, at Philadelphia, to get my commission to negotiate a treaty of commerce annulled, without renewing it to the five commissioners whom they afterwards appointed to negotiate peace. It was intended to keep us embroiled with England as much, and as long as possible, even after a peace. It had that effect for eleven years. The United States never had spirit, decision, and independence, to remove this obstacle to a friendly understanding with England, till 1794, when Mr. Jay sacrificed, and Mr. Washington diminished his popularity, by a treaty which excited the insolent rage of France without a color of justice. The members of Congress who suffered themselves to become the instruments of the Count and of his minister, the Chevalier de la Luzerne, and his secretary, M. Marbois, in this humiliating and pernicious measure of annihilating the power of negotiating on commerce, I am not able to enumerate very exactly. Those who are disposed to investigate the subject are at liberty to do it.

I thought it most prudent at present to conform to the Count's advice, although it was not in this particular satisfactory to me, and wrote him accordingly. Although I could not perceive any candid, equitable, or honorable motives for concealing one of my commissions more than the other, I did not think proper to tell him so.

John Adams

TO THE COUNT DE VERGENNES.

Paris, 25 February, 1780

Sir:—

I had last evening the honor of Your Excellency's letter of yesterday's date, and shall conform myself to your advice.

I shall esteem myself highly honored by a presentation to the King and royal family, and shall wait your Excellency's directions concerning the time of it, and shall not think myself at liberty to make any publication of my powers to treat of peace, until it shall have been announced in the Gazette. After which, I shall transmit to your Excellency any paragraph, which may be thought proper to publish in the gazettes of Holland, and take your advice upon it, before it is sent. My other powers shall be concealed, according to your advice, and I shall have the honor to pay my respects to your Excellency very soon at Versailles.

I have the honor to be, &c.

John Adams.

Having waited from the 25th of February, to the 21st of March, without learning any thing further on the subject, I wrote to the Count again.

John Adams

TO THE COUNT DE VERGENNES.

Paris, 21 March, 1780

Sir:—

In the letter, which you did me the honor to write me on the 24th of February, your Excellency proposed, that the principal object of my mission should be inserted in the Gazette of France, when it should make mention of my presentation to the King and all the royal family.

In the answer to this letter, which I had the honor to write on the 25th of February, I informed your Excellency, that I should not think myself at liberty to make any publication of my powers to treat of peace, until they should have been announced in the Gazette. It was on the 7th of March, that I had the honor to be presented to the King and royal family, but no notice has been taken of it in the Gazette of France. Whether the omission is accidental, or whether it is owing to any alteration in your Excellency's sentiments, I am not able to determine.

Your Excellency will excuse the trouble I give you on this occasion, as it arises wholly from a desire to be able at all times, to render an account to my sovereign, of the motives and reasons of my own conduct.

I have the honor to be, &c.

John Adams.] *Endnote 102*

July 27. Thursday. Setting off on a journey with my two sons to Amsterdam. Lodged at Compiegne. Friday night, lodged at Valenciennes. Saturday, arrived at Brussels.

This road is through the finest country I have anywhere seen. The wheat, rye, barley, oats, peas, beans, and several other grains, the hemp, flax, grass, clover, lucern, sainfoin, &c. The pavements and roads are good. The rows of trees on each side the road, and around many squares of land. The vines, the cattle, the sheep, in short every thing upon this road is beautiful and plentiful. Such immense fields and heavy crops of wheat I never saw anywhere. The soil is stronger and richer than in other parts. I lodged in Brussels at L'Hôtel de l'Impératrice. The cathedral, the park, the ramparts, and canals of this town, are very well worth seeing.

30. Sunday. Went to the cathedral,—a great feast, an infinite crowd. The church more splendidly ornamented than any that I had seen, hung with tapestry. The church music here is in the Italian style. A picture in tapestry was hung up, of a number of Jews stabbing the wafer, the bon Dieu, and blood gushing in streams from the bread. This insufferable piece of pious villany shocked me beyond measure; but thousands were before it, on their knees, adoring. I could not help cursing the knavery of the priesthood and the brutal ignorance of the people; yet, perhaps, I was rash and unreasonable, and that it is as much virtue and wisdom in them to adore, as in me to detest and despise. Spent the afternoon, and drank tea with Mr. W. Lee, Mr. Jenings and his nephew, Mrs. Izard, her two daughters and son, Miss , Mrs. Lee and her children, and an agreeable circle of Americans. In the evening, Mr. Lee, Mr. Jenings and his nephew, &c., my two sons, &c., took a walk to see the canals. Vessels of some burthen come up here in the canal, which reaches to the sea. We afterwards walked upon the ramparts.

In this town is a great plenty of stone, which I think is the same with our Braintree north-common stone. It is equally hard, equally fine grain, capable of a fine polish. I think the color is a little darker than the Braintree stone. There is a new building here, before which is the statue of the late Prince Charles, in front of which are six pillars wholly of this stone; indeed, the steps and the whole front are of the same stone. This town is the capital of Brabant, in the Austrian Netherlands. The late Prince Charles was a brother of the Empress Queen,—l'Impératrice Reine—Uncle of the Emperor and the Queen of France. He was extremely beloved by the people, and has left an excellent character. The Emperor did not like him, it is said. In the late war the Emperor called upon this Prince for money. The Prince wrote to dissuade him from it. The Emperor sent again. The Prince wrote back, that he saw they were determined, and they must appoint another governor of this province, for he could not execute their orders. Upon this the imperial court desisted.

We lodged one night at Antwerp, viewed the Cathedral and the Exchange, &c., and went by Moerdyck to Rotterdam, where we arrived the 4th August.

August 5. Saturday. Lodged at the Maréchal de Turenne's; dined with Mr. Dubbledemuts; went to see the statue of Erasmus, the Exchange, the churches, &c. Mr. Dubbledemuts sent his coach in the evening, and one of his clerks. We rode round the environs of the town; then to his country seat, where we supped. The meadows are very fine; the horses and cattle large; the intermixture of houses, trees, ships, and canals, throughout this town, is very striking; the neatness here is remarkable.

6. Sunday. Went to the English Presbyterian Church, and heard a sensible sermon. The mode of worship differs in nothing from ours but in the organ, whose music joins in the singing.

1781.

January 11. Thursday. Returned from the Hague to Leyden. Was present from 12 to 1 o'clock, when the preceptor gave his lessons in Latin and Greek to my sons. His name is Wensing. He is apparently a great master of the two languages; besides which, he speaks French and Dutch very well; understands little English, but is desirous of learning it; he obliges his pupils to be industrious, and they have both made great progress for the time; he is pleased with them, and they with him. John is transcribing a Greek Grammar, of his master's composition, and Charles, a Latin one; John is also transcribing a treatise on Roman antiquities, of his master's writing. The master gives his lessons in French.

This day Doctor Waterhouse, Mr. Thaxter, and my two sons, dined with me at the Cour de Hollande, and after dinner they went to the Rector Magnificus to be matriculated into the University; Charles was found to be too young, none under twelve years of age being admitted; John was admitted after making a declaration that he would do nothing against the laws of the university, city, or land.

I wish to be informed concerning the constitution and regulations of this university; the number of professors; their characters; the government of the students, both in morals and studies; their manner of living; their privileges, &c. &c.

12. Friday. Mr. Mitchel, Mr. Luzac, Doctor Waterhouse, Mr. Thaxter, and my two sons, supped with me at the Cour de Hollande.

13. Saturday. Returned to Amsterdam; having dined at Haerlem, at the Golden Lion. Went in the evening to see Ingraham, and Sigourney, and Captain Gillon.

14. Sunday. Questions.—How many ships of war are determined to be equipped? How much money have the States-General granted for the navy? Have the States-General resolved to issue letters of marque? Are the letters issued? Is there a disposition to demand them? Will there be many privateers? How many? Will the manifesto be published? When? How many troops are ordered to Zealand? Have the States-General taken any Swedish or Danish men-of-war into their service? How many? On what terms?

When will the decision of the Court of Holland be made upon the conduct of Amsterdam? Will it be this month or next? Who knows what it will be? Why is the decision delayed? What are the reasons, causes, motives, end, and design? Is it not the influence of the English party that still obstructs and retards? Has Zealand proposed or advised to open a negotiation to make up the quarrel? When? What measures does she propose?

The Baron Van der Capellen *Endnote 103* came in. He fears that the Prince, and the proprietors of English funds, will unite in endeavors to make it up by a dishonorable peace. Mr. Van Berckel *Endnote 104* predicts that there will be no war; says it is a rodomontade, a bombine of the English, &c.; that some persons have underwritten upon vessels on the faith of Mr. Van Berckel, &c.

This evening called upon Mr. Van Berckel, who was alone, among a multitude of papers; obliged to go out at five upon business; made many polite excuses, and invited me to call the day after to-morrow at four o'clock; being engaged to-morrow, I agreed. I asked him, however, whether the States-General had resolved to grant letters of marque, and he said, yes; if they were distributed, and he hesitated as if uncertain; I then excused myself from staying longer, and prayed him to keep his chamber, but according to the Dutch fashion, he would accompany me to the door, and make me all the bows which the custom demands, which obliged me to return him as many.

Questions.—Is it certain that the Empress of Russia is well inclined towards America? Who has such information? Has there been any deliberation or consultation between the maritime powers in forming the armed neutrality concerning the American question?

15. Monday. Visited old Mr. Crommelin and Mr. de Neufville. There is a wonderful consternation among the merchants; many houses have great difficulty to support their credit.

February 24. Friday. Went to the Hague in the Trëkschuit. At Leyden, I have seen Mr. Van der Kemp, and Mr.—, and Mr.—; I also visited two large manufactories, one of cloth, another of camlet.

28. Wednesday. At the Arms of Amsterdam. What can be the ground of the malice of so many against America?

1782.

Here occurs another long interval, during which the recognition by Holland of the sovereignty of the United States took place, and a treaty was negotiated, which, at the moment of resumption of this Diary, needed only the forms of execution, to be complete.

September 14. Saturday. Supped last night at Court, in the Maison du Bois. M. Boreel told me he had been to Paris, which he quitted eight days ago. Mr. Franklin had been sick; it was at first reported that he had been struck with an apoplexy; then it was said he had a bilious colic, and afterwards a retention of urine, but that he had got well before he left Paris.

Fell into conversation naturally with Don Joas Theolomico de Almeida, Envoy extraordinary of Portugal. *Endnote 105* He said to me, "The peace is yet a good way off; there will be no peace this winter; there will be another campaign, and no peace until the winter following. Spain will be the most difficult to satisfy of all the powers. Her pretensions will be the hardest for England to agree to. As to the independence of America, that is decided." I said to him, "It is reported that Portugal is about to open her ports to American vessels." "I have not yet received," says he, "any intelligence of that."

The Comte Montagnini de Mirabel, minister plenipotentiary of the King of Sardinia, asked what was the principle of the indecision of Great Britain. "Why don't they acknowledge your independence? They must have some intelligence that is not public." I answered, "I don't believe there is any principle or system in it. It is merely owing to their confusion. My Lord Shelburne, in compliance with the will of his master, refuses to do what all the world sees to be necessary." "Perhaps," says the Comte, "they mean to annex certain conditions to the acknowledgment of your independence." "But," says I, "what if we should annex conditions too? What if we should insist on an acknowledgment of our independence as a preliminary condition to entering into any treaty or conference?" "Ay," says he, "in that case you may have work enough."

Mr. Magis *Endnote 106* said to me afterwards, "I see you often in conversation with M. de Mirabel; he is a great politician; he is very well informed of all affairs in general, but particularly with the affairs and political system of Germany."

M. de Llano, the Spanish Plenipotentiary, said to me afterwards, "Do you know that man you have been in conversation with, this evening, so much, M. de Mirabel?" "Very well," says I. The Baron de Thulemeyer, who was by, said, "Yes, I see Mirabel often attacks him." "I am told," says I, "that he is a great politician." "Ay," says Llano, "I see you know him, but he knows nothing else."

M. Boreel, the Baron de Lynden de Hemmen, and the President of the Grand Committee, all members of the Assembly of their H. M., told me that five copies of the treaties would be made out according to my desire, the English and Dutch side by side upon every page, and the treaty would be signed next week.

The Baron de Thulemeyer [Endnote 107] chatted with me about riding on horseback; says he rides always in the morning at any hour between nine and dinner, but never after dinner.

They showed me this evening the lady who holds at her house an assembly, every evening, where the whole corps diplomatique assist; the lady who used to preside at Sir Joseph Yorke's table, and see that all was in order there.

The Comte de Welderen came as usual and made his compliments to me. The Rhinegrave de Salm, Colonel Bentinck, Mr. Van der Dussen, and other officers; in short, I never spent so social an evening at Court. My party was stronger this evening; Mirabel and Bentinck never play, and there were several others in the same case.

The Count Sarsfield went with me, and returned in my carriage. The Duke de la Vauguyon was not there. Agreed with General Van der Dussen to ride with him this morning at nine. Chatted at supper with one of the Ladies of Honor, Mademoiselle de Staremberg, in English, French, and Dutch.

At nine, took my ride with M. Van der Dussen, Lieutenant-General of cavalry. He was mounted upon a noble English horse, with an embroidered housing, and a white silk net, and with his sword; a servant behind him in livery, upon another fine horse with a white silk net. We made a long ride of three or four leagues; in our way we saw people digging turf out of heaps of sand; upon observing more attentively, I found that they dug away the sand hills to the depth of fifteen or twenty feet, and then came to bodies of peat or turf which they cut up to sell and to burn. The General says at the depth of ten, fifteen, or twenty feet, they find this layer of turf, which is also sometimes ten or fifteen feet deep, and then come to a fine soil upon a level nearly with the general surface of the meadows. The General's hypothesis is this. Before the dikes were built, there were frequent inundations in consequence of storms, which are still frequent. It is supposed that the whole country was originally level, and covered over with thick and heavy forests of woods; in great storms the waves of the sea threw up vast heaps of sand, and carried them sometimes several miles in upon the land, by which means its forests of trees were thrown down, or at least covered up with mountains of sea sand; that the wood of these trees, in the course of many hundreds, perhaps some thousands of years, has putrefied and dissolved into peat and turf, so that you have nothing to do but to dig through the sand hills first, and the turf beds next, to come to the original surface of the earth, which is yet very fertile; many fine meadows have been made in this way. In passing over the spot of downs between the Hague and Leyden, we saw three or four hunters, gunners in search of hares, rabbits, and other game, this being the season of the chase. The General seemed very apprehensive of these sportsmen, that they would not keep a good lookout, but might be so eager for their game as to be inattentive to travellers, and fire upon our bodies. This was a fear that never occurred to me, and I never felt it after it was mentioned.

The General was inquisitive after the American savages, and a great part of our conversation consisted in his questions, and my answers concerning them. The roads, the woods, the forests in America, also occasioned many questions. The General is a relation, as he told me, of the Minister of the same name at the conferences of Gertruidenberg.

Upon inquiry to-day, I find that the lady who was so intimate at Sir Joseph Yorke's, as to oversee his entertainments, is named Madame de Boetzlaar; she holds an assembly every night at her house, to which resort all the corps diplomatique; there they play; she paints, but is horridly ugly.

The Baron de Kruyningen holds an office of intelligence, where the Ministers or Secretaries meet of mornings, as at a kind of coffee house, to exchange with each other the news and compare notes.

Mr. Magis holds such another. What these people get by their assemblies and offices, is a question; perhaps nothing more than a reputation, an acquaintance with foreign ministers, and now and then an invitation to dinner.

The foreign ministers here all herd together, and keep no other company but at Court, and with a few in this way; it is not from choice, but necessity. There is no family but M. Boreel that ever invites any of them to breakfast, dine, or sup; nor do any of the members of the States General, the States of Holland, Bleyswick, Fagel, any of the Lords of the Admiralty, Gecommitteerde Raaden, Council of State, High Council of War, or anybody, ever invite strangers or one another. Hospitality and sociability are no characteristics here.

This day, Mr. Van Asp made me a visit; this gentleman is chargé d'affaires of Sweden, since the departure of the Baron d'Ehrenswerd for Prussia; he is a solid, prudent man.

He very much admired my house, and its situation. I said, smiling, it was very well for a beginning, and that I hoped we should have a house at Stockholm ere long; he smiled in return, but said nothing; his visit was not long; there is not a more sensible, manly, happy, or prudent countenance in the whole diplomatic body; he has desired M. Dumas to inform him as soon as the treaty is signed, that he may write it to his Court before it arrives in the newspapers.

19. Thursday. Went to the comedy; saw the "Sage dans sa Retraite," and "Le jugement de Midas;" both well represented. The music was good, and the show upon the stage splendid. The Princess and all her children were there. The foreign ministers chiefly.

October 1. Tuesday. Dined with M. Boreel, a Deputy to the States-General from the Province of Holland, with Lt. General Van der Dussen, M. de Llano, M. Thulemeyer, M. Renovalis, Mr. Visscher, Mr.—, of the Council of State for the City of Amsterdam, Mr.—, a gentleman of the Court, &c. The dinner was elegant, and a splendid show of plate, as we see at the tables of the rich Dutch families.

A little pleasantry with M. de Thulemeyer about the conduct of the Prussian Minister at Madrid, in notifying to Mr. Carmichael as Chargé des affaires des États Unis de l'Amérique, his presentation to the King and royal family.

Note.—This is the effect of the step I took in notifying my presentation to all the foreign ministers.

2. Wednesday. Walked yesterday to the house in the woods in the rain. To-day will dine with me, Comte Sarsfield, Mr. Visscher, and Mr. Gyzelaer. Received yesterday a volume of the Journals of Congress, with some newspapers, by the post from Lorient, which cost me thirty-seven guilders. The Comte, Mr. Visscher, and Mr. Gyzelaer, dined here. The Comte Sarsfield began, as usual, when we were alone, to give me a lesson of etiquette; this is a trait in his character; no man more attentive to the rules of ceremony and formality; no man more precise. He says, that when I made an entertainment, I should have placed the Ambassador of France at my right hand, and the Minister of Spain at my left, and have arranged the other principal personages; and when I rose from the table, I should have said, Messieurs, voudriez vous, &c., or Monsieur le Duc, voudriez vous, &c. All this, every one sees, is à la Françoise; but it is very little regarded here; and it was because it is generally neglected here, that I neglected it. But the Comte, in every affair of dress, billets, rank, &c., has, from my first acquaintance with him, ever discovered such a minute attention to little circumstances. How is it possible to reconcile these trifling contemplations of a master of ceremonies, with the vast knowledge of arts, sciences, history, government, &c., possessed by this nobleman? A habit of living in the world, however, is necessary, a facility of living with men,—l'habitude de vivre avec les hommes.

It is the fashion among the Dutch, to arrange all the company by putting a card with the name of each gentleman and lady upon the napkins in the plate; this I never saw practised in

France; indeed, they attend but to one person in France; the feast is made in honor of one person; that is the ton. Mr. Visscher, being told by the Count that he and I were to dine to-morrow with General Van der Dussen, appeared surprised, and said that the General, although he had dined with me and rode with me on horseback, would not have dared to have invited me, if he had not met me at M. Boreel's.

I saw the other day Joachimi Hoppii Commentatio Succincta ad Institutiones Justinianas, at Mr. Luzac's.

Mr. Gyzelaer informed me, that the Committee for examining the administration of the Marine, were to-morrow to announce their authority to the Prince. I told him he must make a harangue in order to give dignity and solemnity to his commission. He said it was a delicate thing to make a speech upon the occasion. This I agreed.

I gave the gentlemen an account of the practice of the Provincial Congress of Massachusetts, when they first formed their army. Dr. Warren, their President, made a harangue in the form of a charge, in the presence of the Assembly, to every officer, upon the delivery of his commission; and he never failed to make the officer, as well as all the Assembly, shudder upon those occasions. Count Sarsfield appeared struck and affected with this anecdote. I dare say he has it in his journal. Count Sarsfield told me the news of the destruction of the Spanish floating batteries, by the English red hot bullets. He seemed much affected. Said all Europe would laugh at them, and that they deserved it for attempting a thing so evidently impossible. No governments, says he, but monarchies, are subject to this kind of misfortunes from absurdity. In France, a Madame Pompadour, or Du Barry, may ruin a kingdom. In Spain, an absurd priest, the father confessor of a superstitious king, may so far gain his confidence by working upon his conscience and superstitious fears, as to lead him into such foolish councils. How much mischief, says I, has Spain done in this just cause!

3. Thursday. Dined with Mr. Van der Dussen, Lieutenant-General of the cavalry, in company with Mr. de Llano, Minister of the King of Spain, and Mr. de Renovalis, Secretary of his Legation, Mr. and Madame Boreel, Mr. and Madame Geelvink, Madame Dedel, the Rhinegrave de Salm, Mr. Saumase, a descendant of the famous Salmasius, whom John Milton disputed with. Mr. Boreel is a Deputy to the States-General for the Province of Holland; Mr. Geelvink is a member of the Council of State for Amsterdam.

General Van der Dussen told me he must ask me to take a family dinner with him one of these days, in order to present me to a couple of his friends; one was his brother, and the other was General Ponce; both zealous Americans, he said. I told him he would do me great honor, and give me much pleasure.

Mr. Boreel desired me to send him the American Gazette, which contains the resolution of their High Mightinesses, acknowledging me as Minister, with his name to it. I forgot Mr. Magis, who said to me, "Entre nous, Sir, if I were young, I would endeavor to serve a great power, because one has a chance to be something; but when one serves a small power, one is sure never to be any thing."

Madame Boreel, next to whom I sat at table, asked me if I understood the Dutch. I answered, very little, but that I began to learn it; that I had with me two ingenious young gentlemen, with whom at breakfast I every morning attempted, with the aid of a dictionary, to read the Dutch Gazettes, and that we began to comprehend some paragraphs. Madame Boreel mentioned to the company that I read the Dutch Gazettes. Mr. Geelvink called out to me, pleasantly enough, "Leese Mynheer de Diemermeersche Courant?" "Ja wel, Mynheer," says I, "en de Höllandsche Historiesche Courant, oök." The Dutch part of this company were all high in office and service, and therefore attached to the Court.

The General Van der Dussen said, laughing, that he was ready to wish and to do any thing to the English, for they had almost ruined him. He was Governor of Ipres or Ypres, one of the Barrier Towns, so that he has lost his government by the demolition of the Barriers. I believe, too, they have done him some damage in some estates in the West Indies, &c.

Mr. Boreel promised me to speak to Mr. Fagel, and let him know that I wish to have the treaty signed, that I might be able to send it by several vessels now ready to sail at Amsterdam.

Somebody at table said to Count Sarsfield, that the Americans had laid aside the use of Mr. Franklin's conductors. The Count appealed to me. I said, by no means; on the contrary, the use of them increased, and they were found very useful.

Questions.—What are the powers of the Council of State? How many members? Who appoints them? Are they for life, or years, or at will? Where do they sit? What objects of administration have they? Is their power legislative, executive, or judiciary? Is the Council of State the same body with the Gecommitteerde Raaden? Or are they two?

Answer.—The Council of State, and the Council of Commissioners, are two distinct bodies. De Raad Van Staaten, en de Gecommitteerde Raaden. The first is for the Seven Provinces; the last for the Province of Holland only.

The Hague, October 5, 1782

Saturday. In conference with the Grand Pensionary Bleiswyck, he told me, it was determined to sign the treaty of Commerce on Monday next, at noon. That I should not find the Greffier Fagel, for that being Saturday, he would spend it at his country seat, and not come to town; that the revolution in the Crimea, and the commotions among the Tartars, would probably find employment enough for Russia; that there were some symptoms of Anglomania in Sweden; that there was no news from Paris about peace; that Mr. Brantzen had not, when the last advices came away, had his first audience of the King. I went next to Mr. Fagel's house, but the answer was, that on Saturdays the Greffier never came to town.

There is in the Rotterdamsche Courant of to-day, the following article from Philadelphia, of the 7th of August:

"Het is opmerkelyk dat de Staaten-General, de onafhankelijkheit der Vereenigde Staaten, juist op den 19 April, dezes Jaars erkend hebben, zynde die dag de zevende verjaring van den veldslag by Lexington, en dat deze zaak nog opmerkelyker maakt is, dat de Eerste Memoire van den Heer Adams, die zulk een grooten indruk op de Hollandsche Natie gemaakt heeft, gedagteekend is den 19 April, 1781."

7. Monday. M. Dumas has been out upon the discovery. Neither Mr. Visscher nor Mr. Gyzelaer could guess the reason why their High Mightinesses had sent their agent, De Speeringshoek, to desire me to postpone the signature of the treaty until to-morrow. Mr. Boreel, whom he met in the street, explained it. He says the Prince had sent word to their High Mightinesses that he desired a conference with them to-day, and as the signature would take up some time, they should be obliged to make the Prince or me wait. He learned afterwards from Mr. Visscher, that the council of war of the navy officers at the Texel, have sent an express to day to inform the States that it is impossible for the fleet to go to Brest, according to the resolution of their High Mightinesses, because they were not ready. They are in want of men, of provisions, of stores. Every ship in the fleet is in want of something essential. The blame of this will fall upon the Prince.

The Prince, in his conference to day, has communicated his orders and correspondence relative to the navy.

8. Tuesday. M. Dumas is indefatigable in his way. He visits every day the French Ambassador, M. G—, M. V—, and occasionally M. K—, and sometimes the Prince Galitzin,

M. d'Asp, &c. No American minister could do this; it would ruin his character. I don't know whether it would do for a secretary of legation to do this. I can, however, make an excellent use of him. I can get or communicate intelligence in this, better than any other way, from and to various persons and places. I have been indirectly put upon my guard against "un chien puant;" made use of as a tool in the Friesland affair, which I read of in Count Sarsfield's journal. He now makes his court to both sides. Llano the other day made a grand éloge of the man and his wife, of their peaceable, amiable character, and excellent reputation. Thus it is when parties run high, one side cries, crucify! and the other, hosanna!

At breakfast, Count Sarsfield came in, and put into my hand more of his speculations. I have read through his journal of his journeys into Holland in 1777 and in 1780, and he has promised me that of 1782. The piece he lent me to day is on slavery. He has assembled every appearance of argument in favor of the slavery of the glebe, (villenage,) or domestic slavery, and has refuted them all. *Endnote 108*

At twelve, went to the State House; was received as usual at the head of the stairs by M. de Santheuvel, and M. de Lynden, Deputies from Holland and Zealand, and conducted into the Truce Chamber, where we signed and sealed the treaty of commerce and the convention concerning recaptures.

Waited on the Duke de la Vauguyon, to inform him, as I did, and also, that I had received a letter from Mr. Jay, 28th September, informing me, that the day before, Mr. Oswald received a commission to treat of peace with the Commissioners of the United States of America, and that I believed I should set out, according to Mr. Jay's earnest desire, for Paris, the latter end of next week. The Duke was pleased to say, and with a warmth that proved him sincere, that he rejoiced to hear it, for it seemed by it that Mr. Jay and I were cordial, and he thought further, it was absolutely necessary I should be there, for that the immovable firmness that heaven had given me would be useful and necessary upon this occasion. I could not help laughing at this, and replying, that I had often occasion however for cooler blood than had fallen to my share, to regulate that same firmness.

The Duke then entered into a history of his negotiations with the States and the Prince, to get the fleet to Brest. He thinks there has been a secret communication between Prince and officers to represent the fleet destitute of sails and provisions, &c.

While the clerks were sealing the treaties to-day, I cast an eye on the collection of pictures of Claudius Civilis, and asked the gentlemen who was the painter. Secretary Fagel answered me, that it was Otto Oevenius, a Dutch painter, author of the Emblemata Horatiana; that each of those pictures was formed upon some passage of Tacitus; that his father had been at the pains to transcribe all those passages and affix them to the back of the picture. Upon this, I turned one of them round, and found a paragraph.

9. Wednesday. Went this morning to the Secretary Fagel, and returned him the original treaty, and the original convention which was designed for their High Mightinesses; the others, designed for Congress, I kept. We ran over together the few literal variations, and corrected all; indeed, all the inaccuracies were found to be in my copy which I kept to compare. Mr. Fagel said, that one day this week, he would call upon me with the copies which he and I were to sign, to be sent to Congress. That to-day, the committees would make report, their High Mightinesses would thank them for the pains they had taken, and each province would take the treaty and convention ad referendum, and lay them before their constituents for ratification. He told me that his intelligence from France by the last post, led him to expect peace in the course of this winter. He asked me if mine did not. I answered, smiling, that I could not deny that there appeared some symptoms of it.

About two o'clock, the Count de Sanafée made me a visit, in ceremony, to congratulate me on the signature of the treaty. I told him, I hoped by this time the Count d'Aranda had signed a treaty with Mr. Jay, with equal advantage and satisfaction. He inquired about the twenty-second and twenty-third articles, and said, he understood that I had met with difficulty to get the States to agree with me upon a substitute. I read to him in French the article as it now stands in the treaty, which he was fully satisfied with. He inquired concerning the Prussian Minister at Madrid notifying to Mr. Jay his presentation to the King and Royal family; asked if it was true; observed that Mr. Jay was not at Madrid but at Paris. I answered, the visit was made to Mr. Carmichael, as chargé des affaires, at Mr. Jay's house. He asked me if I told it to Mr. Thulemeyer. I answered in the affirmative. He asked me what I thought of the late behavior respecting the Dutch fleet going to Brest; an order of the States-General, and refusal of obedience on the part of the navy. I answered, it was very extraordinary and very alarming. He said he did not think this people would ever do any thing; but the requisition to send ships to Brest, was very well calculated to try them. I shewed him the paragraph in the London Evening Post which says, that a commission under the royal sign manual has passed the great seal of the court of chancery, authorizing Mr. Oswald, of Philpot Lane, to treat of peace with the United States of America.

Mr. Dumas has learned to-day from our friend, that the two Captains Welderen and Van Hoey, did in truth come with the message, that if the fleet was ordered to Brest, all the officers and crews would resign; but finding that the States were likely to take fire, they were persuaded to soften it down to a want of sails, provisions, stores, &c. This, all agree, must have been a plot. The Prince must be as daring in his system, as his cousin has been. The States of Holland have printed the treaty; a member has given one to Mr. Dumas, who has sent it to-day with his French translation to Leyden, to be inserted in Mr. Luzac's Gazette.

Mr. Thaxter and Mr. Storer have agreed to accompany me to Paris.

10. Thursday. The Comte de Sanafée wrote a card to M. Dumas, desiring a copy in French of the twenty-second article; said that I had read it to him in French, but his memory had not retained it. I desired M. Dumas to send it. M. Dumas, at my desire, had asked the Duke de la Vauguyon what was the usage in my case, who am going to Paris. He brought me answer, to take leave of the President, Secretary Fagel, and Grand Pensionary, and after, of the Prince and Princess. M. Dumas added that I should mention who I left as chargé des affaires, and present him. I told him there was none, and I had not authority to constitute one.

Mr. Van Heukelom has been here. Fourteen hundred persons in Leyden have signed an address of thanks to the regency, for their proposition to inquire into the administration of the navy. Mr. John Luzac is now, he says, universally beloved. A change of system has made a change of circumstances. Mr. Élie Luzac was the most respected, and had the most influence, but his Anglomania had brought him into contempt. Élie Luzac's father and John's father were brothers. Élie's father is dead. He is called at Leyden een Agt en Veertiger. These nick names of Agt en Veertiger and Twee en Agtiger (Eight and Fortyer and Two and Eightyer) are adopted as party distinctions, instead of Whig and Tory, Anglomane and Republican, &c.

Received this day a card from the Baron de Lynden de Blitterswyk, first Noble of Zealand, brother of him who was Envoy in Sweden, and his lady, to dine with them next Wednesday.

As the commerce of Bruges and Ostend have grown out of the American Revolution and the Neutral Confederation, it may be worth while to make the following extract:

Extract from the Journal of Count Sarsfield.

"5 June, 1782. J'ai trouvé Bruges dans un grand mouvement, par le commerce qui y arrive. J'ai compté de vingt à vingt-cinq navires dans le Bassin; il en peut tenir beaucoup plus, et on va l'agrandir. On abat les fortifications; tous les magazins de la ville sont remplis; on en construit de nouveaux, qui seront fort grands. La journée d'un homme qui n'a que ses bras est de 16s. et nourri. 16s. du pays font 1l. 10s. de France. La raison de cela est qu' Ostende est trop petit pour toutes les affaires qui s' y font. Beaucoup de navires viennent à Bruges, ce qui est d'autant plus commode, qu'il faut toujours que les marchandises y payent lors qu'on ne veut pas les expédier par mer. On m'a dit, qu'en particulier les Espagnols expédioient toujours pour Bruges, où ils n'ont point les mêmes lenteurs que le défaut d'emplacement occasione à Ostende. On m'assure que le canal a 21 pieds de profondeur. Tout ce que je viens de dire se fait par les ordres qu'a donnés l'Empereur, lors qu'il est venu ici. Il a declaré qu'on ne devoit regarder Ostende et Bruges que comme la même ville. L'effet de cette augmentation de commerce, se fait sentir sur le prix des maisons, et s'étend sûrement sur tout.

6 Juin. Ostende. Il y a deux chemins pour y aller. L'un suit le canal. Il faut passer le port en bateau pour entrer dans la ville. L'autre est plus long. Distance, deux lieues et demie, à ce qu'on m'a dit. J'ai mis un peu moins de quatre heures et demie à le faire. Il est pavé, et passe par Saint-André, Wassenaar, un autre village dont j'ai oublié le nom, et Gistele. Il y a quelques barrières à payer, excepté sur ce qui depend du Franc de Bruges, qui fait et entretient les chemins à ses frais. On démolit aussi les fortifications d'Ostende, pour y construire des magazins. Le nombre des vaisseaux que j'y ai vus est très considérable, le mouvement prodigieux. On m'a dit à Middelbourg que le commerce se fait très mal à Ostende; les commerçants sont, dit-on, très négligents, quelquefois même infidèles. Il m'a paru dans le détail, qu'il pouvoit bien n'y avoir pas de leur faute; mais les affaires y sont si multipliées qu'ils ne peuvent y satisfaire, et comme les magazins leur manquent, ils ne peuvent empêcher bien des marchandises d'être avariées; ainsi les reproches qu'on leur fait, pourront cesser d'être mérités, mais ceux qu'on fait à leur port ne se dissiperont pas de même. On en dit l'entrée difficile, et effectivement la manière dont on m'en a parlé à Ostende même, me le persuade."

It is an observation in this country, that the wines of the Rhine and Moselle, have in them the principles both of the stone and the gout; but they lose these principles as they advance in age.

Extract from the Journal of Count Sarsfield.

"1 July, at the Hague. Tout ce qui vient de se passer en Hollande, la révolution qui s'y est faite dans les esprits en faveur de la France, la manière dont M. le Duc Louis de Brunswick a été écarté des affaires, au moins en apparence; enfin, cet ouvrage de M. le Duc de la Vauguyon mérite que j'en parle un peu. Je dis un peu, parce qu'il m'est impossible d'en dire tout ce que l'on désireroit d'en savoir, M. de la Vauguyon n'en parlant jamais, et étant d'un secret impénétrable sur lequel d'ailleurs j'ai été fort éloigné de vouloir l'attaquer. Tout le monde connoit les liaisons de ce pays-ci avec l'Angleterre; on n'en connoit pas moins le principe, qui a été si efficace, que pendant long temps on a cru que ces deux nations étoient necessairement attachées l'une à l'autre, de manière à ne pouvoir s'en détacher. On eût dit que cette union étoit l'ouvrage de la nature même; et il y a peut-être encore quelques gens chez lesquels ce préjugé n'est pas entièrement effacé. Le Stathouder n'a, suivant toutes les apparences, aucum autre motif pour être resté dans les intérêts de l'Angleterre au point où il l'est. Les liens du sang ne seroient pas suffisants, puisqu'il a les mêmes, et plus intimes, avec la Prusse, dont le système est tout-à-fait opposé à celui de la prospérité de l'Angleterre. Son abaissement est essentiel à sa sureté. Il faut, donc, que le Prince soit conduit par l'habitude de penser d'une certaine manière, et par le préjugé que je viens de dire. Il se peut aussi, et cela est même vraisemblable, que la crainte des armes Angloises l'y ait engagé. Je remarquerai, à cette occasion, que ce sentiment a opéré certainement sur plusieurs des membres de la République.

Ainsi, voici comme je me la représente. Au commencement de cette guerre-ci, le Chef décide en faveur des Anglois; la plus grande partie des Hollandois mêmes, ayant confusément dans la tête l'idée d'une liaison avec l'Angleterre, nécessaire, impossible à rompre, ou tout au plus, pour des momens, effrayée d'ailleurs des suites d'une conduite hardie, qui pourroit les entrainer dans une guerre, pour laquelle ils n'ont aucunes mesures prises; de grandes difficultés à vaincre; le danger de perdre les jouissances du moment; une très ancienne habitude de paresse, toute la nation semblant dans une sorte d'état de léthargie, qui ne permet que difficilement d'en rien attendre qui réponde à ce qu'elle a été autrefois.

Il n'est pas aussi facile de rendre raison de la conduite de M. le Duc de Brunswick. Il est trop homme d'état, pour que les mêmes causes qui ont engourdi le Stathouder et la nation, aient agi sur lui. On doit croire qu'il est trop éclairé, pour n'avoir pas senti dès le premier moment, combien il étoit important pour elle de se montrer dans cette occasion; et cependant il est toujours resté attaché à l'Angleterre. Il a toujours agi pour elle; il a même manœuvré, suivant toute apparence. Il y a, au moins, un fait de ce genre qu'on ne peut nier: c'est la proposition fait en d'augmenter l'armée de terre, au moment où on alloit commencer une guerre de mer. Quelques gens ont dit qu'il étoit payé par l'Angleterre. J'en ai trouvé qui le defendent sur ce point, et disent qu'il en est incapable; et, quoiqu'ils ne l'aiment pas, rejettent cette idée avec une sort d'indignation. Il faut alors croire que c'est l'attachement qu'il a pour son nom, qui le séduit, et lui fait penser qu'il est de l'intérêt de la Hollande de se soumettre à l'Angleterre, de borner son commerce à la portion à laquelle elle jugera apropos de la réduire, d'être, en un mot, aux termes d'une de ses colonies, et de perdre sa place dans la liste des souverains d'Europe.

C'est, en effet, à quoi les décisions du Ministère Anglois auroient conduit la République, si le Roi avoit envoyé un ministre moins actif, moins pénétrant, moins capable, que M. de la Vauguyon, qui a su, au très grand étonnement des Hollandois même, démonter tous les moyens de leur administration, et ouvrir aux gens bien intentionnés, des routes pour faire parvenir leurs sentiments à l'assemblée des états et la ramener à des principes plus conformes à ses vrais intérêts, on pourroit dire, à la raison, et à leur honneur.

Quelques gens pensent que, malgré tous les talents et tout l'art qu'il a développé, il auroit eu beaucoup de peine à réussir si l'administration n'avoit pas fait des fautes capitales. Je vais en exposer quelques-unes.

1. Elle avoit poussé la pusillanimité jusqu'à défendre aux commandants des escortes, de prendre sous leur protection les navires chargés pour la France d'effets utiles à la marine. Cette résolution secrète fut sue; M. de la V. présenta un mémoire; on y répondit; et par là, on avouoit le fait, qui auroit été bien difficile à prouver si on s'étoit contenté de le nier.

2. Lorsque les Députés d'Amsterdam vinrent présenter au Prince leur mémoire contre M. le Duc de Brunswick, ils annoncèrent eux mêmes que tout ce qu'ils alloient lui dire devoit étre renfermé sous un secret impénétrable. On dit, qu'ils paroissoient fort émus. Si le Prince avoit mis leur mémoire dans sa poche, leur en avoit fait bien des remerciments, et les eût renvoyés en leur faisant sentir la nécessité du secret, que seroit devenue l'affaire? Rien, probablement. Mais il leur rendit ce mémoire; on les ranima; ils le publièrent, ou plûtot le rendirent public; car je ne sache pas qu'il y ait là de publication légale.

3. Alors M. le Duc de Brunswick avoit un parti à prendre, qui étoit de laisser tomber l'affaire, au moins jusqu'au moment où on feroit quelque allégation spéciale contre lui, ce qui auroit été fort difficile. Au lieu de cela, il se plaignit aux États-Généraux; mit les formes contre lui, tant parce qu'au lieu d'une requête ou d'un mémoire il fit une simple lettre, que parce qu'il s'adressa aux États-Généraux pendant que c'étoient les seuls États de Hollande à

qui il appartenoit de connoitre de cette affaire. On a vu les suites qu'elle a eucs; mais si le Duc n'avoit rien dit, s'il avoit laissé aux Magistrats d'Amsterdam le soin de donner le mouvement à cette affaire, ils auroient pu se trouver fort embarrassés.

4. Avant le temps dont je viens de parler, l'administration fit encore une grande faute contre ses vues. Elle vouloit que les Anglois fissent ce qui leur plairoit, et ce qui leur plaisoit étoit, de prendre tous les vaisseaux chargés pour la France de matières propres à l'usage d'une flotte. Il falloit leur dire, de payer aux prix courant les effets qu'ils auroient saisis. Le commerce n'auroit, peut-être, jamais remué. Alors les villes seroient, probablement, restées tranquilles, par les raisons que j'ai indiquées au commencement de cette note. Il est certain que ce ne sont que les négociants qui les ont mis en activité; ou, au moins, ils y ont bien contribués. Ceux qui parini eux avoient le sentiment de la dignité de la République, et qui souffroient de la voir anéantie, se sont fort appuyés sur les pétitions des négociants; mais quand les négociants auroient été bien payés de leurs cargaisons, il auroit été facile au parti Anglois de les écarter, en leur répondant, qu'ils n'avoient aucun droit de se plaindre, aucun fondement légitime pour leurs représentations. Étant payés suivant leurs factures, ils ne pouvoient alors parler que du manque de respect pour le pavillon,—chose qui ne les regardoit pas. Cela auroit été d'autant plus aisé à établir, que les Régences seroient fort fachées qu'on crût que c'est le commerce qui les conduit, ou, si l'on veut, qui les engage à telle ou telle démarche. Plus elles sentent que c'est au commerce que la République doit l'existence qu'elle conserve, et plus elles veulent cacher cette vérité, afin de ne jamais dépendre d'un corps qui leur est à quelques égards étranger. Les magistrats, surtout ceux d'Amsterdam, seroient bien fachés que l'on crût qu'ils font le commerce; ils veulent même cacher que leurs ancêtres aient été commerçants. Et il y a tel homme, qui sauroit fort mauvais gré à celui qui lui diroit que son père ou son grand père avoit le premier comptoir d'Amsterdam.

5. Une autre faute a été dans la célèbre affaire du pensionnaire d'Amsterdam, de rendre aux Députés de cette ville la sentence que la Cour de Hollande avoit prononcée. C'étoit une arme qu'il falloit conserver, quitte a ne jamais s'en servir. Dès qu'on l'eut abandonnée, la Régence d'Amsterdam n'eut plus rien à craindre, et se trouva en liberté d'agir comme elle l'a fait.

Nota.—On ne m'a pas bien expliqué comment cette sentence n'existoit que dans un seul papier, ce que les notaires appellent en brevet. Les Tribunaux ont des registres où sont leurs sentences, et le Public ne peut en avoir que des expéditions. Quand j'ai fait cette question, on ne s'est pas trouvé en état d'y répondre.

Voilà une partie des fautes qu'on reproche à l'Administration. La première de toutes, fort antérieure à celles-ci a été, peut-être, de se laisser voir de trop près, mais certainement de ne s'être pas attaché les gens les plus accrédités dans les provinces pour en former son conseil. Le Duc sait très mauvais gré à ceux qui vont à l'Hôtel de France. Il affecte le contraire, leur dit même non seulement qu'il y faut aller, mais qu'ils feront bien, et cherche ensuite de les desservir.

11. Friday. Count Sarsfield came in familiarly at breakfast, and I had an hour's conversation with him upon the foregoing extract. I showed him some papers. He thinks the American cause ought to come in. Walked to the house in the wood. Near three o'clock Mr. Fagel came in person, and in ceremony, to make me a visit, and delivered to me, the four other copies of the treaty attested by himself, to be sent to America. Complaisant as usual. At six, Mr. Van den Burg van Spieringshoek, the agent of their High Mightinesses, came and delivered me their resolution relative to Mr. Dubbledemuts's vessel, desiring me to transmit it to Congress; which I promised to do. Spent most of the day in signing obligations for the United States. It is hard work to sign one's name sixteen hundred times after dinner.

12. Saturday. Spent the day in signing obligations, and packing the treaties and despatches.

13. Sunday. Sent three copies of the treaty of commerce, and as many of the convention concerning recaptures, by Mr. Storer to Amsterdam, to go by three different vessels. Finished packing my papers for my journey to Paris. Mr. Storer is to prepare every thing for us to set off, from the Arms of Amsterdam, on Friday morning. Mr. Thaxter and I are to be there on Thursday night.

Walked the tour of the wood twice. Met the Court twice.

The names of the Lords the Deputies of the Committee of Foreign Affairs, who signed with me the treaty of commerce, and the convention concerning recaptures, on the eighth of this month, are,—

George Van Randwyck, of Guelderland,
B. Van den Santheuvel of Holland,
Peter Van Bleiswyck, of Holland,
W. C. H. Van Lynden, of Zealand,
D. S. Van Heeckeren, of Utrecht,
Joan Van Kuffeler, of Friesland,
H. Tjassens, of Groningen.

Visscher and Gyzelaer, have been pumping Dumas, to get out of him my secret; *Endnote 109* but luckily, it was not in him. They insinuated to him, that Fitzherbert had received instructions to exchange full powers with the American ministers; that these were about to speak in a high tone—"tenir un haut langage;" that there would be no Congress at Vienna nor Brussels, but the peace would be made at Paris. This they learn, I suppose, from the despatches of their ministers Berkenrode and Brantzen.

14. Monday. Not long after my reception here, I was invited by Mr. Le Vaillant at Amsterdam, to dine with him in company with Mr. Van Berckel, Mr. Bikker, and their connections; when, according to the ton in this country, we came to that period of the feast when the toasts begin, Mr. Le Vaillant produced a beautiful glass, round the rim of which was engraved, Aurea Libertas. He filled it, and first addressing himself to the glass, and then to me, pronounced these words with a profound bow:

Aurea Libertas gaude: pars altera mundi,
Vindice te, renuit subdere colla jugo.
Hæc tibi, legatum quem consors Belga recepit,
Pectore sincero pocula plena fero.
Utraque gens nectet, mox suspicienda Tyrannis,
Quæ libertati vincula sacra precor.

Never was bumper quaffed with more good will.

The Duke de la Vauguyon has invited me and my family to dine with him to-day. He advises me to present Mr. Dumas to the President, Greffier, and Grand Pensionary, as my Chargé des affaires in my absence. As Mr. Dumas has no commission as secretary to this legation, nor any other character than that of correspondent of Mr. Franklin's, or at most, of an ancient committee of Congress, which I suppose has ceased, I have some difficulty about this. Some members of Congress, at least, may think that I advance too fast.

At half-after-nine I waited on Mr. Bleiswyck to give him notice that I intended to set off on Thursday morning for Paris. He cries "C'est un bon augure, Monsieur." "Oui, Monsieur, je m'en vais, avec le rameau d'olivier, dans la bouche, dans le cœur, et à la main." He seemed to be very happy to learn it. I asked him if their ministers at Paris had given them any late information concerning the negotiations for peace. He said, Yes, they had informed him that the court of Great Britain had fully acknowledged the independence of America; that Mr. Fitzherbert was instructed to exchange full powers with the American ministers. I told him that I was invited and pressed by my colleagues to go to Paris, and that I should be happy to take his commands on Wednesday. I went next to Mr. Fagel, and informed him of my intended journey. He seemed really overjoyed. Said "C'est une bonne marque," &c. He repeated to me, that their ministers had written that Mr. Fitzherbert had received such instructions, and that the Count de Vergennes had told them that he was now fully persuaded that Great Britain, that is the British Ministry were now sincerely disposed to peace. Mr. Fagel said, he did not expect that I should have gone so soon. I told him that I was urged by my colleagues to come; that I had the honor to be at the head of this commission; that I was sent to Europe three years ago with a commission as sole minister plenipotentiary for peace; but that, last year, Congress had thought fit to change the plan a little; they had sent me a commission to this republic, and had associated with me in the commission for peace Mr. Franklin, Mr. Jay, Mr. Laurens, and Mr. Jefferson; Mr. Laurens had resigned, or, rather, had not accepted; Mr. Jefferson was in America, so that there remained only Mr. Franklin, Mr. Jay, and myself; that Mr. Franklin was infirm,—had the gout and gravel, or strangury, and could not sleep; so that it became more necessary for me to go. He asked how old Mr. Franklin was? I told him seventy-six; that he was born in 1706. He said, that is my age; I am of 1706; but I have no disorders, no pains, or uneasiness at all; in my youth I was very infirm, had the gravel and several disorders, but they are all worn away with time. I asked him, if he took the air much? He said, Yes, a great deal, and he was very fond of walking; he walked yesterday four hours in the Downs, from ten to two, and he was very well. He asked me when I should return? I answered, that if the negotiations for peace should begin and go on, it was impossible to say; but that otherwise I should return in three weeks. He said, he hoped, then, I should not return before next spring. This gentleman has a very young look, much younger than Mr. Franklin; a countenance fresh and ruddy, clear, unclouded; a small, spare man. Dined with M. de la Vauguyon, with Messrs. de Llano, Renovalis, Sarsfield, Fénelon, Berenger, Dumas, Thaxter, Cremou, Créanci. Very gay and social. Fell into conversation after dinner with Sarsfield, Renovalis, &c. about Biscay, Friesland, &c. Sarsfield said, the genius of certain people had preserved them their privileges. "What is the genius of people?" says I. "It is a manufacture; it is the effect of the government and education," &c. I run on about the Panurge, Pantagruel, &c. of Rabelais, the Romeo and Juliet of Shakspeare, the Mandragore of Machiavel, the Tartuffe of Molière, &c. &c.

15. Tuesday. This morning, at ten, made my visit to the President Van Randwyck, of Guelderland, to take leave of their High Mightinesses, and presented Mr. Dumas as chargé des affaires in my absence. Went next to the Hôtel de Dordrecht, to take leave of Mr. Gyzelaer, and next, to that of Amsterdam, to take leave of Mr. Visscher, who was more bold and open than ever I knew him. Said, it was the Stadtholder, who was the greatest—"le plus g. t.-de ce pays-ci, entêté comme une mule," &c. He showed me a letter from Mr. Brantzen at Paris, which contained, that the Count de Vergennes told him, Mr. Fitzherbert had informed him that the independence of America would meet with no longer difficulty; that he had received a special commission to treat with the ministers of the United States of America.

At twelve, the agent, Van den Burg Spieringshoek, inquired at the house, if I could receive him at one. I answered in the affirmative. Accordingly, at one, he came, and said that he had it in command from their High Mightinesses to inform me, that the President, Mr. Van Randwyck, had informed them of my intention to take a journey to France; that they had charged him to make me their compliments, to wish me a good journey, and a speedy return in good health. At three, I went to the house in the wood, and took leave of the Princess, and afterwards of the Prince. He asked me several questions,—"What were my sentiments of the negotiation at Paris? Whether I thought the King of Great Britain had taken upon himself, without an Act of Parliament, to acknowledge the independence of America? Who were the ministers, on the part of America, to treat of peace?" "Mr. Franklin, Monsieur." "And who is the other?" "Mr. Jay," said I. "He who has been at Madrid?" said he. "The same."

In the evening, Mr. Gyzelaer came in, and we had a long conversation. He told me, that a few weeks ago, Mr. Thulemeyer visited the Duke de la Vauguyon, and informed him that the King of Prussia, his master, would not take it well that the Court of Versailles, or his minister here, should intermeddle with the interior parties and disputes in the Republic. And at the same time, the Duke received a letter from the Count de Vergennes, informing him, that the Prussian Minister at Versailles had said the same things to him; but that he had convinced him that all jealousy of that kind was groundless. He told me that upon this occasion, he entered deep into conversation, and said that he did not desire Versailles to intermeddle, unless as a counterpoise to Prussia's intermeddling. There was an affair of 1714, which had made the Prince absolute in Utrecht, Guilderland, and Overyssel; that if the patriots should attempt to change that, and Prussia should interpose to prevent it, unless they should be supported by France, they must succumb, and pass for the dupes; that he must be sensible, if they determined upon this measure, and France should desert them, they must look out elsewhere. "Ay, where?" "Perhaps to the Emperor." Furious. "Ay, but you must be sensible that I ought not to quit your house without satisfaction upon this point." He says, the Prince has lately said that some foreigner would soon interest himself in the affairs of the Republic. He wished, if I could be useful to them at Versailles, or here, with the Duke, that I would.

16. Wednesday. Dined with the Baron de Lynden de Blitterswyk, the first noble of Zealand. Llano, Almeida, Thulemeyer, Mirabel, Galitzin, and Markow, were all there; Geelvink, Sarsfield, Heyden, Boreel, &c., sixteen in all. Mr. De Lynden, told me that their High Mightinesses had lately consulted with all their admirals and best master-builders, and had endeavored to discover the best possible model of a ship, and that he would send it to me, as he did the next morning. I have desired Mr. Dumas to send it to Congress. Received an invitation from Court to sup, to-morrow night. Sent an excuse.

17. Thursday. Began my journey to Paris from the Hague; dined at Haerlem, and drank tea at five o'clock at Amsterdam. Paid Mr. Bromfield two hundred ducats, ten hundred and fifty guilders, and took his receipt, upon account. Met Mr. Willink upon the road, going to the Hague, with a lady. He has left for me a letter of credit upon Paris, unlimited. He wished my journey to Paris might have a tendency towards peace.

18. Friday. Set off at ten from the Arms of Amsterdam, with Mr. John Thaxter and Mr. Charles Storer; refreshed our horses at Loenen, a village half way to Utrecht; passed the villages Breuekelen, Massen, and Suylem. It is eight hours, stones, or leagues, from Amsterdam to Utrecht. The village of Suylem and its neighborhood, is full of brickkilns; the clay is found in that neighborhood, and they burn the bricks with turf, wood, and coal. Put up at Utrecht, at the new Castle of Antwerp, which is now kept by Oblet, who speaks English very well, although born at Leyden. The grand canal, which runs through this town,

is a great curiosity. The paved street upon each side of it, is a covered way, or rather the cover of a cellar. The cellars of the houses are all continued out, under this paved street, to the canal, and there are doors through which men pass from the canal under the street into the cellars of the houses, and e contra, from the cellars to the canal, and the boats, barks, or schuits in it. The city maintains the pavement, but the vaults underneath are maintained by the proprietors." Oblet tells me, "that the Spanish and Prussian ambassadors were here a few days ago; came in a hired carriage; Lord Stormont and his lady were once here; travelled only with two men servants; very near; my lady had not so much as a maid with her. Peterson is much hated. Oostergo makes a great noise to-day, about the fleet's not going to Brest."

19. Saturday. From Utrecht to Gorcum is eight leagues; here we dined at the Doele, kept by Mr. Van Dongen. He told us, that as soon as we should get out of town, we should come to the river, near the junction of the Maes with the Wahal, a branch of the Rhine; that if we looked up the river, we should have a full view of the castle of Louvestein. We had accordingly a fair view of it. It stands upon an island in the middle of the river. There is a high and large square tower of a church at no great distance from it; Gorichem or Gorcum, is one of the eighteen cities of the Province of Holland. We dined at Gorcum, but as it was impossible to reach Breda before half-after-six, when the gates of that city are shut, my servant rode forward on horseback, and went to the Prince Cardinal, a public house, the keeper of which applied to General Marsdam, the Governor, so that when we arrived at near nine o'clock, we found an officer and a guard at the gate, who said he had orders to admit Mr. Adams, the ambassador of America. I gave the guards four guilders on the spot, and sent them two ducats afterwards. The four last leagues, being sand, were tolerable, but the former four, being clay, were very bad, muddy, and deep.

20. Sunday. Rising early this morning, and ringing for a servant, was told that my servant, and most of those of the house, were gone to mass. The name of the keeper of the Prince Cardinal is Van Opdorp.

Spent the whole day in travelling from Breda to Antwerp, without eating or drinking. The distance is only ten leagues. Put up at the Grand Laboureur, opposite the church with the statue of the prophet Elias upon it. The coaches in great numbers, were driving backwards and forwards upon the Place de Mier, as upon the Boulevards at Paris. It was Sunday evening, and this march and countermarch was for pleasure and for health. Thus four days have been completely consumed in passing from the Hague to Antwerp, and we have seen nothing and conversed with nobody; so bad have been the roads, and so cold and rainy the weather.

21. Monday. Went to the Cathedral, where we saw the Assumption of the Virgin Mary, the famous altar-piece of Rubens—the figures and coloring are beautiful, beyond description,—and the Descent of Jesus from the Cross. Rubens has placed in this piece his three wives and daughter, and his own head. The coloring is all gloomy, accommodated to the subject. In this church each trade has its altar. We remarked the martyrdom of Crispin, patron of the shoemakers. In another part, the martyrdom of Saint Sebastian—shot by arrows. This church is remarkably clean; no dust upon any of the figures. Went next to the church of Saint James, principally to see the tomb of Rubens. There is a picture drawn by Rubens containing in one piece the figures of his grandfather, father, two of his wives, and three of his children; an inscription at the door,—Ostium Monumenti Familiæ Rubenianæ. Rubens was born at Cologne, but removed at the age of ten years, with his family, to Antwerp. He travelled into Italy. Mass is said four times a day at this altar. Went next to see the private collection of Jaques Van Laneker. Here is a head of his second wife, by Rubens, and a larger picture of the Saviour delivering the Keys to Saint Peter. There is a jealousy very

remarkable in the face of one of the apostles. A Christ, by Rubens; a Magdalen, by Paul Veronese, an Italian; a Man and his Wife, by Rembrandt, and several other pieces by him, Vandyke, &c.

We went in the last place to see the private collection of Pilaer and Beekmans, Négocians en Dentelles, Diamans, Tableaux, Desseins, Estampes, &c., Place de Mier. The most remarkable piece in this collection is an old woman, his mother, with a bible on the table before her, by Rembrandt. This is called his master-piece; it is indeed an admirable picture. The son-in-law of this house told me there was a society formed in this town which had begun to send ventures to America.

After dinner we rode to Bruxelles, and put up at the Hôtel de Bellevue. Mr. Jenings *Endnote 110* came in, and we had a very agreeable hour with him. The gate was shut before our arrival. The porter demanded my name and quality, in order to send them to a burgomaster of the city for a billet de poste. The messenger returned with an order to admit Mr. Adams, ministre plénipotentiaire des États Unis, &c. in stronger terms than usual. I did not know but the burgomaster would have omitted the quality in the order. But I am told that everybody here is American.

22. Tuesday. Visited Mr. William Lee in the Place de Saint-Michel with Mr. Jenings. Mr. Lee said, that the swallow was a sign of summer,—my appearance denoted peace.

Mr. Jenings let me into the character of Mr. Fitzherbert. His father was prevailed on by Lord North to vote with him, but he was never easy in his mind about it, and finally cut his own throat. The gentleman at Paris is about thirty-three, wholly dependent on Lord Shelburne; has parts, but very conceited and assuming; not liked by the English while at Brussels, because he did not keep a table. He was only resident, and his appointment small, not more than fifteen hundred pounds. He writes from Paris, that the Count de Vergennes has a great character, but that he sees nothing in him. This is evidence of vanity; for that minister has at least a vast experience, and too much reserve to give proofs of great or little qualities so soon to this young gentleman. His parts are quick, and his education has been good. He has sometimes treated the English with cool contempt, and sometimes with hot pride.

We set off on our journey about twelve, but before we reached Halle, the iron axletree of our fore-wheels snapped off like a piece of glass, our carriage fell, and we were put to great difficulty to drag it to the Porte Verte, a tavern in this village. Being thus detained for the reparation of our carriage, after dinner we walked about the village, and visited the church of Notre-Dame de Halle, but saw nothing but what is very common. The village is dirty and poor. What a contrast to the villages of Holland!

23. Wednesday. Rode to Mons, in a great rain. Dined at the Couronne de l'Empereur; very well and very cheap. Rode to Valenciennes, and found our axletree broken again. Put up at the Post House. Walked about the town,—the churches all shut, and nothing remarkable. All the cities and villages of Brabant are very different from those of Holland. The streets very foul; the houses very dirty; the doors and windows broken; bricks and glass wanting. The people, men, women, and children, filthy and ragged.

24. Thursday. Visited the church at Valenciennes. Saw a Notre-Dame de Halle. A collection of portraits, ancient and modern, and picture of the Virgin Mary in the air, sending by angels a cord round the city, with an inscription, importing Valenciennes surrounded with a cord by the blessed Virgin, and saved from the plague, anno 1008.

Dined at Cambray. Visited the cathedral. Saw the tomb of Fénelon, his statue, picture, &c. Saw the chapter where the chanoines meet twice a week, and saw also the room where are the portraits of all the archbishops and bishops, ancient and modern, and Fénelon among the rest. There is also in this church a curious piece of clock-work, which represents the whole process with Jesus Christ, like that in the seven chapels of Mont Calvaire. Lodged at Péronne.

25. Friday. Dined at Gournay. Carriage broke again. Arrived at night at Pont Saint Maxence, two posts from Chantilly, and one and a half from Senlis.

26. Saturday. Parted from Pont Saint Maxence for Chantilly. The distance is two posts, and we found the road very good. We went to see the stables and horses. I had on my travelling gloves, and one of the grooms ran up to us with three whip-sticks, and presented them to us. This is an air which the grooms give themselves in order to get something to drink. They do the same to the Prince of Condé himself, if he enters the stable with gloves on his hands. I gave them six livres; but if I had been a private character I should have thought twenty-four sous, or even half of it, enough. We went round the castle, and took a look at the statue of the Grand Condé, in marble, half way up the great staircase, and saw the statue on horseback, in bronze, of the Grand Constable Montmorency. Walked round the gardens, fish-ponds, grottos, and water-spouts, and looked at the carps and swans that came up to us for bread. Nothing is more curious than this. Whistle, or throw a bit of bread into the water, and hundreds of carps, large and fat as butter, will be seen swimming near the top of the water towards you, and will assemble all in a huddle before you. Some of them will thrust up their mouths to the surface, and gape at you, like young birds in a nest to their parents for food. While we were viewing the statue of Montmorency, Mademoiselle de Bourbon came out into the round house at the corner of the castle, dressed in beautiful white, her hair uncombed, hanging and flowing about her shoulders, with a book in her hand, and leaned over the bar of iron; but soon perceiving that she had caught my eye, and that I viewed her more attentively than she fancied, she rose up with that majesty and grace which persons of her birth aflect, if they are not taught, turned her hair off both her shoulders with her hands, in a manner that I could not comprehend, and decently stepped back into the chamber, and was seen no more. The book in her hand is consistent with what I heard four years ago at the Palais de Bourbon, in Paris, that she was fond of reading.

The ménagerie, where they exercise the horses, is near the end of the stables, and is a magnificent piece of architecture. The orangery appears large, but we did not look into it. The village of Chantilly appears a small thing; in the forest or park we saw bucks, hares, pheasants, partridges, &c., but not in such plenty as one would expect.

We took a cutlet and glass of wine, at ten, at Chantilly, that we might not be tempted to stop again; accordingly we arrived in very good season at the Hôtel de Valois, Rue de Richelieu, where the house, however, was so full that we found but bad accommodations.

The first thing to be done in Paris, is always to send for a tailor, peruke-maker, and shoemaker, for this nation has established such a domination over the fashion, that neither clothes, wigs, nor shoes, made in any other place, will do in Paris. This is one of the ways in which France taxes all Europe, and will tax America. It is a great branch of the policy of the Court to preserve and increase this national influence over the mode, because it occasions an immense commerce between France and all the other parts of Europe. Paris furnishes the materials and the manner, both to men and women, everywhere else.

Mr. Ridley lodges in the Rue de Cléry, No. 60. Mr. Jay, Rue des petits Augustins, Hôtel d'Orléans.

27. Sunday. Went into the bath upon the Seine, not far from the Pont Royal, opposite the Tuilleries. You are shown into a little room which has a large window looking over the river into the Tuilleries. There is a table, a glass, and two chairs, and you are furnished with hot linen, towels, &c. There is a bell which you ring when you want any thing.

Went in search of Ridley, and found him. He says Franklin has broke up the practice of inviting everybody to dine with him on Sunday, at Passy; that he is getting better; the gout left him weak; but he begins to sit at table; that Jay insists on having an exchange of full powers before he enters on conference or treaty; refuses to treat with D'Aranda, until he has a copy of his full powers; refused to treat with Oswald, until he had a commission to treat with the Commissioners of the United States of America; *Endnote 111* Franklin was afraid to insist upon it; was afraid we should be obliged to treat without; differed with Jay; refused to sign a letter, &c.; Vergennes wanted him to treat with D'Aranda without.

The Ministry quarrel. De Fleury has attacked De Castries, upon the expenses of the marine. Vergennes is supposed to be with De Fleury; talk of a change of ministry; talk of De Choiseul, &c.

Franklin wrote to Madrid at the time when he wrote his pretended request to resign and supposed that I would succeed him at this Court, and obtained a promise that W. should be secretary. Jay did not know but he was well qualified for the place. *Endnote 112*

Went to the Hôtel d'Orléans, Rue des petits Augustins, to see my colleague in the commission for peace, Mr. Jay, but he and his lady were gone out.

Mr. Ridley dined with me, and after dinner we went to view the apartments in the Hôtel du Roi, and then to Mr. Jay, and Mrs. Izard; but none at home. Ridley returned, drank tea, and spent the evening with me. Mr. Jeremiah Allen, our fellow passenger in the leaky Sensible, and our fellow traveller through Spain, came in and spent the evening. He has been home since, and returned.

R. is still full of Jay's firmness and independence; has taken upon himself to act without asking advice, or even communicating with the Count de Vergennes, and this even in opposition to an instruction. This instruction, which is alluded to in a letter I received at the Hague, a few days before I left it, has never yet been communicated to me. It seems to have been concealed designedly from me. *Endnote 113* The commission to William was urged to be filled up, as soon as the commission came to Oswald to treat with the ministers of the United States, and it is filled up and signed. William has lately been very frequently with Jay, at his house, and has been very desirous of persuading Franklin to live in the same house with Jay. Between two as subtle spirits as any in this world, the one malicious, the other, I think honest, I shall have a delicate, a nice, a critical part to act. Franklin's cunning will be to divide us; to this end he will provoke, he will insinuate, he will intrigue, he will manœuvre. My curiosity will at least be employed in observing his invention and his artifice. Jay declares roundly, that he will never set his hand to a bad peace. Congress may appoint another, but he will make a good peace or none.

28. Monday. Dined with Mr. Allen.

29. Tuesday. Dined at the Hôtel du Roi. Mr. Ridley dined with us. In the evening I went out to Passy to make my visit to Franklin.

30. Wednesday. Dined with Mr. Jay.

31. Thursday. Dined with Mr. Oswald, Dr. Franklin, Mr. Jay, Mr. Strachey, Mr. Roberts, and Mr. Whitefoord.

November 1. Friday. Dined at Passy, with Mr. Franklin.

2. Saturday. Mr. Oswald, Mr. Franklin, Mr. Jay, Mr. Strachey, Mr. W. Franklin, dined with me at the Hôtel du Roi, Rue du Carrousel. *Almost every moment of this week has been employed in negotiation with the English gentlemen concerning peace. We have made two propositions; one the line of forty-five degrees; the other, a line through the middle of the lakes. And for the bound between Massachusetts and Nova Scotia, a line from the mouth of Saint Croix to its source, and from its source to the highlands.

3. Sunday. In my first conversation with Franklin, on Tuesday evening last, he told me of Mr. Oswald's demand of the payment of debts and compensation to the tories. He said that their answer had been, that we had not power, nor had Congress. I told him I had no notion

of cheating anybody. The question of paying debts, and that of compensating tories, were two. I had made the same observation that forenoon to Mr. Oswald and Mr. Strachey, in company with Mr. Jay, at his house. I saw it struck Mr. Strachey with peculiar pleasure; I saw it instantly smiling in every line of his face; Mr. Oswald was apparently pleased with it too. In a subsequent conversation with my colleagues, I proposed to them that we should agree, that Congress should recommend it to the States to open their courts of justice for the recovery of all just debts. They gradually fell into this opinion, and we all expressed these sentiments to the English gentlemen, who were much pleased with it; and with reason, because it silences the clamors of all the British creditors against the peace, and prevents them from making common cause with the refugees.

Mr. Jay came in and spent two hours in conversation upon our affairs, and we attempted an answer to Mr. Oswald's letter. He is perfectly of my opinion, or I am of his, respecting Mr. Dana's true line of conduct, as well as his with Spain, and ours with France, Spain, and England.

I learn from him that there has not been a harmony between him and Carmichael. The latter aimed at founding himself upon a French interest, and was more supple to the French ambassador at Madrid, and to Mr. Gérard, than was approved by the former. Gérard endeavored to persuade him to show him his instructions, which he refused, at which offence was taken. Vergennes has endeavored to persuade him to treat with D'Aranda without exchanging powers; he refuses. Vergennes also pronounced Oswald's first commission sufficient, and was for making the acknowledgment of American independence the first article of the treaty. Jay would not treat; the consequence was, a complete acknowledgment of our independence by Oswald's new commission under the great seal of Great Britain, to treat with the commissioners of the United States of America. Thus a temperate firmness has succeeded everywhere, but the base system nowhere.

Ridley says, that Jenings is in easy circumstances, and as he always lives within his income, is one of the most independent men in the world. He remitted him three thousand pounds sterling, when he came over to France. His father left him ten thousand pounds. He kept great company in England, and no other. He is related to several principal families in America, and to several great families in England; was bred to the law in the Temple, and practised as chamber counsel, but no otherwise.

D'Estaing has set off for Madrid and Cadiz. Reste à savoir, what his object is: whether to take the command of a squadron, and in that case where to go; whether to Rhode Island, to join Vaudreuil, and go against New York, or to the West Indies. Will they take New York, or only prevent the English from evacuating it? O. proposed solemnly to all three of us yesterday, at his house, to agree not to molest the British troops in the evacuation, but we did not; this, however, shows they have it in contemplation. Suppose they are going against West Florida; how far are we bound to favor the Spaniards? Our treaty with France must and shall be sacredly fulfilled, and we must admit Spain to accede, when she will; but until she does, our treaty does not bind us to France to assist Spain.

The present conduct of England and America resembles that of the eagle and cat. An eagle scaling over a farmer's yard, espied a creature that he thought a hare; he pounced upon him and took him up in the air; the cat seized him by the neck with her teeth, and round the body with her fore and hind claws. The eagle finding himself scratched and pressed, bids the cat let go and fall down. No, says the cat, I won't let go and fall; you shall stoop and set me down.

4. Monday. Called on Jay, and went to Oswald's, and spent with him and Strachey, from eleven to three, in drawing up the articles respecting debts, and tories, and fishery. I drew up the article anew in this form.

"That the subjects of His Britannic Majesty, and the people of the said United States, shall continue to enjoy unmolested, the right to take fish of every kind, on all the Banks of Newfoundland, in the Gulf of Saint Lawrence, and all other places, where the inhabitants of both countries used, at any time heretofore, to fish; and also to dry and cure their fish on the shores of Nova Scotia, Cape Sable, the Isle of Sable, and on the shores of any of the unsettled bays, harbors, or creeks of Nova Scotia and the Magdalen Islands; and His Britannic Majesty, and the said United States, will extend equal privileges and hospitality to each other's fishermen as to his own."

Dined with the Marquis de Lafayette, with the Prince de Poix, the Viscount de Noailles and his lady, Mr. Jay, Mr. Price and his lady, Mrs. Izard and her two daughters, Dr. Bancroft, Mr. William Franklin. The Marquis proposed to me in confidence, his going out with D'Estaing, to the West Indies. But he is to go, a month hence, in a frigate.

Mem. All the forenoon, from eleven to three, at Mr. Oswald's, Mr. Jay and I—in the evening there again until near eleven. Strachey is as artful and insinuating a man as they could send; he pushes and presses every point as far as it can possibly go; he is the most eager, earnest, pointed spirit. We agreed last night to this:

Whereas certain of the United States, excited thereto by the unnecessary destruction of private property, have confiscated all debts due from their citizens to British subjects, and also, in certain instances, lands belonging to the latter. And whereas it is just that private contracts, made between individuals of the two countries before the war, should be faithfully executed, and as the confiscation of the said lands may have a latitude not justifiable by the law of nations, it is agreed that British creditors, shall, notwithstanding, meet with no lawful impediment, to recovering the full value, or sterling amount, of such bonâ fide debts as were contracted before the year 1775. And also, that Congress will recommend to the said States, so to correct, if necessary, their said acts respecting the confiscation of lands in America belonging to real British subjects, as to render their said acts consistent with perfect justice and equity.

5. Tuesday. Mr. Jay likes Frenchmen as little as Mr. Lee and Mr. Izard did. He says they are not a moral people; they know not what it is; he don't like any Frenchman; the Marquis de Lafayette is clever, but he is a Frenchman. Our allies don't play fair, he told me; they were endeavoring to deprive us of the fishery, the western lands, and the navigation of the Mississippi; they would even bargain with the English to deprive us of them; they want to play the western lands, Mississippi, and whole Gulf of Mexico, into the hands of Spain.

Oswald talks of Pulteney, and a plot to divide America between France and England; France to have New England. They tell a story about Vergennes, and his agreeing that the English might propose such a division, but reserving a right to deny it all. These whispers ought not to be credited by us.

9. Saturday. The Marquis de Lafayette came in and told me he had been to Versailles, and in consultation with him about the affair of money, as he and I had agreed he should. He said he found that the Count de Vergennes and their ministry were of the same opinion with me; that the English were determined to evacuate New York. After some time, he told me, in a great air of confidence, that he was afraid the Count took it amiss that I had not been to Versailles to see him; the Count told him, that he had not been officially informed of my arrival; he had only learned it from the returns of the police.

I went out to Passy to dine with Mr. Franklin, who had been to Versailles, and presented his memorial and the papers accompanying it. The Count said he would have the papers translated, to lay them before the King; but the affair would meet with many difficulties. Franklin brought the same message to me from the Count, and said he believed it would be taken kindly if I went. I told both the Marquis and the Doctor that I would go to-morrow morning.

10. Sunday. Accordingly, at eight this morning I went and waited on the Comte. He asked me how we went on with the English. I told him we divided upon two points,—the Tories and Penobscot; two ostensible points; for it was impossible to believe that my Lord Shelburne or the nation cared much about such points. I took out of my pocket and showed him the record of Governor Pownal's solemn act of burying a leaden plate with this inscription:

"May 23. 1759. Province of Massachusetts Bay. Penobscot, dominions of Great Britain. Possession confirmed by Thomas Pownal, Governor."

This was planted on the east side of the river of Penobscot, three miles above marine navigation. I showed him also all the other records,—the laying out of Mount Desert, Machias, and all the other towns to the east of the river Penobscot; and told him that the grant of Nova Scotia by James I. to Sir William Alexander, bounded it on the river St. Croix; and that I was possessed of the authorities of four of the greatest governors the King of England ever had,—Shirley, Pownal, Bernard, and Hutchinson, in favor of our claim,—and of learned writings of Shirley and Hutchinson in support of it. The Comte said that Mr. Fitzherbert told him they wanted it for the masts; but the Comte said that Canada had an immense quantity. I told him I thought there were few masts there, but that I fancied it was not masts, but tories that again made the difficulty; some of them claimed lands in that territory, and others hoped for grants there. The Comte said it was not astonishing that the British Ministry should insist upon compensation to them, for that all the precedents were in favor of it; that there had been no example of an affair like this, terminated by a treaty, without reëstablishing those who had adhered to the old government in all their possessions. I begged his pardon in this, and said that in Ireland at least there had been a multitude of confiscations without restitution. Here we ran into some conversation concerning Ireland, &c.

Mr. Rayneval, who was present, talked about the national honor and the obligation they were under to support their adherents. Here I thought I might indulge a little more latitude of expression than I had done with Oswald and Strachey; and I answered, if the nation thought itself bound in honor to compensate these people, it might easily do it, for it cost the nation more money to carry on this war one month, than it would cost it to compensate them all; but I could not comprehend this doctrine of national honor; those people, by their misrepresentations, had deceived the nation who had followed the impulsion of their devouring ambition until it had brought an indelible stain on the British name, and almost irretrievable ruin on the nation; and now that very nation was thought to be bound in honor to compensate its dishonorers and destroyers. Rayneval said it was very true.

The Comte invited me to dine. I accepted. When I came, I found the Marquis de Lafayette in conference with him. When they came out, the Marquis took me asidé, and told me he had been talking with the Comte upon the affair of money; he had represented to him Mr. Morris's arguments, and the things I had said to him as from himself, &c.; that he feared the arts of the English; that our army would disband, and our governments relax, &c.; that the Comte feared many difficulties; that France had expended two hundred and fifty millions in this war, and that he talked of allowing six millions, and my going to Holland with the scheme I had projected, and having the King's warranty, &c. to get the rest; that he had already spoken to some of M. de Fleury's friends, and intended to speak to him, &c.

We went up to dinner. I went up with the Comte alone. He showed me into the room where were the ladies and the company. I singled out the Countess, and went up to her to make her my compliments. The Countess and all the ladies rose up; I made my respects to them all, and turned round and bowed to the rest of the company. The Count, who came in after me, made his bows to the ladies, and to the Countess last. When he came to her, he turned round and called out, "Monsieur Adams, venez ici, voilà la Comtesse de Vergennes." A nobleman in company said, "Mr. Adams has already made his court to Madame la Comtesse." I went up again, however, and spoke again to the Countess, and she to me. When dinner was served, the Comte led Madame de Montmorin, and left me to conduct the Countess, who gave me her hand with extraordinary condescension, and I conducted her to table. She made me sit next her on her right hand, and was remarkably attentive to me the whole time. The Comte, who sat opposite, was constantly calling out to me to know what I would eat, and to offer me petits gateaux, claret and madeira, &c. &c. In short, I was never treated with half the respect at Versailles in my life.

In the antechamber, before dinner, some French gentlemen came to me and said they had seen me two years ago; said that I had shown in Holland that the Americans understand negotiation as well as war. The compliments that have been made me since my arrival in France, upon my success in Holland, would be considered as a curiosity if committed to writing. "Je vous félicite sur votre succès," is common to all. One adds, "Monsieur, ma foi, vous avez réussi bien merveilleusement. Vous avez fait reconnoître votre indépendance; vous avez fait un traité, et vous avez procuré de l'argent. Voilà un succès parfait." Another says, "Vous avez fait des merveilles en Hollande: vous avez culbuté le Stathouder et le parti Anglois; vous avez donné bien du mouvement, vous avez remué tout le monde." Another said, "Monsieur, vous êtes le Washington de la négociation." This is the finishing stroke. It is impossible to exceed this. Compliments are the study of this people, and there is no other so ingenious at them.

11. Monday. Mr. Whitefoord, the Secretary of Mr. Oswald, came a second time, not having found me at home yesterday, when he left a card with a copy of Mr. Oswald's commission, attested by himself, (Mr. Oswald.) He delivered the copy, and said Mr. Oswald was ready to compare it to the original with me. I said, Mr. Oswald's attestation was sufficient, as he had already shown me his original. He sat down, and we fell into conversation about the weather, and the vapors and exhalations from Tartary, which had been brought here last spring by the winds, and given us all the influenza; thence, to French fashions, and the punctuality with which they insist upon people's wearing thin clothes in spring and fall, though the weather is ever so cold, &c. I said it was often carried to ridiculous lengths, but that it was at bottom an admirable policy, as it rendered all Europe tributary to the city of Paris for its manufactures. We fell soon into politics. I told him that there was something in the minds of the English and French which impelled them irresistibly to war every ten or fifteen years. He said the ensuing peace would, he believed, be a long one. I said it would, provided it was well made, and nothing left in it to give future discontents; but if any thing was done which the Americans should think hard and unjust, both the English and French would be continually blowing it up and inflaming the American minds with it, in order to make them join one side or the other in a future war. He might well think, that the French would be very glad to have the Americans join them in a future war. Suppose, for example, they should think the tories men of monarchical principles, or men of more ambition than principle, or men corrupted and of no principle, and should, therefore, think them more easily seduced to their purposes than virtuous republicans, is it not easy to see the policy of a French minister in wishing them amnesty and compensation? Suppose a French minister foresees that the presence of the tories in America will keep up perpetually two parties,—a French party and an English party,—and that this will compel the patriotic and independent party to join the French party; is it not natural for him to wish them restored? Is it not easy to see that a French minister cannot wish to have the English

and Americans perfectly agreed upon all points, before they themselves, the Spaniards and Dutch, are agreed too? Can they be sorry, then, to see us split upon such a point as the tories? What can be their motives to become the advocates of the tories?

The French minister at Philadelphia, has made some representations to Congress in favor of a compensation to the royalists, and the Count de Vergennes, no longer than yesterday, said much to me in their favor. The Comte probably knows that we are instructed against it, or rather, have not constitutional authority to do it; that we can only write about it to Congress, and they to the States, who may and probably will deliberate upon it eighteen months, before they all decide, and then every one of them will determine against it. In this way, there is an insuperable obstacle to any agreement between the English and Americans, even upon terms to be inserted in the general peace, before all are ready. It was the constant practice of the French, to have some of their subjects in London, during the conferences for peace, in order to propagate such sentiments there as they wished to prevail. I doubted not such were there now. Mr. Rayneval had been there. Mr. Gérard, I had heard, is there now, and probably others. They can easily persuade the tories to set up their demands, and tell them and the ministers, that the King's dignity and nation's honor are compromised in it.

For my own part, I thought America had been long enough involved in the wars of Europe. She had been a foot-ball between contending nations from the beginning, and it was easy to foresee that France and England both would endeavor to involve us in their future wars. I thought it our interest and duty to avoid as much as possible, and to be completely independent, and have nothing to do, but in commerce, with either of them. That my thoughts had been from the beginning constantly employed to arrange all our European connections to this end, and that they would continue to be so employed, and I thought it so important to us, that if my poor labors, my little estate, or (smiling) sizy blood could effect it, it should be done. But I had many fears.

I said, the King of France might think it consistent with his station, to favor people who had contended for a crown, though it was the crown of his enemy. Whitefoord said, they seem to be, through the whole of this, fighting for reputation. I said, they had acquired it, and more, they had raised themselves high from a low estate by it, and they were our good friends and allies, and had conducted generously and nobly, and we should be just and grateful. But they might have political wishes, which we were not bound by treaty nor in justice or gratitude to favor, and these we ought to be cautious of. He agreed that they had raised themselves very suddenly and surprisingly by it. We had more conversation on the state of manners in France, England, Scotland, and in other parts of Europe, but I have not time to record this.

12. Tuesday. Dined with the Abbés Chalut and Arnoux; the Farmer-General and his daughter, Dr. Franklin and his grandson, Mr. Grand and his lady and niece, Mr. Ridley, and I, with one young French gentleman, made the company. The Farmer's daughter is about twelve years old, and is, I suppose, an enfant trouvée. He made her sing at table, and she bids fair to be an accomplished opera girl, though she has not a delicate ear. The compliment of "Monsieur, vous êtes le Washington de la négociation," was repeated to me by more than one person. I answered, "Monsieur, vous me faites le plus grand honneur, et le compliment le plus sublime possible." "Eh, Monsieur, en vérité, vous l'avez bien mérité." A few of these compliments would kill Franklin, if they should come to his ears.

This evening I went to the Hôtel des Treize États Unis, to see the Baron de Lynden; to the Hôtel d'York, to see the Messrs. Vaughan: and to the Hôtel d'Orleans, to see Mr. Jay; but found neither. Returned through the Rue St. Honoré, to see the decorated shops, which are pretty enough. This is the gayest street in Paris, in point of ornamental shops, but Paris does not excel in this respect.

The old Farmer-General was very lively at dinner; told stories, and seemed ready to join the little girl in songs, like a boy. Pleasures don't wear out men in Paris as in other places. The Abbé Arnoux asked me at table, "Monsieur, où est votre fils cadet, qui chante comme Orphée?" "Il est de retour en Amérique." To Mademoiselle Labhard, he said "Connoissez vous que Monsieur Adams a une demoiselle très aimable an Amérique?"

13. Wednesday. This is the anniversary of my quitting home. Three years are completed. Oh! when shall I return? Ridley dined with me. Captain Barney called in the evening, and took my despatches. One set he is to deliver to Captain Hill, another to Captain —, and the third he takes himself.

15. Friday. Mr. Oswald came to visit me, and entered with some freedom into conversation. I said many things to convince him, that it was the policy of my Lord Shelburne, and the interest of the nation, to agree with us upon the advantageous terms which Mr. Strachey carried away on the 5th; shewed him the advantages of the boundary, the vast extent of land, and the equitable provision for the payment of debts, and even the great benefits stipulated for the tories.

He said he had been reading Mr. Paine's Answer to the Abbé Raynal, and had found there an excellent argument in favor of the tories. Mr. Paine says, "that before the battle of Lexington we were so blindly prejudiced in favor of the English, and so closely attached to them, that we went to war at any time and for any object, when they bid us." Now, this being habitual to the Americans, it was excusable in the tories to behave upon this occasion as all of us had ever done upon all others. He said, if he were a member of Congress, he would show a magnanimity upon this occasion, and would say to the refugees, take your property; we scorn to make any use of it in building up our system.

I replied, that we had no power, and Congress had no power, and, therefore, we must consider how it would be reasoned upon in the several legislatures of the separate States, if, after being sent by us to Congress, and by them to the several States, in the course of twelve or fifteen months, it should be there debated; you must carry on the war six or nine months certainly for this compensation, and consequently spend, in the prosecution of it, six or nine times the sum necessary to make the compensation; for, I presume, this war costs every month to Great Britain a larger sum than would be necessary to pay for the forfeited estates.

"How," said I, "will an independent man in one of our assemblies consider this? We will take a man who is no partisan of England or France, one who wishes to do justice to both and to all nations, but is the partisan only of his own." "Have you seen," says he, "a certain letter written to the Count de Vergennes, wherein Mr. Samuel Adams is treated pretty freely?" "Yes," says I, "and several other papers, in which Mr. John Adams has been treated so too; I don't know what you may have heard in England of Mr. S. Adams; you may have been taught to believe, for what I know, that he eats little children; but I assure you he is a man of humanity and candor, as well as integrity; and further, that he is devoted to the interest of his country, and, I believe, wishes never to be, after a peace, the partisan to France or England, but to do justice and all the good he can to both; I thank you for mentioning him, for I will make him my orator. What will he say when the question of amnesty and compensation to the tories comes before the Senate of Massachusetts, and when he is informed that England makes a point of it, and that France favors her? He will say, here are two old, sagacious courts, both endeavoring to sow the seeds of discord among us, each endeavoring to keep us in hot water, to keep up continual broils between an English party and a French party, in hopes of obliging the independent and patriotic party to lean to its side; England wishes them here and compensated, not merely to get rid of them and to save themselves the money, but to plant among us instruments of their own, to make divisions among us, and between us and France, to be continually crying down the religion, the government, the manners of France, and crying up the language, the fashions, the blood, &c. of England; England also means, by insisting on our compensating these worst of enemies, to obtain from us a tacit acknowledgment of the right of the war, an implicit acknowledgment that the tories have been justifiable, or at least excusable, and that we only, by a fortunate coincidence of events, have carried a wicked rebellion into a complete revolution. At the very time when Britain professes to desire peace, reconciliation, perpetual oblivion of all past unkindnesses, can she wish to send in among us a number of persons, whose very countenances will bring fresh to our remembrance the whole history of the rise and progress of the war, and of all its atrocities? Can she think it conciliatory, to oblige us to lay taxes upon those whose habitations have been consumed, to reward those who have burned them? upon those whose whole property has been stolen, to reward the thieves? upon those whose relations have been cruelly destroyed, to compensate the murderers? What can be the design of France, on the other hand, by espousing the cause of these men? Indeed, her motives may be guessed at. She may wish to keep up in our minds a terror of England, and a fresh remembrance of all we have suffered; or she may wish to prevent our ministers in Europe from agreeing with the British ministers, until she shall say, that she and Spain are satisfied in all points.

I entered largely with Mr. Oswald into the consideration of the influence this question would have upon the councils of the British Cabinet and the debates in Parliament. The King and the old Ministry might think their personal reputations concerned, in supporting men who had gone such lengths, and suffered so much in their attachment to them. The King may say; "I have other dominions abroad,—Canada, Nova Scotia, Florida, the West India Islands, the East Indies, Ireland. It will be a bad example to abandon these men; others will lose their encouragement to adhere to my government." But the shortest answer to this is the best,—let the King, by a message, recommend it to Parliament to compensate them.

But how will my Lord Shelburne sustain the shock of opposition, when Mr. Fox and Mr. Burke shall demand a reason why the essential interests of the nation are sacrificed to the unreasonable demands of those very men who have done this great mischief to the empire, should these orators indulge themselves in philippics against the refugees, show their false representations, their outrageous cruelties, their innumerable demerits against the nation, and then attack the First Lord of the Treasury for continuing to spend the blood and treasure of the nation for their sakes?

17. Sunday. Have spent several days in copying Mr. Jay's despatches.

Mr. Vaughan came to me yesterday, and said that Mr. Oswald had that morning called upon Mr. Jay, and told him if he had known as much the day before as he had since learned, he would have written to go home. Mr. Vaughan said Mr. Fitzherbert had received a letter from Lord Townsend, that the compensation would be insisted on. Mr. Oswald wanted Mr. Jay to go to England; thought he could convince the ministry. Mr. Jay said, he must go with or without the knowledge and advice of this Court, and, in either case, it would give rise to jealousies; he could not go. Mr. Vaughan said, he had determined to go, on account of the critical state of his family, his wife being probably abed; he should be glad to converse freely with me, and obtain from me all the lights and arguments against the tories, even the history of their worst actions, that in case it should be necessary to run them down, it might be done; or at least expose them, for their true history was little known in England. I told him that I must be excused; it was a subject that I had never been desirous of obtaining information upon; that I pitied those people too much to be willing to aggravate their sorrows and sufferings, even of those who had deserved the worst. It might not be amiss to reprint the Letters of Governors Bernard, Hutchinson, and Oliver, to show the rise. It might not be amiss to read the History of Wyoming in the Annual Register for 1778 or 1779, to recollect the prison-ships and the churches at New York, where the garrisons of Fort Washington were starved, in order to make them enlist into refugee corps. It might not be amiss to recollect the burning of cities, and the thefts of plate, negroes, and tobacco.

I entered into the same arguments with him that I had used with Mr. Oswald, to show that we could do nothing, Congress nothing; the time it would take to consult the States, and the reasons to believe that all of them would at last decide against it. I showed him that it would be a religious question with some, a moral one with others, and a political one with more; an economical one, with very few. I showed him the ill effect which would be produced upon the American mind by this measure; how much it would contribute to perpetuate alienation against England, and how French emissaries might, by means of these men, blow up the flames of animosity and war. I showed him how the whig interest and the opposition might avail themselves of this subject in Parliament, and how they might embarrass the minister.

He went out to Passy for a passport, and in the evening called upon me again. Said he found Dr. Franklin's sentiments to be the same with Mr. Jay's and mine, and hoped he should be able to convince Lord Shelburne; he was pretty confident that it would work right; the ministry and nation were not informed upon the subject; Lord Shelburne had told him, that no part of his office gave him so much pain as the levee he held for these people, and hearing their stories of their families and estates, their losses, sufferings, and distresses. Mr. Vaughan said he had picked up here a good deal of information about those people from Mr. Allen and other Americans.

Ridley, Allen, and Mason, dined with me; and in the evening Captain Barney came in, and told me that Mr. Vaughan went off to-day at noon. I delivered to Barney, Mr. Jay's long despatches and the other letters.

In the evening the Marquis de Lafayette came in and told me he had been to see M. de Fleury on the subject of a loan. He told him that he must afford America this year a subsidy of twenty millions. M. de Fleury said France had already spent two hundred and fifty millions in the American war, and that they could not allow any more money to her; that there was a great deal of money in America; that the King's troops had been subsisted and paid there; that the British army had been subsisted and paid there, &c. The Marquis said, that little of the subsistence or pay of the British had gone into any hands but those of the tories within their lines. I said, that more money went in for their goods than came out for provisions or any thing. The Marquis added to M. Fleury that Mr. Adams had a plan for going to the States-General for a loan or subsidy. M. Fleury said he did not want the assistance of Mr. Adams to get money in Holland; he could have what he would. The Marquis said, Mr. Adams would be glad of it; he did not want to go, but was willing to take the trouble if necessary.

The Marquis said he should dine with the Queen to-morrow, and would give her a hint to favor us; that he should take leave in a few days, and should go in the fleet that was to sail from Brest; that he wanted the advice of Mr. Franklin, Mr. Jay, and me, before he went, &c.—said there was a report that Mr. Gérard had been in England, and that M. de Rayneval was gone. I told him I saw Mr. Gérard at Mr. Jay's a few evenings ago. He said he did not believe Mr. Gérard had been; that he had mentioned it to Count de Vergennes, and he did not appear confused at all, but said Mr. Gérard was here about the limits of Alsace. The Marquis said that he believed the reason why Count de Vergennes said so little about the progress of Mr. Fitzherbert with him was, because the difficulty about peace was made by the Spaniards, and he was afraid of making the Americans still more angry with Spain; he knew the Americans were very angry with the Spaniards.

18. Monday. Returned Mr. Oswald's visit. He says, Mr. Strachey, who set out the 5th, did not reach London until the 10th; couriers are three, four, or five days, in going, according as the winds are.

We went over the old ground concerning the tories. He began to use arguments with me to relax. I told him he must not think of that, but must bend all his thoughts to convince and persuade his Court to give it up; that if the terms now before his Court were not accepted, the whole negotiation would be broken off, and this Court would probably be so angry with Mr. Jay and me, that they would set their engines to work upon Congress, get us recalled, and some others sent, who would do exactly as this Court would have them. He said he thought that very probable. In another part of his conversation he said, we should all have gold snuff-boxes set with diamonds; "you will certainly have the picture." I told him, No; I had dealt too freely with this Court; I had not concealed from them any useful and necessary truth, although it was disagreeable; indeed, I neither expected nor desired any favors from them, nor would I accept any; I should not refuse any customary compliment of that sort, but it never had been, nor would be offered me; my fixed principle never to be the tool of any man, nor the partisan of any nation, would forever exclude me from the smiles and favors of courts.

In another part of the conversation, I said, that when I was young, and addicted to reading, I had heard about dancing on the points of metaphysical needles; but, by mixing in the world, I had found the points of political needles finer and sharper than the metaphysical ones. I told him the story of Josiah Quincy's conversations with Lord Shelburne, in 1774, in which he pointed out to him the plan of carrying on the war, which has been pursued this year, by remaining inactive at land, and cruising upon the coast to distress our trade.

He said he had been contriving an artificial truce since he found we were bound by treaty not to agree to a separate truce; he had proposed to the ministry to give orders to their men-of-war and privateers not to take any unarmed American vessels.

I said to him, supposing the armed neutrality should acknowledge American independence, by admitting Mr. Dana, who is now at Petersburg with a commission for that purpose in his pocket, to subscribe the principles of their marine treaty, the King of Great Britain could find no fault with it; he could never hereafter say, it was an affront or hostility; he had done it himself. Would not all neutral vessels have a right to go to America? and could not all American trade be carried on in neutral bottoms?

I said to him, that England would always be a country which would deserve much of the attention of America, independently of all considerations of blood, origin, language, morals, &c.; merely as a commercial country, she would forever claim the respect of America, because a great part of our commerce would be with her, provided she came to her senses, and made peace with us, without any points in the treaty that should ferment in the minds of the people; if the people should think themselves unjustly treated, they would never be easy, and they were so situated as to be able to hurt any power; the fisheries, the Mississippi, the tories, were points that would rankle; and that nation that should offend our people in any of them, would sooner or later feel the consequences.

Mr. Jay, Mr. Le Couteulx, and Mr. Grand came in. Mr. Grand says there is a great fermentation in England, and that they talk of uniting Lord North and Mr. Fox in administration; the Duke of Portland to come in, and Keppel to go out. But this is wild.

"You are afraid," says Mr. Oswald to-day, "of being made the tools of the powers of Europe." "Indeed I am," says I. "What powers?" said he. "All of them," said I. "It is obvious that all the powers of Europe will be continually manœuvring with us, to work us into their real or imaginary balances of power. They will all wish to make of us a makeweight candle, when they are weighing out their pounds. Indeed, it is not surprising; for we shall very often, if not always, be able to turn the scale. But I think it ought to be our rule not to meddle; and that of all the powers of Europe, not to desire us, or, perhaps, even to permit us, to interfere, if they can help it." "I beg of you," says he, "to get out of your head the idea that we shall disturb you." "What!" said I, "do you yourself believe that your ministers, governors, and even nation, will not wish to get us of your side in any future war?" "Damn the governors!" said he, "No! We will take off their heads if they do an improper thing towards you." "Thank you for your good will," said I, "which I feel to be sincere. But nations don't feel as you and I do; and your nation, when it gets a little refreshed from the fatigues of the war, when men and money are become plenty, and allies at hand, will not feel as it does now." "We never can be such sots," says he, "as to think of differing again with you." "Why," says I, "in truth I have never been able to comprehend the reason why you ever thought of differing with us thus far."

19. Tuesday. In the morning Mr. Jay called, and took me with him in his carriage to Versailles. We waited on the Count de Vergennes, and dined with him, in company with all the foreign ministers and others, to the number of forty-four or five. Mr. Berkenrode, the Dutch ambassador, told me, that he thought we should see something very singular in England. The conflicts of parties and contentions for the ministry were such, that he did not know where it would end. It was thought that Lord Shelburne could not support himself without an union with Lord North or Mr. Fox, and that the choice of either would determine the intentions of the Court and Parliament.

Mr. Brantzen told me, that they had begun the negotiations on their part, but were, as yet, very far asunder; but hoped they should approach nearer in a little time. Both he and Berkenrode asked me how we advanced. I told him, Mr. Oswald was waiting for a courier, in answer to his of the 5th, which arrived the 10th. I told them both, that we should not be behind hand of them. That, if it was once said that France, Spain, and Holland were ready, the British Ministry would not hesitate upon any points between us that remained. They both said, they believed we should find less difficulty to arrange our affairs with England than any of the others would.

The Swedish Minister went to a gentleman, and asked him to introduce him to Mr. Jay and me, which he did. The Minister told us he had been here since 1766. The same ministers are here from Russia, Denmark, and Sardinia, whom I knew here formerly. Mr. Jay made his compliment to Count d'Aranda, who invited him to come and see him and dine with him.

I see, by a long conversation at table with the Baron de Lynden, that he has an inclination to go to America; yet he modestly gives place to Mr. Van Berckel. The Marquis de Lafayette took leave of the King to-day in his American uniform and sword. He told me, that the Count de Vergennes told him, the day before, that M. de Rayneval was gone to England again; that he did not think the English so sincere as he wished for a speedy peace. He wished it himself, but could not see a prospect of it suddenly, &c. In returning, I asked Mr. Jay what he thought of the King of Great Britain's sending an ambassador to Congress? "After Mr. Oswald's commission, he might do it, and Congress must receive him." Jay said, "do you think with me upon that point too? If I were King of Great Britain, I would send a minister in the highest character; he should be ambassador extraordinary, and I would accredit him to our dear and beloved friends; and I would instruct that minister to treat Congress with as high respect as any crowned head in Europe."

"But," said I, "he ought to be well instructed, too, in other points, namely, never to hint, or to suffer a hint, against the treaties with France and Holland; never to admit the idea of our failing in our public faith or national honor; and, farther, never to interfere in our parties, general or particular, with our internal policy, or particular governments, and to warn our people not to let the French ministers do it; if the Britons should strike with us, I would agree with you, after the terms are signed, to advise to the measure; if I were the King of Great Britain, I would give orders to all my ambassadors at the neutral courts, to announce to those courts the independence of America; that I had acknowledged it, and given a commission under the great seal to treat with the Ministers of the United States of America; that I recommended to these Courts to follow the example, and open negotiations with the said United States; that I recommended to those neutral States to send their vessels freely to, and receive vessels freely from, all the ports of the United States; I would send the Earl of Effingham ambassador to Congress, instructed to assure them that I would do them my best offices, to secure to them the fisheries, their extent to the Mississippi, and the navigation of that river; that I would favor all their negotiations in Europe, upon their own plan of making commercial treaties with all nations; that I would interpose my good offices with the Barbary States to procure them Mediterranean passes, &c."

20. Wednesday. Dr. Franklin came in, and we fell into conversation; from one thing to another we came to politics. I told him, that it seemed uncertain, whether Shelburne could hold his ground without leaning upon Lord North, on one hand, or Fox, on the other; that if he joined North, or North and company should come in, they would go upon a contracted system, and would join people at this Court to deprive us of the Mississippi and the fisheries, &c.; if Fox came in, or joined Shelburne, they would go upon a liberal and manly system; and this was the only chance they had; no nation had ever brought itself into such a labyrinth; perplexed with the demands of Holland, Spain, France, and America, their funds were failing, and the money undertaken to be furnished was not found. Franklin said, that the bank came in aid, and he learned that large sums of scrip were lodged there. "In this situation," said I, "they have no chance but to set up America very high; and, if I were King of Great Britain, I would take that tone; I would send the first duke of the kingdom ambassador to Congress, and would negotiate in their favor at all the neutral courts, &c.; I would give the strongest assurances to Congress of support in the fisheries, the Mississippi, &c. and would compensate the tories myself."

I asked, what could be the policy of this Court in wishing to deprive us of the fisheries and Mississippi? I could see no possible motive for it, but to plant seeds of contention for a future war; if they pursued this policy, they would be as fatally blinded to their true interests as ever the English were. Franklin said, they would be every bit as blind; that the fisheries and Mississippi could not be given up; that nothing was clearer to him than that the fisheries were essential to the Northern States, and the Mississippi to the Southern, and, indeed, both to all. I told him that Mr. Gérard had certainly appeared to America, to negotiate to these ends, namely,—to persuade Congress to give up both; this was the reason of his being so unpopular in America, and this was the cause of their dislike to Samuel Adams, who had spoken very freely both to Gérard and his Congress on these heads; that Marbois appeared now to be pursuing the same objects. Franklin said, he had seen his letter. I said I was the more surprised at this, as Mr. Marbois, on our passage to America, had often said to me, that he thought the fishery our natural right and our essential interest, and that we ought to maintain it, and be supported in it; yet that he appeared now to be manœuvring against it; I told him that I always considered their extraordinary attack upon me, not as arising from any offence or any thing personal, but as an attack upon the fishery; there had been great debates in Congress upon issuing the first commission for peace, and in settling my instructions; that I was instructed not to make any treaty of commerce with Britain without an express clause acknowledging our right to the fishery; this Court knew that this would be, when communicated to the English, a strong motive with them to acknowledge our right; and, to take away this, they had directed their intrigues against me, to get my commission annulled, and had succeeded; they hoped also to gain some advantage in these points by associating others with me in the commission for peace; but they had failed in this; for the Mississippi and fishery were now much more secure than if I had been alone; that debates had run very high in Congress; that Mr. Drayton and Gouverneur Morris had openly espoused their plan, and Endnote 114 argued against the fishery; that Mr. Laurens and others of the Southern gentlemen had been stanch for them, and contended that, as nurseries of seamen and sources of trade, the Southern States were as much interested as the Northern; that debates had run so high, that the Eastern States had been obliged to give in their ultimatum in writing, and to say they would withdraw if any more was done; and that this point was so tender and important, that if not secured, it would be the cause of a breach of the union of the States; and their politics might, for what I knew, be so profound as to mean to lay a foundation for a rupture between the States, when, in a few years, they should think them grown too big; I could see no possible motive they had, to wish to negotiate the Mississippi into the hands of Spain, but this; knowing the fine country in the neighborhood, and the rapidity with which it would fill with inhabitants, they might force their way down the Mississippi and occasion another war; they had certainly sense enough to know, too, that we could not, and would not, be restrained from the fishery; that our people would be constantly pushing for it, and thus plunge themselves into another war, in which we should stand in need of France; if the old Ministry in England should come in again, they would probably join this Court in attempting to deprive us; but all would not succeed; we must be firm and steady, and should do very well. "Yes," he said, "he believed we should do very well, and carry the points."

I told him I could not think that the King and Council here had formed any digested plan against us upon these points; I hoped it was only the speculation of individuals. I told him, that if Fox should know that Shelburne refused to agree with us, merely because we would not compensate the tories, he would attack the minister upon this ground, and pelt him so with tories as to make him uncomfortable; I thought it would be very well to give Fox a hint. He said he would write him a letter upon it; he had sometimes corresponded with him, and Fox had been in conversation with him here before I arrived.

I walked before dinner to Mr. Jay's, and told him I thought there was danger that the old ministry would come in, or Shelburne unite with North; that the King did not love us, and the old ministry did not love us; but they loved the refugees, and thought, probably, their personal characters concerned to support them; Rayneval was gone to England, and I wanted to have him watched, to see if he was ever in company with North, Germain, Stormont, Hillsborough, Sandwich, Bute, or Mansfield; if the wing-clipping system and the support of the tories should be suggested by this Court to any of them, it would fall in with their passions and opinions, for several of the old ministry had often dropped expressions in the debates in Parliament, that it was the interest of England to prevent our growth to wealth and power; it was very possible that a part of the old ministry might come in, and Richmond, Keppel, Townsend, and Camden go out; and, in this case, though they could not revoke the acknowledgment of our independence, they would certainly go upon the contracted plan of clipping our wings; in this case, it is true, England would be finally the dupe, and it would be the most malicious policy possible against her; it is agreed, that if the whigs go out, and Richmond, Keppel, Townsend, Camden, &c., join Fox and Burke in opposition, there will be great probability of a national commotion and confusion.

Mr. Jay agreed with me in all I had said, and added, that six days would produce the King's speech; if that speech should inform Parliament that he had issued a commission to treat with the United States, and the two houses should thank him for it, it would look as if a good plan was to prevail; but if not, we should then take measures to communicate it far and wide.

I told him I thought, in that case, we should aid opposition as much as we could, by suggesting arguments to those who would transmit them in favor of America, and in favor of those who had the most liberal sentiments towards America, to convince them that the wing-clipping plan was ruinous to England and the most generous and noble part they could act towards America, the only one that could be beneficial to the nation; and to enable them to attack a contracted ministry with every advantage that could be.

I thought it was now a crisis in which good will or ill will towards America would be carried very far in England; a time, perhaps, when the American Ministers may have more weight in turning the tide of sentiment, or influencing the changes of administration, than they ever had before, and, perhaps, than they would have again; that I thought it our duty, upon this occasion, to say every thing we could to the Englishmen here, in order that just sentiments might prevail in England at this moment; to countenance every man well-disposed, and to disabuse and undeceive everybody; to drive out of countenance and into infamy every narrow thought of cramping, stinting, impoverishing, or enfeebling us; to show that it is their only interest to show themselves our friends, to wear away, if possible, the memory of past unkindnesses; to strike with us now upon our own terms, because, though we had neither power nor inclination to make peace without our allies, yet the very report that we had got over all our difficulties, would naturally make all Europe expect peace, would tend to make Spain less exorbitant in her demands, and would make Holland more ardent for peace, and dispose France to be more serious in her importunities with Spain and Holland, and even render France herself easier, though I did not imagine she would be extravagant in her pretensions; to show them the ruinous tendency of the war if continued another year or two. Where would England be if the war continued two years longer? what the state of her finances? what her condition in the East and West Indies, in North America, Ireland, Scotland, and even in England? What hopes have they of saving themselves from a civil war? If our terms are not now accepted they will never again have such offers from America; they will never have so advantageous a line; never, their debts; never, so much for the tories, and, perhaps, a rigorous demand of compensation for the devastations they have committed.

Mr. Jay agreed with me in sentiment, and, indeed, they are the principles he has uniformly pursued through the whole negotiation before my arrival; I think they cannot be misunderstood or disapproved in Congress. There never was a blunder in politics more egregious than will be committed by the present ministry, if they attempt to save the honor of the old ministry and of the tories. Shelburne may be too weak to combat them; but the true policy would be to throw all the odium of the war, and all the blame of the dismemberment of the empire, upon the old ministers and the tories; to run them down, tarnish them with votes, inveigh against them in speeches and pamphlets, even strip them of the pensions, and make them both ridiculous, insignificant, and contemptible; in short, make them as wretched as their crimes deserve; never think of sending them to America. But Shelburne is not strong enough; the old party, with the King at their head, is too powerful and popular yet. I really pity these people, as little as they deserve it; for surely no men ever deserved worse of society. If Fox was in, and had weight enough, and should take this decided part, which is consistent enough with the tenor of his speeches, which have been constant philippics against the old ministry, and frequent sallies against the refugees, and should adopt a noble line of conduct towards America, grant her all she asks, do her honor, and promote her prosperity, he would disarm the hostile mind and soften the resentful heart, recover much of the affection of America, much of her commerce, and, perhaps, equal consideration and profit and power from her as ever; she would have no governor nor armies there, and no taxes; but she would have profit, reputation, and power.

To-day I received a letter from my excellent friend, Mr. Laurens, 12 November, London, in answer to mine of the 6th, agreeing, as speedily as possible, to join his colleagues. "Thank God I had a son who dared to die for his country."

21. Thursday. Paid a visit to Mr. Brantzen, and then to the Count de Lynden. Spent two hours with him. He says the King of Sweden has overwhelmed him with his goodness; is perpetually writing to his ministers to compliment and applaud him for the part he has acted in refusing to go to Vienna, and for the reason he gave for it; says the revolution in Sweden was advantageous to France, in point of economy, for France used to pay very dear for partisans in pensions; that Russia, too, used to have a party there and pay pensions: now, by means of the Court, France predominates more easily. He said that, on Tuesday, he prayed the Introductor of Ambassadors to speak to the Prince de Tingry to put him upon the list to go to the Comedy with the King, Queen, and royal family, in the little Salle de Spectacle; that the King and Queen eyed him the whole evening, and as they came out the Introductor told the King that it was the Comte de Lynden, a man very zealous for the patriotic system; the King said, "Qui je sais son affaire." He says, that there is no man in the Republic who receives any thing from any foreign prince or state; that the law is very strict against it, and obliges every man to take an oath that he has not and will not, and no man dares; he don't believe that the Duke ever did; it would be a blunder in the English to offer it; for he is, by his name and family, enough attached without it. He says, that he has followed the principles which were given him by his Uncle Boetzlaer, who was high in favor at Court, and in great power through the Republic; that his age and family would be an objection against his going to America, but after affairs shall be a little settled, he expects that his friends will ask him what will be agreeable to him; but, if not, he shall take his place in the States-General, and retire to his estate in Zealand.

Ridley and Bancroft came in and spent the evening. Bancroft says, that Mr. Oswald don't feel very well; that he thinks of going home; that the King will bring in some of the old ministers, &c.

22. Friday. Made a visit to Dr. Bancroft, and spent an hour or two with him. Mr. Walpole, he says, is a correspondent of Mr. Fox. I told him I wished I could have two hours time with Fox.

Visited Mr. Mayo, Livingston, Vaughan, Rogers and lady, and Mr. Jay.

Mr. Jay says, that Oswald received a courier from London last evening; that his letters were brought in while he was there; that Oswald read one of them, and said, that "the tories stick; that Strachey is coming again, and may be expected today." Oswald called upon him this morning, but young Franklin was there; so he said nothing, as he would not speak before him. Jay says we had now to consider, whether we should state the question in writing to the Count de Vergennes, and ask his answer. I said to him. "we must be more dry and reserved and short with him, (Oswald,) than we had been." He said, "we must endeavor to discover, whether they agree to all the other points." I asked what he thought of agreeing to some compensation to the tories, if this Court advised to it. He said they would be very mad if we did. He said, that a tract of land, with a pompous preamble, would satisfy the English; but he would call upon Oswald this afternoon, and endeavor to know more, and call upon me in the evening.

Bancroft said to-day, that Fitzherbert was sensible, but conceited; that the Englishmen who were acquainted with him, however, said he was reserved about the secrets of his negotiation; but he expressed openly his feelings when Rayneval went over to England, as it implied, or seemed to imply, a want of confidence in him; he was displeased. That he had dined with him and Mr. Jay, at Mr. Oswald's. He said he found that the Englishmen here were prepared with their quibbles about the acknowledgment of American independence;

that the enabling act did not empower the King to grant such a commission; it enabled him to make peace with the Colonies, and to treat and conclude with any description of men, but not expressly to acknowledge them independent States; so that it might be cast upon the Crown or Ministry as an illegal act. Lord Camden had given his opinion that the act did not authorize the King to acknowledge the independence of America.

To this it may be answered that the King or Crown cannot go back; that an act of Parliament only can annul it; the King would make himself ridiculous in the eyes of all men, sovereigns especially, if he should consent to such an act; that a vote of either house of Parliament, declaring the commission illegal and null, would never pass; it would break off all negotiations, alarm America, and raise a rebellion in England; but the truth is, the Crown of England is absolute in war and peace; there is not even a fundamental law, as there is in France, that the King cannot alienate the domains of the Crown; on the contrary, by the British constitution, the King has power to cede and alienate parts, and, indeed, all his dominions; that is, there is no limitation. Bancroft said, there is an act of Parliament, that the King shall never alienate Gibraltar; so that Gibraltar cannot be ceded to Spain without an act of Parliament.

Bancroft said that Mr. Garnier is in Burgundy upon his estate, where he passes the summer, and comes only to Paris in the winter. He said, if the King in his speech should not announce Mr. Oswald's commission, you, gentlemen commissioners, would do well to take some measures for the publication of it in England and abroad.

I said, I wondered that Mr. Fox had not sent over some friend here, during the conferences, to pick up what he could of intelligence; but, upon recollection, I said his friends, Richmond, Keppel, Townsend, Camden, &c. were in the council and cabinet, and, therefore, no doubt informed him of all intelligence, and let him into all the secret of affairs.

Dr. Franklin, upon my saying the other day that I fancied he did not exercise so much as he was wont, answered, "Yes, I walk a league every day in my chamber; I walk quick, and for an hour, so that I go a league; I make a point of religion of it." I replied, "that as the commandment, 'thou shalt not kill,' forbids a man to kill himself, as well as his neighbor, it was manifestly a breach of the sixth commandment not to exercise; so that he might easily prove it to be a religious point." Bancroft said to-day, that it was often said among the French people, that Mons. de Vergennes loved Spain too well, and was too complaisant to the Spanish Court; that he was ambitious of being made a grandee of Spain, in order to cover his want of birth, for that he was not nobly born. This, I fancy, is a mistake; but such are the objects which men pursue,—titles, ribbons, stars, garters, crosses, keys, are the important springs that move the ambition of men in high life. How poor! how mean! how low! yet, how true! A low ambition, indeed! the pride of nobles and of kings!

"Let us, since life can little more supply
Than just to look about us and to die,
Expatiate free."

•

23. Saturday. Mr. Jay called at ten, and went out with me to Passy to meet the Marquis de Lafayette, at the invitation of Dr. Franklin. The Marquis's business was to show us a letter he had written to the Count de Vergennes on the subject of money. This I saw nettled Franklin, as it seemed an attempt to take to himself the merit of obtaining the loan, if one should be procured. He gave us also a letter to us three, for our approbation of his going out with the Count d'Estaing. He recites in it, that he had remained here by our advice, as necessary to the negotiations. This nettled both Franklin and Jay. I knew nothing of it, not having been here; and they both denied it. This unlimited ambition will obstruct his rise; he grasps at all,

civil, political, and military, and would be thought the unum necessarium in every thing; he has so much real merit, such family supports, and so much favor at Court, that he need not recur to artifice. He said, that Count de Vergennes told him, as the Chevalier de la Luzerne's despatches were not arrived, the Count could do nothing in the aflair of money without something French to go upon; his letter, therefore, was to supply the something French. He told us, that the Count d'Aranda had desired him to tell Mr. Jay, as the lands upon the Mississippi were not yet determined, whether they were to belong to England or Spain, he could not yet settle that matter; so that probably the attempt will be to negotiate them into the hands of the Spaniards from the English. D'Aranda, Rayneval, Grantham, &c. may conduct this without Fitzherbert.

Spent part of the evening at Mrs. Izard's. Mr. Oswald sent for Mr. Jay; desired to meet him at either house. Mr. Jay went, and I came off.

25. Monday. Dr. Franklin, Mr. Jay, and myself, at eleven, met at Mr. Oswald's lodgings. Mr. Strachey told us he had been to London, and waited personally on every one of the King's Cabinet Council, and had communicated the last propositions to them; they, every one of them, unanimously condemned that respecting the tories, so that that unhappy affair stuck, as he foresaw and foretold that it would.

The affair of the fishery too, was somewhat altered. They could not admit us to dry on the shores of Nova Scotia, nor to fish within three leagues of the coast, nor within fifteen leagues of the coast of Cape Breton. The boundary they did not approve; they thought it too extended, too vast a country, but they would not make a difficulty. That if these terms were not admitted, the whole affair must be thrown into Parliament, where every man would be for insisting on restitution to the refugees. He talked about excepting a few, by name, of the most obnoxious of the refugees.

I could not help observing, that the ideas respecting the fishery appeared to me to come piping hot from Versailles. I quoted to them the words of our treaty with France, in which the indefinite and exclusive right to the fishery on the western side of Newfoundland was secured against us, according to the true construction of the treaties of Utrecht and Paris. I showed them the twelfth and thirteenth articles of the treaty of Utrecht, by which the French were admitted to fish from Cape Bona Vista to Cape Riche. I related to them the manner in which the cod and haddock come into the rivers, harbors, creeks, and up to the very wharves, on all the northern coast of America, in the spring, in the month of April, so that you have nothing to do but step into a boat and bring in a parcel of fish in a few hours; but that in May they begin to withdraw; we have a saying at Boston, that when the "blossoms fall, the haddock begin to crawl;" that is, to move out into deep water, so that in summer you must go out some distance to fish. At Newfoundland it was the same; the fish, in March or April, were in shore in all the creeks, bays, and harbors, that is, within three leagues of the coasts or shores of Newfoundland and Nova Scotia; that neither French nor English could go from Europe and arrive early enough for the first fare; that our vessels could, being so much nearer, an advantage which God and nature had put into our hands; but that this advantage of ours had ever been an advantage to England, because our fish had been sold in Spain and Portugal for gold and silver, and that gold and silver sent to London for manufactures; that this would be the course again; that France foresaw it, and wished to deprive England of it, by persuading her to deprive us of it; that it would be a master stroke of policy if she could succeed, but England must be completely the dupe before she could succeed.

There were three lights in which it might be viewed: 1. As a nursery of seamen; 2. As a source of profit; 3. As a source of contention. As a nursery of seamen, did England consider us as worse enemies than France? Had she rather France should have the seamen than

America? The French marine was nearer and more menacing than ours. As a source of profit, had England rather France should supply the markets of Lisbon and Cadiz with fish, and take the gold and silver, than we? France would never spend any of that money in London; we should spend it all very nearly. As a source of contention, how could we restrain our fishermen, the boldest men alive, from fishing in prohibited places? How could our men see the French admitted to fish, and themselves excluded by the English? It would then be a cause of disputes, and such seeds France might wish to sow. That I wished for two hours conversation on the subject with one of the King's council; if I did not convince him he was undesignedly betraying the interest of his sovereign, I was mistaken. Strachey said, perhaps I would put down some observations in writing upon it. I said, with all my heart, provided I had the approbation of my colleagues; but I could do nothing of the kind without submitting it to their judgments, and that whatever I had said, or should say, upon the subject, however strongly I might express myself, was always to be understood with submission to my colleagues. I showed them Captain Coffin's letter, and gave them his character. His words are,—

"Our fishermen from Boston, Salem, Newbury, Marblehead, Cape Ann, Cape Cod, and Nantucket, have frequently gone out on the fisheries to the Straits of Belle-Ile, north part of Newfoundland, and the banks adjacent thereto, there to continue the whole season, and have made use of the north part of Newfoundland, the Labrador coast in the Straits of Belle-Ile, to cure their fish which they have taken in and about those coasts. I have known several instances of vessels going there to load in the fall of the year, with the fish taken and cured at those places for Spain, Portugal, &c. I was once concerned in a voyage of that kind myself, and speak from my own knowledge.

"From Cape Sables to the Isle of Sables, and so on, to the Banks of Newfoundland, are a chain of banks extending all along the coast, and almost adjoining each other, and those banks are where our fishermen go for the first fare in the early part of the season. Their second fare is on the Banks of Newfoundland, where they continue to fish, till prevented by the tempestuous and boisterous winds which prevail in the fall of the year on that coast. Their third and last fare is generally made near the coast of Cape Sables, or banks adjoining thereto, where they are not only relieved from those boisterous gales, but have an asylum to fly to in case of emergency, as that coast is lined, from the head of Cape Sables to Halifax, with most excellent harbors. The sea-cow fishery was, before the present war, carried on to great advantage, particularly from Nantucket and Cape Cod, in and about the river St. Lawrence, at the island St. John's and Anticosti, Bay of Chaleurs, and the Magdalen Islands, which were the most noted of all for that fishery. This oil has the preference to all other, except spermaceti."

Mr. Jay desired to know, whether Mr. Oswald had now power to conclude and sign with us. Strachey said he had, absolutely. Mr. Jay desired to know, if the propositions now delivered us were their ultimatum. Strachey seemed loath to answer, but at last said, No. We agreed these were good signs of sincerity.

Bancroft came in this evening, and said it was reported that a courier had arrived from Mr. Rayneval, in London, and that after it, the Count de Vergennes told the King that he had the peace in his pocket; that he was now master of the peace.

26. Tuesday. Breakfasted at Mr. Jay's with Dr. Franklin, in consultation upon the propositions made to us yesterday by Mr. Oswald. We agreed unanimously to answer him, that we could not consent to the article respecting the refugees, as it now stands. Dr. Franklin read a letter, which he had prepared, to Mr. Oswald, upon the subject of the tories, which we had agreed with him that he should read, as containing his private sentiments. We

had a vast deal of conversation upon the subject. My colleagues opened themselves, and made many observations concerning the conduct, crimes, and demerits of those people.

Before dinner, Mr. Fitzherbert came in, whom I had never seen before, a gentleman of about thirty-three; seems pretty discreet and judicious, and did not discover those airs of vanity which are imputed to him. He came in consequence of the desire which I expressed yesterday, of knowing the state of the negotiation between him and the Count de Vergennes, respecting the fishery. He told us, that the Count was for fixing the boundaries where each nation should fish; he must confess he thought the idea plausible; for that there had been great dissensions between the fishermen of the two nations; that the French marine office had a whole apartment full of complaints and representations of disputes; that the French pretended that Cape Ray was the Point Riche.

I asked him if the French demanded of him an exclusive right to fish and dry between Cape Bona Vista and the Point Riche. He said they had not expressly; and he intended to follow the words of the treaties of Utrecht and Paris without stirring the point. I showed him an extract of a letter from the Earl of Egremont to the Duke of Bedford, March 1, 1763, in which it is said, that by the thirteenth article of the treaty of Utrecht, a liberty was left to the French to fish, and to dry their fish on shore; and, for that purpose, to erect the necessary stages and buildings, but with an express stipulation, "de ne pas séjourner dans la dite ile, au delà du temps nécessaire pour pêcher et sécher les poissons." That it is a received law among the fishermen, that whoever arrives first, shall have the choice of the stations; that the Duke de Nivernois insisted, that by the treaty of Utrecht the French had an exclusive right to the fishery from Cape Bona Vista to Point Riche; that the King gave to his Grace, the Duke of Bedford, express instructions to come to an éclaircissement upon the point with the French ministry, and to refuse the exclusive construction of the treaty of Utrecht, &c. I also showed him a letter from Sir Stanyer Porteen, Lord Weymouth's Secretary, to Lord Weymouth, inclosing an extract of Lord Egremont's letter to the Duke of Bedford, by which it appears that the Duke of Nivernois insisted, "that the French had an exclusive right to the fishery from Cape Bona Vista to Point Riche, and that they had, on ceding the island of Newfoundland to Great Britain, by the thirteenth article of the Treaty of Utrecht, expressly reserved to themselves such an exclusive right, which they had constantly been in possession of, till they were entirely driven from North America in the last war.

For these papers I am obliged to Mr. Izard. Mr. Fitzherbert said it was the same thing now word for word; but he should endeavor to have the treaty conformable to those of Utrecht and Paris. "But," he said, "we had given it up by admitting the word 'exclusive' into our treaty." I said, perhaps not; for the whole was to be conformable to the true construction of the treaties of Utrecht and Paris; and that if the English did not now admit the exclusive construction, they could not contend for it against us; we had only contracted not to disturb them, &c. I said, it was the opinion of all the fishermen in America, that England could not prevent our catching a fish without preventing themselves from getting a dollar; that the first fare was our only advantage; that neither the English nor French could have it; it must be lost if we had it not. He said, he did not think much of the fishery as a source of profit, but as a nursery of seamen. I told him, the English could not catch a fish the more, or make a sailor the more, for restraining us; even the French would rival them in the markets of Spain and Portugal; it was our fish which they ought to call their own, because we should spend the profit with them; that the Southern States had staple commodities; but New England had no other remittance but the fishery; no other way to pay for their clothing; that it entered into our distilleries and West India trade, as well as our European trade, in such a manner that it could not be taken out or diminished, without tearing and rending; that if it should be left to its natural course, we could hire or purchase spots of ground on which to erect stages and buildings; but if we were straightened by treaty, that treaty would be given in instructions to governors and commodores, whose duty it would be to execute it; that it would be very difficult to restrain our fishermen; they would be frequently transgressing and making disputes and troubles.

He said his principal object was, to avoid sowing seeds of future wars. I said, it was equally my object; and that I was persuaded, that if the germ of a war was left anywhere, there was the greatest danger of its being left in the article respecting the fishery. The rest of the day was spent in endless discussions about the tories. Dr. Franklin is very stanch against the tories; more decided a great deal on this point than Mr. Jay or myself.

27. Wednesday. Mr. Benjamin Vaughan came in, returned from London, where he had seen Lord Shelburne. He says he finds the ministry much embarrassed with the tories, and exceedingly desirous of saving their honor and reputation in this point; that it is reputation more than money, &c.

Dined with Mr. Jay, and spent some time before dinner with him and Dr. Franklin, and all the afternoon and evening with them and Mr. Oswald, endeavoring to come together concerning the fisheries and tories.

28. Thursday. This morning I have drawn up the following project:

Article 3. "That the subjects of his Britannic Majesty and the people of the said United States shall continue to enjoy unmolested, the right to take fish of every kind on the Grand Bank and on all the other banks of Newfoundland; also in the Gulf of St. Lawrence, and in all other places where the inhabitants of both countries used at any time heretofore to fish; and the citizens of the said United States shall have liberty to cure and dry their fish on the shores of Cape Sables, and of any of the unsettled bays, harbors, or creeks of Nova Scotia, or any of the shores of the Magdalen Islands and of the Labrador coast; and they shall be permitted, in time of peace, to hire pieces of land for terms of years, of the legal proprietors, in any of the dominions of his said Majesty, whereon to erect the necessary stages and buildings, and to cure and dry their fish."

29. Friday. Met Mr. Fitzherbert, Mr. Oswald, Mr. Franklin, Mr. Jay, Mr. Laurens, and Mr. Strachey, at Mr. Jay's, Hôtel d'Orleans, and spent the whole day in discussions about the fishery and the tories. I proposed a new article concerning the fishery; it was discussed and turned in every light, and multitudes of amendments proposed on each side; and at last the article drawn as it was finally agreed to.

The other English gentlemen being withdrawn upon some occasion, I asked Mr. Oswald if he could consent to leave out the limitation of three leagues from all their shores, and the fifteen from those of Louisburg. He said, in his own opinion he was for it; but his instructions were such that he could not do it. I perceived by this, and by several incidents and little circumstances before, which I had remarked to my colleagues, who were much of the same opinion, that Mr. Oswald had an instruction, not to settle the articles of the fishery and refugees, without the concurrence of Mr. Fitzherbert and Mr. Strachey.

Upon the return of the other gentlemen, Mr. Strachey proposed to leave out the word "right" of fishing, and make it "liberty." Mr. Fitzherbert said the word "right" was an obnoxious expression. Upon this I rose up and said, "Gentlemen, is there or can there be a clearer right? In former treaties,—that of Utrecht and that of Paris,—France and England have claimed the right, and used the word. When God Almighty made the banks of Newfoundland, at three hundred leagues distance from the people of America, and at six hundred leagues distance from those of France and England, did he not give as good a right to the former as to the latter? If Heaven in the creation gave a right, it is ours at least as much as yours. If occupation, use, and possession give a right, we have it as clearly as you. If war, and blood, and treasure give a right, ours is as good as yours. We have been constantly fighting in Canada, Cape Breton, and Nova Scotia, for the defence of this fishery, and have expended beyond all proportion more than you. If, then, the right cannot be denied, why should it not be acknowledged, and put out of dispute? Why should we leave room for illiterate fishermen to wrangle and chicane?"

Mr. Fitzherbert said,—"The argument is in your favor. I must confess, your reasons appear to be good; but Mr. Oswald's instructions were such that he did not see how he could agree with us. And, for my part, I have not the honor and felicity to be a man of that weight and authority in my country that you, gentlemen, are in yours." (This was very genteelly said.) "I have the accidental advantage of a little favor with the present minister; but I cannot depend upon the influence of my own opinion to reconcile a measure to my countrymen. We can consider ourselves as little more than pens in the hands of government at home; and Mr. Oswald's instructions are so particular."

I replied to this,—"The time is not so pressing upon us, but that we can wait till a courier goes to London with your representations upon this subject, and others that remain between us; and I think the ministers must be convinced." Mr. Fitzherbert said, "to send again to London, and have all laid loose before Parliament, was so uncertain a measure—it was going to sea again." Upon this, Dr. Franklin said, that "if another messenger was to be sent to London, he ought to carry something more respecting a compensation to the sufferers in America." He produced a paper from his pocket, in which he had drawn up a claim; and he said, the first principle of the treaty was equality and reciprocity. Now, they demanded of us payment of debts, and restitution or compensation to the refugees. If a draper had sold a piece of cloth to a man, upon credit, and then sent a servant to take it from him by force, and after, bring his action for the debt, would any court of law or equity give him his demand without obliging him to restore the cloth? Then he stated the carrying off of goods from Boston, Philadelphia, and the Carolinas, Georgia, Virginia, &c. and the burning of the towns, &c. and desired that this might be sent with the rest.

Upon this, I recounted the history of General Gage's agreement with the inhabitants of Boston, that they should remove with their effects, upon condition that they would surrender their arms. But as soon as the arms were secured, the goods were forbid to be carried out, and were finally carried off, in large quantities, to Halifax. Dr. Franklin mentioned the case of Philadelphia, and the carrying off of effects there, even his own library. Mr. Jay mentioned several other things; and Mr. Laurens added the plunders in Carolina, of negroes, plate, &c.

After hearing all this, Mr. Fitzherbert, Mr. Oswald, and Mr. Strachey, retired for some time; and, returning, Mr. Fitzherbert said that, upon consulting together, and weighing every thing as maturely as possible, Mr. Strachey and himself had determined to advise Mr. Oswald to strike with us, according to the terms we had proposed as our ultimatum respecting the fishery and the loyalists. Accordingly, we all sat down, and read over the whole treaty, and corrected it, and agreed to meet to-morrow, at Mr. Oswald's house, to sign and seal the treaties, which the secretaries were to copy fair in the mean time.

I forgot to mention that, when we were upon the fishery, and Mr. Strachey and Mr. Fitzherbert were urging us to leave out the word "right" and substitute "liberty," I told them at last,—in answer to their proposal, to agree upon all other articles, and leave that of the fishery to be adjusted at the definitive treaty,—I never could put my hand to any articles without satisfaction about the fishery; that Congress had, three or four years ago, when they did me the honor to give me a commission to make a treaty of commerce with Great Britain, given me a positive instruction not to make any such treaty without an article in the treaty of peace acknowledging our right to the fishery; that I was happy that Mr. Laurens was now present, who, I believed, was in Congress at the time, and must remember it. Mr. Laurens upon this said, with great firmness, that he was in the same case, and could never give his voice for any articles without this. Mr. Jay spoke up, and said, it could not be a peace, it would only be an insidious truce without it.

30. Saturday. St. Andrew's day. We met first at Mr. Jay's, then at Mr. Oswald's; examined and compared the treaties. Mr. Strachey had left out the limitation of time, the twelve months that the refugees were allowed to reside in America, in order to recover their estates if they could. Dr. Franklin said this was a surprise upon us. Mr. Jay said so too. We never had consented to leave it out, and they insisted upon putting it in, which was done.

Mr. Laurens said there ought to be a stipulation that the British troops should carry off no negroes or other American property. We all agreed. Mr. Oswald consented.

Then the treaties were signed, sealed, and delivered, and we all went out to Passy to dine with Dr. Franklin. Thus far has proceeded this great affair.

The unravelling of the plot has been to me the most affecting and astonishing part of the whole piece. As soon as I arrived in Paris I waited on Mr. Jay, and learned from him the rise and progress of the negotiations. Nothing that has happened since the beginning of the controversy in 1761, has ever struck me more forcibly, or affected me more intimately, than that entire coincidence of principles and opinions between him and me. In about three days I went out to Passy and spent the evening with Dr. Franklin, and entered largely into conversation with him upon the course and present state of our foreign affairs. I told him, without reserve, my opinion of the policy of this Court, and of the principles, wisdom, and firmness, with which Mr. Jay had conducted the negotiation in his sickness and my absence, and that I was determined to support Mr. Jay to the utmost of my power in the pursuit of the same system. The Doctor heard me patiently, but said nothing.

The first conference we had afterwards with Mr. Oswald, in considering one point and another, Dr. Franklin turned to Mr. Jay and said, I am of your opinion, and will go on with these gentlemen in the business without consulting this Court. He has, accordingly, met us in most of our conferences, and has gone on with us in entire harmony and unanimity throughout, and has been able and useful, both by his sagacity and his reputation, in the whole negotiation.

I was very happy that Mr. Laurens came in, although it was the last day of the conferences, and wish he could have been sooner; his apprehension, notwithstanding his deplorable affliction under the recent loss of so excellent a son, is as quick, his judgment as sound, and his heart as firm as ever. He had an opportunity of examining the whole, and judging and approving; and the article which he caused to be inserted at the very last, that no property should be carried off, which would most probably in the multiplicity and hurry of affairs have escaped us, was worth a longer journey, if that had been all; but his name and weight is added, which is of much greater consequence. These miserable minutes may help me to recollect; but I have not found time amidst the hurry of business and crowd of visits to make a detail.

I should have before noted, that at our first conference about the fishery I related the facts as well as I understood them; but knowing nothing myself, but as a hearsay witness, I found it had not the weight of ocular testimony; to supply which defect, I asked Dr. Franklin if Mr. Williams of Nantes could not give us light. He said, Mr. Williams was on the road to Paris, and as soon as he arrived he would ask him. In a few days Mr. Williams called on me, and said Dr. Franklin had, as I desired him, inquired of him about the fishery; but he was not able to speak particularly upon that subject; but there was at Nantes a gentleman of Marblehead, Mr. Samuel White, son-in-law to Mr. Hooper, who was master of the subject, and to him he would write.

Mr. Jeremiah Allen, a merchant of Boston, called on me about the same time. I inquired of him. He was able only to give such a hearsay account as I could give myself. But I desired him to write to Mr. White, at Nantes, which he undertook to do, and did. Mr. White answered Mr. Allen's letter by referring him to his answer to Mr. Williams, which Mr. Williams received and delivered to Dr. Franklin, who communicated it to us, and it contained a good account.

I desired Mr. Thaxter to write to Messrs. Ingraham and Bromfield, and Mr. Storer to write to Captain Coffin at Amsterdam. They delivered me the answers; both contained information; but Coffin's was the most particular, and of the most importance, as he spoke as a witness. We made the best use of these letters with the English gentlemen; and they appeared to have a good deal of weight with them.

From first to last I ever insisted upon it with the English gentlemen, that the fisheries and the Mississippi, if America was not satisfied in those points, would be the sure and certain sources of a future war. I showed them the indispensable necessity of both to our affairs, and that no treaty we could make, which should be unsatisfactory to our people upon these points, could be observed; that the population near the Mississippi would be so rapid, and the necessities of the people for its navigation so pressing, that nothing could restrain them from going down, and if the force of arms should be necessary, it would not be wanting; that the fishery entered into our distilleries, our coasting trade, our trade with the Southern States, with the West India Islands, with the coast of Africa, and with every part of Europe, in such a manner, and especially with England,—that it could not be taken from us, or granted us stingily, without tearing and rending; that the other States had staples; we had none but fish; no other means of remittances to London, or paying those very debts they had insisted upon so seriously; that if we were forced off at three leagues distance we should smuggle eternally; that their men-of-war might have the glory of sinking now and then a fishing schooner, but this would not prevent a repetition of the crime; it would only inflame and irritate and enkindle a new war; that in seven years we should break through all restraints and conquer from them the island of Newfoundland itself, and Nova Scotia too.

Mr. Fitzherbert always smiled, and said it was very extraordinary that the British ministry and we should see it in so different a light; that they meant the restriction, in order to prevent disputes and kill the seeds of war, and we should think it so certain a source of disputes, and so strong a seed of war; but that our reasons were such, that he thought the probability of our side.

I have not time to minute the conversations about the sea-cow fishery, the whale fishery, the Magdalen Islands, the Labrador coasts, and the coasts of Nova Scotia; it is sufficient to say, they were explained to the utmost of our knowledge, and finally conceded.

I should have noted before, the various deliberations between the English gentlemen and us, relative to the words "indefinite and exclusive" right, which the Count de Vergennes and Mr. Gérard had the precaution to insert in our treaty with France. I observed often to the English gentlemen, that aiming at excluding us from fishing upon the north side of Newfoundland, it was natural for them to wish that the English would exclude us from the south side; this would be making both alike, and take away an odious distinction; French statesmen must see the tendency of our fishermen being treated kindly and hospitably like friends, by the English on their side of the island, and unkindly, inhospitably, and like enemies, on the French side. I added, further, that it was my opinion, neither our treaty with the French, nor any treaty or clause to the same purpose, which the English could make, would be punctually observed; fishermen, both from England and America, would smuggle, especially the Americans in the early part of the spring before the Europeans could arrive; this, therefore, must be connived at by the French, or odious measures must be recurred to by them or us to suppress it, and, in either case, it was easy to see what would be the effect upon the American mind; they no doubt, therefore, wished the English to put themselves upon as odious a footing, at least, as they had done.

Dr. Franklin said, there was a great deal of weight in this observation, and the Englishmen showed plainly enough that they felt it.

I have not attempted, in these notes, to do justice to the arguments of my colleagues, all of whom were, throughout the whole business, when they attended, very attentive and very able; especially Mr. Jay, to whom the French, if they knew as much of his negotiations as they do of mine, would very justly give the title with which they have inconsiderately decorated me, that of "Le Washington de la négociation"; a very flattering compliment indeed, to which I have not a right, but sincerely think it belongs to Mr. Jay.

December 1. Sunday—2. Monday. Made many visits, &c.

3. Tuesday. Visited Mr. Brantzen, Hôtel de la Chine. Mr. Brantzen asked me, how we went on? I told him we had come to a full stop, by signing and sealing the preliminaries, on the 30th of November. I told him that we had been very industrious, having been at it forenoon, afternoon, and evening, ever since my arrival, either with one another, or with the English gentlemen. He asked if it was definitive and separate. I said, by no means. They were only articles to be inserted in the definitive treaty. He asked if there was to be any truce or armistice in the mean time. I said, again, by no means.

He then said, that he believed France and England had agreed too. That the Count de Vergennes's son was gone to England with Mr. de Rayneval; but he believed the Spaniards had not yet agreed, and the Dutch were yet a great way off, and had agreed upon nothing. They had had several conferences; at the first, he had informed Mr. Fitzherbert, that their High Mightinesses insisted upon the freedom of navigation as a preliminary and a sine quâ non. Mr. Fitzherbert had communicated this to his Court; but the answer received was, that his Court did not approve of conceding this as a sine quâ non, but chose to have all the demands of their High Mightinesses stated together. Mr. Brantzen answered, that his instructions were, not to enter into any conferences upon other points until this was agreed to. That it was the intention of the British Court to agree to this. That he could not consider any changes in the ministry as making any alteration. They were all ministers of the same King, and servants of the same nation. That Mr. Fox, when he was Secretary of State, by his letter to the Russian Minister, had declared the intention of the King to consent to the freedom of navigation, &c.

Mr. Brantzen said, however, that he had, in his private capacity, and without compromising his ministerial character, entered into explanations with Mr. Fitzherbert, and had told him that he should insist upon three points,—the freedom of navigation, the restitution of territories in the East and West Indies, and compensation for damages. The two first points could not be disputed, and the third ought not; for the war against them had been unjust; the pretences for it were groundless; their accession to the armed neutrality must now be admitted, even by Britain's accession to it, to have been an illegitimate cause of war; and the project of a treaty with America could not be seriously pretended to be a just cause of war; and many members of Parliament had, in the time of it, declared the war unjust, and some of those members were now ministers. Even the Prime Minister, my Lord Shelburne himself, had freely declared the war unjust in the House of Peers. And if the war was unjust, the damages and injustice ought to be repaired.

Mr. Fitzherbert said, that there was no precedent of compensation for damages in a treaty of peace. Mr. Brantzen begged his pardon, and thought there had been instances. One example, in particular, which the English themselves had set against the Dutch, which just then came into his head. Cromwell had demanded compensation of them, and they had agreed, as now appears by the treaty, to pay a hundred thousand pounds sterling as a compensation.

Mr. Brantzen was not furnished with a full account of all the losses of individuals, and therefore could not precisely say what the amount would be. That, perhaps, they might not insist upon prompt payment, nor upon a stated sum, but might leave both the sum and time of payment to be ascertained by commissioners, at their leisure, after the peace.

I observed to him, that we intended to write to Mr. Dana, and send him a copy of our preliminaries, that he might commence his negotiations with the neutral powers; and if he succeeded, we could then make common cause with Holland, and insist on an article to secure the freedom of navigation. This idea he received with great pleasure, and said he would write about it to the States. Upon this, I asked him with whom he and the other Dutch Ministers abroad held their correspondence. He answered that the Secretary Fagel was, properly speaking, the Minister of Foreign Affairs. That their principal correspondence was with him; but that they had a correspondence with the Grand Pensionary, Bleiswyck, too. That the letters received by the Secretary were laid before the Besogne Secrète, or Committee of Secrecy. This committee consisted of so many members—one, at least, for each Province—that it was very difficult to keep any thing secret. Foreign ministers were very inquisitive, and the Duke de la Vauguyon would be likely to get at it. So that, if they had any thing to write, which they wished secret, they wrote it to the Grand Pensionary, who is not obliged to lay before the States letters entire. He selects such parts as he judges proper, and prints them, to be taken ad referendum, and laid before the Regencies of the Cities. That they had sometimes a little diffidence of this Court (quelque méfiance,) for this Court was very fine, (diablement fin); and when this happened, they wrote to the Grand Pensionary, that it might not be communicated to the French Minister, and consequently to his Court. "These people are vastly profound. They will not favor the Spaniards in obtaining the Floridas. They will play England against Spain, and Spain against England; England against you, and you against England; and all of you against us, and us against all of you,—according to their own schemes and interests. They are closely buttoned up about Gibraltar; and as to Jamaica, they will not favor Spain in that view. I expect they will get their own affair arranged, and then advise England to agree to the freedom of navigation and a restitution of territory, and then advise us to be easy about compensation." Thus Mr. Brantzen.

I next visited Mr. Jay, to talk about writing to Mr. Dana, and communicating to the neutral powers the preliminary articles. Mr. Jay says, that Mr. Oswald is very anxious that his Court should do that, and he has been writing to the Ministry to persuade them to it. Had a long conversation with Mr. Jay about the manner of settling the western lands; this I cannot now detail.

Went next to Mr. Laurens, upon the subject of writing to Mr. Dana, and found him full in my sentiments; and at my return found answers from Dr. Franklin and Mr. Laurens to the letters I wrote them, both agreeing that this is the critical moment for Dana to commence his negotiations. Dr. Franklin promises to have an authentic copy made to send to Mr. Dana.

In the evening many gentlemen came in, among the rest Mr. Bourse, the agent of the Dutch East India Company, who expressed a good deal of anxiety about their negotiation, and feared they should not have justice in the East Indies.

4. Wednesday. It is proper that I should note here, that in the beginning of the year 1780, soon after my arrival at Paris, Mr. Galloway's pamphlets fell into my hands. I wrote a long series of letters to a friend, in answer to them. That friend sent them to England, but the printers dared not publish them. They remained there until the last summer, when they were begun to be printed, and are continued to this day, not being yet quite finished, in Parker's General Advertiser, but with false dates, being dated in the months of January and February

last, under the title of "Letters from a distinguished American." They appear to have been well received, and to have contributed somewhat to unite the nation in accelerating the acknowledgment of American independence, and to convince the nation of the necessity of respecting our alliances, and of making peace.

I hope it will be permitted to me, or to some other who can do it better, some ten or fifteen years hence, to collect together in one view my little negotiations in Europe. Fifty years hence it may be published, perhaps twenty. I will venture to say, however feebly I may have acted my part, or whatever mistakes I may have committed, yet the situations I have been in, between angry nations and more angry factions, have been some of the most singular and interesting that ever happened to any man. The fury of enemies as well as of elements, the subtilty and arrogance of allies, and, what has been worse than all, the jealousy, envy, and little pranks of friends and copatriots, would form one of the most instructive lessons in morals and politics that ever was committed to paper.

5. Thursday. The Duke de la Vauguyon came in. He says that France and England are agreed, and that there is but one point between England and Spain. England and Holland are not yet so near. I showed him our preliminary treaty, and had some difficulty to prevent his seeing the separate article; but I did prevent him from seeing any thing of it but the words "Separate Article."

Dined at Mr. Jay's, with Messrs. Fitzherbert, Oswald, Franklin, Laurens, and their secretaries, Ellis, Whitefoord, Franklin, and Laurens. Mr. Jenings was there too; he came home and spent the evening with me.

6. Friday. Spent the evening with Mr. Laurens at his own lodgings, Hôtel de York; and on a visit to Mr. Curson, Hôtel de York. Mr. Laurens said that we should very soon raise figs and olives and make oil in America. That he had raised great quantities of figs in his own garden, in Carolina; and that the figs in Carolina and Georgia were the most delicious he had ever tasted. That he had raised in one year, in his own garden in Carolina, between fifty and a hundred bushels of olives. That there were large quantities and a great variety of wild grapes in Carolina and Georgia, of some of which very good wine had been made.

As Mr. Curson talked of going to Marseilles, Mr. Laurens advised him to send to America some Barbary sheep. He says he had one in Carolina, but never could make the American rams go to that sheep. He gives a beautiful description of Marseilles; says it will rival Bordeaux in the wine trade with America. The Levant trade furnishes it with carpets, cottons, silks, raw silks, and drugs, and it has a large manufactory of Castile soap.

Mr. Laurens's apartments, at the Hôtel de York, are better than mine, at the Hôtel du Roi, au Carrousel; yet he gives but twelve louis, and I am obliged to give eighteen. He has two large rooms, besides a large commodious bed-chamber and a large ante-chamber for servants. He says there will be an outrageous clamor in England, on account of the fisheries and the loyalists; but what is done is irrevocable.

7. Saturday. Dined with my family at the Place Vendome,—the Abbé Chalut's. An Abbé there cries, "Voilà la semence d'une autre guerre."

8. Sunday. At home all day. Mr. Jenings, M. Grand, père et fils, Mr. Mason, and Mr. Hooper called upon me.

9. Monday. Visited Count Sarsfield, who lent me his Notes upon America. Visited Mr. Jay. Mr. Oswald came in. We slided from one thing to another into a very lively conversation upon politics. He asked me what the conduct of his Court and nation ought to be in relation to America. I answered, "The alpha and omega of British policy towards America was summed up in this one maxim:

"See that American independence is independent; independent of all the world; independent of yourselves, as well as of France; and independent of both, as well as of the rest of Europe. Depend upon it, you have no chance for salvation but by setting up America very high. Take care to remove from the American mind all cause of fear of you. No other motive but fear of you will ever produce in the Americans any unreasonable attachment to the House of Bourbon."

"Is it possible," said he, "that the people of America should be afraid of us or hate us?" "One would think, Mr. Oswald," said I, "that you had been out of the world for these twenty years past. Yes, there are three millions of people in America, who hate and dread you more than any thing in the world." "What!" said he, "now we are come to our senses?" "Your change of system is not yet known in America," said I. "Well," said he, "what shall we do to remove these fears and jealousies?" "In one word," said I, "favor and promote the interest, reputation, and dignity of the United States in every thing that is consistent with your own. If you pursue the plan of cramping, clipping, and weakening America, on the supposition that she will be a rival to you, you will make her really so; you will make her the natural and perpetual ally of your natural and perpetual enemies." "But, in what instance," said he, "have we discovered such a disposition?" "In the three leagues from your shores, and the fifteen leagues from Cape Breton," said I, "to which your ministry insisted so earnestly to exclude our fishermen. Here was a point that would have done us great harm, and you no good, on the contrary, harm; so that you would have hurt yourselves to hurt us. This disposition must be guarded against." "I am fully of your mind about that," said he; "but what else can we do?" "Send a minister to Congress," said I, "at the peace,—a clever fellow, who understands himself, and will neither set us bad examples, nor intermeddle in our parties. This will show that you are consistent with yourselves; that you are sincere in your acknowledgment of American independence; and that you don't entertain hopes and designs of overturning it. Such a minister will dissipate many fears, and will be of more service to the least obnoxious refugees than any other measure could be. Let the King send a minister to Congress, and receive one from that body. This will be acting consistently, and with dignity, in the face of the universe."

"Well, what else shall we do?" said he. "I have more than once already," said I, "advised you to put your ministers upon negotiating the acknowledgment of our independence by the neutral powers." "True," said he, "and I have written about it; and in my answers,"—laughing,—"I find myself charged with speculation. But I don't care; I will write them my sentiments. I won't take any of their money. I have spent already twelve or thirteen hundred pounds; and all the reward I will have for it shall be the pleasure of writing as I think. My opinion is, that our court should sign the armed neutrality, and announce to them what they have done with you, and negotiate to have you admitted to sign too. But I want to write more fully upon the subject; and I want you to give me your thoughts upon it, for I don't understand it so fully as I wish. What motives can be thrown out to the Empress of Russia? Or what motives may she be supposed to have, to acknowledge your independence? And what motives can our Court have to interfere, or intereede, with the neutral powers to receive you into their confederation?"

"I will answer all these questions," said I, "to the best of my knowledge, and with the utmost candor. In the first place, there has been, with very little interruption, a jealousy between the Courts of Petersburg and Versailles, for many years. France is the old friend and ally of the Sublime Porte, the natural enemy of Russia. France, not long since, negotiated a peace between Russia and the Turks; but upon the Empress's late offers of mediation, and especially her endeavors to negotiate Holland out of the war, France appears to have been piqued; and, as the last revolution in the Crimea happened soon after, there is reason to suspect that French emissaries excited the revolt against the new, independent government which the Empress had taken so much pains to establish. Poland has been long a scene of competition between Russian and French politics; both parties having spent great sums in pensions to partisans, until they have laid all virtue and public spirit prostrate in that country. Sweden is another region of rivalry between France and Russia, where both parties spent such sums in pensions as to destroy the principles of liberty, and prepare the way for that revolution, which France favored from a principle of economy rather than any other. These hints are sufficient to show the opposition of views and interests between France and Russia; and we see the consequence of it, that England has more influence at Petersburg than France. The Empress, therefore, would have two motives; one, to oblige England, if they should intercede for an acknowledgment of American independence; and another, to render America less dependent on France. The Empress, moreover, loves reputation; and it would be no small addition to her glory, to undertake a negotiation with all the neutral Courts, to induce them to admit America into their confederacy. The Empress might be further tempted; she was bent upon extending her commerce; and the commerce of America, if it were only in hemp and duck, would be no small object to her. As to the motives to your Court; princes often think themselves warranted, if not bound, to fight for their glory; surely they may lawfully negotiate for reputation. If the neutral powers should acknowledge our independence now, France will have the reputation, very unjustly, of having negotiated it; but if your Court now takes a decided part in favor of it, your Court will have the glory of it in Europe and America, and this will have a good effect upon American gratitude."

"But," said he, "this would be negotiating for the honor and interest of France: for, no doubt, France wishes all the world to acknowledge your independence." "Give me leave to tell you, sir," said I, "you are mistaken. If I have not been mistaken in the policy of France, from my first observation of it to this hour, they have been as averse to other powers acknowledging our independence as you have been." Mr. Jay joined me in the same declaration. "God!" says he, "I understand it now; there is a gentleman going to London this day,—I will go home and write upon the subject by him."

10. Tuesday. Visited Mr. Oswald, to inquire what news from England. He had the Courier de l'Europe, in which is Mr. Secretary Townsend's letter to the Lord Mayor of London, dated the third of this month, in which he announces the signature of preliminaries on the thirtieth of November, between the Commissioner of his Majesty and the Commissioners of the United States of America. He had also received the King's speech announcing the same thing. Mr. Oswald said, that France would not separate her affairs from Spain; that he had hoped that America would have assisted them somewhat in compromising affairs with France, &c. Dr. Franklin, who was present, said he did not know any thing of the other negotiations. He said, that neither Mr. Fitzherbert, nor the Count de Vergennes, nor the Count d'Aranda communicated any thing to him; that he understood the Dutch were the farthest from an agreement. Upon this I said, "Mr. Oswald, Mr. Fitzherbert can't, I think, have any difficulty to agree with Mr. Brantzen.

There are three points:

1. The liberty of navigation; 2. restitution of possessions; 3. compensation for damages. The liberty of navigation, I suppose, is the point that sticks. But why should it stick? When all nations are agreed in the principle, why should England stand out? England must agree to it; she has already, in effect, agreed to it as it affects all nations but Holland and America; and, if she were disposed, she could not prevent them from having the benefit." Upon this, Dr. Franklin said, "the Dutch would be able in any future war to carry on their commerce even of naval stores in the bottoms of other neutral powers." "Yes," said Mr. Oswald, "and I am of opinion that England ought to subscribe the armed neutrality." "Very well," said I, "then let Mr. Fitzherbert agree this point with Mr. Brantzen, and let Mr. Harris, at Petersburg, take Mr. Dana in his hand, and go to the Prince Potemkin or the Count

d'Osterman, and say, 'the King, my master, has authorized me to subscribe the principles of the armed neutrality, and instructed me to introduce to you Mr. Dana, Minister from the United States of America, to do the same; let him subscribe his name under mine.' "

At this, they all laughed very heartily. Mr. Oswald, however, recollecting himself, and the conversation between him and me yesterday on the same subject, very gravely turned it off, by saying, "he did not see a necessity to be in a hurry about that; America was well enough." I said, as to restitution of the Dutch territories, I suppose your Court will not make much difficulty about that, if this Court does not, as it is not probable they will; and, as to compensation for damages, the Dutch will probably be as easy as they can about that. Dr. Franklin said, "he was for beginning early to think about the articles of the definitive treaty; we had been so happy as to be the first in the preliminaries, and he wished to be so in the definitive articles." Thus we parted.

It may be proper for me to minute here some points to propose in the definitive treaty.

1. The liberty of navigation.

2. That no forts shall be built, or garrisons maintained, upon any of the frontiers in America, or upon any of the land boundaries.

3. That the island of Bermuda be ceded to us, or independent, or not fortified, or that no privateers be fitted or sent out from thence, or permitted to enter there, or prizes carried in.

4. That the Isle of Sables remain the property of its present owner, and under the jurisdiction of the United States or Massachusetts.

5. That the account of prisoners be balanced, and the sums due for their subsistence, &c. be paid, and the balance of prisoners paid for, according to the usages of nations.

11. Wednesday. Dined with Mr. Laurens.

12. Thursday. Met at Mr. Laurens's, and signed the letter I had drawn up to Mr. Dana, which I sent off inclosed with a copy of the preliminaries, and consulted about articles to be inserted in the definitive treaty. Agreed that Mr. Jay and I should prepare a joint letter to Congress. At seven o'clock I met Mr. Jay at his house, and we drew a letter.

13. Friday. I went first to Mr. Jay, and made some additions to the joint letter, which I carried first to Mr. Laurens, who made some corrections and additions, and then to Passy, to Dr. Franklin, who proposed a few other corrections, and showed me an article he has drawn up for the definitive treaty, to exempt fishermen, husbandmen, and merchants, as much as possible, from the evils of future wars. This is a good lesson to mankind at least. All agreed to meet at my house at eleven to-morrow to finish the joint letter. *Endnote 115*

16. Monday. Mr. Fitzherbert and Mr. Oswald, Mr. Laurens, &c. dined with me.

17. Tuesday. The four commissioners dined with Mr. Fitzherbert. Lord Mountnorris, a celebrated speaker in the Irish House of Lords dined there, and several English gentlemen. The rock-salt is taken out of the salt-pits in England, Lord Mountnorris said. He gave me a description of the caverns, and the kind of architecture with which they support them, like the pillars of a temple.

We met at Mr. Laurens's, at Dr. Franklin's summons or invitation, at eleven o'clock. He produced a letter to him from the Count de Vergennes, and a project of an answer which he had drawn up, which we advised him, unanimously, to send.

19. Thursday. Visited M. Louis, Secretary of the Royal College of Surgery, in order to form a correspondence between it and the Medical Society at Boston. Was very politely received, and promised every thing that the college could do. M. Louis talked a great deal, and very ingeniously and entertainingly.

Spent the evening at the Abbé Chalut's with the Abbé de Mably, two other abbés, and two academicians. The Abbé de Mably has just published a new work,—Sur la Manière d'écrire l'Histoire. He is very agreeable in conversation, polite, good-humored, and sensible;

spoke with great indignation against the practice of lying, chicaning, and finessing, in negotiations; frankness, candor, and probity, were the only means of gaining confidence. He is seventy-four or seventy-five years old. Mr. Laurens told me this morning, that the salt-pits in England are directly under the river Dee, and that ships sail over the heads of the workmen. Bay-salt is such as is made in France and Spain, round the Bay of Biscay. Rock-salt from Sal, Tortugas.

20. Friday. Dined with Mr. Laurens.

21. Saturday. Visited Mr. Jay, and then went out to Passy to show Dr. Franklin Mr. Dana's letter. The Doctor and I agreed to remit Mr. Dana the money to pay the fees to the Russian ministers, according to the usage, upon the signature of a treaty, six thousand rubles to each minister who signs the treaty.

The Count de Lynden told me the other day, that the King of Sweden was the first inventor and suggester of the plan of the armed neutrality; that his minister first proposed it to the Count Panin, where it slept some time. Lynden says, that the King of Sweden has penetration and ambition; and that his ambition to be the first power to propose an alliance with us, is perfectly in character. This step, however, I conjecture, was suggested to his minister here, in order to support Dr. Franklin, by the Count de Vergennes. The Count de Lynden showed me his gold snuff-box, set with diamonds, with the miniature of the King of Sweden, presented to him on taking leave of that Court. The King is like Mr. Hancock. Dr. Franklin went to Versailles yesterday, and was assured of the six millions, and all is fair weather; all friendly and good-humored; so may it remain! I suspect, however, and have reason, but will say nothing. Our country is safe, Mr. Jay is uneasy about the French troops in America; afraid that more are going, and that they will overawe our councils; that France is agreed with England upon her points, and that the war will be continued for Spanish objects only. In that case we are not obliged to continue it.

22. Sunday. Made several visits, &c.

23. Monday. Received from Monsieur Geoffroy, Docteur Régent de la Faculté de Médecine, de Paris, a letter of thanks from the Société Royale de Médecine, for my letter to him proposing a correspondence between that Society and the Medical Society at Boston.

Made several visits, &c. Went to the Italian comedy. Saw Les Troqueurs, the Two Harlequins, &c.

24. Tuesday. There are men who carry the countenance and air of boys through life.

This evening Mr. Jay told me an extraordinary story of Lord Mount Steuart, the British Minister at Turin, which he had from Mr. Oswald.

25. Wednesday, Christmas.

- **Lady Lucan's Verses on Ireland.**

"Hear this, ye great, as from the feast ye rise,
Which every plundered element supplies'
Hear, when fatigued, not nourished, ye have dined;
The food of thousands is to roots confined.

Eternal fasts that know no taste of bread,
Nor where who sows the corn by corn is fed;
Throughout the year, no feast e'er crowns his board—
Four pence a day, ah' what can that afford?

Open our ports at once, with generous minds,
Let commerce be as free as waves and winds;
Seize quick the time, for now, consider well,
Whole quarters of the world at once rebel."

26. Thursday. Mr. Brantzen called upon me at one. He says that Mr. Fitzherbert and he are yet a great way asunder; the first point, of the freedom of navigation, sticks; the other points they have agreed on, or may agree on, not being far off. Mr. F. has no answer from London to the Dutch propositions. I told him he might make himself very easy about the freedom of navigation, for that the English must come into it. I suspected my Lord Shelburne was manœuvring to save a little pride; that he thought it would be less humiliating to the English, and less flattering to the Dutch, to concede that point to the armed neutrality first: I knew it had been recommended to his Lordship by Mr. Oswald and other English gentlemen here, and I had seen, in the English papers, that couriers had been sent off from the Secretary of State's office to all the foreign Courts. Combining these circumstances together, I suspected that they had given orders to their minister at Petersburg to sign the treaty of armed neutrality, as France and Spain have done; and after this negotiation shall be accomplished, they will have no difficulty to agree with the Dutch, for they demand no more than the principle of the armed neutrality. Mr. Brantzen said this never had occurred to him, but that he thought it possible and natural. I gave him Mr. Higginson's letter and papers, and a copy of our treaty, in confidence, all but the separate article. He says Mr. Bourse will not do for minister to America; he is of the wrong side, and will not be goûté du tout.

The Duke de la Rochefoucauld made me a visit to-day, and desired me to explain to him some passages in the Connecticut Constitution which were obscure to him, which I did. Sir James Jay too came in from the Hague, full of projects of burning towns, and making fifty-gun ships equal to hundred-and-tengun ships. I told him that this country abounded so much with projects and projectors, that there would be a presumption and prejudice against him at first blush; but he is going to the Marquis de Castrics.

Mr. Vaughan and Mr. Brantzen both told me to-day, that the Count de Vergennes sent off a courier to London the night before Christmas. Mr. Brantzen told me, that he had twice seen Dr. Franklin, once at Versailles, and once at Mr. Grand's; that he appeared to him heavy and inactive, and that if he had been alone, America would not have obtained such good terms. I said he was right, for if he had been alone, we should not, at this moment, have had any terms at all; that our negotiations would have trained on as heavily and confusedly as all the rest; that if his advice and that of Count de Vergennes had been followed, we should now have been treating under Mr. Oswald's first commission. It was the refusal of Mr. Jay and me to treat under that commission, against the opinion and advice of V. and F., that produced Mr. Oswald's new commission, acknowledging our independence. "That was a noble triumph for you," said Mr. Brantzen.

Mr. Vaughan showed me to-day a parcel of new French books,—Le Système Naturel, Le Système Moral, Le Système Social, Le Système Politique. There is one shop tolerated in selling forbidden books. Vaughan has a brother in Philadelphia, who has written him a long letter about the Constitutionalists and the Republicans. *Endnote 116* They have chosen Mr. Dickinson Governor, and Mr. Mifflin into Congress.

1783.

Paris, January 1. Went to Versailles; made my visit and compliments of the season to Monsieur le Comte de Vergennes, and delivered him a copy of our Treaty and Convention with the States-General. He received me with politeness, made me the compliments of the season très-sincèrement, and was sensibly obliged to me for the copies, and invited me to dine. I went to see the ceremony of the Knights of the Saint-Esprit, in the chapel, where the Queen shone in great splendor; dined with an immense company at the Count's, and returned to Paris.

One of these first days of January, I had a conversation with Mr. Benjamin Vaughan upon the liberty of navigation, as claimed by the confederated neutral powers and the Dutch. I showed him the necessity England was in of acceding to it, and the importance of doing it soon, that they might have it to say that they had arranged their affairs with the Dutch as well as with the United States. He said he saw the importance of pulling at the hairs, one by one, when you could not pull out the whole tail at once. That he had written, and would write again, to my Lord Shelburne upon the subject; "But," says he, "you cannot blame us for endeavoring to carry this point to market, and get something by it. We cannot prevent the French from getting some territory in the East Indies more than they had, and perhaps we may buy this of the Dutch for this point." The same day I called upon Mr. Jay, and asked him to speak with Mr. Oswald upon the same subject; called next upon Mr. Laurens, and mentioned the same idea to him; called at Mr. Oswald's, to talk with him upon it, but he was gone out.

5. Sunday. Dined with Mr. Vaughan, in company with the Abbés de Mably, Chalut, Arnoux, and Tersaint. Had more conversation with De Mably than at any time before; he meditates a work upon our American Constitutions. He says, the character he gives of Herodian in his last work, "Sur la Manière d'écrire l'Histoire," has procured to his bookseller purchasers for all the copies of that historian which he had in his shop. Arnoux said, that Rousseau, by his character of Robinson Crusoe, helped his bookseller to the sale of a whole edition of that romance in a few days.

11. Saturday. Mr. W. T. Franklin came in to talk with me about a subject which he said he did not talk often about, and that was, himself. He produced a commission, drawn up for Messrs. Franklin and Jay to sign, when they, only, were here, before I arrived, and, in fact, signed by them. I took the commission and read it. He asked me to sign it. I told him, that I considered myself as directly affronted in this affair; that, considering that I came out to Europe, without any solicitation of mine, single in the commission for peace, and considering that Congress had done me the honor to place me at the head of the new commission, I had a right to be consulted in the appointment of a Secretary to the Commission; but that, without saying or writing a word to me, Dr. Franklin had written to Mr. Jay, at Madrid, and obtained a promise from him; *Endnote 117* that, considering the relation to me in which Mr. Thaxter came out, and his services and sufferings in the cause, and the small allowance he had received, I thought he had a better right to it; that I thought myself ill treated in this, as in many other things; that it was not from any disrespect to him, Mr. W. T. Franklin, that I declined it; that I should not, if my opinion had been asked, have named Mr. Thaxter, but another gentleman. He told me, how his grandfather was weary; that he had renewed his solicitation to Congress to be relieved; that he wanted to be with his family at Philadelphia, &c., &c., &c. I told him I was weary too, and had written an unconditional resignation of all my employments in Europe; that an attack had been made on me by the Count de Vergennes, and Congress had been induced to disgrace me; that I would not bear this disgrace, if I could help it; that I would wear no livery with a spot upon it; the stain should be taken out, or I would not wear the coat; that Congress had placed me now in a situation that I could do nothing without being suspected of a sinister motive,—that of aiming at being restored to the mission to Great Britain; the conduct of the American cause in Europe had been a constant scramble for offices, and was now likely to be a new and more passionate scene of factions for places; that I would have nothing to do with it; had

not been used to it. He said, that Congress would have now a number of places, and would provide for Mr. Thaxter; that they would undoubtedly give me full satisfaction, &c. I told him, that the first wish of my heart was to return to my wife and children, &c.

He showed me an extract of a letter of Dr. Franklin to Congress concerning him, containing a studied and long eulogium,—sagacity beyond his years, diligence, activity, fidelity, genteel address, facility in speaking French; recommends him to be secretary of some mission; thinks he would make an excellent minister, but does not propose him for it as yet. *Endnote 118*

This letter and other circumstances convince me that the plan is laid between the Count de Vergeunes and the Doctor, to get Billy made minister to this Court, and, not improbably, the Doctor to London. Time will show.

12. Sunday. Mr. Benjamin Vaughan came in. I told him, I had some facts to communicate to him in confidence; they affected my personal interest, character, and feelings so intimately, that it was impossible for me to speak of them without being suspected of personal resentments and sinister motives; but that these facts were, at the same time, so connected with public affairs, with the interests of the House of Bourbon, and with the essential interests of Great Britain and America, and the true system of policy which the two last ought in future to pursue towards each other, that it was my indispensable duty to communicate them to some English gentleman, who might put their Government upon their guard; the two facts I should now mention, were two instances of the policy of the Count de Vergennes, to defeat the good intentions of Congress towards Great Britain. I then showed him my two original commissions, one, as minister plenipotentiary for making peace; the other, as minister plenipotentiary to make a treaty of commerce with the ambassador or plenipotentiary of his Britannic Majesty, vested with equal powers: "and whatever shall be so agreed and concluded for us and in our name to sign, and thereupon make a treaty of commerce, and to transact every thing that may be necessary for completing, securing, and strengthening the same, in as ample form, and with the same effect, as if we were personally present and acted therein. 29 September, 1779."

Mr. Vaughan said, he was astonished at my secrecy and patience, in never communicating this before; that they never had any idea of this in London. I told him, the Count de Vergennes had required me, in the name of the King, not to communicate it. I then showed him the resolution of Congress of 12 July, 1781, by which the commission and instructions for negotiating a treaty of commerce between the United States and Great Britain, given me on the 29th day of September, 1779, were revoked.

I then read to him the following part of my instructions of 16 October, 1779, to wit,—

"That the common right of fishing shall in no case be given up; that it is essential to the welfare of all these United States that the inhabitants thereof, at the expiration of the war, should continue to enjoy the free and undisturbed exercise of their common right to fish on the banks of Newfoundland and the other fishing banks and seas of North America; that our faith be pledged to the several States, that without their unanimous consent, no treaty of commerce shall be entered into, nor any trade or commerce whatever carried on with Great Britain, without the explicit stipulation hereinafter mentioned. You are, therefore, not to consent to any treaty of commerce with Great Britain, without an explicit stipulation on her part not to molest or disturb the inhabitants of the United States of America in taking fish on the banks of Newfoundland and other fisheries in the American seas," &c. Here I stopped.

"You see here," said I, "Mr. Vaughan, a proof of a great confidence in me; and what was the cause of it? No other than this: my sentiments were known in Congress to be unalterable for independence, our alliance, fisheries, and boundaries; but it was known also to be a fixed principle with me, to hurt Great Britain no farther than should be necessary to secure our independence, alliance, and other rights.

"The Count de Vergennes knew my character, both from his intelligences in America, and from my conversation and correspondence with him; he knew me to be a man who would not yield to some of the designs he had in view; he accordingly sets his confidential friend, M. Marbois, to negotiating very artfully with Congress; they could not get me removed or recalled, and the next scheme was, to get the power of the commission for peace into the hands of Dr. Franklin; to this end, the choice was made to fall upon him and four other gentlemen who could not attend; they have been, however, mistaken, and no wrestler was ever so completely thrown upon his back as the Count de Vergennes.

"But their policy did not stop here. I had still a parchment to make a treaty of commerce with Great Britain, and an instruction annexed to it, which would be a powerful motive with Great Britain to acknowledge our right to the fisheries. This commission and these instructions were to be and were revoked."

Mr. Vaughan said this was very important information, and entirely new; that he was much enlightened, and had sentiments upon the occasion; that he would write it to the Earl of Shelburne, and his Lordship would make great use of it, without naming me, &c.

13. Monday. Mr. Oswald came to take leave, and showed me a letter from the Secretary of State for him to come home. He goes off on Wednesday. I told him, if he was going home, I would communicate to him what I had not intended. I told him what I told yesterday to Vaughan, and gave him some short account of my correspondence with the Count de Vergennes, upon the question whether I should communicate to Lord G. Germaine my commissions, and his requisition from the King not to do it, &c.

19. Sunday. Received a note from Mr. Franklin, that the Count de Vergennes had written to him to desire me to meet him at his office to-morrow at ten. Went out to Passy. Told Mr. Franklin, that I had been informed last night, that the Count was uneasy at Mr. Oswald's going away, because he expected to sign the preliminaries in a day or two.

20. Monday. Mr. Franklin and I met the Count de Vergennes at his office at ten. He told us he was going to sign preliminaries and an armistice. At eleven, the Count d'Aranda came in, and Mr. Fitzherbert. After examining the papers, D'Aranda and Fitzherbert signed the preliminary treaty between the Crowns of Great Britain and Spain. De Vergennes and Fitzherbert that between Britain and France. Then Fitzherbert on one part, and Adams and Franklin on the other, signed, sealed, and exchanged declarations of an armistice between the Crown of Great Britain and the United States of America. Previous to the signature, all the original commissions were shown. The Count d'Aranda showed his; the Count de Vergennes his; Mr. Fitzherbert his; and Adams and Franklin theirs. Fitzherbert agreed to exchange copies with us. Thus was this mighty system terminated with as little ceremony, and in as short a time, as a marriage settlement.

Before the British and Spanish ministers came in, I asked the Count de Vergennes what was to become of Holland. He smiled, and said that we had nothing to do with that. I answered, with a smile too, it was very true we had nothing to do with it, but that I interested myself very much in the welfare and safety of that people. He then assumed an affected air of seriousness, and said he interested himself in it too a good deal; and then told me, that the English had first wished to retain Demarara and Essequibo, but the King would not hear to that; then they wanted Trincomalee in the East Indies, but the King would not agree to that; then they wanted Negapatnam; this the King left them to settle with the Dutch, but insisted on a declaration from the King of Great Britain that he would restore all the other possessions. Fitzherbert told me, afterwards, it was the severity of the Spaniards, that obliged his Court to be so hard with the Dutch; the Spaniards would do nothing without Minorca and the Floridas.

Returned to Paris, and dined with the Duchess d'Enville and the Duke de la Rochefoucauld.

21. Tuesday. Went to Versailles, to pay my respects to the King and royal family, upon the event of yesterday. Dined with the foreign ambassadors at the Count de Vergennes'. The King appeared in high health and in gay spirits; so did the Queen. Madame Elizabeth is grown very fat. The Comte d'Artois seems very well. Mr. Fitzherbert had his first audience of the King and royal family, and dined, for the first time, with the Corps Diplomatique.

23. Thursday. Mr. Whitefoord made me a visit. He said it was the fatal policy of the Earl of Chatham, in supporting the King of Prussia against the House of Austria, that had given an Austrian Queen to France; that the French had contrived to marry the King's two brothers to princesses of Savoy, by which they had damped the zeal of another of the allies of England, the King of Sardinia. I told him the story of my correspondence with the Count de Vergennes, in 1780, about communicating my mission to Lord George Germaine. He said, if I had followed my own opinion, and written to his Lordship, and published the letter, it would have turned out the old ministry. I told him I was restrained by a requisition from the King; besides, the defeat of D'Estaing and Langara had turned the heads of the people of England at that time.

February 18. Tuesday. Received a letter from my son John, dated at Gottenburgh, the first of February. This letter gave me great joy; it is the first I have received from him since he left Petersburg, and the first news I have had of him since the beginning of December, when he was at Stockholm. I have suffered extreme anxiety on his account. I have omitted my Journal and several things of some consequence; but I am weary, disgusted, affronted, and disappointed. This state of mind I must alter, and work while the day lasts. I have been injured, and my country has joined in the injury; it has basely prostituted its own honor by sacrificing mine. But the sacrifice of me was not so servile and intolerable as putting us all under guardianship. Congress surrendered their own sovereignty into the hands of a French minister. Blush! blush! ye guilty records! blush and perish! It is glory to have broken such infamous orders. Infamous, I say, for so they will be to all posterity. How can such a stain be washed out? Can we cast a veil over it and forget it?

24. Monday. Dined in company with M. Malesherbes, the famous first president of the Court of Aids, uncle of the Chevalier de la Luzerne, and son of the Chancelier de Lamoignon. He is about half way, in appearance, between Mr. Otis and Mr. A. Oliver.

Franklin, this morning, mentioned to me the Voyage de la Fonté, who mentions a Captain Shapley and a Seymour Gibbons. Franklin thinks it is translated from the Spanish, and that the translator or printer has put Seymour for Señor. He had once a correspondence about this voyage; and Mr. Prince found there had been a Captain Chapelet at Charlestown, and a Gibbons, but not named Seymour. Endnote 119

25. Tuesday. Mr. Samuel Vaughan says, that Cook's Voyage will be three volumes, sixty plates, and will not be out these twelve months. The plates are of islands discovered, &c. He mentions a new sort of bark, much redder and much stronger than any known before.

27. Thursday. Dined at the Farmer-General's in company with the Comte de Polastron, father of the Duchesse de Polignac; no friend of D'Estaing. Spent the evening in company with the Abbé de Mably, some other abbés and academicians.

De Mably says, there are in France three orders of citizens,—the first order is of the clergy; 2. the second of the nobility; 3. and the third is called Le Tiers État. There are several classes in the order of the clergy; seven or eight classes in the order of nobles; and thirty classes in the Tiers État. The nobles all believe that their nobility is from God; and therefore, the nobles are all equal, and that the King cannot confer nobility.

March 7. Friday. In the Morning Chronicle of Saturday, February 22, Mr. Secretary Townsend, in the debate upon the five propositions of Lord John Cavendish, is represented to have said,—"He was willing to give his full assent to the first proposition, because such a declaration from Parliament was, after the address voted on Monday last, indispensably necessary. To the second and to the third resolutions, likewise, he had no objections. The fourth he certainly should resist, because it conveyed a direct censure upon ministers, reprobated and condemned the peace, would give alarm and umbrage to the foreign powers with whom the peace had been made, and be attended with a variety of bad consequences. With regard to the fifth, that respecting the loyalists, it would produce much evil. It would totally defeat the recommendations which Congress were pledged to make in favor of the loyalists, and put them in a worse predicament than they already stood in by the treaty. In order to support this assertion, Mr. Townsend reasoned a good deal on the great danger arising at all times from creating jealousies and suspicions in parties negotiating; but if there was any party more prone to jealousy, any state more liable to catch suspicion sooner than another, it must be the United States of America, on account of their having been little accustomed to the business of negotiating, and being obliged to trust their first and dearest interests in the hands of persons of whose fidelity they had scarcely any pledge of security. Mr. Townsend concluded with saying, that for these reasons he should resist the fifth resolution as well as the fourth."

9. Saturday. Dined at Passy; the Spanish ambassador, the Count de Rochambeau, the Chevalier de Chastellux, Mr. Jay, &c., present. Chastellux said to the Abbé Morlaix, that I was the author of the Massachusetts Constitution, and that it was the best of them all, and that the people were very contented with it.

10. Sunday. Mercure de France, 1 February, 1783, page 26, Académie Royale de Musique:—

"Lorsqu'un homme entre dans la carrière des arts, n'ayant pour guide et pour appui que son génie, lorsque l'intrigue et la charlatanerie, ces deux grandes ressources des petits talens, lui sont étrangères, il doit s'attendre à être long temps perséeuté méconnu, arrété à chaque pas. Mais qu'il ne perde point courage; tous les obstacles s'aplanissent peu-à-peu devant lui; ses ennemis se lassent ou deviennent odieux et suspects; et le public, éclairé par ces mêmes productions qu'il n'avoit pas d'abord appreciées, rend enfin justice à leur auteur.

"Il est vrai, qu'un artiste qui se présente après vingt-cinq ans de gloire et de succès, ne devroit pas éprouver les mêmes dégoûts; son nom fameux dans l'empire des arts, paroitroit fait pour en imposer à ses détracteurs. Mais si dans le nouveau pays ou il arrive, son art est encore ignoré; s'il y regne un faux savoir, pire que l'ignorance; si l'on y a la manie des préférences, des préférences exclusives, et que l'on ait déjà choisi l'objet de ces préférences, son nom lui devient inutile, ou même dangereux; et la réputation qui le précéde, en éveillant l'envie, n'est pour lui qu'un obstacle de plus."

"On se rappelle aujourd'hui, avec une espèce de honte, les excès où l'on se porta d'abord contre l'auteur de Roland. Les quolibets, les plates epigrammes, les comparaisons injurieuses—rien ne fut épargné." Mr. Piccini is the author of Roland.

In this country the demon of monarchy haunts all the scenes of life. It appears in every conversation, at every table, and upon every theatre. These people can attend to no more than one person at a time; they can esteem but one; and to that one their homage is adulation and idolatry.

I once heard the Baron Van der Capellen de Pol say, that the demon of aristocracy appeared everywhere in that republic; that he had collected together a number of merchants to sign a requête; they agreed upon the measure, but insisted upon appointing a committee to sign it. Many of them declared, they would not sign it with a crowd—avec une foule. Thus it is that the human mind contracts habits of thinking from the example of the government; accustomed to look up to a few as all, in an aristocracy, they imitate the same practice in private life and in common things; accustomed, in monarchies, to look up to one man in great affairs, they contract a similar disposition in little ones.

In the same manner, in democracies, we contract a habit of deciding every thing by a majority of votes; we put it to vote whether the company will sing a song or tell a story. In an aristocracy, they ask two or three of the better sort; in a monarchy, they ask the lady or the gentleman in whose honor the feast is made.

I dined with the Comte de Pilo, under the incognito name of M. d'Olavide, heretofore Intendant of Seville, who established the colony of Sierra Morena in Spain; Mr. Boystel, Consul-General of France in Spain; the Comte de Jaucourt, Maréchal de Camp; the Comte de Lusignan, Maréchal de Camp; and the Comte de Langeron, Maréchal de Camp, Commandant à Brest,—at Count Sarsfield's.

Paris, April 27. Mr. Hartley met Franklin, Laurens, Jay, and me, at my lodgings, and showed us an instruction, under the King's privy seal, and signed George Rex, in which his Majesty recites, that he had appointed Mr. Hartley, his Minister Plenipotentiary, to treat with us, &c.

The American Ministers unanimously required a commission under the great seal, and promising to ratify what he should do. Mr. Hartley was chagrined.

Much conversation passed which might as well have been spared. Mr. Hartley was as copious as usual. I called on Mr. Jay in the evening, and we agreed to meet at my house next morning, at ten.

28. Monday. At ten, Mr. Jay came in, and I showed him a variety of projects which I had drawn up last night, concerning the removal of the troops, opening the ports, tranquillizing the tories now within the lines; articles for commerce, in explanation of the provisional treaty, &c. We drew, together, a proposition for withdrawing the troops, opening the ports, and quieting the tories, and went with it in my carriage to Mr. Laurens, who thought it might do. I said to my brothers, I shall be very ductile about commerce. I would agree at once to a mutual naturalization, or to the article, as first agreed on, by Dr. Franklin and Mr. Jay, with Mr. Oswald; or, I would agree to Mr. Hartley's propositions, to let the trade go on as before the war, or as with Nova Scotia; I could agree to any of these things, because that time and the natural course of things will produce a good treaty of commerce. Great Britain will soon see and feel the necessity of alluring American commerce to her ports by facilities and encouragements of every kind. We called at Mr. Hartley's, Hôtel de York, he was out; at Mr. Jay's, Mr. Hartley came in; we told him, we thought of making him a proposition to-morrow, and would meet him at Mr. Laurens's, at one; wrote to Dr. Franklin and W. T. Franklin, desiring their attendance at Mr. Laurens's, Hôtel de l'Empereur, at eleven to-morrow; received an answer that they would attend. Mr. Hartley desired of me letters of introduction for Il Conte di Fermé, a cousin of the Neapolitan ambassador in London, who is going to America, which I promised him, and wrote in the evening.

29. Tuesday. At eleven, we all met at Mr. Laurens's, near the new French Comedy, and agreed upon a proposition to open the ports as soon as the United States should be evacuated. At one, Mr. Hartley came and we showed it to him, and after some conversation with him, we agreed upon three propositions:

1. To open the ports as soon as the States should be evacuated;

2. To set all confined tories at liberty at the same time; and

3. To set all prisoners of war at liberty, upon the same terms respecting the accounts of their expenses as those between France and England.

30. Wednesday. Mr. Hartley did me the honor of a visit, to assure me, as he said, of the satisfaction he had in reflecting upon what passed yesterday, and upon what we had agreed upon. He thought it was exactly as it should be. I was glad to hear of his satisfaction and expressed my own.

I told him, that I was so convinced that Great Britain and America would soon feel the necessity and convenience of a right plan of commerce, that I was not anxious about it; that it was simply from a pure regard to Great Britain, and to give them an opportunity of alluring to themselves as much of our commerce as, in the present state of things, would be possible, that I should give myself any trouble about it; that I had never had but one principle and one system concerning this subject, before, during, or since the war, and that had generally been the system of Congress, namely, that it was not our interest to hurt Great Britain, any further than was necessary to support our independence and our alliances; that the French Court had sometimes endeavored to warp us from this system, in some degrees and particulars; that they had sometimes succeeded with some American ministers and agents, Mr. Deane particularly, and I must add, that Dr. Franklin had not adhered to it at all times with so much firmness as I could have wished; and indeed Congress itself, from the fluctuations of its members, or some other cause, had sometimes appeared to lose sight of it; that I had constantly endeavored to adhere to it, but this inflexibility had been called stubborness, obstinacy, vanity, &c., and had exposed me to many attacks and disagreeable circumstances; that it had been to damp the ardor of returning friendship, as I supposed, which had induced the French minister to use his influence to get the commission to make a treaty of commerce with Great Britain revoked without appointing another; that I did not care a farthing for a commission to Great Britain, and wished that the one to me had never existed; but that I was very sorry it was revoked without appointing another; that the policy of this Court he might well think would be to lay every stumbling block between Great Britain and America; they wished to deprive us of the fisheries and western lands for this reason; they espoused the cause of the tories for this reason.

I told him the Comte de Vergennes and I were pursuing different objects; he was endeavoring to make my countrymen meek and humble, and I was laboring to make them proud; I avowed it was my object to make them hold up their heads, and look down upon any nation that refused to do them justice; that, in my opinion, Americans had nothing to fear but from the meekness of their own hearts; as Christians, I wished them meek; as statesmen, I wished them proud; and I thought the pride and the meekness very consistent. Providence had put into our hands such advantages, that we had a just right, and it was our duty to insist upon justice from all courts, ministers, and nations; that I wished him to get his commission as soon as possible, and that we might discuss every point, and be perfectly ready to sign the definitive treaty. He said his commission would come as soon as the courier could go and return; and that he would prepare his propositions for the definitive treaty immediately. He said he had not imagined that we had been so stout as he found us. But he was very silent and attentive. He has had hints, I suppose, from Laurens and Jay, and Franklin too. He never before discovered a capacity to hearken. He ever before took all the talk to himself.

I am not fond of talking; but I wanted to convey into his mind a few things for him to think upon. None of the English gentlemen have come here apprized of the place where their danger lay.

May 1. Thursday. Dined with the Marquis de Lafayette, with the other American ministers, and others. Visited the Duke and Duchess de la Vauguyon at the Petite

Luxembourg. The Duke is to stay here some time. I told him he and I were in the same case, and explained to him my situation, and gave him my frank sentiments of a certain minister. He said he was véritablement touché.

2. Friday. Mr. Hartley came in to introduce to me his Secretary, Mr. Hammond, whom he introduced also to mine, Mr. Thaxter and Storer.

He told me that the Comte de Vergennes had been treating with Mr. Fitzherbert about the post of Panmure at the Natches, which is within the limits which England has acknowledged to be the bounds of the United States; the Spaniards want to keep it, and the Comte de Vergennes wants to make a merit of procuring it for them, with a few leagues round it. I told Mr. Hartley that this subject was within the exclusive jurisdiction of Mr. Jay; that the ministers for peace had nothing to say in it.

I told Mr. Hartley the story of my negotiation with the Comte de Vergennes, about communicating my mission to Lord George Germaine, three years ago, and the subsequent intrigues and disputes, &c. It is necessary to let the English ministers know where their danger lies, and the arts used to damp the ardor of returning friendship.

Mr. Jay came with several pieces of intelligence:

1. The story of Panmure.

2. The Marquis de Lafayette told him that no instructions were ever sent by the Count de Vergennes to the Count Montmorin to favor Mr. Jay's negotiations at Madrid, and that Montmorin told Lafayette so.

Mr. Jay added, that the Marquis told him that the Count de Vergennes desired him to ask Mr. Jay why he did not come and see him. Mr. Jay says he answered, "How can he expect it, when he knows he has endeavored to play us out of the fisheries and vacant lands?" Mr. Jay added, that he thought it would be best to let out by degrees, and to communicate to some French gentlemen the truth, and show them Marbois' letter; *Endnote 120* he particularly mentioned Count Sarsfield.

Mr. Jay added, "Every day produces some fresh proof and example of their vile schemes. He had applied to Montmorin to assist him, countenance him, support him, in his negotiation at Madrid, and showed him a resolution of Congress, by which the King of France was requested to aid him. Montmorin said he could not do it without instructions from his Court; that he would write for instructions. But Mr. Jay says he never heard any farther about it; but, yesterday, Lafayette told him, that Montmorin told him, no such instructions had ever been sent him. *Endnote 121*

The commissions of the Comtes de Vergennes and D'Aranda, on the 20th of January, were plainer than ours, and upon paper. The French reserve their silver boxes to the exchange of ratifications.

3. Saturday. When we met Mr. Hartley, on Tuesday last, at Mr. Laurens's, I first saw and first heard of Mr. Livingston's letter to Dr. Franklin upon the subject of peace, dated January 7, 1782. The peace is made, and the negotiations all passed, before I knew of this letter, and at last by accident. Such is Dr. Franklin.

Visited Mr. Jay. Found him, his lady, Miss Laurens, and the Marquis de Lafayette at breakfast, going out of town. Visited Mr. Laurens. Not at home. Duke de la Vauguyon not at home. Mr. Hartley at home. Mr. Laurens came in soon after. I agreed to make a visit to the Duke of Manchester this evening. His rank, as duke and as ambassador, and the superiority of the State he represents, make it unnecessary to attend to the rule in this town, which is, that the last comer make the first visit, or to inquire very nicely what the sublime science of etiquette dictates upon this occasion.

Mr. Hartley proposes that we should agree that the English should continue their garrisons in Detroit, Niagara, and Michilimackinac, for a limited time, or that Congress should put garrisons into those places to protect their people, traders, and troops, from the insults of the Indians; the Indians will be enraged to find themselves betrayed into the hands of those people against whom they have been excited to war.

Mr. Hartley proposes also, that we should agree that all the carrying places should be in common. This is a great point. These carrying places command the fur trade. Mr. Laurens hinted to me, between us, that this was the complaint in England against the ministry who made the peace; that they had thrown the whole fur trade into the hands of the United States, by ceding all the carrying places, and that the lakes and waters were made useless to them by this means.

Mr. Laurens quoted a Creek king, who said he would not be for quarrelling with either side, especially with us Americans, for we were all born of the same mother, and sucked at the same breasts. But, turning to his young men, he said, with tears in his eyes, whichever side prevails, I see that we must be cut off.

Mr. Hartley talked about Passamaquoddy and the islands at the mouth of the river St. Croix. He is for settling this matter so as to prevent questions.

Between five and six I made my visit to the Duke of Manchester, the British ambassador, upon his arrival. Not at home. Left my card. The next day, or next but one, the Duke returned my visit, came up to my apartment, and spent a half hour in familiar conversation. He is between fifty and sixty, a composed man, plain Englishman.

One day this week, I visited the Duke de la Vauguyon upon his arrival from the Hague, who returned my visit in a day or two.

5. Monday. Dined with my family at Count Sarsfield's. The Dukes de la Vauguyon and De la Rochefoucauld, Mr. Jay, &c. of the party.

6. Tuesday. Dined at Mr. Jay's. Lieutenant-General Melville, who is here to solicit for the inhabitants of Tobago the continuance of their assembly and trials by jury, was there.

7. Wednesday. Dined at M. de Calonne's.

8. Thursday. The Duke de la Vauguyon and Mr. Hartley, Mr. Laurens and Jay, Mr. Barclay and Ridley, dined with me.

9. Friday. Dined with Mr. Laurens, with a large company. The Marquis de Lafayette showed me the beginning of an attack upon the Chancellor, &c. &c.

10. Saturday. Dined with the Marquis de Lafayette, with a large American company.

19. Monday. The American ministers met Mr. Hartley at my house; and he showed us his commission, and we showed him ours. His commission is very magnificent; the great seal, in a silver box, with the King's arms engraven on it, with two large gold tassels, &c. as usual. Dined with Mr. Laurens and Mr. Jay, at Mr. Hartley's, Hôtel de York. We are to meet of evenings, at six o'clock, de die in diem, at my house.

Mr. Hartley informed us to-day that the King's council had not agreed to our proposition, of putting Britons upon the footing of Americans in all American ports, rivers, &c., and Americans on the footing of Britons in all British ports, rivers, &c. He says he is very sorry for this, because he thinks it just and politic, and that he shall ever be, in Parliament, for bringing things to that point.

20. Tuesday. Saw Philadelphia papers to the 12th of April. The corvette despatched from Cadiz, by the Comte d'Estaing, carried the first news of the preliminaries of the 20th of January. Mr. Livingston wrote it to Carlton and Digby; but they thought it, however respectable, not authentic for them. Soon after, the February packet arrived at New York, from whence English newspapers were sent out, and the provisional and preliminary treaties all published in the Philadelphia papers.

Visited Mr. Hartley. He said he thought the Dutch negotiation in a bad way, and that there would be a civil contest in Holland; a struggle between the Stadtholder and the States.

Mr. Hartley said, that some Dutch friends he had in London had told him there would be a civil dissension in Holland, and he was now more convinced of it. He said the King of Prussia and the King of England would take the part of the Stadtholder. I answered, they would do well to consider, whether, in that case, France and the Emperor would not assist the republicans, and thus throw all Europe into a flame.

I told him I thought the English policy towards the republic all wrong; they were wrong to make themselves partisans of the Stadtholder against the Republicans; that they ought to be impartial; that they were interested in the conservation of the liberties of that country; if that spot should be annexed to the Empire or to France, it would be fatal to Great Britain; that without its liberty it could not maintain its independency; human life in that country struggling against the sea, and in danger from so many quarters, would be too painful and discouraging without liberty; that the King of England and the Stadtholder would make a fatal mistake, if they thought of making the latter sovereign, or of increasing his power; the country would not be worth the governing; that the families of Orange and Brunswick owed their grandeur to the cause of liberty, and if they now engaged in a conspiracy against it, they must go to Italy after the Stuarts. I added, that Sir Joseph Yorke had been wrong to attach himself so closely to the Court, and declare war so decidedly against the patriots; that he should have kept upon good terms with the Capellens, Van Berckel, Gyzelaer, Visscher, &c.; I had reflected much upon this subject; I had always been ready to acknowledge that I could not distinctly foresee what would be the consequence of our independence in Europe; it might depress England too much, and elevate the House of Bourbon too high; if this should be the case, neither England nor America could depend upon the moderation of such absolute monarchies and such ambitious nations; America might find France and Spain demanding of her things which she could not grant; so might England; both might find it necessary to their safety to join, and, in such a case, it would be of great importance to both to have Holland join them; whereas the policy of the British Court, if pursued, would drive the Dutch into the arms of France, and fix them there; that I hoped the case put would never happen; but England would have a stronger reason than ever, now, to cultivate the friendship of Holland; that, in my opinion, she ought to give up Negapatnam and the liberty of navigation; give satisfaction to the Dutch, and carry an even hand in future between the Court and the States; that the British minister ought to seek the acquaintance and friendship of the principal patriots in all the Provinces, and give them the assurances of his Court, that nothing should be attempted against their constitution.

Mr. Hartley said he was of my mind, and had said as much to Mr. Fox before he left London; but the King would stand by the Stadtholder. "The King," says he, "will go wrong in Holland, and in Ireland and Scotland too; but it will all work against himself; there are discontents in Scotland as well as Ireland; we shall have struggles, but I don't dread these; we shall have settled with America, and the American war was all that I dreaded."

21. Wednesday. What is it in the air which burns? When we blow a spark with the bellows, it spreads. We force a current of air to the fire, by this machine, and in this air are inflammable particles. Can it be in the same manner that life is continued by the breath? Are there any particles conveyed into the blood of animals through the lungs which increase the heat of it? or is the pulse caused by rarefying the blood or any part of it into vapor, like the experiment made with spirits of wine in a glass tube, with a globule at each end? If one end or globule is placed in a position a little warmer than the other, you see a pulsation caused by repeated rarefications of the spirits of wine into vapor at one end, which flows to the other, and then flows again to its former position, where it is again rarefied and protruded.

The external air drawn into the lungs in breathing through the mouth or nostrils, either leaves some particles behind in the lungs or in the blood, or carries some particles off with it;

it may do both, that is, carry in some particles that are salubrious, and carry out others which are noxious. The air once breathed is certainly altered; it is unfit to be breathed again. The body is said to render unfit for respiration a gallon of air in a minute. Four persons in a coach would render unfit four hogsheads of air in an hour, which is more than the coach would hold; which shows the necessity of keeping the windows open, and of frequently airing your dining rooms, keeping rooms, and bed-chambers. I suspect that the health of mankind is much injured by their inattention to this subject.

Mr. Hartley, Mr. Franklin, Mr. Jay, Mr. Laurens, met me at my house, Hôtel du Roi, au Carrousel, this evening; and we exchanged with Mr. Hartley full powers, and entered into conferences.

Mr. Hartley made us the following proposition in writing, namely,—

"Whereas it is highly necessary that an intercourse of trade and commerce should be opened between the people and territories belonging to the Crown of Great Britain, and the people and territories of the United States of America; and whereas it is highly expedient that the intercourse between Great Britain and the said United States should be established on the most enlarged principles of reciprocal benefit to both countries; but, from the distance between Great Britain and America, it must be a considerable time before any convention or treaty for establishing and regulating the trade and intercourse between Great Britain and the said United States of America upon a permanent foundation, can be concluded. Now, for the purpose of making a temporary regulation of the commerce and intercourse between Great Britain and the said United States of America, it is agreed, that all the citizens of the United States of America shall be permitted to import into, and export from, any part of his Britannic Majesty's dominions, in American ships, any goods, wares, and merchandises, which have been so imported or exported by the inhabitants of the British American Colonies, before the commencement of the war, upon payment of the same duties and charges as the like sort of goods or merchandise are now, or may be, subject and liable to, if imported by British subjects in British ships from any British island or plantation in America; and that all the subjects of his Britannic Majesty shall be permitted to import and to export from any part of the territories of the thirteen United States of America, in British ships, any goods, wares, and merchandises, which might have been so imported or exported by the subjects of his Britannic Majesty before the commencement of the war, upon payment of the same duties and charges as the like sort of goods, wares, and merchandises, are now, or may be, subject and liable to, if imported in American ships by any of the citizens of the United States of America.

"This agreement to continue in force until.

"Provided always, That nothing contained in this agreement shall, at any time hereafter, be argued on either side in support of any future demand or claim."

Mr. Hartley withdrew, and we entered into consultation upon his proposition.

We agreed to write a line to Mr. Hartley, to inquire if he thought himself authorized to sign that agreement without further orders from St. James's. The gentlemen proposed that I should write it, as first in the commission. I answered, that in that case I must have their sanction to the letter. They desired me to draw one. I sat down to the table, and wrote,—

Sir,—The American ministers have done me the honor to direct me to present you their compliments, and desire to be informed whether you think yourself sufficiently authorized to agree and subscribe to the proposition you have made them this evening, without further instructions or information from your Court.

Dr. Franklin moved that the secretary should sign and send it, which was agreed, the letter being approved in the foregoing words.

The gentlemen desired me to draw an answer to Mr. Grand's letter, and a letter to the bankers in Amsterdam, which I agreed to do, and lay it before them at their next meeting.

22. Thursday. This morning I drew the following letters, to be laid before the ministers this evening:—

John Adams

TO M. GRAND.

Paris, 22 May, 1783

Sir.—

We have received the letter you did us the honor to write us on the day of this month, containing a brief state of the affairs of the United States in your hands. We see the difficulties you are in, and are sorry to say that it is not in our power to afford you any relief.

We have, &c.

Messrs. Wilhem and Jan Willink, Nicolas and Jacob Van Staphorst, and De la Lande and Fynje, Bankers of the United States of America, at Amsterdam.

Gentlemen,—

Mr. Grand has laid before us a state of the affairs of the United States under his care; and the demands upon him for money to discharge the bills drawn upon him are such as to require some assistance from you, if the demands upon you will admit of it. If, therefore, the state of the cash in your hands, compared with the draughts made upon you, will allow of it, we advise you to remit to Mr. Grand, on account of the United States, the amount of five millions of livres tournois; and we doubt not that Congress and their minister of finances will approve of it, although we have not, in strictness, authority to give orders for it.

We have, &c.

This morning I also drew the following, to be laid before the gentlemen this evening:—

ARTICLES ***Endnote 122***

Agreed upon by and between David Hartley, Esquire, Minister Plenipotentiary of his Britannic Majesty for , in behalf of his said Majesty, on the one part, and John Adams, Benjamin Franklin, John Jay, and Henry Laurens, Ministers Plenipotentiary of the United States of America, for treating of peace with the Minister Plenipotentiary of his said Majesty, on their behalf, on the other part;

IN ADDITION

to those agreed upon, on the 30th day of November, 1782, by and between Richard Oswald, Esquire, the Commissioner of his Britannic Majesty for treating of peace with the Commissioners of the United States of America, in behalf of his said Majesty, on the one part, and the said John Adams, Benjamin Franklin, John Jay, and Henry Laurens, Commissioners of the said States for treating of peace with the Commissioner of his said Majesty, on their behalf, on the other part.

Whereas, it is expedient that an intercourse and commerce should be opened between the people and territories subject to the Crown of Great Britain, and those of the United States of America; and that this intercourse and commerce should be established on the most enlarged principles of reciprocal benefit to both countries:

1. It is agreed, that ministers shall be forthwith nominated, and vested with full powers to treat, agree, and conclude upon a permanent treaty of commerce between the two powers and their respective citizens, subjects, and countries.

2. For the purpose of a temporary regulation of such intercourse and commerce, it is agreed, that the citizens of the United States shall import into, and export from, any part of the dominions subject to the Crown of Great Britain, in American ships, any goods, wares, and merchandises, which have been so imported, or exported, by the inhabitants of the British American Colonies before the commencement of the late war, paying only the same duties and charges as the like sort of goods, wares, and merchandises are now or may be subject to, if imported by British subjects, in British ships, from any British island or plantation in America; and that the subjects of his Britannic Majesty shall import to and export from any part of the territories of the United States of America, in British ships, any goods, wares, and merchandise, which might have been so imported, or exported, by the subjects of his Britannic Majesty before the commencement of the war, paying the same duties and charges as the like sort of goods, wares, and merchandises are now, or may be subject to, if imported in American ships, by any of the citizens of the said United States.

This agreement to continue in force for all vessels which shall sail from any port of either party on or before the day of and no longer.

Provided always, that nothing in this agreement shall at any time hereafter be argued on either side, in support of any proposition which may be made in the future negotiation of a permanent treaty of commerce.

It was observed last evening, that all the laws of Great Britain for the regulation of the plantation trade, were contrived solely for the benefit of Great Britain.

These laws, therefore, ought not now to be the regulation, which ought to be for the reciprocal benefit of both. The new system of commerce, the permanent treaty, ought to be framed for the benefit of the United States as much as for that of Great Britain. Will not this temporary revival of the old partial system encourage British merchants and statesmen to aim at the perpetuation of it in the treaty? Will not our making such a convention be a temptation to the British Court to postpone the definitive treaty—perhaps to be indifferent about ever signing a definitive treaty?

By this project of Mr. Hartley's, American manufactures are excluded from the British dominions, but British manufactures are not excluded from the United States; Americans are excluded from carrying the productions of other countries to the British dominions, but Britons are not excluded from carrying the productions of other countries to America,—two instances of partiality and inequality which may be seeds of discord. Men's minds cannot be contented under partiality among equals; they think it, as it is, injustice; it is humiliating; it is thought disgraceful.

The Dutch will allow Americans to bring their manufactures and those of other countries to Amsterdam, and this attraction will draw our ships to that market. We may carry hats, spermaceti candles, &c., from America; wines from Portugal, Spain, or France, to Holland; sugars, &c., from the West India Islands, to Holland, &c.

If other nations allow Americans to carry any thing to them which Britain forbids, this will allure them to foreign ports and drive them from those of Britain.

At 10, this morning, Mr. Hartley called upon me; said he had received our note of last night, and had reflected upon our question, reviewed his instructions, and called upon the

Duke of Manchester, to consult with him, and, upon the whole, he thought he must wait the return of a courier, which he should send off to-morrow.

I told him, that his Court must be sensible, if the trade was renewed upon the old system it must be upon that system entire; and even then, it would be a reciprocity all on one side,—all in favor of Great Britain. That if they thought of excluding us from the West India trade, they must think it would obstruct our agreement; and I was afraid, if he mentioned it, and thus put it into the heads of the council, they would embarrass him with some wrong orders about it. He said, he should support what was right, as we wished it, in his despatches, and so would the Duke of Manchester; but they thought it most prudent to send to London for orders.

He then said, he had heard a story, in which the Marquis de Lafayette was named, that the French Court had applied to the American Ministers, to know if they would come into the definitive treaty under the mediation of the two Imperial Courts; *Endnote 123* that we answered, that such a thing might be very well, but we could not help observing, that those Courts had not acknowledged our independence as yet. The reply was, that accepting the mediation would be acknowledging our independence. Whence came this story? Secrets will always be thus kept, while negotiations are carried on by such circuitous messages.

At eleven, returned visits to Mr. Fitch and Mr. Boylston, and then to the Baron de Waltersdorf, chamberlain of the King of Denmark, who remarked to me, that he was surprised that his Court had never been informed that Mr. Dana had powers to treat with Denmark. I told him, that Mr. Dana had been advised against communicating it; but that his Court might send a full power to their minister at Petersburg, to treat and conclude with any minister of the United States, vested with equal powers; and the conferences might begin as soon as they please. He said, that he hoped the Dutch would not regain all their trade, but that the northern nations would retain some of it; that he thought St. Eustatia would be of no value in future, as the King had made St. Thomas a free port; that vessels might he in safety at St. Thomas in the hurricane months, but not at St. Eustatia. He said, that some Danish vessels had gone to America, loaded with linens, duck, sail-cloth, &c.

The following is a copy of the Order in Council of the 14th May, 1783, delivered to us last night by Mr. Hartley. *Endnote 124*

23. Friday. Last evening, the American ministers and secretary met again at my house, and signed the letters to Mr. Grand and to the bankers at Amsterdam.

Mr. Laurens gave it as his opinion, that the balance of trade for the future, between Great Britain and America, would be in favor of the latter. I asked him, what in that case would become of the former. He replied, "She must be humble. She has hitherto avoided trading with any nation when the balance was against her. This is the reason why she would not trade with France."

This morning Mr. Laurens called on me, to introduce to me a West India gentleman, from Jamaica, a Mr.—.

Mr. Laurens says, the English are convinced that the method of coppering ships is hurtful. The copper corrodes all the iron, all the bolts, spikes, and nails, which it touches. The vessel falls to pieces all at once. They attribute the late losses of so many ships to this. That Mr. Oswald made an experiment, twenty years ago, which convinced him that copper was fatal. He lost a ship by it.

Mr. Laurens, Mr. Jay, and Mr. Jarret and Mr. Fitch, two West India gentlemen, said to be very rich, dined with me. Mr. Fitch is a native of Boston,—holds an office of Receiver-General, I think, in Jamaica. Ward Nicholas Boylston was to have dined with me, but was taken sick.

Mr. Jay told me, that the Count de Vergennes turned to him and Mr. Franklin, and asked, "Où est M. Adams?" Franklin answered, "Il est à Paris." Then, turning to Jay, he said, "Ce monsieur a beaucoup d'esprit, et beaucoup de tête aussi." Jay answered, "Oui, Monsieur, Monsieur Adams a beaucoup d'esprit."

25. Sunday. Mr. Hartley came in, and showed me a letter concerning his beloved sister, whose case is very dangerous, and keeps him in deep affliction. She is his housekeeper and friend. She examines his writing, and proposes corrections. She has transcribed his papers, his American letters, &c. She has labored much for America, &c.

I made a transition, and asked, what news from England. He said, "None." I told him, I had heard that it was expected by some, that Shelburne would come in. He said, "No." I asked him, "Why can't you coalesce with Shelburne as well as North?" He said, "Shelburne is an Irishman, and has all the impudence of his nation. He is a palaverer, beyond all description. He palavers everybody, and has no sincerity."

Mr. Barclay dined with me, after having been out to see Dr. Franklin. The Doctor, he says, is greatly disappointed in not having received letters from Congress, containing his dismission. He wants to get out of this, and to be at home with his family. He don't expect to live long.

26. Monday. I hope for news to-day, from the Hague.

June, 1. Sunday. The loadstone is in possession of the most remarkable, wonderful, and mysterious property in nature. This substance is in the secret of the whole globe. It must have a sympathy with the whole globe. It is governed by a law, and influenced by some active principle, that pervades and operates from pole to pole, and from the surface to the centre and the antipodes. It is found in all parts of the earth. Break the stone to pieces, and each morsel retains two poles, a north and a south pole, and does not lose its virtue. The magnetic effluvia are too subtle to be seen by a microscope; yet they have great activity and strength. Iron has a sympathy with magnetism and electricity, which should be examined by every experiment which ingenuity can devise.

Has it been tried, whether the magnet loses any of its force in vacuo,—in a bottle charged with electrical fire, &c.? This metal called iron may one day reveal the secrets of nature. The primary springs of nature may be too subtle for all our senses and faculties. I should think, however, that no subject deserved more the attention of philosophers, or was more proper for experiment, than the sympathy between iron and the magnetical and electrical fluid.

It would be worth while to grind the magnet to powder, and see if the dust still retained the virtue,—steep the stone or the dust in wine, spirits, oil, and other fluids, to see if the virtue is affected, increased, or diminished. Is there no chemical process, that can be formed upon the stone or the dust, to discover what it is that the magnetic virtue resides in, whether boiling or burning the stone destroys or diminishes the virtue,—see whether earth, air, or fire, anywise applied, affects it, and how.

Mr. Laurens came in, in the morning; and we had a long conversation upon his proposed journey to England, to borrow some money. I explained to him the manner and conditions of my loan in Holland.

Dined at the Spanish ambassador's, with the Corps diplomatique. M. Markow was there, and was very civil. D'Aranda lives now in the end of the new buildings which compose the Façade de la Place de Louis XV. From the windows at the end you look into the Grand Chemin, the Champs Élysées, and the road to Versailles. From the windows and gallery in the front, you see the Place de Louis XV., the gardens of the Tuilleries, the river, and the fine row of houses beyond it, particularly the Palais de Bourbon and the dome of the Invalids. It is the finest situation in Paris.

Mr. Fitzherbert told me, I might depend upon it, the present ministry would continue at least until the next meeting of Parliament. He says there is little to be got in the company of the Corps diplomatique. They play deep, but there is no conversation.

Mr. De Stutterheim, the minister from Saxony, came to me and said, he had received orders from his Court to propose a treaty of commerce with the United States. He said he had spoken to Mr. Franklin about it. I asked him if Mr. Franklin had written to Congress upon it. He said he did not know. I told him, that I thought Mr. Dana, at Petersburg, had power to treat, though not to conclude. He said, he would call upon me some morning at my house, to consult about it. Herrera dined there, and the Duke of Berwick.

Went to Versailles on the day of Pentecôte.

17. Tuesday. Went to Versailles; had a conference with the Count de Vergennes; made my court, with the Corps diplomatique, to the King, Queen, Monsieur, Madame, the Comte d'Artois, Madame Elizabeth, Mesdames Victoire and Adelaide. Dined with the ambassadors. Had much conversation with the ambassadors of Spain, Sardinia, M. Markow, from Russia, the Dutch ambassadors, &c. It was to me, notwithstanding the cold and rain—the equinoctial storm at the time of the solstice, when all the rooms had fires like winter—the most agreeable day I ever saw at Versailles. I had much conversation, too, with the Duke of Manchester and Mr. Hartley, Dr. Franklin and his son, Mr. Waltersdorf, &c., Mr. Madison, and Mr. Shirley, &c. The Count de Vergennes observed, that Mr. Fox was startled at every clamor of a few merchants. I answered, "C'est exactement vrai;" and it is so. The Count recommended to us to discuss and complete the definitive treaty, and leave commerce to a future negotiation. Shall we gain by delay? I ask myself. Will not French politics be employed to stimulate the English to refuse us in future things that they would agree to now? The Count observed, that to insist on sending British manufactures to America, and to refuse to admit American manufactures in England, was the convention léonine.

The Duke of Manchester told me, that the Dutch had offered them Sumatra and Surinam for Negapatnam; "but we know," says the Duke, "that both those settlements are a charge, a loss." Brantzen told me, he had not displayed his character of ambassador, because it would be concluded from it, that he was upon the point of concluding the peace.

The Count d'Aranda told me, he would come and see me. He said, "Tout, en ce monde, a été révolution." I said, true; universal history was but a series of revolutions. Nature delighted in changes, and the world was but a string of them. But one revolution was quite enough for the life of a man; I hoped never to have to do with another. Upon this he laughed very heartily, and said he believed me.

The Sardinian Ambassador said to me, "It was curious to remark the progress of commerce; the furs which the Hudson Bay Company sent to London, from the most northern regions of America, were sent to Siberia, within one hundred and fifty leagues of the place where they were hunted." He began to speak of La Fonté's Voyage, and of the Boston story of Seymour, or Señor Gibbons; but other company came in, and interrupted the conversation.

18. Wednesday. Visited the Duke de la Vauguyon, and had a long conversation with him. He was glad to hear I had been plusieurs fois à Versailles dernièrement. The Duke said, he had conversed with the Count de Vergennes, and had told him, he thought it would be for the good of the common cause if there were more communication between him and me. I told him, that I had expressed to the Count a desire to be informed of the intentions of the King, concerning the communication between the United States and his islands; and that the Count had answered, that if I would give him a note, he would consult with the Marquis de Castries, and give me an answer. He added, smiling, "You will leave to us the regulation of

that; and let us take a little care of our marine and our nurseries of seamen, because we cannot go to your assistance (secours) without a marine."

The Duke said, it would be very difficult to regulate this matter. They could not let us bring their sugars to Europe, neither to France nor any other port. This would lessen the number of French ships and seamen. But he thought we should be allowed to purchase sugars for our own consumption. (How they will estimate the quantity, and prevent our exceeding it, I know not.) He said, there were provinces in France, as Guienne and Provence, which depended much upon supplying their islands with provisions, as wheat and flour, &c. I asked him if we should be allowed to import into their islands wheat, flour, horses, live stock, lumber of all sorts, salt-fish, &c. He said it would be bien difficile for wheat and flour, &c.

19. Thursday. Fête-Dieu. The processions were less brilliant than ordinary, on account of the storm.

Went with Mr. Hartley in his carriage to Passy, where he made his propositions for the definitive treaty. We had had a long conversation about De Fonté's voyage from Peru to Hudson's Bay. He says he found an inlet and a river, which he entered, and navigated until he came to a lake, in which he left his ship, and followed the course of a river, which descended with falls in it, or rather rapids, in his boats, until he came to Hudson's Bay, where he found Seimor Gibbons or Señor Gibbons,—Major-General Edward Gibbons of Boston, as Dr. Franklin supposes. Dr. Franklin had once a correspondence with Mr. Prince upon this voyage; and perhaps Mr. Gill, in the Journal of Mr. Prince, has some information about it. The trade to Hudson's Bay was carried on by Boston people from its first discovery until after the restoration of Charles II. from whom the Hudson's Bay Company obtained their charter; and there are several families in New England descended from persons who used that trade, (namely, the Aldens.) De Fonté's Voyage was printed in English, in a collection called Miscellanca Curiosa, in 1708, and has been lately printed in French in a large collection of voyages, in twenty volumes.

Dr. Franklin once gave to Lord Bute his reasons, in writing, for believing this a genuine voyage. De Fonté was either a Spaniard or Portuguese; inquiry has been made at Madrid, but no traces could be discovered there of De Fonté or his voyage. *Endnote 125*

Cook, in one of his voyages, anchored in the latitude of Philadelphia, forty degrees, on the west side of the continent of America, and ascertained the longitude, from whence Dr. Franklin computes the distance from Philadelphia to the South Sea to be two thousand miles. Cook saw several inlets, and he entered that between America and Asia, Kamschatka, where the passage is not wider than that between Calais and Dover.

The separation of America from Asia is between the sixtieth and seventieth degree of north latitude, precisely at the Arctic polar circle. It is called in the French maps, Détroit du Nord,—the Northern Strait, or Strait of the North; it is near the Archipel du Nord or Northern Archipelago. The point of land in Asia is under the dominion of Russia, and is called Russian Tartary. The Strait forms the communication between the Eastern and the Frozen Oceans,—the Mer Orientale and the Mer Glaciale. There are a number of islands in the Archipelago, and one in the Strait itself, called on the map Alaska Island. There is a sea and a promontory called Kamschatka, situated on the Eastern Ocean, within ten or twelve degrees of the Strait. The three Tartarys,—Independent Tartary, Chinese Tartary, and Russian Tartary, form a vast country, extending from Persia, Hindostan, and China, to the point of Asia at the Straits of the North, which divide Asia from America.

What should hinder the Empress of Russia from establishing a trading city on the sea of Kamschatka, and opening a commerce with Pekin, Nankin, and Canton,—the cities of

China? It is so near the islands of Japan, the Philippines, the Moluccas, that a great scene may one day be opened here.

Lima, the capital of Peru, is in ten degrees of south latitude. So that De Fonté must have sailed by the isthmus of Panama, Mexico, California, New Mexico, Cape Mendocin, Canal du Roi George, and entered the river, at the mouth of which is the isle San Carlos. About half way between the South Sea and Hudson's Bay is a great lake. Here it is to search for a north-west passage to the East Indies. Baffin's Bay, Baffin's Strait, Davis's Strait, Hudson's Bay, Hudson's Strait, are all one great inlet of water, the entrance of which is a strait, formed by Greenland on one side, and Labrador on the other.

Paris, September 14. Mr. Thaxter took his leave of me to return to America, with the definitive treaty of peace and the original treaty with the States-General. I had been some days unwell, but soon fell down in a fever. Sir James Jay, who was my physician, prescribed for me, &c. &c.

On the 22d of September I removed from the grand Hôtel du Roi to Mr. Barclay's, at Auteuil, where I have continued to this sixth day of October, 1783.

Mr. Thaxter sailed in the packet from Lorient, or rather from the island of Groix, on the 26th of September, with a good wind.

At first, I rode twice a day in my carriage, in the Bois de Boulogne; but, afterwards, I borrowed Mr. Jay's horse, and have generally ridden twice a day, until I have made myself master of this curious forest.

The pavillon of Bagatelle, built by Monseigneur Comte d'Artois; the castle of Madrid; the outlet of the forest near Pont Neuilly; the porte which opens into the grand chemin; the castle of la Muette, at Passy; the porte which opens to the great road to Versailles; the other porte which opens into a large village, nearly opposite to St. Cloud,—are the most remarkable objects in this forest.

Auteuil, October 7. Tuesday. I am now lodged in Mr. Barclay's house, which he hires of the Comte de

There is a large garden, full of all vegetables and fruits, as grapes, pears, peaches; there is, besides, a large flower-garden.

From the windows in my chamber, and more distinctly from those of the chambers one story higher, you have a view of the village of Issy, of the castle royal of Meudon, of the palace of Bellevue, of the castle of the Duke of Orleans at St. Cloud, and of Mont Calvaire. Upon the bank of the river Seine, at the foot of the hill on which stands the palace of Bellevue, is a glass-house which smokes night and day; but in the night it blazes at every window, and exhibits a very gay appearance.

Opposite to St. Cloud is the village of Boulogne, from whence the grove or forest takes its name. This wood merits a particular description.

From Mr. Barclay's house, where I now am, I go to the gate, by which you enter the Bois de Boulogne from the village of Auteuil; I turn to the left, and follow the path which runs in sight of the stone wall of twelve feet high, which bounds the forest, until I come to a gate which they call Porte Royale, out of which you go to Versailles; from this gate I follow the path which runs near the boundary stone wall, until I come to the gate which opens into the village of Boulogne; I pursue this path by the wall, until I come to the pavillon of Bagatelle belonging to the Comte d'Artois. The estate of the Comte is separated from the forest only by a treillage or a kind of picketed wooden fence. Having passed the Bagatelle, you come to the royal castle of Madrid; passing this, you go out of the wood into the grand chemin, by the gate called Porte de Neuilly, near the new bridge of that name; but, by following the path in sight of the stone wall, which separates the forest from the grand chemin, you come to the gate which is called Porte Maillot, at the Plaine de Sablons; by following the grand road from this gate, you come to the royal castle of Muette, at Passy, near which is the gate by which you enter the forest from Passy; by following the path near the stone wall, which bounded the wood, you come to the gate at Auteuil, by which we first entered the forest; near the centre of the forest is a circle of clear ground, on which are no trees or shrubs; from the centre of this circle proceed avenues in all directions; one goes to the Porte Royale, another to the village of Boulogne, another to the castle of Madrid, another to the castle of Muette at Passy, and another to the gate of Auteuil. In riding over this forest, you see some neat cattle, some horses, a few sheep, and a few deers, bucks, does, and fawns, now and then a hare, and sometimes a few partridges; but game is not plenty in this wood.

In this village of Auteuil, is the seat of the famous Boileau; it is in the Rue des Garennes. I have been twice to see it. The gardener has not the keys of the apartments, so that I could not see the inside of the house; but the gardener showed me the stables, coach-house, and all the out-houses, and the garden, which is very large, containing, perhaps, five or six acres; it is full of flowers and of roots and vegetables of all kinds, and of fruits; grapes of several sorts, and of excellent quality, pears, peaches, &c.; but every thing suffers for want of manure. There is an acre or two of ground without the garden fence which belongs to the estate, which affords pasture for a cow; but the land is poor. There is a head of Boileau over the door, behind the house, and the heads of two children,—one on each side of [384a] the door, which are said to be the heads of two children of his gardener that he was fond of, and which he ordered to be placed there near him. The estate now belongs to Madame Binet, who advertises it for sale, and, it is said, asks forty-five thousand livres for it. She declines letting it, or I should have hired it. The principal people in this village of Auteuil are Madame Helvétius, who lives but a few doors from this house; Madame Boufflers, who lives opposite, &c.

20. Monday. Set out, with my son and one servant, Levêque, on a journey to London. We went from Auteuil, through the Bois de Boulogne, and went out at the Porte de Maillot to Saint-Denis, where we took post-horses. We dined at Chantilly, and lodged at night at Saint-Just.

21. Tuesday. Dined at Amiens, and put up at night at Abbeville. The roads are the best I have ever seen in France; they are not paved, or if they are, the pavement is covered with flint stones. They pick up in the neighboring fields a species of small flint stones, which they lay along in heaps on the side of the road; and with these they mend their highways from time to time. The wheels of the carriages crush them to dust, and they make admirable roads.

There are no vines on this road. The country is all sown with wheat. They are everywhere cutting up by the roots the elms and other forest trees which were formerly planted on the sides of the roads, and introducing apple-trees in their stead. We found tea apparatus generally in the public houses, and the andirons, tongs, &c., and several other things, more in the English style than you find in other parts of France.

22. Wednesday. Went to Calais. Dined at Boulogne sur Mer. Put up at Mr. Dessein's.

23. Thursday. Went on board the packet at nine; put off from the wharf at ten; but had such contrary winds and calms, that we did not arrive at Dover until three o'clock next morning. I was eighteen hours on the passage; the packet was seventeen. She could not come into the harbor. Made signals for a boat, which carried us ashore for five shillings a head. I was never before so sea-sick, nor was my son; my servant was very bad; almost all the passengers were sick; it is a remarkable place for it. We are told that many persons, masters of vessels and others who were never sea-sick before, have been very bad in making this passage.

24. Friday. We are lodged at Dover, at the Royal Hotel Inn, kept by Charles Meurice. On the back of his house is one of the Dover Cliffs; it is a high mountain, and at this place is perpendicular; and there is an appearance of danger that the rocks at top might split off by their own weight, and dash to pieces some of the small brick houses at its foot, white stone. I walked round with my son to the coach road, and ascended to the top of this mountain. It is very steep; it is covered with a thick sward, and with a verdure quite to the top. Upon the top of the mountain there is a ploughed field, sown with turnips, which look very vigorous. I went into the ploughed ground to examine its composition, and found it full of flint stones, such as the road from Chantilly to Calais is made of, and all the fields on that road are full of. In short, the white stones of the cliffs, and the flint stone of the fields, convince me that the lands here are the same with those on the other side the channel, and but a continuation of the same soil. From this mountain we saw the whole channel, the whole town and harbor of Dover. The harbor is but a basin, and the town but a little village. We saw three small vessels on the stocks, building or repairing, and fifteen or twenty small craft, fishing sloops and schooners, chiefly in the harbor. It has not the appearance of a place of any business at all. No manufacture, no commerce, and no fishery of any consequence here.

The sheep here are very large; and the country all around has a face of verdure and fertility beyond that of France in general; but this is owing no doubt to the difference of cultivation. The valleys only in France look rich; plains and mountains look meagre. Here the mountain is rich.

The channel between this and Calais is full of vessels, French and English, fishing for herrings. The sardines are not caught here.

25. Saturday. Went in a postchaise, from Dover through Canterbury, Rochester, &c., to Dartford, where we lodged.

26. Sunday. Went to London; and the postboy carried us to the Adelphi Buildings in the Strand to John's Street. We are at Osborne's Adelphi Hotel. I am obliged here to give thirteen shillings a day for a parlor, a bedchamber, and another bedchamber over it for my son, without any dining-room or antechamber. This is dearer than my lodgings at the Hôtel du Roi in Paris. Half a guinea for my bedchamber and parlor, and half a crown for my son's bedchamber; my servant's lodging is included in the half guinea. The rooms and furniture are more to my taste than in Paris, because they are more like what I have been used to in America.

27. Monday. Went to see Mr. Jay, who is lodged with Mr. Bingham in Harley Street, Cavendish Square, No. 30; and, in the afternoon, went to see Mr. Johnson, Great Tower Hill, who informed me that a vessel with one thousand hogsheads of tobacco is passed by, in the channel, from Congress to Messrs. Willinks. I gave Mr. Johnson his letter, as I had left Mr. Hartley's for him at his house, who is gone into the country, to Bath, as he says.

These Adelphi Buildings are well situated on the Thames. In sight of the terrace is Westminster Bridge one way, and Blackfriars Bridge on the other; St. Paul's is by Blackfriars Bridge.

1784.

The Hague, June 22. Tuesday. Last night, at Court, one of the ladies of honor told me that the supper was given in a great measure for Mrs. Bingham. There was great inquiry after her, and much admiration expressed by all who had seen her of her beauty. As the Princess of Orange was inquiring of me concerning her, and her journey to Spain, Paris, Italy, the Spanish minister said, "She would form herself at Paris." I replied, very quick, but smiling, "J'espère qu'elle ne se formera pas à Paris, qu'elle est déja formée." This produced as hearty a laugh as is permitted at Court, both from the Princess and the Comte. The Princess asked me immediately, if I had not been pleased at Paris. I answered that I had; that there was something there for every taste; but that such great cities as Paris and London were not good schools for American young ladies at present. The Princess replied, that Mrs. Bingham might learn there the French language.

I made acquaintance with Mr. Kempar, of Friesland, once a professor at Franequer, who says there are but two millions of people in the seven provinces. He quoted to me two authors who have written upon the subject,—one twenty years ago, and the other ten, and they have decided this subject; stated the numbers in each province, city, village; accurate accounts are kept of births and deaths, baptisms and funerals; the midwives and undertakers are obliged to make returns of all they bring in or carry out of the world. This last fact I had from Lynden de Blitterswyck, the first noble of Zealand.

Mirabel reported what he had said often before, as well as Reischach and Calichef, that their Courts expected a letter from Congress, according to the rules and precedents, to inform them of their independence.

Mem. "I think Congress should inform them that on the 4th July, 1776, they assumed their sovereignty; that on the day of France made a treaty; on the 7th of October, 1782, Holland ; on the Great Britain ; on the day of Sweden." Endnote 126

July 10. Saturday. May not the ascent of vapors be explained, or rather accounted for, upon the principle of the air balloon? Is not every bubble of vapor that rises an air balloon? Bubbles are formed at the bottoms of canals, rivers, ponds,—rise to the top and mount up; these bubbles are particles, or small quantities of inflammable air, surrounded with a thin film of water.

Champagne wine, bottled porter, &c., are full of air bubbles or balloons. Set a decanter or tumbler of water in the sun, and thousands of air balloons are formed in the water at the bottom and on the sides of the glass; turn the glass aside, so as to expose these bubbles to the air, many of them burst in an instant; others do not, but continue some time covered with a thin film of water; inflammable air, being lighter than common air, rises in it.

In the common experiment, with which boys amuse themselves, the air which is blown through the tobacco-pipe into the soap suds is common air, of equal weight with that which surrounds the bubble, and, therefore, will not ascend very high; but if inflammable air were blown through the pipe, instead of common air, we should have a series of balloon aerostatics, which would ascend like those of Montgolfier.

August 4. Set off for London. Had a tedious passage from Helvoet of near two days; obliged to put in at Lowestoff and ride from thence twenty-four miles in a cart.

7. Arrived at the Adelphi Buildings, and met my wife and daughter, after a separation of four years and a half; indeed, after a separation of ten years, excepting a few visits. Set off the next day for Paris.

13. Arrived at Paris at the Hôtel de York on the

17. Removed to Auteuil the at the house of the Comte de Rouault, opposite the Conduit. The house, the garden, the situation, near the Bois de Boulogne, elevated above the river Seine and the low grounds, and distant from the putrid streets of Paris, is the best I could wish for.

1785.

January 31. Monday. Last evening the Marquis de Lafayette, lately returned from America, called upon me, on his way home from Versailles. He gave me a very pleasing account of the commerce, the union, &c., in America, and then began to discourse of another subject. He interrogated me, whether I had any correspondents in Holland; whether

I received letters from week to week and from post to post from thence? Who were the heads of the republican party? Whether I knew any thing of the intentions of the States-General, to place M. de Maillebois at the head of their armies? He then talked of Maillebois; said he had great abilities, and that he had heard him justify himself very well in the affair of D'Estrées; *Endnote 127* said that Monsieur de Vergennes was his friend. I said that I knew it, for that I had once, in 1778, heard the Comte wish that M. de Maillebois had the command of our army in America. He said that the Comte de Broglie wished for the command in America at the same time.

As he went out, he took me aside, and whispered, that although he would not serve a foreign prince, he would serve a republic, and although he should hurt himself with the Queen and her party to a great degree, yet, if the States-General would invite him, without his soliciting or appearing to desire it, he would accept the command. Maillebois loved money, and demanded splendid appointments. He did not regard money so much, and would be easy about that: I was the first mortal to whom he had suggested the idea; he wished I would think of it, and he would call and see me again in a few days.

March 19. Saturday. Met Mr. Franklin and Mr. Jay at Passy. Read the letter from Mr. Carmichael at Madrid, with the letters from Count de Florida Blanca, the letters from Morocco to Mr. Harrison at Cadiz, and the letters from Morocco to Dr. Franklin, concerning the vessel of Mr. Fitzsimmons, of Philadelphia, taken by a Morocco frigate.

I asked for books and collections of treaties; they were brought. I looked for, and read the treaty between Louis XIV. and Algiers, and the treaties between Holland and Algiers, and found a multitude of treaties between Algiers and Morocco and the Christian States, as France, Holland, England, &c., with the passes in the Corps Diplomatique.

We came to no resolution, but that I should go to-morrow to Versailles, and ask the advice of the Comte de Vergennes. Dr. Franklin being confined by his stone could not go; and Mr. Jefferson being worse with his disorder cannot go. I was for writing a letter to the Count, but my colleagues were not. Franklin and Jay are confident that England has no right to appoint a consul without a treaty or convention for that purpose. I think they have a right by the law of nations.

Auteuil, near Paris, March 20. Sunday. Went early to Versailles, and found the Comte de Vergennes. Communicated to him my errand and papers. He read those in Italian, Spanish, and French, and Mr. Carmichael's letter in English. I asked him whether the French treaty with Algiers was renewed. He said it was upon the point of expiring; but he could not tell me whether it was renewed, as it was not in his department, but in that of the M. de Castries. I asked him if he would be so good as to inform me what presents were sent annually to the several Barbary Powers by the King, in what they consisted, and to what they amounted. He said he did not know; but if we would make an office of it, he would communicate it to the minister of marine, and obtain for us all the information he could.

I told him I had obtained information authentically from Holland, from Mr. Bisdom and Mr. Vanderhope. I asked him if he would be so good as to convey a letter from us to the Emperor of Morocco, by means of the French consul. He said that I might depend upon it, whenever we made an office, it should be punctually attended to. But, that Cadiz would be the best place from whence to send presents; that the Emperor of Morocco was the most interested man in the world, and the most greedy of money. He asked if we had written to Congress and obtained their instructions. I told him we had received full powers to treat with Morocco, Algiers, Tunis, Tripoli, and all the rest, and had written for instructions upon the article of money and presents.

He said that there was a frequent communication between Marseilles and the coast of Barbary; but that as these things were not in his department, we must state our desires in writing, which I agreed to do. I asked him if he thought it advisable for us to send any one to Morocco. He said, Yes; but as we could neither go, nor were authorized to substitute, we should write to the Emperor until Congress could send a consul. I asked what he thought of our leaving it, by our letter, in the option of the Emperor to send a minister here to treat with us, or to wait until we could write to Congress, and recommend to them to send him a consul. He said, by no means; for the expense of receiving his minister here would be much greater; for we must maintain him and pay all his expenses. He said that the King of France never sent them any naval stores; he sent them glaces and other things of rich value, but never any military stores.

Auteuil, May 3. Tuesday. At Versailles, the Count de Vergennes said he had many felicitations to give me upon my appointment to England. I answered, that I did not know but it merited compassion more than felicitation. "Ay, why?" "Because, as you know, it is a species of degradation in the eyes of Europe, after having been accredited to the King of France, to be sent to any other Court." "But permit me to say," replies the Count, "it is a great thing to be the first ambassador from your country to the country you sprang from. It is a mark." I told him that these points would not weigh much with me; it was the difficulty of the service, &c.

I said to him, as I would not fail in any point of respect or duty to the King, nor any of our obligations to this country, I wished to be advised, whether an audience in particular of congé was indispensable. He said he would inform himself.

The Duke of Dorset said to me, that if he could be of any service to me, by writing either to public or private persons, he would do it with pleasure. I told his Grace that I should be glad of half an hour's conversation with him in private. "I will call upon you at Auteuil," said he, "any morning this week." I answered that any morning and any hour, agreeable to him, should be so to me. "Saturday," said he, "at twelve o'clock." "I shall be happy to receive you," said I. He repeated, that if he could be of any service, he would be glad. I said, it might probably be in his Grace's power to do great service to me, and, what was of infinitely more importance, to his country as well as mine, if he thought as I did upon certain points; and, therefore, I thought it was proper we should compare notes. He said he believed we did think alike, and would call on Saturday. He said that Lord Carmarthen was their minister of foreign affairs; that I must first wait upon him, and he would introduce me to his Majesty; but that I should do business with Mr. Pitt very often. I asked him Lord Carmarthen's age. He said, thirty-three. He said I should be stared at a great deal. I told him I trembled at the thoughts of going there; I was afraid they would gaze with evil eyes. He said, No, he believed not.

One of the foreign ambassadors said to me, "You have been often in England." "Never, but once in November and December, 1783." "You have relations in England, no doubt." "None at all." "None, how can that be? you are of English extraction?" "Neither my father or mother, grandfather or grandmother, great grandfather or great grandmother, nor any other relation that I know of, or care a farthing for, has been in England these one hundred and fifty years; so that you see I have not one drop of blood in my veins but what is American." "Ay, we have seen," said he, "proof enough of that." This flattered me, no doubt, and I was vain enough to be pleased with it.

Auteuil, May. Monday. The posts within the limits of the United States not yet surrendered by the English are,—

Oswegatchy, in the River St. Lawrence. Oswego, Lake Ontario. Niagara and its dependencies. Presqu' Isle, east side of Lake Erie. Sandusky, ditto. Detroit. Michilimakinac. St. Mary's, south side of the strait between Lakes Superior and Huron, bottom of the Bay des Puantz. St. Joseph, bottom of Lake Michigan. Ouitanon. Miamis.

1786.

Grosvenor Square, Westminster, March 26. Sunday. Dined in Bolton street, Picadilly, at the Bishop of Saint Asaph's. Mr. and Mrs. Sloper, the son-in-law and daughter of the bishop; Mrs. and Miss Shipley, the wife and daughter; Mr. and Mrs. Vaughan, Mr. Alexander and Mrs. Williams, Mr. Richard Peters and myself, were the company. In the evening, other company came in, according to the fashion in this country.

Mrs. Shipley, at table, asked many questions about the expense of living in Philadelphia and Boston. Said she had a daughter who had married less prudently than they wished, and they thought of sending them to America.

29. Wednesday. Dined at Mr. Blake's. Mr. Middleton and wife, Mr. Alexander and Mrs. Williams, Mr. Jefferson, Colonel Smith, and my family.

30. Thursday. Presented Mr. Hamilton to the Queen at the drawing-room.

Dined at Mr. Paradise's. Count Woronzow and his gentleman and chaplain, M. Soderini, the Venetian minister, Mr. Jefferson, Dr. Bancroft, Colonel Smith, and my family. Went at nine o'clock to the French ambassador's ball, where were two or three hundred people, chiefly ladies. Here I met the Marquis of Lansdown and the Earl of Harcourt. These two noblemen ventured to enter into conversation with me. So did Sir George Young. But there is an awkward timidity in general. This people cannot look me in the face; there is conscious guilt and shame in their countenances when they look at me. They feel that they have behaved ill, and that I am sensible of it.

London, April. Mr. Jefferson and myself went in a postchaise to Woburn farm. Caversham, Wotton, Stowe, Edgehill, Stratford upon Avon, Birmingham, the Leasowes, Hagley, Stourbridge, Worcester, Woodstock, Blenheim, Oxford, High Wycombe, and back to Grosvenor Square.

Edgehill and Worcester were curious and interesting to us, as scenes where freemen had fought for their rights. The people in the neighborhood appeared so ignorant and careless at Worcester, that I was provoked, and asked, "And do Englishmen so soon forget the ground where liberty was fought for? Tell your neighbors and your children that this is holy ground; much holier than that on which your churches stand. All England should come in pilgrimage to this hill once a year."

This animated them, and they seemed much pleased with it. Perhaps their awkwardness before might arise from their uncertainty of our sentiments concerning the civil wars.

Stratford upon Avon is interesting, as it is the scene of the birth, death, and sepulture of Shakspeare. Three doors from the inn is the house where he was born, as small and mean as you can conceive. They showed us an old wooden chair in the chimney corner where he sat. We cut off a chip according to custom. A mulberry tree that he planted has been cut down, and is carefully preserved for sale. The house where he died has been taken down, and the spot is now only yard or garden. The curse upon him who should remove his bones, which is written on his gravestone, alludes to a pile of some thousands of human bones which lie exposed in that church. There is nothing preserved of this great genius which is worth knowing; nothing which might inform us what education, what company, what accident, turned his mind to letters and the drama. His name is not even on his gravestone. An illsculptured head is set up by his wife, by the side of his grave in the church. But paintings and sculpture would be thrown away upon his fame. His wit, fancy, his taste and judgment, his knowledge of nature, of life and character, are immortal.

At Birmingham we only walked round the town, and viewed a manufactory of paintings upon paper. The gentlemen's seats were the highest entertainment we met with. Stowe, Hagley, and Blenheim, are superb; Woburn, Caversham, and the Leasowes are beautiful. Wotton is both great and elegant, though neglected. Architecture, painting, statuary, poetry, are all employed in the embellishment of these residences of greatness and luxury. A national debt of two hundred and seventy-four millions sterling, accumulated by jobs, contracts, salaries, and pensions, in the course of a century might easily produce all thimagnificence. The pillars, obelisks, &c., erected in honor of kings, queens, and princesses, might procure the means.

The temples to Bacehus and Venus are quite unnecessary, as mankind have no need of artificial incitement to such amusements. The temples of ancient Virtue, of the British worthies, of Friendship, of Concord and Victory, are in a higher taste. I mounted Lord Cobham's Pillar, one hundred and twenty feet high, with pleasure, as his Lordship's name was familiar to me from Pope's works.

Lord Littleton's seat interested me, from a recollection of his works, as well as the grandeur and beauty of the scenes. Pope's pavilion and Thomson's seat made the excursion poetical. Shenstone's Leasowes is the simplest and plainest, but the most rural of all. I saw no spot so small that exhibited such a variety of beauties.

It will be long, I hope, before ridings, parks, pleasure grounds, gardens, and ornamented farms, grow so much in fashion in America; but nature has done greater things and furnished nobler materials there; the oceans, islands, rivers, mountains, valleys, are all laid out upon a larger scale. If any man should hereafter arise to embellish the rugged grandeur of Pen's Hill he might make something to boast of, although there are many situations capable of better improvement.

Since my return I have been over Blackfriar's Bridge to see Viny's manufacture of patent wheels made of bent timber. Viny values himself much upon his mechanical invention; is loud in praise of Franklin, who first suggested to him the hint of a bent wheel. Franklin once told me he had scen such a wheel in Holland before he set Viny to work. Viny says that Franklin said to him,—

"Mankind are very superficial and very dastardly; they begin upon a thing, but meeting with a difficulty they fly from it discouraged; but they have capacities if they would but employ them."

"I," says Viny, "make it a rule to do nothing as others do it. My first question is, How do others do this? And whenever I have found out, I resolve to do it another way and a better way. I take my pipe and smoke like a limeburner's kiln, and I find a pipe is the best aid to thinking."

This man has genius. But has genius always as much vanity? It is not always so open; it is really modest and humble sometimes; but in Viny it is very vain. His inventions for boiling and bending his timber, and for drilling his irons, are very ingenious. The force requisite for bending a stick of ash into a hoop, suitable for a large wheel or a small one, is prodigious.

15. Saturday. Dined with Mr. Brand Hollis, in Chesterfield Street. His mantle-trees are ornamented with antiques, Penates, little brazen images of the gods,—Venus, Ceres, Apollo, Minerva, &c. Hollis is a member of the Antiquarian Society. Our company were Price, Kippis, Bridgen, Romilly, and another, besides Jefferson, Smith, and myself.

18. Tuesday. Yesterday, dined here Mr. Jefferson, Sir John Sinclair, Mr. Heard, Garter King at Arms, Doctor Price, Mr. Brand Hollis, Mr. Henry Lloyd of Boston, Mr. Jenings, Mr. Bridgen, Mr. Vaughan, Mr. Murray, Colonel Smith.

19. Wednesday. This is the anniversary of the battle of Lexington, and of my reception at the Hague by their High Mightinesses.

This last event is considered by the historians and other writers and politicians of England and France as of no consequence; and Congress and the citizens of the United States in general concur with them in sentiment.

I walked to the booksellers,—Stockdale, Cadel, Dilly, Almon, and met Dr. Priestley for the first time. The Conquest of Canaan, the Vision of Columbus, and the History of the Revolution in South Carolina, were the subjects. I wrote a letter to John Luzac for Dilly.

This day I met Dr. Priestley and Mr. Jenings, with the latter of whom I had a long walk. I spent the day upon the whole agreeably enough. Seeds were sown this day which will grow.

20. Thursday. Went with Mr. Jefferson and my family to Osterly, to view the seat of the late banker, Child. The house is very large; it is three houses, fronting as many ways; between two is a double row of six pillars, to which you rise by a flight of steps; within, is a square, a court, a terrace paved with large slate. The green-house and hot-house were curious. Blowing roses, ripe strawberries, cherries, plums, &c., in the hot-house.

The pleasure grounds were only an undulating gravel walk, between two borders of trees and shrubs; all the evergreens, trees, and shrubs, were here. There is a water for fish ponds and for farm uses, collected from the springs and wet places in the farm and neighborhood. Fine flocks of deer and sheep, wood doves, guinea hens, peacocks, &c.

The verdure is charming; the music of the birds pleasant; but the ground is too level. We could not see the apartments in the house, because we had no ticket. Mrs. Child is gone to Newmarket, it seems, to the races.

The beauty, convenience, and utility of these country seats are not enjoyed by the owners. They are mere ostentations of vanity; races, cocking, gambling, draw away their attention.

On our return we called to see Sion House, belonging to the Duke of Northumberland. This farm is watered by a rivulet drawn by an artificial canal from the Thames. A repetition of winding walks, gloomy evergreens, sheets of water, clumps of trees, green-houses, hot-houses, &c. The gate which lets you into this farm from the Brentford road, is a beautiful thing, and lays open to the view of the traveller a very beautiful green lawn, interspersed with clumps and scattered trees.

The Duke of Marlborough owns a house upon Sion Hill, which is only over the way.

Osterly, Sion Place, and Sion Hill, are all in Brentford, within ten miles of Hyde Park corner. We went through Hyde Park and Kensington to Brentford. We passed, in going and returning, by Lord Holland's house, which is a modern building in the Gothic manner.

23. Sunday. Heard Dr. Priestley at Mr. Lindsey's in Essex Street.

24. Monday. Viewed the British Museum. Dr. Grey, who attended us, spoke very slightly of Buffon. Said "he was full of mauvaise foi; no dependence upon him; three out of four of his quotations not to be found; that he had been obliged to make it his business to examine the quotations; that he had not found a quarter of them.

"That Linnæus was quoted from early editions, long after the last edition was public, of 1766, the twelfth,—which was inexcusable. He did not think Buffon superior to Dr. Hill; both had imagination," &c. This is partly national prejudice and malignity, no doubt.

London, June 26. Monday. On Saturday night returned from a tour to Portsmouth, in which we viewed Painshill in Surrey as we went out, and Windsor as we returned. We were absent four days. Painshill is the most striking piece of art that I have yet seen. The soil is a heap of sand, and the situation is nothing extraordinary. It is a new creation of Mr. Hamilton; all made within thirty-five years. It belongs to Mr. Hopkins, who rides by it, but never stops. The owners of these enchanting seats are very indifferent to their beauties. The country from Guilford to Portsmouth is a barren heath, a dreary waste.

July 1. Saturday. Last night Colonel Smith and his lady *Endnote 128* took their leave of us, and went to their house in Wimpole Street.

Yesterday visited Desenfan's Collection of Pictures. A Port in Italy, by Claude Lorraine, is the best piece that remains. A Samson Sleeping in the Lap of Delilah, while the Philistines cut off his Locks, is said to be by Rubens; but Mr. Copley, who was present, doubts it; supposes it to be by some one of Rubens's school. Fine colors, and the air of one of Rubens's wives is given to Delilah.

This art shows us examples of all the various sorts of genius which appear in poetry,—the epic poet, the tragedian, the comedian, the writer of pastorals, elegies, epigrams, farces, and songs.

The pleasure which arises from imitation we have in looking at a picture of a landscape, a port, a street, a temple, or a portrait. But there must be action, passion, sentiment, and moral, to engage my attention very much. The story of the prince, who lost his own life in a bold attempt to save some of his subjects from a flood of water, is worth all the paintings that have been exhibited this year.

Copley's Fall of Chatham, or Pierson, West's Wolf, Epaminondas, Bayard, &c., Trumbull's Warren and Montgomery, are interesting subjects and useful. But a million pictures of flowers, game, cities, landscapes, with whatever industry and skill executed, would be seen with much indifference. The sky, the earth, hills, and valleys, rivers and oceans, forests and groves and cities, may be seen at any time.

July 6. Thursday. Dined at Clapham, at Mr. Smith's. Dr. Kippis, Dr. Reese, Dr. Harris, Mr. Pais, Mr. Towgood and his two sons, Mr. Channing,—were the company. Mr. Pais told a story admirably well of a philosopher and a Scotchman:—

The wit attempted to divert himself, by asking the Scot if he knew the immense distance to heaven? It was so many millions of diameters of the solar system, and a cannon ball would be so many thousand years in running there. "I don't know the distance nor the time," said the Scot; "but I know it will not take you a millionth part of the time to go to hell." The Scottish dialect and accent were admirably imitated. The conversation was uniformly agreeable; nothing to interrupt it.

8. Saturday. In one of my common walks along the Edgeware road there are fine meadows, or squares of grass land belonging to a noted cow-keeper. These plats are plentifully manured. There are, on the side of the way, several heaps of manure, a hundred loads perhaps in each heap. I have carefully examined them, and find them composed of straw, and dung from the stables and streets of London; mud, clay, or marl, dug out of the ditch along the hedges; and turf, sward, cut up with spades, hoes, and shovels, in the road. This is laid in vast heaps, to mix. With narrow hoes they cut it down at each end, and with shovels throw it into a new heap, in order to divide it and mix it more effectually. I have attended to the operation, as I walked, for some time. This may be good manure, but is not equal to mine, which I composed in similar heaps upon my own farm.

16. Sunday. At Hackney heard a nephew of Dr. Price, who is settled at Yarmouth. It may be of use to minute miscellaneous thoughts, like Selden, Swift, &c.

It is an observation of one of the profoundest inquirers into human affairs, that a revolution of government successfully conducted and completed is the strongest proof that can be given by a people of their virtue and good sense. An enterprise of so much difficulty can never be planned and carried on without abilities; and a people without principle cannot have confidence enough in each other.

Mr. Langbourne, of Virginia, who dined with us on Friday at Colonel Smith's, dined here yesterday. This gentleman, who is rich, has taken the whim of walking all over Europe, after having walked over most of America. His observations are sensible and judicious. He walks forty-five or fifty miles a day. He says he has seen nothing superior to the country from New York to Boston. He is in love with New England; admires the country and its inhabitants. He kept company with the King of France's retinue, in his late journey to Cherbourg. He says the Virginians have learned much in agriculture, as well as in humanity to their slaves, in the late war.

20. Thursday. "Every act of authority of one man over another, for which there is not an absolute necessity, is tyrannical."

"Le pene che oltre passano la necessita di conservare il deposito della salute pubblica, sono ingiuste di lor natura." Beccaria.

The sovereign power is constituted to defend individuals against the tyranny of others. Crimes are acts of tyranny of one or more on another or more. A murderer, a thief, a robber, a burglar, is a tyrant. Perjury, slander, are tyranny too, when they hurt any one.

21. Friday. Major Langbourne dined with us again. He was lamenting the difference of character between Virginia and New England. I offered to give him a receipt for making a New England in Virginia. He desired it; and I recommended to him town meetings, training days, town schools, and ministers, giving him a short explanation of each article. The meeting-house and school-house and training field are the scenes where New England men were formed. Colonel Trumbull, who was present, agreed that these are the ingredients.

In all countries and in all companies, for several years, I have, in conversation and in writing, enumerated the towns, militia, schools, and churches, as the four causes of the growth and defence of New England. The virtues and talents of the people are there formed; their temperance, patience, fortitude, prudence, and justice, as well as their sagacity, knowledge, judgment, taste, skill, ingenuity, dexterity, and industry. Can it be now ascertained whether Norton, Cotton, Wilson, Winthrop, Winslow, Saltonstall, or who, was the author of the plan of town schools, townships, militia laws, meeting-houses, and ministers, &c.?

24. Monday. Went with Mr. Bridgen, Colonel Smith, Mrs. Smith, to the Hyde in Essex, the country seat of Brand Hollis, Esq. We breakfasted at Rumford, and turned out of the way to see the seat of Lord Petre, at Thorndon. Mr. Hollis prefers the architecture of this house to that at Stow, because it is more conformable to Palladio,—his Bible for this kind of knowledge. There are in the back front six noble Corinthian pillars. There is a grand saloon unfinished in which are many ancient pictures,—one of Sir Thomas More, his wife and two daughters, with a group of other figures. There is in another apartment a picture of the Cornaro family, by Titian.

This house is vast, and the apartments are grand, and the prospects from the windows are extensive and agreeable. The furniture is rich and elegant. The pictures of King James II., of Lord Derwentwater, who was beheaded in 1715, as well as many others, besides that of Sir Thomas More, show that the family is Catholic; the library shows this more fully, as the books are generally of that kind; but the chapel furnishes full proof. The library is semicircular, with windows and mahogany colonnades, very elegant, but contrived more as an ornamental passage to the chapel than for study. There are two stoves; but at neither of them could a student be comfortable in cold weather.

I might talk of glades and forests, groves and clumps, with which this house is surrounded, like all other palaces of the kind.

We dined at the Hyde, with Mr. Brand Hollis and his sister, Miss Brand. This is a curious place. The house is the residence of an antiquarian, as most of the apartments, as well as the great hall, sufficiently show. I will, perhaps, take a list of all the antiques in this hall. The most interesting to me is the bust of my friend as well as Mr. Brand's friend, the late Thomas Hollis, Esq., in beautiful white marble.

This house, which is a decent, handsome one, was the seat of Mr. Brand's father; and the chamber where we lodge is hung round with the portraits of the family. It is at the end of the house; and from two windows in front, and two others at the end, we have a pleasant view of lawns and glades, trees and clumps, and a piece of water full of fish. The borders by the walks, in the pleasure grounds, are full of rare shrubs and trees, to which collection America has furnished her full share. I shall here have a good opportunity to take a list of these trees, shrubs, and flowers. Larches, cypresses, laurels, are here as they are everywhere. Mr. Brand Hollis has planted near the walk, from his door to the road, a large and beautiful fir, in honor of the late Dr. Jebb, his friend. A tall cypress in his pleasure grounds he calls General Washington, and another his aide-de-camp, Colonel Smith.

25. Tuesday. Mr. Brand Hollis and Mr. Brand, Mr. and Mrs. Smith, and Mr. and Mrs. Adams, took a ride to Chelmsford. Stopped at a bookseller's, the printer of a newspaper, in which Mr. B. Hollis had printed the late act of Virginia in favor of equal religious liberty. We then went to Moulsham Hall, built originally by Lord Fitzwalter, but lately owned by Sir William Mildmay, one of the commissioners with Governor Shirley at Paris, in 1754, for settling the boundaries between the French and English in America. Lady Mildmay owns it at present, but is not yet come down from London. Mr. Brand Hollis admires the architecture of this house, because it is according to the principles of Palladio. The apartments are all well proportioned in length, breadth, and height. There is here a Landscape of Rembrandt. The words, halls, parlors, saloons, and drawing rooms, occur upon these occasions; but to describe them would be endless. We returned by another road through the race-grounds to the Hyde; and, after dinner, made a visit to the gardener's house, to see his bees. He is bee mad, Mr. Brand Hollis says. He has a number of glass hives, and has a curious invention to shut out the drones; he has nailed thin and narrow laths at the mouth of the hive, and has left spaces between them barely wide enough for the small bees to creep through; here and there he has made a notch in the lath large enough for a drone to pass; but this notch he has covered with a thin light clapper which turns easily upwards upon a pivot. The drone easily lifts up the clapper and comes out, but as soon as he is out the clapper falls and excludes the drone, who has neither skill nor strength to raise it on the outside; thus shut out from the hive, the gardener destroys them, because he says they do nothing but eat honey.

The gardener, who is a son of liberty, and was always a friend to America, was delighted with this visit. "Dame," says he to his wife, "you have had the greatest honor done you to-day that you ever had in your life." Mr. Brand Hollis says he is a proud Scotchman, but a very honest man and faithful servant.

After tea, Mr. Brand Hollis and I took a circular walk round the farm. He showed us a kind of medallion, on which was curiously wrought a feast of all the heathen gods and goddesses sitting round a table. Jupiter throws down upon the middle of it one of his thunderbolts flaming at each end with lightning, and lights his own pipe at it, and all the others follow his example; Venus is whiffing like a Dutchman; so is Diana and Minerva, as well as Mars, Bacchus, and Apollo.

Mr. Brand Hollis is a great admirer of Marcus Aurelius. He has him in busts and many other shapes. He observed to me, that all the painters of Italy, and from them most others, have taken the face of Marcus Aurelius for a model in painting Jesus Christ. He admires Julian too; and has a great veneration for Dr. Hutcheson, the moral writer, who was his tutor or instructor. He has a number of heads of Hutcheson, of whom he always speaks with affection and veneration. Lord Shaftsbury too is another favorite of his.

In the dining-room are two views of that estate in Dorsetshire, which the late Mr. Hollis gave to Mr. Brand. There is only a farm-house upon it. Here are to be seen Hollis mead and Brand pasture. In Hollis mead Mr. Hollis was buried ten feet deep, and then ploughed over; a whim to be sure; but singularity was his characteristic; he was benevolent and beneficent, however, throughout. In the bondoir is a dagger made of the sword which killed Sir

Edmunbury Godfrey. An inscription,—Memento Godfrey, proto-martyr. pro religione Protestantium. Mr. Hollis's owl, cap of liberty, and dagger, are to be seen everywhere; in the boudoir, a silver cup with a cover, all in the shape of an owl, with two rubies for eyes. This piece of antiquity was dug up at Canterbury from ten feet depth. It was some monkish conceit.

26. Wednesday. Mr. Brand Hollis, Miss Brand, Mrs. Adams, Mrs. Smith, and I, walked to Mill Green, or Mill Hill, the seat of a Mr. Allen, a banker of London. We walked over the pleasure grounds and kitchen garden and down to Cocytus,—a canal or pond of water surrounded with wood in such a manner as to make the place gloomy enough for the name. This is a good spot; but Mr. Allen has, for want of taste, spoiled it by new picket fences at a great expense. He has filled up the ditches, and dug up the hedges, and erected wooden fences and brick walls, a folly that I believe in these days is unique. They are very good, civil people, but have no taste.

27. Thursday. Went with Mrs. Adams to Braintree, about eight miles from the Hyde.

As our objects were fresh air, exercise, and the gratification of curiosity, I thought we ought to make a little excursion to the town after which the town in New England where I was born and shall die, was originally named. The country between Chelmsford and Braintree is pleasant and fertile, though less magnificent in buildings and improvements than many other parts of England; but it is generally tillage land, and covered with good crops of barley, oats, rye, wheat, and buckwheat.

Braintree is a market town, and fairs are held here at certain seasons. I went to the church, which stands in the middle of a triangular piece of ground; and there are, parallel to each side of the triangle, double rows of handsome lime trees, which form the walks and avenues to the church. The church is a very old building, of flint stone; workmen were repairing it, and I went all over it; it is not much larger than Mr. Cleverly's church at Braintree, in New England. I examined all the monuments and gravestones in the church and in the churchyard, and found no one name of person or family of any consequence, nor did I find any name of any of our New England families, except Wilson and Joslyn, Hawkins, Griggs, and Webb. I am convinced that none of our Braintree families came from this village, and that the name was given it by Mr. Coddington, in compliment to the Earl of Warwick, who, in the beginning and middle of the seventeenth century had a manor here, which, however, at his death, about 1665, went out of his family. The parish of Bocking has now more good houses. Braintree is at present the residence only of very ordinary people,—manufacturers only of baizes. Chelmsford was probably named in compliment to Mr. Hooker, who was once minister of that town in Essex, but afterwards in Holland, and after that minister at "Newtown" (Cambridge,) and after that at Hartford, in New England.

We returned to dinner, and spent the evening in examining the curiosities of Mr. Thomas Brand Hollis's house. His library, his Miltonian cabinet, his pictures, busts, medals, coins, Greek, Roman, Carthaginian, and Egyptian gods and goddesses, are a selection of the most rare and valuable. It would be endless to go over the whole in description.

We have had with Alderman Bridgen an agreeable tour and an exquisite entertainment.

I should not omit Alderman Bridgen's nuns and verses. About thirty years ago, Mr. Bridgen, in the Austrian Netherlands, purchased a complete collection of the portraits of all the orders of nuns, in small duodecimo prints. These he lately sent as a present to the Hyde; and Mr. Hollis has placed them in what he calls his boudoir,—a little room between his library and drawing-room. Mr. Bridgen carried down with him a copy of verses of his own composition to be hung up with them. The idea is, that banished from Germany by the Emperor they were taking an asylum at the Hyde, in sight of the Druid, the portico of Athens, and the venerable remains of Egyptian, Greek, Roman, and Carthaginian antiquities.

28. Friday. Returned to Grosvenor Square to dinner.

1787.

August 5. At Kingsbridge, the southerly point of the county of Devonshire, the birthplace of my brother Cranch.

Went yesterday to church in the morning. Dined with Mr. Burnell. Went to the Presbyterian meeting in the afternoon. Drank tea with Mr. Trathan, and went to the Baptist meeting in the evening. Lord Petre is the lord of this manor. The nephew of my brother Cranch possesses the family estate, which I saw very near the church,—four lots of very fine land in high cultivation. The nephews and nieces are married and settled here; all tradesmen and farmers in good business and comfortable circumstances, and live in a harmony with each other that is charming. On Saturday we passed through Plympton and Modbury. From the last town emigrated my brother Cranch with Mr. Palmer. It is a singular village, at the bottom of a valley formed by four high and steep hills. On Friday, we went out from Plymouth to Horsham to see Mr. Palmer, the nephew of our acquaintance in America. His sister only was at home. This is a pleasant situation. We had before seen Mr. Andrew Cranch at Exeter, the aged brother of my friend, and Mr. William Cranch, another brother, deprived by a paralytic stroke of all his faculties.

Mr. Bowring, at Exeter, went with me to see Mr. Towgood, the author of the dissenting gentlemen's Answer to Mr. Wade's Three Letters, eighty-seven years of age.

Brook is next door to Swainstone and Strachleigh, near Lee Mill Bridge, about two miles from Ivy Bridge. Strachleigh did belong to the Chudleighs, the Duchess of Kingston's family.

Haytor Rock is at the summit of the highest mountain in Dartmoor Forest. Bren Tor is said by some to be higher.

6. Monday. Dined at Totness, through which the river Dart runs to Dartmouth. Slept at Newton Bushel.

NOTES OF A DEBATE IN THE SENATE OF THE UNITED STATES.

A few very brief and fragmentary notes of one or two debates held in the Senate, during the first session after the adoption of the Constitution, have been found intermixed with the latest pages of the Diary. The interest that attaches to them grows out of the fact that, during this period, and even until 1795, the doors of the Senate were kept closed, with a single exception, through all legislative as well as executive transactions, and therefore nothing has been reported. The resemding of the rule has changed the character of the body; whether for the better or for worse, time alone can fully determine.

The discussions which took place in the first Congress have a peculiar interest, from the fact that they were held between persons, many of whom had been engaged in framing the Constitution, upon vital measures of organization. Of these measures, none were of more consequence than those creating the offices subordinate to the President,—the great executive departments of the government. It was during the progress of one of these through both Houses, that the question was agitated of the President's constitutional power of removing from office. A brief recital of the prominent steps taken will facilitate the comprehension of the succeeding notes.

On the 19th of May, the House of Representatives being then in committee of the whole, Mr. Madison, of Virginia, moved a resolution organizing the Department of Foreign Affairs, &c., and terminating with these words,—"who shall be appointed by the President, by and with the advice and consent of the Senate, and to be removable by the President."

A long debate upon the power of removal ensued. Mr. Madison taking the lead in defence of the words of the resolution. Mr. Bland proposed to add "by and with the advice and consent of the Senate." But his motion failed, and the language objected to was retained by a considerable majority.

In accordance with this decision, a bill to organize the Department was subsequently reported, and was again debated in committee from the 16th to the 22d of June. A motion to strike out the words was lost, twenty voting for it against thirty-four in the negative. The objection then seems to have occurred to the majority, that they might be construed as conferring a power by the House, which the same authority might at any time withdraw. To escape this construction, when the bill was returned to the House, they consented to the erasure of the words which had caused the debate, and in lieu of them inserted in the second enacting clause the words "whenever the said principal officer shall be removed from office by the President of the United States." This movement, acknowledging the power as conferred by the Constitution on the President, was sustained by thirty votes against eighteen in the negative. A day or two afterwards, the bill passed the House by twenty-nine affirmative against twenty negative votes.

The bill went to the Senate. On the 14th of July it was taken up for consideration, and was debated until the 18th. It is of a portion of this debate that the following notes were taken. Mr. Adams was then Vice-President; and it is probable that he took them for the sake of guiding his judgment in the contingency which happened of his being called to decide the disputed question by his casting vote. A motion was made to strike out the words marked in italics, which had been inserted in the last stages of the bill in the House; and the senators were found equally divided, nine on each side. The Vice-President then recorded his vote in the negative, and the words remained a part of the bill.

The country acquiesced in this decision; and the power of absolute removal has been exercised by the President ever since. The question has been agitated, however, at intervals, and it is liable to be whenever a majority of the Senate may be in political opposition to a new President coming in on a revolution of popular opinion. It is, therefore, not without its use, to accumulate as much of the contemporaneous construction of the Constitution on this point as possible. Among the papers of Mr. Adams, is what would seem to be the original of a paper defining the powers of the Senate on the subject of appointments, drawn up by Mr. Jefferson, as one of the Cabinet of General Washington, in the spring of the next year. It will be found in the Appendix to the present volume, A.

POWER OF REMOVAL.

July 15. Carroll. *Endnote 129* The executive power is commensurate with the legislative and judicial powers.

The rule of construction of treaties, statutes, and deeds.

The same power which creates must annihilate. This is true where the power is simple, but when compound, not.

If a minister is suspected to betray secrets to an enemy, the Senate not sitting, cannot the President displace nor suspend?

The States-General of France demanded that offices should be during good behavior.

It is improbable that a bad president should be chosen—but may not bad senators be chosen?

Is there a due balance of power between the executive and legislative, either in the General Government or State governments?

Montesquieu.

English liberty will be lost when the legislative shall be more corrupt than the executive. Have we not been witnesses of corrupt acts of legislatures, making depredations? Rhode Island yet perseveres.

Ellsworth. *Endnote 130*

We are sworn to support the Constitution.

There is an explicit grant of power to the President, which contains the power of removal. The executive power is granted; not the executive powers hereinafter enumerated and explained.

The President, not the Senate, appoint; they only consent and advise.

The Senate is not an executive council; has no executive power.

The grant to the President express, not by implication.

Butler. *Endnote 131*

This power of removal would be unhinging the equilibrium of power in the Constitution.

The Stadtholder withheld the fleet from going out, to the annoyance of the enemies of the nation.

In treaties, all powers not expressly given, are reserved.

Treaties to be gone over, clause by clause, by the President and Senate together, and modelled.

The other branches are imbecile; disgust and alarm; the President not sovereign; the United States sovereign, or people or Congress sovereign.

The House of Representatives would not be induced to depart, so well satisfied of the grounds.

Ellsworth.

The powers of this Constitution are all vested; parted from the people, from the States, and vested, not in Congress, but in the President.

The word sovereignty is introduced without determinate ideas. Power in the last resort. In this sense the sovereign executive is in the President.

The United States will be parties to a thousand suits. Shall process issue in their name versus or for themselves?

The President, it is said, may be put to jail for debt.

Lee. *Endnote 132*

United States merely figurative, meaning the people.

Grayson. *Endnote 133*

The President is not above the law; an absurdity to admit this idea into our government. Not improbable that the President may be sued. Christina II. of Sweden committed murder. France excused her. The jurors of our lord the President, present that the President committed murder. A monarchy by a side wind. You make him vindea injuriarum. The people will not like "the jurors of our lord, the President," nor "the peace of our lord, the President," nor his dignity; his crown will be left out. Do not wish to make the Constitution a more unnatural, monstrous production, than it is. The British Court is a three-legged stool; if one leg is longer than another, the stool will not stand.

Unpalatable; the removal of officers not palatable. We should not risk any thing for nothing. Come forward like men, and reason openly, and the people will hear more quietly than if you attempt side winds. This measure will do no good, and will disgust.

Lee.

The danger to liberty greater from the disunited opinions and jarring plans of many, than from the energetic operations of one. Marius, Sylla, Cæsar, Cromwell trampled on liberty with armies.

The power of pardon; of adjourning the legislature.

Power of revision sufficient to defend himself. He would be supported by the people.

Patronage gives great influence. The interference more nominal than real.

The greater part of power of making treaties in the President.

The greatest power is in the President; the less in the Senate.

Cannot see responsibility in the President or the great officers of State.

A masked battery of constructive powers would complete the destruction of liberty.

Can the executive lay embargoes, establish fairs, tolls, &c.?

The federal government is limited; the legislative power of it is limited; and, therefore, the executive and judicial must be limited.

The executive not punishable but by universal convulsion, as Charles I.

The legislative in England not so corrupt as the executive.

There is no responsibility in the President or ministry.

Blackstone.

The liberties of England owing to juries. The greatness of England owing to the genius of that people.

The Crown of England can do what it pleases, nearly.

There is no balance in America to such an executive as that in England.

Does the executive arm mean a standing army?

Willing to make a law that the President, if he sees gross misconduct, may suspend pro tempore.

Patterson. *Endnote 134*

Laments that we are obliged to discuss this question; of great importance and much difficulty.

The executive coextensive with the legislative. Had the clause stood alone, would not there have been a devolution of all executive power?

Exceptions are to be construed strictly. This is an invariable rule.

Grayson.

The President has not a continental interest, but is a citizen of a particular State. A. K. of E. otherwise; K. of E. counteracted by a large, powerful, rich, and hereditary aristocracy. Hyperion to a satyr.

Where there are not intermediate powers, an alteration of the government must be to despotism.

Powers ought not to be inconsiderately given to the executive without proper balances.

Triennial and septennial parliaments made by corruption of the executive.

Bowstring. General Lally. Brutus's power to put his sons to death.

The power creating shall have that of uncreating. The minister is to hold at pleasure of the appointer.

If it is in the Constitution, why insert it in the law? brought in by a side wind, inferentially.

There will be every endeavor to increase the consolidatory powers; to weaken the Senate, and strengthen the President.

No evil in the Senate's participating with the President in removal.

Read. *Endnote 135*

The President is to take care that the laws be faithfully executed. He is responsible. How can he do his duty or be responsible, if he cannot remove his instruments?

It is not an equal sharing of the power of appointment between the President and Senate. The Senate are only a check to prevent impositions on the President.

The minister an agent, a deputy to the great executive.

Difficult to bring great characters to punishment or trial.

Power of suspension.

Johnson. *Endnote 136*

Gentlemen convince themselves that it is best the President should have the power, and then study for arguments.

Exceptions. Not a grant. Vested in the President would be void for uncertainty. Executive power is uncertain. Powers are moral, mechanical, material. Which of these powers? what executive power? The land; the money; conveys nothing. What land? what money?

Unumquodque dissolvitur eodem modo quo ligatur.

Meddles not with the question of expediency.

The executive wants power by its duration and its want of a negative, and power to balance. Federalist.

Ellsworth.

What is the difference between a grant and a partition?

Izard. *Endnote 137*

Cujus est instituere, ejus est abrogare. *Endnote 138*

ON THE PERMANENT SEAT OF GOVERNMENT.

No question was more vehemently contested in the first Congress than that of fixing the place for the seat of government. The records of both Houses show the spirit of rivalry which existed among the respective advocates of a position somewhere on the Susquehanna, on the Delaware, and on the Potomac. After a long debate, the House finally settled upon a bill authorizing the appointment of a commission to select a site on the banks of the Susquehanna, in the State of Pennsylvania. This bill went up to the Senate on the 22d of September, when the remarks that follow appear to have been made.

September 22. Grayson. No census yet taken, by which the centre of population—

We have markets, archives, houses, lodgings. Extremely hurt at what has passed in the House of Representatives. The money,—is your army paid? Virginia offered one hundred thousand dollars towards the federal buildings. The buildings may be erected without expense to the Union. Lands may be granted; these lands laid out in lots, and sold to adventurers.

Butler.

The recent instance in France shows that an attempt to establish a government against justice and the will of the people, is vain, idle, and chimerical.

23. Wednesday. Lee. Navigation of the Susquehanna.

Grayson.

Antwerp and the Scheldt. Reasons of state have influenced the Pennsylvanians to prevent the navigation from being opened. *Endnote 139* The limiting the seat of empire to the State of Pennsylvania, on the Delaware, is a characteristic mark of partiality. The Union will think that Pennsylvania governs the Union, and that the general interest is sacrificed to that of one State. The Czar Peter took time to inquire and deliberate before he fixed a place to found his city.

We are about founding a city which will be one of the first in the world, and we are governed by local and partial motives.

Morris moves to expunge the proviso. *Endnote 140*

Carroll against the motion to expunge the proviso; considers the western country of great importance. Some gentlemen in both houses seem to undervalue the western country, or despair of commanding it. Government on the Potomac would secure it.

Butler.

The question is not whether Pennsylvania or Maryland shall be benefited, but how are the United States benefited or injured.

Maclay. *Endnote 141*

Pennsylvania has altered the law this month respecting the navigation of the Susquehanna.

24. Thursday. Grayson moves to strike out the words "in the State of Pennsylvania."

Butler.

The centre of population the best criterion. The centre of wealth and the centre of territory.

Lee.

The centre of territory is the only permanent centre. *Endnote 142*

1790. UNFINISHED BUSINESS

At the commencement of the second session of the first Congress, the question occurred upon the revival of the business of the preceding session, or beginning anew. A joint committee raised to consider the matter reported on the 22d. "That the business unfinished between the two Houses ought to be regarded as if it had not been passed upon by either."

On the 25th, a motion was made to postpone the report of the committee.

January 25. Monday. *Endnote 143* It was not the sense of either House, or of any member of either, that the business pending at the adjournment should be lost.

Where is the economy of repeating the expense of time?

Can this opinion be founded on the law of Parliament? The King can prorogue the Parliament, but there is no such power here.

The rule of Parliament, that business once acted on and rejected, shall not be brought on again the same session, is a good rule, but not applicable to this case.

Ellsworth.

In legislative assemblies, more to be apprehended from precipitation than from delay. *Endnote 144*

Williamson.

Great numbers emigrate to the back part of North and South Carolina and Georgia, for the sake of living without trouble. The woods, such is the mildness of the climate, produce grass to support horses and cattle, and chestnuts, acorns, and other things, for the food of hogs; so that they have only a little corn to raise, which is done without much labor. They call this kind of life following the range. They are very ignorant, and hate all men of education; they call them pen and ink men. *Endnote 145*

1795.

A few entries in the Diary, made in the years 1795 and 1796, remain. They principally relate to agriculture, and to the improvements undertaken by the writer upon the farm purchased by him after his return from Europe, and which became his residence during the remainder of his life. A selection from them closes this portion of the work.

June 21. Lime dissolves all vegetable substances, such as leaves, straws, stalks, weeds, and converts them into an immediate food for vegetables; it kills the eggs of worms and seeds of weeds. The best method is to spread it in your barnyard among the straw and dung; it succeeds well when spread upon the ground. Burning limestones or shells diminishes their weight; but slaking the lime restores that weight. The German farmers say that lime makes the father rich, but the grandson poor; that is, exhausts the land. This is all from Mr. Rutherford. Plaster of Paris has a vitriolic acid in it which attracts the water from the air, and operates like watering plants. It is good for corn; not useful in wet land. You sprinkle it by hand as you sow barley, over the ground; five bushels powdered to an acre: carry it in a bag, as you would grain to sow.

Mr. Meredith, at Mr. Vaughan's, explained to me his method. He takes a first crop of clover early; then breaks up the ground, cross-ploughs and harrows it, then plants potatoes. He only ploughs a furrow, drops the potatoes a foot asunder, and then covers them with another furrow. He ploughs now and then between these rows, but never hoes. As soon as the season comes for sowing his winter barley, he digs the potatoes, ploughs and harrows the ground, sows the winter barley with clover seeds and orchard-grass seeds; and the next spring he has a great crop of barley, and afterwards a great burthen of grass. He prefers orchard-grass to herds-grass, as much more productive.

1796.

Quincy, July 12. Tuesday. Yesterday mowed all the grass on Stony-field Hill. To-day ploughing for hilling among the corn over against the house. Briesler laying the foundation of the new barn, which is to be raised to-morrow at the east end of my father's barn. Puffer and Sullivan Lathrop ploughing among potatoes in the lower garden.

This Journal is commenced to allure me into the habit of writing again, long lost. This habit is easily lost, but not easily regained. I have, in the course of my life, lost it several times, and regained it as often; so I will now. I can easily credit the reports I have heard of Dr. Robertson, the Scottish historian, who is said to have lost the habit of writing for many years; but he reacquired it before his death, and produced his Inquiry into the Knowledge of the Ancients of India.

13. Wednesday. B. went out to hoe this morning, but soon came in. Said he had sprained his arm, and could not work. He soon went out towards Captain Beale's. P., one of my workmen from Stoughton, came home late last night. Said Captain L. had called him in and given him a bottle of brandy. By what sympathy do these tipplers discover one another?

This day my new barn was raised, near the spot where the old barn stood, which was taken down by my father when he raised his new barn in 1737.

14. Thursday. The wind northwest, after a fine rain. A firing of cannon this morning in the harbor. I arose by four o'clock, and enjoyed "the charm of earliest birds;" their songs were never more various, universal, animating, or delightful.

My corn this year has been injured by two species of worms,—one of the size and shape of a caterpillar, but of a mouse color, lies at the root, eats off the stalk, and then proceeds to all the other plants in the hill, till he frequently kills them all; the other is long and slender as a needle, of a bright yellow color; he is found in the centre of the stalk near the ground, where he eats it off, as the Hessian fly eats the wheat. My brother taught me the method of finding these vermin and destroying them. They lie commonly near the surface.

I have been to see my barn, which looks very stately and strong. Rode up to Braintree, and saw where T. has been trimming red cedars. He has not much more to do. He was not at work. He has probably worked two days since I was there last.

It rains at eleven o'clock. The barley is growing white for the harvest. My men are hilling the corn over the road. A soft fine rain in a clock calm is falling as sweetly as I ever saw in April, May, or June; it distils as gently as we can wish; will beat down the grain as little as possible, refresh the gardens and pastures, revive the corn, make the fruit grow rapidly, and lay the foundation of fine rowen and after feed.

15. Friday. A very heavy shower of rain. Thunder in the morning.

Went with three hands to Braintree, and cut between forty and fifty red cedars, and with a team of five cattle brought home twenty-two of them at a load. We have opened the prospect, so that the meadow and western mountains may be distinctly seen.

B. has two hands employed in heaping up manure in his barnyard. The cattle have broken into his cornfield, through the gap which we left unfinished in the great wall, and eaten a hundred hills.

The new barn is boarded on the roof, and the underpinning is finished.

17. Sunday. Warm, but clear. B. at home, but running down cellar for cider.

We are to have a Mr. Hilliard.

Yesterday, Dr. Tufts and Mr. Otis and family dined with me. Otis *Endnote 146* was very full of elections, and had many things to say about Pinckney and Henry, Jefferson and Burr. He says there was a caucus at Philadelphia; that they agreed to run Jefferson and Burr; that Butler was offended and left them. Otis takes it for granted the President will retire. Pickering has given out publicly that he will. Mrs. W. takes it for granted he will. Collections, packages, and removals of clothes and furniture of their own, have been made. When the electors are chosen, the declaration is to be made.

Mr. Otis confirms the account of the nomination and appointment of my son to be minister plenipotentiary of the United States at the court of Portugal. He also confirms the adjournment of Congress to the constitutional day, the first Monday in December. Mrs. W. is not to return to Philadelphia till November.

Mr. Hilliard of Cambridge preached for us. He is the son of our old acquaintance, minister of Barnstable, and afterwards at Cambridge. Mr. Quincy and Mr. Sullivan drank tea with us.

18. Monday. B. is at hoe. The kitchen-folk say he is steady. A terrible, drunken, distracted week he has made of the last. A beast associating with the worst beasts in the neighborhood, running to all the shops and private houses, swilling brandy, wine, and cider, in quantities enough to destroy him. If the ancients drank wine as our people drink rum and cider, it is no wonder we read of so many possessed with devils.

Went up to Pen's Hill. Trask has the rheumatism in his arm, and is unable to work. He told me that rattlesnakes began to appear,—two on Saturday; one killed, the other escaped. He told me, too, of another event that vexed, provoked, and alarmed me much more, namely,—that my horses were yesterday in such a frenzy at the church door, that they frightened the crowd of people, and frightened a horse, or the people in the chaise, so that they whipped their horse till he ran over two children. The children stooped down, or fell down, so that the chaise went over them without hurting them; but it must have been almost a miracle that they were not killed or wounded. I know not when my indignation has been more excited at the coachman for his folly and carelessness, and, indeed, at others of the family, for the carriage going to meeting at all. As Mrs. A. could not go, the coach ought not to have gone. The coachman and footman ought to have gone to meeting, and the girls to have walked. I scolded at the coachman first, and afterwards at his mistress, and I will scold again and again; it is my duty. There is no greater tyranny or insolence than sporting with horses and carriages among crowds of people.

19. Tuesday. A plentiful shower of rain, with thunder and lightning, this morning. Took a teaspoonful of bark in spirits. B. steady, but deep in the horrors, gaping, stretching, groaning.

20. Wednesday. Commencement. Rode to the swamp at the top of Pen's Hill. T. is mowing the bushes, cutting the trees, and leaves only the white oaks, which he trims and prunes as high as he can reach. My design is to plough up a cornfield for Burrill, against next year, in that inclosure. Walked in the afternoon over the hills and across the fields and meadows, up to the old plain. The corn there is as good as any I have seen, excepting two or three spots. Briesler and Sullivan cutting sleepers for the barn. My beautiful grove, so long preserved by my father and my uncle, proves to be all rotten. More than half the trees we cut are so defective as to be unfit for any use but the fire. I shall save the white oaks and cut the rest. I was overtaken with the rain at the end of my walk, and returned home in it.

21. Thursday. S. L. and B. carting earth into the yard from the ground which is to be thrown into the highway, over against my house. The old apple-tree, probably a hundred years of age, is to fall. B. and T. L. mowing in the meadow. Six hogsheads of lime, fifty gallons each, were brought home yesterday for manure. I have it of Mr. Brackett, at fifteen shillings the hogshead.

I am reading Dr. Watson's Apology for the Bible, in Answer to T. Paine's Second Part of the "Age of Reason."

That apple-tree over the way, to which the beauty and convenience of the road have been sacrificed for a hundred years, has now, in its turn, with apples enough upon it to make two barrels of cider, fallen a sacrifice to the beauty and convenience of the road. It has been felled this morning, never to rise again; and the road is to be widened and enlarged. The stump and roots are to be dug out of the ground, and the wall to be removed back and made a ha-ha. B. had a mind to go upon wall. I went with him from place to place, and could resolve on nothing. I then set him to split and mortise some posts for the fence against Mrs. Veazie's. We went up, carried the posts, but when we came there we found that the wall was too heavy and stones too large for two hands; four at least were necessary. B. was wild; and we came to some explanation. He must go off, &c. Mrs. Adams paid him, and then he thought he would not go. After long conversations, B. came to a sort of agreement to stay a year from this day, at forty-five pounds. He declared he would not drink spirit nor cider for the whole year. He reserved, however, twelve days for himself. We shall see to-morrow morning how he behaves.

22. Friday. B. sober and steady, persevering in his declaration that he will not drink these twelve months. Paid Trask in full, sixteen dollars for twenty-four days' work. He insisted on four shillings a day. He has finished clearing the swamp on Pen's Hill this day.

23. Saturday. Rode down to the barley and black-grass at the beach. The barley is better than I hoped. The clover has taken pretty well in general; parts where the tide has flowed are killed. Weeds very thick round the margin of the salt meadow, or rather black-grass meadow. Twitch-grass, scattering and thin. B. sober, composed as ever; B. and B. mowing with him. James, the coachman, enjoying the pleasures of a sportsman, shooting marsh birds instead of mowing.

Still reading Bishop Watson's Apology; finished.

My men mowed the black-grass and barley at the beach, came home and split all the red cedars into posts, and mortised some of them. Sullivan mortised, after having assisted Burrill to get in all his fresh hay.

Began the Life of Petrarch, by Susanna Dobson.

24. Sunday. We are to have for a preacher a Mr. Whitcomb. B. is still cool and steady. In the first volume of the Life of Petrarch, p. 52, it is said that Pope John XXII. believed that the souls of the just would not enjoy the vision of God till after the universal judgment and the resurrection of their bodies. This opinion is Priestley's, and Price was much inclined to it. This Pope's imprudent endeavors to establish this doctrine, produced an insurrection of the cardinals and court of Rome, divisions of the doctors in theology, at Paris, &c., and obliged the Pope to retract. Petrarch appears to have favored his opinion concerning the vision of God.

Went to church forenoon and afternoon, and heard Mr. Whitcomb of Bolton.

25. Monday. Dull weather, but no rain. The L. with the team are going to the swamp on Pen's Hill for a load of wood that T. has cut. Rode up to the swamp on Pen's Hill. S. and B. loaded up a cord of wood, and S. drove it home. B. staid, and cut down and cut up an old walnut, murdered by the women and children for their dye-pots.

26. Tuesday. Cloudy, and begins to rain; the wind at northeast. The men gone up the hill to rake the barley. In conformity to the fashion, I drank this morning and yesterday morning about a gill of cider; it seems to do me good.

The Christian religion is, above all the religions that ever prevailed or existed in ancient or modern times, the religion of wisdom, virtue, equity, and humanity, let the blackguard Paine say what he will; it is resignation to God, it is goodness itself to man.

27. Wednesday. B. and S. making and liming a heap of manure. They compounded it of earth carted in from the ground opposite the garden, where the ha-ha wall is to be built, of salt hay and sea weed trodden by the cattle in the yard, of horsedung from the stable, and of cowdung left by the cows. Over all this composition they now and then sprinkle a layer of lime. Bass and Thomas hoeing potatoes in the lower garden.

I rode up to the barn, which Mr. Pratt has almost shingled, and over to the plain, but found my tenants were at work in my father's old swamp, which I could not reach without more trouble than I was willing to take.

Dr. W. came up, with two young gentlemen from New York, Mr. John and Mr. Henry Cruger, the youngest of whom studies with my son Charles, as a lawyer, who gives him an excellent character. They are journeying eastward as far as Portland, and return by Albany. The eldest of them has lately returned from the East Indies.

28. Thursday. B. and S. are gone to the beach for a load of sea-weed to put into their hill of compost. B. and T. hoeing still in the lower garden. James sick of a surfeit of fruit. I

continue my practice of drinking a gill of cider in the morning, and find no ill, but some good effects.

It is more than forty years since I read Swift's comparison of Dryden in his translation of Virgil, to the Lady in a Lobster, but, until this day, I never knew the meaning of it. To-day, at dinner, seeing lobsters at table, I inquired after the Lady, and Mrs. B. rose and went into the kitchen to her husband, who sent in the little lady herself, in the cradle in which she resides. She must be an old lady; she looks like Dr. Franklin, that is, like an Egyptian mummy. Swift's droll genius must have been amused with such an object. It is as proper a subject, or rather allusion or illustration for humor and satire, as can be imagined. A little old woman in a spacious habitation as the cradle is, would be a proper emblem of a President in the new house at Philadelphia.

B. and S. brought up in the morning a good load of green sea-weed. B. and B. have been carting dirt and liming the heap of compost. S. and T. thrashing barley at the little barn.

29. Friday. Hot, after thunder, lightning, and an hour's rain. The two Lathrops threshing. B. and B. brought up a third load of sea-weed. They go on making the heap of compost with lime, sea-weed, earth, &c. &c. Still reading the second volume of Petrarch's Life.

31. Sunday. A fine northwest wind, pure air, clear sky, and bright sun. Reading the second volume of Petrarch's Life. This singular character had very wild notions of the right of the city of Rome to a republican government, and the empire of the world. It is strange that his infatuation for Rienzi did not expose him to more resentment and greater danger. In the absence of the Pope at Avignon, and the people having no regular check upon the nobles, these fell into their usual dissensions, and oppressed the people till they were ripe to be duped by any single enthusiast, bold adventurer, ambitious usurper, or hypocritical villain who should, with sufficient impudence, promise them justice, elemency, and liberty. One, or all of these characters belonged to Rienzi, who was finally murdered by the people whom he had deceived, and who had deceived him. Tacitus appears to have been as great an enthusiast as Petrarch for the revival of the republic and universal empire. He has exerted the vengeance of history upon the emperors, but has veiled the conspiracies against them, and the incorrigible corruption of the people which probably provoked their most atrocious cruelties. Tyranny can scarcely be practised upon a virtuous and wise people.

August 4. Thursday. Of all the summers of my life, this has been the freest from care, anxiety, and vexation to me, the sickness of Mrs. A. excepted. My health has been better, the season fruitful, my farm was well conducted. Alas! what may happen to reverse all this? But it is folly to anticipate evils, and madness to create imaginary ones.

6. Saturday. Omnium rerum domina, virtus. Virtue is the mistress of all things. Virtue is the master of all things. Therefore a nation that should never do wrong must necessarily govern the world. The might of virtue, the power of virtue, is not a very common topic, not so common as it should be.

7. Sunday. I am reading a work of Cicero, that I remember not to have read before. It is intituled, M. Tullii Ciceronis, si Deo placet, Consolatio; *Endnote 147* remarkable for an ardent hope and confident belief of a future state.

10. Wednesday. Mr. Howell, of Rhode Island, came up to see me, and conversed the whole evening concerning the St. Croix and his commission for settling that boundary.

11. Thursday. Mr. Howell lodged with us, and spent the whole morning in conversation concerning the affairs of his mission. He said, by way of episode, that the President would resign, and that there was one thing which would make Rhode Island unanimous in his successor, and that was, the funding system. He said they wanted Hamilton for Vice-President. I was wholly silent.

13. Saturday. Three loads of salt hay yesterday from the beach marsh. Got in fifty-one bushels of barley, winnowed and raddled. T. burning bushes on Pen's Hill. Reading Tully's Offices. It is a treatise on Moral Obligation. Our word obligation answers nearer and better than duty to Cicero's word, officium.

14. Sunday. One great advantage of the Christian religion is, that it brings the great principle of the law of nature and nations,—Love your neighbor as yourself, and do to others as you would that others should do to you,—to the knowledge, belief, and veneration of the whole people. Children, servants, women, and men, are all professors in the science of public and private morality. No other institution for education, no kind of political discipline, could diffuse this kind of necessary information, so universally among all ranks and descriptions of citizens. The duties and rights of the man and the citizen are thus taught from early infancy to every creature. The sanctions of a future life are thus added to the observance of civil and political, as well as domestic and private duties. Prudence, justice, temperance, and fortitude, are thus taught to be the means and conditions of future as well as present happiness.

26. Friday. "Inflexible to preserve, virtuous to pursue, and intelligent to discern the true interests of his country." Flattering expressions of a toast, the more remarkable as they originated in New York. God grant they may never be belied, never disproved!

Mr. Sedgwick and Mr. Barrell came up to see me, and give a sanguine account of the future elections of senators and representatives.

September 8. Thursday. B. and P. laying wall. B. and J. picking apples and making cider. S. widening the brook.

I think to christen my place by the name of Peacefield, in commemoration of the peace which I assisted in making in 1783, of the thirteen years peace and neutrality which I have contributed to preserve, and of the constant peace and tranquillity which I have enjoyed in this residence.

ESSAYS AND CONTROVERSIAL PAPERS OF THE REVOLUTION.

ESSAYS.

The three Essays that follow, are the earliest printed productions known to have come from Mr. Adams. In a letter dated in 1819, he says, "There were many flickerings in the newspapers between Mr. Sewall and me, the precise dates of which I cannot recollect. Sewall wrote under the signature of Philanthropos sometimes, and at other times under the signature of a long J.; and I wrote under that of a great U., and, perhaps, other signatures that I do not remember. All these trifles of mine were printed in the Boston Gazette. There were several papers written by me on occasion of the assault of Colonel Murray upon General Brattle, on the council stairs of the old town house."

The first and third papers relate to this event, which caused some excitement at the moment, and led to a legal prosecution that continued it. All three bear the peculiar mental and moral characteristics of the author, and are therefore preserved.

ON PRIVATE REVENGE. NO. I. *ENDNOTE 148*

Man is distinguished from other animals, his fellow inhabitants of this planet, by a capacity of acquiring knowledge and civility, more than by any excellency, corporeal, or mental, with which mere nature has furnished his species. His erect figure and sublime countenance would give him but little elevation above the bear or the tiger; nay, notwithstanding those advantages, he would hold an inferior rank in the scale of being, and would have a worse prospect of happiness than those creatures, were it not for the capacity of uniting with others, and availing himself of arts and inventions in social life. As he comes originally from the hands of his Creator, self-love or self-preservation is the only spring that moves within him; he might crop the leaves or berries with which his Creator had surrounded him, to satisfy his hunger; he might sip at the lake or rivulet to slake his thirst; he might screen himself behind a rock or mountain from the bleakest of the winds; or he might fly from the jaws of voracious beasts to preserve himself from immediate destruction. But would such an existence be worth preserving? Would not the first precipice or the first beast of prey that could put a period to the wants, the frights, and horrors of such a wretched being, be a friendly object and a real blessing?

When we take one remove from this forlorn condition, and find the species propagated, the banks of clams and oysters discovered, the bow and arrow invented, and the skins of beasts or the bark of trees employed for covering,—although the human creature has a little less anxiety and misery than before, yet each individual is independent of all others. There is no intercourse of friendship; no communication of food or clothing; no conversation or connection, unless the conjunction of sexes, prompted by instinct, like that of hares and foxes, may be called so. The ties of parent, son, and brother, are of little obligation. The relations of master and servant, the distinction of magistrate and subject, are totally unknown. Each individual is his own sovereign, accountable to no other upon earth, and punishable by none. In this savage state, courage, hardiness, activity, and strength, the virtues of their brother brutes, are the only excellencies to which men can aspire. The man who can run with the most celerity, or send the arrow with the greatest force, is the best qualified to procure a subsistence. Hence, to chase a deer over the most rugged mountain, or to pierce him at the greatest distance, will be held, of all accomplishments, in the highest estimation. Emulations and competitions for superiority in such qualities, will soon commence; and any action which may be taken for an insult, will be considered as a pretension to such superiority; it will raise resentment in proportion, and shame and grief will prompt the savage to claim satisfaction or to take revenge. To request the interposition of a third person to arbitrate between the contending parties, would be considered as an implicit acknowledgment of deficiency in those qualifications, without which, none in such a barbarous condition would choose to live. Each one, then, must be his own avenger. The offended parties must fall to fighting. Their teeth, their nails, their feet, or fists, or, perhaps, the first club or stone that can be grasped, must decide the contest, by finishing the life of one. The father, the brother, or the friend, begins then to espouse the cause of the deceased; not, indeed, so much from any love he bore him living, or from any grief he suffers for him dead, as from a principle of bravery and honor, to show himself able and willing to encounter the man who had just before vanquished another. Hence arises the idea of an avenger of blood, and thus the notions of revenge, and the appetite for it grow apace. Every one must avenge his own wrongs when living, or else lose his reputation, and his near relation must avenge them for him after he is dead, or forfeit his. Indeed, nature has implanted in the human heart a disposition to resent an injury when offered; and this disposition is so strong, that even the horse treading by accident on a gouty toe, or a brickbat falling on the shoulders, in the first twinges of pain, seems to excite the angry passions, and we feel an inclination to kill the horse and to break the brickbat. Consideration, however, that the horse and brick were without design, will cool us; whereas the thought that any mischief has been done on purpose to abuse, raises revenge in all its strength and terrors; and the man feels the sweetest, highest gratification, when he inflicts the punishment himself. From this source arises the ardent desire in men to judge for themselves, when, and to what degree they are injured, and to carve out their own remedies for themselves. From the same source arises that obstinate disposition in barbarous nations to continue barbarous, and the extreme difficulty of introducing civility and Christianity among them. For the great distinction between savage nations and polite ones, lies in this,—that among the former every individual is his own judge and his own executioner; but among the latter all pretensions to judgment and punishment are resigned to tribunals erected by the public; a resignation which savages are not, without infinite difficulty, persuaded to make, as it is of a right and privilege extremely dear and tender to an uncultivated nature.

To exterminate from among mankind such revengeful sentiments and tempers, is one of the highest and most important strains of civil and humane policy. Yet the qualities which contribute most to inspire and support them may, under certain regulations, be indulged and encouraged. Wrestling, running, leaping, lifting, and other exercises of strength, hardiness, courage, and activity, may be promoted among private soldiers, common sailors, laborers, manufacturers, and husbandmen, among whom they are most wanted, provided sufficient precautions are taken that no romantic, cavalier-like principles of honor intermix with them, and render a resignation of the right of judging, and the power of executing, to the public, shameful. But whenever such notions spread so inimical to the peace of society, that boxing, clubs, swords, or firearms, are resorted to for deciding every quarrel, about a girl, a game at cards, or any little accident that wine or folly or jealousy may suspect to be an affront,—the whole power of the government should be exerted to suppress them.

If a time should ever come when such notions shall prevail in this Province to a degree, that no privileges shall be able to exempt men from indignities and personal attacks, not the privilege of a counsellor, nor the privilege of a House of Representatives of "speaking freely in that assembly, without impeachment or question in any court or place," out of the

General Court—when whole armed mobs shall assault a member of the House, when violent attacks shall be made upon counsellors, when no place shall be sacred, not the very walls of legislation, when no personages shall overawe, not the whole General Court added to all the other gentlemen on 'Change, when the broad noon-day shall be chosen to display before the world such high, heroic sentiments of gallantry and spirit, when such assailants shall live unexpelled from the legislature, when slight censures and no punishments shall be inflicted,—there will really be danger of our becoming universally ferocious, barbarous, and brutal, worse than our Gothic ancestors before the Christian era.

The doctrine, that the person assaulted "should act with spirit," "should defend himself by drawing his sword and killing, or by wringing noses, and boxing it out with the offender," is the tenet of a coxcomb and the sentiment of a brute. The fowl upon the dunghill, to be sure, feels a most gallant and heroic spirit at the crowing of another, and instantly spreads his cloak, and prepares for combat. The bull's wrath enkindles into a noble rage, and the stallion's immortal spirit can never forgive the pawings, neighings, and defiances of his rival. But are cocks and bulls and horses the proper exemplars for the imitation of men, especially of men of sense, and even of the highest personages in the government!

Such ideas of gallantry have been said to be derived from the army. But it was injuriously said, because not truly. For every gentleman, every man of sense and breeding in the army, has a more delicate and manly way of thinking, and from his heart despises all such little, narrow, sordid notions. It is true that a competition, and a mutual affectation of contempt, is apt to arise among the lower, more ignorant, and despicable, of every rank and order in society. This sort of men, (and some few such there are in every profession,) among divines, lawyers, physicians, as well as husbandmen, manufacturers, and laborers, are prone, from a certain littleness of mind, to imagine that their labors alone are of any consequence to the world, and to affect a contempt for all others. It is not unlikely, then, that the lowest and most despised sort of soldiers may have expressed a contempt for all other orders of mankind, may have indulged a disrespect to every personage in a civil character, and have acted upon such principles of revenge, rusticity, barbarity, and brutality, as have been above described. And, indeed, it has been observed by the great Montesquieu, that "From a manner of thinking that prevails among mankind," (the most ignorant and despicable of mankind, he means,) "they set a higher value upon courage than timorousness, on activity than prudence, on strength than counsel. Hence, the army will ever despise a senate, and respect their own officers; they will naturally slight the orders sent them by a body of men whom they look upon as cowards, and therefore unworthy to command them." This respect to their own officers, which produces a contempt of senates and councils, and of all laws, orders, and constitutions, but those of the army and their superior officers, though it may have prevailed among some soldiers of the illiberal character above described, is far from being universal. It is not found in one gentleman of sense and breeding in the whole service. All of this character know that the common law of England is superior to all other laws, martial or common, in every English government, and has often asserted triumphantly its own preëminence against the insults and encroachments of a giddy and unruly soldiery. They know, too, that civil officers in England hold a great superiority to military officers, and that a frightful despotism would be the speedy consequence of the least alteration in these particulars. And, knowing this, these gentlemen, who have so often exposed their lives in defence of the religion, the liberties, and rights of men and Englishmen, would feel the utmost indignation at the doctrine which should make the civil power give place to the military, which should make a respect to their superior officers destroy or diminish their obedience to civil magistrates, or which should give any man a right in conscience, honor, or even in punctilio and delicacy, to neglect the institutions of the public, and seek his own remedy for wrongs and injuries of any kind.

ON SELF-DELUSION. NO. II.

to the printers. Endnote 149

My worthy and ingenious friend, Mr. J., having strutted his hour upon the stage, and acquired as well as deserved a good reputation, as a man of sense and learning, some time since made his exit, and now is heard no more.

Soon after Mr. J.'s departure, your present correspondent made his appearance, but has not yet executed his intended plan. Mr. J. enlisted himself under the banners of a faction, and employed his agreeable pen in the propagation of the principles and prejudices of a party, and for this purpose he found himself obliged to exalt some characters, and depress others, equally beyond the truth. The greatest and best of all mankind deserve less admiration, and even the worst and vilest deserve more candor, than the world in general is willing to allow them. The favorites of parties, although they have always some virtues, have always many imperfections. Many of the ablest tongues and pens have, in every age, been employed in the foolish, deluded, and pernicious flattery of one set of partisans, and in furious, prostitute invectives against another; but such kinds of oratory never had any charms for me; and if I must do one or the other, I would quarrel with both parties and with every individual of each, before I would subjugate my understanding, or prostitute my tongue or pen to either.

To divert men's minds from subjects of vain curiosity, or unprofitable science, to the useful, as well as entertaining speculations of agriculture; to eradicate the Gothic and pernicious principles of private revenge that have been lately spread among my countrymen, to the debasement of their character, and to the frequent violation of the public peace, and to recommend a careful attention to political measures, and a candid manner of reasoning about them, instead of abusive insolence or uncharitable imputations upon men and characters, has, since I first undertook the employment of entertaining the public, been my constant and invariable view. The difficulty or impracticability of succeeding in my enterprise, has often been objected to me by my friends; but even this has not wholly disheartened me. I own it would be easier to depopulate a province, or subvert a monarchy, to transplant a nation, or enkindle a new war; and that I should have a fairer prospect of success in such designs as those. But my consolation is this,—that if I am unable by my writings to effect any good purpose, I never will subserve a bad one. If engagements to a party are necessary to make a fortune, I had rather make none at all; and spend the remainder of my days like my favorite author, that ancient and immortal husbandman, philosopher, politician, and general, Xenophon, in his retreat, considering kings and princes as shepherds, and their people and subjects like flocks and herds, or as mere objects of contemplation and parts of a curious machine in which I had no interest, than to wound my own mind by engaging in any party, and spreading prejudices, vices, or follies. Notwithstanding this, I remember the monkish maxim,—fac officium taliter qualiter, sed sta bene cum priore; and it is impossible to stand well with the abbot without fighting for his cause through fas and nefas.

Please to insert the foregoing and following, which is the last deviation I purpose to make from my principal and favorite views of writing on husbandry and mechanic arts. u.

There is nothing in the science of human nature more curious, or that deserves a critical attention from every order of men so much, as that principle which moral writers have distinguished by the name of self-deceit. This principle is the spurious off-spring of self-love;

and is, perhaps, the source of far the greatest and worst part of the vices and calamities among mankind.

The most abandoned minds are ingenious in contriving excuses for their crimes, from constraint, necessity, the strength or suddenness of temptation, or the violence of passion, which serve to soften the remordings of their own consciences, and to render them by degrees insensible equally to the charms of virtue and the turpitude of vice. What multitudes in older countries discover, even while they are suffering deservedly the most infamous and terrible of civil punishments, a tranquillity and even a magnanimity like that which we may suppose in a real patriot dying to preserve his country! Happy would it be for the world if the fruits of this pernicious principle were confined to such profligates. But, if we look abroad, shall we not see the most modest, sensible, and virtuous of the common people, almost every hour of their lives, warped and blinded by the same disposition to flatter and deceive themselves? When they think themselves injured by any foible or vice in others, is not this injury always seen through the magnifying end of the perspective? When reminded of any such imperfection in themselves, by which their neighbors or fellow-citizens are sufferers, is not the perspective instantly reversed? Insensible of the beams in our own eyes, are we not quick in discerning motes in those of others? Nay, however melancholy it may be, and how humbling soever to the pride of the human heart, even the few favorites of nature, who have received from her clearer understandings and more happy tempers than other men, who seem designed, under Providence, to be the great conductors of the art and science, the war and peace, the laws and religion of this lower world, are often snared by this unhappy disposition in their minds, to their own destruction, and the injury, nay, often to the utter desolation of millions of their fellow-men. Since truth and virtue, as the means of present and future happiness, are confessed to be the only objects that deserve to be pursued, to what imperfection in our nature, or unaccountable folly in our conduct, excepting this of which we have been speaking, can mankind impute the multiplied diversity of opinions, customs, laws, and religions that have prevailed, and are still triumphant, in direct opposition to both? From what other source can such fierce disputations arise concerning the two things which seem the most consonant to the entire frame of human nature?

Indeed, it must be confessed, and it ought to be with much contrition lamented, that those eyes, which have been given us to see, are willingly suffered by us to be obscured, and those consciences, which by the commission of God Almighty have a rightful authority over us, to be deposed by prejudices, appetites, and passions, which ought to hold a much inferior rank in the intellectual and moral system. Such swarms of passions, avarice and ambition, servility and adulation, hopes, fears, jealousies, envy, revenge, malice, and cruelty, are continually buzzing in the world, and we are so extremely prone to mistake the impulses of these for the dictates of our consciences,—that the greatest genius, united to the best disposition, will find it hard to hearken to the voice of reason, or even to be certain of the purity of his own intentions.

From this true, but deplorable condition of mankind, it happens that no improvements in science or literature, no reformation in religion or morals, nor any rectification of mistaken measures in government, can be made without opposition from numbers, who, flattering themselves that their own intentions are pure, (how sinister soever they may be in fact) will reproach impure designs to others, or, fearing a detriment to their interest or a mortification to their passions from the innovation, will even think it lawful directly and knowingly to falsify the motives and characters of the innocent.

Vain ambition and other vicious motives were charged by the sacred congregation upon Galileo, as the causes of his hypothesis concerning the motion of the earth, and charged so often and with so many terms, as to render the old man at last suspicious, if not satisfied, that the charge was true, though he had been led to this hypothesis by the light of a great genius and deep researches into astronomy. Sedition, rebellion, pedantry, desire of fame, turbulence, and malice, were always reproached to the great reformers, who delivered us from the worst chains that were ever forged by monks or devils for the human mind. Zosinius and Julian could easily discover or invent anecdotes to dishonor the conversion of Constantine, and his establishment of Christianity in the empire.

For these reasons we can never be secure in a resignation of our understandings, or in confiding enormous power either to the bramble or the cedar; no, nor to any mortal, however great or good; and for the same reasons we should always be upon our guard against the epithets and reflections of writers and declaimers, whose constant art it is to falsify and blacken the characters and measures they are determined to discredit.

These reflections have been occasioned by the late controversies in our newspapers about certain measures in the political world. *Endnote 150* Controversies that have this in common with others of much greater figure and importance, and, indeed, with all others, (in which numbers have been concerned,) from the first invention of letters to the present hour; that more pains have been employed in charging desire of popularity, restless turbulence of spirit, ambitious views, envy, revenge, malice, and jealousy on one side; and servility, adulation, tyranny, principles of arbitrary power, lust of dominion, avarice, desires of civil or military commissions on the other; or, in fewer words, in attempts to blacken and discredit the motives of the disputants on both sides, than in rational inquiries into the merits of the cause, the truth, and rectitude of the measures contested.

Let not writers nor statesmen deceive themselves. The springs of their own conduct and opinions are not always so clear and pure, nor are those of their antagonists in politics always so polluted and corrupted, as they believe, and would have the world believe too. Mere readers and private persons can see virtues and talents on each side; and to their sorrow they have not yet seen any side altogether free from atrocious vices, extreme ignorance, and most lamentable folly. Nor will mere readers and private persons be less excusable if they should suffer themselves to be imposed on by others, who first impose upon themselves. Every step in the public administration of government concerns us nearly. Life and fortune, our own and those of our posterity, are not trifles to be neglected or totally entrusted to other hands; and these, in the vicissitudes of human things, may be rendered in a few years either totally uncertain, or as secure as fixed laws and the British constitution well administered can make them, in consequence of measures that seem at present but trifles, and to many scarcely worth attention. Let us not be bubbled then out of our reverence and obedience to government on one hand; nor out of our right to think and act for ourselves in our own department on the other. The steady management of a good government is the most anxious, arduous, and hazardous vocation on this side the grave. Let us not encumber those, therefore, who have spirit enough to embark in such an enterprise, with any kind of opposition that the preservation or perfection of our mild, our happy, our most excellent constitution, does not soberly demand.

But, on the other hand, as we know that ignorance, vanity, excessive ambition and venality, will, in spite of all human precautions, creep into government, and will ever be aspiring at extravagant and unconstitutional emoluments to individuals, let us never relax our attention, or our resolution, to keep these unhappy imperfections in human nature, out of which material, frail as it is, all our rulers must be compounded, under a strict inspection and a just control. We electors have an important constitutional power placed in our hands; we have a check upon two branches of the legislature, as each branch has upon the other two; the power I mean of electing, at stated periods, one branch, which branch has the power of electing another. It becomes necessary to every subject then, to be in some degree a statesman, and to examine and judge for himself of the tendency of political principles and measures. Let us examine, then, with a sober, a manly, a British, and a Christian spirit; let us neglect all party virulence and advert to facts; let us believe no man to be infallible or impeccable in government, any more than in religion; take no man's word against evidence, nor implicitly adopt the sentiments of others, who may be deceived themselves, or may be interested in deceiving us. u.

ON PRIVATE REVENGE. NO. III.

Impiger, iracundus, inexorabilis, acer,
Jura neget sibi nata, nihil non arroget armis.
Hor.
Rebuke the spearmen, and the troops
Of bulls that mighty be.
Novang.

to the printers. *Endnote 151*

It seems to be necessary for me, (notwithstanding the declaration in my last) once more to digress from the road of agriculture and mechanic arts, and to enter the list of disputation with a brace of writers in the Evening Post, one of whom has subscribed himself X, and the other W. I shall agree with the first of these gentlemen, that "to preach up non-resistance with the zeal of a fanatic," would be as extraordinary as to employ a bastile in support of the freedom of speech or the press, or an inquisition in favor of liberty of conscience; but if he will leave his own imagination, and recur to what I have written, he will not find a syllable against resistance. Resistance to sudden violence, for the preservation not only of my person, my limbs and life, but of my property, is an indisputable right of nature which I never surrendered to the public by the compact of society, and which, perhaps, I could not surrender if I would. Nor is there any thing in the common law of England, (for which Mr. X supposes I have so great a fondness,) inconsistent with that right. On the contrary, the dogmas of Plato, the maxims of the law, and the precepts of Christianity, are precisely coincident in relation to this subject.

Plato taught that revenge was unlawful, although he allowed of self-defence. The divine Author of our religion has taught us that trivial provocations are to be overlooked; and that if a man should offer you an insult, by boxing one ear, rather than indulge a furious passion and return blow for blow, you ought even to turn the other also. This expression, however, though it inculcates strongly the duty of moderation and self-government upon sudden provocations, imports nothing against the right of resistance or of self-defence. The sense of it seems to be no more than this: that little injuries and insults ought to be borne patiently for the present, rather than run the risk of violent consequences by retaliation.

Now, the common law seems to me to be founded on the same great principle of philosophy and religion. It will allow of nothing as a justification of blows, but blows; nor will it justify a furious beating, bruising, and wounding, upon the provocation of a fillip of the finger, or a kick upon the shins; but if I am assaulted, I can justify nothing but laying my hands lightly upon the aggressor for my own defence; nothing but what was absolutely necessary for my preservation. I may parry or ward off any blow; but a blow received is no sufficient provocation for fifty times so severe a blow in return. When life, which is one of the three favorites of the law, comes into consideration, we find a wise and humane provision is made for its preservation. If I am assaulted by another, sword in hand, and if I am even certain of his intention to murder me, the common law will not suffer me to defend myself, by killing him, if I can avoid it. Nay, my behavior must absolutely be what would be called cowardice, perhaps, by Mr. X and W, though it would be thought the truest bravery, not only by the greatest philosophers and legislators, but by the best generals of the world; I must run away from such an assailant, and avoid him if I have room, rather than stand my ground and defend myself; but if I have no room to escape, or if I run and am pursued to the wall or into a corner where I cannot elude his fury, and have no other way to preserve my own life from his violence, but by taking his there, I have an indisputable right to do it, and should be justified in wading through the blood of a whole army, if I had power to shed it and had no other way to make my escape.

What is said by Mr. W, that "if a gentleman should be hurried by his passions so far as to take the life of another, the common law will not adjudge it murder or manslaughter, but justifiable homicide only,"—by which he must mean, if in truth he had any meaning at all, that killing upon a sudden provocation is justifiable homicide,—is a position in comparison of which the observations of the grave-digger upon the death of the young lady, in Shakspeare's Hamlet, ought to be ranked among the responsa prudentium.

Every catechumen in law, nay, every common man, and even every porter upon the dock, that ever attended a trial for murder, knows that a sudden provocation raising a violent passion, where there is no precedent malice, is, in consideration of human frailty, allowed to soften killing from murder down to manslaughter; but manslaughter is a heinous crime, and subjected to heavy punishments.

Such is the wisdom and humanity of English law; upon so thorough a knowledge of human nature is it founded, and so well is it calculated to preserve the lives and limbs of men and the interior tranquillity of societies! I shall not dispute with Mr. X my affection for this law, in preference to all other systems of law that have ever appeared in the world. I have no connection with parishioners, nor patients, nor clients, nor any dependence upon either for business or bread; I study law as I do divinity and physic; and all of them as I do husbandry and mechanic arts, or the motions and revolutions of the heavenly bodies; or as I do magistracy and legislation; namely, as means and instruments of human happiness. It has been my amusement for many years past, as far as I have had leisure, to examine the systems of all the legislators, ancient and modern, fantastical and real, and to trace their effects in history upon the felicity of mankind; and the result of this long examination is a settled opinion that the liberty, the unalienable, indefeasible rights of men, the honor and dignity of human nature, the grandeur and glory of the public, and the universal happiness of individuals, were never so skilfully and successfully consulted as in that most excellent monument of human art, the common law of England; a law that maintains a great superiority, not only to every other system of laws, martial or canon, or civil and military, even to majesty itself; it has a never-sleeping jealousy of the canon law, which in many countries, Spain in particular, has subjected all officers and orders, civil and military, to the avarice and ambition, the caprice and cruelty of a clergy; and it is not less watchful over the martial law, which in many cases and in many countries, France in particular, is able to rescue men from the justice of the municipal laws of the kingdom; and I will own, that to revive in the minds of my countrymen a reverence for this law, and to prevent the growth of sentiments that seemed to me to be in their tendency destructive of it, especially to revive a jealousy of martial laws and cavalier-like tempers, was the turn which I designed to serve for myself and my friends in that piece which has given offence to X and W.

A certain set of sentiments have been lately so fashionable, that you could go into few companies without hearing such smart sayings as these,—"If a man should insult me, by kicking my shins, and I had a sword by my side I would make the sun shine through him;"—

"if any man, let him be as big as Goliah, should take me by the nose, I would let his bowels out with my sword, if I had one, and if I had none, I would beat his brains out with the first club I could find." And such tempers have been animated by some inadvertent expressions that have fallen from persons of higher rank and better sentiments. Some of these have been heard to say, that "should a man offer a sudden insult to them, they could not answer for themselves, but they should lay him prostrate at their feet in his own blood." Such expressions as these, which are to be supposed but modest expressions of the speaker's diffidence of his own presence of mind, and government of his passions, when suddenly assaulted, have been taken for a justification of such returns to an insult, and a determination to practise them upon occasion. But such persons as are watching the lips of others for wise speeches, in order to utter them afterwards as their own sentiments, have generally as little of understanding as they have of spirit, and most miserably spoil, in reporting, a good reflection. Now, what I have written upon this subject was intended to show the inhumanity of taking away the life of a man, only for pulling my nose or boxing my ear; and the folly of it too, because I should be guilty of a high crime, that of manslaughter at least, and forfeit all my goods, besides receiving a brand of infamy.

But I have not yet finished my history of sentiments. It has been said by others that "no man ought to receive a blow without returning it;" "a man ought to be despised that receives a cuff without giving another in return." This I have heard declared for a sober opinion by some men of figure and office and importance. But I beg leave to repeat it,—this is the tenet of a coxcomb and the sentiment of a brute; and the horse, the bull, and the cock, that I mentioned before, daily discover precisely the same temper and the same sense of honor and decency. If, in walking the streets of this town, I should be met by a negro, and that negro should lay me over the head with his cudgel, should I think myself bound in honor or regard to reputation to return the blow with another cudgel? to put myself on a level with that negro, and join with him in a competition which was most expert and skilful at cudgels? If a mad dog should meet me and bite me, should I think myself bound in honor, (I mean before the poison had worked upon me enough to make me as mad as the dog himself,) to fall upon that dog and bite him again? It is not possible for me to express that depth of contempt that I feel for such sentiments, and for every mortal that entertains them; and I should choose to be "the butt, the jest, and contempt" of all companies that entertain such opinions, rather than to be in their admiration or esteem. I would take some other way to preserve myself and other men from such insolence and violence for the future; but I would never place myself upon a level with such an animal for the present.

Far from aiming at a reputation for such qualities and accomplishments as those of boxing or cuffing, a man of sense would hold even the true martial qualities, courage, strength, and skill in war, in a much lower estimation than the attributes of wisdom and virtue, skill in arts and sciences, and a true taste to what is right, what is fit, what is true, generous, manly, and noble, in civil life. The competition between Ajax and Ulysses is well known.

> "Tu vires sine mente geris, mihi cura futuri,
> Tu pugnare potes:
> Tu tantum corpore prodes,
> Nos animo;
> Pectora sunt potiora manu.
> Vigor omnis in ills." *Endnote 152*

And we know in whose favor the prize was decreed.

I shall not be at the pains of remarking upon all the rodomontade in the two pieces under consideration, and Mr. X and Mr. W, and the whole alphabet of writers may scribble as many volumes as the twenty-four letters are capable of variations, without the least further notice from me, unless more reasoning and merit appear in proportion to the quantity of lines than is to be found in those two pieces. But since I have made some remarks upon them, it will, perhaps, before I conclude, be worth my while to mention one thing more in each. Mr. X tells us "that cases frequently occur where a man's person or reputation suffer to the greatest degree, and yet it is impossible for the law to make him any satisfaction."

This is not strictly true; such cases but seldom occur, though it must be confessed they sometimes do; but it seldom happens, very seldom indeed, where you know the man who has done you the injury, that you can get no satisfaction by law; and if such a case should happen, nothing can be clearer than that you ought to sit down and bear it; and for this plain reason, because it is necessary, and you cannot get satisfaction in any way. The law, by the supposition, cannot redress you; and you cannot, if you consider it, by any means redress yourself. A flagellation in the dark would be no reparation of the injury, no example to others, nor have any tendency to reform the subject of it, but rather a provocation to him to contrive some other way to injure you again; and of consequence would be no satisfaction at all to a man even of that false honor and delicacy of which I have been speaking, unless he will avow an appetite for mere revenge, which is not only worse than brutal, but the attribute of devils; and to take satisfaction by a flagellation in public would be only, in other words, taking a severe revenge upon yourself; for this would be a trespass and a violation of the peace, for which you would expose yourself to the resentment of the magistrate and the action of the party, and would be like running your sword through your own body to revenge yourself on another for boxing your ears; or like the behavior of the rattle-snake that will snap and leap and bite at every stick that you put near him, and at last when provoked beyond all honorable bearing, will fix his sharp and poisonous teeth into his own body.

I have nothing more to add, excepting one word of advice to Mr. W and all his readers, to have a care how they believe or practise his rule about "passion and killing," lest the halter and the gibbet should become their portion; for a killing that should happen by the hurry of passion would be much more likely to be adjudged murder than justifiable homicide only. Let me conclude, by advising all men to look into their own hearts, which they will find to be deceitful above all things and desperately wicked. Let them consider how extremely addicted they are to magnify and exaggerate the injuries that are offered to themselves, and to diminish and extenuate the wrongs that they offer to others. They ought, therefore, to be too modest and diffident of their own judgment, when their own passions and prejudices and interests are concerned, to desire to judge for themselves in their own causes, and to take their own satisfactions for wrongs and injuries of any kind. u.

A DISSERTATION ON THE CANON AND FEUDAL LAW.

The occasion of the production of this Dissertation, has already been explained in the Diary of the author. Endnote 153 It was printed in the month of August of the year 1765, in the Boston Gazette, there divided into four numbers, and without any title whatever. It attracted much attention in Massachusetts and in England, where it was attributed to Jeremy Gridley, then well known as at the head of the bar in the Colony. Thomas Hollis immediately procured it to be reprinted in the London Chronicle, and three years later, in 1768, caused it to be published by Almon, at the end of a small octavo volume, entitled "The True Sentiments of America," with the caption by which it has ever since been known. In this volume, it is ascribed to Mr. Gridley; but Mr. Hollis afterwards endeavored to correct his mistake by writing at the end of his copy these words: "This Dissertation on the Canon and Feudal Law was written by John Adams, Esq., a young gentleman of the law, who lately removed from the country to Boston. He has a large practice, and will probably be soon at the head of his profession." So great was the admiration it excited in him, that at another time, he made the following memorandum, which is found transcribed by Dr. Andrew Eliot, in his copy of the book, now in the possession of Mr. Everett.— Endnote 154

"The Dissertation on the Canon and Feudal Law is one of the very finest productions ever seen from North America.

"By a letter from Boston, in New England, signed Sui Juris, inserted in that valuable newspaper, the London Chronicle, July 19, it should seem the writer of it, happily, yet lives. T. H."

This Dissertation was reprinted in London, though without date of any kind, probably in the year 1782, and in Philadelphia, by Robert Bell, at the end of a tract upon another subject, in 1783.

It appears to merit consideration rather as a searching, analytical sketch, than as a complete performance. In the brief compass of a few pages are crowded thoughts sufficient to furnish as much material as is found in some thick quartos. But they are justly denominated by the author, hints for future inquiries, rather than a satisfactory theory. They should be weighed in connection with his remote position, the time of writing, and the general current of thought of even the educated society around him. By this only can the natural energy and expansion of the author's mind be estimated. Nor yet can it be said, that the reflections contained in the production were thrown off hastily and with little consideration. There is evidence to show that they were slowly and carefully matured and developed. It has already been mentioned, that the first draught is found incorporated in the writer's Diary for the month of February, 1765. But no publication took place until July and August; the result then discloses the extent of the changes, enlargements, and improvements, which the work had in the interval undergone. As not infrequently happens, however, in this process, one strong passage was lost by it, which at this time must be regarded as the most deserving of any to be remembered. This will be found appended as a note to the place where it belonged.

"Ignorance and inconsideration are the two great causes of the ruin of mankind." This is an observation of Dr. Tillotson, with relation to the interest of his fellow men in a future and immortal state. But it is of equal truth and importance if applied to the happiness of men in society, on this side the grave. In the earliest ages of the world, absolute monarchy seems to have been the universal form of government. Kings, and a few of their great counsellors and captains, exercised a cruel tyranny over the people, who held a rank in the scale of intelligence, in those days, but little higher than the camels and elephants that carried them and their engines to war.

By what causes it was brought to pass, that the people in the middle ages became more intelligent in general, would not, perhaps, be possible in these days to discover. But the fact is certain; and wherever a general knowledge and sensibility have prevailed among the people, arbitrary government and every kind of oppression have lessened and disappeared in proportion. Man has certainly an exalted soul; and the same principle in human nature,—that aspiring, noble principle founded in benevolence, and cherished by knowledge; I mean the love of power, which has been so often the cause of slavery,—has, whenever freedom has existed, been the cause of freedom. If it is this principle that has always prompted the princes and nobles of the earth, by every species of fraud and violence to shake off all the limitations of their power, it is the same that has always stimulated the common people to aspire at independency, and to endeavor at confining the power of the great within the limits of equity and reason.

The poor people, it is true, have been much less successful than the great. They have seldom found either leisure or opportunity to form a union and exert their strength; ignorant as they were of arts and letters, they have seldom been able to frame and support a regular opposition. This, however, has been known by the great to be the temper of mankind; and they have accordingly labored, in all ages, to wrest from the populace, as they are contemptuously called, the knowledge of their rights and wrongs, and the power to assert the former or redress the latter. I say rights, for such they have, undoubtedly, antecedent to all earthly government,—Rights, that cannot be repealed or restrained by human laws—Rights, derived from the great Legislator of the universe.

Since the promulgation of Christianity, the two greatest systems of tyranny that have sprung from this original, are the canon and the feudal law. The desire of dominion, that great principle by which we have attempted to account for so much good and so much evil, is, when properly restrained, a very useful and noble movement in the human mind. But when such restraints are taken off, it becomes an encroaching, grasping, restless, and ungovernable power. Numberless have been the systems of iniquity contrived by the great for the gratification of this passion in themselves; but in none of them were they ever more successful than in the invention and establishment of the canon and the feudal law.

By the former of these, the most refined, sublime, extensive, and astonishing constitution of policy that ever was conceived by the mind of man was framed by the Romish clergy for the aggrandisement of their own order. Endnote 155 All the epithets I have here given to the Romish policy are just, and will be allowed to be so when it is considered, that they even persuaded mankind to believe, faithfully and undoubtingly, that God Almighty had entrusted them with the keys of heaven, whose gates they might open and close at pleasure; with a power of dispensation over all the rules and obligations of morality; with authority to license all sorts of sins and crimes; with a power of deposing princes and absolving subjects from allegiance; with a power of procuring or withholding the rain of heaven and the beams of the sun; with the management of earthquakes, pestilence, and famine; nay, with the mysterious, awful, incomprehensible power of creating out of bread and wine the flesh and blood of God himself. All these opinions they were enabled to spread and rivet among the people by reducing their minds to a state of sordid ignorance and staring timidity, and by infusing into them a religious horror of letters and knowledge. Thus was human nature chained fast for ages in a cruel, shameful, and deplorable servitude to him, and his subordinate tyrants, who, it was foretold, would exalt himself above all that was called God, and that was worshipped.

In the latter we find another system, similar in many respects to the former; Endnote 156 which, although it was originally formed, perhaps, for the necessary defence of a barbarous people against the inroads and invasions of her neighboring nations, yet for the same purposes of tyranny, cruelty, and lust, which had dictated the canon law, it was soon adopted by almost all the princes of Europe, and wrought into the constitutions of their government. It was originally a code of laws for a vast army in a perpetual encampment. The general was invested with the sovereign propriety of all the lands within the territory. Of him, as his servants and vassals, the first rank of his great officers held the lands; and in the same manner the other subordinate officers held of them; and all ranks and degrees held their lands by a variety of duties and services, all tending to bind the chains the faster on every order of mankind. In this manner the common people were held together in herds and clans in a state of servile dependence on their lords, bound, even by the tenure of their lands, to follow them, whenever they commanded, to their wars, and in a state of total ignorance of every thing divine and human, excepting the use of arms and the culture of their lands.

But another event still more calamitous to human liberty, was a wicked confederacy between the two systems of tyranny above described. It seems to have been even stipulated between them, that the temporal grandees should contribute every thing in their power to maintain the ascendency of the priesthood, and that the spiritual grandees in their turn, should employ their ascendency over the consciences of the people, in impressing on their minds a blind, implicit obedience to civil magistracy.

Thus, as long as this confederacy lasted, and the people were held in ignorance, liberty, and with her, knowledge and virtue too, seem to have deserted the earth, and one age of darkness succeeded another, till God in his benign providence raised up the champions who began and conducted the Reformation. From the time of the Reformation to the first settlement of America, knowledge gradually spread in Europe, but especially in England; and in proportion as that increased and spread among the people, ecclesiastical and civil tyranny, which I use as synonymous expressions for the canon and feudal laws, seem to have lost their strength and weight. The people grew more and more sensible of the wrong that was done them by these systems, more and more impatient under it, and determined at all hazards to rid themselves of it; till at last, under the execrable race of the Stuarts, the struggle between the people and the confederacy aforesaid of temporal and spiritual tyranny, became formidable, violent, and bloody.

It was this great struggle that peopled America. It was not religion alone, as is commonly supposed; but it was a love of universal liberty, and a hatred, a dread, a horror, of the infernal confederacy before described, that projected, conducted, and accomplished the settlement of America.

It was a resolution formed by a sensible people,—I mean the Puritans,—almost in despair. They had become intelligent in general, and many of them learned. For this fact, I have the testimony of Archbishop King himself, who observed of that people, that they were more intelligent and better read than even the members of the church, whom he censures warmly for that reason. This people had been so vexed and tortured by the powers of those days, for no other crime than their knowledge and their freedom of inquiry and examination, and they had so much reason to despair of deliverance from those miseries on that side the ocean, that they at last resolved to fly to the wilderness for refuge from the temporal and spiritual principalities and powers, and plagues and scourges of their native country.

After their arrival here, they began their settlement, and formed their plan, both of ecclesiastical and civil government, in direct opposition to the canon and the feudal systems. The leading men among them, both of the clergy and the laity, were men of sense and learning. To many of them the historians, orators, poets, and philosophers of Greece and Rome were quite familiar; and some of them have left libraries that are still in being, consisting chiefly of volumes in which the wisdom of the most enlightened ages and nations is deposited,—written, however, in languages which their great-grandsons, though educated in European universities, can scarcely read. *Endnote 157*

Thus accomplished were many of the first planters in these colonies. It may be thought polite and fashionable by many modern fine gentlemen, perhaps, to deride the characters of these persons, as enthusiastical, superstitious, and republican. But such ridicule is founded in nothing but foppery and affectation, and is grossly injurious and false. Religious to some degree of enthusiasm it may be admitted they were; but this can be no peculiar derogation from their character; because it was at that time almost the universal character not only of England, but of Christendom. Had this, however, been otherwise, their enthusiasm, considering the principles on which it was founded and the ends to which it was directed, far from being a reproach to them, was greatly to their honor; for I believe it will be found universally true, that no great enterprise for the honor or happiness of mankind was ever achieved without a large mixture of that noble infirmity. Whatever imperfections may be justly ascribed to them, which, however, are as few as any mortals have discovered, their judgment in framing their policy was founded in wise, humane, and benevolent principles. It was founded in revelation and in reason too. It was consistent with the principles of the best and greatest and wisest legislators of antiquity. Tyranny in every form, shape, and appearance was their disdain and abhorrence; no fear of punishment, nor even of death itself in exquisite tortures, had been sufficient to conquer that steady, manly, pertinacious spirit with which they had opposed the tyrants of those days in church and state. They were very far from being enemies to monarchy; and they knew as well as any men, the just regard and honor that is due to the character of a dispenser of the mysteries of the gospel of grace. But they saw clearly, that popular powers must be placed as a guard, a control, a balance, to the powers of the monarch and the priest, in every government, or else it would soon become the man of sin, the whore of Babylon, the mystery of iniquity, a great and detestable system of fraud, violence, and usurpation. Their greatest concern seems to have been to establish a government of the church more consistent with the Scriptures, and a government of the state more agreeable to the dignity of human nature, than any they had seen in Europe, and to transmit such a government down to their posterity, with the means of securing and preserving it forever. To render the popular power in their new government as great and wise as their principles of theory, that is, as human nature and the Christian religion require it should be, they endeavored to remove from it as many of the feudal inequalities and dependencies as could be spared, consistently with the preservation of a mild limited monarchy. And in this they discovered the depth of their wisdom and the warmth of their friendship to human nature. But the first place is due to religion. They saw clearly, that of all the nonsense and delusion which had ever passed through the mind of man, none had ever been more extravagant than the notions of absolutions, indelible characters, uninterrupted successions, and the rest of those fantastical ideas, derived from the canon law, which had thrown such a glare of mystery, sanctity, reverence, and right reverend eminence and holiness, around the idea of a priest, as no mortal could deserve, and as always must, from the constitution of human nature, be dangerous in society. For this reason, they demolished the whole system of diocesan episcopacy; and, deriding, as all reasonable and impartial men must do, the ridiculous fancies of sanctified effluvia from episcopal fingers, they established sacerdotal ordination on the foundation of the Bible and common sense. This conduct at once imposed an obligation on the whole body of the clergy to industry, virtue, piety, and learning, and rendered that whole body infinitely more independent on the civil powers, in all respects, than they could be where they were formed into a scale of subordination, from a pope down to priests and friars and confessors,—necessarily and essentially a sordid, stupid, and wretched herd,—or than they could be in any other country, where an archbishop held the place of a universal bishop, and the vicars and curates that of the ignorant, dependent, miserable rabble aforesaid,—and infinitely more sensible and learned than they could be in either. This subject has been seen in the same light by many illustrious patriots, who have lived in America since the days of our forefathers, and who have adored their memory for the same reason. And methinks there has not appeared in New England a stronger veneration for their memory, a more penetrating insight into the grounds and principles and spirit of their policy, nor a more earnest desire of perpetuating the blessings of it to posterity, than that fine institution of the late Chief Justice Dudley, of a lecture against popery, and on the validity of presbyterian ordination. This was certainly intended by that wise and excellent man, as an eternal memento of the wisdom and goodness of the very principles that settled America. But I must again return to the feudal law. The adventurers so often mentioned, had an utter contempt of all that dark ribaldry of hereditary, indefeasible right,—the Lord's anointed,—and the divine, miraculous original of government, with which the priesthood had enveloped the feudal monarch in clouds and mysteries, and from whence they had deduced the most mischievous of all doctrines, that of passive obedience and non-resistance. They knew that government was a plain, simple, intelligible thing, founded in nature and reason, and quite comprehensible by common sense. They detested all the base services and servile dependencies of the feudal system. They knew that no such unworthy dependencies took place in the ancient seats of liberty, the republics of Greece and Rome; and they thought all such slavish subordinations were equally inconsistent with the constitution of human nature and that religious liberty with which Jesus had made them free. This was certainly the opinion they had formed; and they were far from being singular or extravagant in thinking so. Many celebrated modern writers in Europe have espoused the same sentiments. Lord Kames, a Scottish writer of great reputation, whose authority in this case ought to have the more weight as his countrymen have not the most worthy ideas of liberty, speaking of the feudal law, says,—"A constitution so contradictory to all the principles which govern mankind can never be brought about, one should imagine, but by foreign conquest or native usurpations." *Endnote 158* Rousseau, speaking of the same system, calls it,—"That most iniquitous and absurd form of government by which human nature was so shamefully degraded." *Endnote 159* It would be easy to multiply authorities, but it must be needless; because, as the original of this form of government was among savages, as the spirit of it is military and despotic, every writer who would allow the people to have any right to life or property or freedom more than the beasts of the field, and who was not hired or enlisted under arbitrary, lawless power, has been always willing to admit the feudal system to be inconsistent with liberty and the rights of mankind.

To have holden their lands allodially, or for every man to have been the sovereign lord and proprietor of the ground he occupied, would have constituted a government too nearly like a commonwealth. They were contented, therefore, to hold their lands of their king, as their sovereign lord; and to him they were willing to render homage, but to no mesne or subordinate lords; nor were they willing to submit to any of the baser services. In all this they were so strenuous, that they have even transmitted to their posterity a very general contempt and detestation of holdings by quitrents, as they have also a hereditary ardor for liberty and thirst for knowledge.

They were convinced, by their knowledge of human nature, derived from history and their own experience, that nothing could preserve their posterity from the encroachments of the two systems of tyranny, in opposition to which, as has been observed already, they erected their government in church and state, but knowledge diffused generally through the whole body of the people. Their civil and religious principles, therefore, conspired to prompt them to use every measure and take every precaution in their power to propagate and perpetuate knowledge. For this purpose they laid very early the foundations of colleges, and invested them with ample privileges and emoluments; and it is remarkable that they have left among their posterity so universal an affection and veneration for those seminaries, and for liberal education, that the meanest of the people contribute cheerfully to the support and maintenance of them every year, and that nothing is more generally popular than projections for the honor, reputation, and advantage of those seats of learning. But the wisdom and benevolence of our fathers rested not here. They made an early provision by law, that every town consisting of so many families, should be always furnished with a grammar school. They made it a crime for such a town to be destitute of a grammar schoolmaster for a few months, and subjected it to a heavy penalty. So that the education of all ranks of people was made the care and expense of the public, in a manner that I believe has been unknown to any other people ancient or modern.

The consequences of these establishments we see and feel every day. A native of America who cannot read and write is as rare an appearance as a Jacobite or a Roman Catholic, that is, as rare as a comet or an earthquake. It has been observed, that we are all of us lawyers, divines, politicians, and philosophers. And I have good authorities to say, that all candid foreigners who have passed through this country, and conversed freely with all sorts of people here, will allow, that they have never seen so much knowledge and civility among the common people in any part of the world. It is true, there has been among us a party for some years, consisting chiefly not of the descendants of the first settlers of this country, but of high churchmen and high statesmen imported since, who affect to censure this provision for the education of our youth as a needless expense, and an imposition upon the rich in favor of the poor, and as an institution productive of idleness and vain speculation among the people, whose time and attention, it is said, ought to be devoted to labor, and not to public affairs, or to examination into the conduct of their superiors. And certain officers of the crown, and certain other missionaries of ignorance, foppery, servility, and slavery, have been most inclined to countenance and increase the same party. Be it remembered, however, that liberty must at all hazards be supported. We have a right to it, derived from our Maker. But if we had not, our fathers have earned and bought it for us, at the expense of their ease, their estates, their pleasure, and their blood. And liberty cannot be preserved without a general knowledge among the people, who have a right, from the frame of their nature, to knowledge, as their great Creator, who does nothing in vain, has given them understandings, and a desire to know; but besides this, they have a right, an indisputable, unalienable, indefeasible, divine right to that most dreaded and envied kind of knowledge, I mean, of the characters and conduct of their rulers. Rulers are no more than attorneys, agents, and trustees, for the people; and if the cause, the interest and trust, is insidiously betrayed, or wantonly trifled away, the people have a right to revoke the authority that they themselves have deputed, and to constitute abler and better agents, attorneys, and trustees. And the preservation of the means of knowledge among the lowest ranks, is of more importance to the public than all the property of all the rich men in the country. It is even of more consequence to the rich themselves, and to their posterity. The only question is, whether it is a public emolument; and if it is, the rich ought undoubtedly to contribute, in the same proportion as to all other public burdens,—that is, in proportion to their wealth, which is secured by public expenses. But none of the means of information are more sacred, or have been cherished with more tenderness and care by the settlers of America, than the press. Care has been taken that the art of printing should be encouraged, and that it should be easy and cheap and safe for any person to communicate his thoughts to the public. And you, Messieurs printers, [*Endnote 160*] whatever the tyrants of the earth may say of your paper, have done important service to your country by your readiness and freedom in publishing the speculations of the curious. The stale, impudent insinuations of slander and sedition, with which the gormandizers of power have endeavored to discredit your paper, are so much the more to your honor; for the jaws of power are always opened to devour, and her arm is always stretched out, if possible, to destroy the freedom of thinking, speaking, and writing. And if the public interest, liberty, and happiness have been in danger from the ambition or avarice of any great man, whatever may be his politeness, address, learning, ingenuity, and, in other respects, integrity and humanity, you have done yourselves honor and your country service by publishing and pointing out that avarice and ambition. These vices are so much the more dangerous and pernicious for the virtues with which they may be accompanied in the same character, and with so much the more watchful jealousy to be guarded against.

"Curse on such virtues, they've undone their country."

Be not intimidated, therefore, by any terrors, from publishing with the utmost freedom, whatever can be warranted by the laws of your country; nor suffer yourselves to be wheedled out of your liberty by any pretences of politeness, delicacy, or decency. These, as they are often used, are but three different names for hypocrisy, chicanery, and cowardice. Much less, I presume, will you be discouraged by any pretences that malignants on this side the water will represent your paper as factious and seditious, or that the great on the other side the water will take offence at them. This dread of representation has had for a long time, in this province, effects very similar to what the physicians call a hydropho, or dread of water. It has made us delirious; and we have rushed headlong into the water, till we are almost drowned, out of simple or phrensical fear of it. Believe me, the character of this country has suffered more in Britain by the pusillanimity with which we have borne many insults and indignities from the creatures of power at home and the creatures of those creatures here, than it ever did or ever will by the freedom and spirit that has been or will be discovered in writing or action. Believe me, my countrymen, they have imbibed an opinion on the other side the water, that we are an ignorant, a timid, and a stupid people; nay, their tools on this side have often the impudence to dispute your bravery. But I hope in God the time is near at hand when they will be fully convinced of your understanding, integrity, and courage. But can any thing be more ridiculous, were it not too provoking to be laughed at, than to pretend that offence should be taken at home for writings here? Pray, let them look at home. Is not the human understanding exhausted there? Are not reason, imagination, wit, passion, senses, and all, tortured to find out satire and invective against the characters of the vile and futile fellows who sometimes get into place and power? The most exceptionable paper that ever I saw here is perfect prudence and modesty in comparison of multitudes of their applauded writings. Yet the high regard they have for the freedom of the press, indulges all. I must and will repeat it, your paper deserves the patronage of every friend to his country. And whether the defamers of it are arrayed in robes of scarlet or sable, whether they lurk and skulk in an insurance office, whether they assume the venerable character of a priest, the sly one of a scrivener, or the dirty, infamous, abandoned one of an informer, they are all the creatures and tools of the lust of domination.

The true source of our sufferings has been our timidity.

We have been afraid to think. We have felt a reluctance to examining into the grounds of our privileges, and the extent in which we have an indisputable right to demand them, against all the power and authority on earth. And many who have not scrupled to examine for themselves, have yet for certain prudent reasons been cautious and diffident of declaring the result of their inquiries.

The cause of this timidity is perhaps hereditary, and to be traced back in history as far as the cruel treatment the first settlers of this country received, before their embarkation for America, from the government at home. Everybody knows how dangerous it was to speak or write in favor of any thing, in those days, but the triumphant system of religion and politics. And our fathers were particularly the objects of the persecutions and proscriptions of the times. It is not unlikely, therefore, that although they were inflexibly steady in refusing their positive assent to any thing against their principles, they might have contracted habits of reserve, and a cautious diffidence of asserting their opinions publicly. These habits they probably brought with them to America, and have transmitted down to us. Or we may possibly account for this appearance by the great affection and veneration Americans have always entertained for the country from whence they sprang; or by the quiet temper for which they have been remarkable, no country having been less disposed to discontent than this; or by a sense they have that it is their duty to acquiesce under the administration of government, even when in many smaller matters grievous to them, and until the essentials of the great compact are destroyed or invaded. These peculiar causes might operate upon them; but without these, we all know that human nature itself, from indolence, modesty, humanity, or fear, has always too much reluctance to a manly assertion of its rights. Hence, perhaps, it has happened, that nine tenths of the species are groaning and gasping in misery and servitude.

But whatever the cause has been, the fact is certain, we have been excessively cautious of giving offence by complaining of grievances. And it is as certain, that American governors, and their friends, and all the crown officers, have availed themselves of this disposition in the people. They have prevailed on us to consent to many things which were grossly injurious to us, and to surrender many others, with voluntary tameness, to which we had the clearest right. Have we not been treated, formerly, with abominable insolence, by officers of the navy? I mean no insinuation against any gentleman now on this station, having heard no complaint of any one of them to his dishonor. Have not some generals from England treated us like servants, nay, more like slaves than like Britons? Have we not been under the most ignominious contribution, the most abject submission, the most supercilious insults, of some custom-house officers? Have we not been trifled with, brow-beaten, and trampled on, by former governors, in a manner which no king of England since James the Second has dared to indulge towards his subjects? Have we not raised up one family, in them placed an unlimited confidence, and been soothed and flattered and intimidated by their influence, into a great part of this infamous tameness and submission? "These are serious and alarming questions, and deserve a dispassionate consideration."

This disposition has been the great wheel and the mainspring in the American machine of court politics. We have been told that "the word rights is an offensive expression;" "that the king, his ministry, and parliament, will not endure to hear Americans talk of their rights;" "that Britain is the mother and we the children, that a filial duty and submission is due from us to her," and that "we ought to doubt our own judgment, and presume that she is right, even when she seems to us to shake the foundations of government;" that "Britain is immensely rich and great and powerful, has fleets and armies at her command which have been the dread and terror of the universe, and that she will force her own judgment into execution, right or wrong." But let me entreat you, sir, to pause. Do you consider yourself as a missionary of loyalty or of rebellion? Are you not representing your king, his ministry, and parliament, as tyrants,—imperious, unrelenting tyrants,—by such reasoning as this? Is not this representing your most gracious sovereign as endeavoring to destroy the foundations of his own throne? Are you not representing every member of parliament as renouncing the transactions at Runing Mede, (the meadow, near Windsor, where Magna Charta was signed;) and as repealing in effect the bill of rights, when the Lords and Commons asserted and vindicated the rights of the people and their own rights, and insisted on the king's assent to that assertion and vindication? Do you not represent them as forgetting that the prince of Orange was created King William, by the people, on purpose that their rights might be eternal and inviolable? Is there not something extremely fallacious in the common-place images of mother country and children colonies? Are we the children of Great Britain any more than the cities of London, Exeter, and Bath? Are we not brethren and fellow subjects with those in Britain, only under a somewhat different method of legislation, and a totally different method of taxation? But admitting we are children, have not children a right to complain when their parents are attempting to break their limbs, to administer poison, or to sell them to enemies for slaves? Let me entreat you to consider, will the mother be pleased when you represent her as deaf to the cries of her children,—when you compare her to the infamous miscreant who lately stood on the gallows for starving her child,—when you resemble her to Lady Macbeth in Shakspeare, (I cannot think of it without horror,) who

"Had given suck, and knew
How tender 't was to love the babe that milked her,"

but yet, who could

"Even while 't was smiling in her face,
Have plucked her nipple from the boneless gums,
And dashed the brains out."

Let us banish for ever from our minds, my countrymen, all such unworthy ideas of the king, his ministry, and parliament. Let us not suppose that all are become luxurious, effeminate, and unreasonable, on the other side the water, as many designing persons would insinuate. Let us presume, what is in fact true, that the spirit of liberty is as ardent as ever among the body of the nation, though a few individuals may be corrupted. Let us take it for granted, that the same great spirit which once gave Cæsar so warm a reception, which denounced hostilities against John till Magna Charta was signed, which severed the head of Charles the First from his body, and drove James the Second from his kingdom, the same great spirit (may heaven preserve it till the earth shall be no more) which first seated the great grandfather of his present most gracious majesty on the throne of Britain,—is still alive and active and warm in England; and that the same spirit in America, instead of provoking the inhabitants of that country, will endear us to them for ever, and secure their good-will.

This spirit, however, without knowledge, would be little better than a brutal rage. Let us tenderly and kindly cherish, therefore, the means of knowledge. Let us dare to read, think, speak, and write. Let every order and degree among the people rouse their attention and animate their resolution. Let them all become attentive to the grounds and principles of government, ecclesiastical and civil. Let us study the law of nature; search into the spirit of the British constitution; read the histories of ancient ages; contemplate the great examples of Greece and Rome; set before us the conduct of our own British ancestors, who have defended for us the inherent rights of mankind against foreign and domestic tyrants and usurpers, against arbitrary kings and cruel priests, in short, against the gates of earth and hell. Let us read and recollect and impress upon our souls the views and ends of our own more immediate forefathers, in exchanging their native country for a dreary, inhospitable wilderness. Let us examine into the nature of that power, and the cruelty of that oppression, which drove them from their homes. Recollect their amazing fortitude, their bitter sufferings,—the hunger, the nakedness, the cold, which they patiently endured,—the severe labors of clearing their grounds, building their houses, raising their provisions, amidst dangers from wild beasts and savage men, before they had time or money or materials for commerce. Recollect the civil and religious principles and hopes and expectations which constantly supported and carried them through all hardships with patience and resignation. Let us recollect it was liberty, the hope of liberty for themselves and us and ours, which conquered all discouragements, dangers, and trials. In such researches as these, let us all in our several departments cheerfully engage,—but especially the proper patrons and supporters of law, learning, and religion!

Let the pulpit resound with the doctrines and sentiments of religious liberty. Let us hear the danger of thraldom to our consciences from ignorance, extreme poverty, and dependence, in short, from civil and political slavery. Let us see delineated before us the true map of man. Let us hear the dignity of his nature, and the noble rank he holds among the works of God,—that consenting to slavery is a sacrilegious breach of trust, as offensive in the sight of God as it is derogatory from our own honor or interest or happiness,—and that God Almighty has promulgated from heaven, liberty, peace, and good-will to man!

Let the bar proclaim, "the laws, the rights, the generous plan of power" delivered down from remote antiquity,—inform the world of the mighty struggles and numberless sacrifices made by our ancestors in defence of freedom. Let it be known, that British liberties are not the grants of princes or parliaments, but original rights, conditions of original contracts, coequal with prerogative, and coeval with government; that many of our rights are inherent and essential, agreed on as maxims, and established as preliminaries, even before a parliament existed. Let them search for the foundations of British laws and government in the frame of human nature, in the constitution of the intellectual and moral world. There let us see that truth, liberty, justice, and benevolence, are its everlasting basis; and if these could be removed, the superstructure is overthrown of course.

Let the colleges join their harmony in the same delightful concert. Let every declamation turn upon the beauty of liberty and virtue, and the deformity, turpitude, and malignity, of slavery and vice. Let the public disputations become researches into the grounds and nature and ends of government, and the means of preserving the good and demolishing the evil. Let the dialogues, and all the exercises, become the instruments of impressing on the tender mind, and of spreading and distributing far and wide, the ideas of right and the sensations of freedom.

In a word, let every sluice of knowledge be opened and set a-flowing. The encroachments upon liberty in the reigns of the first James and the first Charles, by turning the general attention of learned men to government, are said to have produced the greatest number of consummate statesmen which has ever been seen in any age or nation. The Brookes, Hampdens, Vanes, Seldens, Miltons, Nedhams, Harringtons, Nevilles, Sidneys, Lockes, are all said to have owed their eminence in political knowledge to the tyrannies of those reigns. The prospect now before us in America, ought in the same manner to engage the attention of every man of learning, to matters of power and of right, that we may be neither led nor driven blindfolded to irretrievable destruction. Nothing less than this seems to have been meditated for us, by somebody or other in Great Britain. There seems to be a direct and formal design on foot, to enslave all America. This, however, must be done by degrees. The first step that is intended, seems to be an entire subversion of the whole system of our fathers, by the introduction of the canon and feudal law into America. The canon and feudal systems, though greatly mutilated in England, are not yet destroyed. Like the temples and palaces in which the great contrivers of them once worshipped and inhabited, they exist in ruins; and much of the domineering spirit of them still remains. The designs and labors of a certain society, to introduce the former of them into America, have been well exposed to the public by a writer of great abilities; [Endnote 161] and the further attempts to the same purpose, that may be made by that society, or by the ministry or parliament, I leave to the conjectures of the thoughtful. But it seems very manifest from the Stamp Act itself, that a design is formed to strip us in a great measure of the means of knowledge, by loading the press, the colleges, and even an almanack and a newspaper, with restraints and duties; and to introduce the inequalities and dependencies of the feudal system, by taking from the poorer sort of people all their little subsistence, and conferring it on a set of stamp officers, distributors, and their deputies. But I must proceed no further at present. The sequel, whenever I shall find health and leisure to pursue it, will be a "disquisition of the policy of the stamp act." In the mean time, however, let me add,—These are not the vapors of a melancholy mind, nor the effusions of envy, disappointed ambition, nor of a spirit of opposition to government, but the emanations of a heart that burns for its country's welfare. No one of any feeling, born and educated in this once happy country, can consider the numerous distresses, the gross indignities, the barbarous ignorance, the haughty usurpations, that we have reason to fear are meditating for ourselves, our children, our neighbors, in short, for all our countrymen and all their posterity, without the utmost agonies of heart and many tears.

INSTRUCTIONS OF THE TOWN OF BRAINTREE TO THEIR REPRESENTATIVE, 1765.

An account of the author's agency in the proceedings which led to the instructions here given, is to be found in the second volume, page 153.

Boston,

14 October. Endnote 162

We hear from Braintree, that the freeholders and other inhabitants of that town, legally assembled, on Tuesday, the twenty-fourth of September last, unanimously voted, that instructions should be given their representative for his conduct in General Assembly on this great occasion. The substance of these instructions is as follows:—

John Adams

TO EBENEZER THAYER, ESQ.

Sir,—

In all the calamities which have ever befallen this country, we have never felt so great a concern, or such alarming apprehensions, as on this occasion. Such is our loyalty to the King, our veneration for both houses of Parliament, and our affection for all our fellow-subjects in Britain, that measures which discover any unkindness in that country towards us are the more sensibly and intimately felt. And we can no longer forbear complaining, that many of the measures of the late ministry, and some of the late acts of Parliament, have a tendency, in our apprehension, to divest us of our most essential rights and liberties. We shall confine ourselves, however, chiefly to the act of Parliament, commonly called the Stamp Act, by which a very burthensome, and, in our opinion, unconstitutional tax, is to be laid upon us all; and we subjected to numerous and enormous penalties, to be prosecuted, sued for, and recovered, at the option of an informer, in a court of admiralty, without a jury.

We have called this a burthensome tax, because the duties are so numerous and so high, and the embarrassments to business in this infant, sparsely-settled country so great, that it would be totally impossible for the people to subsist under it, if we had no controversy at all about the right and authority of imposing it. Considering the present scarcity of money, we have reason to think, the execution of that act for a short space of time would drain the country of its cash, strip multitudes of all their property, and reduce them to absolute beggary. And what the consequence would be to the peace of the province, from so sudden a shock and such a convulsive change in the whole course of our business and subsistence, we tremble to consider. We further apprehend this tax to be unconstitutional. We have always understood it to be a grand and fundamental principle of the constitution, that no freeman should be subject to any tax to which he has not given his own consent, in person or by provy. And the maxims of the law, as we have constantly received them, are to the same effect, that no freeman can be separated from his property but by his own act or fault. We take it clearly, therefore, to be inconsistent with the spirit of the common law, and of the essential fundamental principles of the British constitution, that we should be subject to any tax imposed by the British Parliament; because we are not represented in that assembly in any sense, unless it be by a fiction of law, as insensible in theory as it would be injurious in practice, if such a taxation should be grounded on it.

But the most grievous innovation of all, is the alarming extension of the power of courts of admiralty. In these courts, one judge presides alone! No juries have any concern there! The law and the fact are both to be decided by the same single judge, whose commission is only during pleasure, and with whom, as we are told, the most mischievous of all customs has become established, that of taking commissions on all condemnations; so that he is under a pecuniary temptation always against the subject. Now, if the wisdom of the mother country has thought the independency of the judges so essential to an impartial administration of justice, as to render them independent of every power on earth,—independent of the King, the Lords, the Commons, the people, nay, independent in hope and expectation of the heir-apparent, by continuing their commissions after a demise of the crown, what justice and impartiality are we, at three thousand miles distance from the fountain, to expect from such a judge of admiralty? We have all along thought the acts of trade in this respect a grievance; but the Stamp Act has opened a vast number of sources of new crimes, which may be committed by any man, and cannot but be committed by multitudes, and prodigious penalties are annexed, and all these are to be tried by such a judge of such a court! What can be wanting, after this, but a weak or wicked man for a judge, to render us the most sordid and forlorn of slaves?—we mean the slaves of a slave of the servants of a minister of state. We cannot help asserting, therefore, that this part of the act will make an essential change in the constitution of juries, and it is directly repugnant to the Great Charter itself; for, by that charter, "no amerciament shall be assessed, but by the oath of honest and lawful men of the vicinage;" and, "no freeman shall be taken, or imprisoned, or disseized of his freehold, or liberties of free customs, nor passed upon, nor condemned, but by lawful judgment of his peers, or by the law of the land." So that this act will "make such a distinction, and create such a difference between" the subjects in Great Britain and those in America, as we could not have expected from the guardians of liberty in "both."

As these, sir, are our sentiments of this act, we, the freeholders and other inhabitants, legally assembled for this purpose, must enjoin it upon you, to comply with no measures or proposals for countenancing the same, or assisting in the execution of it, but by all lawful means, consistent with our allegiance to the King, and relation to Great Britain, to oppose the execution of it, till we can hear the success of the cries and petitions of America for relief.

We further recommend the most clear and explicit assertion and vindication of our rights and liberties to be entered on the public records, that the world may know, in the present and all future generations, that we have a clear knowledge and a just sense of them, and, with submission to Divine Providence, that we never can be slaves. Endnote 163

Nor can we think it advisable to agree to any steps for the protection of stamped papers or stamp-officers. Good and wholesome laws we have already for the preservation of the peace; and we apprehend there is no further danger of tumult and disorder, to which we have a well-grounded aversion; and that any extraordinary and expensive exertions would tend to exasperate the people and endanger the public tranquillity, rather than the contrary. Indeed, we cannot too often inculcate upon you our desires, that all extraordinary grants and expensive measures may, upon all occasions, as much as possible, be avoided. The public money of this country is the toil and labor of the people, who are under many uncommon difficulties and distresses at this time, so that all reasonable frugality ought to be observed.

And we would recommend particularly, the strictest care and the utmost firmness to prevent all unconstitutional draughts upon the public treasury.

THE EARL OF CLARENDON TO WILLIAM PYM.

On the 20th of August, 1765, there appeared in the London Evening Post an article, under the somewhat singularly-chosen signature of Pym, the purport of which seems to have been to avow to the people of the Colonies a settled design in Great Britain to overthrow whatever they had been in the habit of regarding as safeguards to their liberties. The writer of this article is not known; but his style, which is clear and forcible, indicates confidence and connection with the sources of power. The drift of his argument may be gathered from the statement of his position in these words: "Let me inform my fellow-subjects in America, that a resolution of the British Parliament can at any time set aside all the charters that have ever been granted by our monarchs." Starting in this manner, it is not surprising his consequences should be, that the rights of the colonists were wholly at the mercy of Great Britain.

This article was deemed of such importance as to gain immediate admittance into the columns of the Boston Evening Post, in which it appeared on the 25th of November following. It at once roused a host of writers on the Colonial side, among whom the most conspicuous were James Otis, as Hampden, and John Adams, as Clarendon. However singular the assumption of this last title may appear in the latter, his letters clearly show how much he had studied the character of the man to whom the name had belonged, and of the age in which he lived.

Clarendon

William Pym

THE EARL OF CLARENDON TO WILLIAM PYM. Endnote 164 NO. I.

Sir,—

The revolution which one century has produced in your opinions and principles is not quite so surprising to me as it seems to be to many others. You know very well, I had always a jealousy that your humanity was counterfeited, your ardor for liberty cankered with simulation, and your integrity problematical at least.

I must confess, however, that such a sudden transition from licentiousness to despotism, so entire a transformation from a fiery, furious declaimer against power, to an abject hireling of corruption, though it furnishes a clue to the labyrinth of your politics in 1641, gives me many painful reflections on the frailty, inconstancy, and depravity of the human race. These reflections, nevertheless, are greatly mollified, by the satisfaction I feel in finding your old friend and coadjutor, Mr. Hampden, unaltered and unalterable in the glorious cause of liberty and law. His inflexibility has confirmed the great esteem my Lord Falkland and I always had of his wisdom, magnanimity, and virtue; and we are both of us at present as well convinced of his excellency, as a subject and citizen, as we were formerly of his amiable accomplishments in private life. But your apostasy has confirmed our belief of what was formerly suspected, namely,—your subornation of witnesses, your perjuries, briberies, and cruelties; and that though your cunning was exquisite enough to conceal your crimes from the public scrutiny, your heart was desperately wicked and depraved.

Can any thing less abominable have prompted you to commence an enemy to liberty,—an enemy to human nature? Can you recollect the complaints and clamors, which were sounded with such industry, and supported by such a profusion of learning in law and history, and such invincible reasoning, by yourself and your friends, against the Star-Chamber and High Commission, and yet remain an advocate for the newly-formed courts of admiralty in America? Can you recall to your memory the everlasting changes which were rung, by yourself and your party, against ship-money, and the other projects of that disgraceful reign, and on the consent of the subject as indispensably necessary to all taxations, aids, reliefs, talliages, subsidies, duties, &c., and yet contend for a taxation of more than five million subjects, not only without their consent, expressed or implied, but directly against their most explicit and determined declarations and remonstrances?

You, of all mankind, should have been the last to be hired by a minister to defend or excuse such taxes and such courts,—taxes more injurious and ruinous than Danegeld of old, which our countryman Speed says, "emptied the land of all the coin, the kingdom of her glory, the commons of their content, and the sovereign of his wonted respects and observance;"—courts which seem to have been framed in imitation of an ancient jurisdiction, at the bare mention of which I have often seen your eyes lighten, I mean the court of the masters of the king's forfeitures. I cannot omit so fair an opportunity of repeating the history and unfolding the powers of that court, as it seems to have been the very antitype of the new courts of admiralty in America, and to have been created and erected with the same powers and for the same purposes. *Endnote 165* It was in the reign of King Henry VII. that a British Parliament was found to be so timid, or ignorant, or corrupt, as to pass an act, that justices of assize, as well as justices of peace, without any finding or presentment of twelve men, upon a bare information for the king, should have full power and authority to hear and determine, by their discretions, all offences against the form, ordinance, and effect of certain penal statutes. This unconstitutional act was passed in the eleventh year of that reign; and thus the commons were found to sacrifice that sacred pillar, that fundamental law, that everlasting monument of liberty, the Great Charter, in complaisance to the ravenous avarice of that monarch. In pursuance of this act, Sir Richard Empson and Edmund Dudley were made justices throughout England, and "masters of the king's forfeitures." The old sage, Coke, says, that act was against and in the face of that fundamental law, Magna Charta, and that it is incredible what oppressions and exactions were committed by Empson and Dudley upon this unjust and injurious act, shaking that fundamental law. "And that, in the first year of the reign of King Henry VIII. the Parliament recited that unconstitutional act, and declared it void." And those two vile oppressors fell a sacrifice to the righteous indignation of an injured and exasperated nation. And he closes with an admonition, that the fearful end of these two oppressors should deter others from committing the like, and admonish parliaments that, instead of this ordinary and precious trial, per pares et per legem terræ, they bring not in absolute and partial trials by discretion.

Give me leave, now, to ask you, Mr. Pym, what are the powers of the new courts of admiralty in America? Are the trials in these courts per pares or per legem terræ? Is there any grand jury there to find presentments or indictments? Is there any petit jury to try the fact, guilty or not? Is the trial per legem terræ, or by the institutes, digests, and codes and novels of the Roman law? Is there not a judge appointed, or to be appointed, over all America? Is not this a much more extensive jurisdiction than that of Empson and Dudley, as justices over all England? Will you say, that no Empsons and Dudleys will be sent to America? Perhaps not; but are not the jurisdiction and power given to the judges greater than that to those oppressors? Besides, how can you prove that no Empsons will be sent there? Pray, let me know, are not the forfeitures to be shared by the governors and the informers? Are we not to prophesy the future by the experience of the past? And have not many governors been seen in America whose avarice was at least as ravenous as that of Henry VII.? Have not many of their tools been as hungry, restless, insolent, and unrelenting as Empson and

Dudley, in proportion to their power? Besides, are not the Americans at such a distance from their king, and the august council of the mother country, and, at the same time, so poor, as to render all redress of such insolence and rapacity impracticable?

If you consider the nature of these new American taxations, the temper and manners of the people in that country, their religious and civil principles; and if you recollect the real constitution of Great Britain, and the nature of the new courts of admiralty, you will not wonder at the spirit that has appeared in that country. Their resistance is founded in much better principles, and aims at much better ends, than I fear yours did in Charles's reign; though I own you were much nearer the truth and right of the cause then than now. And you know, if you had lived in America, and had not been much changed, you would have been the first to have taken arms against such a law, if no other kind of opposition would do. You would have torn up the foundations, and demolished the whole fabric of the government, rather than have submitted; and would have suffered democracy, aristocracy, monarchy, anarchy, any thing or nothing, to have arisen in its place.

You may, perhaps, wonder to hear such language as the foregoing from me, as I was always in an opposite faction to yours while we lived on earth. I will confess to you, that I am in many respects altered since my departure from the body; my principles in government were always the same, founded in law, liberty, justice, goodness, and truth; but in the application of those principles, I must confess, my veneration for certain churchmen, and my aspiring, ambitious temper, sometimes deceived me and led me astray. This was a source of remorse, at times, through my life; and, since my separation, and the sublimation of my faculties, and the purification of my temper, the detestation of some parts of my conduct has been greatly increased. But as these are subjects of very great importance, I shall make them the materials of a correspondence with you for some time to come.

Clarendon.

Clarendon

William Pym

THE EARL OF CLARENDON TO WILLIAM PYM. *Endnote 166* NO. II.

Sir,—

You and I have changed sides. As I told you in my last, I can account for your tergiversation, only on the supposition of the insincerity, baseness, and depravity of your heart. For my own part, as the change in me is not so great, neither is it so unaccountable. My education was in the law, the grounds of which were so riveted in me that no temptation could induce me, knowingly, to swerve from them. The sentiments, however, which I had imbibed in the course of my education from the sages of the law, were greatly confirmed in me by an accident that happened to me in my youth. This is an anecdote relative to my father and me which I presume you must have heard. A scene which will remain with indelible impressions on my soul throughout my duration. I was upon that circuit which led me down to my native county, and on a visit to my aged father, who gave me an invitation to take a walk with him in the field. I see the good old gentleman, even at this distance of time, and in his venerable countenance that parental affection to me, that zeal for the law, that fervent love of his country, that exalted piety to God and good-will to all mankind, which constituted his real character. "My son," said he, "I am very old, and this will probably be the last time I shall ever see your face; your welfare is near my heart; the reputation you have in your profession for learning, probity, skill, and eloquence, will, in all probability, call you to manage the great concerns of this nation in parliament, and to counsel your king in some of the greatest offices of state; let me warn you against that ambition which I have often observed in men of your profession, which will sacrifice all to their own advancement; and I charge you, on a father's blessing, never to forget this nation, nor to suffer the hope of honors or profits, nor the fear of menaces or punishments from the crown, to seduce you from the law, the constitution, and the real welfare and freedom of this people." And these words were scarcely pronounced, before his zeal and concern were too great for his strength, and he fell upon the ground before me, never to rise more! His words sunk deep into my heart, and no temptation, no bias or prejudice, could ever obliterate them. And you, Mr. Pym, are one witness for me, that, although I was always of the royal party, and for avoiding violence and confusion, I never defended what could be proved to be real infringements on the constitution. While I sat in parliament with you, I was as heartily for rectifying those abuses, and for procuring still further security of freedom, as any of you; and after the restoration, when the nations were rushing into a delirium with loyalty, I was obliged, in order to preserve even the appearance of the constitution, to make a stand; and, afterwards, in the reign of my infamous and detestable, though royal son-in-law, James II., I chose to go into banishment, rather than renounce the religion and liberties of my country.

I have made these observations to excuse my conduct in those reigns, in some degree, though I must confess there were many parts of it which admit of no excuse at all. I suffered myself to be blindly attached to the king and some of his spiritual and temporal minions, particularly Laud and Strafford, in some instances, and to connive at their villanous projects, against my principles in religion and government, and against the dying precepts of my father. Besides, my intimacy with that sort of company had gradually wrought into me too great a reverence for kingly and priestly power, and too much contempt of the body of the people, as well as too much virulence against many worthy patriots of your side of the question, with whom, if I had coöperated instead of assisting the court, perhaps all the confusions and bloodshed which followed might have been prevented, and all the nation's grievances redressed.

These reflections were a source of remorse at times, through my life; and since my departure from the earth I have revolved these things so often, and seen my errors so clearly, that were I to write a history of your opposition now, I should not entitle it a rebellion; nay, I should scarcely call the protectorate of Cromwell a usurpation.

With such principles as these, and divested as I am of all views and motives of ambition, as well as attachment to any party, you may depend upon it, the conduct of Barbadoes has given me great uneasiness. *Endnote 167* That island was settled in the Oliverian times by certain fugitives of the royal party, who were zealous advocates for passive obedience; and I suppose a remnant of the servile spirit of their ancestors and of that ruinous doctrine has prevailed on them to submit. I own it is a severe mortification to me to reflect that I ever acted in concert with a people with such sentiments, a people who were capable of so mean and meaching a desertion of the cause both of liberty and humanity. *Endnote 168* But the gallant struggle in St. Christopher's and on the continent of North America, is founded in principles so indisputable in the moral law, in the revealed law of God, in the true constitution of Britain, and in the most apparent welfare of the British nation, as well as of the whole body of the people in America, that it rejoices my very soul. When I see that worthy people, even in the reign of a wise and good king fettered, chained, and sacrificed by a few abandoned villains, whose lust of gain and power would, at any time, fasten them in the interest of France or Rome or hell, my resentment and indignation are unutterable.

If ever an infant country deserved to be cherished it is America. If ever any people merited honor and happiness they are her inhabitants. They are a people whom no character can flatter or transmit in any expressions equal to their merit and virtue; with the high sentiments of Romans, in the most prosperous and virtuous times of that commonwealth, they have the tender feelings of humanity and the noble benevolence of Christians; they have the most habitual, radical sense of liberty, and the highest reverence for virtue; they are descended from a race of heroes, who, placing their confidence in Providence alone, set the seas and skies, monsters and savages, tyrants and devils, at defiance for the sake of religion and liberty.

And the present generation have shown themselves worthy of their ancestors. Those cruel engines, fabricated by a British minister, for battering down all their rights and privileges, instead of breaking their courage and causing despondency, as might have been expected in their situation, have raised and spread through the whole continent a spirit that will be recorded to their honor with all future ages. In every colony, from Georgia to New Hampshire inclusively, the executioners of their condemnation have been compelled by the unconquerable and irresistible vengeance of the people to renounce their offices. Such and so universal has been the resentment, that every man who has dared to speak in favor of them, or to soften the detestation in which they are held, how great soever his character had been before, or whatever had been his fortune, connections, and influence, has been seen to sink into universal contempt and ignominy. The people, even to the lowest ranks, have become more attentive to their liberties, more inquisitive about them, and more determined to defend them, than they were ever before known or had occasion to be; innumerable have been the monuments of wit, humor, sense, learning, spirit, patriotism, and heroism, erected in the several provinces in the course of this year. Their counties, towns, and even private clubs and sodalities have voted and determined; their merchants have agreed to sacrifice even their bread to the cause of liberty; their legislatures have resolved; the united colonies have remonstrated; the presses have everywhere groaned; and the pulpits have thundered; and such of the crown officers as have wished to see them enslaved, have everywhere trembled, and all their little tools and creatures been afraid to speak and ashamed to be seen· *Endnote 169* Yet this is the people, Mr. Pym, on whom you are contributing, for paltry hire, to rivet and confirm everlasting oppression.

Clarendon.

Clarendon
William Pym

THE EARL OF CLARENDON TO WILLIAM PYM· *Endnote 170* NO. III.

Sir,—

You are pleased to charge the colonists with ignorance of the British constitution; but let me tell you there is not ever a son of liberty among them who has not manifested a deeper knowledge of it, and a warmer attachment to it, than appears in any of your late writings; they know the true constitution and all the resources of liberty in it, as well as in the law of nature, which is one principal foundation of it, and in the temper and character of the people much better than you, if we judge by your late impudent pieces, or than your patron and master, if we judge by his late conduct.

The people in America have discovered the most accurate judgment about the real constitution, I say, by their whole behavior, excepting the excesses of a few, who took advantage of the general enthusiasm to perpetrate their ill designs; though there has been great inquiry and some apparent puzzle among them about a formal, logical, technical definition of it. Some have defined it to be the practice of parliament; others, the judgments and precedents of the king's courts; but either of these definitions would make it a constitution of wind and weather, because the parliaments have sometimes voted the king absolute, and the judges have sometimes adjudged him to be so. Some have called it custom, but this is as fluctuating and variable as the other. Some have called it the most perfect combination of human powers in society which finite wisdom has yet contrived and reduced to practice for the preservation of liberty and the production of happiness. This is rather a character of the constitution and a just observation concerning it, than a regular definition of it, and leaves us still to dispute what it is. Some have said that the whole body of the laws, others that king, lords, and commons, make the constitution. There has also been much inquiry and dispute about the essentials and fundamentals of the constitution, and many definitions and descriptions have been attempted; but there seems to be nothing satisfactory to a rational mind in any of these definitions; yet I cannot say that I am at a loss about any man's meaning when he speaks of the British constitution or the essentials and fundamentals of it.

What do we mean when we talk of the constitution of the human body? what by a strong and robust, or a weak and feeble constitution? Do we not mean certain contextures of the nerves, fibres, and muscles, or certain qualities of the blood and juices, as sizy or watery, phlegmatic or fiery, acid or alkaline? We can never judge of any constitution without considering the end of it; and no judgment can be formed of the human constitution without considering it as productive of life or health or strength. The physician shall tell one man that certain kinds of exercise or diet or medicine are not adapted to his constitution, that is, not compatible with his health, which he would readily agree are the most productive of health in another. The patient's habit abounds with acid and acrimonious juices. Will the doctor order vinegar, lemon juice, barberries, and cranberries, to work a cure? These would be unconstitutional remedies, calculated to increase the evil which arose from the want of a balance between the acid and alkaline ingredients in his composition. If the patient's nerves are overbraced, will the doctor advise to jesuits'-bark? There is a certain quantity of exercise, diet, and medicine, best adapted to every man's constitution, which will keep him in the best health and spirits, and contribute the most to the prolongation of his life. These determinate quantities are not perhaps known to him or any other person; but here lies the proper province of the physician, to study his constitution and give him the best advice what and how much he may eat and drink; when and how long he shall sleep; how far he may walk or ride in a day; what air and weather he may improve for this purpose; when he shall take physic, and of what sort it shall be, in order to preserve and perfect his health and prolong his life.

But there are certain other parts of the body which the physician can, in no case, have any authority to destroy or deprave; which may properly be called stamina vitæ, or essentials and fundamentals of the constitution; parts, without which, life itself cannot be preserved a moment. Annihilate the heart, lungs, brain, animal spirits, blood, any one of these, and life will depart at once. These may be strictly called fundamentals of the human constitution. Though the limbs may be all amputated, the eyes put out, and many other mutilations practised to impair the strength, activity, and other attributes of the man, and yet the essentials of life may remain unimpaired many years.

Similar observations may be made, with equal propriety, concerning every kind of machinery. A clock has also a constitution, that is a certain combination of weights, wheels, and levers, calculated for a certain use and end, the mensuration of time. Now, the constitution of a clock does not imply such a perfect constructure of movement as shall never go too fast or too slow, as shall never gain nor lose a second of time in a year or century. This is the proper business of Quare, Tomlinson, and Graham, to execute the workmanship like artists, and come as near to perfection, that is, as near to a perfect mensuration of time, as the human eye and finger will allow. But yet there are certain parts of a clock, without which it will not go at all, and you can have from it no better account of the time of day than from the ore of gold, silver, brass, and iron, out of which it was wrought. These parts, therefore, are the essentials and fundamentals of a clock. Let us now inquire whether the same reasoning is not applicable in all its parts to government. For government is a frame, a scheme, a system, a combination of powers for a certain end, namely,—the good of the whole community. The public good, the salus populi, is the professed end of all government, the most despotic as well as the most free. I shall enter into no examination which kind of government, whether either of the forms of the schools, or any mixture of them, is best calculated for this end. This is the proper inquiry of the founders of empires. I shall take for granted, what I am sure no Briton will controvert, namely,—that liberty is essential to the public good, the salus populi. And here lies the difference between the British constitution and other forms of government, namely, that liberty is its end, its use, its designation, drift, and scope, as much as grinding corn is the use of a mill, the transportation of burdens the end of a ship, the mensuration of time the scope of a watch, or life and health the designation of the human body.

Were I to define the British constitution, therefore, I should say, it is a limited monarchy, or a mixture of the three forms of government commonly known in the schools, reserving as much of the monarchical splendor, the aristocratical independency, and the democratical freedom, as are necessary that each of these powers may have a control, both in legislation and execution, over the other two, for the preservation of the subject's liberty.

According to this definition, the first grand division of constitutional powers is into those of legislation and those of execution. In the power of legislation, the king, lords, commons, and people are to be considered as essential and fundamental parts of the constitution. I distinguish between the house of commons and the people who depute them; because there is in nature and fact a real difference, and these last have as important a department in the constitution as the former—I mean the power of election. The constitution is not grounded on "the enormous faith of millions made for one." It stands not on the supposition, that kings are the favorites of heaven, that their power is more divine than the power of the people, and unlimited but by their own will and discretion. It is not built on the doctrine, that a few nobles or rich commons have a right to inherit the earth, and all the blessings and pleasures of it; and that the multitude, the million, the populace, the vulgar, the mob, the herd, and the rabble, as the great always delight to call them, have no rights at all, and were made only for their use, to be robbed and butchered at their pleasure. No, it stands upon this principle, that the meanest and lowest of the people are by the unalterable, indefeasible laws of God and nature, as well entitled to the benefit of the air to breathe, light to see, food to eat, and clothes to wear, as the nobles or the king. All men are born equal; and the drift of the British constitution is to preserve as much of this equality as is compatible with the people's security against foreign invasions and domestic usurpation. It is upon these fundamental principles that popular power was placed, as essential, in the constitution of the legislature; and the constitution would be as complete without a kingly as without a popular power. This popular power, however, when the numbers grew large, became impracticable to be exercised by the universal and immediate suffrage of the people; and this impracticability has introduced from the feudal system an expedient which we call representation. This expedient is only an equivalent for the suffrage of the whole people in the common management of public concerns. It is in reality nothing more than this, the people choose attorneys to vote for them in the great council of the nation, reserving always the fundamentals of the government, reserving also a right to give their attorneys instructions how to vote, and a right at certain, stated intervals, of choosing a-new; discarding an old attorney, and choosing a wiser and better. And it is this reservation of fundamentals, of the right of giving instructions, and of new elections, which creates a popular check upon the whole government which alone secures the constitution from becoming an aristocracy, or a mixture of monarchy and aristocracy only.

The other grand division of power is that of execution. And here the king is, by the constitution, supreme executor of the laws, and is always present, in person or by his judges, in his courts, distributing justice among the people. But the executive branch of the constitution, as far as respects the administration of justice, has in it a mixture of popular power too. The judges answer to questions of fact as well as law; being few, they might be easily corrupted; being commonly rich and great, they might learn to despise the common people, and forget the feelings of humanity, and then the subject's liberty and security would be lost. But by the British constitution, ad quæstionem facti respondent juratores,—the jurors answer to the question of fact. In this manner, the subject is guarded in the execution of the laws. The people choose a grand jury, to make inquiry and presentment of crimes. Twelve of these must agree in finding the bill. And the petit jury must try the same fact over again, and find the person guilty, before he can be punished. Innocence, therefore, is so well protected in this wise constitution, that no man can be punished till twenty-four of his neighbors have said upon oath that he is guilty. So it is also in the trial of causes between party and party. No man's property or liberty can be taken from him till twelve men in his neighborhood have said upon oath, that by laws of his own making it ought to be taken away, that is, that the facts are such as to fall within such laws.

Thus, it seems to appear, that two branches of popular power, voting for members of the house of commons, and trials by juries, the one in the legislative and the other in the executive part of the constitution, are as essential and fundamental to the great end of it, the preservation of the subject's liberty, to preserve the balance and mixture of the government, and to prevent its running into an oligarchy or aristocracy, as the lords and commons are to prevent its becoming an absolute monarchy. These two popular powers, therefore, are the heart and lungs, the mainspring and the centre wheel, and without them the body must die, the watch must run down, the government must become arbitrary, and this our law books have settled to be the death of the laws and constitution. In these two powers consist wholly the liberty and security of the people. They have no other fortification against wanton, cruel power; no other indemnification against being ridden like horses, fleeced like sheep, worked like cattle, and fed and clothed like swine and hounds; no other defence against fines, imprisonments, whipping-posts, gibbets, bastinadoes, and racks. This is that constitution which has prevailed in Britain from an immense antiquity. It prevailed, and the house of commons and trials by jury made a part of it, in Saxon times, as may be abundantly proved by many monuments still remaining in the Saxon language. That constitution which has been for so long a time the envy and admiration of surrounding nations; which has been no less than five and fifty times since the Norman conquest, attacked in parliament, and attempted to be altered, but without success; which has been so often defended by the people of England, at the expense of oceans of their blood; and which, cooperating with the invincible spirit of liberty inspired by it into the people, has never failed to work the ruin of the authors of all settled attempts to destroy it.

What a fine reflection and consolation is it for a man, that he can be subjected to no laws which he does not make himself, or constitute some of his friends to make for him,—his father, brother, neighbor, friend, a man of his own rank, nearly of his own education, fortune, habits, passions, prejudices, one whose life and fortune and liberty are to be affected, like those of his constituents, by the laws he shall consent to for himself and them! What a satisfaction is it to reflect, that he can lie under the imputation of no guilt, be subjected to no punishment, lose none of his property, or the necessaries, conveniencies, or ornaments of life, which indulgent Providence has showered around him, but by the judgment of his peers, his equals, his neighbors, men who know him and to whom he is known, who have no end to serve by punishing him, who wish to find him innocent, if charged with a crime, and are indifferent on which side the truth lies, if he disputes with his neighbor!

Your writings, Mr. Pym, have lately furnished abundant proofs that the infernal regions have taken from you all your shame, sense, conscience, and humanity; otherwise I would appeal to them, who has discovered the most ignorance of the British constitution,—you who are for exploding the whole system of popular power with regard to the Americans, or they who are determined to stand by it, in both its branches, with their lives and fortunes.

Clarendon.

GOVERNOR WINTHROP TO GOVERNOR BRADFORD

Governor Hutchinson, in the third volume of his History, has the following paragraph, at the close of the year 1766:—

"The publications, in the newspapers, against the Governor, (Sir Francis Bernard) were abusive and licentious to a great degree. Attempts were made to destroy his character, by false and groundless charges, which easily obtain credit with the people when brought against a governor. At length a very sensible and fair writer, under the signature of Philanthropos, undertook his vindication, and, in a series of papers, much attended to, refuted the calumnies brought against him, and silenced his calumniators."

In a note to this passage, the name of the writer is given. It was Jonathan Sewall, the old friend of Mr. Adams, who was now rapidly coming to the point where the paths of the two were to diverge, never again to join. The two following papers, manifesting the progress of party asperity, seem to have been written to counteract the effect produced by Philanthropos.

Governor Winthrop

GOVERNOR WINTHROP TO GOVERNOR BRADFORD. *Endnote 171* NO. I.

We have often congratulated each other, with high satisfaction, on the glory we secured in both worlds by our favorite enterprise of planting America. We were Englishmen; we were citizens of the world; we were Christians. The history of nations and of mankind was familiar to us; and we considered the species chiefly in relation to the system of great nature and her all-perfect Author. In consequence of such contemplations as these, it was the unwearied endeavor of our lives to establish a society on English, humane, and Christian principles. This, (although we are never unwilling to acknowledge that the age in which we lived, the education we received, and the scorn and persecution we endured, had tinctured our minds with prejudices unworthy of our general principles and real designs,) we are conscious, was our noble aim. We succeeded to the astonishment of all mankind; and our posterity, in spite of all the terrors and temptations which have from first to last surrounded them, and endangered their very being, have been supremely happy. But what shall we say to the principles, maxims, and schemes, which have been adopted, warmly defended, and zealously propagated in America, since our departure out of it,—adopted, I say, and propagated, more by the descendants of some of our worthiest friends than by any others? You and I have been happier, in this respect, than most of our contemporaries. If our posterity have not without interruption maintained the principal ascendency in public affairs, they have always been virtuous and worthy, and have never departed from the principles of the Englishman, the citizen of the world, and the Christian. You very well remember the grief we felt, for many years together, at the gradual growth and prevalence of principles opposite to ours; nor have you forgotten our mutual joy at the very unexpected resurrection of a spirit which contributed so much to the restoration of that temper and those maxims which we have all along wished and prayed might be established in America. Calamities are the caustics and cathartics of the body politic. They arouse the soul. They restore original virtues. They reduce a constitution back to its first principles. And, to all appearance, the iron sceptre of tyranny, which was so lately extended over all America, and which threatened to exterminate all for which it was worth while to exist upon earth, terrified the inhabitants into a resolution and an ardor for the noble foundations of their ancestors.

But how soon is this ardor extinguished! In the course of a few months they have cooled down into such a tame, torpid state of indolence and inattention, that the missionaries of slavery are suffered to preach their abominable doctrines, not only with impunity, but without indignation and without contempt. What will be the consequence if that (I will not say contemptible but abominable) writer, Philanthrop, is allowed to continue his wicked labors? I say allowed, though I would not have him restrained by any thing but the cool contempt and dispassionate abhorrence of his countrymen; because the country whose interior character is so depraved as to be endangered from within by such a writer, is abandoned and lost. We are fully persuaded, that New England is in no danger from him, unless his endeavors should excite her enemies abroad, of whom she has many, and extremely inveterate and malicious, and enable them, in concert with others within her own bosom, whose rancor is no less malignant and venomous, to do her a mischief. With pleasure I see that gentlemen are taking measures to administer the antidote with the poison.

As the sober principles of civil and ecclesiastical tyranny are so gravely inculcated by this writer, as his artifices are so insidious, and his mis-affirmations so numerous and egregious, you will excuse me if I should again trouble you with a letter upon these subjects from your assured and immutable friend,

Winthrop.

In the Boston Gazette of the 2d of February is found the following notice:—

"We have received a second letter from Governor Winthrop to Governor Bradford, and are very sorry it came to hand too late for a place in this day's paper. But the learned and unlearned, the wise and virtuous, lovers of their country, of all denominations, may depend on a delicious regalement next week."

The paper of Philanthropos to which this is an answer, is found in the Evening Post of the 26th of January, 1767. It is written with great skill, in order to defend the conduct of Sir Francis Bernard in one particular case, called in the letter below, the Concord anecdote, which may be briefly explained thus,—Sir Francis had received instructions from the government at home not to give his assent to any bill passed by the General Court to divide an old town. The motive assigned for this was that the town representation was already too great for convenient despatch of business in the legislative department, and every subdivision of towns tended to increase it. In 1763, however, there arose out of an unhappy dispute in the old town of Newbury an application to the General Court for a division. So strong were the interests enlisted in its behalf that the Governor was finally induced to transcend his instructions, on the condition, however, that the number of representatives from the two towns should not exceed that of the old one before the division. Notwithstanding this proviso the new town of Newburyport sent two representatives to the General Court which met at Concord in 1764, instead of one, to which only it was entitled. The Governor, taking offence, assumed the responsibility of specially excepting the names of the two representatives in the Dedimus potestatem, or form of power to administer the usual oaths to the members at the commencement of a session. The right of the Governor to do this constituted the ground of the dispute.

Governor Winthrop

GOVERNOR WINTHROP TO GOVERNOR BRADFORD. Endnote 172 NO. II.

That the Hypocrite reign not, lest the People be ensnared.

Job.

Sir,—

You have my promise of another letter, concerning the maxims, arts, and positions of Philanthrop; whose performances of the last week I shall proceed to consider, without any formal apology for departing from the plan I proposed at first.

The art employed by this writer, in the introduction to his account of the Concord anecdote, is worth observation, before we undertake an examination of the account itself, and his reasonings upon it. God forbid that I should trifle with religion, or blame any man for professing it publicly. But there is a decency to be observed in this. True religion is too modest and reserved to seek out the market-places and corners of the streets, party newspapers and political pamphlets, to exhibit her prayers and devotions. Besides, there is so much in the temper of times and manners of ages, that ostentation of this kind may be more excusable in one century than another. The age in which you and I lived was religious to enthusiasm. Yet we may safely say, that canting and hypocrisy were never carried to so shameless a pitch, even by a Sir Henry Vane, an Oliver St. John, an Oliver Cromwell or a Hugh Peters, as Philanthrop in his last Monday's paper has carried them. True religion, my friend Bradford, was the grand motive, with you and me, to undertake our arduous and hazardous enterprise, and to plant a religion in the world, on the large and generous principles of the Bible, without teaching for doctrines the commandments of men, or any mixture of those pompous rituals, and theatrical ceremonies, which had been so successfully employed to delude and terrify men out of all their knowledge, virtue, liberty, piety, and happiness. A religion that should never be made subservient to the pride, ambition, avarice, or lust, of an assuming priesthood, or a cruel and usurping magistracy, was our incessant aim, and unwearied endeavor. And we have now the happiness to reflect on our success; for at least we have approached nearer to such an institution than any others have done since the primitive ages of Christianity. And although stiffness, formality, solemnity, grimace, and cant, very common in our times, have worn off, in a great measure, from New England; yet true religion, on the plan of freedom, popular power, and private judgment, remains and prospers. This, we are fully persuaded, is truth, though the deluded Philanthrop seems to be so far given up to blindness of mind, as to think that his quotations from Scripture, his affected meekness, charity, benevolence, and piety, his formal stiffness, and hypocritical grimace, will divest his countrymen of their senses, and screen him from their jealousy, while he is tearing up, by his principles and practices, conversation and writings, the foundations of their constitution, both in church and state.

But it is not only by attempting to throw around himself the rays of religion, that this writer has attempted to deceive his countrymen; he has labored to possess their minds with principles in government utterly subversive of all freedom, tending to lull them into an indolent security and inattention. In one of his late papers he has a paragraph to this purpose,—"A brave and free people, who are not through luxury enervated and sunk to that degree of effeminate indolence, which renders them insensible to the difference between freedom and slavery, can never fail to perceive the approaches of arbitrary power. The constitution of all free governments, especially that of the English, is of such a nature, the principles of it are so familiar, and so interwoven with the human mind, and the rulers are so circumscribed with positive laws, for the directing and controlling their power, that they can never impose chains and shackles on the people, nor even attempt it, without being discovered. In such a government, and among such a people, the very first act in pursuance of a design to enslave or distress the subjects in general, must be so obvious, as to render all false coloring totally unnecessary to arouse the public attention; a simple narration of facts, supported by evidence, which can never be wanting in such a case, will be sufficient, and will be the surest means to convince the people of their danger."

What conclusion shall a candid reader draw by a fair interpretation from this wordy, cloudy passage? Would he not conclude that a free government, especially the English, was a kind of machine, calculated for perpetual motion and duration; that no dangers attended it; and that it may easily preserve and defend itself, without the anxiety or attention of the people?

The truth is precisely the reverse of this. Though a few individuals may perceive the approaches of arbitrary power, and may truly publish their perceptions to the people, yet it is well known, the people are not persuaded without the utmost difficulty to attend to facts and evidence. Those who covet such power, always have recourse to secrecy and the blackness of darkness to cover their wicked views, and have always their parties and instruments and minions at hand, to disguise their first approaches, and to vilify and abuse,—as turbulent destroyers of the public peace, as factious, envious, malicious pretenders to patriotism, as sowers and stirrers of sedition,—all those who perceive such approaches, and endeavor to inform and undeceive their neighbors. Liberty, instead of resting within the intrenchment of any free constitution of government ever yet invented and reduced to practice, has always been surrounded with dangers, exposed to perils by water and by fire. The world, the flesh, and the devil, have always maintained a confederacy against her, from the fall of Adam to this hour, and will, probably, continue so till the fall of Antichrist. Consider the commonwealths of Greece. Were not the wisest of them so sensible of it as to establish a security of liberty, I mean the ostracism, even against the virtues of their own citizens,—that no individual, even by his valor, public spirit, humanity, and munificence, might endear himself so much to his fellow citizens as to be able to deceive them and engross too much of their confidence and power? In Rome, how often were the people cheated out of their liberties, by kings, decemvirs, triumvirs, and conspirators of other denominations! In the times when Roman valor, simplicity, public spirit, and frugality, were at the highest, tyranny, in spite of all the endeavors of her enemies, was sometimes wellnigh established, and even a Tarquin could not be expelled but by civil war. In the history of the English nation, which Philanthrop is pleased to distinguish from all others, how many arbitrary reigns do we find since the conquest! Sometimes, for almost a whole century together, notwithstanding all the murmur, clamor, speeches in the senate, writings from the press, and discourses from the pulpit, of those whom Philanthrop calls turbulent destroyers of the public peace, but you and I think the guardian angels of their country's liberties, the English nation has trembled and groaned under tyranny.

For reasons like these, the spirit of liberty is and ought to be a jealous, a watchful spirit. Obsta principiis is her motto and maxim, knowing that her enemies are secret and cunning, making the earliest advances slowly, silently, and softly, and that, according to her unerring oracle, Tacitus, "the first advances of tyranny are steep and perilous, but, when once you are entered, parties and instruments are ready to espouse you." It is one of these early advances, these first approaches of arbitrary power, which are the most dangerous of all, and, if not prevented but suffered to steal into precedents, will leave no hope of a remedy without recourse to nature, violence, and war, that I now propose to consider.

And, in the first place, let us see how far the court writer and his opponents are agreed in the facts. They seem to agree that two gentlemen, chosen and returned as members of the house, were expressly excepted by the Governor in the dedimus, or power of administering the usual oaths to the members of the house; that the house, that is, the gentlemen returned from the other towns besides Newbury, would not receive the dedimus with this exception, that is, refused themselves to be sworn by virtue of it. I say, by the way, that Philanthrop agrees to this fact, though he seems to endeavor, by the obscurity of his expression, to disguise it; because the house itself must have considered the exception as an infraction of their right, though Philanthrop only says it was so considered by some among them; otherwise the house would not have chosen a committee to remonstrate against the exception. That the Governor erased the exception, or gave a new dedimus, upon the remonstrance of the committee; that the Governor, however, gave it up only for that time, expressly reserving the claim of right to except members out of the commission, and told the committee he should represent the case home for further instructions concerning it. This being the acknowledged state of facts, trifling with the instance in the reign of king James the First, is as good a proof of Philanthrop's knowledge in history and the constitution as his shrewd suggestion, that Cassius and B. B. are the same person, is of his sagacity. It is with real sorrow that I now observe and propose hereafter to demonstrate, that both Philanthrop and his idol are too much enamored with the fine example of the Jemmys and Charleys, and too much addicted to an awkward imitation of their conduct. One example of such an imitation is this of the dedimus at Concord, this memorable attempt to garble the house of representatives, which bears so exact a resemblance to the conduct of that self-sufficient innovator, that pedantical tyrant, that I own it seems more probable to me to have been copied designedly from it than to have happened by accident. For the gentleman whose conduct and character Philanthrop defends, cannot be denied to be well read in the reigns of the Stuarts, and therefore cannot be supposed to have been ignorant of James's conduct. That a solid judgment may be formed of the nature of the privilege for which I contend, and whether it has been invaded or not, I shall produce a short sketch of the history of that transaction, and will then produce the opinion of writers quite impartial, or to be sure not partial in my favor, concerning it.

If we go back so far as the reign of Elizabeth, we find her, on one occasion, infringing on this privilege of the commons, of judging solely of their own elections and returns. This attempt was, however, so warmly resented by the commons that they instantly voted,—"That it was a most perilous precedent, when two knights of a county were duly elected, if any new writ should issue out, for a second election, without order of the house itself. That the discussing and adjudging of this and such like differences belonged only to the house; and that there should be no message sent to the Lord Chancellor, not so much as to inquire what he had done in the matter; because it was conceived to be a matter derogatory to the power and privilege of the house." After this vote, which had in it something of the spirit of liberty and independency, we hear of no more disputes upon that subject till we come to the reign of James the First, whose whole life was employed in endeavoring to demolish every popular power in the constitution, and to establish the awful and absolute sovereignty of kingship, that, as he expressed himself to the convocation, Jack and Tom and Dick and Will might not meet and censure him and his council. And in order to accomplish the important purpose of his reign, he thought that nothing could be more useful than to wrest from the commons into his own hands, or those of his creature, the chancellor, the adjudication of their elections and returns. Outlaws, whether for misdemeanors or debts, had been declared by the judges, in the reign of Henry the Sixth, incapable by law of a seat in the house, where they themselves must be lawgivers. Sir Francis Goodwin was now chosen for the county of

Bucks; and his return was made as usual into chancery. The chancellor decreed him an outlaw, vacated his seat, and issued writs for a new election. Sir John Fortescue was chosen in his room. But the first act of the house was to reverse the decree of the chancellor, and restore Goodwin to his seat. At James's instigation, the lords desired a conference on this subject, but were absolutely refused by the commons, as the question regarded entirely their own privileges. They agreed, however, to make a remonstrance to the king, by their speaker; where they maintained that though the returns were by form made into chancery, yet the sole right of judging with regard to elections belonged to the house itself. James was not satisfied, and ordered a conference between the house and the judges. The commons were in some perplexity. Their eyes were now opened; and they saw the consequences of that power which had been assumed, and to which their predecessors had in some instances blindly submitted. This produced many free speeches in the house. "By this course," said one member, "the free election of the counties is taken away; and none shall be chosen but such as shall please the king and council. Let us therefore with fortitude, understanding, and sincerity, seek to maintain our privileges. This cannot be construed any contempt in us, but merely a maintenance of our common rights, which our ancestors have left us, and which is just and fit for us to transmit to our posterity." Another said,—"This may be called a quo warranto, to seize all our liberties." "A chancellor," added a third, "by this course may call a parliament consisting of what persons he pleases. Any suggestion, by any person, may be the cause of sending a new writ. It is come to this plain question, whether the chancery or parliament ought to have authority." The commons, however, notwithstanding this watchful spirit of liberty, appointed a committee to confer with the judges before the king and council. There the question began to appear a little more doubtful than the king had imagined; and, to bring himself off, he proposed that Goodwin and Fortescue should both be set aside, and a writ be issued by the house for a new election. Goodwin consented; and the commons embraced this expedient, but in such a manner that, while they showed their regard for the king, they secured for the future the free possession of their seats, and the right which they claimed of judging solely of their own elections and returns. Hume, who will not be suspected of prejudice against the Stuarts, and very nearly in whose words this story is related, remarks at the conclusion,—"A power like this, so essential to the exercise of all their other powers, themselves so essential to public liberty, cannot fairly be deemed an encroachment in the commons, but must be regarded as an inherent privilege, happily rescued from that ambiguity which the negligence of former parliaments had thrown upon it." Smollett concludes his account of this affair with this reflection,—"Thus the commons secured to themselves the right of judging solely in their own elections and returns." And my Lord Bolingbroke, whose knowledge of the constitution will not be disputed, whatever may be justly said of his religion and his morals, remarks upon this transaction of James thus,—"Whether the will of the prince becomes a law independently of parliament, or whether it is made so upon every occasion by the concurrence of parliament, arbitrary power is alike established. The only difference lies here. Every degree of this power which is obtained without parliament, is obtained against the forms, as well as against the spirit of the constitution, and must, therefore, be obtained with difficulty, and possessed with danger. Whereas, in the other method of obtaining and exercising this power, by and with parliament, if it can be obtained at all, the progress is easy and short, and the possession of it so far from being dangerous, that liberty is disarmed as well as oppressed by this method; that part of the constitution, (namely, the house of commons,) which was instituted to oppose the encroachments of the crown, the maladministration of men in power, and every other grievance, being influenced to abet these encroachments, to support this maladministration, and even to concur in imposing the grievances."

Now, if we compare the attempt of King James with the attempt of the governor, who can discern a difference between them? James would have vacated the seat of Sir Francis Goodwin, because his election was against law; that is, because Sir Francis was an outlaw. The governor would have vacated the seats of Colonel Gerrish and Captain Little, because their election was against law, that is, because they were both chosen and returned by a town which by law was to choose and return but one. The king in one case, the governor in the other, made himself judge of the legality of an election, and usurped authority to vacate the seats of members. I consider the power of the chancellor here, which the king contended for, as the power of the king; because there is no great difference in such cases, as has been very well known from the time of James to this day, between the power of the creator and that of the creature. And I say, vacate the seats, because an exception from the dedimus is an absolute annihilation of a gentleman's seat; because by charter no man can vote or act as a representative till he has taken the oaths. It is as entire an exclusion from the house as an expulsion would be.

We will now, if you please, throw together a few reflections upon the soothing, amazing, melting solution of this arduous difficulty with which Philanthrop has entertained the public.

He begins with an instruction to the governor from his majesty not to consent to the division of towns. There has often been conversation during the administration of several late governors, concerning such a royal instruction, which, for any thing I know, may be a good one; but let it be good or evil, or whether there is any such or not, it has been found in experience, that when the division of a town would make way for the election of a friend, this instruction has been no impediment; and I need not go further than Concord and Newbury for two examples of this. Though I must go as far as the celebrated Berkshire for an instance of another member and favorite chosen and returned as expressly against the instruction and law of the province, and knowingly suffered by the governor to be sworn, without any exception in the dedimus, and to vote for the council; and finally left to the house, without any exception, caveat, message, or hint, to judge of their privilege, and vacate his seat. But to return to the instruction, is it a command to the governor to take upon himself to judge of the legality or illegality of the choice, returns, or qualifications of the members of the house? No man will pretend this, or dare throw such an infamous affront upon his majesty or his ministers, who perfectly know that even his majesty himself has no right or authority whatever to judge in this matter; and that for the king himself to attempt to judge of the elections, returns, or qualifications of the members of the house of commons, or of the house of representatives, would be an invasion of their privilege as really, as for them to coin money, or issue commissions in the militia, would be an encroachment on the royal prerogative. If Newbury had sent ten, and Boston forty, members, has the common law, or any act of parliament, or any law of the province, or this, his majesty's instruction, made the governor the judge, that those towns have not a right by law to send so many? The only question is, who shall judge? Is it the purport of that instruction, that the governor should except the forty and the ten out of the dedimus? Would it not be as much as the king would expect of the governor, if he should give the dedimus in the usual form, that is, to swear all the members, and leave it to the house to judge who the members were? And if the governor really supposed, as Philanthrop says he did, that the house would be jealous of the honor of their own laws, why should he have taken that jealousy away from them? Why did he not leave it to them to vindicate their own cause? If he had known any facts in this case, of which the house was not apprized, it would have been friendly and constitutional in him to have hinted it privately to some member of the house, that he might have moved it there. But there was no pretence of this, the case of Newbury being as well known to the house as to the governor. Or if he must have inserted himself in the business publicly, he might have sent the necessary information to the house in a message, recommending it to their consideration, not giving his own opinion, for this would have been an infraction of their privilege, because they are the sole judges in the matter, and ought not to be under the influence even of a message from his Excellency, expressing his opinion, in deciding so very delicate a point as elections and returns, a point on which all the people's liberties depend. Five members chosen and returned by Boston would be an illegal election; but how should the governor come by his knowledge, that Boston had chosen and returned five? How should the precepts and returns come into his hands? It is no part of his excellency's duty to examine the returns which are made to the sheriff, and lodged in the secretary's office. There can be no objection to his looking over them to satisfy his curiosity; but to judge of them belongs wholly to another department. Suppose him to have inspected them, and found five returned for Boston; would not this be as manifestly against the spirit of the instruction, and the standing law of the province, as the case of Newbury? And what pretence would he have to judge of this illegal election, any more than of any other? Suppose, for instance, it was proved to his excellency, that twenty members returned were chosen by corruption, that is, had purchased the votes of the electors by bribery; or let it be proved that any members had taken Rhode Island or New Hampshire bills, were outlaws, or chosen by a few inhabitants of their towns without any legal meeting, these would be equally illegal elections, equally against the instructions and the law of the land; but shall the governor judge of these things, and vacate all such seats, by refusing them their oaths? Let it be suggested that a member is an infant, an idiot, a woman in man's clothing, a leper, a petit-maître, an enemy to government, a friend to the governor's enemies, a turbulent destroyer of the public peace, an envious, malicious pretender to patriotism, any one of these or a thousand other pretences, if the governor is once allowed to judge of the legality or illegality of elections and returns, or of the qualifications or disqualifications of members, may soon be made sufficient to exclude any or all whom the governor dislikes. The supposition that Boston should send forty, and all the other towns ten, is possible; but it is not less improbable than that the governor, and all others in authority, should be suddenly seized with a delirium, negative every counsellor chosen, dissolve the house, call another, dissolve that, command all the militia to muster and march to the frontiers, and a thousand other raving facts; and all that can be said is, that when such cases shall happen, the government will be dissolved, and individuals must scramble as well as they can for themselves, there being no resource in the positive constitution for such wild cases. But surely, a negative, a right of exception in the dedimus, would be of no service to him in such a case. So that no justification or excuse for the governor's apprehensions or conduct, can be drawn from such supposed cases.

How the governor's conduct in signing the bill for dividing Newbury came to be considered as so very friendly and highly obliging, is not easily comprehended, unless every act of the governor is to be considered in that light. If he signed the bill to oblige any particular friend, or in order that a friend's friend might get into the house, it was friendly and obliging no doubt to such friends; but if he signed it because he thought it for the general good, as I suppose he did, it was a part of his general duty, as governor, and no more obliging than any other act of equal importance. I suppose here, that such conduct was not inconsistent with what he knew to be the intention of his instructions; for surely no man will call it friendly and obliging wilfully to break his instructions for so small a benefit to the province as dividing a town. So that he can't be imagined to have run any risk in this case, any more than in any other instance of his duty.

It is asserted that the governor had been misinformed concerning the custom of the house. How far this is true, I know not. But had he been informed that they had a custom to let the governor judge of their elections and returns; a custom to let him pick out whom he would to be sworn, and whom he would to send home? Unless he had been informed of such a custom, I cannot see that any other misinformation can defend or even palliate his taking that part upon himself. But surely, he had opportunity enough to have had the truest information. There were gentlemen enough of both houses ready to acquaint him with the customs, nay, the journals of the house would have informed him that the returns were all read over the first day before they proceeded to the choice of counsellors. And he ought, one would think, to have been very sure he was right before he made so direct an onset on so fundamental a privilege. Besides, it has been, and is very credibly reported, and I believe it to be true, that he gave out, more than a week before that election, what he would do and did, and that some of his friends, fearing the consequences, waited on him, on purpose to dissuade him from such an attempt, but without success. So that it was no sudden thought, nor inadvertency, nor rashness of passion. I report this, as I have before some other things, from credible information and real belief, without calling on witnesses by name; as such evidence has lately come in fashion and is thought alone sufficient to support narratives and depositions, sent to the boards at home, charging the blackest crimes on the country and some of the most respectable characters in it. But admitting he was misinformed of the custom, I can't see that this is of any weight at all in the dispute. Whether the house examined any returns at all the first day, or not, he could have no pretence to interpose. If he thought the custom was to examine no returns till the second day, and that such a custom was wrong, and ought to be altered, he might, for aught I know unexceptionably, have sent a message recommending this matter to the consideration of the house, not dictating to them how they should decide; much less should he have decided himself without consulting them; much less should he have taken from them the opportunity of judging at all, as, by excepting the gentlemen out of the dedimus, in fact he did.

Philanthrop makes it a problematical point, whether his excellency's apprehensions or the custom of the house be most consonant to reason and our constitution. I confess myself at a loss to know, from his account, what his excellency's apprehensions were. If he means, that his excellency apprehended that the house ought to change their custom, and decide upon all elections and returns before they proceed to the choice of counsellors, I agree with him that such a point is immaterial to the present dispute; but if he means, that his excellency apprehended he had a right to except such members out of the dedimus as he pleased, or any members at all, he begs the question, and assumes that it is problematical whether he is or is not the sole judge of elections, has or has not the same cathartic negative to administer, when he thinks proper, to the house, as he has to the board; which, according to all the authorities I have cited before, and according to common sense, is to make it problematical whether the governor has or has not plenary possession of arbitrary power.

It is asserted by our writer that the two gentlemen were sworn, and voted, or might have voted. As to their being sworn, there could not possibly any harm accrue from any gentleman's taking the oaths of allegiance, subscribing the declaration, &c. and if the committee had been pleased to swear the whole country on that occasion, no damage would have been done; and from whence the governor's dread of administering the oaths of allegiance to those gentlemen could arise, I can't conceive. From scruples of conscience it could not be, because he has often taken those oaths himself. As to the gentlemen's voting, I believe Philanthrop is mistaken; because I have been strongly assured they did not, but that they stood by till the elections were over, as it was expected by the other members that they should. However, I do not affirm this. The gentlemen themselves can easily determine this matter.

Philanthrop is often complaining of "skulking, dark insinuations," &c.; but I know of no man who deals in them so much as he. Witness, among a thousand others, his base insinuations about the senate and Gazette, Endnote 173 in his first piece, and what he says in his last about such a thing "being given out from a certain quarter, from what principle he will not say," a very dark, unintelligible insinuation of nobody knows what, against nobody knows whom, which leaves everybody at liberty to fix what he will on whom he will, and tends only to amuse and mislead. And nearly of the same character is a curious expression somewhere in the piece, calling the exception of the two gentlemen out of the dedimus, a "caveat to the house;" which is about as sensible as it would be to cut off a man's legs and chain him fast to a tree, and then give him a caution, a caveat, not to run away.

That the governor did not succeed in his attempt is no proof that he did not make it. Our thanks are not due to him, but to the house, that this dedimus was not received, all the members sworn by virtue of it, and itself lodged on file, as a precedent, to silence all envious and revengeful declaimers, both for himself and all his successors. It is equally true, that King James did not succeed in his attempt, but gave it up. Yet all historians have recorded that attempt, as a direct and formidable attack on the freedom of elections, and as one proof that he aimed at demolishing the constitution, at stretching prerogative beyond its just bounds, and at abridging the constitutional rights and liberties of the nation. What should hinder, but that a governor's attempt should be recorded too? I doubt not a Bacon quibbling and canting his adulation to that monarch, in order to procure the place of attorney-general or lord chancellor, might celebrate his majesty's friendly, modest, obliging behavior in that affair; yet even the mighty genius of Bacon could never rescue his sordid soul from contempt for that very adulation, with any succeeding age.

Winthrop.

INSTRUCTIONS OF THE TOWN OF BOSTON TO THEIR REPRESENTATIVES, 17 JUNE, 1768.

The history of the seizure of Mr. Hancock's sloop Liberty, for a violation of the revenue laws, and of the riots that followed, is given at large by Hutchinson Endnote 174 and by Gordon. Endnote 175 It is sufficient for the present purpose, to state, that the event led to a crowded town meeting held on the 13th of June, 1768, at which James Otis was made chairman, and a committee of twenty-one persons was appointed to wait on the governor with an address and remonstrance, ascribed by Governor Hutchinson to Otis's pen. At the same time another committee was appointed to prepare instructions to the representatives, then newly chosen, for their regulation "at this alarming crisis." That committee reported the following paper to an adjourned meeting on the 17th, when it was unanimously adopted.

These instructions were written by Mr. Adams. They, as well as the address, are given in full by Mr. Hutchinson in the appendix to the third volume of his history.

John Adams
James Otis
Thomas Cushing
Samuel Adams
John Hancock

TO THE HON. JAMES OTIS, AND THOMAS CUSHING, ESQUIRES; MR. SAMUEL ADAMS, AND JOHN HANCOCK, ESQUIRE.

Gentlemen,—

After the repeal of the late American Stamp Act, we were happy in the pleasing prospect of a restoration of that tranquillity and unanimity among ourselves, and that harmony and affection between our parent country and us, which had generally subsisted before that detestable act. But with the utmost grief and concern, we find that we flattered ourselves too soon, and that the root of bitterness is yet alive. The principle on which that act was founded continues in full force, and a revenue is still demanded from America.

We have the mortification to observe one act of parliament after another passed for the express purpose of raising a revenue from us; to see our money continually collecting from us, without our consent, by an authority in the constitution of which we have no share, and over which we have no kind of influence or control; to see the little circulating cash that remained among us for the support of our trade, from time to time transmitted to a distant country, never to return, or, what in our estimation is worse, if possible, appropriated to the maintenance of swarms of officers and pensioners in idleness and luxury, whose example has a tendency to corrupt our morals, and whose arbitrary dispositions will trample on our rights.

Under all these misfortunes and afflictions, however, it is our fixed resolution to maintain our loyalty and duty to our most gracious Sovereign, a reverence and due subordination to the British parliament, as the supreme legislative in all cases of necessity, for the preservation of the whole empire, *Endnote 176* and our cordial and sincere affection for our parent country; and to use our utmost endeavors for the preservation of peace and order among ourselves; waiting with anxious expectation, for a favorable answer to the petitions and solicitations of this continent for relief. At the same time, it is our unalterable resolution, at all times, to assert and vindicate our dear and invaluable rights and liberties, at the utmost hazard of our lives and fortunes; and we have a full and rational confidence that no designs formed against them will ever prosper.

That such designs have been formed, and are still in being, we have reason to apprehend. A multitude of placemen and pensioners, and an enormous train of underlings and dependents, all novel in this country, we have seen already. Their imperious tempers, their rash, inconsiderate, and weak behavior, are well known.

In this situation of affairs, several armed vessels, and among the rest his majesty's ship-of-war, the Romney, have appeared in our harbor; and the last, as we believe, by the express application of the board of commissioners, with the design to overawe and terrify the inhabitants of the town into base compliances and unlimited submission, has been anchored within a cable's length of the wharves.

But passing over other irregularities, we are assured that the last alarming act of that ship, namely,—the violent, and, in our opinion, illegal seizure of a vessel lying at a wharf, the cutting off her fasts, and removing her with an armed force in hostile manner, under the protection of the king's ship, without any probable cause of seizure that we know of, or indeed any cause that has yet been made known, no libel or prosecution whatever having yet been instituted against her, was by the express order or request in writing of the board of commissioners to the commander of that ship.

In addition to all this, we are continually alarmed with rumors and reports of new revenue acts to be passed, new importations of officers and pensioners to suck the life-blood of the body politic while it is streaming from the veins; fresh arrival of ships-of-war to be a still severer restraint upon our trade, and the arrival of a military force to dragoon us into passive obedience; orders and requisitions transmitted to New York, Halifax, and to England, for regiments and troops to preserve the public peace.

Under the distresses arising from this state of things, with the highest confidence in your integrity, abilities, and fortitude, you will exert yourselves, gentlemen, on this occasion, that nothing be left undone that may conduce to our relief; and, in particular, we recommend it to your consideration and discretion, in the first place, to endeavor that impresses of all kinds may, if possible, be prevented. There is an Act of Parliament in being which has never been repealed, for the encouragement of the trade to America. We mean by the 6th Anne chap. xxxvii. sect. 9, it is enacted, "That no mariner or other person who shall serve on board, or be retained to serve on board any privateer or trading ship or vessel that shall be employed in any part of America, nor any mariner, or other person, being on shore in any part thereof, shall be liable to be impressed or taken away by any officer or officers, of or belonging to any of her majesty's ships-of-war, impowered by the lord high admiral or any other person whatsoever, unless such mariner shall have before deserted from such ship-of-war belonging to her majesty, at any time after the fourteenth day of February, 1707, upon pain that any officer or officers so impressing or taking away, or causing to be impressed or taken away, any mariner or other person, contrary to the tenor and true meaning of this act, shall forfeit to the master or owner or owners of any such ship or vessel, twenty pounds for every man he or they shall so impress or take, to be recovered, with full costs of suit, in any court within any part of her majesty's dominions." So that any impresses of any mariner from any vessel whatever, appear to be in direct violation of an act of parliament. In the next place, it is our desire that you inquire and use your endeavors to promote a parliamentary inquiry for the authors and propagators of such alarming rumors and reports as we have mentioned before; and whether the commissioners or any other persons whatever have really wrote or solicited for troops to be sent here from New York, Halifax, England, or elsewhere, and for what end; and that you forward, if you think it expedient, in the house of representatives, resolutions that every such person who shall solicit or promote the importation of troops at this time, is an enemy to this town and province, and a disturber of the peace and good order of both.

INSTRUCTIONS OF THE TOWN OF BOSTON TO THEIR REPRESENTATIVES, 15 MAY, 1769.

In the spring of 1769, an unusual number of British troops were stationed in Boston. The main guard, "unluckily," as Hutchinson expresses it, and "without any design to give offence, had been stationed in a house which was before unoccupied, opposite to the door of the court house; and, as is usual, some small field pieces were placed before the door of the guard-house, and thus happened to point to the door of the court house." Endnote 177 However usual this may have been elsewhere, it was so unprecedented an event in Boston as to give rise to a reasonable suspicion of some design to overawe the legislature about to assemble there. At the annual town meeting, it was decided to appoint a committee to draw up instructions to their representatives, suitable for the emergency. Mr. Adams was placed at the head of this committee, and reported the following paper. Mr. Bradford gives the substance of it in his history, and says it "was an expression of feelings worthy of freemen, and deserving perpetual remembrance." Endnote 178

At the adjournment of the meeting of the freeholders, and other inhabitants of this town, on Monday last, the committee appointed for that purpose reported the following draft of instructions, which, being several times distinctly read, was accepted by the town, nemine contradicente:—

John Adams
James Otis
Thomas Cushing
Samuel Adams
John Hancock

TO THE HONORABLE JAMES OTIS, AND THOMAS CUSHING, ESQUIRES; MR. SAMUEL ADAMS, AND JOHN HANCOCK, ESQUIRE.

Gentlemen,—

You have once more received the highest testimony of the confidence and affection of your constituents, which the constitution has empowered them to exhibit,—the trust of representing them in the great and general court, or assembly of this province. This important trust is committed to you at a time when your country demands the exertion of all your wisdom, fortitude, and virtue, and therefore, it is presumed, a free communication of our sentiments cannot but be agreeable to you.

The first object of your attention is the privilege of that assembly of which you are now chosen to be members. The debates there must be free. You will therefore exert yourselves to remove every thing that may carry the least appearance of an attempt to awe or intimidate. As the assembly is called to sit in the usual place, common decency as well as the honor and dignity of a free legislative, will require a removal of those cannon and guards, as well as that clamorous parade which has been daily around the court house since the arrival of his majesty's troops, and at some times while the highest court of judicature has been sitting there, on the trial even of capital causes. When this grievance shall be removed, and the debates of the assembly shall be free, it will be natural to inquire into all the grievances we have suffered from the military power; why they have been quartered in the body of the town, in contradiction to the express words, and, as we conceive, the manifest intention of an act of parliament; why the officers who have thus violated our rights have not been called to an account, and dealt with as the law required; whether the measure taken by the governor of the province, in appointing an extraordinary officer to provide quarters for the troops, was not an evasion of the act of parliament made for the billeting and quartering his majesty's troops in America, (the professed rule of their conduct,) and a design to elude the clause of said act purposely providing for the convenience of American subjects, and their security against an excess of military power? Why the repeated offences and violences committed by the soldiery, against the peace, and in open defiance and contempt of the civil magistrate and the law, have escaped punishment in the courts of justice? And whether the attorney-general has not, in some late instances, unduly exercised a power of entering nolle prosequi upon indictments, without the concurrence of the court, in obstruction to the course of justice, and to the great encouragement of violence and oppression?

And, as the quartering troops here has proved the occasion of many evils, we do earnestly recommend to you to use your utmost endeavors for a speedy removal of them.

Should the expense that has been incurred for providing barracks for the troops, and supplying them with necessaries, be required of the house of representatives, we do in the most solemn and express manner enjoin you, by no means to comply with such a requisition. If the general court is a free assembly, no power upon earth has authority to compel it to pay this money. Should it ever be deprived of its freedom, it shall never, with our consent, be made an engine to drain us of the little money we have left.

Another object of great importance, and which requires your earliest attention, is a late flagrant and formal attack upon the constitution itself,—an attempt not only to deprive us of the liberties, privileges, and immunities of our charter, but the rights of British subjects. We have seen copies of letters published here, authenticated by the clerk of the papers to the honorable house of commons, the contents of which must have awakened the jealousy of the country. Endnote 179 The design of the writer is sufficiently apparent. And, considering his station as representative of the first person in the empire, and the rank of the minister to whom he addressed himself, we cannot wonder that credit has been given to his letters in Great Britain, and that they have already produced effects alarming to the colonies, and dangerous to both countries. It is therefore expected, that you use the whole influence you may have, that the injurious impressions which they have unhappily made may be removed, and that an effectual antidote may be administered, before the poison shall have wrought the ruin of the constitution.

It is unnecessary for us, at this time, to repeat our well-known sentiments concerning the revenue which is continually levied upon us, to our great distress, and for no other end than to support a great number of very unnecessary placemen and pensioners. We have only to add, that our sentiments on this subject are in no respect changed, and we expect that you will pursue with firm resolution and unremitted ardor, every measure that may tend to procure us relief, never yielding your consent to, or connivance at the least encroachment on our rights.

Next to the revenue itself, the late extensions of the jurisdiction of the admiralty are our greatest grievance. The American courts of admiralty seem to be forming by degrees into a system that is to overturn our constitution and to deprive us entirely of our best inheritance, the laws of the land. It would be thought in England a dangerous innovation, if the trial of any matter upon land was given to the admiralty; it would be thought more threatening still, if the power of confiscation over ships and cargoes for illicit trade was committed to the court; but if the forfeitures of ships and cargoes, large penalties upon masters, and such exorbitant penalties as the treble value of cargoes upon every person concerned in landing uncustomed goods were, by act of parliament, appointed to be tried by the admiral, the nation would think their liberties irrecoverably lost.

This, however, is the miserable case of North America! In the forty-first section of the statute of the fourth of George III. chap. xv. we find that "all the forfeitures and penalties inflicted by this or any other act of parliament, relating to the trade and revenues of the British colonies or plantations in America, which shall be incurred there, may be prosecuted, sued for, and recovered in any court of admiralty in the said colonies." Thus these extraordinary penalties and forfeitures are to be heard and tried, not by a jury, nor by the law of the land, but by the civil law of a single judge! Unlike the ancient barons who answered with one voice, "We will not that the laws of England be changed, which of old have been used and approved," the barons of modern times seem to have answered that they are willing those laws should be changed with regard to America in the most tender point and fundamental principle.

And this hardship is the more severe, as we see in the same page of the statute, and the section immediately preceding,—"That all penalties and forfeitures which shall be incurred in Great Britain shall be prosecuted, sued for, and recovered in any of his majesty's courts of record in Westminster, or in the court of exchequer in Scotland respectively." Here is a contrast that stares us in the face! A partial distinction that is made between the subject in Great Britain and the subject in America! The parliament in one section guarding the people of the realm and securing to them the benefit of a trial by jury and the law of the land, and by the next section depriving Americans of those important rights. Is not this distinction a brand of disgrace upon every American—a degradation below the rank of an Englishman? Is it not with respect to us a repeal of the twenty-ninth chapter of Magna Charta? "No freeman shall be taken or imprisoned or disseised of his freehold or liberties or free customs or outlawed or exiled or any otherwise destroyed, nor will we pass upon him nor condemn him, but by lawful judgment of his peers or the law of the land." Englishmen are inviolably attached to the important right expressed in this clause, which for many centuries has been the noblest monument and firmest bulwark of their liberties. One proof of this attachment, given us by a great sage of the law, we think proper to mention, not for your information, but as the best expression of the sense of your constituents. "Against this ancient and fundamental law, and in the face thereof," says Lord Coke, "I find an act of parliament made, that as well justices of assize as justices of peace, without any finding or presentment of twelve men, upon a bare information for the king before them made, should have full power and authority by their discretions to hear and try men for penalties and forfeitures." His lordship, after mentioning the repeal of this statute, and the fate of Empson and Dudley, who received the full weight of the national vengeance for acting under it, concludes with a reflection, which, if well considered, might be sufficient to discourage such attacks upon fundamental principles: "The ill-success of this statute, and the fearful end of these two oppressors, should deter others from committing the like, and should admonish parliaments, that instead of this ordinary and precious trial by the law of the land, they bring not in absolute and partial trials by discretion." Such are the feelings and reflections of an Englishman upon a statute not unlike the statute now under consideration, and upon courts and judges not unlike the courts and judges of admiralty in America!

The formidable power of these courts, and their distressing course of proceedings, have been severely felt within the year past; many of your fellow-citizens having been worn out with attendance upon them, in defence against informations for extravagant and enormous penalties. And we have the highest reason to fear, from past experience, that if no relief is obtained for us, the properties and liberties of this unhappy country, and its morals too, will be ruined by these courts and the persons employed to support them.

We, therefore, earnestly recommend to you, by every legal measure, to endeavor that the power of these courts may be confined to their proper element, according to the ancient

English statutes; and that you petition and remonstrate against the late extensions of their jurisdiction; and, we doubt not, the other colonies and provinces who suffer with us under them will cheerfully harmonize with this in any justifiable measures that may be taken for redress.

We need not here take occasion to instruct you, that while you in the most ample manner testify your loyalty to our gracious sovereign, you strenuously assert and maintain the right of the subject, jointly or severally to petition the king, or to declare it as our clear opinion that the house of representatives in any one province has an undeniable right, whenever a just occasion shall offer, to communicate their sentiments upon a common concern to the assemblies of any or all the other colonies, and to unite with them in humble, dutiful, and loyal petitions for redress of a general grievance.

THE INDEPENDENCE OF THE JUDICIARY; A CONTROVERSY BETWEEN WILLIAM BRATTLE AND JOHN ADAMS 1773

INDEPENDENCE OF THE JUDICIARY.

The origin of the following controversy is given in the Diary of Mr. Adams· *Endnote 180* The assumption of the payment of the judges' salaries by the king, in conjunction with the natural and general tendency, in all ages and countries, of the legal profession to side with authority, threatened to put the administration of the law completely under the control of government. The people of Massachusetts, greatly alarmed at this state of things, which was not relieved by the signs of temporizing visible in some leading quarters, first resorted, at this moment, to the expedient, which afterwards proved so effective, of a regular organization of committees of correspondence in the towns. Among those who had given signs of a disposition to change his course, was General William Brattle, of Cambridge, senior member of the council, who seized the opportunity of a town meeting, called to remonstrate against the measure, to make a speech designed to reconcile the popular sentiment to it. Relying upon the silence of the bar, it would seem that he ventured so far as to challenge the patriotic party, and even Mr. Adams by name as the most prominent lawyer attached to it, to dispute his positions. The following papers were the result. They are given in series, rather as a curious specimen of the controversial skill and professional learning of Mr. Adams, than as involving any points of great present interest. Although it must be admitted that, by the revolution of sentiment, the question underlying the controversy bids fair to rise again in a modified shape, for decision in America.

Cambridge,
21 December, 1772

.

At a legal meeting of the freeholders, and other inhabitants of the town of Cambridge, on Monday the 14th instant, the following vote passed, namely,—

Voted, That a committee be appointed to write to the committee appointed by the town of Boston, and acknowledge the vigilance and care, discovered by the metropolis, of the public rights and liberties; acquainting them that this town will heartily concur in all salutary, proper, and constitutional measures for the redress of those intolerable grievances which threaten, and, if continued, must overthrow the happy civil constitution of this province; and that said committee take under consideration the rights, as stated by the committee of correspondence of the town of Boston, and the infringements and violations of the same, and make report at the adjournment of this meeting.

After which the town voted the following instructions to their representative, Captain Thomas Gardner, namely,—

Sir,—We, his majesty's most dutiful and loyal subjects, freeholders and other inhabitants of the town of Cambridge, in town meeting legally assembled this fourteenth day of December, 1772, to consult upon such measures as may be thought most proper to be taken at this alarming crisis, and most conducive to the public weal,—do, therefore, with true patriotic spirit declare, that we are and ever have been ready to risk our lives and fortunes in defence of his majesty, King George the Third, his crown and dignity, and in the support of constitutional government. So, on the other hand, we are as much concerned to maintain and secure our own invaluable rights and liberties, and that glorious inheritance, which was not the gift of kings or monarchs, but was purchased at no less price than the precious blood and treasure of our worthy ancestors, the first settlers of this province, who for the sake of those rights left their native land, their dearest friends and relations, goodly houses, pleasant gardens, and fruitful fields, and in the face of every danger settled a wild and howling wilderness, where they were surrounded with an innumerable multitude of cruel and barbarous enemies; and destitute of the necessaries of life, yet aided by the smiles of indulgent heaven, by their heroic fortitude (though small in number) they subdued their enemies before them, and by their indefatigable labor and industry cultivated this land, which is now become a fruitful field, which has much enriched our mother country, and greatly assisted in raising Great Britain to that state of opulence it is now in, that if any people on earth are entitled to the warmest friendship of a mother country, it is the good people of this province and its sister colonies. But, alas! with what ingratitude are we treated—how cruelly oppressed! We have been sighing and groaning under oppression for a number of years; our natural and charter rights are violated in too many instances here to enumerate; our money extorted from us, and appropriated to augment our burdens; we have repeatedly presented our most decent, dutiful, and loyal petitions to our most gracious sovereign for a redress of our grievances, but no redress has as yet been obtained; whereby we have been almost driven to despair; and in the midst of our distress, we are still further alarmed with seeing the governor of the province made independent of the people, and the shocking report that the judges of the superior court of judicature, and other officers, have salaries affixed to their offices, dependent on the crown and ministry, independent of the grants of the commons of this province. By this establishment, our lives and properties will be rendered very precarious; as there is the utmost danger that through an undue influence the streams of public justice will be poisoned. Can we expect the scales will be held equal between all parties? Will such judges be unmoved by passion or prejudice, fear or favor? What a miserable situation will the man be in, under a corrupt administration, who shall dare to oppose their vile measures? Must he not expect to feel the keenest resentment of such administration, by judges thus bribed to pursue the plan of the ministry?

In fine, we look upon this last innovation as so great a grievance, especially when added to the many other grievances we have been so long groaning under, as to be almost insupportable. We therefore think it seasonable and proper to instruct you, our representative in general assembly, that you use your greatest influence at the next session of the general court for a speedy redress of all our grievances.

And, inasmuch as it has been for some years past thought, that the judges of the superior court, especially since their circuits have been enlarged, have not had salaries adequate to their important services, we desire you would make due inquiry into this matter; and, if you shall find it to be a fact, that you would use your utmost endeavors that their salaries may be enlarged, and made adequate to their merit and station. And in all our difficulties and distress, we depend upon your prudence and firmness.

A true copy,

Attest, ANDREW BOARDMAN, *Town Clerk.*

From the Massachusetts Gazette, 4 January, 1773.

to the printers.

Finding in the papers of the 21st instant, sundry votes passed at a legal town meeting held at Cambridge the 14th instant, I thought it proper to give the public the true state of the case, by desiring the same might be printed, that the world may judge whether the inhabitants there convened, had any right to act upon the resolves and letter of the town of Boston. I do this without any design to consider whether what was then voted is right or wrong, provided there had been any thing in the warrant that could have justified the inhabitants in taking the same under their consideration. There was a petition presented to the selectmen, signed by a considerable number of respectable freeholders, inhabitants of Cambridge, desiring that we would call a meeting of the town, to consider what was most proper to be done relative to the salaries granted to the justices of the superior court, by the king, dependent upon him, independent upon the people, and to act and do thereon as the inhabitants should think best; this was the sole prayer of their petition. The selectmen met and voted that a meeting should be called at the time the town did meet, and inserted in the warrant the desire of said inhabitants, which is in the following words: "To hear a motion of a very large number of the inhabitants of this town for calling a town meeting soon as may be, to take under consideration the current report we have of late, that the honorable judges of the superior court have salaries affixed to their offices dependent on the crown and ministry, independent on the people, and to act relating to the same as they shall think proper." There were two other articles in the warrant, but they related only to the particular business of the town. The town met accordingly; the warrant read; a moderator was chose. I spake my mind very freely upon said clause. I said, in my opinion we were too premature in acting upon this matter at present. The packet was expected daily that might give us more light in the affair, than we now had; and that I was not alone in this sentiment, having heard at sundry times some very respectable gentlemen of Boston, as true sons of liberty as any I know of in the province, express themselves in the same words. I observed that no man in the province could say whether the salaries granted to the judges were durante bene placito, or quamdiu bene se gesserint, as the judges of England have their salaries granted them. I supposed the latter, though these words are not expressed, but necessarily implied; and that there was an essential difference between the one and the other; that I always thought the judges' salaries should be independent both upon the king and the people; that there was great danger to a commission arising from their dependency upon either; but their grant was only during the king's pleasure. There was no one living could be more offended at it than myself, or that would exert himself in a constitutional way more heartily, openly, and perseveringly to prevent the grants taking place. And I took the freedom to propose a method, which, if adopted, I have not the least doubt would answer the purpose aforesaid, namely,—to vote the judges an ample and honorable support, suitable to the dignity and importance of their station and the vast trouble that attended it, quamdiu bene se gesserint, and that I doubted not but that his excellency the governor, and the judges themselves, would be our advocates and intercessors; and that his majesty would be graciously pleased to withdraw his grant. The grant not arising from any desire the king had to make the judges dependent upon him, but because they who have the same powers with the king's bench, common bench, and exchequer, at home, have no more than one hundred and twenty pounds a year. Had there been an adequate salary granted, I believed we should have never heard of any grant from the king to them. I was very far from thinking there was any necessity of having quamdiu bene se gesserint in their commissions; for they have their commissions now by that tenure as truly as if said words were in. That by the charter and common law of England, there is no necessity of their having any commission at all; a nomination and appointment recorded is enough; nomination and appointment are the words of the charter, a commission for them not so much as mentioned in it. Their commission is only declarative of their nomination and appointment. A civil commission by the common law can give no new powers. This is what I am persuaded the governor and council disclaim; it would be most dangerous to suppose and allow it, and tyranny in them to assume it. The great and general court of this province, and they only, have determined what powers and authorities unto the judges do appertain. What right, what estate vests in them, in consequence of their nomination and appointment, the common law of England, the birthright of every man here as well as at home, determines, and that is, an estate for life, provided they behave well. Wherever there is an office there is a trust, whenever there is a material breach of trust there is a forfeiture, and not otherwise. These points of law have been settled and determined by the greatest sages of the law, formerly and more lately. It is so notorious that it becomes the common learning of the law; my Lord Chief Justice Holt settled it so, not long before the statute of William and Mary, that enacts that the words quamdiu bene se gesserint shall be in the judges' commissions. Upon this it is naturally enough thought and said, if that was law before, what occasion was there for the parliament to have said any thing about it? I answer, the parliament often makes acts which introduce no new law, but in affirmance of the old law, that which was really law before, and there might possibly be a reason for it. It must be remembered this act was not to take place during the lives of King William, Queen Mary, and the Princess Anne, and the commissions I apprehend were without these words inserted in them during their reigns. It took place by said act, upon the accession of King George I. then Elector of Hanover, a sovereign prince.

For these reasons I was for suspending the consideration of the judges' salaries till we had more evidence and more light than generally arises from a current report.

As to acting upon the letter and resolves aforesaid, which were distinctly read by order of the inhabitants, I observed there was not a single clause in the warrant that could justify any vote to act thereon; then I read the law, which is in the words following,—"That no matter or thing whatsoever shall be voted or determined, but what is inserted in the warrant for calling said meeting." It was answered that they knew that law very well, but they had a right to act and determine upon such interesting subjects as were contained in said letter and resolves, founded upon the law of nature. I answered that there were plain standing laws of this province that might have been attended to, and yet were not (for what reason I never could conjecture). I thought they ought rather to be attended to and complied with, than to view ourselves in a state of nature, and be governed by any law now existing; because there was not one equal in authority and right to the statute law of this province, touching the point in controversy, and that I, in the most public manner, protested against their proceedings. That, for my own part, I did not look upon myself in a state of nature, and that it was a pity anybody should in this case, where (upon their own principles) they could have so easily removed all these difficulties without placing themselves in so bad a situation as to be in a state of nature, and to be governed by the laws of nature in direct repugnancy and opposition to the well known standing law of the province, founded upon the eternal reason and nature of things, the safety of every town in the government; but, notwithstanding, the votes passed, as mentioned in your paper.

Upon the true principles of liberty I gave my sentiments, apprehending every one hath a right, both natural and constitutional so to do, provided it is with decency and good manners; which I hope I have not deviated from in this narration.

W. Brattle.

Cambridge, 16 December, 1772

.

From the Boston Gazette, 11 January, 1773.

to the printers.

General Brattle, by his rank, station, and character, is entitled to politeness and respect even when he condescends to harangue in town meeting or to write in a newspaper; but the same causes require that his sentiments, when erroneous and of dangerous tendency, should be considered with entire freedom, and the examination be made as public as the error. He cannot, therefore, take offence at any gentleman for offering his thoughts to the public with decency and candor, though they may differ from his own.

In this confidence I have presumed to publish a few observations which have occurred to me upon reading his narration of the proceedings of the late town meeting at Cambridge. It is not my intention to remark upon all things in that publication which I think exceptionable, but only on a few which I think the most so.

The General is pleased to say, "That no man in the province could say whether the salaries granted to the judges were durante beneplacito, or quamdiu bene se gesserint, as the judges of England have their salaries granted them. I supposed the latter, though these words are not expressed, but necessarily implied." This is said upon the supposition that salaries are granted by the crown to the judges.

Now it is not easy to conceive how the General or any man in the province could be at a loss to say, upon supposition that salaries are granted, whether they are granted in the one way or the other. If salaries are granted by the crown, they must be granted in such a manner as the crown has power to grant them. Now it is utterly denied that the crown has power to grant them in any other manner than durante beneplacito.

The power of the crown to grant salaries to any judges in America is derived solely from the late act of parliament, and that gives no power to grant salaries for life or during good behavior. But not to enlarge upon this at present.

The General proceeds,—"I was very far from thinking there was any necessity of having quamdiu bene se gesserint in their commissions; for they have their commissions now by that tenure as truly as if said words were in."

It is the wish of almost all good men that this was good law. This country would be forever obliged to any gentleman who would prove this point from good authorities to the conviction of all concerned in the administration of government here and at home. But I must confess that my veneration for General Brattle's authority by no means prevails with me to give credit to this doctrine; nor do his reasons in support of it weigh with me even so much as his authority. He says, "What right, what estate vests in them, (that is, the judges,) in consequence of their nomination and appointment, the common law of England, the birthright of every man here as well as at home, determines, and that is an estate for life, provided they behave well." I must confess I read these words with surprise and grief; and the more I have reflected upon them, the more these sentiments have increased in my mind.

The common law of England is so far from determining that the judges have an estate for life in their offices, that it has determined the direct contrary; the proofs of this are innumerable and irresistible. My Lord Coke, in his fourth Institute, 74, says, "Before the reign of Edward I. the chief justice of this court was created by letters-patent, and the form thereof (taking one example for all) was in these words:—

"Rex, &c., archiepiscopis, episcopis, abbatibus, prioribus, comitibus, baronibus, vice-comitibus, forestariis, et omnibus aliis fidelibus regni Angliæ, salutem. Cum pro conservatione nostrâ, et tranquillitatis regni nostri, et ad justitiam universis et singulis de regno nostro exhibendam constituerimus dilectum et fidelem nostrum Philippum Basset justiciarium Angliæ quamdiu nobis placuerit capitalem, &c." And my Lord Coke says afterwards in the same page,—"King Edward I. being a wise and prudent prince, knowing that, cui plus licet quam par est, plus vult quam licet, (as most of these summi justiciarii did) made three alterations. 1. By limitation of his authority. 2. By changing summus justiciarius to capitalis justiciarius. 3. By a new kind of creation, namely, by writ, lest, if he had continued his former manner of creation, he might have had a desire of his former authority; which three do expressly appear by the writ yet in use, namely,—Rex, &c. E. C. militi salutem. Sciatis quod constituimus vos justiciarium nostrum capitalem ad placita coram nobis tenenda, durante beneplacito nostro. Teste, &c." Afterwards, in the same page, Lord Coke observes, "It is a rule in law, that ancient offices must be granted in such forms and in such manner as they have used to be, unless the alteration were by authority of parliament. And continual experience approveth, that for many successions of ages without intermission, they have been, and yet are called by the said writ." His lordship informs us also in the same page that "the rest of the judges of the king's bench have their offices by letters-patent in these words,—Rex omnibus ad quos presentes literæ pervenerint salutem. Sciatis quod constituimus dilectum et fidelem Johannem Doderidge militem unum justiciariorum ad placita coram nobis tenenda durante beneplacito nostro. Teste, &c."

His lordship says, indeed, that these judges are called perpetui by Bracton, because "they ought not to be removed without just cause." But the question is not what the crown ought to do, but what it had legal power to do.

The next reason given by the General, in support of his opinion, is that "these points of law have been settled and determined by the greatest sages of the law, formerly and more lately." This is so entirely without foundation, that the General might, both with safety and decency, be challenged to produce the name of any one sage of the law, ancient or modern, by whom it has been so settled and determined, and the book in which such determination appears. The General adds, "It is so notorious that it becomes the common learning of the law." I believe he may decently and safely be challenged again to produce one lawyer in this country who ever before entertained such an opinion or heard such a doctrine. I would not be misunderstood. There are respectable lawyers who maintain that the judges here hold their offices during good behavior; but it is upon other principles, not upon the common law of England. "My Lord Chief Justice Holt settled it so, not long before the statute of William and Mary, that enacts that the words quamdiu bene se gesserint shall be in the judges' commissions;" and afterwards he says, that the commissions, as he apprehends, were without these words inserted in them during the reigns of King William, Queen Mary, and Queen Anne.

This, I presume, must have been conjectured from a few words of Lord Holt, in the case of Harcourt against Fox, which I think are these. I repeat them from memory, having not the book before me at present. "Our places as judges are so settled, determinable only upon misbehavior."

Now from these words I should draw an opposite conclusion from the General, and should think that the influence of that interest in the nation, which brought King William to the throne, prevailed upon him to grant the commissions to the judges expressly during good behavior. I say this is the most natural construction, because it is certain their places were not at that time, namely, 5 William and Mary, determined, by an act of parliament, to be determinable only upon misbehavior; and it is as certain, from Lord Coke and from all history, that they were not so settled by the common law of England.

However, we need not rest upon this reasoning because we happen to be furnished with the most explicit and decisive evidence that my conclusion is just, from my Lord Raymond. In the beginning of his second volume of Reports, his lordship has given us a list of the chief officers in the law at the time of the death of King William III., 8 March, 1701-2. And he says in these words, that "Sir John Holt, Knight, chief justice of the king's bench, holding his office by writ, though it was quamdiu se bene gesserit, held it to be determined by the demise of the king, notwithstanding the act of 12 and 13 William III. And, therefore, the queen in council gave orders that he should have a new writ, which he received accordingly, and was sworn before the lord keeper of the great seal the Saturday following, namely, the 14th of March, chief justice of king's bench." From this several things appear: 1. That General Brattle is mistaken in apprehending that the judges' commissions were without the clause, quamdiu bene se gesserint, in the reign of King William and Queen Mary, and most probably also in the reign of Queen Anne; because it is not likely that Lord Holt would have accepted a commission from the queen during pleasure, when he had before had one from King William during good behavior; and because if Queen Anne had made such an alteration in the commission, it is most likely Lord Raymond would have taken notice of it. 2. That Lord Holt's opinion was, that by common law he had not an estate for life in his office; for, if he had, it could not expire on the demise of the king. 3. That Lord Holt did not think the clause in the statute of 12 and 13 William III. to be a declaration of what was common law before, nor in affirmance of what was law before, but a new law, and a total alteration of the tenure of the judges' commissions established by parliament, and not to take place till after the death of the Princess Anne. 4. That in Lord Holt's opinion it was not in the power of the crown to alter the tenure of the judges' commissions, and make them a tenure for life, determinable only upon misbehavior, even by inserting that express clause in them, quamdiu se bene gesserint.

I have many more things to say upon this subject, which may possibly appear some other time.

Meanwhile, I am, Messrs. Printers,
Your humble servant,
John Adams.

From the Boston Gazette, 18 January, 1773.

to the printers.

It has been said already that the common law of England has not determined the judges to have an estate for life in their offices, provided they behaved well. The authorities of Lord Coke and Lord Holt have been produced relative to the judges of the king's bench; and, indeed, authorities still more ancient than Coke might have been adduced. For example, the learned Chancellor Fortescue, in his book in praise of the laws of England, chap. 51, says, "When any one judge of the king's bench dies, resigns, or is superseded, the king, with the advice of his council, makes choice of one of the sergeants-at-law, whom he constitutes a judge by his letters-patents in the room of the judge so deceased, resigning, or superseded." And afterwards he says, "It is no degree in law, but only an office and a branch of magistracy determinable on the king's good pleasure." I have quoted a translation in this place, as I choose to do whenever I can obtain one; but I do not venture to translate passages myself, lest I should be charged with doing it unfairly. The original words of Fortescue are unusual and emphatical: "Ad regis nutum duratura."

The judges of the court of common pleas held their offices by a tenure as precarious. "The chief justice of the common pleas is created by letters-patents,—Rex, &c. Sciatis quod constituimus dilectum et fidelem E. C. militem, capitalem justiciarium de communi banco. Habendum quamdiu nobis placuerit, cum vadiis et feodis ab antiquo debitis et consuetis. In cujus rei testimonium has literas nostras fieri fecimus patentes. Teste, &c. And each of the justices of this court hath letters-patents. Sciatis quod constituimus dilectum et fidelem P. W., militem, unum justiciariorum nostrorum de communi banco," *Endnote 181* &c.; and this &c. implies the habendum quamdiu nobis placuerit, as in the patent of the chief justice.

It is true that in the same Fourth Institute, 117, we read, that "the chief baron" (that is, of the exchequer) "is created by letters-patents, and the office is granted to him quamdiu se bene gesserit, wherein he hath a more fixed estate (it being an estate for life) than the justices of either bench, who have their offices but at will. And quamdiu se bene gesserit must be intended in matters concerning his office, and is no more than the law would have implied if the office had been granted for life. And in like manner are the rest of the barons of the exchequer constituted; and the patents of the attorney-general and solicitor are also quamdiu se bene gesserit."

It is also true, that by the law of this province a superior court of judicature, court of assize, and general jail delivery is constituted over this whole province, to be held and "kept by one chief justice and four other justices to be appointed and commissionated for the same; who shall have cognizance of all pleas, real, personal, or mixed, as well all pleas of the crown, &c.; and generally of all other matters, as fully and amply to all intents and purposes whatsoever, as the courts of king's bench, common pleas, and exchequer, within his majesty's kingdom of England, have, or ought to have," &c.

Will it be said that this law, giving our judges cognizance of all matters of which the court of exchequer has cognizance, gives them the same estate in their offices which the barons of exchequer had? or will it be said that by "the judges," General Brattle meant the barons of the exchequer?

The passages already cited will afford us great light in considering the case of Harcourt and Fox. Sir Thomas Powis, who was of counsel in that case for the plaintiff, indeed says, "I take it, by the common law and the ancient constitution of the kingdom, all officers of courts of justice, and immediately relating to the execution of justice, were in for their lives, only removable for misbehavior in their offices. Not only my lords the judges of the courts in Westminster Hall were anciently as they now are, since the revolution, quamdiu se bene gesserint, but all the officers of note in the several courts under them were so, and most of them continue so to this day, as the clerks of the crown in this court, and in the chancery, the chief clerk on the civil side in this court, the prothonotaries in the common pleas, the master of the office of pleas in the exchequer, and many others. I think, speaking generally, they were all in for their lives by the common law, and are so still to this day."

"And in this particular the wisdom of the law is very great; for it was an encouragement to men to fit and prepare themselves for the execution and performance of those offices, that when by such a capacity they had obtained them, they might act in them safely, without fear or dependence upon favor. And when they had served in them faithfully and honestly, and done their duty, they should not be removable at pleasure. And on the other side, the people were safe; for injustice, corruption, or other misdemeanors in an office were sufficient causes for removal and displacing the offender."

And Sergeant Levinz says, "If any judicial or ministerial office be granted to any man to hold, so long as he behaves himself well in the office, that is an estate for life, unless he lose it for misbehavior. So was Sir John Waller's case, as to the office of chief baron of the exchequer; and so was Justice Archer's case in the time of King Charles the Second. He was made a judge of the common pleas quamdiu se bene gesserit; and though he was displaced as far as they could, yet he continued judge of that court to the time of his death; and his name was used in all the fines, and other records of the court; and so it is in all cases of grants from the king, or from any other person." And afterwards,—"It is a grievance that runs through the whole common law, as to ministerial offices; for all the offices in this court, in the chancery, in the exchequer, in the common pleas, and generally all over the kingdom, relating to the administration of justice, and even the judges themselves, are officers for life;

and why there should be more of a grievance in this case than in theirs, I do not see. In general, they are all for life, though some few particular ones may be excepted indeed."

I have repeated at length these sayings of Sir Thomas Powis and Sergeant Levinz, because they are music in my ears; and I sincerely wish they were well supported; and because I suspect that General Brattle derived much of his learning relative to the judges' offices from them.

But, alas! so far as they make for his purpose, the whole stream of law and history is against them. And, indeed, Mr. Hawles, who was of counsel for Mr. Fox, seems to have given a true and sufficient answer to them in these words:—"Whatsoever the common law was as to offices that were so ancient, is no rule in this matter; though it is we know, that, as our books tell us, some offices were for life. And the office of chancellor of England, my Lord Coke says, could not be granted to any one for life. And why? Because it never was so granted. Custom and nothing else prevails, and governs in all those cases; of those offices that were usually granted for life, a grant of such an office for life was good, and of those that were not usually granted for life, a grant of such an office for life was void."

The judges, indeed, did not expressly deny any of those sayings of Sir Thomas Powis, or of Sergeant Levinz, who spoke after him on the same side; but the reason of this is plain; because it was quite unnecessary, in that case, to determine what was common law; for both the office of custos rotulorum, and that of clerk of the peace, were created by statute, not erected by common law, as was clearly agreed both on the bench and at the bar.

Nevertheless, my Lord Holt seems to have expressed his opinion when he said, "I compare it to the case which my Lord Chief Justice Hobart puts of himself in his book, 153, Colt and Glover's case. Saith he, 'I cannot grant the offices of my gift as chief justice for less time than for life;' and he puts the case there of a man's assigning a rent for dower out of the lands dowable, that it must be for no less estate than life; for the estate was by custom, and it cannot be granted for a lesser estate than what the custom appoints; and in that case of the chief justice, in granting offices in his gift, all that he had to do was to point out the person that should have the office, the custom settled his estate in it."

Thus, we see that the sentiments of Lord Coke and of Lord Holt concur with those of Mr. Hawles, that the custom was the criterion, and that alone. So that, if the king should constitute a baron of the exchequer during pleasure, he would have an estate for life in his office, or the grant would be void. Why? Because the custom had so settled it. If the king should constitute a judge of the king's bench, or common bench, during good behavior, he would have only an estate at will of the grantor. Why? Because the custom hath determined it so. And that custom could not be annulled or altered but by act of parliament.

But I go on with my delightful work of quotation. "In order to maintain both the dignity and independency of the judges in the superior courts, it is enacted by the stat. 13 W. III. c. 2, that their commissions shall be made, not, as formerly, durante beneplacito, but quamdiu se bene gesserint, and their salaries ascertained and established; but that it may be lawful to remove them on the address of both houses of parliament. And now, by the noble improvements of that law in the statute of 1 G. III. c. 23, enacted at the earnest recommendation of the king himself from the throne, the judges are continued in their offices during their good behavior, notwithstanding any demise of the crown, which was formerly held (see Lord Raym. 747) immediately to vacate their seats; and their full salaries are absolutely secured to them during the continuance of their commissions,—his majesty having been pleased to declare, that he looked upon the independence and uprightness of the judges as essential to the impartial administration of justice; as one of the best securities of the rights and liberties of his subjects; and as most conducive to the honor of the crown."
Endnote 182

It would be endless to run over all the passages in English history relating to this subject, and the examples of judges displaced by kings. It may not be amiss to turn our attention to a very few, however. The oracle himself was silenced by this power in the crown. "Upon the 18th November, this term, Sir Henry Montague was made chief justice of the king's bench, in the place of Sir Edward Coke, the late chief justice, who, being in the king's displeasure, was removed from his place by a writ from the king, reciting that whereas he had appointed him by writ to that place, that he had now amoved him, and appointed him to desist from the further execution thereof. And now this day, Egerton, lord chancellor, came into the king's bench; and Sir Henry Montague, one of the king's sergeants, being accompanied with Sergeant Hutten and Sergeant Francis Moore, came to the middle of the bar; and then the lord chancellor delivered unto him the king's pleasure, to make choice of him to that place." *Endnote 183*

There is a passage in Hume's History of England which I cannot forbear transcribing. "The Queen's (Elizabeth's) menace," says he, "of trying and punishing Hayward for treason, could easily have been executed, let his book have been ever so innocent. While so many terrors hung over the people, no jury durst have acquitted a man when the court was resolved to have him condemned. And, indeed, there scarcely occurs an instance during all these reigns, that the sovereign or the ministers were ever disappointed in the issue of a prosecution. Timid juries, and judges who held their offices during pleasure, never failed to second all the views of the crown."

Sergeant Levinz, in the argument of Harcourt against Fox, speaking of the first parliament under King William, says,—"The parliament might observe, that some years before there had been great changing of offices that usually were for life into offices quamdiu placuerit. This is very well known in Westminster Hall; and I did know some of them myself, particularly the judges of the courts of common law; for I myself (among others) lost my judge's place by it," &c.

Mr. Hume, in the reign of James the Second, says,—"The people had entertained such violent prepossessions against the use which James here made of his prerogative, that he was obliged, before he brought on Hales's cause, to displace four of the judges, Jones, Montague, Charlton, and Nevil."

There is not in history a more terrible example of judges perishing at the royal nod than this, nor a stronger evidence that the power and prerogative of removing judges at pleasure were allowed to be, by law, in the crown. It was loudly complained of as a grievance, no doubt, and an arbitrary exertion of prerogative; but it was allowed to be a legal prerogative still. And it cannot be doubted, that the legality of it would have been denied everywhere, if the sense of the nation, as well as the body of the law, had not been otherwise, when the circumstances of that case of Sir Edward Hales are considered. And they ought to be remembered, and well considered by every wellwisher to the public; because they show the tendency of a precarious, dependent tenure of the judges' offices. Sir Edward Hales was a papist; yet the king gave him a commission as a colonel of foot; and he refused to receive the sacrament, and to take the oaths and test, within the time prescribed by an act of parliament, 25 Car. II. c. 2, by which refusal, and that statute, he forfeited five hundred pounds. By concert between King James and Sir Edward, his coachman was employed to bring an action against him upon that statute, for the penalty. Sir Edward appears, and pleads a dispensation under the broad seal, to act non obstante that statute. To this the plaintiff demurs. When this action was to be brought to trial, the judges were secretly closeted by the king, and asked their opinions. Such as had scruples about judging as the court directed, were plainly told by the king himself, that he would have twelve judges of his own opinion, and turned out of their offices. The judges mentioned by Hume were thus displaced, to their lasting honor; and one of them, Jones, had the fortitude and integrity to tell the king to his face, that he might possibly make twelve judges, but he would scarcely find twelve lawyers of his opinion. Bedingfield, Atkins, Lutwyche, and Heath, to their disgrace and infamy, were created judges. And Westminster Hall thus garbled became the sanctuary of despotism and injustice. All the judges excepting one gave their opinions for the king, and made it a general rule in law,—1. That the laws of England are the king's laws. 2. That, therefore, it is an incident, inseparable prerogative of the kings of England, as of all other sovereign princes, to dispense with all penal laws in particular cases, and upon particular, necessary reasons. 3. That of these reasons and necessities the king is the sole judge. Consequently, 4. That this is not a trust invested in and granted to the king, but the ancient remains of the sovereign power of the kings of England, which never was yet taken from them, nor can be." In consequence of this decision, the papists, with the king's permission, set up everywhere in the kingdom in the free and open exercise of their religion. To enumerate all the struggles of the people, the petitions and addresses to kings, praying that the judges' commissions might be granted during good behavior, the bills which were actually brought into one or the other house of parliament for that purpose, which failed of success until the final establishment in the 12 & 13 William III., would be too tedious; *Endnote 184* and, indeed, I anxiously fear I have been so already.

I also fear the proofs that the common law of England has not determined the judges to have estates for life in their offices, appear to be very numerous, and quite irresistible. I very heartily wish General Brattle success in his researches after evidence of the contrary position; and while he is thus engaged, if I should find neither business more profitable nor amusement more inviting, I shall be preparing for your press a few other observations on his first publication.

John Adams.

From the Boston Gazette, 25 January, 1773.

Cambridge,18 January, 1773

.

to the printers.

As the lines of men's minds are as various as the features of their faces, they can no more, upon every subject, think alike than they can look alike, and yet both be equally honest. Consequently, they ought respectively to be treated with good manners, let their stations in life be what they may, by all excepting those who think they have infallibility on their side. For the public peace and good order, I should be willing to be mistaken in my law, as John Adams, Esq., in his letter of last week, supposes I am, if the writers upon political controversy would follow his example in his decent, polite writing. As to his knowledge and learning in the law, I can't expect their imitation till they have his genius and accomplishments, which I sincerely believe are rare. It appears to me, that Mr. Adams's sentiments upon the estate that the justices of the superior court here, by virtue of their nomination and appointment, have,—namely, that they may be legally displaced, merely by the arbitrary will and pleasure of the governor and council,—are tory principles. But as I am convinced to draw the consequence therefrom, that he is one, would be injurious and false, I hope his sentiments (though however mistaken) will not be improved to his prejudice. I, on the other hand, have said, and now declare as my opinion, that the governor and council can no more constitutionally and legally remove any one justice of the superior court, as the commissions now are, unless there is a fair hearing and trial, and then a judgment that he hath behaved ill, than they can hang me for writing this my opinion; and the latter (if it went no further) would not be of one half the public mischief and damage as the former, notwithstanding I am very sensible that this hath been the case in one or two arbitrary administrations. I recollect but two since the charter; but these were arbitrary, illegal, unconstitutional measures, and do not determine what the law is, any more than the arbitrary, illegal measures of the Stuart kings determine that their measures were legal and ought to be the rule of his present majesty's conduct. Arbitrary measures never did, after people had come to their senses, and I hope never will, determine what the law is.

Further I observe, that supposing a corrupt governor and a corrupt council, whether the words in the commission are, so long as the governor and council please, or, during good behavior, will just come to the same thing, the security as to the public will be just the same. But this is not our unhappy case. I am convinced that nothing would induce his excellency Governor Hutchinson, to nominate, or one member of the council to consent to a nomination in the room of any one justice of the superior court (however disagreeable he might be), till he had, after an impartial trial, been first adjudged to have behaved ill, and so forfeited his estate by a breach of trust. The first thing Mr. Adams expresses his great surprise at is, that I should be at any loss, or any man in the province should be at a loss, for what time the grant is made to the judges. He says the king cannot grant salaries in any other manner than durante beneplacito; and that the king's power to grant salaries to any judges in America is derived solely from the late act of parliament; and that gives no power to grant salaries for life or good behavior. The above assertions,—without the least color of proof, but Mr. Adams's word for it,—I deny. The parliament grants no salaries to the judges of England. The king settles the salaries, and pays his judges out of the civil list; and I challenge Mr. Adams to show one instance of any judge who was continued in office, though at the same time most disagreeable to the king, that his salary was taken from him; to suppose this, is frustrating the act of parliament that enacts that their commissions should be during good behavior. For what if they are during good behavior? What good will it do them; or what safety will it be to the community, if it is in the power of the king to take away their salaries, and starve them? Will they not in this case be as dependent upon the crown as if their commissions were to determine by the will of the king? Again, this act of parliament with respect to the judges' salaries was made for no other reason than this, that the king might not pay them out of the civil list, but out of another fund, namely, out of the revenue; here the above-mentioned act says nothing about durante beneplacito; and therefore, if there is a grant made to the judges, that grant stands upon the same footing with the salaries granted by the king to the judges in England. Mr. Adams challenges me to produce one lawyer that ever was, or now is, in the country, that entertained such an opinion as I have advanced,—namely, that, by the common law of England, the judges' commissions are, so long as they behave well. He acknowledges there may be respectable lawyers in this country that hold that the judges' commissions are during good behavior, though not expressly mentioned in their commission; but it is on other principles. I answer, if they are of that opinion, it must be upon my principles; for there is no statute law about it which extends to the plantations; the canon law or civil law says nothing about it; and therefore if they are in sentiments with me, they can found their opinion on the common law only; and this I do solemnly declare, the Honorable Mr. Read did, who was, to every lawyer, as highly esteemed for reforming and correcting the law and the pleadings as Justinian was at Rome. He was my friend, my father, under whose direction I studied the law. I have heard him often and often declare it as his opinion, and I have living witnesses to prove it. The late Judge Auchmuty was of the same mind. I have asked no gentlemen at the bar, now on the stage, their opinion, and do not know it; but this I know, that it is the opinion of the greatest lawyers, who are not at the bar, in the province, that I am right in what I have advanced. Mr. Adams makes a further challenge, and denies that I can produce the name of one of the sages of the law by whom it hath been settled as I contend for; or, in other words, that I am alone in my sentiments. This surprises me much, that a gentleman of Mr. Adams's learning should be so extremely mistaken, and forgetful. Sir Thomas Powis, one of the sages of the law, gives his opinion in the words following: "I take it, by the common law and the ancient constitution of the kingdom, all officers of courts of justice, and immediately relating to the execution of justice, were in for their lives, only removable for misbehavior in their offices. Not only my lords the judges of the courts in Westminster Hall were anciently as they now are, since the revolution, quamdiu se bene gesserint, but all the officers of note in the several courts under them were so; and most of them continue so to this day, as the clerks of the crown in this court, and in the chancery, the chief clerk on the civil side in this court, the prothonotaries in the common pleas, master of the office of pleas in the exchequer, and many others. I think, speaking generally, they were all in for their lives, by the common law, and are so to this day."

"I shall not enlarge upon this matter: I need not, it being so well known," says Sir Thomas. Sergeant Levinz expressly says that in the time of King Charles II., Justice Archer was made a judge of the common pleas quamdiu bene se gesserit. If it never was the common law of England that the judges' commissions run during their good behavior, as Mr. Adams affirms, and there was an act of parliament formerly, that they should be during the king's pleasure, (which, let it be observed, Lord Coke never said there was a statute relating to it) unless that statute was repealed,—and I challenge Mr. Adams, and so I would my Lord Coke if he was alive, to show that it was, and even that there ever was such a statute,—I query how it came about that King Charles II. did not conform to said statute; how, in the face of an act of parliament or the common law, or both, to give commissions to the judges to continue during good behavior, and thereby lessen their dependence on him; this can't well be reconciled with the history of his reign. And how came it about that ever since the revolution to George I.'s time, the commissions were during good behavior? This, I agree with Mr. Adams, was the case, and am quite obliged to him for correcting my mistake, when, in my harangue, I said otherwise. According to Mr. Adams's doctrine, and according to the law, they were ipso facto null and void, because they were directly against law; provided Mr. Adams is right, that both common law and statute law formerly obliged the king to give the judges their commissions during good pleasure only. But I conceive that King William and Queen Mary, that came over to save an almost ruined and undone people by the tyranny of their predecessors and their acting directly contrary to the laws of the land, that they should begin their reign by going directly against the law, and thereby violate their coronation oath, this is not credible. What the law was before their reign was better known; and the law, which was often fluctuating by the arbitrary power of some former princes, was put upon a more solid basis since the revolution than it was before. And we are to inquire what the law was formerly, by the resolutions, the judgments of court, and the practice, since the revolution, and the tenure of the judge's commission since the revolution being during good behavior, to the reign of George I.; and when the act of King William was to take place, and not before,—namely, that during good behavior should be in their commissions, plainly proves what I have advanced to be law, is law, or else great dishonor is reflected upon King William, Queen Mary, and Queen Anne. I am obliged to Mr. Adams for quoting the following passage out of my Lord Coke, which fully justifies my reasoning upon the judges' commissions; the words are these: "It is a rule in law that ancient offices must be granted in such forms and in such manner as they have used to be, unless the alteration was by authority of parliament."

It is manifest to every one that doth not depend upon their memory, that Lord Chief Justice Holt, one of the sages of the law, apprehended that for the judges' commissions being during good behavior, was upon the rule of the common law. He says, after a cause had been argued upon a special verdict, after Sir T. Powis and Sergeant Levinz had most positively affirmed that this was the rule of the common law, not denied by the counsel on the other side, but rather conceded to, that in giving his opinion upon the whole matter. "We all know it," says that great lawyer, "and our places as judges are so settled, only determinable upon misbehavior." Settled by—whom? Not by an act that was not to take place till the accession of George I. Not by any statute then existing. Where is it? who ever heard of it? let it be produced. If not by statute, certainly, then, by common law. And can any man think that Lord Chief Justice Holt would have taken a commission from King William and Queen Mary, if they had offered him one, supposing it had been contrary to law, or rather if it had not been consonant to law; or can we suppose that all the judges of the king's bench would have heard the before-mentioned gentlemen with respect to the tenure of the judges' commissions, without a reproof, or at least without telling them it was not law, if all the judges had not thought it was law? I leave the world to determine.

Mr. Adams says, and says truly, that Sir John Holt, knight, chief justice of the king's bench, holding his office by writ, though it was quamdiu bene se gesserit, held it to be determined by the demise of the king, and therefore Queen Anne ordered a new writ. And what then? Every civil officer's commission holden quamdiu bene se gesserit, died with the demise of the king, till the act made in the present king's reign. Wherefore, there was an act of parliament that all officers should be continued a certain time after the demise of the king, to prevent the total stagnation of justice.

Mr. Adams supposes a material difference between an estate that the judges have as such for life, or so long as they behave well. The following judges, his equals at least, differ from him. Sergeant Levinz: "I take it clear law, that if an office be granted to hold so long as he behaves himself well in the office, that is an estate for life, unless he lose it for misbehavior; for it hath an annexed condition to be forfeited upon misdemeanor, and this by law is annexed to all offices, they being trusts; and misdemeanor in an office is a breach of trust; and with his opinion agree the judges of the king's bench, in the case of Harcourt against Fox. Eyre, Justice, says, "I do think there is plainly given an estate for life in his office, determinable upon his good behavior." Gregory, Justice, says the same. Dolben, Justice, says, that "if any man is to enjoy an office so long as he behaves well in it, no one will doubt but the grantee hath an estate for life in it." My Lord Chief Justice Holt says, "I do agree with my brothers in opinion." Upon the whole, using Mr. Adams's own words, my haranguing in the town meeting in Cambridge hath not received any sufficient legal answer; and notwithstanding my veneration for Mr. Adams's authority, it by no means prevails with me to give credit to his doctrine. Nor do his reasons in support of it weigh with me even so much as his authority.

W. Brattle.

From the Boston Gazette, 25 January, 1773.

to the printers.

Another observation which occurred to me upon reading General Brattle's first publication was upon these words:—"That by the charter and common law of England, there is no necessity of having any commission at all; a nomination and appointment recorded is enough; nomination and appointment are the words of the charter, a commission for them not so much as mentioned in it. Their commission is only declarative of their nomination and appointment." Two questions arise upon this paragraph; and the first is, what provision is made by our charter? and the next is, what was necessary to the creation of a judge at common law?

As to our charter. The king thereby grants and ordains,—"That it shall and may be lawful for the said governor, with the advice and consent of the council or assistants, from time to time to nominate and appoint judges, commissioners of oyer and terminer, sheriffs, provosts, marshals, justices of the peace, and other officers to our council and courts of justice belonging."

It is obvious from this, that there is no superior court of judicature, court of assize and general jail delivery, nor any inferior court of common pleas, or any court of exchequer, expressly erected by the charter. Commissioners of oyer and terminer, the governor, with the advice and consent of the council, is empowered to nominate and appoint; but it will not follow from hence that a nomination and appointment will alone constitute and empower commissioners of oyer and terminer. For the judges, whom the governor with the advice of council is empowered to nominate and appoint, are not vested with any powers at all by the charter; but by another clause in it, the great and general court or assembly "shall forever have full power and authority to erect and constitute judicatories and courts of record, or other courts, to be held in the name of us, our heirs and successors, for the hearing, trying, and determining of all manner of crimes, offences, pleas, processes, plaints, actions, matters, causes, and things, whatsoever, arising or happening within our said province or territory, or between persons inhabiting and residing there, whether the same be criminal or civil, and whether the said crimes be capital or not capital, and whether the said pleas be real, personal, or mixt, and for the awarding and making out execution thereupon."

In pursuance of this authority, our legislature, in 1699, by a law, 2 William III. c. 3, have established "a superior court of judicature, court of assize, and general jail delivery within this province, to be held by one chief justice and four other justices, to be appointed and commissionated for the same," &c. Is not General Brattle, then, greatly mistaken when he says, that "a nomination and appointment recorded is enough?" Enough for what? Enough to constitute judges of our superior court, for they alone can be meant by the General, because the General himself determines his own meaning to be, "they who have the same powers with the king's bench, common bench, and exchequer;" and no other judges have those powers but the judges of our superior court, &c., and they have them, not by charter, but by the law of the province. If the governor should nominate and appoint, with advice and consent, &c. A to be a judge, or A, B, and C to be judges, in the words of the charter, what powers would this nomination and appointment convey? None at all. It would be nugatory and void; for, according to Lord Coke, Endnote 185 a "new court cannot be erected but by act of parliament. And when a new court is erected, it is necessary that the jurisdiction and authority of the court be certainly set down. And that the court can have no other jurisdiction than is expressed in the erection." And he there mentions the case of a letter-patent granted by Edward IV. in these words: "We will and ordain that Richard Beauchampe, &c., should have it (that is, the office of the chancellor of the garter) for his life, and after his decease, that his successors should have it forever"; and "it was resolved unanimously that this grant was void; for that a new office was erected, and it was not defined what jurisdiction or authority the officer should have; and, therefore, for the uncertainty, it was void."

Let us next inquire whether, by the common law of England, there is or is not a necessity of the judges having any commissions at all. The authorities cited before seem to show very plainly that the judges, either of the king's bench, common bench, or exchequer, can be created only by writ, or by letters-patent; and although these may be said not to be commissions, yet they are surely something more than nomination and appointment.

However, writs and letters-patent are commissions, I presume; and should never have doubted it, if I had never read a newspaper. But if I had doubted, I might easily have resolved the doubt; for we read Endnote 186 that "all judges must derive their authority from the crown by some commission warranted by law. The judges of Westminster are (all except the chief justice of the king's bench, who is created by writ) appointed by patent, and formerly held their places only during the king's pleasure, &c." Endnote 187

And Lord Coke observes, that "the creation of the office of chief justice was first by writ, and afterwards by letters-patents." "As all judges must derive their authority from the crown by some commission warranted by law, they must also exercise it in a legal manner." Endnote 188

In order to see whether writs and letters-patent are not commissions, let us look into any common dictionary or interpreter of law terms. "Commission, commissio," (says Cowell, and after him, in the same words, Cunningham,) "is for the most part, in the understanding of the law, as much as delegatio with the civilians, Endnote 189 and is taken for the warrant, or letters-patent, that all men exercising jurisdiction, either ordinary or extraordinary, have for their power to hear or determine any cause or action."

Thus it seems to be very clear that, by the common law of England, a commission was absolutely necessary for all the judges known at common law; and as to others, erected by statute, let the statute speak. By 27 H. 8, c. 24, it is enacted: "That no person or persons, of what estate, degree, or condition soever they be, shall have any power or authority to make any justices of eyre, justices of assize, justices of peace, or justices of jail delivery; but that all such officers and ministers shall be made by letters-patent, under the king's great seal, in the name and by the authority of the king's highness, in all shires, counties palatine, Wales, &c., or any other his dominions, &c., any grants, usages, allowance, or act of parliament to the contrary notwithstanding."

I shall add no more upon this point but this. We find in Jenkin's Centuries, 123, this question determined by all the judges of England in the exchequer chamber: "A writ of admittas in association is directed to the justices of assize; A. shows this writ of admittas in association to them, but does not show the patent by which he is made justice. In this case, both ought to be shown to the justices of assize.

By all the Judges in the Exchequer Chamber."

The judges of the king's bench and common pleas, and the barons of the exchequer are made by patent, in which the word constituimus is used. The chief justice of the king's bench is constituted only by writ."

John Adams.

From the Boston Gazette, 1 February, 1773.

One thing at one time.
—De Witt.

to the printers.

The question is, in the present state of the controversy, according to my apprehension of it, whether, by the common law of England, the judges of the king's bench and common bench had estates for life in their offices, determinable on misbehavior, and determinable also on the demise of the crown. General Brattle still thinks they had; I cannot yet find reason to think so. And as whether they had or had not is the true question between us, I will endeavor to confine myself to it without wandering.

Now, in order to pursue my inquiry regularly, it is necessary to determine with some degree of precision what is to be understood by the terms "common law." Out of the

Mercian laws, the laws of the West Saxons, and the Danish law, King Edward the Confessor extracted one uniform digest of laws, to be observed throughout the whole kingdom, which seems to have been no more than a fresh promulgation of Alfred's code, or Dome Book, with such improvements as the experience of a century and a half had suggested, which is now unhappily lost. This collection is of higher antiquity than memory or history can reach; they have been used time out of mind, or for a time whereof the memory of man runneth not to the contrary. General customs, which are the universal rule of the whole kingdom, form the common law in its stricter and more usual signification. This is that law which determines that there shall be four superior courts of record, the chancery, the king's bench, the common pleas, and the exchequer, among a multitude of other doctrines, that are not set down in any written statute or ordinance, but depend merely upon immemorial usage, that is, upon common law, for their support. Judicial decisions are the principal and most authoritative evidence that can be given of the existence of such a custom as shall form a part of the common law. The law and the opinion of the judge are not always convertible terms; though it is a general rule, that the decisions of courts of justice are the evidence of what is common law. *Endnote 190*

I have endeavored to ascertain what is meant by the common law of England, and the method of determining all questions concerning it, from Blackstone. Let us now see what is said upon the same subject, by Justice Fortescue Aland, in the preface to his Reports. "Our judges," says he, "do not determine according to their princes, or their own arbitrary will and pleasure; but according to the settled and established rules and ancient customs of the nation, approved for many successions of ages. . . . . . . King Alfred, who began his reign in 871, magnus juris Anglicani conditor, the great founder of the laws of England, with the advice of his wise men, collected out of the laws of Ina, Offa, and Æthelbert, such as were the best, and made them to extend equally to the whole nation, and therefore very properly called them the common law of England, because those laws were now first of all made common to the whole English nation. This jus commune, jus publicum, or folcright, that is, the people's right, set down in one code, was probably the same with the Doom-Book, or liber judicialis, which is referred to in all the subsequent laws of the Saxon kings, and was the book that they determined causes by. And in the next reign, that of Edward the elder, the king commands all his judges to give judgment to all the people of England according to the Doom-Book. And it is from this origin that our common law judges fetch that excellent usage of determining causes, according to the settled and established rules of law, and that they have acted up to this rule for above eight hundred years together, and continue to do so to this very day. Edward the Confessor was afterwards but the restorer of the common law founded by Alfred, and William the Conqueror confirms and proclaims these to be the laws of England, to be kept and observed under grievous penalties, and took an oath to keep them inviolable himself. King Henry I. promised to observe them; King Stephen, King Henry II., and Richard I. confirmed them; King John swore to restore them; King Henry III. confirmed them; Magna Charta was founded on them, and King Edward I. in parliament, confirmed them." *Endnote 191*

Now I apprehend General Brattle's opinion to be, that the common law of England, the birthright of every subject, or, in the language of the Saxons, the folkright, determines the judges of the king's bench and common pleas to have estates for life in their offices, determinable only on misbehavior, or the demise of the crown. And this, I suppose, was the meaning of Sir Thomas Powis, when he said, "I take it, by the common law and the ancient constitution of the kingdom, all officers of courts of justice, &c., were in for their lives, &c.; not only my lords the judges of the courts in Westminster Hall were anciently, as they now are since this revolution, quamdiu se bene gesserint."

I have never expressed any disrespect to the character of Sir Thomas Powis, and I have no disposition to harbor any; it is enough for me to say, that these expressions were used by him when arguing a cause for his client at the bar, not when he was determining a cause as a judge; that they were entirely unnecessary for the support of his cause, which was a very good one, let these expressions be true or otherwise,—that is, whether the judges were anciently in for their lives, or only at pleasure; that they depend wholly upon his affirmation, or rather his opinion, without the color or pretence of an authority to support them; and that I really believe them to be untrue. And I must add, it appears to me extraordinary, that a gentleman educated under that great Gamaliel, Mr. Read, should ever adduce the simple dictum of a counsel at the bar, uttered arguendo, and as an ornament to his discourse too, rather than any pertinent branch of his reasoning, as evidence of a point "settled and determined by the greatest sages of the law formerly and more lately." Does Sir Thomas Powis produce the Dome-Book itself in support of his doctrine? That was irrecoverably lost for ages before he had a being. Does he produce any judicial decision, ancient or modern, to prove this opinion? No such thing pretended. Does he produce any legal authority, a Hengham, Britton, Fleta, Fortescue, Coke; or any antiquarian, Matthew Paris, Dugdale, Lambard, or any other; or even the single opinion of one historian, to give a color to his doctrine? No such matter. Nay, I must inquire further, can General Brattle draw from any of these sources a single iota to support this opinion? But, in order to show, for the present, the improbability that any such authority will be found, let us look a little into history. Mr. Rapin, in his Dissertation on the Government of the Anglo-Saxons, says, "One of the most considerable of the king's prerogatives was the power of appointing the earls, viscounts, judges, and other officers, as well civil as military. Very probably it was in the king's power to change these officers, according to his pleasure, of which we meet with several instances in history." By this it appears to have been Mr. Rapin's opinion, that very probably the kings, under the ancient Saxon constitution, had power to change the judges according to their pleasure. I would not be understood, however, to lay any great stress on the opinions of historians and compilers of antiquities, because it must be confessed that the Saxon constitution is involved in much obscurity, and that the monarchical and democratic factions in England, by their opposite endeavors to make the Saxon constitutions swear for their respective systems, have much increased the difficulty of determining, to the satisfaction of the world, what that constitution, in many important particulars, was. Yet Mr. Rapin certainly was not of that monarchical faction; his bias, if he had any, was the other way; and therefore his concession makes the more in my favor.

Mr. Hume, in his Feudal and Anglo-Norman Government and Manners, *Endnote 192* says: "The business of the court was wholly managed by the chief justiciary and the law-barons, who were men appointed by the king, and wholly at his disposal." And since I am now upon Hume, it may be proper to mention the case of Hubert de Burgh, who, "while he enjoyed his authority, had an entire ascendant over Henry III., and was loaded with honors and favors beyond any other subject, . . . and, by an unusual concession, was made chief justiciary of England for life." *Endnote 193* Upon this I reason thus: If his being made justiciary for life was an "unusual concession," it could not be by the immemorial, uninterrupted usage and custom, which is the criterion of common law. And the very next words of Hume show how valid and effectual this grant of the office for life was then esteemed. "Yet Henry, in a sudden caprice, threw off this faithful minister;" which implies that he was discarded and displaced in both his capacities, because the summus justiciarius or chief justiciary, was in those reigns supreme regent of the kingdom, and first minister of state, as well as of the law; and this seems to show that the grant for life was void, and not binding on the king, in the sense of those times, ancient as they were (1231). This summus justiciarius is the officer whose original commission I gave the public from Lord Coke, in my first paper, which was expressly during pleasure. And my Lord Coke's account of the change of the chief justice's commission and authority may receive some additional light from Lord Gilbert's Historical View of the Court of Exchequer. Towards the latter end of the Norman period, the power of the justiciar was broken, so that the aula regis, which was before one great court, only distinguished by several offices, and all ambulatory with the king before Magna Charta, was divided into four distinct courts,—chancery, exchequer, king's bench, and common pleas. The justiciary was laid aside, lest he should get into the throne, as Capet and Pepin, who were justiciars in France, had done there. *Endnote 194* Now, from the exorbitant powers and authority of these justiciaries arises a proof, from the frame of the government and the balance of the estates, that the office in those ages was always considered as dependent on the pleasure of the king, because the jealousy between the kings and nobles, or between the monarchical and aristocratical factions, during the whole Norman period, was incessant and unremitted; and therefore it may be depended on, that kings never would have come into the method of granting such an office usually for life. For such a grant, if it had been made, and been valid, must have cost the grantor his throne, as it made the justiciar independent of the king, and a much more powerful man than himself. And if, during the whole Norman period, and quite down to the death of Sir Edward Coke, a course of almost six hundred years, the offices of judges were held during pleasure, what becomes of the title to them for life, which General Brattle sets up, by immemorial, uninterrupted usage, or common law?

Sir Thomas Powis, however, has not determined whether, by the ancient constitution of the kingdom, he meant under the Norman or the Saxon period; and in order to show the improbability that the judges held their offices during good behavior, in either of those periods, I must beg the pardon of your readers if I lead them into ages, manners, and government more ancient and barbarous than any mentioned before. Our Saxon ancestors were one of those enterprising northern nations, who made inroads upon the provinces of the Roman empire, and carried with them, wherever they went, the customs, maxims, and manners of the feudal system; and although, when they intermingled with the ancient Britons, they shook off some part of the feudal fetters, yet they never disengaged themselves from the whole. They retained a vast variety of the regalia principis of the feudal system, from whence most branches of the present prerogatives of our kings are derived; and, among other regalia, the creation and annihilation of judges was an important branch. For evidence of this, we must look into the feudal law. It was in consequence of this prerogative that the courts were usually held in the aula regis, and often in the king's presence, who often heard and determined causes in person; and in those ages the justiciary was only a substitute or deputy to the king, whose authority ceased entirely in the king's presence. This part of the prerogative has a long time ago been divested from the crown, and it has been determined that the king has delegated all his authority to his judges. The power of the king in the Saxon period was absolute enough, however, and he sometimes treated them with very little ceremony. Alfred himself is said, in the Mirror of Justices, to have hanged up forty-four of his judges in one year for misdemeanors.

To some of these facts and principles Bracton is a witness. "Dictum est," (says he,) "de ordinaria jurisdictione, quæ pertinet ad regem, consequenter dicendum est de jurisdictione delegata, ubi quis ex se ipso nullam habet auctoritatem, sed ab alio sibi commissam, cum ipse qui delegat non sufficiat per se omnes causas sive jurisdictiones terminare. Et si ipse dominus rex ad singulas causas terminandas non sufficiat, ut levior sit illi labor, in plures personas partito onere, eligere debet de regno suo viros sapientes et timentes Deum. . . Item justiciariorum, quidam sunt capitales, generales, perpetui et majores a latere regis residentes, qui omnium aliorum corrigere tenentur injurias et errores. Sunt etiam alii perpetui, certo loco residentes, sicut in banco, . . . qui omnes jurisdictionem habere incipiunt præstito sacramento. . . Et quamvis quidam eorum perpetui sunt, ut videtur, finitur tamen eorum jurisdictio multis modis, s. mortuo eo qui delegavit, &c. Item cum delegans revocaverit jurisdictionem," &c. Bracton, chap. 10, lib. 3.

Sergeant Levinz says, "If any judicial or ministerial office be granted to any man to hold, so long as he behaves himself well in the office, that is an estate for life, unless he lose it for misbehavior. So was Sir John Waller's case, as to the office of chief baron of the exchequer." To all this I agree, provided it is an office that by custom, that is, immemorial usage, or common law, (as that of the chief baron of the exchequer was,) or by an express act of parliament, (as that of clerk of the peace, in the case of Harcourt against Fox, was,) has been granted in that manner, but not otherwise; and therefore these words have no operation at all against me. But the Sergeant goes on: "And so was Justice Archer's case, in the time of King Charles II. He was made a judge of the common pleas quamdiu se bene gesserit; and though he was displaced as far as they could, yet he continued judge of that court to the time of his death; and his name was used in all the fines and other records of the court." General Brattle thinks these words are full in his favor; and he cannot reconcile this patent to Judge Archer with the history of Charles II.'s reign, &c. We shall presently see if a way to reconcile it cannot be discovered: but before I come to this attempt, as it is my desire to lay before the public every thing I know of, which favors General Brattle's hypothesis, and to assist his argument to the utmost of my power, I will help him to some other authorities, which seem to corroborate Sergeant Levinz's saying; and the first is Justice Fortescue Aland: *Endnote 195* "Justice Archer was removed from the common pleas; but his patent being quamdiu se bene gesserit, he refused to surrender his patent without a scire facias, and continued justice, though prohibited to sit there; and in his place Sir William Ellis was sworn." The next is Sir Thomas Raymond, 217: "This last vacation, Justice Archer was amoved from sitting in the court of common pleas, pro quibusdam causis mihi incognitis; but the judge having his patent to be judge quamdiu se bene gesserit, refused to surrender his patent without a scire facias, and continued justice of that court, though prohibited to sit there; and in his place Sir William Ellis, Knight, was sworn."

But will any man from these authorities conclude that King Charles II. had power by the common law to grant Judge Archer an estate for life in his office? If he had, how could he be prohibited to sit? how came Justice Ellis to be sworn in his stead? Was not the admission of Ellis by his brother judges an acknowledgment of the king's authority? Will any man conclude from these authorities that it had before been the custom, time out of mind, for kings to grant patents to the judges, quamdiu se bene gesserint? If we look into Rushworth, 1366, we shall find some part of this mystery unriddled: "After the passing of these votes against the judges, and transmitting of them unto the house of peers, and their concurring with the house of commons therein, an address was made unto the king shortly after, that his majesty for the future would not make any judge by patent during pleasure, but that they may hold their places hereafter quamdiu se bene gesserint, and his majesty did readily grant the same, and in his speech to both houses of parliament, at the time of giving his royal assent to two bills, one to take away the high commission court, and the other the court of star-chamber, and regulating the power of the council table, he hath this passage,—'If you consider what I have done this parliament, discontents will not sit in your hearts; for I hope you remember that I have granted that the judges hereafter shall hold their places, quamdiu se bene gesserint.' And likewise his gracious majesty, King Charles II. observed the same rule and method in granting patents to judges, quamdiu se bene gesserint, as appears upon record in the rolls, namely,—to Sergeant Hyde, to be lord chief justice of the king's bench, Sir Orlando Bridgeman to be lord chief baron, and afterwards lord chief justice of the common pleas, to Sir Robert Foster, and others. Mr. Sergeant Archer, now living, (notwithstanding his removal,) still enjoys his patent, being quamdiu se bene gesserit, and receives a share in the profits of that court, as to fines and other proceedings, by virtue of his said patent, and his name is used in those fines &c. as a judge of that court."

This address of the two houses of parliament which was in 1640, was made in consequence of a general jealousy conceived of the judges, and the general odium which had fallen upon them, for the opinion they gave in the case of ship money and other cases, and because there had been, not long before, changes and removals in the benches. To mention only one: "Sir Randolph Crew, not showing so much zeal for the advancement of the loan as the king was desirous he should, was removed from his place of lord chief justice, and Sir Nicholas Hyde succeeded in his room." And King Charles, in 1640, began to believe the discontents of his subjects to be a serious affair, and think it necessary to do something to appease them. *Endnote 196*

But will it do to say that he had power to give away the prerogative of the crown, that had been established in his ancestors for eight hundred years, and no man can say how many centuries longer, without an act of parliament, against the express words of Lord Coke, which the General thanks me for quoting? "It is a rule in law that ancient offices must be granted in such forms and in such manner as they have used to be, unless the alteration was by authority of parliament."

As to King Charles II. his character is known to have been that of a man of pleasure and dissipation, who left most kinds of business to his ministers, and particularly in the beginning of his reign, to my Lord Clarendon, who had, perhaps, a large share in procuring that concession from Charles I., and therefore chose to continue it under the Second.

But notwithstanding all this, Charles II. soon discovered that by law his father's concession and his own had not divested him of the power of removing judges, even those to whom he had given patents quamdiu se bene gesserint, and he actually reassumed his prerogative, displaced Judge Archer and many others in the latter end of his reign, and so did his successor. *Endnote 197* These examples show that those kings did not consider these concessions as legally binding on them; they also show that the judges in Westminster Hall were of the same mind, otherwise they would not have admitted the new judges in the room of those displaced; and it seems that even the judges themselves who were then displaced, Judge Archer himself, did not venture to demand his place, which he might have done if he had an estate for life in his office. Nay, it may be affirmed that the house of commons themselves were of the same mind; for in the year 1680, in the reign of Charles II. after the removal of Archer and many other judges, the commons brought in a bill to make the office of judge during good behavior. *Endnote 198* Now I think they would not have taken this course if they had thought Archer had an estate for life in his office, but would have voted his removal illegal, and would have impeached the other judges for admitting another in his room.

Archer "continuing judge," and "receiving fees for fines," and "his name being used in the fines," I conjecture are to be accounted for in this manner. He refused to surrender his patent without a scire facias. The king would not have a scire facias brought, because that would occasion a solemn hearing, and much speculation, clamor, and heat, which he chose to avoid; and as his patent remained unsurrendered and uncancelled, and as by law there might be more judges of the common pleas than four, and therefore the appointment of another judge might not be a supersedeas to Archer, they might think it safest to join his name in the fines, and give him a share in the fees. And no doubt this might be done in some instances to keep up the appearance of a claim to the place, and with a design to provoke the king's servants and friends to bring a scire facias, and so occasion an odium on the administration, and hasten a revolution.

I have hazarded these conjectures unnecessarily, for it is incumbent upon General Brattle to show from good authorities, for the affirmative side of the issue is with him, that by common law the judges had estates for life in their offices. In order to do this, he ought to show that the king at common law, that is, from time immemorial, granted patents to these judges during good behavior, or that he, the king, had his election to grant them either durante beneplacito, or quamdiu se bene gesserint, as he pleased. Nay, it is incumbent on him to show that a patent without either of these clauses conveys an estate for life. None of these things has he done, or can he do.

It was never denied nor doubted by me, that a grant made in pursuance of immemorial custom, or of an act of parliament, to a man to hold, so long as he should behave himself well, would give him an estate for life. The unanimous judgment of the court in that case of Harcourt against Fox proves this. But then, in that case, an express act of parliament empowered the custos rotulorum to constitute a clerk of the peace for so long time as he should behave himself well. Nor have I any doubt that the patents to the barons of the exchequer, which are by immemorial usage, quamdiu se bene gesserint, convey to them an estate for life; but my difficulty lies here; no custom, no immemorial usage, no act of parliament, enabled the king to grant patents to the judges of king's bench, and common pleas, expressly quamdiu se bene gesserint; and therefore, if Lord Coke's rule is right, "that ancient offices must be granted in such forms and in such manner as they have used to be, unless the alteration be by authority of parliament," the king's grant at common law, to a judge of king's bench or common pleas, of his office, for life in terms, or during good behavior, which is tantamount, would have been void—void, I mean quoad an estate for life or good behavior, but good, as an estate at will; and I conceive, when we read that the king cannot make a lord chancellor for life, but that such a grant would be void, the meaning is, that the habendum for life or good behavior shall be void; but that this shall not vitiate the other parts of the patents, but that they shall convey such estate, and such estate only, as the king had power by custom or by statute to grant. I do not suppose that the writ to Lord Holt, or the patents to his brothers in the reign of King William were void, but I fear that, had the king seen fit to have removed them by writ, it would have been legally in his power, notwithstanding that clause in their commissions.

John Adams.

From the Boston Gazette, 8 February, 1773.

to the printers.

Two or three anecdotes were omitted in my last for want of room, which may be here inserted, in order to show that General Brattle's "rule of the common law of England" originated in the reign of King Charles I. I say originated, because the example of Hubert de Burgh is so ancient and so uncertain that it is even doubted by Baron Gilbert whether he was ever chief justiciary or not.

In 1641, King Charles I. finding his affairs in a desperate condition, was obliged to consent to an act of the Scottish parliament, that no member of the privy council, no officer of state, none of the judges, should be appointed but by advice and approbation of parliament; and all the officers of state were to hold their places quamdiu se bene gesserint. Four of the present judges, who had been active on the side of prerogative, were displaced.

In 1642, the parliament of England transmitted to the king, at York, nineteen propositions, in order for an accommodation of the differences then subsisting, the twelfth of which was, that the judges should hold their places quamdiu se bene gesserint. *Endnote 199*

This was but about two years after the king had given orders, at the instance of parliament, and his royal promise in his public speech, that the judges' commissions should for the future be granted quamdiu se bene gesserint. And it proves incontestably one of these things, either that the parliament thought the king's promise was void, as being what he had not power by law to promise; or that the grants so made would be void, at least as to the habendum during good behavior; or, at least, that the crown had its election by law to make judges, at pleasure or at will, as it should see fit. Now, if either of these apprehensions was just, it could not be true that at common law the judges had their commissions quamdiu se bene gesserint, nor could it be true that by common law the judges had estates for life in their offices, whether quamdiu se bene gesserint was in their commissions or not.

I believe enough has been said concerning these dark sayings of Powis and Levinz. Let us now proceed to consider what was said by Lord Holt. And I must think, the General has discovered a degree of art in managing his lordship's words that is very remarkable; and I beg the reader's patience while I develop in some detail this complicated mystery. In order to this, I must state the case of Harcourt against Fox; for this will show that the decision of that case is no proof of any thing that I have ever denied, and that General Brattle has unaccountably misinterpreted Lord Holt's words.

The act of parliament made in the first year of William and Mary, says "the custos rotulorum, or other, having right to nominate a clerk of the peace, shall nominate and appoint a fit person for the same, for so long time only as such clerk of the peace shall demean himself well in his office."

The earl of Clare is made custos according to that statute. By his deed, he constituted the plaintiff, Harcourt, to be clerk of the peace, "to have and execute that office so long as he did well behave himself in it."

After this the earl of Clare was removed, and my lord of Bedford was made custos; and he, by his deed, appointed Fox, the defendant, to be clerk of the peace for so long time as he should continue custos, if the said Fox did behave himself well in the office. And the question, as stated by Lord Holt, was "whether or no by the motion of my lord of Clare from the office of custos, Harcourt ceased to be clerk of the peace; for then, the law was for the defendant; otherwise, it was for the plaintiff."

Lord Holt concurred with his brothers, that judgment should be for the plaintiff, and that he was still clerk of the peace; and, after explaining his reasons at great length, and with great learning and perspicuity, he hath these words,—

"All that the custos hath to do in reference to this office of clerk of the peace, is to point out the person that should have it; and as the other" (that is, the officer appointed by the chief justice) "is in by custom, so here he is in by act of parliament; the custos, when he hath named him, he hath executed his authority, and cannot qualify the interest which passeth by the act. I am the more inclined to be of this opinion, because I knew the temper and inclination of the parliament at the time when this act was made; their design was, that men should have places not to hold precariously or determinable upon will and pleasure, but have a certain, durable estate, that they might act in them without fear of losing them; we all know it, and our places as judges are so settled, only determinable upon misbehavior."

Now, I would ask any impartial person, to what those words, "we all know it," refer? We all know it; know what?—that such was the temper and inclination of that parliament, and that such was their design. Can it be said that these words refer to words that follow? We all know it; know what?—that our places as judges are so settled! Some new kind of grammar, logic, and common sense, must be invented, and applied to this paragraph, before this construction can be adopted.

I will now repeat the words of General Brattle:—"It is manifest to every one that doth not depend upon their memory, that Lord Chief Justice Holt, one of the sages of the law, apprehended that for the judges' commissions being during good behavior, was upon the rule of the common law. He says, after a cause had been argued upon a special verdict, after Sir T. Powis and Sergeant Levinz had most positively affirmed that this was the rule of the common law, not denied by the counsel for the other side, but rather conceded to, that, in giving his opinion upon the whole matter. 'We all know it,' says that great lawyer, 'and our places as judges are so settled, only determinable by misbehavior.' "

Now, I will ask the same impartial person, to what those words, "we all know it," appear to refer, in the foregoing words of General Brattle. We all know it;—know what? That this was the rule of the common law, as Powis and Levinz had most positively affirmed.

In Lord Holt's own mouth, they referred to the temper, inclination, and design, of parliament; in General Brattle's writings, they are made to refer, seemingly, if not necessarily, to the sayings of Powis and Levinz, and to the rule of the common law. I hope this was the effect of haste, inadvertence, any thing rather than design in the General.

I must entreat every gentleman to look into that case of Harcourt and Fox, which is reported in Shower, at great length, and he must be convinced that, taken all together, it makes against General Brattle rather than for him. It was determined in that case, as it had been long before, that to hold an office during good behavior was to hold it for life, determinable upon misbehavior. This was never, and will never be, denied by me. But it was not determined that the judges' offices were held so, or that the king had power to grant them so. What was said by Lord Holt concerning the judges' offices had no direct relation to the point then in judgment before him, which concerned only the office of clerk of the peace. It was only said incidentally, and not explained. It might, and probably did, mean no more than it was so settled by King William in the patents he had given the judges, so far as it was in his power to settle it, and that it was the inclination and design of the parliament, and the then governing interest in the nation, that it should be so settled by act of parliament, as soon as it would bear. For it should be here observed, that although the friends of King William were most numerous and powerful, yet James had friends too, many and powerful friends, and the government was then weak; the revolution was so recent that they all had their fears. And the most sagacious of King William's friends might not choose to have this matter settled very suddenly; they might choose that the judges should remain subject to a revocation of their patents if they should fail in supporting King William; although they chose to have their patents granted quamdiu bene se gesserint, that they might have some hold of the royal word and honor, in order to obtain in due time a settlement of it by act of parliament.

Let me subjoin to this the authority of a very modern, though a very able and upright judge; I mean Sir Michael Foster: "The king, (Richard II.) and his ministers, soon after the dissolution of the parliament, entered into measures for defeating this commission. One expedient was to take the opinion of the judges upon the whole proceeding; a refuge constantly open to a corrupt administration, though—be it spoken to the honor of the profession—not always a sure one, even while the judges' commissions were determinable at the pleasure of the crown." And in page 396, we find the eighth question propounded by the king to those judges was this:—"Since the king can, whenever he pleaseth, remove any of his judges and officers, and justify or punish them for their offences, whether the lords and commons can, without the will of the king, impeach in parliament any of the said judges or officers for any of their offences?" to which the judges answered unanimously, that "they cannot; and if any one should do so, he is to be punished as a traitor." *Endnote 200*

It was said in a former paper, that the supreme jurisdiction in all causes, and the power of creating and annihilating magistrates, was an important branch of the jura regalia principis of the feudal law. These regalia were distributed into two principal divisions, the regalia majora and minora. The majora were those "quæ personam et dignitatem principis et administrationem reipublicæ concernunt, ut collatio dignitatum regalium, et jurisdictio summa in causis ecclesiasticis et secularibus, as well as the jus belli et pacis &c.; et hæc alias jura majestatis dicuntur. *Endnote 201*

Supreme, sovereign jurisdiction, therefore, in all causes temporal and spiritual, was one of the greater royalties, or sublimest prerogatives of the feudal princes, was inseparable from the feudal majesty, and could not be granted away by the prince to any subject, so as to be irrevocable. And the feudal law says expressly, if an infeudation of these regalia majora should be made, "majestas divisionem non recipiat, nec jura ab ea separari possint; distinguendum est inter ipsum jus, et exercitium hujus juris;—hoc alteri concedi potest, ut eodem utatur, dependenter: illud, vero, penes principem remanet." *Endnote 202*

That this was one of the regalia majora, see the Consuetudines Feudorum, tit. 56: "Quæ sint Regalia. Potestas constituendorum magistratuum ad justitiam expediendam."

It was this old feudal idea that such prerogatives were inseparable from majesty, and so incident and essential to the kingly office, that not even an act of parliament could divest it of them, which puzzled the heads of the two Jameses and the two Charleses, and cost them and the nations they governed very dear. It was this which was intended by Sir Edward Herbert and his brothers, who determined for Sir Edward Hales's case, mentioned in a former paper, and gave their opinions, and made it a general rule in law, that the dispensing power was an incident, inseparable prerogative of the kings of England, as of all other sovereign princes; and that this was not a trust invested in and granted to the king, but the ancient remains of the sovereign power of the kings of England, which was never yet taken from them, nor can be.

The way is now prepared for the most important question of all.

General Brattle declares his opinion in very strong terms, "that the governor and council cannot legally or constitutionally remove a justice of the superior court, as the commissions now are, unless there is a fair hearing and trial, and then a judgment that he hath behaved ill."

This I am content to make a question, after premising that we ought, in such inquiries, always to obtain precise ideas, and to give exact definitions of the terms we use, in order to arrive at truth. The question, then, appears to me to be different from what it would be, if we were to ask whether a justice of that court can be constitutionally removed, without a trial and judgment. Many people receive different ideas from the words legally and constitutionally. The law has certainly established in the crown many prerogatives, by the bare exertion of which, in their utmost extent, the nation might be undone. The prerogatives of war and peace, and of pardon, for examples, among many others. Yet it would be absurd to say that the crown can constitutionally ruin the nation, and overturn the constitution. The British constitution is a fine, a nice, a delicate machine; and the perfection of it depends upon such complicated movements, that it is as easily disordered as the human body; and in order to act constitutionally, every one must do his duty. If the king should suffer no parliament to sit for twelve years, by reason of continual prorogations, this would be an unconstitutional exercise of prerogative. If the commons should grant no supplies for twelve years, this would be an unconstitutional exertion of their privilege. Yet the king has power legally to do one, and the commons to do the other. I therefore shall not contend with

General Brattle what the governor and council can constitutionally do, about removing justices, nor what they can do in honor, integrity, conscience, or Christianity: these things I shall leave to the internal sentiments of future governors and councils, and shall confine myself to the question, whether they can legally remove a judge.

And it is with great reluctance that I frankly say, I have not been able hitherto to find sufficient reason to convince me that the governor and council have not, as the law now stands, power to remove a judge, as the commissions now are, without a trial and judgment for ill behavior.

I believe it to be true that the judges in all King William's reign had their commissions quamdiu se bene gesserint. Our charter and our province law, erecting the superior court, were made in that reign. In the charter, the king grants power to the governor, with advice and consent of council, to nominate judges, &c., and to the general court to erect judicatories, &c.; "and that all and every of the subjects of us, our heirs and successors, which shall go to and inhabit within our said province and territory, and every of their children which shall happen to be born there, or on the seas in going thither or returning from thence, shall have and enjoy all liberties and immunities of free and natural subjects, within any of the dominions of us, our heirs and successors, to all intents, constructions, and purposes whatsoever, as if they and every of them were born within this our realm of England."

Now, admitting, for argument's sake, that the judges in England in that reign held their offices legally for life, determinable upon misbehavior, and that it was by law, in that reign, a liberty of free and natural subjects, born within the realms, that the judges should hold such an estate in their offices, what will be the consequence? Will it not be, that the governor and council have power, by charter and by law, to grant their commissions quamdiu se bene gesserint? and that, if the governor and council should grant their commissions in that manner, the judges would have estates for life in their offices? But will it follow that they have such estates, if the governor and council do not grant them in that manner? Here, then, if these principles are all just, let the just consequence be drawn. Let the governor and council—I speak with humble deference and submission—issue the commissions to the judges, quamdiu se bene gesserint; and if that is declined, let the province—I speak with all possible respect again—make their humble supplications to his majesty, that his governor may be permitted, or instructed, if you will, to grant them in that manner. I fear there is too much reason to think, as no judicature can be created but by the legislature, and the jurisdiction must appear in the erection, and as no judge at common law, or by the law of the province, can hold an office but by commission, that the duration of the judge's office or estate must appear in the commission itself.

However, all this reasoning in favor of an estate for life in our judges, is built upon the principle that Lord Holt, and the judges in England under King William, had estates for life, by law, in their offices. And this principle implies that the crown, at common law, had authority to make judges to hold for life or at will, at its pleasure; which is a problematical doctrine, at least. Some of the passages of law and history which I have quoted in former papers, seem to be evidence that, at some times, the houses of parliament and some of the ministers of the law had such an apprehension; but a multitude of others, produced in the same papers, betray an apprehension of the contrary; but I do not recollect a single circumstance, in law or history, that favors the opinion that a judge there had an estate for life, without the words quamdiu se bene gesserit in his commission.

General Brattle took the right way of establishing the independency of our judges, by affirming that they had estates for life by their nomination and appointment, and by common law, whether their commissions expressed quamdiu se bene gesserint or not, or whether they had any commissions at all or not; and if he could have proved these allegations, he would have got his cause. But he has been extremely unfortunate in having Bracton, Fortescue, Coke, Foster, Hume, Rapin, and Rushworth directly against him, and nothing in his favor but the say of a lawyer in arguing a cause for his client, and that say by no means so extensive as the General's assertions; for Powis himself does not say the judges at common law were in for their lives, without the clause quamdiu se bene gesserint in their commissions. The questions that have been considered are liberal, and of much importance. I have done little more than labor in the mines of ore and the quarries of stones. The materials are at the service of the public; and I leave them to the jeweller and lapidary, to refine, fabricate, and polish them.

John Adams.

From the Boston Gazette, 15 February, 1773.

to the printers.

We are now upon the commissions of our own judges; and we ought to examine well the tenure by which they are holden.

It may be depended on, that all the commissions of judges throughout America are without the words quamdiu se bene gesserint in them; and, consequently, that this horrid fragment of the feudal despotism hangs over the heads of the best of them to this hour. If this is the case, it is a common and a serious concern to the whole continent, and the several provinces will take such measures as they shall think fit to obtain a better security of their lives, liberties, and properties. One would think there never could happen a more favorable opportunity to procure a stable tenure of the judges' offices than the present reign, which was begun with his majesty's most gracious declaration from the throne, "that the independency and uprightness of the judges were essential to the impartial administration of justice." However, let us return and confine ourselves to this province. Our judges' commissions have neither the clause quamdiu se bene gesserit, nor the clause durante beneplacito in them. By what authority, and for what reasons, both these clauses were omitted, when the commission was first formed and digested, I know not; but the fact is certain, that they are not in it. But will it follow that, because both clauses are omitted, therefore the judges are in for life? Why should it not as well follow that they are in only at pleasure? Will it be said that the liberty of the subject and the independency of the judges are to be favored, and therefore, as there is no express clause to determine it otherwise, it must be presumed to be intended for life? If this is said, I answer that, by all rules, common law is to be favored; and, therefore, whatever was the rule at common law must be favored in this case; and if the judges at common law were in only at pleasure, it will follow that ours are so too, without express words; for there is no rule more established than this, that the prerogative is not to be taken away without express words, and that the king's grant is to be construed most favorably for the king, when it has not the clause ex mero motu, speciali gratia, et certa scientia, in it, as these commissions have not.

Why should the omission of both clauses make the commissions during good behavior, in the case of a superior judge, any more than in the case of a justice of the peace? The commission of a justice of the peace here is without both clauses, as much as the commission of a judge; yet it never was pretended here that a justice of peace might not be removed at pleasure by the governor and council, and without a hearing and judgment that he had misbehaved.

And I suppose it to be clearly settled so in England. By the form of the commission of the peace in England, *Endnote 203* we find that both these clauses are omitted out of that commission, which was settled and reformed as it there stands by Sir Christopher Wray, Chief Justice of England, and all the other judges of England, in the 32 and 33 Elizabeth, upon perusal of the former commission of the peace, and upon conference within themselves.

Yet these commissions are determinable at pleasure. Endnote 204 "These commissioners of the peace, their authority doth determine by divers means, yet more usually by three means: 1. By the death of the king, or by his resignation of his crown; for by the commission he maketh them justiciarios nostros; so that, he being once dead, or having given over his crown, they are no more his justices, and the justices of the next prince they cannot be, unless it shall please him afterwards so to make them. 2. At the king's pleasure, and that in two sorts. 1. Either by the king's pleasure, expressed, (as the king by express words may discharge them by his writ under the great seal,) or by supersedeas; but the supersedeas doth but suspend their authority, which may be revived by a procedendo. 2. Or by implication; as by making other commissioners of the same kind, and within the same limits, leaving out the ancient commissioners' names."

Thus, the argument arising from the omission of the clause in our judges' commissions, of durante beneplacito, seems to have no weight in it, because the same clause is omitted from the commission of the peace both at home and here, and yet the commission has been settled at home to be determinable at the pleasure of the king, and here, at the pleasure of the governor and council, particularly in a late instance, which General Brattle may possibly remember.

Let us now proceed to consider with more particular attention the principle upon which all colorable pretension of establishing the independency of our judges is founded. The principle is this, that Lord Holt and his brothers, under King William, had legal estates for life in their offices, determinable only on misbehavior and the demise of the crown; though, I apprehend, that even this principle will not serve the purpose. It is true that, if this principle is admitted, it will follow, that the governor and council here have power to issue the commissions quamdiu se bene gesserint; but it will not follow, that by law they are bound to do that, because King William was not bound by law to do it in England. If King William had his election to grant commissions quamdiu se bene gesserint, or durante beneplacito, then the natural subjects, born within the realm, had not a right to have the judges' patents granted quamdiu se bene gesserint, unless the king pleased. It is true, upon this supposition, that they had a right to have them granted so, if they were happy enough to persuade the crown to grant them so, not otherwise.

The same right and liberty will belong to the subject in this province. Not a right absolutely to have the judges' commissions granted quamdiu se bene gesserint; but to have them granted so, if the governor and council saw fit, and could be prevailed on to do it.

And, on the other hand, if King William had power to grant the commissions either way as he pleased, it will follow, that the governor and council have power to grant them either way. And if this is true, it is to be hoped General Brattle will have influence enough to prevail that the commissions, for the future, may be granted expressly quamdiu se bene gesserint; but until that is done, even upon these principles, our judges hold their places only at will.

However, we must examine yet further, whether the crown, in King William's time, or any other, ever had its election to grant the patents either way.

Lord Coke's authority has been quoted before several times, and it seems to be very explicit, that a grant of a judicial office for life, which had usually been granted at will, is void. "Nay, it is said by some, that the king is so far restrained by the ancient forms, in all cases of this nature, that his grant of a judicial office for life, which has been accustomed to be granted only at will, is void." "And the law is so jealous of any kind of innovation, in a matter so highly concerning the safety of the subject, as not to endure any the least deviation from the old known stated forms, however immaterial it may seem, as will be more fully shown, c. 5, s. 1." Endnote 205

I have not been able to find any direct adjudication of any of the courts of common law, or any absolute determination of all the judges in the exchequer chamber, that a grant to a judge of king's bench or common bench, quamdiu se bene gesserit, is void; but, besides what is before cited, from Coke and Hawkins, it is certain that, whenever such a grant has been made, the king who made it considered it as void. King Henry thought it was void, when he threw off his faithful Hubert de Burgh. Charles I. thought it void, and so did his parliament, in 1642, as appears by the twelfth article transmitted by them to the king at York; and Charles II. and James II. thought it void, as appears many ways,—by their displacing Judge Archer and others; and it appears also by King Charles's displacing the Earl of Clarendon; for there is no reason why a grant of the office of chancellor for life should be void, as Lord Coke says expressly that it is, and a grant of the office of chief justice, in the same manner, be good. "Note, that this vacation, Sir Edward Hyde, Earl of Clarendon and Lord Chancellor of England, was deposed by the king from being chancellor, although he had a patent for his life, because the taking away of the seal is a determination of the office, as 4 Inst." Endnote 206

Here the grant for life is considered as void, and Lord Coke's authority is quoted for it, I suppose where he says, a grant of the office of chancellor for life is void, because it never was so granted, that is, as I understand it, never was customarily so granted; for it is not literally true that it never was so granted. It has been granted for life almost if not quite as often as the judges' offices ever were before the revolution. It may be proper to show this.

Thomas, Lord Ellesmere, in his Observations concerning the office of the lord chancellor, says: "The election or creation of chancellors and keepers, &c. was of more than one sort. Sometimes, and for the most part, the chancellor was elected by the king, durante beneplacito, and put in power of his office by the delivery of the seal; and sometimes the chancellor was made by patent to hold that place or office during his life, as Walter Grey, Bishop of Chester, in the time of King John, and others; some, and the most part, elected by the king only; some had patents of the king, and were confirmed chancellors by consent of the three estates, as were Ralph Nevil, Bishop of Chester, in the time of King Henry III., with whom the prince being offended, as reports Matthew Paris, and demanding the seal at his hands, he refused to yield the same unto him, affirming that, as he had received it by the common consent of the nobility, so he would not, without like warrant, resign the same; and in the days of the same king, it was told him by all the lords, spiritual and temporal, that of ancient time the election and disposition of the chief justice, chancellor, and treasurer belonged to the parliament; and, although the king in displeasure did take the seal from him, and deliver the same to the custody of others, yet did the aforesaid Nevil remain chancellor notwithstanding, and received the profits thereof, to whom the king would have restored the seal, but he refused to receive it."

Here, let me observe, that I have a long time expected from General Brattle some such authority as this; for I believe it was in the mind of Sir Thomas Powis, when he said, by the ancient constitution my lords the judges were in for their lives. But let it be considered, that there is no remaining record that the lords spiritual and temporal told the king so, nor any legal authority to prove it, nor any other authority for it but Matthew Paris, whose writings are not sufficient evidence of this; let it also be considered, that this King Henry would probably have been obliged to insert a clause in his Magna Charta to secure this privilege, if the claim of it had been then thought to be well founded; and, as this was not done, it is most likely (admitting Matthew Paris's fact to be true) that the lords spiritual and temporal meant no more than this, that some king of ancient time had, in some few instances, condescended to take the advice of his wittenagemote, or assembly of wise men, concerning the appointment and removal of such officers. But a few particular examples of royal condescension could form no established rule, and according to the notions of those feudal ages, could never alienate from the prince any of his regalia majora.

Lord Ellesmere goes on: "And let us note, by the way, three several patents were granted unto this Ralph Nevil, two whereby he is ordained to be chancellor, and the third for the custody of the seal, all remaining among the records of the tower in hæc verba:

"Henricus Rex, &c. Archiepiscopis, &c. Sciatis, nos dedisse, concessisse, et hac charta nostra confirmasse, venerabili Randolpho cicestrensi episcopo cancellariam nostram habendam et tenendam toto tempore vitæ suæ, cum omnibus pertinentibus, &c."

His second patent was of this form:—"Henricus, &c. Archiepiscopis, &c. Sciatis nos concessisse, et hac charta nostra confirmasse, pro nobis et hæredibus nostris venerabili Randolpho cicestrensi episcopo, cancellario nostro, cancellariam Angliæ, toto tempore vitæ suæ, cum omnibus pertinentibus, &c. Quare volumus et firmiter præcipimus pro nobis, et hæredibus nostris, quod prædictus episcopus habeat ipsam cancellariam, toto tempore vitæ suæ, &c."

This is the transcript of his third patent, the same day and year:—"Henricus, &c. Archiepiscopis, &c. Sciatis nos concessisse, et hac charta nostra confirmasse venerabili patri Randolpho cicestrensi episcopo cancellario nostro, custodiam sigilli nostri toto tempore vitæ suæ, cum omnibus, &c. ita quod sigillum portat et custodiat, in propria persona sua, quamdiu valuerit."

And in page 18, Lord Ellesmere says: "Sometimes the chancellors of England were elected by the nobility, as Nicolas of Eli was made chancellor by the barons, but this seemed a usurpation by them, for they were afterwards, the most of them, most sharply chastised, and the said Nicolas deprived by Henry III., disdaining to have officers of that estate appointed him by his subjects."

Thus we see that a few examples of appointments for life to the office of chancellor, have not been sufficient to establish the power of the crown to grant it in that manner, but it is often said in our books to be void, and in the case of Lord Clarendon was presumed to be so. Why, then, should a few examples of judges constituted quamdiu se bene gesserint, in the reigns of Charles I. and II., and King William, determine them to be good?

I think it has been determined by all the judges in England that time of memory should be limited to the reign of King Richard I.; and every rule of common law must be beyond the time of memory, that is, as ancient as the reign of that king, and continued down generally until it is altered by authority of parliament.

Sir James Dyer, at the end of his Reports, has given us the names of all the chief justices of the king's bench, from the twenty-second year of Edward III. to the sixteenth year of Queen Elizabeth, namely,—Thorpe, Shareshull, Greene, Knyvett and Cavendish, under Edward III.; Tresilian and Clopton under Richard II.; Gascoigne under Henry IV.; Hankford under Henry V.; Cheyne, Ivyn, and Fortescue, under Henry VI.; Markham and Billing under Edward IV.; Hussey under Richard III.; Fineux under Henry VII.; Montague, Lyster, and Cholmley, under Henry VIII.; Bromley, Portmore, and Saunders under Queen Mary; Catlyne and Wray under Elizabeth.

And also the names of all the chief justices of the common pleas from the year 1399, namely,—the last year of the reign of Richard II. to the twenty-fourth of Queen Elizabeth, namely,—Thirninge under Henry IV.; Norton under Henry V.; Ivyn, Cottesmore, Newton, and Prisot, under Henry VI.; Danby and Brian, under Edward IV.; Woode, Frowicke and

Rede, under Henry VII.; Erneley, Brudnell, Norwiche, Baldwin, Montague, under Henry VIII.; Morgan, Brooke and Browne, under Philip and Mary; Dyer and Anderson, under Elizabeth.

The writs or patents of all these chief justices remain enrolled in the courts of king's bench and common pleas, and also enrolled in chancery, and every one of them is durante beneplacito, as I conclude, because Dyer has given us the tenure of his own commission: "Ego, Jac. Dyer, constitutus fui unus justiciariorum ad placita coram rege et regina tenenda, per L. patentes gerentes datum apud Greenwich, 23 die Aprilis, durante beneplacito Regi, &c."; and because the foregoing lists, and the records from whence they were taken, were familiarly known to Sir Edward Coke; and he says, that form had been used and approved without any variation for many successions of ages, even from the time of Edward I. and long before. It may, therefore, be safely affirmed, that there is no record of any justiciary or chief justice of king's bench or common pleas whose writ or patent was not durante beneplacito, quite down to the year 1640, in the reign of Charles I. I say there is no record of any, because the story of Hubert de Burgh has no record extant to prove it, and rests upon no better evidence than Matthew Paris, *Endnote 207* which, in our present view of the matter, is no evidence at all, because he is no legal authority.

If there is no record, therefore, extant to warrant the crown in granting patents to the judges quamdiu se bene gesserint, anterior to 1640, it is in vain to look for any adjudged case, that a patent so granted is good anterior to that period, and I am equally confident to say there has been none since.

There is a case in the Year-Books, which was quoted by the attorney-general, in the argument of the case of Harcourt against Fox, to prove that a grant quamdiu se bene gesserit conveyed a frank tenement. But common sense, without a judicial decision, would be sufficient to determine that. It is but the necessary, natural import of the words. If a man has a lease of a house as long as he behaves well, if he behaves well as long as he lives, he must hold the house as long as he lives. That case is in 3 Ass. 4. pl. 9. That part of it which is to our present purpose is no more than this: "Note, that a grant of rent to be paid to another, as long as he wills or pleases, is a freehold clearly enough. Sicut dominus rex concessit alicui aliquam ballivam vel hujusmodi, donec bene et fideliter se gesserit in officio illo."

It is easy to see that this is no adjudication that the king's grant to a judge of king's bench or common pleas quamdiu se bene gesserit is good and valid, and I believe it may be depended on, that there never was such a judgment in Westminster Hall.

I have heretofore mentioned several instances of great, wise, and honest judges falling victims at the royal nod, and giving place to others, much their inferiors in all respects. To these let me add the case of the learned, firm, and upright Chief Justice Pemberton, who, in the thirty-fourth year of Charles II., was obliged to descend from the chief seat in the king's bench into the common pleas, to make way for the cunning chicanery of Saunders, who was elevated to his place in order to carry some court-points; and in the next year that great and honest man was deposed from his place in the common pleas, and after having been chief justice of both benches, was necessitated to take a place again at the bar, and to bear the sneers and railleries of young mooting barristers, who thought to recommend themselves at court by insulting him.

And here I cannot forbear introducing a curiosity. It is the speech of the Lord Chancellor to Sir Henry Montague, when he was sworn chief justice of the king's bench in the room of a man much greater and better; I mean Lord Coke. It is found at length in Sir Francis Moore's Reports, and I mention it because it is fraught with lessons of instruction. It shows the tendency of holding offices at pleasure. It shows what sordid, nauseous, and impious adulations to superiors, what malicious, envious, and cruel invectives against honest Coke, or any other brave and honest man whom the courtiers are determined to hunt down, are inspired by this dependent state of mind. It shows what a deep and lively sense they had upon their minds of their dependence, every moment of their existence, upon the royal will, and how carefully they cultivated in one another, as the highest virtue, this base servility of spirit.

"The king's majesty," (says the Chancellor to Sir Henry Montague,) "in the governing of his subjects, representeth the divine majesty of Almighty God; for it is truly said of God, that, infima per media ducit ad summa, &c." "You are called to a place vacant, not by death or cession, but by amotion and deposing of him that held the place before you, by the great King James, the great King of Great Britain; wherein you see the prophet David's words are true: 'He putteth down one and setteth up another;' a lesson to be learned of all, and to be remembered and feared of all that sit in judicial places, &c. It is dangerous, in a monarchy, for a man holding a high and eminent place, to be ambitiously popular; take heed of it."

"Remember Sir Edward Montague, your worthy grandfather. You are called to succeed him in this high place, and called thereunto upon amotion and deposing of another by the great judgment and wisdom of the great King of Great Britain, whose royal virtues will be admired to all posterity." Then follows much abuse upon honest Coke.

"Your grandfather doubted not but if the king, by his writ under the great seal, commanded the judges that they should not proceed rege inconsulto, then they were dutifully to obey, and to consult with the king, not in this court but in another, that is, the court of chancery.

"Remember also the removing and putting down of your late predecessor, and by whom, which I often remember unto you,—that is, by the great King of Great Britain, whose great wisdom, royal virtues, and religious care for the weal of his subjects, and for the due administration of justice, can never be forgotten, but will remain admirable to all posterity." Who would think that this were a James? "Comfort yourself with this, that sithe the king's majesty hath enabled you, who shall or can disable you?"

Let us here subjoin a few clauses more from Hawkins: "All such justices must derive their authority from such instruments as are of a known, stated, and allowed form, warranted by ancient precedents," &c. "It seems clearly to be agreed, by all these books, that the best rule of judging of the validity of any such commissions, is their conformity to known and ancient precedents." "Such commissions may be determined expressly or impliedly; expressly by an absolute repeal or countermand from the king," &c.

John Adams.

From the Boston Gazette, 22 February, 1773.

to the printers.

In all General Brattle's researches hitherto, aided and assisted as he has been by mine, we have not been able to discover either that the judges at common law had their commissions quamdiu se bene gesserint, or for life, or that the crown had authority to grant them in that manner. Let us now examine, and see whether estates for life, determinable only on misbehavior or the demise of the crown, can be derived to the Massachusetts judges from any other source. If they can, they must be from the charter, from the nomination and appointment of the governor, with the advice and consent of council, from the judges' commissions, or from the law of the province; from one or more, or all these together, they must be derived, if from any thing. For, as the judges of the king's bench and common bench are in by the king's grant or by custom, or both; as justices of oyer and terminer, jail delivery, &c., are in by the king's grant; as the clerk of the peace is said by Lord Holt, in the case of Harcourt against Fox, to be in by the act of parliament, 1 William and Mary; and the officers, whose places are in the gift of the chief justice, are in by the custom; so the Massachusetts justices are in by one or more, or all of the four titles mentioned before.

And here the first inquiry is, what is meant by an officer's being in by custom or by statute, &c.? And I suppose the true answer to be this: he is invested with his powers, is obligated to his duties, and holds his estate by that custom or statute, &c. And the next inquiry is, by what are our judges in? that is, by what act or instrument are they clothed with their powers, bound to their duties, and entitled to their estates?

By the charter, there are no certain powers given them, no certain duties prescribed to them, nor any certain estate conferred upon them. The charter empowers the governor, with advice and consent of council, to nominate and appoint them, that is, to designate the persons; nothing more.

There are three sorts of officers in the charter. Those reserved to the nomination of the king, as the governor, lieutenant-governor, secretary, and judge of admiralty. And it is not limited how long they shall continue, excepting the first secretary, Addington, and he is constituted expressly during pleasure; and the duration of all these officers has been limited ever since expressly, by their commissions, to be during pleasure. The second sort of officers in the charter are those which the general court are to name and settle; and the charter expressly says they shall be named and settled annually, so that their duration is ascertained in the charter. The third sort are those which the governor, with advice and consent of council, is to nominate and appoint; and there are no duties imposed, no powers given, no estates limited to these, in the charter. But the power of erecting judicatories, stating the rights and duties, and limiting the estates, of all officers to the council and courts of justice belonging, is given to the general court; and the charter expressly requires that all these courts shall be held in the king's name, and that all officers shall take the oaths and subscribe the declarations appointed to be taken and subscribed, instead of the oaths of allegiance and supremacy. And it is in observance of this requisition in the charter,—namely, that all courts shall be held in the king's name,—that the judges' commissions are in the king's name. The governor and council designate a person, not to be the governor and council's justice, but the king's justice; not of the governor and council's court, but of the king's court. And the law of the province requires that the justices of the superior court should have a particular species of evidence of their nomination and appointment, namely, a commission; otherwise, as General Brattle says, a nomination and appointment recorded would be enough. And here I cannot refuse myself the pleasure of observing, that the opinion of Mr. Read concurred with, and, I humbly conceive, was founded on, these principles. Governor Belcher persuaded the council that, upon the appointment of a new governor, it was necessary to renew all civil commissions, and the same thing "was proposed in council by his successor; but Mr. Read, who was then a member of the council, brought such arguments against the practice, that the majority of the board refused to consent to it," and it never has been done since. *Endnote 208* This was an important service rendered his country by that great lawyer and upright man, and it was grounded upon the principles I have mentioned. Civil officers are not nominated to be the governor's officers; they don't hold their courts nor commissions in his name, but in the king's; and therefore governors may come and go, as long as the same king reigns, and they continue the same officers. And, in conformity to the same principles, upon the demise of the crown, the commissions must be renewed, because the charter requires they should be in the king's name. The words are, "in the name of us, our heirs and successors;" and therefore, upon the accession of an heir apparent, that is, after six months from his accession, the commissions must be renewed, otherwise they cannot be held in his name, nor the requisition in the charter complied with. I said in six months, because the statute of 6 Anne, c. 7, s. 8, not the statute of the present king's reign, (as General Brattle supposes,) has provided, that "no office, place, or employment, civil or military, within the kingdoms of Great Britain or Ireland, dominion of Wales, town of Berwick-upon-Tweed, isles of Jersey, Guernsey, Alderney, or Sark, or any of her majesty's plantations, shall become void by reason of the demise or death of her majesty, her heirs or successors, kings or queens of this realm; but every person, &c., shall continue in their respective offices, places, and employments, for the space of six months next after such demise or death, unless sooner removed and discharged by the next in succession as aforesaid."

But, to return; our judges are not in merely by nomination and appointment of the governor and council, because they are not bound to their duties nor vested with their powers by the charter immediately, nor by that nomination and appointment. They are not in by the grant of the king merely, or by their commissions, because their court is not erected, their powers are not derived, their duties are not imposed, and no estate is limited by that grant. But their commission is nothing more than a particular kind of evidence, required by the province law, to show their conformity to the charter, in holding their court in the king's name, and to show their nomination and appointment, or the designation of their persons to those offices, by the governor and council.

It is the law of the province which gives them all the powers, and imposes upon them all the duties, of the courts of king's bench, common pleas, and exchequer; but it does not limit to them any estate in their offices. If it had said, as it ought to have said, that they shall be commissionated, quamdiu se bene gesserint, they would have been so commissionated, and would have held estates for life in their offices.

Whence, then, can General Brattle claim for them an estate for life in their offices? No such estate is given them by the charter, by their nomination and appointment, by their commissions, nor by the law of the province.

I cannot agree with General Brattle, that "supposing a corrupt governor and a corrupt council, whether the words in the commission are, so long as the governor and council please, or, during good behavior, will just come to the same thing." Because in the one case a judge may be removed suddenly and silently, in a council of seven only; in the other not without a hearing and trial, and an opportunity to defend himself before a fuller board, knowing his accuser and the accusation. And this would be a restraint even to corruption itself; for in the most abandoned state of it there is always some regard shown to appearances.

It is no part of my plan, in this rencounter with the General, to make my compliments to his excellency Governor Hutchinson, and the present council; but I may be permitted to say, that the governor differs in sentiment from his Major-General about the power of the governor and council. In a note in the second volume of the History of the Massachusetts Bay, we have these words:—"The freedom and independency of the judges of England is always enumerated among the excellencies of the constitution." The Massachusetts judges are far from independent. In Mr. Belcher's administration they were peculiarly dependent upon the governor. Before and since, they have been dependent upon the assembly for their salary granted annually, which sometimes has been delayed, sometimes diminished, and which rarely escapes being a subject of debate and altercation. The dependency in Mr. Belcher's time is attributed to the pusillanimity of the council, as no appointment can be made without their advice.

And we are told, too, that the emoluments of a Massachusetts counsellor are very small, and can be but a poor temptation to sacrifice virtue. All this, however, has been found in many instances, by experience, to be but a poor consolation to the people. Four gentlemen, a majority of seven, have, since Mr. Belcher's day, been found under the influence of the same pusillanimity, and, for the sake of those emoluments, small as they are, or some other emoluments, have been seen to sacrifice virtue. And it is highly probable men will be composed of the same clay fifty years hence as they were forty years ago; and therefore they ought not to be left exposed to the same temptations.

The next thing observable in the General's last publication, is this. "The parliament grants," says he, "no salaries to the judges of England. The king settles the salaries, and pays his judges out of the civil list." How is it possible this gentleman should make such mistakes? What is the king's civil list? Whence do the moneys come to discharge it? Is it a mine of gold,—a quarry of precious stones? The king pays the judges! Whence does he get the money? The crown, without the gift of the people, is as poor as any of the subjects. But, to dwell no longer upon an error so palpable and gross, let us look into the book. The act of parliament of the 12 & 13 William III. expressly enacts, that the judges' salaries shall be ascertained and established, meaning, no doubt, at the sums which had then usually been allowed them. And another act of parliament was made in the thirty-second year of George II. c. 35, augmenting the salaries of the puisne judges five hundred pounds each, and granting and appropriating certain stamp duties to the payment of it. With what color of truth, then, can the General say, that parliament grants no salaries, but that the king settles the salaries?

Another thing that follows is more remarkable still. "The act of parliament," says the General, (meaning the late act empowering the crown to appropriate moneys for the administration of justice in such colonies where it shall be most needed,) "was made for no other reason than this, that the king might not pay them (that is, the judges) out of the civil list, but out of another fund, the revenue." The General seems to have in his mind a notion that the king's civil list is a magazine of gold and silver, and the crown a spot where diamonds grow. But I repeat it, the crown has no riches but from the gifts of the people. The civil list means an enumeration of the king's civil officers and servants, and the sums usually allowed them as salaries, &c. But the money to discharge these sums is, every farthing of it, granted by parliament. And without the aid of parliament the crown could not pay a porter. Near the beginning of every reign, the civil list revenue is granted by parliament. But are the Massachusetts judges in the king's civil list? No more than the Massachusetts Major-General is. If a minister of state had taken money from the civil list revenue to pay our judges, would it not have been a misapplication of the public money? Would it not have been peculation? And in virtuous times, would not that minister have been compelled to refund it out of his own pocket? It is true, a minister who handles the public money may apply it to purposes for which it was never intended or appropriated. He may purchase votes and elections with it; and so he may rob the treasury-chests of their guineas; and he has as good a right to do one as the other, and to do either, as to apply moneys appropriated to the king's civil list to the payment of salaries to the Massachusetts judges.

Without the late act of parliament, therefore, as the king could not pay our judges out of the civil list, because the king can do no wrong, he could not pay them at all, unless he had given them presents out of his privy purse. The act must, therefore, have been made to enable the king to pay them, with what views of policy I leave to be conjectured by others.

I am very nearly of a mind with the General, that a lawyer who holds the judges' offices here to be during good behavior, must do it upon his principles; because I can see none much more solid to ground such an opinion upon. But I believe his principles appear by this time not to be infallible.

The General solemnly declares, that Mr. Read held this opinion and upon his principles. Mr. Read's opinion deserves great veneration, but not implicit faith; and, indeed, if it was certain that he held it, what resistance could it make against the whole united torrent of law, records, and history? However, we see, by the report the General was pleased to give the public of Lord Holt's words, that it is possible for him to mistake the words and opinion of a sage; and therefore it is possible he may have mistaken Mr. Read's words as well as his lordship's.

I believe the public is weary of my speculations, and the subject of them. I have bestowed more labor upon General Brattle's harangue in town meeting, and his writings in the newspaper, than was necessary to show their imperfection. I have now done with both,—and subscribe myself, Your, General Brattle's, and the Public's, well-wisher, and very humble servant,

John Adams.

APPENDIX.

A.

The following paper is in the handwriting of Mr. Jefferson. It bears on the back the following endorsement by the hand of General Washington:—"Construction of the powers of the Senate with respect to their agency in appointing ambassadors, &c., and fixing the grade."

How this came into the possession of Mr. Adams, does not appear.

ON THE POWERS OF THE SENATE.

The constitution having declared, that the president "shall nominate, and by and with the advice and consent of the senate shall appoint, ambassadors, other public ministers, and consuls," the president desires my opinion whether the senate has a right to negative the grade he may think it expedient to use in a foreign mission, as well as the person to be appointed.

I think the senate has no right to negative the grade.

The constitution has divided the powers of government into three branches, legislative, executive, and judiciary, lodging each with a distinct magistracy. The legislative it has given completely to the senate and house of representatives; it has declared that "the executive powers shall be vested in the president," submitting only special articles of it to a negative by the senate; and it has vested the judiciary power in the courts of justice, with certain exceptions also in favor of the senate.

The transaction of business with foreign nations is executive altogether; it belongs, then, to the head of that department, except as to such portions of it as are specially submitted to the senate. Exceptions are to be construed strictly; the constitution itself, indeed, has taken care to circumscribe this one within very strict limits; for it gives the nomination of the foreign agent to the president, the appointment to him and the senate jointly, and the commissioning to the president. This analysis calls our attention to the strict import of each term. To nominate must be to propose; appointment seems that act of the will which constitutes or makes the agent; and the commision is the public evidence of it. But there are still other acts previous to these, not specially enumerated in the constitution,—to wit, 1. The destination of a mission to the particular country where the public service calls for it, and, 2. The character or grade to be employed in it. The natural order of all these is, 1. destination, 2. grade, 3. nomination, 4. appointment, 5. commission. If appointment does not comprehend the neighboring acts of nomination or commission, (and the constitution says it shall not, by giving them exclusively to the president,) still less can it pretend to comprehend those previous and more remote of destination and grade. The constitution, analyzing the three last, shows they do not comprehend the two first. The fourth is the only one it submits to the senate, shaping it into a right to say that "A or B is unfit to be appointed." Now, this cannot comprehend a right to say that "A or B is indeed fit to be appointed, but the grade fixed on is not the fit one to employ," or "our connections with the country of his destination are not such as to call for any mission." The senate is not supposed by the constitution to be acquainted with the concerns of the executive department. It was not intended that these should be communicated to them; nor can they, therefore, be qualified to judge of the necessity which calls for a mission to any particular place, or of the particular grade, more or less marked, which special and secret circumstances may call for. All this is left to the president; they are only to see that no unfit person be employed.

It may be objected, that the senate may, by continual negatives on the person, do what amounts to a negative on the grade, and so indirectly defeat this right of the president; but this would be a breach of trust, an abuse of the power confided to the senate, of which that body cannot be supposed capable. So, the president has a power to convoke the legislature, and the senate might defeat that power, by refusing to come. This equally amounts to a negative on the power of convoking; yet nobody will say they possess such a negative, or would be capable of usurping it by such oblique means. If the constitution had meant to give the senate a negative on the grade or destination, as well as the person, it would have said so in direct terms, and not left it to be effected by a sidewind. It could never mean to give them the use of one power through the abuse of another.

Th. Jefferson.

New York,

April 24, 1790

ENDNOTES:

Endnote 002

From the records of the town of Braintree, it appears that in the year 1775, Mr. Adams was again elected one of the Selectmen.

His name is also found upon the town committees raised this year to prepare a non-importation agreement, and to procure enlistments of minute men, and as associated with the committees of correspondence and observation.

Endnote 003

See the Journals of Congress for 1775, p. 238. Wednesday, November 8th, 1775, and the note. (Also the Secret Journals since printed, vol. 1. pp. 26. 33.)

Endnote 004

See Journals of Congress for the year 1775, pp. 272, 273.

Endnote 005

See the Journals, vol. ii. pp. 24, 25.

Endnote 006

8th of March, 1805.

Endnote 007

An interesting letter of Mr. Jay, in reply to one by Mr. Adams on this subject, is found in the Life of John Jay, by his son William Jay, vol. ii. pp. 380-384.

Endnote 008

Vol. ii. page 209, of the Journals.

Endnote 009

See the Journals.

Endnote 010

A slight idea of the character of this discussion is given in the notes of debates in this Congress, vol. ii. page 463. Governor Ward of Rhode Island in his letters to his brother, alludes to the obstacles interposed to the adoption of the resolution. Gammell's Life of Ward, in Sparks's American Biography, vol. xix. p. 316.

Endnote 011

See, for the rest of these resolutions, Journals of Congress, first edition, vol. i. pp. 259-261.

Endnote 012

These regulations are to be found in pages 262-271 of the Journals of Congress for 1775; they are too long to transcribe.

Endnote 013

Journals of Congress, p. 112.

Endnote 014

In the first part of Almon's Remembrancer, for the year 1776, is an article purporting to be the "Fragment of a Speech made in the General Congress of America, by one of the Delegates, in 1775." By whom this was furnished, or whence obtained, does not appear. Mr. Austin, in his Life of Gerry, inserts it in a note to page 188, vol. i., with the intimation of his belief that it was made by John Adams. If genuine, the ownership probably lies between him, Patrick Henry, Richard Henry Lee, and Edward Rutledge, as there were no other eloquent men on that side of the question in this Congress. The difficulties are, that it has too much rhetoric for Mr. Adams, too much learning for Patrick Henry, and too much vigor for R. H. Lee, whilst its political tone is too high for Rutledge. With these comments, the reader will be left to form his own opinion from the perusal.

"FRAGMENT OF A SPEECH MADE IN THE GENERAL CONGRESS OF AMERICA, BY ONE OF THE DELEGATES IN 1775.

"The great God, sir, who is the searcher of all things, will witness for me, that I have spoken to you from the bottom and purity of my heart. We have heard that this is an arduous consideration. And surely, sir, we have considered it earnestly. I may think of every gentleman here, as I know of myself, that, for seven years past, this question has filled the day with anxious thought, and the night with care. The God to whom we appeal must judge us. If the grievances, of which we complain, did not come upon us unprovoked and unexpected, when our hearts were filled with respectful affection for our parent state, and with loyalty to our King, let slavery, the worst of human ills, be our portion. Nothing less than seven years of insulted complaints and reiterated wrongs could have shaken such rooted sentiments. Unhappily for us, submission and slavery are the same; and we have only the melancholy alternative left—of ruin or resistance.

"The last petition *Endnote 015* of this Congress to the King contained all that our unhappy situation could suggest. It represented our grievances, implored redress, and professed our readiness to contribute for the general want, to the utmost of our abilities, when constitutionally required.

"The apparently gracious reception it met with, promised us a due consideration of it, and that consideration relief. But, alas! sir, it seems at that moment the very reverse was intended. For it now appears, that in a very few days after this specious answer to our agents, a circular letter was privately written by the same Secretary of State to the Governors of the Colonies, before Parliament had been consulted, pronouncing the Congress illegal, our grievances pretended, and vainly commanding them to prevent our meeting again. Perhaps, sir, the ministers of a great nation never before committed an act of such narrow policy and treacherous duplicity. They found Parliament, however, prepared to support every one of their measures.

"I forbear, sir, entering into a detail of those acts, which, from their atrociousness, must be felt and remembered forever. They are calculated to carry fire and sword, famine and desolation, through these flourishing Colonies. They 'cry, Havoc, and let slip the dogs of war.' The extremes of rage and revenge, against the worst of enemies, could not dictate measures more desperate and destructive.

"There are some people who tremble at the approach of war. They fear that it must put an inevitable stop to the further progress of these Colonies, and ruin irretrievably those benefits which the industry of centuries has called forth from this once savage land. I may commend the anxiety of these men, without praising their judgment.

"War, like other evils, is often wholesome. The waters that stagnate, corrupt. The storm that works the ocean into rage, renders it salutary. Heaven has given us nothing unmixed. The rose is not without the thorn. War calls forth the great virtues and efforts which would sleep in the gentle bosom of peace.

Paulúm sepuliæ distat mettæ
Celata virtus.'

It opens resources which would be concealed under the inactivity of tranquil times. It rouses and enlightens. It produces a people of animation, energy, adventure, and greatness. Let us consult history. Did not the Grecian republics prosper amid continual warfare? Their prosperity, their power, their splendor, grew from the all-animating spirit of war. Did not the cottages of shepherds rise into imperial Rome, the mistress of the world, the nurse of heroes, the delight of gods! through the invigorating operation of unceasing wars?

Per damna, per cædes, ab ipso
Ducit opes animumque terro

How often has Flanders been the theatre of contending powers, conflicting hosts, and blood! Yet what country is more flourishing and fertile? Trace back the history of our parent state. Whether you view her arraying Angles against Danes; Danes against Saxons; Saxons against Normans; the Barons against the usurping Princes, or the civil wars of the red and white roses, or that between the people and the tyrant Stuart, you see her in a state of almost continual warfare. In almost every reign, to the commencement of that of Henry VII., her peaceful bosom (in her poet's phrase) was gored with iron war. It was in the peaceful reigns of Henry VII., Henry VIII., and Charles II., that she suffered the severest extremities of tyranny and oppression. But, amid her civil contentions, she flourished and grew strong. Trained in them, she sent her hardy legions forth, which planted the standard of England upon the battlements of Paris, extending her commerce and her dominion.

'Those noble English, who could entertain
With half their topics the fuel power of France,
And let another half stand laughing by,
All out of work, and cold for action

"'The beautiful fabric of her constitutional liberty was reared and cemented in blood. From this fulness of her strength those scions issued, which, taking deep root in this delightful land, have reared their heads and spread abroad their branches like the cedars of Lebanon.

"Why fear we then to pursue, through apparent evil, real good? The war, upon which we are to enter, is just and necessary. 'Justum est bellum, ubi necessarium; et pia arma, quibus nulla, nisi in armis, relinquitur spes.' It is to protect these regions, brought to such beauty through the infinite toil and hazard of our fathers and ourselves, from becoming the prey of that more desolating, cruel spoiler than war, pestilence, or famine—absolute rule and endless extortion.

"Our sufferings have been great, our endurance long. Every effort of patience, complaint, and supplication, has been exhausted. They seem only to have hardened the hearts of the ministers who oppress us, and double our distresses. Let us, therefore, consult only how we shall defend our liberties with dignity and success. Our parent state will then think us worthy of her, when she sees that with her liberty we inherit her rigid resolution of maintaining it against all invaders. Let us give her reason to pride herself in the relationship.

"And thou, great Liberty! inspire our souls.
Make our lives happy in thy pure embrace
Or our deaths glorious in thy just defence!"

Endnote 015

In 1774, presented last Christmas.

Endnote 016

The following singularly worded letter is found among Mr. Adams's papers. The difficulty in assigning the authority under which the Council could act is obvious, and is evaded in the way recommended by the resolve of Congress. See p. 16-17.

Perez Morton
Council Chamber,

Watertown, October 28, 1775

Sir:—

I am directed by the major part of the Council of this Colony, to acquaint you that by virtue of the power and authority in and by the royal charter, in the absence of the Governor and Lieutenant Governor, lodged in them, they have seen fit to appoint you, with the advice and consent of Council, to be first or Chief Justice of the Superior Court of Judicature, &c., for this Colony.

The inclosed is a list of your brethren of the Bench, who are to hold their seats in the order therein arranged. I am further directed to request your Honor to signify to the Board, in writing, your acceptance of, or refusal of, said appointment, as soon as may be.

In the name and by order of the Council.
Perez Morton, Deputy Secretary.
Hon. John Adams, Esq.
List Inclosed.
Hon. John Adams, Esq.
William Cushing, Esq.
Hon. William Read, Esq.
Robert Treat Paine, Esq.
Nathaniel Sargent, Esq.

The answer to this letter is now in the Archives of the State, in the State House, in Boston. Though belonging to another portion of this work, it may, from its connection with the personal history of the writer, properly find a place here.

John Adams
24 November, 1775
Philadelphia
Perez Morton

John Adams to Perez Morton, Deputy Secretary, to be communicated to the Honorable Board.

Philadelphia,24 November, 1775

I had the honor of receiving your letter of the twenty-eighth of October last, by Mr. Revere, in which you acquaint me that the major part of the Honorable Council, by virtue of the power and authority, in and by the Royal Charter of the Massachusetts Bay, in the absence of the Governor and Lieutenant Governor, lodged in them, have seen fit to appoint me, with the advice and consent of Council, to be a Justice of the Superior Court of Judicature, &c. for that Colony, inclosing a list of the Honorable gentlemen, who are to hold seats on the same bench, and requesting me to signify in writing my acceptance or refusal of said appointment as soon as might be.

I am deeply penetrated, sir, with a sense of the high importance of that office, at all times difficult, but under those distresses in which our country is involved, exposed to greater hazard and embarrassments than were ever known in the history of former times.

As I have ever considered the confidence of the public the more honorable in proportion to the perplexity and danger of the times, so I cannot but esteem this distinguished mark of the approbation of the Honorable Board, as a greater obligation, than if it had been bestowed at a season of greater ease and security; whatever discouraging circumstances, therefore, may attend me in point of health, of fortune or experience, I dare not refuse to undertake this duty.

Be pleased then to acquaint the Honorable Board, that as soon as the circumstances of the Colonies will admit an adjournment of the Congress, I shall return to the Honorable Board, and undertake to the utmost of my ability, to discharge the momentous duties to which they have seen fit to appoint me.

Although I am happy to see a list of gentlemen appointed to the Bench, of whose abilities and virtues I have the highest esteem, and with whom I have long lived in friendship, yet the rank in which it has pleased the Honorable Board to place me, perplexes me more than any other circumstance; but as I ought to presume that this was done upon the best reasons, I must submit my private opinion to the judgment of that Honorable body, in whose department it is to determine.

With the most devout wishes for the peace and prosperity of the Colonies, and of the Massachusetts Bay in particular, and with the greatest respect to the Honorable Board,

I am, Sir,

Your most obedient, humble servant.

John Adams.

Although Mr. Adams accepted this post, he never took his seat on the bench. In order to complete the history of this transaction, the following letter of resignation is here subjoined.

John Adams

To the Honorable, the Council of the State of Massachusetts Bay.

Baltimore,10 February, 1777

May it please your Honors:—

I find myself under a necessity of resigning my appointment to a seat in the Superior Court; and I do accordingly hereby resign it, and request that some other gentleman may be forthwith appointed to that most honorable station.

I am your Honors' Most obliged and obedient humble servant,

John Adams.

Appended to this letter in the copy book is this note:

10 February. Informed Portia [his wife] of the above resignation, and that I was determined, whilst I was ruining my constitution, both of mind and body, and running daily risks of my life and fortune in defence of the independence of my country, I would not knowingly resign my own.

Endnote 017

"The thought of independence had not yet become at all palatable in Maryland" The instruction is inserted in full in the Life of Thomas Stone, in Sanderson's Biography. Much of it appears to be distinctly levelled at the three great measures advocated by Mr. Adams in Congress. The passage alluded to in the text is in these words:

"And we further instruct you to move for, and endeavor to obtain a resolve of Congress, that no person who holds any military command in the continental, or any provincial regular forces, or marine service, nor any person who holds or enjoys any office of profit under the Continental Congress, or under any government assumed since the present controversy with Great Britain began, or which shall hereafter be assumed, or who directly or indirectly receives the profits, or any part of the profits of such command or office, shall, during the time of his holding or receiving the same, be eligible to sit in Congress."

Endnote 018

This interesting letter will be found in the correspondence, under date of 14 June, 1775, in another volume. The name of the mover of the resolution is not given, though it is said that he was a colleague of Mr. Chase. The delegates from Maryland at this time, were Matthew Tilghman. Thomas Johnson, Robert Goldsborough, William Paca, Samuel Chase, John Hall, Robert Alexander, and John Rogers.

Endnote 019

First Edition, Vol. ii. pp. 67, 68.

Endnote 020

As it is more than once intimated in this record that Charles Thomson was some what biased in his action as secretary by his connection with Mr. Dickinson, it is fair to give his own explanation:—

"I was married to my second wife on a Thursday; on the next Monday, I came to town to pay my respects to my wife's aunt and the family. Just as I alighted in Chestnut Street, the door-keeper of Congress (then first met) accosted me with a message from them, requesting my presence. Surprised at this, and not able to divine why I was wanted, I however bade my servant put up the horses, and followed the messenger myself to the Carpenter's Hall, and entered Congress. Here was indeed an august assembly, and deep thought and solemn anxiety were observable on their countenances! I walked up the aisle, and standing opposite to the President I bowed, and told him I awaited his pleasure. He replied, 'Congress desire the favor of you, sir, to take their minutes.' I bowed in acquiescence, and took my seat at the desk. After a short silence, Patrick Henry arose to speak. I did not then know him; he was dressed in a suit of parson's gray, and from his appearance I took him for a Presbyterian clergyman, used to haranguing the people. He observed, that we were here met in a time and on an occasion of great difficulty and distress; that our public circumstances were like those of a man in deep embarrassment and trouble, who had called his friends together to devise what was best to be done for his relief:—one would propose one thing, and another a different one, whilst perhaps a third would think of something better suited to his unhappy circumstances, which he would embrace, and think no more of the rejected schemes with which he would have nothing to do. 'I thought,' continued the venerable narrator, 'that this was very good instruction to me, with respect to the taking the minutes. What Congress adopted, I committed to writing; with what they rejected, I had nothing farther to do; and even this method led to some squabbles with the members who were desirous of having their speeches and resolutions, however put to rest by the majority, still preserved upon the minutes.' " American Quarterly Review, vol. i. p. 30.

Endnote 021

It is rather singular that Mr. Jefferson should have ascribed, even though in vague language, to Patrick Henry, a young man, not of the aristocracy, and just upon the threshold of public life, the origination of this bold measure. See Wirt's Life of Henry, p. 52. Mr. Lee, though also young at the time, had been for several years in the House of Burgesses, and naturally acted with more confidence, from knowing himself to be sustained by a strong and extensive family connection. His grandson and biographer states the facts almost exactly as they are given by Mr. Wythe in the text; and he further asserts, that among the manuscripts to which he had access is a letter from a gentleman of a distant county to Mr. Lee, thanking him for the part he had taken in the matter. Life and Correspondence of R. H. Lee, vol. i. p. 23. Yet it is not unlikely that Mr. Henry should have supported the motion, after it had been made by Mr. Lee. Mr. Jefferson's inclination to disparage the Lees is obvious enough in his writings.

Endnote 022

The particulars of this agency of Lord Drummond are to be found in the Appendix No. XIII. to the third volume of the writings of Washington. It would seem from his letter that he had been busy among the members of Congress, at Philadelphia, as early as the beginning of January.

Endnote 023

These resolutions are inserted in the report of the Debates. See vol. ii. p. 486.

Endnote 024

For the rest of these resolutions, see Journals of Congress, vol. ii. pp. 107, 108.

Endnote 025

This letter is printed, together with a private letter addressed by Mr. Adams to General Washington at the same time, in the Appendix, No. xiv. to the third volume of Mr. Sparks's edition of the Washington Papers.

Endnote 026

See the Journal.

Endnote 027

The curious reader will find a corroboration of these views in the strong letters of Elbridge Gerry written to his friends at home. Austin's Life of Gerry, vol. i. pp. 176-181.

Endnote 028

General Wooster's defect was his age. He gave what remained of his natural life to his country, in the action at Danbury, in 1777. Few of the brave officers in the French war sustained their reputation in the revolutionary struggle. The same remark may be made of the revolutionary officers engaged in the war of 1812.

Endnote 029

This is a mistake. Marshall refers to the final resolutions of the seventh of June.

Endnote 030

The decisive effect of this measure is well described in Mr. Reed's Life of Joseph Reed, vol. i. pp. 185-7. Pennsylvania was the battle ground of the movement at this time. The timidity even of the friends of independence is remarkably developed in the letters of Mr. Reed himself, and of Robert Morris. pp. 199-202. It seems that even Patrick Henry was staggering.

Endnote 031

See Notes of Debates. Mr. Duane's Speech, vol. ii. pp. 488-9.

Endnote 032

Mr. Graydon's experience of recruiting in Pennsylvania, is given in his Memoirs, Littel's edition, pp. 135-137.

Endnote 033

The resolutions reported and adopted may be seen on the Journal.

Endnote 034

See for the names of this board, of which Mr. Adams was chairman, page 6.

Endnote 035

For the remainder, see Journals for 1776, p. 209.

Endnote 036

The following letter, first published in Gordon's History, without the name of the person to whom it was addressed, is not without interest in this connection.

Samuel Chase

SAMUEL CHASE TO JOHN ADAMS.

Annapolis,28 June, 1776. Friday Eve, 9 o'clock

Dear Sir:—

I thank you for your two letters of the 17th and 24th instant. They were handed to me in Convention.

I shall offer no other apology for concluding, than that I am this moment from the House, to procure an express to follow the post, with a unanimous vote of our Convention for independence, &c. &c. See the glorious effects of county instructions. Our people have fire if not smothered. Poor General Thompson!

I charge you to write to me. Now for a government.

Jubeo te bene valere. Adieu.

Your friend,

S. Chase.

Endnote 037

This must be a mistake. No trace of it has been found.

Endnote 038

Mr. Sedgwick, in his Memoir of the Life of William Livingston, relies upon a passage in Samuel Adams's letter to R. H. Lee, printed in the Memoir of R. H. Lee, vol. i. p. 183, to prove that the new delegates from New Jersey did not arrive until after the Declaration was signed, but that they were allowed to affix their names to it. The language of his authority is certainly equivocal enough to justify his interpretation. Yet, on the other hand, nothing is better established in history than the fact that those delegates arrived in season to hear the conclusion of the debate, and were present to vote upon the final question.

Mr. Adams was in constant communication with the leading men who were pushing for independence in the Middle States, where the cause was weakest. Mr. Chase's note of triumph has already been given, but Mr. Adams had received the following equally cheering lines, thirteen days earlier, from one of the most active friends of the measure in New Jersey.

Jonathan D. Sergeant
Burlington,
15 June, 1776

Dear Sir:—

Jacta est alea. We are passing the Rubicon, and our delegates in Congress, on the first of July, will vote plump. The bearer is a staunch Whig, and will answer any questions you may need to ask. I have been very busy here, and have stolen a minute from business to write this.

In haste, yours,

Jona. D. Sergeant.

For a long time the struggle between the friends and the opponents of decided measures had been severe in New Jersey. The scale is said to have been at last turned, in the Provincial Congress, by the information received of Governor Tryon's plot against Washington, in New York; but, from a comparison of dates, it is clear that this event could only have come in, to complete what was already determined on. The new delegates were elected a week after the date of Mr. Sergeant's note, and nearly a week later, that is, on the 28th of June, the Journals of Congress show that Mr. Francis Hopkinson, one of the number, attended and produced the credentials of the whole. He was immediately placed upon the committee for preparing a plan of confederation.

The instructions given to the new members were not however, peremptory, in respect to their action in favor of a declaration of independence. Power was given them to join with the delegates of the other Colonies in that act, if they should judge it necessary or expedient to the support of the just rights and liberties of America. In the Life of Richard Stockton, in Sanderson's Collection, it is said that he was so far doubtful that his mind was not absolutely made up until after he had heard Mr. Adams. This corroborates the statement of the text. But, in addition, there is a letter written many years afterwards by his son, the late Richard Stockton, to Mr. Adams, which contains the following voluntary tribute of reminiscence. It is dated in 1821, and says,—

"I well remember that on my father's first return home from Congress, in the summer of 1776, after the fourth of July, he was immediately surrounded by his anxious political friends, who were eager for minute information in respect of the great event which had just taken place. Being then a boy of some observation, and of very retentive memory, I remember these words, addressed to his friends. 'The man to whom the country is most indebted for the great measure of independence is Mr. John Adams, of Boston. I call him the Atlas of American independence. He it was who sustained the debate, and by the force of his reasoning demonstrated not only the justice, but the expediency, of the measure.' This I have often spoken of to others, and distinctly remember the very language which he used."

George Walton, a delegate from Georgia, in a letter dated the seventh of November, 1789, fixes the day upon which the greatest impression was made upon his mind by Mr. Adams in the debate. He says,—

"I can truly assure you that since the first day of July, 1776, my conduct in every station in life has corresponded with the result of that great question which you so ably and faithfully developed on that day—a scene which has ever been present to my mind. It was then that I felt the strongest attachments, and they have never departed from me."

The strength of the resistance made to the declaration at this time is now very little understood. It gained ground through the temporizing spirit of that large class who in times of political contention are by temperament averse to a final measure, though often willing to favor an intermediate step tending the same way. Of this class a very large number were found in the States of New York, New Jersey, Pennsylvania, and Maryland, including many of their most distinguished men. They had formed a party in the very first Congress of 1774, which continued to act with great force until dispersed by the decisive measure of independence. The speakers were almost all of that side. Among them Mr. Jefferson enumerates Dickinson, Wilson, R. R. Livingston, and E. Rutledge, whilst on the other side he mentions only R. H. Lee, who was called home on the tenth of June, Wythe, and John Adams. From this it is tolerably plain how large a share of the active support of the measure must have fallen on the last named.

Mr. Jefferson's testimony at a later day is emphatic on this point. In a letter addressed in February, 1813, to Mr. W. P. Gardner, a gentleman at Washington, who was then meditating the publication of an ornamented copy of the Declaration of Independence, he says,—

"No man better merited than Mr. John Adams to hold a most conspicuous place in the design. He was the pillar of its support on the floor of Congress, its ablest advocate and defender against the multifarious assaults it encountered; for many excellent persons opposed it on doubts, whether we were provided sufficiently with the means of supporting it, whether the minds of our constituents were yet prepared to receive it, &c., who, after it was decided, united zealously in the measures it called for."

Governor McKean's testimony, given to the same gentleman at an earlier period, is to the same effect. Mr. Madison, though not himself present, writes to Mr. G. A. Otis the impressions which he received from those who were. "I well recollect," he says, "that the reports from Mr. Adams's fellow laborers in the cause, from Virginia, filled every mouth in that State with the praises due to the comprehensiveness of his views, the force of his arguments, and the boldness of his patriotism."

This fact respecting Mr. Adams being abundantly established, it would seem superfluous to dwell upon it, were it not for the equally certain fact that up to a comparatively late period, most if not all of those who have undertaken to write concerning the Revolution, either overlooked or misrepresented it. The Italian, Botta, though generally well informed, so far as researches made in Europe could avail, and under no temptation to pervert the facts, was so misguided by his authorities as to present Richard Henry Lee, because the mover of the first proposition, as the type of the whole argument for independence. But, if Mr. Jefferson's evidence be trusted, Mr. Lee, though a zealous, was a florid and verbose, rather than a strong speaker; and his exertions, undoubtedly of great value when those of all were needed, were suspended, three days after the presentation of his resolution, by his departure for Virginia. Singularly enough, Botta, after this mistake, falls into another, more remarkable, as it involves something of an anachronism. He represents John Dickinson, as addressing himself, not to the Continental Congress, in which he did speak, but to the revolutionary convention of Pennsylvania, an organization by no means then completed, which had been resorted to by the popular party as the only means of stemming the resistance instigated by him in the Assembly of the Province, and one, the validity of which he would have been slow to recognize. The convention did ultimately throw him and some of his associates out, and bring in another set, whose names appear attached to the declaration. But it is very certain that this did not happen, as Botta states, before the fourth of July, neither was it the cause of the change in the votes of the delegation favorable to independence; for the new members were not elected until the 20th, nearly three weeks afterwards. See p. 61. Mr. Dickinson, with three more out of seven old delegates of Pennsylvania, voted in committee of the whole, against independence on the first instant. On the second, he and Mr. Robert Morris absented themselves, which reversed the condition of parties and determined the favorable vote of the State.

This is not the place to treat of the causes which led to the mode of writing American history in the early part of the present century. No more striking instance of the effect, however, can be adduced, than Mr. Wirt's Life of Patrick Henry, a book which tacitly assumes for Virginia and Virginians the origin of the Revolution. At the time of writing. Mr. Wirt was comparatively a young man, fully imbued with the prejudices of his favorite State.

His biographer, Mr. Kennedy, has given the evidence both of the extent to which he carried his horror of New England at one time, and of the frank manner in which he confessed his error at a later period. To Mr. Adams's remonstrances, firmly but gently made, it was owing, in a great degree, that the public mind did not completely imbibe the impressions which the Life of Henry was calculated to give.

It was the moment of this publication that another Virginian, who had been active in political hostility to Mr. Adams through the violent scenes of his Presidency, the mover of the celebrated "resolutions of '98," selected to place his voluntary testimony on record in his hands. Perhaps his opinion of Patrick Henry may have been somewhat influenced by what he regarded as the excessive eulogy of Mr. Wirt. Of this, impartial posterity will judge, with whom it rests to make up its calmest judgment from the comparison of conflicting testimony. The following is the letter.

John Taylor

JOHN TAYLOR, OF CAROLINE, TO JOHN ADAMS.

Virginia, Port Royal, 20 February, 1819

"Respectable Sir:—

Permit me to express my concurrence with your remarks in relation to Mr. Wirt's History of Mr. Henry. I was old enough to serve often in our Legislature with this gentleman, to know him and many other patriots of the Revolution personally, and to take a deep interest in its progress from beginning to end; and although Mr. Henry possessed very popular talents as an orator, yet I know that he had but little celebrity as a statesman, and none as a soldier or a writer. He had certainly some merit as a revolutionary patriot, but I sincerely believe that its efficiency in promoting that event was not one tenth part of that resulting from the efforts of many other gentlemen, among whom I cordially and conscientiously class yourself, as an offering to justice, and in some degree (should this letter reach future times) to supply your forbearance to vindicate your own claim.

"This testimony is, I confess, from a source too inconsiderable to be very important; but as it comes from a contemporary witness, who has subsequently differed from you in several political opinions, its integrity may perhaps give it some weight.

"I am, with great respect, sir,
"Your most obedient servant,
"John Taylor."

It would be a curious subject of inquiry to consider what might have been the result of the mission of Lord Howe, and the disastrous campaign of 1776-7, had the Rubicon not been crossed on the Fourth of July.

Endnote 039

See the Resolutions in the Journal.

Endnote 040

See their names in the Journal. Among them are those of Franklin, Clymer, Morris, Wilson, and Rush.

Endnote 041

Mr. Cooper seems to justify Hopkins. History of the Navy, vol. i. p. 107.

Endnote 042

This is a mistake. The record does contain the motions, the yeas and nays, and the alterations proposed; but it was kept secret until the publication of the Secret Journals, ordered by Congress, in 1820.

Endnote 043

The following reminiscence of one of the scenes that took place, is taken from a letter of Mr. Henry Marchant, a delegate of Rhode Island, written to Mr. Adams, in 1789, just as the new constitution was going into operation:—

"You wish me to give you a particular account of the prophetic declaration made on the floor of Congress, just as the former confederation was concluded.

"When my friend has all his feelings wound up upon an important subject, and vent must be given, he has a manner of expression so peculiar to himself, and so striking to the hearers, that the impression, as from a stroke of lightning, is left behind, while the flash and sound, the mode of expression, is lost or forgotten. His words I will not engage to recollect with exactness.

"The articles of confederation being completed, the members by rotation were called to place their signatures to them. This being concluded, a pause and perfect calm succeeded. He sat and appeared full of thought. He rose. 'Mr. President.' His cane slipped through his thumb and forefinger, with a quick tap upon the floor; his eyes rolled upwards, his brows were raised to their full arch.

" 'This business, sir, that has taken up so much of our time seems to be finished. But, sir, I now, upon this floor, venture to predict that, before ten years, this confederation, like a rope of sand, will be found inadequate to the purpose, and its dissolution will take place. Heaven grant that wisdom and experience may then avert what we have most to fear!'

"I never knew a greater solemnity upon the minds of the members. It was near the usual time of adjournment. Congress was adjourned."

Mr. Adams, in his reply, makes some correction.

"Your account of the prophecy is humorous enough, but you must be mistaken in the point of time. I left Congress on the 11th of November, 1777, that year which the Tories said, had three gallowses in it, meaning the three sevens, just as Congress had gone through the confederation, but before it was signed. My name is not to that confederation; so that the prediction must have been uttered either at Yorktown, a day or two before I left it, or before, at Philadelphia.

"I recollect some expressions of that sort, on the floor of Congress, in Philadelphia, immediately after the determination that the votes should be by States, and not by numbers, a point which Wilson and I labored with great zeal. After that determination and some others, I own I gave up that confederation in despair of its efficacy or long utility."

The decisive vote, to which Mr. Adams alludes, was upon the following motion:

"That each State shall have a right to send one delegate to Congress for every thirty thousand of its inhabitants; and, in determining questions in Congress, each delegate shall have one vote."

In favor of this motion, but seven ayes are recorded. That of John Adams, from Massachusetts, the four Virginia delegates, Messrs. Harrison, Jones, F. L. and R. H. Lee, Mr. Penn, of North Carolina, and Mr. Middleton, of South Carolina, made up the number.

At this day, there can be little doubt that, even if the confederation could have survived its other defects, the rejection of the principle contained in this proposition sealed its fate.

Endnote 044

Which see in the Journal.

Endnote 045

Mr. Adams's name had already been inserted in a bill of attainder commenced in one house of Parliament. Tucker's Life of T. Jefferson, vol. i. p. 61, note.

Endnote 046

The letters are inserted, under the proper dates, in the General Correspondence.

Endnote 047

See the Journal.

Endnote 048

The resolutions, which may be seen in the Journal, contain the whole plan of an army of eighty-eight battalions, to be enlisted as soon as possible, to serve during the war.

Endnote 049

The Secret Journal was published in 1820, but it gives little clue to individual action. The draught of the treaties is stated in a former volume to have been made by Mr. Adams. See vol. ii. p. 516. The only other instance in which his name appears, is as one of the committee appointed on the 26th of September to prepare a draught of letters of credence to the commissioners, and to report the ways and means of providing for their subsistence.

Endnote 050

The 7th of June, 1805.

Endnote 051

Which may be seen, pages 357, 358, of the Journal of 1776.

Endnote 052

Since published by order of Congress.

Endnote 053

These resolutions fill two pages of the Journal.

Endnote 054

Mr. W. B. Reed, in his valuable life of his grandfather, has endeavored to do away the impression of the time, as recorded by Gordon in his History, that his grandfather, when acting as Adjutant-General, was deeply imbued with the prevailing prejudices against the New England troops. Possibly this might in his case have been exaggerated, although it must be conceded that the weight of evidence lies the other way. It would be surprising if Mr. Reed should have been an exception to a feeling almost universal among the officers out of New England. Mr. Graydon has stated the case with fairness in his Memoirs. It had very much to do with the hostility to General Schuyler among the New England troops, a circumstance which seems to have been unnecessarily puzzling to some writers upon American affairs.

This matter merits a closer analysis than it has met with. In speaking of the origin of the revolutionary movement in Virginia and Pennsylvania, Mr. Wirt and Mr. Graydon alike trace it to the more favored and wealthy classes of society. Such was not the case in New England. The persons of considerable property who entered into it are so few that they can readily be counted. Mr. Adams's Diary and the catalogue of the graduates at Harvard college sufficiently show how many of that class in Massachusetts, a community remarkable at that time for the equalization of property, refused to join it, and became exiles in consequence. Probably the social system of New England more nearly approximated theoretical democracy in 1776, than that of any other Colony then did, or than it has ever itself done since. The effect was visible in the military organization around Boston, which was that of an armed community, and not of what is understood in a military sense to be an army. The relation between officers and privates was one inspired by preference and not by authority. Of course the prevailing ideas of discipline were very different from those acquired by men coming to them as officers from an opposite condition of society. It is only a right conception of this state of things that can fully illustrate at once the fitness of Washington's appointment to command the army before Boston, and the peculiarities of his character which enabled him, in so delicate a position, to acquit himself with so much honor.

It is the province of the historian to show the influence which the prejudices imbibed in the army against the New England troops in 1776, have had upon subsequent events.

Endnote 055

By the Diary, the 13th. See vol. ii. p. 432.

Endnote 056

This assertion has found higher authority than Paine. In the army, the impression that it was true, so far prevailed, that General Lafayette seems to have caught it at the time and retained it all his life. In the publication of his papers, made by his family, in 1837, is the following statement:—

"Gates étoit à Yorktown, où il en imposait par son ton, ses promesses, et ses connoissanees Européennes. Parmi les députés qui s'unirent à lui, on distingue les Lees, Virginiens, ennemis de Washington, et les deux Adams."

Mémoires de ma main.

By reference to the Diary, it appears that Mr. John Adams left Congress, at Yorktown, on the 11th of November, never to return. At that time General Gates was still in the North, having barely got through with the capitulation of Burgoyne. Congress received the news of that great event through his aid-de-camp, Colonel Wilkinson, on the 3d of November, five days before leave of absence was granted to Mr. Adams, and eight days before he departed. It only remains to remark, that the importance of General Gates, as a rival of Washington, arose after, and in consequence of, his success in the North.

Endnote 057

The following special instructions were given to Captain Tucker, by the commissioners of the navy board.

James Warren
William Vernon

TO SAMUEL TUCKER.

Navy Board—Eastern Department, Boston,February, 1778

Sir:—

Notwithstanding the general instructions given you, you are now to consider the Hon. John Adams, Esq. (who takes passage in the Boston) as one of the commissioners with the Hon. Benjamin Franklin and Arthur Lee, Esquires; and therefore, any applications or orders received from him, as valid as if received from either of the other two. You are to afford him, on his passage, every accommodation in your power, and to consult him, on all occasions, with respect to your passage and general conduct, and the port you shall endeavor to get into, and on all occasions have great regard to the importance of his security and safe arrival.

We are your humble servants,
William Vernon,
James Warren.

Endnote 058

"Seeing no probability of going to sea. I gave two midshipmen, two mates, and the purser, liberty to go on shore. At two, P. M., the wind got round to the northward. I ordered preparation for sea, fired several signal guns, for my officers on shore to come on board, but without effect. I was obliged to go myself and get them on board, not without a great deal of trouble." Extract from the Log Book.

Endnote 059

"At 6, A. M., saw three large ships bearing east, standing to the northward. I mistrusted they were cruising for me. I hauled my wind to the southward; found they did chase me. I consulted my officers whether it was not best to give them chase. We agreed in opinion. Wore ship to the north, and gave them chase one hour. I then discovered one of the ships to be as large as myself, the other a twenty gun ship; the third out of sight almost. A man at the mast head cried out, 'A ship on our weather-quarter;' the other two under our lee, and I under small sail. I then consulted the Honorable John Adams and my officers what was best to do, not knowing the best of my ship's sailing. They, one and all, consented to stand to the southward from them. The two that were under my lee were before me, and stood after me. I then wore, and at meridian, the small ship out of sight, the other at three leagues to leeward." Log Book. 19 February.

Endnote 060

"Ship still in chase, but being poorly manned, dare not attack her. For this, and sundry other reasons, at 6, P. M., lost sight of the chase. Hauled my wind. The next morning saw the same ship ahead, standing to the southward and westward. I could not weather her on that tack. After running three hours to the westward, the wind favoring me, I then hove in stays, and came to windward of the ship, about four miles. Was satisfied it was the same ship; she tacked, and continued chasing me all day, but I rather gain upon her." Log Book. 20 February.

Endnote 061

"21. Still chased by the ship. At 4 P. M. variable winds, and calm; at 7 P. M. sprung up a small breeze to the westward; run E. S. E. till 10 P. M. Heavy thunder and sharp lightning. At midnight the ship was struck by lightning at the mainmast and topmast, and wounded twenty-three men, and struck down three. Although we were in the greatest danger, received but little damage. Lost sight of the ship. Heavy and hard gales; we scudding."

"22. Heavy gales and head sea. One thing and another continually giving way on board the ship. Lay by under mainsail. Down top gallant yards; at 4 P. M. carried away slings and chains of mizzen yards; at 4 A. M. somewhat moderate; made sail, and began to repair the rigging." Log Book.

Endnote 062

"Saw a ship to the south-east standing to the westward. Asked the favor of the Hon. John Adams to chase, which was immediately granted. Made sail and gave chase. At 3 P. M. came up with the chase, gave her a gun and she returned me three, one shot of which carried away my mizzen yard. She immediately struck. Out boat. Got the prisoners on board. She proved the ship Martha from London, bound to New York. I ordered a prize-master on board, intending to send her to France, but on consulting Mr. Adams, he thought most advisable to send her to America." Log-book.

Endnote 063

It must be to this occasion, being the only one upon which a shot was fired by an enemy, that Mr. Sprague, in his Eulogy of Adams and Jefferson, refers, in the following anecdote. He doubtless had it from Tucker in his latest days, when a sailor's stories commonly lose nothing in the telling.

"Discovering an enemy's ship, neither Commodore Tucker nor Mr. Adams could resist the temptation to engage, although against the dictates of prudent duty. Tucker, however, stipulated that Mr. Adams should remain in the lower part of the ship, as a place of safety. But no sooner had the battle commenced, than he was seen on deck, with a musket in his hands, fighting as a common marine. The Commodore peremptorily ordered him below; but called instantly away, it was not until considerable time had elapsed, that he discovered this public minister still at his post, intently engaged in firing upon the enemy. Advancing, he exclaimed, 'Why are you here, sir? I am commanded by the Continental Congress to carry you in safety to Europe, and I will do it,' and, seizing him in his arms, forcibly carried him from the scene of danger."

Endnote 064

"After finding the papers necessary and giving Mr. Adams time to pack them, I consulted him about sending one of my lieutenants to command her, as she was a commissioned ship and in the King's service, mounting sixteen nine and six pound cannon; her cargo insured at £72,000 in London. At 3 P. M. I sent her by Mr. Welch, my third lieutenant, by the consent of the Hon J. Adams, with fourteen good men and four prisoners for Boston or any port adjacent."

Log-Book.

Endnote 065

17. Tuesday. At 2 P. M. discovered two large ships under courses, in full chase of me. When they came within about a half mile, made one a two-decker; the other, I could not tell what she was. I then set my mainsail, and left them. Log-Book.

Endnote 066

The French term for flags.

Endnote 067

The log-book fixes this upon the fifteenth of March, as appears from the following entry:

"At 8 P. M. saw two ships on my starboard bow, standing to the westward. I crossed them about half a mile under their lee. Discovering them to be British ships, one a two-decker, the other a frigate, I then bore away from them, by order of Hon. John Adams. One of the gentleman passengers informed me, they were boarded the day before I took them, by three men-of-war boats; that there were six two-deckers and frigates in company. At 9 A. M. lost sight of them."

Endnote 068

Probably Mr. Champagne, mentioned the next day.

Endnote 069

"At 2 P. M. came to sail up the river to town. Saluted a small town called Blaye, with the Independent salute." Log-Book.

Endnote 070

"I sent the pinnace to town with the Hon. John Adams, son, and the two gentlemen passengers; likewise the cutter with the French gentlemen passengers. At 1 P. M. came within one mile of the town. A number of gentlemen and ladies came on board, who seemed much pleased with the ship." Log-Book.

Endnote 071

"At 6 P. M. took my leave of Hon. John Adams. They set off for Paris, my Captain of marines and Doctor accompany him." Log-Book.

The log-book continues to the 9th of September, 1779; and at the end is a list of prizes captured in the latest voyage. Captain Tucker, though not a polished, was an energetic and successful commander. Mr. Cooper has scarcely done him justice in his History.

Endnote 072

Here follow two letters to Mr. Dumas, one of them covering the draught of a letter to the Grand Pensionary of Holland, which, having been since printed in the Diplomatic Correspondence of the American Revolution, vol. i. pp. 376-378, are now omitted. In the copy book of the commission, for 1778, left in Mr. Adams's hands, almost all the letters appear to have been drawn up by him. The two above-mentioned are noted as having been drawn by Dr. Franklin, and a few others are in the handwriting of Mr. Lee.

Endnote 073

Mr. Deane's character of this gentleman is to be found in the first volume of the Diplomatic Correspondence of the Revolution, p. 150, a work in which much information respecting the action of all the persons here mentioned can be obtained. Of De Lauraguais, the wit, the spendthrift, and the roué, many traces are visible in the Correspondance Littéraire de Grimm et Diderot, vol. iii. pp. 297-302, vol. viii. and elsewhere.

Endnote 074

This happened in 1775. It ought in justice to be added that, even then, the individual was driven off the ground by the public indignation. Perhaps the supposed insult to the Queen had as much to do with it, however, as the cause of morals. The anecdote is told in that curious repertory of Parisian manners and opinions, during the reign of Louis XVI., the Correspondance Secrète of Bachaumont, vol. i. p. 314.

Endnote 075

He is stated to have left only daughters. Dictionnaire Universel, &c.

Endnote 076

This opinion is entirely confirmed by the letters of Mr. Hartley, published in the Works of Franklin, Sparks's Edition, vol. viii. pp. 267-8, 312.

Endnote 077

William Carmichael. Mr. Sparks says that he returned to America. Dipl. Corresp. of the Rev. vol. ix. p. 4.

Endnote 078

He was eighty-four. His death took place on the thirtieth of the succeeding month.

Endnote 079

Here follow two entries made in French, not sufficiently good to merit publication. Perhaps the following remark may serve as an example of the whole. "Je crois qu'on riroit si on verroit mon françois!"

Endnote 080

An extract from one of these letters, dated 6 December, 1776, is given by Dr. Gordon. It refers more particularly to Marshal Broglie.

"I submit the thought to you, whether if you could engage a great general of the highest character in Europe, such for instance as Prince Ferdinand, or M. B., or others of equal rank, to take the lead of your armies, such a step would not be politic, as it would give a character and credit to your military, and strike perhaps a greater terror into our enemies. I only suggest the thoughts, and leave you to confer with Baron (Kalb) on the subject at large." History, vol. iii. p. 221.

Endnote 081

This anecdote is told in the Life of Voltaire, by Condorcet. Œuvres Complètes, vol. c. p. 161.

Endnote 082

This story of a family council, respecting Lafayette's departure to America, is believed to be a mistake. Lafayette expressly says, "Quelques circonstances, inutiles à rapporter, m'avaient appris à n'attendre sur cet objet, de ma famille, que des obstacles." Mémoires de ma Main. See also the Writings of Washington, vol. v. Appendix No. I.

Endnote 083

Here is inscrted the whole of a letter to Samuel Adams, dated 21 May, 1778. But inasmuch as it has been printed in the Diplomatic Correspondence of the Revolution, vol. iv. pp. 244-248, only that portion is here retained, necessary to the immediate subject discussed.

Endnote 084

Mr. Deane never succeeded in throwing much light upon his mode of doing business in France. But his personal expenses have been ascertained by the banker's accounts.

Endnote 085

It is very much to be regretted that this was not done by the writer; as the history is indispensable to a correct understanding of the relations between France and the United States, which followed.

Endnote 086

The letter signed, Charles de Weissenstein, and the copy of the answer to it. transmitted to Count de Vergennes, were found in the French Archives, by Mr. Sparks, and the answer was printed by him in his edition of Franklin's Works, vol. viii. pp. 278-286. The style, which is pointed and bitter towards the King, treats him as the source of the application. It is now well known that George III. was the real mover of the American war.

For the better understanding of the record of this period, it is scarcely necessary to say, that the work to which reference is here made, is of the greatest possible service. The Life and Correspondence of Arthur Lee may also be consulted with advantage.

Endnote 087

The Address of Silas Deane to the people of America, in November, 1778, already alluded to in the preceding page, which first published to the world the extent of the differences that had taken place, and which deeply agitated the parties in Congress and in the country. It is almost needless to say that Mr. Arthur Lee, Mr. Izard, and Dr. Franklin, are the persons referred to.

Endnote 088

Mr. Joshua Johnson, afterwards employed in the settlement of the accounts of the United States in France, and still later, as consul in London. He was the father of the lady who was subsequently married to the writer's eldest son, John Quincy Adams.

Endnote 089

It is a singular fact that throughout the Revolution, the naval commanders seem, as a class, to have caused the greatest embarrassment both at home and abroad. Captain Landais, after manitesting his utter incapacity for command, was at last discharged from the service as insane. Cooper's History of the Navy, vol. i. p. 208.

Endnote 090

An arrangement had been made by Dr. Franklin to send the Alliance directly home as a convoy to the trade at Nantes. Mr. Adams was to go in her. But this plan was changed by the desire of the French government, which offered to provide a passage for him in the ship about to take out the new French minister. This occasioned a delay of three months. Franklin's Writings, vol. viii. p. 352; Diplomatic Correspondence of the Revolution, vol. iv. p. 308.

Endnote 091

The Bonhomme Richard, afterwards made famous by the engagement with the Serapis.

Endnote 092

Mr. Cooper's character of John Paul Jones, though favorable, seems to be summed up with impartiality. History, vol. i. p. 209, note.

Endnote 093

In the roll of the ship he is entered as Laurence Brooks, of New Hampshire. Most of the persons here mentioned are more or less noticed in the Life and Character of J. P. Jones, by John Henry Sherburne.

Endnote 094

He was a supernumerary in the ship, acting as secretary.

Endnote 095

See p. 146. Mr. Deane's letter is not found in the Diplomatic Correspondence of the Revolution.

Endnote 096

It is scarcely necessary to say that the writer subsequently changed his sentiments respecting Mr. Jay, whose political character took a bolder development after his departure from Congress, on his mission to Spain. In the violent dispute of that body respecting Silas Deane's conduct, Mr. Jay had taken a very active part in his favor; and the resignation of Mr. Laurens, as President, as well as his election to that post, had turned upon the question of hearing Deane's charges against Mr. Lee, in the form in which he chose to present them. All these circumstances contributed to raise expectations in the French and Spanish agents, at Philadelphia, which secured their cooperation in promoting his nomination as minister to Spain. But in this they were completely disappointed by Mr. Jay's later, which, like his earlier conduct, was prompted only by his conscientious convictions. He outlived his confidence in Mr. Silas Deane. Gordon's History, vol. iii. p. 218; Life of J. Jay, by his son, W. Jay, vol. i. p. 99, 129.

Endnote 097

A singular slip of the memory. Mr. Sherman and Mr. R. R. Livingston were of the committee, and Mr. Harrison was not.

Endnote 098

Probably Dr. Bancroft, a sketch of whom is given page 140.

Endnote 099

Le Ray de Chaumont.

Endnote 100

Francis Dana, of Massachusetts, went out as Secretary of Legation to Mr. Adams; he afterwards received a commission as minister to Russia. After his return, he was made Chief Justice of the Supreme Court in Massachusetts, in which post he died, in 1811.

His life deserves a more extended notice than has yet been taken of it.

Endnote 101

This seems to have been forgotten. Florez in his great work on Spain, says, "that the peculiar genius, customs, manners, &c., of those people, would require a volume, at least, to describe them."

Endnote 102

Here terminates the last fragment of the autobiography, and at a moment when it would have been of great value to the elucidation of a much disputed point in the subsequent history, if it had been extended. The rest of the letters upon the subject of the treaty of commerce, are all printed in the fifth volume of the Diplomatic Correspondence of the Revolution.

Endnote 103

John Derk, Baron Van der Capellen tot de Pol, of Overyssel, was a man of marked character, and one whose services, rendered to the cause of America during the struggle for recognition in Holland, deserve to be remembered. As early as the year 1775, he made earnest opposition to the request of the King of Great Britain, for the loan of the Scotch regiments in the service of the Stadtholder. Not long afterwards, though himself a nobleman, he distinguished himself by an endeavor to put an end to certain feudal burdens that weighed upon the people of his neighborhood, the confirmation of which had been eagerly sought by many of his own class. This drew upon him their indignation, which showed itself in the States of Overyssel, by the adoption of a decree censuring him for sedition and slander, and demanding of him a humble apology, and promise of amendment, on penalty of exclusion from the position in the States to which his rank entitled him, in case of refusal. He declined the condition, and remained excluded four years, and until the popular voice demanded his restoration in a manner it was not deemed safe to neglect. His triumph was complete, and it took place at the same time with that of the United States over the resistance of Great Britain in Holland. A medal was struck upon the occasion, and distributed among his friends. One of these was presented to Mr. Adams, and is now in the possession of the Editor.

Baron Van der Capellen and the active interest he took in American affairs, are frequently mentioned in the Diplomatic Correspondence of the Revolution.

Endnote 104

Engelbert Francis Van Berckel, Pensionary of the City of Amsterdam, was another prominent friend of America, in Holland. Under his auspices, a plan of a commercial treaty was secretly in train of negotiation, until the moment when the capture of Henry Laurens and of his papers, disclosed the whole proceeding to the British Ministry. They immediately demanded, through their minister, Sir Joseph Yorke, the exemplary punishment of M. Van Berckel, which not having been promptly decided upon, was the principal cause assigned in the declaration of Great Britain for the war that ensued. A clear and connected idea of these events, may be gathered from the letters of Mr. Adams in the fifth volume of the Diplomatic Correspondence of the American Revolution.

Endnote 105

"A young gentleman glittering with stars, and, as they say, very rich. He has twice, once at Court, and once at the Spanish Minister's, entered familiarly into conversation with me upon the climates of America and Portugal, and the commerce that has been and will be between our countries, and upon indifferent subjects; but there is no appearance that he is profoundly versed in political subjects, nor any probability that he could explain himself, until all the neutral powers do, of whom Portugal is one." Letter of J. A. in Dipl. Corresp. of the Am. Rev. vol. vi. p. 392.

Endnote 106

"He has been eight-and-twenty years Envoy at the Hague from the Bishop of Liege, and converses more with all of the foreign ministers here, than any other." Dipl. Corresp. vol. vi. p. 414.

Endnote 107

"The Minister from Prussia, M. de Thulemeyer, is very civil, attacks me, (as he expresses it,) in English, and wishes to meet me on horseback, being both great riders; will converse freely with me upon astronomy, or natural history, or any mere common affairs; will talk of news, battles, sieges, &c.; but these personages are very reserved in politics and negotiations; they must wait for instructions." Letter of J. A. in Dipl. Corresp. vol. vi. p. 390.

Endnote 108

This, and a large number of other essays upon various subjects by the same author, were found in manuscript among the papers of Mr. Adams. The relations which he maintained with this agreeable and intelligent gentleman during his residence on the Continent, were of the most friendly description.

Endnote 109

Of the reason why he was going to Paris.

Endnote 110

Edmund Jenings, of Maryland, with whom the author was in close correspondence during the greater part of his residence in Europe.

Endnote 111

See Mr. Jay's letter to R. R. Livingston of the 13th October. Dipl. Corresp. of the Amer. Rev. vol. viii. p. 128.

Endnote 112

This is an error, which Mr. Jay himself subsequently corrected. His vote in favor of Mr. W. T. Franklin was voluntary and unsolicited. Franklin's Writings, vol. ix. p. 473.

Endnote 113

This is probably the instruction to the commissioners, "ultimately to govern themselves by the advice and opinion of the French Ministry," carried through Congress on an amendment, and after a severe struggle.

Endnote 114

Note in the margin by the author: "A mistake, as Mr. Jay tells me."

Endnote 115

Here ends that portion of the Diary, beginning at the place marked with an asterisk on page 300, from which extracts were made by Mr. Adams, and sent home to one of the delegates of Massachusetts in the Congress of the Confederation, Mr. Jonathan Jackson, for the sake of furnishing unofficial, but interesting information, respecting the negotiation. By some mistake in sealing up the packages, these went with the despatches to Mr. Livingston, and not with the letter to Mr. Jackson; and they were deemed so valuable that they were not given up to that gentleman when he went to claim them, and thus became official papers. This statement is necessary to explain the facts which were eighteen years afterwards made the ground of a political and personal attack upon the author, involving an insinuation even against his veracity, by Mr. Hamilton. The letter to Mr. Jackson will be found in the General Correspondence.

Endnote 116

The names of the parties into which the people of Pennsylvania were at this time divided. Mr. Dickinson was of the Republican party.

Endnote 117

This error has already been pointed out, see page 299.

Endnote 118

This letter is of an early date, 12 March, 1781. It is inserted in Mr. Sparks's edition of Dr. Franklin's Writings, vol. ix. pp. 1-6.

Endnote 119

This is the celebrated voyage of Bartolomeo de Fuente, in 1640, to the northwestern coast of America, first printed in 1708, which furnished for a long period a topic for controversy among geographers in England, Germany, and France. The material part of it is now regarded as a fiction, though founded on a veritable narrative.

Endnote 120

This alludes to the well known intercepted despatch of M. de Marbois, which had so powerful an effect on the negotiation of the treaty, and the force of which is scarcely impaired by time. This subject, the discussion of which has of late been revived, is examined at large in the first volume of the present work, in connection with some new matter appertaining to the history of that negotiation.

Endnote 121

Here follows in the margin of the Diary a draught of three articles proposed by the American ministers, at Mr. Laurens's rooms, and delivered to Mr. David Hartley, 29 April, 1783. As they are inserted in the second volume of the Diplomatic Correspondence of the Revolution, among the letters of Henry Laurens, vol. ii. pp. 499-500, they are omitted here. The record of the 28th explains the mode in which they were prepared. See p. 363.

Endnote 122

This proposal is also found in the Diplomatic Correspondence of the Am. Revolution, vol. x. pp. 151-153.

Endnote 123

See the letter of the Marquis de Lafayette to the Commissioners. Dipl. Corresp. of the Am. Revolution, vol. x. p. 141.

Endnote 124

The Order, Mr. Hartley's full power, exchanged with the American ministers, 19 May, 1783, and his observations and propositions left with them, 21 May, 1783, are omitted, as they may be readily found elsewhere. See Dipl. Corresp. of the Am. Revolution, vol. x. pp. 140-146; vol. ii. pp. 500-505.

Endnote 125

See page 360, note.

Endnote 126

This memorandum of the language of the Sardinian minister had been transmitted to Mr. Livingston, the Secretary of Foreign Affairs, in the month of July preceding. See his letter in the Dipl. Corresp. of the Revolution, vol. 7. p. 122.

Endnote 127

The Count de Maillebois had been charged with a design to injure his commanding officer, Maréchal d'Estrées, by his action and advice at the battle of Hastenbeck, in 1757. He published a pamphlet in his justification which threw much blame upon the commander, who replied, and pursued Maillebois before the tribunal of the Marshals of France. They gave in a sealed verdict to the King, Louis XV., who immediately deprived Maillebois of all his employments, and had him confined in the castle of Doullens. Sismondi draws a very unfavorable character of him. Histoire des Français, vol. xxix. p. 127; Correspondance Littéraire de Grimm, vol. ii. p. 230.

Endnote 128

Mr. Adams's daughter, just married to Colonel W. S. Smith, at that time Secretary of Legation.

Endnote 129

Charles Carroll of Carrollton, Senator of Maryland.

Endnote 130

Oliver Ellsworth, Senator of Connecticut. Afterwards Chief Justice of the Supreme Court of the United States.

Endnote 131

Pierce Butler, Senator of South Carolina.

Endnote 132

Richard Henry Lee, Senator of Virginia.

Endnote 133

William Grayson, Senator of Virginia.

Endnote 134

William Patterson, Senator of New Jersey. Afterwards Associate Justice of the Supreme Court of the United States.

Endnote 135

George Read, Senator of Delaware.

Endnote 136

William S. Johnson, Senator of Connecticut.

Endnote 137

Ralph Izard, Senator of South Carolina.

Endnote 138

The yeas and nays upon this question were, in support of the President's unqualified power of removal,—Messrs. Bassett, Carroll, Dalton, Elmer, Henry, Morris, Patterson, Read, Strong.

Against it,—Messrs. Few, Grayson, Green, Johnson, Izard, Langdon, Lee, Maclay, Wingate.

Endnote 139

A motion had been made when the bill was in the House of Representatives to add a proviso requiring the Legislatures of Pennsylvania and Maryland to make provision for removing all obstructions to the navigation of the Susquehannah, below the seat to be selected, and it had failed. Ayes, 24. Nays, 25.

Endnote 140

It would seem from this that the proviso had been inserted in the Senate.

Endnote 141

William Maclay, Senator of Pennsylvania.

Endnote 142

The motion was lost, and the bill was subsequently lost at this session, by a disagreement between the Houses, and a consequent postponement of the subject.

Endnote 143

The name of the speaker appears to have been accidentally omitted.

Endnote 144

The report of the committee was sustained. Ten yeas, eight nays.

Endnote 145

A single entry in the Diary occurs in 1791, as follows. Philip Freneau afterwards became noted in the political struggles of the time, as a friend of Mr. Jefferson, who in his turn sheltered him from the indignation of Washington. Memoirs of T. Jefferson, vol. iv. p. 485.

"November 11. Friday. Yesterday a number of the National Gazette was sent to me by Philip Freneau, printed by Childs and Swaine. Mr. Freneau, I am told, is made interpreter."

Endnote 146

Samuel Allyne Otis, Secretary of the Senate.

Endnote 147

Generally conceded to be spurious.

Endnote 148

From the Boston Gazette, No. 435, 1 August, 1763.

Endnote 149

From the Boston Gazette, No. 439, 29 August, 1763.

Endnote 150

Hutchinson mentions the year 1763, as the time when parties in Massachusetts began to take their form. "Men took sides in New England upon mere speculative points in government, when there was nothing in practice which could give any grounds for forming parties." The next paragraph, however, betrays his sense of the connection these speculative points had with grounds for forming parties which all instinctively felt to be about to be furnished by the mother country. It was the ripple on the face of the still water, indicative of the storm that was soon to follow. History of Massachusetts, vol. iii. pp. 103-105.

Endnote 151

From the Boston Gazette, 5 September, 1763.

Endnote 152

From the speech of Ulysses, in Ovid. Metamorphos. lib. iii. l. 363-368.

Endnote 153

See volume ii. p. 150.

Endnote 154

Orations and Speeches on Various Occasions, by Edward Everett, vol. i. p. 140, note.

Endnote 155

Robertson's History of Charles V. ch. v. pp. 54, 141, 315.

This work did not appear until the year after the publication of this Dissertation in England. The two references are in the handwriting of Mr. Adams, in the margin of his printed copy.

Endnote 156

Rob. Hist. ch. v. pp. 178-9, &c.

Endnote 157

"I always consider the settlement of America with reverence and wonder, as the opening of a grand scene and design in Providence for the illumination of the ignorant, and the emancipation of the slavish part of mankind all over the earth."

Endnote 158

Brit. Ant. p. 2.

Endnote 159

Social Compact, page 164.

Endnote 160

Edes and Gill, printers of the Boston Gazette.

Endnote 161

The late Rev. Dr. Mayhew.

Endnote 162

Printed from the Boston Gazette, of Monday, 14 October, 1765.

Endnote 163

A Cambridge correspondent of the Evening Post, in October, 1765, enters into a comparison of these instructions with some of an opposite nature, coming from Marblehead, and published at the same time, and picks out this paragraph, as "worthy to be wrote in letters of gold."

Endnote 164

From the Supplement to the Boston Gazette, Monday, 13 January, 1766.

Endnote 165

"Fearing that the local courts would not be inclined to execute the Stamp Act, penalties incurred in America were made recoverable in any court of record or in any court of admiralty in the Colony, where the offence should be committed, or in any court of vice-admiralty, which might be appointed over all America, at the election of the informer or prosecutor." Minot's History of Massachusetts, vol. ii. p. 167-8.

The eighth resolve adopted by the Convention at New York, in 1765, is levelled at this clause of the Stamp Act.

Endnote 166

From the Boston Gazette, 20 January, 1766.

Endnote 167

The indignation of the writer at the submission of Barbadoes to the stamp act is expressed in the Diary, vol. ii. p. 173.

Endnote 168

Nova Scotia, Quebec, Pensacola, &c., are more excusable on account of their weakness and other peculiar circumstances.

Endnote 169

The curious reader will notice that this paragraph is almost a literal transcript from the Diary of the 18th of December, 1765, vol. ii. p. 154.

Endnote 170

From the Boston Gazette, 27 January, 1766.

Endnote 171

From the Boston Gazette, 26 January, 1767.

Endnote 172

From the Boston Gazette of Monday 9, and Monday 16, February 1767.

Endnote 173

"It must, it cannot but be evident to all who are willing to see and judge for themselves, notwithstanding the slander of Paskalos scribbling in the Gazette, or Tertullus, haranguing in the senate, that we never had a governor in the chair, who discovered more mildness, &c. than Governor Bernard has discovered."

Philanthrop, 1 December, 1766.

Who the writer in the Gazette, signing himself Paskalos was, it is not easy now to say. Tertullus was probably James Otis.

Endnote 174

History, vol. iii. pp. 189-193.

Endnote 175

History of the American War, vol. i. pp. 231-236.

Endnote 176

Hutchinson comments upon this passage as "aiming at independency." In a note he says, "this is a singular manner of expressing the authority of parliament." History, vol. iii. p. 193. The curious reader can compare this proposition with the fourth article of the Declaration of Rights and Grievances, made by the congress of 1774, and with Mr. Adams's account of the origin of that article. See vol. ii. p. 374, and appendix C.

Endnote 177

History, vol. iii. p. 231.

Endnote 178

History, vol. i. p. 180.

Endnote 179

Copies of six letters of Sir Francis Bernard to the government at home, had been obtained through the agency of Alderman Beckford, a member of parliament, and had been transmitted by the colonial agent, Mr. Bollan, to the council of Massachusetts. The suggestions of changes necessary to be made in the government were well calculated to aggravate the popular irritation already existing.

Endnote 180

Vol. ii. pp. 315, 317. See also Bradford's History of Massachusetts, vol. i. pp. 262-264.

Endnote 181

4 Inst. 100.

Endnote 182

1 Blackstone's Comm. 267-8.

Endnote 183

Croke, Jac. 407.

Endnote 184

See Rapin, Burnet, Skinner, Comberbach, State Trials, and Sir Edward Herbert's Vindication of Himself.

Endnote 185

4 Inst. 200.

Endnote 186

1 Bacon's Abr. 555.

Endnote 187

4 Inst. 75. "Where, in 5 E. 4. it is holden by all the chief justices in the exchequer chamber that a man cannot be justice by writ, but by patent or commission, it is to be understood of all the judges, saving the chief justice of this court (that is, the king's bench); but both the chief justice and the rest of the judges may be discharged by writ under the great seal."

Endnote 188

Bacon's Abr. 555.

Endnote 189

See Brooke and Lit. Commission.

Endnote 190

See 1 Blackst. Comm. 65-73.

Endnote 191

This is rather an abstract than a quotation from the first ten pages of the preface to the reports of Lord Fortescue, printed in 1748, and signed with the initials J. F. A.

Endnote 192

History of England, vol. i. Appendix II.

Endnote 193

2 Hume, 162.

Endnote 194

See also Gilbert's History and Practice of the High Court of Chancery.

Endnote 195

Reports, 394, known as Lord Fortescue's.

Endnote 196

See Rushworth, 420; 2 Rush. Append. 266.

Endnote 197

See Skinner's Reports, and Raymond, 251.

Endnote 198

See 8 Hume, 143.

Endnote 199

See Rapin and Mrs. Macaulay.

Endnote 200

See 1 State Trials,—the proceedings against Chief Justice Tresilian and others.

Endnote 201

Strykii, Examen Juris Feudalis.

Endnote 202

Stryk. 173.

Endnote 203

Which we have in Dalton, c. 5; and in 3 Burn, tit. Justices of the Peace; 1 Shaw's Inst. 13, 16, 17.

Endnote 204

See Dalton's Justice, c. 3.

Endnote 205

2 Hawkins's P. C. 2, ss. 5, 6.

Endnote 206

1 Sid. 338, Mich. 19, Car. II. B. R.

Endnote 207

Lord Campbell, in his late work, speaks of this case as an exception, thus:

"In the vain hope of perpetuating his power, he obtained a grant for life of chief justiciar, which hitherto had always been held during pleasure."

Lives of the Chief Justices, vol. i. p. 49.

Endnote 208

Hutchinson's History of Massachusetts, vol. 2, p. 375-6, note.

49958389R00201

Made in the USA
Middletown, DE
25 October 2017